ESCAPING THE HOLOCAUST

STUDIES IN JEWISH HISTORY
Jehuda Reinharz, General Editor

OTHER VOLUMES ARE IN PREPARATION

ESCAPING THE HOLOCAUST

Illegal Immigration to
the Land of Israel,
1939–1944

DALIA OFER

New York   Oxford
Oxford University Press
1990

Oxford University Press

Oxford New York Toronto
Delhi Bombay Calcutta Madras Karachi
Petaling Jaya Singapore Hong Kong Tokyo
Nairobi Dar es Salaam Cape Town
Melbourne Auckland

and associated companies in
Berlin Ibadan

Library of Congress Cataloging-in-Publication Data
Ofer, Dalia. [Derekh ba-yam. English]
Escaping the Holocaust : illegal immigration to the land
of Israel, 1939-1944 / Dalia Ofer.
p. cm.—(Studies in Jewish history)
Translation of: Derekh ba-yam
Includes bibliographical references.
ISBN 0-19-506340-6
1. Palestine—Emigration and immigration.
2. Holocaust, Jewish (1939-1945)
3. World War, 1939-1945—Jews—Rescue—Palestine.
4. Immigrants—Palestine.   Title.
II. Title: Illegal immigration to Palestine, 1939-1944.
III. Series.
JV8749.P303413 1990
325.5694—dc20 89-72138

1 3 5 7 9 8 6 4 2

Printed in the United States of America
on acid-free paper

Preface

Aliyah bet—illegal Jewish immigration to Palestine before the state of Israel was established—is one of the most fascinating chapters in the history of Zionism. It is a unique episode, a saga of national and personal resistance in the face of unprecedented adversity. Bringing Jews from Europe to Palestine by land and by sea, in defiance of restrictive immigration policies imposed by the British government, was partly an undertaking of national rescue and partly a calculated strategy of political and diplomatic brinkmanship. More than 100,000 immigrants reached Palestine in this way until May 1948.

Aliyah bet is a multidimensional story: of the immigrants themselves, the organizers and supporters; of forces that worked to stop the flow of refugees and those that sought to exploit it. The variety of names given illegal aliyah (immigration) reflects its many facets: *ha'apala,* connoting surmounting obstacles to reach the high ground; aliyah bet—"class B immigration"—to designate an underground operation; "independent" or "special" aliyah—terms used to emphasize the positive validity of Jewish immigration to Palestine, regardless of British laws; and finally, illegal immigration—the preferred British designation. This story also constitutes one of the most dramatic encounters between the Jewish Diaspora and the Jews of prestate Palestine (the Yishuv).

As in any good drama, there is a plot, central characters, and internal and external conflict. As the story develops, so do the lives of the characters, the locations, and the background. This drama, however, is one that has multiple final acts, ranging from the tragic to the almost classic "happy ending." Like a Greek drama, the aliyah bet story also has its "chorus" representing Fate, driving the characters onward and directing the course of events without itself being alterable or controllable. The characters in this story were conscious of this immovable force, and indeed pitted themselves against it with their very last ounce of strength, without knowing in advance what the outcome would be. During the Second World War, the Nazis through their policies and their plans for a "Final Solution" (as they put it) to the "Jewish problem" took the role of the chorus.

This study, which is a revised English version of the Hebrew book *Derech Bayam,* published in Jerusalem by Yad Ben Zvi in 1988, strives to preserve the human essence of the story, the individual details of thought, emotion, and deed. In researching and writing this book, I have been guided by a desire to remain faithful to the events themselves and to the context in which they took place, and to retain the original voices of the past. Over the years, the stories of aliyah bet have become part of the Israeli national myth, so that the voices of the past, more often than not, reach us through the filter of special effects and melodramatic fanfare. Yet, in the two generations that have passed since the end of aliyah bet, there has been a growing desire to look back at the past objectively, to take advantage of the perspective of time to carefully—but not impersonally—reconstruct events.

Was aliyah bet a wave of immigration, a concept of Zionism, a certain kind of national liberation struggle, or a popular movement with its roots in these and other historical factors? What were the forces behind aliyah bet both in Europe and in Palestine, and what were the forces that tried to stop it? Is the significance of aliyah bet measured best against the goals set by the Zionist movement during the war and the results obtained? Did illegal aliyah grow out of the historical values of Zionism and the standards of Jewish political behavior in modern times, or did the phenomenon mark a transition to a new pattern? Was it an expression of the responsibility felt by Palestinian Jewry (the Yishuv) toward the Jews of the Diaspora and, in particular, a sense of obligation to rescue the Jews from the Nazis and their collaborators?

This book takes up these questions and discusses how the concept of rescue changed over the course of the war, thus altering the character of aliyah bet. An asymmetry existed between the forces pushing the Jews out of Europe, on the one hand, and the means at the Jews' disposal, on the other. To assess the extent to which Zionist policy affected the dimensions of immigration to Palestine, we must take into account this asymmetry. In addition, the evolution of German policy on the Jewish question must be analyzed in terms of its impact on the efforts of Jews to leave Europe. The interrelationship of the factors that led Britain to formulate its policies vis-à-vis Palestine, refugee victims of Nazi persecution, and the question of illegal immigration constitutes a major segment of the historical analysis.

In seeking to elucidate these points, I highlight some aspects and central events of the aliyah bet story, including the saga of the refugees of the "Kladovo-Sabac group," the history of the S.S. *Struma*, and the vicissitudes in the course of Jewish refugee emigration from Rumania and Bulgaria in 1944 and 1945.

Circumstances changed rapidly during the war period, and this was reflected in the developing Zionist response. The mood of the Yishuv in Palestine shifted from relative calm at the outset to heightened anxiety and fear of a German invasion (or destruction of the country by German-backed forces). This accompanied a shift from grave concern for the fate of European Jewry to a focus on the logistics of defending Palestine itself. Then, the easing of tensions in the wake of Britain's victory in North Africa coincided with the arrival of the terrible news of the Holocaust in Nazi Europe (the fall of 1942).

At that time, too, the Zionist leadership formulated the political demands it would seek to achieve when the war was over. The leaders viewed the new conditions created by the war as a basis for tactical maneuvering and political planning aimed at ensuring the survival of the Jewish people—at the very moment that the Jewish people were being destroyed. How did the Zionist leadership, and indeed, the public at large, react to these developments? Did they continue to conform to the same approach and ideological beliefs that had dominated Zionist thought before the war; or were there substantive changes in the way they viewed themselves, their relations with the rest of the world, the activities they were willing to undertake, and the time frame in which they worked to put the Zionist program into effect? This study on aliyah bet adds another layer and perspective to the efforts of Israeli historians to portray and evaluate, in the historical context and perspective, the politics of the Yishuv in Palestine during the war years and the politics of the democracies facing the Holocaust.

Ironically, the total number of immigrants to Palestine in aliyah bet until 1945 did not exceed 36,000. Yet the historic significance of aliyah bet goes beyond mere numbers, as indicated by the weighty historical issues that it raises.

Finally, there is the problem of sources that such a work must confront. Despite the limited time span (1939–45), the material examined to research this study is particularly diverse, both geographically and politically. The historical narrative itself had to be pieced together through a painstaking comparison of different and conflicting versions. The archival material, in a number of languages, has been published only in part, and generally does not offer a complete picture. Given the nature of illegal immigration activity, much of it remained secret, and orderly records were not kept, except in code and by indirect allusion. In addition, wartime conditions prevented people from spending a great deal of time keeping proper records and notes. Letters did not always reach their destinations. A great deal of material that was held by the aliyah bet agents themselves was lost when they moved from country to country, or was destroyed in the interests of security. It is fortunate for the historian that the matter was of concern to the authorities in the immigrants' countries of origin, to those in the countries that served as transit points, and, in particular, to the British, whose records were of great help not only in understanding the British role, but also that of other countries.

Much information was gleaned from letters and diaries kept by those who were directly involved. More information was obtained from recent studies of the Jewish communities of Europe before, during, and after the Holocaust, which allowed me to place Zionist wartime activity and aliyah within their local context. I was thus able to see them in light of the special problems affecting each community. These studies also helped to understand the attitudes taken with regard to the personalities involved in aliyah work and to secret aliyah itself, with all its risks and opportunities. Of equal importance were studies of the war period dealing with the belligerent powers and their policies on the Jewish issue. These enabled me to gain a greater appreciation of the political impact of aliyah and of how it was perceived by the various governments.

Nevertheless, I found it necessary to turn to memoirs and oral documentation in order to fill in certain gaps. Memoirs express primarily the point of view of their authors. There are often contradictory accounts about the same events, some of which aroused a great deal of controversy. I therefore occasionally had to make a judgment, after comparing varying versions of activists and immigrants, and these versions with the facts recorded elsewhere. In this I took into account questions of motive, interest, and the general attitude of memoirists, their ideological outlook, political standing, and the positions they took on other issues at the time. I thus tried to see their aliyah work within the context of their personality and career.

Some of the oral documentation was prepared specifically for this study. There are many limitations in using oral documentation as a historical source, and I need list only a few. The selective and changing memory of the interviewee introduces discrepancies between the events of the past and the account of those events. The perspective gained by the individual and by his society regarding the past may alter the memory of the past, even unconsciously—certainly with respect to the relationship between actions, intentions, and considerations that guided the actions. These problems become magnified for the topic studied here, because it has become part of a national myth over which various groups seek to establish proprietary rights.

In many ways, the events of the aliyah bet story took on special significance at the moment they happened, and participants on all sides were aware of the implications of their actions. For many, their historical consciousness was inseparable from their work. This self-consciousness, along with social and ideological changes affecting Israeli society, have shaped the memory of those times. One may say that the events of the war, once the war ended, acquired special significance, to say nothing of how they came to be perceived in the wake of the establishment of the state of Israel and the ensuing wave of immigration. In spite of the best intentions and their utmost integrity, the witnesses to the events struggle to free themselves of these layers of consciousness. This is especially true for those central figures whose activities came to be "historically appreciated" so soon after the events themselves—sometimes after a few years or even months.

None of this means, however, that we should not use oral documentation. Indeed, it has special importance for our topic, not only because of the human and dramatic element it adds to a historic description, but also because of the depth it gives to the historian's probing for the unseen and unrecorded aspects of experience.

*

I would like to express my appreciation to those who have helped me. The many archivists in Israel and abroad, though I cannot mention them all by name, displayed endless patience and were always ready to show me yet another document, to advise me on the location of further material, and to search until they could answer each of my requests. I am deeply grateful to them.

My husband, Gur, deserves a special note of thanks, as do our daughters, who did not stop loving history. They remained my true partners, dedicated readers, and first critics as various passages and chapters passed through first drafts.

Yehuda Bauer, in directing my doctoral research, encouraged me to continue this work. I owe special thanks, too, to Shmuel Almog, who, as colleague and friend, read the manuscript with care and made thoughtful and helpful comments. Michael Waltzer, Jonathan Frankel, and Debora Dash Moore read the English manuscript, and each of them enriched it with important remarks. I am grateful to the Institute of Contemporary Jewry for providing financial support for the English translation, and to the faculty of the Humanities Department at the Hebrew University for its support in editing the English text. And I had the privilege of working with Eli Lederhendler. He is not only an excellent translator, but a fine historian and a friend. It is with special pleasure that I extend my gratitude to Naomi Laufer, who spared neither time nor effort in helping me with many passages in German and in deciphering difficult handwritings. Without her dedicated help, this study would have been much more difficult. And finally, thanks to my good friend Nurit, whose loyalty, wisdom, and fine sense of the line between criticism and encouragement helped me at so many stages of this project.

In addition, I should like to thank the staff of the Library of Congress for the study desk and the good services of the personnel, in particular of the Jewish and Hebrew section, during my sabbatical year in Washington, D.C. And last but not least, I thank Sussane Lane and Sharon Fliesher, without whose assistance and dedicated work the final stages of editing the English text would have been impossible.

I wish to acknowledge the willingness, confidence, and interest of those at Yad Ben-Zvi who were responsible for publishing the Hebrew original, and to the staff of Oxford University Press for publishing this book. I want to thank Professor Jehuda Reinharz in particular for his important and valuable suggestions for the English edition.

Washington, D.C.   D. O.
January 1990

Contents

ESCAPING THE
HOLOCAUST

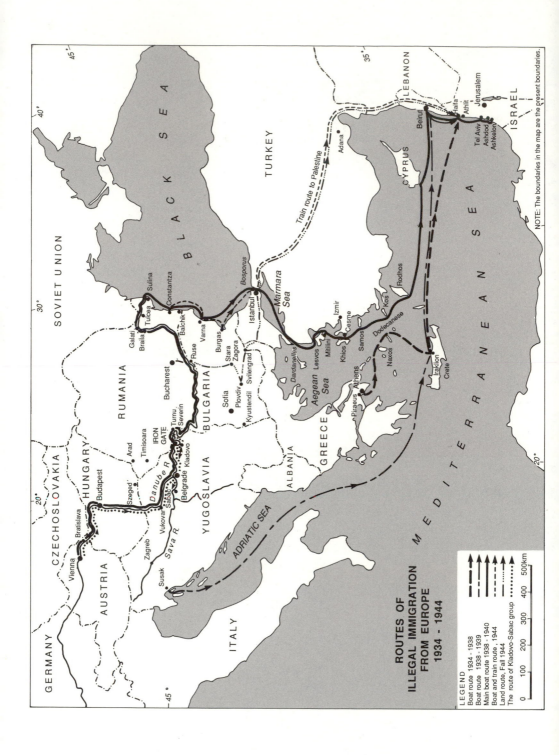

ROUTES OF
ILLEGAL IMMIGRATION
FROM EUROPE
1934 - 1944

LEGEND

Boat route 1934 - 1938	
Boat route 1938 - 1939	
Main boat route 1938 - 1940	
Boat and train route, 1944	
Land route, Fall 1944	
The route of Kladovo-Sabac group	

0 100 200 300 400 500km

NOTE: The boundaries in the map are the present boundaries.

GERMANY

SOVIET UNION

BLACK SEA

CZECHOSLOVAKIA

Vienna

Bratislava

AUSTRIA

HUNGARY

Budapest

Szeged

Arad

Timisoara

RUMANIA

Bucharest

Zagreb

Susak

YUGOSLAVIA

Vukovar

Sabac

Belgrade

Kladovo

Turnu-Severin

IRON
GATE

Danube R.

Sava R.

ADRIATIC SEA

ITALY

ALBANIA

BULGARIA

Sofia

Plovdiv

Kyustendil

Svilengrad

Stara
Zagora

Ruse

Galati

Braila

Tulcea

Sulina

Constantza

Balchik

Varna

Burgas

Istanbul

Marmara
Sea

Bosporus

TURKEY

Train route to Palestine

Adana

Dardanelles

Lesvos

Izmir

Cesme

Khios

Samos

Mitilini

Naxos

GREECE

Piraeus

Athens

Aegean
Sea

Dodecanese

Kos

Rodhos

Iraklion

Crete

MEDITERRANEAN SEA

CYPRUS

LEBANON

Beirut

Haifa

Athlit

Jerusalem

Tel Aviv

Ashdod

Ashkelon

ISRAEL

45°

40°

35°

30°

20°

45°

20°

35°

20°

1

Illegal Immigration before World War II

Jewish clandestine, illegal entry into and residence in Palestine prior to the establishment of the state of Israel in 1948 has its roots in the earliest days of Zionist immigration to Palestine. Even prior to the first Zionist Congress in 1898 and its adoption of the political goal of establishing a Jewish state in Palestine, Jews had established settlements in Ottoman-ruled Palestine—at times legally, but more often illegally. The Ottoman Empire viewed all national movements as potential threats to its hegemony, and these Jewish settlers came mostly from Russia, a long-standing enemy of the Empire, making them undesirable on two counts. Even prior to the 1898 Zionist declaration, Jewish settlers in Palestine saw their destinies as tied to the creation of a Jewish state in Palestine.

Within the Zionist worldview, the right of every Jew to immigrate to the land of Israel is elemental and undeniable. As such, the notion of "illegal" or "irregular" aliyah (immigration), as the British called it, is a contradiction in terms. Consequently, immigration carried out in violation of the laws of the governing authority came to be known as independent, or type B, Aliyah (aliyah bet), in the Zionist lexicon.

From the beginnings of modern Jewish settlement in Palestine in 1882 and throughout the British Mandate period ending in 1948, independent entry took place over land and sea. Immigrants were in most cases aided by emissaries from the Yishuv (the prestate Jewish settlers in Palestine) to the European Jewish communities. These were at first unaffiliated visionaries and later the envoys of the developing Zionist political parties and their youth groups, who raised funds, espoused the cause of Zionism to sympathizers and others in Europe, and facilitated would-be settlers' passage to Palestine. In many cases, emissaries escorted and arranged sea journeys, and specially trained squads arranged for disembarkation from boats. Sea passage was the predominant means of clandestine entry into Palestine.

Other means were used as well, and in the case of overland entry, organized assistance was also arranged. Travelers would be met by guides at designated contact points, whence they were secreted across Palestine's borders from Syria and Lebanon. During the British Mandate period, entry was

3

at times secured legally through tourist visas, and upon expiration of these visas, those holding them stayed on illegally. The most notable instance of the use of tourist visas to gain residence in Palestine took place in 1932, on the occasion of the Maccabiah tournament (an international Jewish athletic competition), for which some 25,000 tourist visas were issued. The Mandate authorities later estimated that some 20,000 of those who entered Palestine failed to leave. (The British legalized all unauthorized immigrants in 1936.) Fictitious marriages constituted yet another means of evading restrictions, and thousands of people gained residence in Palestine in this way during the 1930s. However, from 1934 on, the principal illegal route to Palestine was by secretly organized sea transport.

It has been posited that type B aliyah accounted for the major part of Jewish settlement in Palestine and that authorized, legal immigration was the exception to the rule.[1] In fact, however, the vast majority of Jews who entered prior to 1948 immigrated legally. British records show a total immigration of 485,800 for the period 1919 to 1948. Of these, some 77,000 entered illegally. In addition, another 30,000 people (including those who entered as tourists) were never entered into the records, bringing the total of illegal immigrants to just over 100,000—less than 25 percent of all immigration to Palestine.[2]

The impression that aliyah bet accounted for the major share of immigration to Palestine led to the image cast on it by contemporaries—often precisely those activists responsible for bringing these immigrants to Palestine. In the aftermath of the Holocaust, aliyah bet became a symbol of Jewish survival as well as the primary expression and vehicle of the Zionist movement's capacity for independent action and determination to bring about its goals. Writers who took down testimonies during the events and were part of the active echelon of emissaries involved in aliyah bet overestimated its role as an immigration drive in their effort to place it in the national legacy.

In prestate Palestine of the 1930s, illegal ships came to be organized as a result of internal pressures within the Zionist movement and of external pressures, especially the restrictions increasingly imposed on immigration by the British. These forces, combined with the escalating anti-Semitism in Europe over the course of the decade, propelled Zionist activists to organize the first clandestine sea voyages.

British Policy on Jewish Immigration

The official British commitment to create a Jewish national home in Palestine began with the issue of the Balfour Declaration in November 1917, in the midst of the First World War. At the end of the war, Palestine went from Ottoman Turk rule to British, and the substance of the Balfour Declaration was incorporated into the League of Nations Mandate for Palestine. The British were to be responsible for the economic development and security of the land and its inhabitants, which was to eventually result in a Jewish national home. The governing authorities in the Mandate were to be a bureaucracy of British civil servants headed by a high commissioner. In the interests of creating a viable community, Article 4 of the Mandate for Palestine set forth a contingency for establishing a Jewish agency to represent the interests of the Jewish national home vis-à-vis the Mandate administration and to serve as an incipient governing body. The executive of the Zionist Organization, the international, democratically controlled body established at the first Zionist Congress in 1898, initially filled this role. In 1929, the Jewish Agency was established.

The text of the Mandate contains no reference to limits on immigration or to any mechanism by which immigration at a later stage might be restricted. However, even before the League of Nations' formal ratification of the British Mandate, the White Paper of June 1922 (issued by then-Colonial Secretary Winston Churchill) set forth certain limitations on its scope, principally based on the economic capacity of Palestine's economy. In response, the Zionist Executive submitted a letter of understanding to the British government, stating that the "economic capacities" of Palestine should be interpreted maximally—that is, as an expansive concept whereby increased immigration would generate greater demand, in turn requiring a larger economic base to be strengthened by continued population growth. This formulation was accepted by the British in practice until political considerations were later brought to bear.

The British established immigration criteria in terms of economic standing: the financially secure, those sponsored by public institutions, candidates for entry into the work force, and the dependents of the above.[3] During most of the Mandatory period, entry for persons in the first, second, and fourth categories was almost automatic. For the third category (termed by the Zionists "labor aliyah"), a quota was set by the high commissioner every six months (and later every three months). The quota was based on detailed information on employment opportunities in all sectors submitted by the Zionist Organization (and later the Jewish Agency) to the Mandatory administration. The quota governing labor aliyah varied greatly from year to year. It was of utmost importance to the Zionists since the entry of youth, the mainstay of the agricultural economy and the polity, was almost wholly contingent on it.

Immigration was a central source of friction among the British authorities, the Yishuv (the Jewish community in Palestine), and the Arab community. The Arabs viewed immigration as the linchpin of the Jewish effort to gain control of the country. Arab rioting erupted in Hebron and elsewhere in the summer of 1929, and in its wake, the British began to limit Jewish immigration by applying the economic capacity clause in a restrictive sense. The White Paper of 1930 made this policy official. According to its terms, Palestine's economic capacity to absorb immigrants was to be based not on the needs of the Jewish sector's planned-growth economy, as before, but on Palestine's employment as a whole. The White Paper introduced unemployment among Arabs as grounds for halting aliyah, which would resume only after the reentry of unemployed Arabs into the work force.

The Jews argued that in the Arab economy (which was predominantly agricultural) seasonal unemployment was common; consequently, Arab workers turned to urban employment only during the off-season, making it difficult to accurately determine the extent of unemployment. Moreover, given the imbalance in size of the Arab and Jewish sectors and the slow modernization of the Palestine economy, the possibility existed that the Arab work force could supply all the manpower needs of the Jewish sector in developing the country, a possibility made all the more likely by the frequent migrations of large numbers of Arabs from neighboring countries. The impact of the 1930 White Paper would be to curtail Jewish labor immigration entirely.

In 1931, the British acceded to the Jewish request that the two economies be treated independently, as before. The Zionist Organization rallied British public opinion and the British press and successfully persuaded the government to retract its stated position. In a letter to Chaim Weizmann, the president of the Zionist Organization, Prime Minister Ramsay MacDonald, confirmed that Britain intended to fulfill the policy first enunciated in the Balfour Declaration, in effect nullifying the restrictions introduced in the 1930 White Paper.

The 1930 White Paper provoked the Zionist leadership further in its introduction of the concept of "political limits to Jewish immigration." The White Paper claimed that previous immigration policy had intensified Arab distrust of Britain and aggravated Arab suspicion of Zionist intentions, thus hindering a reconciliation between Jews and Arabs. In so doing, the White Paper assigned Jewish immigration a political weight, though at this stage measures addressing it as such had not been proposed.

During the 1930s, the British authorities and the Jewish Agency clashed repeatedly over the absorptive capacity of the labor market in Palestine and over the labor aliyah quota dependent on it. In years of economic depression as well as in prosperous ones, British approval of immigration certificates fell far short of Jewish Agency requests; at most 50 percent and as little as 20 percent of requests were granted. With the outbreak of the Arab Revolt (1936–38), economic considerations gave way to political ones. The Mandatory government set out to restructure the immigration schedules as a whole, fixing as a maximum limit 4,450 certificates for the six-month period March to September 1936—a substantial decrease compared to the total of 18,000 set for the previous six months.

The Peel Commission report, published in July 1937, imposed explicitly political considerations on further aliyah. In a special regulation, it enabled the high commissioner to set an absolute maximum on the number of immigrants and to establish limits within each category. This regulation was intended to remain in force for one year (from July 1937 to August 1938). The Peel Commission report also recommended a partition plan for Palestine, though it was never realized. In 1938, the Woodhead Commission was formed to investigate the feasibility of implementing the partition plan, but concluded that a different approach altogether would have to be found to resolve the conflict over Palestine.

This conclusion prepared the way for a third White Paper on Palestine, the White Paper of May 1939, issued by Colonial Secretary Malcolm Mc-Donald. It placed a ceiling of 75,000 immigrants for the following five-year period, following which further Jewish immigration would require Arab consent. The White Paper also limited the sale of land to Jews and called for the election of a representative body, composed of both Jews and Arabs, at the end of this period. The 1939 White Paper was dubbed "the Paper of Treachery" by the Zionists. It was the culmination of British retrenching throughout the 1930s from the goals expressed in the League of Nations Mandate. To the Zionists it represented an abandonment of the Balfour Declaration and its goal of establishing a Jewish national home in Palestine. The 1939 White Paper in effect became the official British policy on Jewish immigration throughout the war years and until the Palestine problem was placed in discussion before the United Nations in 1947.

The Zionist Leadership and Aliyah bet in the Early 1930s

The immediate victims of British immigration restrictions were the Jewish communities of Central, Eastern, and Southern Europe, and in particular Poland and Nazi Germany. Their status steadily deteriorated throughout the 1930s. Their worsening plight was well known to the Zionist leaders. The central questions of what action to take and how to fulfill their responsibilities gave rise to heartfelt reevaluations of previous attitudes. Berl Katznelson, a leader of the labor Zionist party, Mapai, and editor of its newspaper, *Davar,* visited Europe in 1933. Katznelson, who commanded great moral sway, returned to Palestine imbued with the conviction that the conditions of European Jewry required immediate support and action on the part of the Yishuv. In an address to an assembly of workers in Tel Aviv, he spoke at length of the worsening conditions for Jews in Central and Eastern Europe, describing how the once affluent and self-confident Jews of Germany had suffered an unimaginable blow, and how in Poland, growing anti-Semitism had rendered the Jews' position in society untenable. He continued:

> There was a time when we had to try to forget the Diaspora, to bury ourselves in work on Palestinian soil, to turn the dream of a homeland into a reality. Our way of assisting Diaspora Jewry was to settle in the land of Israel, to make ourselves into what we are. That was all we were able to do, and that is what we did. We took from the Diaspora practically all that there was to take, and we were entitled to every last bit of it. We took from the Diaspora every able-bodied person we could find. But now times have changed. Today

it is we who are strong, settled, materially secure. We also possess spiritual riches that the Diaspora lacks. Today, for our own sake, not simply out of pity for others, we must turn our faces back toward the Diaspora. We must understand that the Diaspora of today is the land of Israel of tomorrow.[4]

Katznelson reiterated that the aid Palestinian Jewry had to offer was a home for immigrants but that providing this home would require a struggle against the British and economic sacrifices demanded by the absorption of great numbers of immigrants. These would be but material sacrifices, in exchange for "spiritual riches." The Yishuv could enable European Jewry not only to find security but also to fulfill the Zionist ideal. The unprecedented stability and prosperity of the Yishuv enabled it to take the leading role in solving the Jewish question in Europe, and to establish the Yishuv's position in world Jewish affairs.

Katznelson's message marked a revolutionary change in the perception of the relative viability of the Diaspora vis-à-vis the Yishuv. The Jewish community of Palestine was generally considered fragile and dependent. Zionist immigration policy had been characterized by great caution—with a goal of securing the settlement of Palestine in order to offer a large-scale solution to the Diaspora at a later date. Past experiences during the larger waves of immigration—the severe unemployment during the Third Aliyah (1918–22) and the economic crisis following the Fourth Aliyah (1923–27)—pushed Zionist leaders to a careful planning of the rate of immigration based on the Yishuv's economic growth. Furthermore, they felt that immigration should not be viewed as a general solution for all; instead, only those who had prepared themselves adequately—acquired skills necessary for a rugged agricultural existence and accustomed themselves to its hardships—should immigrate at this time.

Others echoed Katznelson's call for large-scale illegal immigration at this time, though for many different reasons. In September 1934, Yitzhak Tabenkin, the leading figure of Hakibbutz Hameuhad (the United Kibbutz federation), vigorously advocated large-scale immigration, even in the face of British regulations. The British approach to immigration, he argued, was a disappointment. It was thus left to the Yishuv to take care of the needs of the Diaspora through independent initiative.[5]

Both Katznelson and Tabenkin commanded a great deal of moral leadership; however, neither of them held posts in the Jewish Agency itself. Those in charge, David Ben-Gurion, chairman of the Jewish Agency executive, and Moshe Shertok, head of the Jewish Agency political department, opposed taking a stance that would bring the Yishuv into direct confrontation with the British over immigration. Although the Jewish Agency and the Mandatory government consistently disagreed over the total number of certificates to be allotted, the growing number of immigrants permitted into the country in 1934 and 1935 (42,359 and 61,854) indicated to them that a sound practical basis of mutual understanding existed. Therefore, they were unwilling to condone illegal immigration or to aid those who continued to organize it despite their disapproval and who sometimes encountered difficulties.[6]

Hehalutz and Betar: First Attempts
at Organized Aliyah bet, 1934

Those who showed the greatest determination to make their way to Palestine were the youth groups of the Zionist movements in Poland: Hehalutz and Betar. The two were rivals. Hehalutz was affiliated with the labor wing of Zionism (which held sway in the Jewish Agency) and was closely connected to the kibbutz movement. Betar was the youth group of the Revisionist movement, which strongly opposed labor and saw itself as representing the interests and Zionist aspirations of the Jewish middle class in the Diaspora. Immigration to Palestine held a great allure for these youth—it was the fulfillment of their Zionist ideal. They were more radical in overall attitude than their elders and could break their ties to their home countries more easily. Moreover, the chance to change their future through action, a fundamental element of both youth groups' philosophies, held a stirring appeal. Between 1929 and 1934, Hehalutz and Betar membership increased sevenfold.

For Hehalutz, developments in Palestine in the early 1930s seemed to brighten their immigration prospects. In 1932, the British had permitted a significant increase in the overall immigration quota (from 350 in 1931 to 4,500 in 1932). Moreover, the increased demand for labor resulting from a growth spurt in the Palestinian economy and the gradual improvement in living conditions (which made resettlement easier) both served to render immigration more attractive. Membership in Hehalutz grew in Poland as well as in other centers of the movement—Lithuania and Rumania. Enrollment in *hachshara,* the movement's training farms, spiraled. (For Hehalutz members, a six-month to one-year period of training was required before eligibility for immigration.)

Yet immigration from within the ranks of Hehalutz did not keep pace with the growth in membership. The first Class-C (labor) schedule of 1934 allowed for only 6,800 certificates, yet the *hachshara* contained some 7,500 youth awaiting permits. Moreover, Hehalutz's share in labor aliyah declined throughout the 1930s—from 83 percent to 39 percent. The number of working-class and lower-middle-class Jews seeking entry to Palestine had grown in the wake of the Depression and filled the allowed quotas quickly. Another factor contributing to Hehalutz's decreased share in the quota was the allegation of favoritism on the part of the Jewish Agency toward Hehalutz. This charge was leveled at the Zionist Congress of 1933, where a strident confrontation between labor and Revisionist wings took place that finally resulted in a Revisionist split from the movement as a whole in 1935. The labor leaders agreed to reduce the Hehalutz share in aliyah by 50 percent as part of a coalition agreement made between the General Zionist party and the Mizrahi religious party.

Hehalutz's expectation of being able to transfer all those on the *hachshara* went unfulfilled. Anxiety and depression set in among Hehalutz members and training-farm workers in Poland, and Hehalutz leaders grew concerned that members would desert the farms and the local clubs.[7] Thus, Hehalutz members decided to try to solve the problem on their own—to arrange an immigration effort independently, despite the lack of certificates. The support of Hehalutz emissaries from Palestine was a crucial factor in their decision to attempt this mission, since the emissaries represented the moral and practical support of the kibbutz movement and the Histadrut, the general federation of labor, who constituted the final authority for Hehalutz. The first illegal Hehalutz voyage, that of the *Velos,* was to be the result of this decision.

In early 1934, two members who were already resident in Palestine were designated by the Polish Hehalutz movement to travel to Greece and arrange for a suitable vessel. These were Yosef Barpal from kibbutz Ayanot, and Yosef Baratz of kibbutz Degania.[8] Their mission was carried out in great secrecy; all the parties involved used aliases to protect themselves should the British uncover the plan. It also lacked official Zionist sanction, though some highly placed individuals did support it, in particular Eliyahu Golomb, head of the Haganah (the Jewish defense organization in Palestine). Barpal and Baratz, aided by Victor Meyer, a German Jew who had lived in Greece since World War I, purchased a ship, the *Velos,* and prepared it to accommodate 340 passengers. Once the arrangements for the ship had been concluded, Yehuda Braginsky of kibbutz Givat Hashlosha and Ze'ev Shind of kibbutz Ayelet Hashahar traveled to Poland to recruit candidates to attempt the clandestine entry. The group organized by Braginsky and Shind arrived in Athens in July 1934. They embarked on the *Velos* and arrived off the coast of Palestine after a few days' sail. The passengers landed safely without attracting the attention of the British.

The complete success of the first voyage of the *Velos* prompted its organizers to attempt another. Braginsky and Barpal, apprehensive of British surveillance, changed the port of embarkation from Athens to Varna, Bulgaria. The boat left port and sailed through the Dardanelles, whereupon the British discovered it and trailed it to Palestine. The British forced the ship back to sea, and after several foiled landing attempts the *Velos* returned to Greece. For several months it wandered from one port to another, but the passengers were barred from landing. At last the Polish government accepted the would-be immigrants back. After spending a period of time in Zleszciki, a resort village on the Polish-Rumanian border, the passengers of the failed second voyage traveled to Palestine in small groups and entered legally with certificates obtained through the Jewish Agency. The failure of the second voyage of the *Velos* was a financial disaster for Hehalutz in Poland. Four years would pass before Hehalutz attempted to send another group of illegal immigrants to Palestine.

The youth group of the Revisionists, Betar, felt compelled to immigrate illegally because they perceived that they were discriminated against in the Jewish Agency's recommendations for certificates.[9] The Revisionists charged the Jewish Agency's aliyah department with attempting to achieve hegemony within the Yishuv by preventing the settlement of Revisionists in Palestine. Though Betar had claimed a membership of 30,000 in 1934, it received but a handful of certificates. The Revisionists actively promoted illegal immigration during the Maccabiah tournament, and by 1934 they had organized a network of operatives that guided groups of illegals overland (via Beirut and Damascus) on a regular basis. The overland aliyah effort was directed by Avraham Stavsky, a prominent member of the movement in Poland.

Principal figures in the Revisionist movement supported this network— and clandestine immigration in general—unlike the status of Hehalutz's efforts. Indeed, illegal aliyah was central to Revisionism. Ze'ev Jabotinsky, the movement's leader, had published articles as early as 1932 publicly avowing Zionist "adventurism"—the fulfillment of the ideal of settling in Palestine through outlandish and daring means—against whatever odds or legal obstacles. The articles were an inducement to independent aliyah.[10] The voyage of the *Union* in September 1934 was undertaken in just such a spirit and was entirely successful. It was arranged by Betar members from Poland and Lithuania and received the assistance of the Revisionist leadership in Warsaw and Danzig. Spurred by the *Union*'s success, the movement purchased and prepared a second boat, the *Wanda,* which was to set sail from Danzig. However, the *Wanda* sank while still in the harbor, though all its passengers survived. Its failure discouraged other large operations by Betar in this period, though small boats carrying twenty to thirty people continued to be organized by people affiliated with Betar.[11]

There were other setbacks at this time as well. Eliyahu Glazer (a Betar leader in Danzig), working with Stavsky (a Betar member who was already engaged in overland aliyah efforts), proved unsuccessful in their attempts to smuggle Jewish students from Latvia into Palestine via the overland network. The combined failures of their operations and of others at the time aroused harsh criticism within the movement that weighed against further activities. A delay of three years ensued before the Revisionists again participated in organized aliyah efforts. In retrospect, these years were crucial ones for European Jews.

Renewed Illegal Immigration, 1937 to 1939

Organized aliyah bet activities resumed in 1937. Three factors were responsible for the renewed effort: the crisis of Hehalutz in Poland, the worsening situation of Jews under Nazi rule, and the political strife in Palestine over the Peel Commission's partition plan.

In Poland, conditions for Jews had deteriorated. Following the death of Marshall Pilsudski in May 1935, the Polish government had instituted an official policy of discrimination against Jews, and incidents of violence increased.[12] Many Polish Jews wished to immigrate to Palestine but were dismayed at conditions there following the Arab Revolt of 1936–38. Within

Hehalutz, many sought to immigrate but were still unable to obtain certificates. The organization was on the verge of collapse as a result. Membership declined by 25 percent, and life on the training farms was increasingly difficult. Members were unable to secure employment because of anti-Semitic sentiment and had to be supported by their families to avoid starvation. The hardships and lack of hope for immigration were extremely discouraging. Bezalel Schwartz, a member of Hehalutz, observed that, based on the number of certificates granted Hehalutz in the preceding years—200 in 1936, 250 in 1937, and 363 in 1938—it would take twenty years for those on the training farms to immigrate legally.[13]

Thus, illegal immigration was reconsidered in order to save the movement. In November 1936, the central council of Hehalutz demanded that the Jewish Agency espouse a policy supportive of independent aliyah. Eliyahu Dobkin, assistant head of the Jewish Agency aliyah section, took part in the central council meeting and promised to raise the matter before the Agency's leadership. Yehuda Braginsky, who was at that time an emissary in Hehalutz, also promised to press for support for organized illegal immigration following his return to Palestine in April 1937.[14]

At that time, however, little support could be mustered. Palestine was gripped by the Arab Revolt. It constituted one of the most difficult points in the history of the Yishuv. The Zionist leadership was widely criticized, by the labor movement and the Haganah as well as by the Revisionists and centrists for restraining its reaction to Arab assaults. The Jewish Agency was pressed to mobilize all its resources for defense, which required cooperation with the British. Those who had supported illegal immigration earlier—Tabenkin, the leaders of Hakibbutz Hameuhad, and Golomb (the leader of the Haganah)—were solely preoccupied with the daily problems of defense.

Despite the leadership's efforts to deal with the revolt, criticism grew within labor Zionist ranks following the 1937 Peel Commission partition proposal. Those opposing partition were convinced that Britain had become implacably hostile to the creation of a Jewish national home and that further cooperation with Britain was useless. As a means of strengthening their numbers in the Palestinian electorate, they set out to aid Hehalutz members who wished to immigrate.

As a renewed illegal aliyah effort was being contemplated, the successes of Moshe Galili exerted an electrifying impact on members of Hehalutz and the Hakibbutz Hameuhad movement. Galili's efforts came to be known as "despite-it-all" aliyah.[15] Moshe Galili (Krivosheyn) was a young Palestinian Jew who harbored Revisionist sympathies (though he remained politically neutral). Galili committed himself to the cause of clandestine immigration after encounters with German Jewish refugees in Paris. He believed that a vigorous Zionist campaign of secret immigration could restore to these morally and materially destitute people their sense of human dignity and instill in them the capacity to cope with their fate. He set out to persuade them by example that illegal immigration was a feasible solution to their plight.

Enlisting the support of the leaders of the Maccabi, a Zionist athletic organization in Paris, and of prominent Revisionists in Vienna (among them a young lawyer, Willi Perl), Galili organized his first illegal voyage in April 1937. Among the passengers were fifteen Betar members. The boat's landing in Palestine was arranged by members of the Revisionist party and Irgun, an underground military organization in Palestine that opposed the views of the Haganah and was allied with the Revisionist movement. The plan elicited the support of Eri Jabotinsky (Ze'ev Jabotinsky's son), the leader of Betar in Palestine. The success of his first attempt won Galili broad support among the Revisionists in Vienna, who arranged for Galili to meet with Mordecai Katz, Betar's chief in Vienna. Galili and Katz agreed on a system for bringing Betar members to Palestine, under which Galili arranged the details of transport and Betar organized the groups of immigrants.

Galili and the Revisionists in Austria worked together until the summer of 1938, during which time five voyages were undertaken, all of them successful. Differences of opinion over financial arrangements and the composition of the immigrant groups caused Galili to break off his activity, even though he had not yet begun to act on his original goal of transporting German Jewish refugees in Paris. The Revisionists continued the operation, which reached significant proportions and became well known among Jewish communities.

Galili's successes electrified the Hehalutz leaders and aliyah activists. The first Hehalutz vessel of this second period, *Poseidon,* sailed in January 1938, seven months after Galili's first transport. However, Hehalutz's determination to renew illegal immigration was tentative; wholesale adoption of a policy of illegal immigration would have transgressed the movement's tradition of identification with and obedience to the political leadership of the Yishuv. Within Zionist and Labor Federation circles, Galili and the Revisionists' recent operations were considered yet another form of Revisionist political demonstration from which they ought to distance themselves. Other voyages were arranged by Hehalutz in this period—the second voyage of *Poseidon* in May 1938 and two voyages of the *Artemis* in April and July 1938—but little operational support for them was offered by the labor Zionist organizations in the Yishuv.

Despite the ambiguous situation, operational routines began to be established: David Nameri of the Haganah instituted disembarkation techniques and coordinated landings with escorts assigned to each illegal vessel, usually men from the Haganah. Nameri also formed a working group made up mostly of Hakibbutz Hameuhad members. The successes of the *Poseidon* and the *Artemis* were a very persuasive factor in the later decision to continue and expand operations, not least because they boosted the morale and thereby the commitment of the aliyah activists.

That Hehalutz succeeded in establishing an illegal immigration operation was in large measure due to its character as a movement of revolution in Jewish life, such that its members were prevented from being absorbed into the adult Jewish communities surrounding them. In a similar way, Betar adopted a rebellious stance toward Jewish life in the Diaspora and gave expression to its ideology through individual and collective activism. Betar fulfilled Jabotinsky's calls for "adventurism" through the appearance of boats on the horizon. In the last analysis, it was in the Zionist idea itself and in the youth movements' uninhibited credo of action on its behalf that the seeds of aliyah bet were planted. Illegal immigration was their response to the situation in the Diaspora on the one hand, and to immigration restrictions in Palestine on the other—whether imposed by the British or devised by the Zionist establishment.

Toward the end of 1938 and the first months of 1939, aliyah bet came to be adopted as policy by both Hehalutz and the Revisionists, and formal bodies were established to organize it. Two factors were decisive in bringing about this development: the intensified pressure on Jews to leave the Reich following the Anschluss between Austria and Nazi Germany in March 1938 and the Kristallnacht, and the wavering British policy toward the Jewish national home, which came to be embodied in the White Paper of 1939, and which spurred the Zionists to replace cooperation with protest and rebellion. As the situation of Jews in Germany and Austria became more urgent than that of Polish Jewry, aliyah bet became a movement of rescue per se, even before the Final Solution became a reality. Aliyah bet at this time came to be understood as a mission undertaken to save Jews from violence and persecution as well as from situations in which they could neither work nor maintain themselves economically.

The Revisionist movement organized the Center for Aliyah in January 1939 in Paris, and leading figures in the movement, such as Shlomo Yaakobi, Hillel Kook, and Eri Jabotinsky, took part in its establishment. The Haganah created the Aliyah bet Agency (Mossad), based in Paris. Its personnel was drawn from Hehalutz and movement representatives from Palestine who had acquired experience organizing aliyah bet. Its staff included Shaul Meirov-Avigur, and a leading member of the Haganah was nominated to head it. At this time, numerous individuals began to organize illegal voyages as well. These came from various Jewish communities, and most had Revisionist connections.

The expanded activity in 1938 and 1939 represented a considerable proportion of the great Jewish exodus from Nazi Germany. From 1938 until the outbreak the war in August 1939, 257,878 Jews left their home countries; of these 103,379 were German Jews, 119,409 Austrian, and 35,000 Czechoslovakian. Of this total, 40,147 reached Palestine, and 17,240 of these, or almost one-half, were illegal. Illegal immigrants to Palestine made up 7.4 percent of all Jewish emigrants during this period.[16] The Revisionists (and private individuals) were responsible for the transport of some 12,000 illegal immigrants, and Hehalutz and the Mossad for some 5,500. At least 80 percent of the passengers on Revisionist and private boats were German and Austrian Jews. Some 52 percent of the legal and illegal immigrants to Palestine were German and Austrian Jews, yet they constituted more than 70 percent of all illegal immigrants. Hehalutz and Mossad vessels predominantly carried Jews from Poland, who constituted 25 percent of all Jewish immigrants to Palestine

The *Atrato*, spring 1939.

Refugees on the *Atrato*, spring 1939.

Refugees on the *Colorado*, spring 1939.

during this period. Jews from the Reich constituted only 15 percent of those traveling on board Hehalutz and Mossad boats.

The chief target of Mossad and Hehalutz transport operations remained Polish Zionist youth, although a growing number of German and Austrian Jews began to be included in the voyages (amounting to about 30 percent of the passengers). The discipline and preparation of the youth ameliorated the often harsh conditions at sea. For these, illegal aliyah constituted the final, climactic step toward personal fulfillment of their Zionist ideal, and therefore they bore up well under the inconvenience, hardship, and danger of this concluding stretch of their journey. The sea passages organized by Hehalutz and the Mossad were efficient, well planned, and brief, usually lasting from ten to fourteen days (except for the voyage of the *Tiger Hill*). Disembarkation was arranged through communication with Haganah squads on shore, and two-thirds of the Mossad vessels landed without attracting notice of the British.

Conditions on Revisionist and privately operated boats were often difficult. On boats carrying groups of Betar members, a sense of order and organization prevailed. However, later voyages contained fewer and fewer Betar members, and refugees from the Reich made up the majority of passengers—well over 80 percent. The greater the social differences among passengers, the more strenuous the voyages, exacerbated as they were by conditions of extreme overcrowding and grossly inadequate sanitary facilities. Provisions were in short supply on many voyages as well (on board *Liesel, Aster,* and *Ageus Nicolaus,* for example). Transfer of passengers to shore, in the case of the Revisionists, was coordinated with the Irgun command onshore, and two Irgun escorts were aboard each vessel to facilitate landing. The Revisionists often operated without the necessary secrecy, and the British came to know of their plans weeks in advance. Consequently, almost 90 percent of their boats were intercepted by British authorities, and the boats were forced to pull away from the coast time and again, adding weeks to the journey. Privately chartered boats suffered from an inordinate amount of engine trouble and in some cases sank (*Rim, Prosula,* and the second voyage of the *Geppo*). Some passengers on private boats and on Revisionist boats were charged exorbitant sums.

The route most often used by privately operated and Revisionist boats was down the Danube to the Black Sea. The Danube's status as an international waterway eliminated the need for transit visas. At first, the Mossad avoided this route because of the difficulty of concealing operations on the river. But as transit visas to cross Europe grew harder to obtain, the Mossad also began to take the Danube route. (The *Tiger Hill* and *Colorado* passengers sailed this way.) Ports in Greece, Yugoslavia, and Italy were also used as points of embarkation until British pressure on these governments caused them to prohibit their use by illegal immigrant boats.

The clandestine aliyah organized by the Revisionists and by private individuals came about in direct response to the plight of the Jews of the Reich. Its *modus operandi* and scope were shaped by developments in the predicament of the German Jews. The more extreme Nazi policy became, the greater was the number of illegal immigrants brought out. Thus, the total conveyed by the Revisionists was more than double that of Hehalutz and the Mossad, who reacted much more slowly to the changing reality.

Both the Mossad and the Revisionist movements suffered from a lack of resources, preventing them from buying or chartering larger and better ships and from further expanding the immigration program. Both movements had plans to purchase ships that came to naught because they lacked the necessary funds. Yehuda Braginsky conjectured that had the Mossad been able to command the necessary resources, it could have organized the immigration of 100,000 people. The Revisionists, too, were convinced that much more could have been done given the proper support.

The Zionist Political Leadership, 1938 to 1939

The Jewish Agency leadership's opposition to illegal immigration began to falter in 1938. The severe limits on immigration, the partition recommendations of the Peel Commission, and the drastic proposals of the Woodhead Commission signaled to them that British deviations from the goals set out in the Balfour Declaration were not temporary measures, but instead marked a major shift in direction—amounting to a retreat from the establishment of a Jewish national home in Palestine. At this stage (prior to the publication of the 1939 White Paper), Ben-Gurion and Moshe Shertok began to support illegal immigration. Ben-Gurion saw illegal immigration as a tool in the struggle to change British policy—one that would force it to end concessions to the Arabs. He envisioned an immigration rebellion against Britain that would be based on the fate of Jewish refugees, one of the central moral components of the Zionist cause.[17] In a meeting of the Jewish Agency on 11 November 1938, Ben-Gurion stated:

> What we need is neither a selective aliyah nor a broad-based aliyah, but a mass aliyah of hundreds of thousands. . . . Without a mass aliyah Zionism is liable to fail, and we are liable to lose this country. . . . [We must] wage a battle not *for* aliyah, but *through* aliyah. . . .
>
> We must try to find a way to join the refugee question and the question of [the Yishuv in] Palestine, and to block England's obstinate attempt to separate the two.

Ben-Gurion's idea was to organize dozens of boats to arrive in broad daylight, and thus force the British to appear before the world as they denied entry to Jewish refugees fleeing Nazi persecution. In this sense, Ben-Gurion's approach was similar to Jabotinsky's. Both saw illegal immigration as a weapon of provocation in the struggle against Britain.

Ben-Gurion put forth his plan to the Mossad leadership in early 1939 while in London to attend the St. James roundtable conference on Palestine. The immigration activists welcomed the idea of expanding their efforts, but assigning such means and ends for aliyah bet disturbed them. To make a spectacle of it for the sake of the media or the British government would compromise their *modus operandi,* their organization, and the identities of those involved. Just such tactics—an exploitation of the rescue effort for political ends—were the chief criticism that the Mossad leveled against the Revisionist Center for Aliyah.

Ben-Gurion had hoped to raise enough support in London to finance a thoroughly revamped illegal immigration campaign on a mass scale. Eliyahu Golomb and Shaul Avigur had accompanied him there to help raise funds, but the fruits of their efforts were meager. Considerable dissent existed over whether endorsement of aliyah bet was an appropriate course of action. Chaim Weizmann and labor moderates led by Yosef Sprinzak felt that brazenly flouting the law of the land was incompatible with Zionism's nature as a moral force. Moreover, they regarded an open confrontation with the British over illegal immigration as rash and ill-advised. They proposed instead to apply pressure on the British and to resist the White Paper of 1939 on the grounds that in it Britain had violated its solemn duties sworn to in the League of Nations Mandate. They held fast to the view of Britain as the traditional ally of the Zionist enterprise, whose role no other country could fill, especially given the current international crises that threatened to deteriorate into war.

Richard Lichtheim, the head of the Jewish Agency's office adjacent to the League of Nations, trusted that an agreement to expand the legal immigration quotas might yet be reached if plans for illegal immigration were abandoned. Lichtheim's objections were grounded in fears that aliyah bet would discredit Zionism among Diaspora Jewish communities and non-Jews. It would invite charges of exploitation and irresponsibility for the entire movement, as it had for the Revisionists. The fact of who organized which voyages would not be apparent; all those who supported aliyah bet would be open to criticism.[18]

Despite the controversy, the approval of eminent figures such as Shertok and Ben-Gurion tremendously encouraged the Mossad's aliyah bet activists. In their eyes, it legitimated previous operations as well as the tactics in place—the Haganah's disembarkation routines, training of escorts, and long-range planning—crucial elements of successful rescue operations.

In contrast to the debate that raged over the propriety or impropriety of aliyah bet with regard to British policy, Berl Katznelson accorded the effort a formulation based on the historical fate of the Jews. Katznelson had supported aliyah bet since 1933. He spoke at the Twenty-First Zionist Congress, held in Geneva in August 1939 on the eve of the Second World War. The international congress was not to reconvene until after the war was finished.

Katznelson spoke of the current emergency in Europe as "expulsion." His choice of the term directly linked current events to the Jewish expulsions of the past and assigned both events a common historical context, the continuation of one fate.[19] Seen in this light, aliyah bet could no longer be seen as the task of one movement or group within the Jewish people; it was a reflection of and a response to the Jewish fate in its entirety. Secret immigration—whatever its organizational background—ought to be the inspiration guiding the nation at that hour. Katznelson phrased this imperative in moving terms:

> We do not determine the course of history, and neither can we foresee what it will bring. We may ask why it is that history did not choose free, wealthy and well-behaved Jews to be the bearers of its mission, but preferred instead the Jewish refugees, the most wretched of all humankind, cast adrift on the seas. But this is a fact we cannot change. This is what history has determined, and it is left to us to accept its choice and to follow the refugee.[20]

Katznelson broke with his own movement's past insistence on a selective approach to aliyah and stressed that the task at hand was not to decide who should immigrate, but how to arrange to bring over whoever was able to, legally or illegally. Through settlement in Palestine, the Land of Israel, Zionism had created a new reality, one that held out "real, practical help in the midst of the great catastrophe," unlike the situation at the turn of the century when masses of Jews fled the pogroms in Russia but no organized Jewish community existed in Palestine to come to their aid. Katznelson continued, asking, "What, after all, is Zionism all about? Summer camps? Sabbath eve gatherings? Had not its aim always been, since Pinsker and Herzl, to provide a true salvation for the Jewish people?"

Katznelson insisted that responsibility for the stream of illegal immigrants lay with the entire Jewish leadership—Zionist and non-Zionist alike—and that united it must rally all possible support in keeping with the traditional Jewish values of mutual responsibility and assistance.[21] Their standard-bearer would be the refugee himself.

Katznelson spoke of the crisis in terms of the historical continuity of Jewish fate and went on to liken it to shared experiences in modern Jewish history. He compared the decision now confronting the Jews to the decision over the Uganda Scheme at the beginning of the century, which nearly dissolved the World Zionist Organization. The Uganda Scheme, debated at the Sixth and Seventh Zionist Congresses, had pitted Zionists against each other over the question of whether to accept Uganda as a Jewish national home, and the offer of immediate asylum it represented, or to continue toward the dream of acquiring the land of Israel for the Jewish people. Katznelson reflected:

> The Uganda crisis occurred when there was almost no Yishuv, no Jewish Palestine to speak of. Despite all that has been destroyed since then in the Jewish world, at least now there is the basic foundation of a nation in its own land, the vanguard of a nation that is ready to fight for its freedom and its homeland and stands with open arms to welcome its brethren. In and around Palestine we have built up the kind of strength that we have lacked throughout the history of the Exile.

Katznelson's speech laid the basis for widespread support of illegal aliyah in the Yishuv. It is impossible to judge whether or not Katznelson's ideas might have been translated into a full-fledged plan of action, political and diplomatic. The war intervened, rendering it impossible to maintain an organized program of aliyah bet, even though the need had never been greater.

I

ILLEGAL IMMIGRATION IN THE FIRST YEARS OF WORLD WAR II

2

An Ambivalent Zionist Leadership

Primary Considerations

Britain's declaration of war against Nazi Germany in September 1939 complicated the Zionist position toward aliyah bet. It created paradoxes of basic interests: an opposition to British White Paper policy and a strong support and identification with Great Britain in its war against Nazi Germany. Since aliyah bet was the principal means of Zionist opposition to British policy, its continuation following the start of the war was a source of debate among Zionists. Many favored full cooperation with Britain and felt that any actions that would divert British resources from the war effort were unethical.[1] More important and more interesting, however, is the position of the Zionist leadership in Palestine who recognized and tried to reconcile the fact that adopting one position or the other closed off vital concerns, ultimately forcing a choice between Zionist interests and Jewish values, one, which we will see, the leadership avoided making because of its fundamental contradictions to their basic values.

In the early days of the war, Ben-Gurion gave what was to be the guiding formulation of the Zionist position toward Britain and aliyah. In discussions of the Mapai central committee session of 12 September 1939, he stated that "We must aid the [British] army as if there were no White Paper, and fight the White Paper as if there were no war." Five days later he again voiced his view, this time to the Jewish Agency Executive: "As to our position vis-à-vis the English, we clearly must offer absolute loyalty and full cooperation in the war effort—but as Jews, not as English subjects. Our duty is to stand up and be counted as the Jewish nation, not as individuals, and at the same time [to stress] our uncompromising opposition to the White Paper. . . . Our first duty is to the future of the Jewish people."[2] Just how the fight against the White Paper was to be waged changed with the circumstances of the war.

But how was it possible to be both for and against Britain at the same time, on an issue that cut to the very heart of Jewish interests? It certainly did not help matters that at this stage Nazi Germany still favored a mass emigration of Jews from Europe. Great Britain opposed the immigration of German Jews to British territories on the grounds that they were enemy aliens, and furthermore that among the groups of refugees the Nazis were planting

23

spies. Yet the flow of Jewish refugees from Poland and the Reich into Slo-vakia, Yugoslavia, Rumania, and Hungary continued. The need for assistance and immigration certificates mounted, but it became quite clear from the first weeks of the war that Britain would not ease its immigration regulations. Thus the need to bring people to the country in irregular ways became more acute; and for Jews from Nazi-held territories, it was their sole hope.

The Jewish Agency executive and other Zionist political bodies confronted these problems and searched for a way to resolve them without disturbing their political goals. The dilemma faced by the Zionist leadership pitted Jewish and ethical values against political considerations. Morally, aliyah bet was justifiable because it meant saving Jews; in these terms criticism of illegal immigration was unthinkable. Economically and politically, one had to be willing to weigh aliyah bet against a variety of other factors, reckoning its contribution to the Zionist cause in a rational manner. The scope of the Jewish refugee problem was simply overwhelming in relation to the size and resources of the Yishuv. The Yishuv was capable of, and obligated to building the national home for the sake of the future of the Jewish people. Only in that way could it hope to provide a solution in the future. But in the interim, this required placing priority on the problems facing the Jews in Palestine, rather than those of the Diaspora.

Zionism saw itself, above all, as bearing the primary responsibility for the fate of the Jewish people. Aliyah bet posed a problem of conscience for the Zionist leadership, and its intractability was a function of the ideological and emotional block against admitting the possibility that Zionist interests and basic Jewish values could be in conflict with each other. The conflict was much more profound than simply the arguments for and against. Illegal im-migration was the cause of deep personal ambivalence and inner conflict—sometimes never truly resolved—and it was not unusual to harbor favorable and unfavorable views at the same time.

Because of the Jewish Agency's status as an official body responsible to the British Mandatory authorities, discussions on aliyah bet—an act of direct defiance to the British—were entered into the minutes only indirectly—in general deliberations on Zionist policy regarding immigration taken in re-sponse to concrete, pressing problems. This helps explain how individuals sometimes expressed different and conflicting views. Discussions on the sub-ject also took place in the labor party bodies—in the Mapai committee meet-ings and in meetings of the Histadrut, which played an important role in internal political matters as well as in relations with Diaspora Jewry. State-ments are also found in letters and private diaries, and these are more clear and candid. The issue was also widely discussed in the press, though many facts were concealed on account of British censorship. Indeed, newspapers were often temporarily closed for publishing information or editorials hostile to the British. The most telling evidence of individuals' actual standpoints on aliyah bet is revealed in concrete decisions, actions taken, and budgetary support for it.

Formal discussion of aliyah bet took place mainly during two limited periods: during the early months of the war, in response to many pressing requests for aid to immigrants and refugees, and from November 1940 to January 1941, in response to the arrival of three ships—the *Milos,* the *Pacific,* and the *Atlantic*—an illegal transport of over 3,000 people. In fact, however, it never ceased being of compelling relevance. The arguments for and against aliyah bet in the early stages of the war were basically given on economic, moral, and political grounds. An investigation of the arguments posed provides a better understanding of the circumstances that confronted the Zionist leadership and why it was impossible for them to declare themselves for or against.

Eliezer Kaplan, treasurer of the Jewish Agency, voiced the classic position linking immigration to the economic absorptive capacity of the country in a Jewish Agency debate of 30 October 1939.[3] The discussion concerned a plan proposed to the executive for the immigration of 2,600 persons, including refugees from Poland who had reached Rumania as well as refugees from Nazi-held territories who were facing expulsion back to the Reich. The plan was an expression of the Yishuv's concern given the needs that had arisen during the first months of war. Kaplan demanded that any decision to bring the refugees to Palestine be accompanied by an allocation to cover two months' resettlement costs for all. He contended that it was simply impossible to absorb a mass immigration, given the ongoing economic crisis and high unemployment.

Kaplan argued that neither the kibbutzim nor private industry was capable of accepting scores of new arrivals. All of Palestine's resources were stretched to the breaking point: the kibbutzim had already lowered the daily subsistence budget of their members to a bare minimum. In addition, the refugees already in the country imposed a massive burden on the treasury; the Agency was already spending large sums on relief for immigrants (about ten percent of its budget). The hostels for new immigrants were crowded with illegals who had no place to go. Kaplan maintained that only by providing for resettlement costs could Palestine absorb the refugees in question; however, to allocate such a sum would drain the treasury and require the cessation of all other Agency programs.

He concluded that a decision in favor of mass immigration at this time would be unconscionable and irresponsible. The situation of the Jews in Austria under the heel of the Gestapo was indeed grave, but, he pointed out, there were others in the same position in Prague and in other places. Palestine was in no position to attempt to offer a solution to the entire Jewish Diaspora. He warned the Jewish Agency executive against precipitous decisions that invited disaster. The executive turned down Kaplan's demand, and he threatened to resign. As a compromise, the executive decided to allocate funds for the immigration of 1,200 people and refused to accept Kaplan's tendered resignation.

The economic argument, extreme as it was, received the backing of others in the Jewish Agency. Rabbi Fishman stated that the threat of hunger was serious among the Yishuv. Dr. Emil Shmorek, representing the General

Zionists, also argued that further immigration should not proceed as long as the pressing economic situation continued. He recommended that money for European refugee relief be paid out of funds in European accounts earmarked for Palestine that were now blocked because of wartime currency-transfer restrictions.

Indeed, Palestine was in the midst of an economic recession that continued to worsen during the first years of the war. It had been in an economic recession since the end of 1937, and income per capita had decreased since then at a rate of ten percent per year. The economic situation deteriorated further in the first months of the war because it was almost impossible to export goods to Europe—especially citrus, the economy's chief cash crop.[4] The Jewish Agency's treasury was quite limited. It depended primarily on contributions given to the national funds and on special fund-raising drives in the Diaspora. It had no authority to tax the Yishuv population; sales tax and other forms of taxation went to the Mandate government. The Jewish Agency could propose voluntary taxation of the Jewish community, which it had done since the summer of 1938, and it could also ask the government to support it in special loans. Once the war started, however, its treasury budgets shrank from 811,514 Palestinian pounds in 1939 to 799,117 in 1940.

Ben-Gurion, for his part, disagreed with Kaplan's conclusions. However, he understood Kaplan's reasoning given his responsibility as treasurer and his reading of Palestine's economic constraints.[5] In a report to the Mapai political committee, he characterized the Agency debate as being of fundamental significance, pitting pragmatic Zionists against visionary Zionists.[6] Among the visionaries, Ben-Gurion noted, were those who argued that aliyah was not a means, but rather an end in itself with the purely humane purpose of saving lives.

Among the members of Mapai, this view was echoed. Yitzhak Ben-Aharon rebuked the kibbutz movement for yielding to economic considerations rather than accept new immigrants and called these actions a grotesque distortion of Zionism.[7] Aaron Zisling noted that Palestine was relatively well off, with but a few actually threatened with hunger. He contended that "Anyone who calls for a halt in immigration at a time [like this] negates our very right to stand on this soil." Shmuel Dayan reiterated this view, arguing that continued aliyah took precedence over the Yishuv's economic development, even should it jeopardize that drive. He stated that "We here are no more privileged nor entitled to any more than Jews elsewhere. . . . There is no choice; aliyah must continue."[8] Berl Katznelson objected to the discussion of aliyah bet in terms of utilitarian calculations. Aliyah and rescue, he argued, had to be viewed as a historic movement, an expression of instinctive feelings of national unity, common destiny, and mutual responsibility. Rescue and immigration could not be judged in terms of success or failure. They were their own justification.[9]

The Yishuv had put forth the plan to aid the 2,600 refugees in response to the new needs arising from the war in late 1939. However, those opposing and supporting the plan on economic and ethical grounds were not of a single mind on the issue of aliyah bet in general. These were their stances in this specific, concrete plan. Kaplan, though he voiced strong opposition on economic grounds in this case and in others, did not rule out aid for aliyah entirely. On several other occasions, he released funds for it. On the other hand, the proponents of the ethical argument for aliyah bet in this case chose to see it in terms of political calculations in later episodes and denied it their support.

The Political Approach

Parallel with these considerations, the question of support for aliyah bet was also weighed in terms of the political goal of establishing a Jewish state after the war. When the war ended, the prewar balance of power would be upset. The Zionist movement's position and influence at that time would affect the outcome of any reevaluation of policy and goals by the British—regarding both immigration and statehood. As Moshe Shertok put it:

> Our general assumption must be that the world's fate, the Jewish people's fate and our fate here in Palestine are inseparable. All will be affected by the outcome of this war, and we want to be in a position to influence that outcome.[10]

Political conditions were in a state of flux throughout the first years of the war, and perceptions of how the movement could influence them to its advantage changed with them. In the war's early months, many believed that supporting a large-scale aliyah, which would provide the Yishuv with strength in numbers in postwar bargaining, was the preferred course of action. Eliezer Liebenstein, a member of Mapai, stressed in September 1939 that although a swift victory for Britain was vitally important for the Jewish people, it was also liable to impede the creation of a Jewish state in Palestine. Therefore, as long as sea travel remained possible (before Italy's impending entry into the war), networks and mechanisms for organizing aliyah bet had to be established in neutral countries and the maximum number of immigrants transported.[11]

Menachem Ussishkin, one of the senior members of the Jewish Agency executive and a founding father of the Zionist movement, maintained that a million hungry Jews in Palestine would be a far more potent force for Zionism than a hundred thousand well-fed ones. He stressed that the end of aliyah would spell the end of Zionism.[12] Other leaders saw aliyah bet as necessary in obtaining American Jewry's support for Zionism.[13] (Later, in 1941, Eliyahu Golomb posed another political argument for continuing secret immigration work: that it would aid in preparing the Jews of Palestine to wage a political struggle at war's end, when there would be no alternative but an organized mass immigration.)

Hence support for aliyah bet was strong when, in fall 1939, the British announced that no immigration quota would be issued for the next six-month period (October to April). The Mossad, which had virtually dismantled its operations following the outbreak of the war, reorganized itself for secret aliyah work as a result of this British action (and of a decision reached by the Yishuv that though conditions were dangerous, its emissaries were vital to support European Jews at this time). Thus, the Mossad established bases in Geneva and in other centers.

However, by early 1940 support for illegal immigration had declined, and a policy of cooperation with the British came to be favored.[14] In January 1940, key members of the Jewish Agency—Ben-Gurion, Shertok, Kaplan, and several others—held an unofficial meeting in which the Agency's role in illegal aliyah was debated—whether the Agency could support this activity in the open, in secret, or at all; and what the political and economic ramifications would be of any of these choices.

The meeting went unrecorded, but from the little evidence that exists, it appears that the opponents of aliyah bet gained the upper hand.[15] Shertok's actions shortly thereafter seem to confirm this. He informed the Mossad's Geneva office in February 1940 that aliyah bet operations were to be suspended. The Mossad members protested and emphasized the absence of any alternative for the Jews whom Hitler was forcing from Europe.[16] Entries in Shertok's diary show that he was moved and convinced by the Mossad's arguments, yet he did little to advance this point of view among his colleagues.

In May 1940, Zvi Yehieli, of the Mossad office in Geneva, met with Ben-Gurion, Kaplan, Weizmann, and Shertok in London, to advocate for continued support of aliyah bet operations and received an ambiguous response.[17] Kaplan claimed that the decision to withdraw from these activities had already been reached in Jerusalem (in the unofficial meeting). Ben-Gurion maintained that a decision had been made but it was somewhat different: though the Agency had agreed to disclaim responsibility for secret aliyah, all material and other support for it had not necessarily been canceled. Throughout 1940, this uncertainty prevailed.

The main factor tending to weaken support for aliyah bet at this time was the plan to create a Jewish army from among the Yishuv and Jewish volunteers from neutral countries to participate in the war under British high command. In early 1940, Ben-Gurion and others were quite optimistic that the plan's goals would be realized. Talks about the possibility of Jews assisting the British in the event of a war had been held in the months prior to September 1939 between Zionists and British politicians sympathetic to Zionism. In December, further discussions were held with British army officials. The support of Field Marshal Ironside (the Imperial Army chief of staff) and Orde Wingate (whose connection with the Yishuv was long-standing) created an auspicious outlook for the plan's success. With Winston Churchill's election as prime minister in May 1940, the plan seemed to gain considerable support among British politicians. (Churchill had for long been greatly supportive of Zionism.) Discussions progressed quite well and reached a very advanced stage: different forms of organization, training programs, and special fields of action for the Jewish army were elaborated. In fall 1940, however, the opposition in the British Cabinet managed to block the plan's realization.

The Zionist leadership's decision to cooperate with the British to the detriment of aliyah bet operations seemed rational given their knowledge of the circumstances. In 1940, there was no way of knowing how long the war would last and in what direction the fate of European Jewry was developing. The accounts of violence against Jews that reached Palestine from Poland and other European countries were understood as part of the horrors and atrocities of war—the results, some believed, of the chaos that reigned. The situation of the Jews under Nazi anti-Semitism did not seem to be uniquely different from that of the Poles. One should keep in mind that the Final Solution—the deliberate plan to exterminate all European Jewry—did not commence until the summer of 1941, after the war with the Soviet Union had begun.

Ben-Gurion's and Shertok's Ambivalence

The attitudes of Ben-Gurion and Moshe Shertok are of great importance here, since their respective roles as Jewish Agency chairman and political department head gave them most responsibility for policy. In the early months of the war, Ben-Gurion had argued that aliyah and the ongoing efforts to sustain it were essential to the fate of the Zionist enterprise in Palestine. He held that aliyah would shape the future of the Yishuv: its strength and, moreover, its character. However, as the year 1940 wore on, successful aliyah operations grew fewer and the costs of maintaining them began to appear to outweigh their results. Ben-Gurion began to doubt the advisability of jeopardizing the opportunity to cooperate with the British for such a risky enterprise. Uppermost in his mind was the peace settlement at the end of the war, where a Yishuv that had fought alongside Britain in its hour of crisis could bargain from a strong position and demand independent statehood in Palestine as its reward.

According to Ben-Gurion, however, cooperation with the British war effort ought not to be done at the expense of obscuring the Zionist character of the Yishuv for the duration of the war. "Our role in this war is determined first of all by what we do here. . . . We make our contribution as an independent force—endowed with its own will, its own values, its own goals—and never for an instant serving only the goals of another."[18] But he concluded at this time that if the struggle for Jewish immigration entailed a weakening of British capabilities, it would have to be carefully reconsidered.

Ben-Gurion raised the issue of the role and character Zionism should take given the political realities of wartime in a session of the Agency executive on 14 April 1940. He criticized the Agency's position toward the British as unnecessarily passive—a tacit acceptance of the White Paper. He suggested a more assertive resistance—a new "fighting Zionism," in the broadest sense.[19] In his remarks he asserted that aliyah would have been the chosen weapon of fighting Zionism, but since the seas were now under British control, it had to be ruled out. He suggested instead to continue the struggle to defend

Zionist interests in other ways: through a campaign of settlement to subvert the White Paper's land regulations and through efforts to gain residency for refugees who arrived in the country illegally. At that time, many had arrived in Palestine without organized assistance; Ben-Gurion contended that intervention on their behalf was an entirely legitimate role for the Jewish Agency to play.

Thus, in Ben-Gurion's view, aliyah was not primarily a matter of rescue; rather, it was part of a greater task undertaken by the Yishuv on its own behalf, to eventually benefit the Jewish people as a whole. Thus in November 1939, for example, when the Jewish Agency was called upon to press for the entry of 2,900 German Jews who had been issued immigration certificates before war broke out, Ben-Gurion chose to give priority to political considerations instead. (The British opposed allowing the refugees to proceed on the grounds that they were now enemy aliens and that there were likely to be spies among them.) He preferred to put priority on the chances of successful negotiations with the British; the importance of a one-time rescue could not be equated with the possibility of winning significant concessions from the British.[20] Nevertheless, Ben-Gurion did not agree with Kaplan's position either—that the Agency should take no part in aid and support for illegal immigration. Ben-Gurion was ambivalent: his pragmatism as a political strategist did not entirely eclipse his deep commitment to basic Zionist and Jewish values, and he was thus unable to ignore the aliyah activists or the plight of the refugees. He was truly torn between the two.

Like Ben-Gurion, Moshe Shertok believed that the way to win concessions for Zionism lay in cooperation and negotiations with the British. He, too, put priority on supporting Britain in its virtually solitary battle against Hitler. However, he opposed taking a firm line of opposition toward Britain, and in this respect believed Ben-Gurion acted with insufficient caution. He preferred to maintain constant political pressure in London over the issues of aliyah and settlement rather than promote resistance among the Yishuv.

Aliyah bet, for Shertok, was a matter of rescue rather than a means of building up the political strength of the Yishuv. From a political standpoint, he believed that immigrants had to be well prepared and thus preferred an Agency-supervised immigration.[21] However, he did not trust in British intimations that restrictions might be eased if illegal immigration were to cease.[22] Moreover, he was fully aware that the forces driving the Jews to flee Nazi-occupied Europe were considerably more powerful than any other factor. This determined his position on the matter of the 2,900 German Jewish certificate holders: this was something concrete that could be done for German Jewry, whereas anything to be gained out of negotiations with the British was, at that point, still academic. Shertok also opposed the idea of bidding for British favor by having the Jewish Agency officially announce an end to illegal immigration. Such a course had been proposed to him in February 1940 by Richard Lichtheim, the Agency's representative to the League of Nations in Geneva.[23]

Nevertheless, ambivalence prevailed in Shertok's stance as well. Though he recognized the question of aliyah bet as one of utmost urgency, he did not in fact advance that position in party or Agency discussions. Time and again, he hesitated and instead looked for a modification of British policy to come about as the result of the new wartime Cabinet's changed political profile.[24] It was not clear to him that it was worth embarking on a provocative campaign for illegal immigration at that juncture. At times he supported the idea and at others rejected it. On other occasions, he was unable to decide at all. He was thus even more ambivalent then Ben-Gurion was.

This failure to make a decisive choice characterized Zionist policy over an extended period of time. Since very few immigrant boats arrived during 1940, the leadership was not confronted with the task of addressing the issue in an unequivocal, precise fashion. The Agency did not oppose the organization of Mossad bases in Geneva and elsewhere in the fall of 1939, but neither did it render the requisite support; the ambiguity of their situation did not go unnoticed by Mossad members.[25] Their principal support came from American Zionists and the American Jewish Joint Distribution Committee (the JDC).[26] The Agency acted in a few specific cases, but otherwise it restricted its role to obtaining legal entry for Zionist movement stalwarts in Nazi-occupied lands. We find little general information about the situation in Europe in records of the Agency executive or party bodies.

The Debate Over the Three Ships

It was the arrival of three ships—the *Milos,* the *Pacific,* and the *Atlantic*—that brought about serious questioning and reappraisal in the Zionist establishment. The ships arrived off Palestine in November 1940 and were immediately seized by the British. The transport had been organized by Berthold Storfer, who had organized Jewish emigration from Austria and Germany with the approval of the Jewish community and the consent of Nazi authorities.[27] The ships carried many active Zionists from Germany and Czechoslovakia and many who had children in Palestine and who had invested heavily in the country. All had lived through the Nazi threat over the first year of the war; some had experienced concentration camps and others had been saved from deportation to Poland. All were eager to leave the Reich. It was an unquestioned case of rescue, of life or death.

However, the timing of the arrival was inauspicious: Britain was then in its loneliest hour in its heroic fight against Hitler's Reich. It was a time of absolute solidarity between the British public and government. The British had feared a large-scale organized exodus of Jews from the Reich, and the transport was seen as the beginning of a massive wave, not as one of the last in an all-too-short series of successes, as it turns out to have been.

By November 1940, none of the plans for the Yishuv's participation as a political entity in the war effort had been satisfactorily realized, nor had there been any softening of the British line on the White Paper. Furthermore, though the number of illegal immigrants in 1940 had been insignificant, no immigration quota had been issued for the first half of 1941.[28] The British shortly unveiled a plan to deport the ships' passengers from Palestine. The plan epitomized British immigration policy in general and posed the question once again of how the Yishuv leadership would respond.

On 3 November 1940, twelve days before the first of the ships, the *Pacific,* arrived in Haifa Harbor, Moshe Shertok reported to the Jewish Agency executive that an illegal immigrant ship carrying one thousand passengers would soon arrive offshore and that others would soon follow.[29] He noted that there was reason to fear that the British would not grant new entry permits for the period October 1940 to April 1941, and thus the arrival of an illegal ship was a partial consolation. The British practice since the summer of 1939 had been to subtract illegal entrants from the quota of permits (or from future quotas in the case of the many periods for which no schedules were issued), thus allowing them to remain in the country. However, before the three ships even arrived in port, the British revealed a seemingly draconian plan to discourage further immigration: to transfer the illegal immigrants on an old vessel, the *Patria,* to Mauritius, an island under British control that had been prepared as a center for detainees—political exiles and refugees.

The new British policy constituted a strict formulation of the White Paper, against which the Zionist leadership felt compelled to protest vigorously. Shertok, in an effort to prevent the pending deportation, contacted Berl Locker, head of the Agency's political office in London, on November 7. Shertok urged that the Zionist leaders in London make representations to the Cabinet, recruit the aid of public figures and friendly members of Parliament, and attempt to rally public opinion against the scheme.[30] (Similar requests to arouse public opinion were also made to the American Zionists.) However, Shertok felt pessimistic about the chances of success. From his talks with British officials, he knew quite well that the plan to send Jewish refugees to Mauritius would cause little or no outcry in government circles and among the British public while London was in the middle of the Blitz. British officials informed Shertok to that effect, stating that their consciences were perfectly clear on the issue of the deportations to Mauritius. The lives of the refugees were certainly not being placed at risk.[31]

Shertok was also aware that Chaim Weizmann, the president of the Zionist Organization and its most influential member in London, looked askance on illegal immigration and would be reluctant to provoke the British at such a time. Shertok voiced his doubts about Weizmann's effectiveness in this matter at a meeting of the Mapai political committee on November 7:

> Weizmann has always recoiled at the idea of illegal immigration, and he still does. It was always a burden to him, and he never speaks of it in meetings with the government. He will likely tell us that he is in the midst of delicate talks with the government on an issue of prime concern . . . and cannot take issue with them now over refugees who left Germany two months ago.[32]

Weizmann was not alone in his reluctance to press the British government on the issue of illegal immigration. Many among the Jewish Agency executive agreed that no action should be taken that might widen the breach in British-Jewish relations. Kaplan argued that the objective capabilities of the Yishuv at this time barred them from waging an isolated struggle. He acknowledged the bitter reality of the situation, but insisted that the Yishuv's scarce resources and the ships' unpropitious timing made it impossible to conduct a campaign of resistance to British policy. Kaplan opposed any public demonstration or strike and saw their only available recourse as lying in diplomatic channels.

In Kaplan's opinion Ben-Gurion's policy, "with Britain against Hitler, against Britain on the White Paper," had failed to prove itself. The war had convinced him that unqualified cooperation with Britain was called for. The arrival of two thousand illegal immigrants did not dissuade him from this conviction. Other members of the Jewish Agency executive joined Kaplan in calling for complete cooperation with the British and opposed any act of public defiance, such as the proposed strike, or other demonstrative act. All shared the concern that any further breach in relations might bring about a dangerous weakening of the Agency's standing—leaving the Yishuv vulnerable to the disastrous possibility of the British pursuing other purposes in Palestine.[33]

Shertok himself was pessimistic that British intentions could be altered by any means. Nevertheless, he criticized the timidity of the Zionist leadership and the Yishuv in a meeting of the political committee of Mapai on 21 November (after the arrival of the *Pacific* and the *Milos*).[34] Shertok favored convening a demonstrative session of the Yishuv's leading institutions—a joint meeting of the Jewish Agency executive and the National Council—to arouse public opinion and protests in the Yishuv. He also urged that pressure on London be increased. He proposed activating Mapai's connections with the British Labour party and suggested that a special emissary of the Zionist Labor party be dispatched to meet with Ernest Bevin and Clement Attlee, Labour party members of the British Cabinet. As Shertok saw it, the whole issue of illegal immigration was at stake; hence all these measures were called for.

Nonetheless, Shertok refused to consider activities beyond ones directly focused on the White Paper: he hoped to avoid a rupture of relations with Britain and thus opposed any anti-British actions as such. The proposed general strike, he felt, should be conducted as a demonstration of public mourning and must not be permitted to turn violent. He wished to calm those staging a hunger strike on board ship and reassure them of the Agency's continuing support. The next stage, accordingly, ought to be a campaign to replace high commissioner Harold MacMichael. All these steps—the general strike, demonstrations, and a joint session of Zionist public institutions—were carried out in the manner Shertok proposed.

All avenues were tried to prevent the deportation. The chief rabbis paid visits to MacMichael and pleaded with him on the passengers' behalf. Shertok himself met a few times during the month of November with Mr. McPherson, the general secretary of the Mandate administration (Shertok's usual channel of communication). In these meetings he took a restrained line, noting that he feared a great public outcry in the event of deportation, but that he was attempting to calm aroused passions. He also stressed that there was no problem with spies among the refugees, an abiding British fear, and that, as in the past, the Jewish Agency would cooperate fully with the government in this matter.[35] Yet Shertok was not encouraged by these meetings; if anything, they convinced him of Britain's determination to carry out the deportation policy. Likewise, the responses to his frequent telegrams to London asking for intervention with the Cabinet gave him little cause to hope.[36] Believing that all possible appeals had been exhausted, Shertok proposed no further or more militant action on the part of the Yishuv.

A letter from Shertok to Weizmann, written in mid-December, describes the atmosphere of tension at the time.[37]

> The Yishuv and its constituted bodies accepted the verdict. After a series of tense meetings and angry sessions of the Zionist Executive and the Delegates' Council, and after the illegal publication of pamphlets aimed at defying censorship regulations . . . there was a peaceful and dignified strike on 20 November as a sign of protest and of mourning, a sign of identification with the sad fate of those to be deported *rather than a declaration of war* [emphasis added].

Shertok refused to consider any further actions even after the government announced on November 24 that the deportees were to be banned from ever entering Palestine.

Within the Zionist leadership, there were those who championed the idea of militancy and mass actions as a means of resisting British policy. Yitzhak Gruenbaum, head of the Agency's settlement department, thought that the Agency should pledge itself to a full-scale anti-British campaign to prevent the deportation. The most extreme position was taken by Eliyahu Golomb, the head of the Haganah. Golomb called for firm action—not just diplomacy— to stop the deportation and expressed his views both in meetings of the Mapai political committee and in telegrams to his colleagues in London. To the latter he indicated that the Yishuv's response was unpredictable and that Britain would bear sole responsibility for any consequences. He instructed the London Zionists to convey this message to the British authorities.[38]

The plan to sabotage the *Patria* was put into effect on November 25, after it became clear that all diplomatic efforts to abort the deportation had failed. The plan was to prevent the ship from sailing by placing a bomb on board; the ship would be disabled and forced to remain in Palestine.[39] The operation was organized in absolute secrecy—not only from the British, but from the Zionist establishment as well. Neither the Agency executive nor the political committee of Mapai was permitted to know of it. The decision was apparently made by the top leaders of the Haganah: Golomb along with Shaul Avigur and Yisrael Galili, and with the support of Katznelson. There was no true consultation with the Agency leadership.

From the evidence available, it seems that even Shertok was unaware of the details of the plan. In the summer of 1977, Shaul Avigur related that while the arguments were taking place over the proper Zionist response to the British deportation order, in the very midst of the political and diplomatic efforts, he and Golomb went to Jerusalem to meet their colleagues at the Jewish Agency. They instead met with Katznelson, and it was he who supported the idea of sabotaging the ship. Without further consultation with members of the executive, not even with Shertok, the two took Katznelson's support as tantamount to a go-ahead order.[40] (This is revealed in Golomb's cable to London of 21 November.)

The conduct of the operation demonstrates the degree of Haganah independence from the official Zionist leadership as well as its awareness of the divisions within it. Further, it shows how the more militant faction of the leadership made use of the Haganah in order to implement its own approach when it was blocked by lack of a majority within the Yishuv's political bodies.

The Haganah members in Haifa took responsibility for carrying out the operation. Munia Mardor, a central figure in the Haifa Haganah, disguised himself as a dockworker and boarded the *Patria*. Mardor spoke with Hans Wandel and Erich Frank, the Hehalutz leaders on the ship, and together they planned the method and timing of the explosion. Executing the plan was very difficult, since the ship was heavily guarded by the British army. The first explosive that was put on the ship failed to go off; the second one was too great for the weak body of the *Patria* to sustain, and the ship sank within minutes. Utter panic broke out as the ship began to sink. Passengers leaped into the water and were unable to swim; many were trapped in the hold of the ship and screamed for help that could not get there fast enough. British soldiers risked their lives to rescue the victims of the sinking ship; they tried to free those trapped inside and to save those who had jumped overboard. In spite of their efforts, 267 people lost their lives and another 172 were injured.

For weeks afterward, Palestine's newspapers published the names of victims as they were pulled from the sea, a long and painful memorial to the tragedy and the failure. British public opinion and Weizmann's intervention with Churchill forced the high commissioner to agree to allow the survivors of the *Patria* to remain in Palestine.

The tragic results of the operation provoked a mixed reaction among the Yishuv and the leadership. Many, like Shertok, took a cautious line—neither condemning nor supporting the action—but noting the positive results that stemmed from it. In his letter to Weizmann of December 17, Shertok wrote:

> It appears that there were those among us who did not accept the conclusions we had reached, and the tragedy then took place on the morning of the twenty-fifth. . . . It is hard to imagine that those who planned the operation were deliberately aiming to sink the ship. It is even harder to imagine that they were prepared for such a cruel and heavy loss of life. After the fact, though, with all the differences of opinion and varied judgments of this shocking event, the general tendency in the Yishuv has been to view the permission granted to the survivors to remain in the country as a justification for the tragedy and for the sacrifice that was made.[41]

Militants and moderates alike pointed to the results of the *Patria* affair as proof of the validity of their own positions. The moderates—who opposed resorting to extreme measures in order to change British policy—saw the tragedy as support for their view. Militants such as Golomb, Katznelson, and their supporters found a positive side to the incident.

Shortly after the *Patria* episode, the struggle over the deportation of the *Atlantic* passengers commenced. (The *Atlantic* was the third of the ships to arrive, and most of its passengers had not been transferred to the *Patria*.) Shertok felt that High Commissioner MacMichael would be adamant in denying entry to the *Atlantic* passengers. MacMichael had been forced to grant permits to the *Patria* survivors against his will, contrary to a decision he had supported from the first—an offense to his authority and personal dignity. Golomb sent a panic-stricken wire to London, demanding superhuman efforts.[42] The Zionist leadership feared yet another violent incident and wanted to avert it. There was, again, a great desire to avoid an open confrontation with the British. Weizmann and the London office tried to offer the British a way out in a policy formulation whereby future illegal immigrant ships would be seized outside the territorial limit and the refugees sent to a British colony, but for humanitarian reasons ships that had entered the territorial waters and refugees who were already in the country would be allowed to stay. Weizmann was even ready to commit the Jewish Agency to play a part in bringing illegal immigration operations to a halt if, as the British believed, tens of thousands of refugees were on the verge of streaming to Palestine illegally.[43]

And still Shertok remained unconvinced that all possible diplomatic and political avenues in London had been explored. He felt that the *Patria* affair and the reversed deportation decree had induced a certain passivity among the Zionist representatives in London. Shertok expressed the misgivings the Yishuv leaders felt at the time in his letter to Weizmann.

> We told ourselves that our only chance lay with [those in] London. So we turned to you once again. We are not entirely clear here on what happened: were further efforts attempted and they were not successful, or did you feel unable to carry on, realizing that even the *Patria* permits were achieved only through extreme circumstances? . . . It is likely that we somehow failed to get across to you just how much this matter of permits for the *Atlantic* people mattered to us, even after our victory in the case of the *Patria*.[44]

The British government and Mandatory authorities refused to yield. On the night of 5 December, the *Atlantic* passengers were forcibly removed from the detention camp at Atlit where they had been interned. They were loaded onto trucks bound for Haifa, where they were put aboard a ship and sent to Mauritius. The deportation was in all aspects conducted as a military operation. Surprise was total; local police contingents had been reinforced; troops had blocked the roads. The camp itself had been divided into sectors, each one assigned to a specific unit. Resistance was met with force; many were beaten, dragged, and injured.[45] Eyewitness accounts agree that the experience was one of sheer terror.

The Zionist leadership, hardly recovered from the effects of the *Patria,* now had to face the issue of the forced deportation. However, Shertok's fear that public outrage would lead to mobs in the streets, blocking roads and preventing British movements, did not materialize. Indeed, the leadership was taken aback by the absence of public outcry. The silence in the streets bespoke an abandonment of the struggle for those in need of rescue—of Zionist ideals. Such an anticlimax evoked profound doubts among the leadership. Had they failed in their mission to provide direction to the Yishuv? A wave of self-criticism surged among the leaders, led by Katznelson. He decried the seeming impotence of the Yishuv, which had stood by silently while Jews were dragged under cover of night and expelled from the Land of Israel. He held the leadership responsible for the Yishuv's betrayal of their Zionist mission.

At the Histadrut labor federation's convention on 9 December 1940, Katznelson stated that only militancy might have prevented the deportation from being carried out and called for militancy as the only hope, regardless of risks.[46]

> We are fighting all over the world, on every front; our blood is being spilled everywhere . . . but for ourselves, for our own liberation, we stop, we deliberate and we weigh the pros and cons so carefully, more than we ever had for any problem, great or small.

Katznelson charged that agreeing to a policy that was aimed from the start at preventing violent attempts at rescue had been a great mistake. It had crippled further efforts for aliyah and for rescue.

Katznelson's speech aroused a great storm within the labor movement over the concept of militancy and its implications. Impassioned debate raged over the sinking of the *Patria,* over its significance as a case of Jewish resistance, and over the meaning of illegal aliyah during the war. The controversy spilled over into the Mapai central committee meeting of 15 December 1940.[47] Kaplan led the opposition to a policy of militant activism. His remarks stressed political wisdom—knowing when to respond vigorously and when to exercise restraint. "Even powerful nations must choose carefully when to act and when to remain silent. We as a weak nation must be all the more careful. . . . " Kaplan contended furthermore that the sinking of the *Patria* had undermined the authority of the constituted political bodies of the Yishuv, because the decision had not been made by the proper authorities and, in fact, had gone against their will. In his opinion, the Yishuv ought to be satisfied with Britain's willingness to send refugees to British colonies, since it was a way of saving them; the outstanding question of their immigration to Palestine was one that could be resolved after the war.

Kaplan was supported by those among the central committee members who saw the sinking of the *Patria* as a moral blot on illegal immigration as a whole. Joseph Lofban, one of the editors of the Histadrut daily *Davar,* deemed the sinking an irresponsible and immoral act, "in comparison to which the actions of the Revisionists, with their unorganized aliyah, are *just and honorable*." [Emphasis in the original.][48]

Within Mapai, Golomb led the attack on the moderates. The timidity of the Zionist politicians, he charged, was partially responsible for the deportation. He claimed that the British had probed again and again, in Jerusalem and in London, to determine what the Yishuv's reaction might be. The proper answer had never been given. It was quite likely, Golomb contended, that had they been sufficiently warned of the likelihood of an uncontrollable outburst, the British would have abandoned their plan. He criticized the policy of withholding information from the public as a means of preventing spontaneous unsupervised reactions. (The Jewish Agency had not released all the information it had about the failure of the diplomatic efforts to prevent the deportation of the *Atlantic* passengers, since they feared extremist reactions.) Golomb echoed Katznelson's conviction that any view of illegal immigration that did not make allowance for risks and even tragedies was one that would prevent illegal immigration from taking place at all. Tragedy was part and parcel of this work, he asserted. There had been victims: refugees had drowned, had been beaten by British police. But these were not sacrifices made in vain.

Berl Raptor, a member of Mapai, charged the leadership with having caused the Yishuv's paralysis while the refugees were expelled.

> The fact is that for forty days, while the *Patria* rode at anchor in Haifa bay, we just stood by like so many mutes. That is why the Yishuv has no understanding of the importance of aliyah for itself and for the Zionist movement. . . . When they expelled the *Asimi*, and when they tried to deport the passengers of the *Hilda*, there was an outcry. But now there was silence. That is only a logical extension of the policy that says that we dare not engage at this time in activating the masses, and that we restrict ourselves to what Kaplan calls "Cabinet activity" [diplomatic efforts].

Raptor framed the question to be faced as "the epitome of simplicity." In short, "Will we during the war encourage secret aliyah and fight for it or not?"[49]

There were many more extreme statements on both sides. Some considered the lack of activism a sign of failure; others saw activism as failure. The essential question remained: What would the attitude to illegal immigration be? Did aliyah bet in December 1940 still represent an ideal tool in the just struggle of a weak people against a great power that had abandoned justice; or should illegal immigration have different goals in the new circumstances? Perhaps the most striking aspect of the entire episode was that after a combination of such shocking events, the Zionist leadership remained exactly where it had been before, with each side more deeply entrenched in its own position. The group that viewed it as possible and indeed necessary to give up illegal immigration, including Weizmann and Kaplan, was now willing to accept detention of refugees in British colonies as a means of rescuing Jews from Nazism. The other group called for militant activism and saw illegal immigration as its only hope for rescuing and strengthening the Zionist enterprise in Palestine.[50]

Zionist Policy in 1941

The *Patria* affair continued to disturb the Yishuv. Some regarded it as an example of Zionist heroism and sought to make it a symbol of national struggle; others recoiled at the way it was being used to promote national ideals.[51] Yet even those, like Shertok, who considered the incident in a relatively favorable light did not see it as an opening to a radically broadened campaign of illegal immigration activity. Too many practical obstacles stood in the way: inadequate funding and political instability prevented continued planning of new operations.

The British, in keeping with their hardened policy line, had issued no new immigration quota in the winter of 1941. Yet none of the more "militant" Zionist leaders—Golomb, Katznelson, Ben-Gurion—suggested increasing aliyah bet activities in order to fight for Zionist interests. Golomb had no specific plan to offer for the present. Ben-Gurion and Katznelson stressed the need for renewing Zionist committedness within the Yishuv and for redefining the goals of the movement for the postwar era. In the wake of the *Patria* affair (discussed primarily in terms of policy failures and the loss of public responsiveness), it seemed to them that aliyah bet would simply not be possible as long as the war lasted. While they were aware that it might be possible for Jews to leave some European countries like Rumania and Hungary—a prospect that aroused a certain amount of hope—Zionist leaders tended to anchor their war policy in the chance of mobilizing Jewish military forces, either as individuals serving in the British army or else as Jewish units organized in Palestine to fight alongside British forces.

All active opposition to the White Paper and to British land policy was directed specifically at the high commissioner and not at the British government as such. Within the Mapai central committee, Shertok charged that it was High Commissioner MacMichael who was responsible for the hardening of British policy on both Jewish settlement and illegal immigration. Shertok saw some hope for advancing Zionist interests if the high commissioner were replaced, and declared that Zionist protest ought to be directed at having him removed from the post. At the same time, he also stressed that much cooperative activity was occurring between the Zionists and the British army in the Middle East in intelligence work, in discussions over Jewish units, and in other matters still pending. These matters, once decided, would provide a more favorable context for the resolution of outstanding issues. Shertok admitted that this policy had not yet produced the expected results, but he had no alternative to offer.[52]

On 19 March 1941 the *Darien* arrived in Haifa with 789 unauthorized immigrants on board. The leadership again undertook to determine a course of action in the event the British authorities should prepare to expel the refugees. Golomb hinted at violent action in his comments to the Mapai political committee on the day of the boat's arrival.[53] These intimations provoked great opposition and with it the demand that any action be expressly authorized by the constituted political bodies of the Yishuv—an outright rejection of the manner in which the *Patria* decision had been reached.[54]

Contrary to Zionist fears, the British announced that they intended to intern the illegal immigrants on Mauritius, but for the present they were to stay in detention in Atlit, because transport was unavailable. Keeping the refugees in Atlit provided the Zionists with an opportunity to exert whatever pressure they could muster in lobbying the authorities in both Jerusalem and London. The British decision encouraged the moderates and gave them time to pursue their strategy of cooperation and negotiation: to obtain the release of the detainees by having the British agree to subtract their number from the next quota of certificates. In June 1942, after a year and a half, the British gave their consent.

The British reaction to the arrival of the *Darien* is also open to another interpretation; it could be understood as a response to the militancy of the Haganah and a desire to avoid a repetition of the *Patria*. Such a reading of events would seem to indicate the need to continue illegal aliyah and violent resistance of expulsions. But the events did not transpire toward such a course. Despite vocal declamations of illegal immigration as the embodiment of Zionist heroism, the Zionist leadership took no practical steps to further aliyah bet operations.[55] No unified and defined group existed to press for continued activity in the face of the practical obstacles and the wavering of the political leadership.

The Soviet Union's entry into the war in June 1941 proved to be an initial turning point toward the serious consideration of a renewal of aliyah operations. Although the Nazi invasion of the Soviet Union meant that the Jewish catastrophe was spreading over additional vast territories, Soviet involvement meant that certain new opportunities presented themselves for the transit of refugees, via Iran, to Palestine. In June and July, Katznelson proposed to Mapai's political bodies that a base of operations be established in Istanbul to function as a relay point for communicating with the Jews of occupied Europe and as a center for organizing aliyah.[56] Kaplan and Eliyahu Dobkin (assistant head of the Agency's immigration section) suggested that the British ought now to take into account the improved economic conditions in Palestine: unemployment had vanished and labor was in demand. Moreover, aliyah would provide more young men to fill the ranks of the British armed forces.

Nevertheless, these arguments did not win the approval of the Zionist leadership. Ben-Gurion considered the Istanbul idea premature. Instead, he determined that the Jewish Agency's chief efforts regarding aliyah were to remain focused on diplomacy, to attempt to obtain British approval for the transfer of Jewish refugees from Soviet central Asia via Iran, for certificates to refugees in the Balkans, and for entry of unaccompanied children (Youth Aliyah).[57] The worsening situation of Jews in Rumania and the Balkan States following the Nazi invasion of the Soviet Union did not alter this basic position. As late as January 1942, Shertok stated that "Reports have reached us that the government has information on some illegal immigrant boats en route to Palestine. If true, this could make it more difficult for us to secure the release of the *Darien* passengers."[58]

Thus, political orientation came to dominate official Zionist thinking on the question of illegal aliyah in 1941. It was judged according to criteria of interests and priorities, losses and gains. Aliyah was one of a number of political alternatives, to be chosen or not according to estimates of relative utility. Partly because the logistic and material difficulties involved in aliyah were enormous and because results could not be guaranteed, it did not rank highly among political alternatives. Illegal aliyah was not yet viewed primarily as a rescue operation, nor as an absolute moral imperative. This approach was a reflection of the leadership's inability to come to grips with the true nature of what was happening to the Jews in Europe.

The aliyah operations of the Mossad, the Haganah, and Hehalutz body that looked to the Zionist leadership in Palestine for authority, guidance, and support were directly influenced by the leadership's stance. Their interrelationship pertains directly to the Mossad's efforts and failures during the first years of the war. We now turn to this aspect of Yishuv-sponsored aliyah bet.

3

The Mossad and the
Kladovo *Darien* Incident

News of the outbreak of the war reached most of the Mossad agents in Paris. There they gathered following the Zionist Congress in Geneva in late August. The Congress had left a profound impression. Katznelson's resounding plea on behalf of aliyah bet stirred them, and their encounters with aliyah activists from Germany, Austria, and Czechoslovakia rekindled their sense of urgency. They began to discuss new efforts, both to initiate additional operations and to persuade potential funders, in order to launch the largest aliyah campaign possible. Even as they spoke, the *Tiger Hill* was en route to Palestine carrying several hundred refugees from Poland and Rumania. Groups had been organized in Germany, Austria, and Bratislava and awaited departure. The issue of using the Danube route to the Black Sea was discussed. The Mossad had avoided this route, since it greatly compromised secrecy; it was accepted now after extensive debate because of its logistical convenience, a crucial factor in a large-scale campaign.

Yet at this point as war broke out, the head of Mossad's Paris bureau, Yehuda Braginsky, ordered Mossad representatives in Holland and Germany to return to Palestine. It is unclear whether Braginsky reached this decision on his own or after consulting the leadership in Palestine. (On 25 August, the final night of the Congress, a special meeting of Histadrut delegates had reached decision that Yishuv emissaries should return to the communities in Europe.)[1] However, because of Braginsky's order the Mossad activity broke off for a period of five to six weeks, perhaps the most crucial ones for organizing groups, given that the onset of winter and the freezing of the Danube would severely hamper operations shortly thereafter.

However, the decision seemed the wisest course at the time. Pino Ginsburg, at the time a Hehalutz emissary and Mossad agent in Germany, noted that the emissaries, as citizens of Palestine (part of the British empire), were now enemy aliens and were perceived as being in greater danger than the resident Jews. Also, communication beyond the boundaries of those countries became very difficult and risky—all in all, a very dangerous situation.[2] Zvi Yehieli and Ze'ev Shind, both key Mossad activists, returned to Palestine for consultation. Braginsky, too, prepared for his own return. Nevertheless, continuing operations from countries not yet involved in the war—the Nether-lands, France, the Balkan countries, and others—could still be possible. The fate of those groups awaiting transport was not addressed.

In Geneva, Moshe Agami, who had served as Hehalutz emissary and Mossad agent in Austria until he was expelled by Eichmann in May 1939, also made plans to depart. All the while, however, communications that Agami received from the heads of the Jewish communities in Germany, Austria, and Slovakia insisted that greater decision, daring, and activity were needed more urgently than ever before—not a halt to clandestine immigra-tion. Agami therefore delayed his plans to return to Palestine.

In Palestine, the emissaries' exit from Europe was debated as well, and a group of Mossad operatives was reorganized. At Agami's request, a number of assignments were made: Zvi Yehieli, one of the most capable and seasoned aliyah bet activists, was sent to work with Agami. Shmarya Tsameret, who had a great deal of experience in hiring ships, was posted to Athens. Yosef Barpal returned to Rumania, and Gideon Rufer (Raphael) went to Italy to investigate its suitability as an alternate staging area. Ze'ev Shind, an aliyah bet veteran since the voyage of the *Velos* in 1934, was assigned as a roving agent responsible for acquiring ships. By the end of November, agents had returned to Greece, Geneva, and Italy, and operations had begun anew. The center of operations now shifted to Geneva. Switzerland's neutral status made it secure, and the offices of international Jewish organizations located there made them convenient and logical for lobbying purposes.

The Mossad's Organization of Aliyah bet

From its beginnings in spring 1939, the Mossad functioned in a centralized fashion (as had the Hehalutz operations that preceded it). Principal policy decisions were made by Mossad leaders in Tel Aviv, who were under the direct authority of the Haganah. Eliyahu Golomb, the head of the Haganah, and Shaul Avigur, a Mossad member and a leading figure in the Haganah, maintained very close ties. Policy on aliyah bet was set in meetings of the Haganah and Mossad, and political leaders such as Ben-Gurion and Shertok, Histadrut members involved in Hehalutz, and Berl Katznelson took part in these. However, there were no formal ties between the Mossad and the Jewish Agency. The meetings were under no institutional framework, and authority in decision-making was never formalized. In numerous cases, decisions were reached in private meetings involving Golomb, Avigur, Katznelson, Ben-Gurion, and sometimes Shertok.

Mossad operations across Europe were directed from Paris (and, after November 1939, from Geneva). There, the needs of individual communities were assessed and emissaries' proposals evaluated. Mossad representatives from Palestine were assigned to the main Jewish communities in Europe. Some agents, such as Yosef Barpal in Rumania and Shmarya Tsameret in Greece, were dispatched expressly for the Mossad's purposes. Others played a dual role as emissaries of Hehalutz and as Mossad representatives (Pino Ginsburg, Moshe Agami, and others). In both cases, no work was carried out without prior consultation with Paris.

Mossad representatives managed all logistical activities: finding ships, arranging travel and departure dates, and obtaining funds (the amounts contributed by the would-be immigrants fell far short of actual costs). The local Palestine offices and Hehalutz groups selected the candidates for immigration and were responsible for organizing groups of potential immigrants—obtaining travel documents and informing them of travel dates, how much luggage they could bring, and how much each would pay. In general, the selection criteria used were much the same as those of the Zionist authorities in Palestine: ability to adjust to life in Palestine, vocational training, health, age, and so on. In countries under Nazi rule, an individual's degree of personal danger was a decisive criterion. The net result was that most of those chosen tended to be youthful members of Hehalutz who had undergone some training on *hachshara*.

Thus, locally, the Mossad played mainly an advisory role—in the selection process and in other respects. Yet their importance to the local Hehalutz members was great. Hehalutz members tended to be young (under twenty-five), without financial means, and lacking in influence and professional contacts that elder Zionists had. Without the aid of the Mossad, Hehalutz members had little chance of immigrating, whereas older, better-established Jews had a few other options—privately arranged voyages and so forth. Mossad agents were also young (Braginsky, who was about thirty-five, was considered old by his colleagues). Yet by virtue of their status as members of the Yishuv, they commanded a great deal of respect and were able to acquire funds, arrange logistics, and exercise influence where Hehalutz members were powerless. Local Hehalutz members completely depended on the Mossad.

The Mossad's funds came almost entirely from the Zionist Organization, who raised them inside and outside Europe. These were disbursed centrally, from the Zionist Organization to the Mossad on behalf of particular groups or Jewish communities. (For certain operations, the American Joint Distribution Committee [the JDC, the main American institution aiding European Jewish communities under Nazism in the 1930s] also provided funds.) Virtually all the costs of the Mossad's aliyah operations were subsidized; passengers' contributions covered but a small portion of a transport's expenses. At the end of 1939, it was decided to include more veteran Zionists among the groups of passengers; these could generally afford to contribute more toward expenses.

While the Mossad was being reorganized after the outbreak of the war, Moshe Agami urged that less centralized procedures be adopted in order to give those in the field greater flexibility in making decisions. It was not always possible to wait for decisions from Tel Aviv and Geneva—especially under wartime conditions. He asked the leadership in Palestine for far greater autonomy for agents than there had been in the past.[3] No change in policy was considered at this time, however. Indeed, the authority of the Mossad central office was never deviated from during its long years of operation. A certain tension existed between center and periphery, since in a few cases decisions had been made by the main office despite the objections of agents in the field, but established procedures were held to and central authority respected nonetheless. No serious challenge to the central office arose until the events surrounding the *Darien,* at the end of 1940 and early 1941.

The Mossad's Logistical Difficulties

The political realities of wartime complicated the work of the Mossad and of all illegal aliyah activists. Because of restrictions and legal use of ships, the Mossad usually commissioned ships through an agent rather than purchasing them outright. The agent, in turn, hired captain and crew and arranged ship's papers and other details. The demand for shipping was such that only those vessels retired from service because of age or poor condition were available. These required extensive repairs and refitting for use as passenger ships. Prices soared, and vessels judged to be no better than scrap by governments during wartime doubled and tripled in value.

Aliyah activists were very much at the mercy of shipping agents and owners, even should they prove dishonest. All involved knew that the transport of refugees often violated conventions or laws, and in the event of fraud or breach of faith the Mossad agents had little recourse, legal or otherwise. Regardless of the ship's condition or the shipping agent's integrity, all ships were insured at exorbitantly high rates to guarantee some return for the owner, increasing the Mossad's expenses yet again. Ships were sometimes deliberately damaged before journey's end or even while still in port so the owners could collect on their insurance. The organizers had to bear the huge costs of delays or failure.[4] Also, shipping agents often demanded last-minute bank guarantees, which were very difficult to obtain at short notice, again threatening delays and raising costs.

Shipping agents, as well as captains and crews, became increasingly hard to hire and of deteriorating quality. The Balkan governments, Rumania— Bulgaria, Greece, and Yugoslavia—increasingly put pressure on shipping agents and captains to dissuade them from cooperating with activists as the result of repeated British requests to prohibit the passage of Jewish refugees to Palestine. Because of this, some arrangements fell through even after all details had been concluded and money had changed hands. Crews were also discouraged from cooperating by British policies: illegal ships began to be seized off Palestine and their crews arrested.[5] Rumors also circulated among seamen about attempts at secret landings that endangered all on board. Given the risks entailed, the pool of those willing to sign on as crew members was reduced to those most in need of work—frequently men with criminal records or questionable backgrounds. Crews often demanded the entire journey's wages in advance, when in ordinary circumstances a small portion of these would have sufficed. Furthermore, the low caliber of crews at times gave rise to tensions aboard ship.

Bringing the refugees to their port of embarkation also became more difficult and much more costly. Legally obtaining transit visas through the countries along the way proved near to impossible, and forged visas or illegally acquired ones became rarer and ever more expensive. Some governments sought to avoid an influx of impoverished refugees and others succumbed to British pressure to restrict the flow of Jews. The impact of the numerous obstructions was to increase the hardships of the journey for the refugees. Delays on land and aboard ship caused anxiety and turmoil. The only thing to inspire confidence was the prospect of eventual arrival in Palestine.

In short, arranging illegal immigration entailed overcoming virtually insurmountable obstacles. In the face of these, Mossad agents, even at this early stage, raised the idea of buying ships outright and training Jewish crews. "All of these failures involving non-Jews," Agami wrote in January 1940, "show that we must find some other way so that we can be sure the tents [ships] will really be at our disposal and so that we will not be at the mercy of these cheats and scoundrels."[6] Such a scheme was not seriously considered at the time, however.

A picture emerges of competition in a volatile and uncertain market. Many groups sought to arrange illegal transports: the Mossad, the Revisionists, private organizers such as Baruch Konfino, who organized aliyah privately from Bulgaria, and Berthold Storfer, a Jewish businessman from Vienna engaged by the Jewish community to organize Jewish emigration from the Reich. All bid for the same ships in ports in Rumania, Greece, Italy, Bulgaria, and Turkey. Some used the same shipping agent;[7] and the names of the same ships appear again and again in the accounts of their dealings: *Maria Luda, Sirus, Popi, Asimi, Wetan,* and a Greek-Rumanian barge. In Turkey, controls on shipping were the strictest by far, and all the organizers approached the same Panamanian consuls seeking its flag of registry for their vessels. Thus, the various organizers were competing against each other even while trying to accomplish the same thing for the same people, roughly speaking. This situation certainly compounded their own problems and indirectly contributed to the refugees' sufferings.

Mossad Activities after the Renewal of Operations

The Mossad's task after resuming operations in October and November 1939 was to arrange the transportation of four groups of illegals that had been organized before the outbreak of hostilities. In one group, there were 725 members of Young Maccabi and other Zionists. These were waiting aboard the *Hilda* in Rumania, but the Mossad feared that the ship was unseaworthy and hoped to obtain another for the group. A second group of about 1,100 people, composed of the remainder of Hehalutz in Vienna, youth groups and *hachshara* trainees from Germany, and refugees from Danzig were on riverboats at the port of Kladovo in Yugoslavia waiting for orders to depart for the Black Sea. A third contingent of 300 farm trainees from Prague and Berlin and 150 refugees from Danzig waited in Bratislava. Another group, 600 Jews from Germany, Danzig, and Austria was also ready to depart from Bratislava. Meanwhile, they were at the mercies of the local police.[8] In addition, there were now many people who descended upon the Hehalutz offices and the Palestine Offices in Berlin and in Prague, as well as on shipping agencies in Vienna, seeking a way out of Europe.

Zvi Yehieli arrived in Greece at the end of November and contacted shipping agents he had worked with in the past. He was informed that costs had now doubled. Nevertheless, Yehieli instructed them to arrange the charter of the *Maria Luda* to transport 500 people at a cost per head of £17 (as compared with the £9–10 paid in August for the *Tiger Hill*). The *Dora* was to be assigned to the group aboard the *Hilda*.[9] The ship had already been under contract to the Mossad, and its owners claimed it was en route to Rumania from Marseilles, as agreed. It had actually been sent to North Africa and its owners seeking other business. Only in December was it clear that the *Dora* was lost.[10]

It was imperative, however, that the *Hilda* group leave Rumania. Its presence in Rumania complicated additional efforts. The government had barred the entry of new groups of refugees until those already in the country left, and now it added two other stipulations: that a ship be standing by in port to await each group entering Rumania, and that 15 to 20 percent of the passengers of each ship consist of refugees already in Rumania or of Rumanian Jews. Furthermore, as winter approached conditions on the *Hilda* deteriorated. The group threatened to publicize its plight, and the Mossad feared a furor in the press.[11] Revisionist-organized groups had provoked such a storm in the local press and in European newspapers after having been left waiting for weeks on frail river craft in Rumania.[12] The Mossad proposed the hire of a boat with Panamanian registry, the *Asimi*, despite the still higher cost demanded by its owners, now amounting to £20 per person.

It thus seemed that two ships, the *Maria Luda* and the *Asimi*, were available, allowing the evacuation of the *Hilda* group and the groups that were in Bratislava and Kladovo. However, on December 3 the Greek government, under British pressure, announced a prohibition on the use of Greek ships to transport refugees, and the shipping agent assigned to hire the *Asimi* was threatened with arrest. The owner was warned not to get involved in transporting Jewish refugees, and the ship was placed under Greek registry. Hopes of acquiring the *Maria Luda* vanished as well. Attempts to transfer it to Panamanian registry failed on account of a government order forbidding changes of registry for passenger vessels. By mid-December, all the Mossad's efforts thus far had been in vain. Agami wrote to Golomb:

Things have gotten worse than they were before. The truth is that we have suffered a major setback, and that in the entire time since the war began we have not been able to save even one "tent" [shipload], despite the fact that we do have funds. There have, of course, been reasons. The [British] are interfering with us wherever there is a market in ships. Still, others have succeeded in obtaining one [the *Sakariya*, acquired by the Revisionists], while we are stuck in the bargaining stage. I am not qualified to give you a firm judgment on this, but those are the sad facts.[13]

Given this situation, Yosef Barpal and Ruth Klueger Aliav, the Mossad's agent assigned to Rumania, made the decision to sail the *Hilda* itself to Palestine, despite fears of its unseaworthiness. An agreement was reached with the ship's owner in January 1940, and an exorbitant sum was paid. Yet, as Agami wrote to a comrade in the U.S. Zionist Organization, further problems remained:

> Things here are very trying. The first contingent has not yet left and is under Kadmon's [Barpal's] care. This is costing us dearly, both in lives and in expenses. After much effort, we had found "drivers" (the main reason why they hadn't left yet). The officers were brought from Greece, and the men from Turkey as well as some locals. A few hours before sailing, a fight broke out between the Turks and the local men, and we had to get rid of all of them. Only the officers remained. Maybe things will move in a few days if we can get other crewmen.[14]

The *Hilda* sailed on 8 January and arrived offshore in fairly short order, on 18 January. The ship was impounded and the crew brought to trial. Its passengers were seized, brought to Haifa, and interned. After a few months, however, they were released and their numbers subtracted from the next three-month schedule of legal immigrants (March to May 1940).

During winter 1939–40, the Mossad was kept from further operations by the frozen Danube, preventing transport of the groups in Bratislava and Kladovo. The Mossad spent the period strengthening its network, consolidating their main base in Geneva, and establishing others in Bucharest and Athens. In Rotterdam, Amsterdam, and Paris, Ze'ev Shind pursued the owners of vessels who had reneged on agreements and tried to recoup lost funds. He also approached the JDC in an effort to gain financial support. Mossad agents communicated daily, in meetings or by telephone and letters. They also kept in touch with leaders of the Berlin and Prague communities, and with Sima Spitzer, secretary of the Union of Jewish communities in Yugoslavia, who bore responsibility for the maintenance of the group at Kladovo as well as for thousands of other Jewish refugees.

The Mossad worked in many directions simultaneously. It primarily focused on acquiring ships and reestablishing a network of contacts among the shipping agents. They even went so far as to renew liaisons with Germans who had aided illegal aliyah before the war, especially through contacts in the German government. Among these was Alexander von Hoepfner (known as "the aristocrat"). Von Hoepfner had maintained a link to Pino Ginsburg in Germany, at some risk to himself. In December, Yehieli, Agami, and Shind met von Hoepfner in Italy, where he was seeking means to help German Jews gain passage to Palestine.[15]

The Mossad attempted to reestablish contact with the movement in Poland and to send money via von Hoepfner, but to no avail. A plan was also discussed of offering some sort of agreement to the Germans in order to organize an evacuation from Poland. Yehieli also proposed cooperating with Revisionist groups in order to maintain the flow of immigrants.[16] He had also suggested that the Mossad cooperate with private aliyah organizers and on several occasions had met with Baruch Konfino in Italy, Belgrade, and Bucharest.

The Mossad agents saw their work as dictated by circumstances. Their constant contacts with the European Jewish communities convinced and compelled them. It was clear to them that the Jews of Europe would flee whether they were given organizational assistance or not. The Mossad saw itself as a facilitator. In one sense, it hoped that it could deter the Nazis in their extreme measures—such as expulsion to Lublin—by organizing large numbers of refugees and, as it were, offering the regime a simpler alternative.[17] In addition, it acted as a vehicle to mobilize the funds of various Jewish communities and agencies, centralizing funds and putting them to use. Yet the scarcity of funds and the lack of decisive support on the part of the Zionist leadership plagued them. They were far removed from the policymakers' concerns over political implications and absorption difficulties. For the Mossad, Jewish and Zionist values coincided. In its practical operations, the Mossad agents were mindful of anxieties in Palestine—of possible German infiltration of the immigrant groups and of the difficulties and risks involved in aliyah bet. In their organizing efforts they strictly guarded against possible infiltration. Insofar as risks were concerned, the Mossad gave great care to refugees' safety. Yet they also recognized the necessity of taking chances, as in the sailing of the *Hilda*. In such cases, however, decisions were made only as a last resort.

For the Mossad, the important question was not *whether,* but rather *how,* to pursue aliyah bet. Their conclusions were that the operations of the many disparate aliyah bet organizers should be concentrated under the Mossad's direction to ameliorate logistical difficulties and avoid counterproductive competition. (Leaders of the Jewish communities, Paul Epstein in Germany and Jacob Edelstein in Prague, stressed this in their communications with the Mossad and expressed their preference to cooperate with the Mossad over any other organization.)[18] The activists also strongly believed that the Nazi regime would permit an organized effort to go on if that effort produced significant results—evacuating large numbers of Jews. In sum, their approach became one of looking beyond the solution of immediate problems, such as that of the Kladovo contingent or of the other groups awaiting transport, to a broader and more comprehensive effort. Their outlook was one of openness to all proposals, of taking chances on many plans at once and of accepting a higher level of risk than before.

The Kladovo *Darien* Incident

All of the several attempts made to bring the group of refugees in Kladovo, Yugoslavia, to Palestine failed. Finally, most of the people in the group were killed by the Nazis.[19] The group's story is one of the saddest episodes in the history of clandestine aliyah. The incident became a painful issue between the Diaspora Jewish communities and the leaders of the Yishuv and was raised time and again as an example of Mossad and Jewish Agency irresponsibility.

The chances to rescue the Kladovo group and the issue of how the ship *Darien* was to be used—whether for war or for rescue work—are directly related to the fundamental question for Zionist policy: How was the leadership to choose? In favor of an immediate rescue operation with some probability of success, or instead in favor of small steps in a political strategy calculated to enable a much larger rescue effort at a later time? An accurate assessment of this episode requires a thorough examination of events beginning in summer 1939, when the group was first organized for an illegal journey to Palestine.

Ehud Ueberall (Avriel) was responsible for organizing the initial group, composed of 1,000 Hehalutz members (who mostly came from Austria), as well as approximately 200 others from Germany and Danzig. The plan was that the group would travel by train to Bratislava, proceed to the Black Sea via the German Danube Line (DDSG), then sail to Palestine on a vessel arranged by the Mossad.

Originally, in summer of 1939, the group was intended to sail either on the *Dora* or the *Holm,* but the outbreak of the war interrupted the plans of the Mossad.[20] It became imperative to get the group out of German-controlled territory as soon as possible—it was unclear whether Jews would continue to be allowed to leave the Reich or whether the Lublin expulsion plan would be attempted on a large scale. In late November, Ueberall learned of the horrible conditions facing the deported Jews from Vienna community leaders who had visited the Lublin camps. Ueberall resolved that the group must exit Austria at once. Between 24 and 26 November, the group left Vienna for Bratislava. Ueberall had obtained temporary visas for Slovakia with the aid of Storfer and through bribes paid to the Slovak consul in Vienna (with whom the Mossad had had prewar ties).[21] The group stayed at a hotel waiting for word of the arrival of their ship in Sulina before setting out on the next leg of their journey. Ueberall urged his comrades in Geneva and Rumania to find them a ship quickly. The DDSG refused to transport the group to Rumania until a ship was stationed in Sulina. After repeated requests, Ueberall realized that in fact the Mossad had no ships at its disposal.

The Slovak police began to threaten to send the refugees back to the Reich. Ueberall engaged in stalling tactics to put them off. The Mossad, however, believed it was better for the group to wait in Bratislava rather than Rumania, which was flooded with refugees. Furthermore, the Mossad felt it could do no more to ensure the group's safety in Rumania than could Ueberall in Bratislava. Ueberall demanded that the group move on, no matter what; funds were exhausted on provisions and bribes, and the situation was growing ever more critical.[22] Yehieli remained opposed, knowing that there was no ship to transport them. He believed that as long as the group stayed in Bratislava, he had a better chance of obtaining financial assistance from the JDC. Agami, however, fully appreciated the seriousness of Ueberall's arguments and took upon himself the responsibility for issuing the go-ahead. Agami turned for help to Sima Spitzer, secretary of the Union of Jewish communities in Yugoslavia. With Spitzer's aid and after paying large sums of money, they hired three Yugoslavian riverboats to take the group from the Yugoslavian border to Sulina, Rumania.[23] By mid-December, the boats had arrived near the Rumanian border, a few days' sail from Sulina.

Yet it remains unclear why anyone involved assumed the Rumanian authorities would clear the boats for entry when no ships were available to transport the group from Rumania. It seems that the Mossad members themselves had little idea of how this problem would be solved; the necessity of moving on had overridden all other considerations. They had probably hoped to improvise tactics—they had succeeded in this way before and were at that very moment doing just this with the *Hilda* group.[24]

However, even prior to receiving word about proceeding to Sulina, the boats were instructed to halt. The Danube had frozen early that year. They entered a small port in Yugoslavia—Kladovo. There they were meant to remain until the spring thaw. However, the Yugoslavian authorities barred the passengers from going ashore, forcing them to remain on the boats under dire conditions. There was no heat, since the boats were not designed for winter operation, and they lacked facilities for extended residence on board. Through great efforts Sima Spitzer obtained a river barge (without power) on which two kitchens, an eating area, a sick bay, and berths were set up, somewhat relieving the overcrowding. The Union of Jewish communities of Yugoslavia took it upon itself to supply the group (at a time when 10,000 other Jewish refugees were already in the country).

Supplying Kladovo was difficult. It was located some eighty miles from the nearest town, and in winter it could be reached only by sled. Under these conditions, a supply line and communications had to be maintained. But life on the river was harder by far. Cold, monotony, and despondency plagued the stranded refugees. In an effort to overcome these, the group's leaders established a regimen of order and discipline and organized cultural activities. Throughout the period, the members of the group demonstrated impressive stamina and spirit.[25]

The Wetan

The Mossad's search for a vessel began in Genoa, Italy, where Shind, Yehieli, and Gideon Rufer tried to locate a ship through various agents. Meanwhile, in Athens, Shmarya Tsameret bargained for a small boat, and Barpal and Klueger Aliav negotiated for a Turkish ship, the *Wetan*, which could carry 3,000 passengers. Baruch Konfino, the private aliyah organizer, was approached to try to acquire a boat in Bratislava.[26]

The Mossad's goal was to hire or purchase enough vessels to transport 3,000 people in the months to come. In addition to the 1,100 waiting in Kladovo, there were other groups waiting in ever more precarious situations in Bratislava and Rumania totaling more than a thousand people, as well as concentrations of Jewish refugees in Venice and Genoa who had requested the Mossad's help. There was growing pressure on the remaining Jews in Danzig, and the Mossad sought to aid them as well. In addition, the Mossad promised to help some 2,000 Czech Jews leave Prague. The commitment to this last group had come about after meetings in Geneva with the Berlin and Prague leaders—Jacob Edelstein, Fritz Ullmann, and Paul Epstein—in January and February. The Czech Jewish community was able to obtain foreign currency for emigration, and they offered funds equivalent to £25 per person to purchase a ship and to cover the costs of travel.

Negotiations for several vessels were conducted simultaneously to increase the chances of success. The practice was risky—it was costly and invited the possibility of provoking some agents in the end. However, the state of the market demanded such dubious methods, and the Mossad had to guard against the possibility of fraud. By early March, the *Wetan* seemed the most attractive solution.[27] Its large capacity would allow the transport of the groups in Kladovo and Bratislava, a major step toward fulfilling the overall plan. A successful precedent encouraged them: the Revisionists had used a Turkish vessel, the *Sakariya,* to convey refugees out of Sulina. The Mossad was confident that it, too, could circumvent Turkish restrictions.

After several setbacks, a contract was ready, and three Mossad representatives—Klueger Aliav, Barpal, and Yehieli—traveled to Istanbul, arriving 1 March 1940. They were greeted with news in the press of a new law prohibiting the transfer of Turkish vessels to foreign ownership and instituting tighter controls on shipping. Upon further inquiry, however, it appeared that the law applied only during a state of emergency and therefore was not applicable for the present.[28] The group met with the owner of the *Wetan,* who had received an advance of $12,000. He announced that he was raising his asking price from $30,000 to $60,000. The Mossad representatives were unwilling to let the ship slip through their fingers and agreed to the price. The additional costs, they reasoned, could be offset by including more passengers, and Yehieli asked Edelstein in Prague to send more money.

At this point there began a series of delays in the transfer of the needed funds, delays whose true nature was unclear to the Mossad at the time. (It was later revealed that the delays were the work of Storfer, who was engaging in a struggle with the Zionist leaders over the control of aliyah. The Mossad, whose information came mostly from the Zionist leadership, was not fully aware of Storfer's influence and power.)[29] When the Czech funds had failed to arrive, the Mossad began to search feverishly for others. In the meantime, $35,000 that had been raised by American Zionist organizations for relief to the Kladovo group arrived in Geneva. The Mossad was thrown into a moral quandary. The amount would cover the cost of purchasing a smaller ship, large enough to carry the Kladovo group, but it was not enough to buy or even to pay for refitting the *Wetan,* whose procurement was part of the Mossad's plan for a large-scale aliyah. In addition to the question of the propriety of using funds sent for one purpose for another—which was not merely a technicality—there were further considerations. Under Turkish currency restrictions, dollars deposited in Turkey could not be taken out again. In the event that the Czech funds did not arrive or if for some reason the *Wetan* transaction fell through, the money might be unavailable for the purchase of a smaller ship.

There was no simple answer to the Mossad's dilemma—to risk the *Wetan* by waiting for money from Prague or to risk the Kladovo money by putting it toward purchase of the *Wetan*. But a fine line separated a reasonable gamble from a disastrous speculation. The Mossad decided to try to win some time. Yehieli returned to Geneva and tried to offer the owners short-term bank guarantees in lieu of actual payment. These were refused, however. Klueger Aliav and Barpal, who had remained in Istanbul, pressed Yehieli to make a decision. They feared that the *Wetan*'s owners would cancel the deal if there were too many more delays. There was still no clear word out of Prague. Meanwhile, from the information gathered by Yehieli it became evident that Storfer's intervention was a factor in the delay, and Yehieli realized that some way to win his cooperation had to be found. Yehieli contacted Storfer, who demanded to inspect the ship, but the Mossad rejected this, arguing that it would require too long a wait. They finally compromised on an inspection in Rumania prior to boarding. The Mossad was to release the money it had ($42,000), enough for the ship's purchase but not enough for refitting. The Mossad decided to proceed with the deal even though the final arrangements were still in doubt. As Yehieli summed up the matter:

> Even though we were agreed on the importance of not allowing the vessel to be lost, it was difficult to go through with the transfer of funds. We contacted Kadmon [Barpal] and Dani [Shind] again in Istanbul. They assured us that the deal was dangling by a thread, and unless we signed at once it would be lost. On that understanding, we sent all the money we had, including $6,000 we had from the JDC for Danzig. . . . I want to stress that we all took responsibility for the decision, some of us with more misgivings than others. We knew that under the circumstances we had no choice. The transfer was made toward the end of March.[30]

In a letter to the United States of March 25, Agami spoke of the acquisition of the *Wetan* as a very real possibility.[31] But soon after, a new obstacle materialized—as they had feared all along—barring the transfer of the *Wetan* to their Greek agent, Pandelis.[32] Whether or not this obstacle was the new Turkish law forbidding the sale of Turkish shipping to foreign nationals remains unclear from the documents; nor is it clear why, if this was indeed the case, the law could not have been circumvented through a fictitious sale or a lease arrangement. What was quite clear was that the Mossad was now left with no money and no ship.

The fiasco brought a chain of repercussions in its wake. In the United States, Zionist supporters were angered at the Mossad's seeming irresponsibility. The reaction hampered additional fund-raising efforts. The JDC, which had supported the Mossad in the Kladovo case with considerable reservations, became even more uncertain. In Yugoslavia, the refugees sunk into a profound depression, and the rift between the Mossad and the Yugoslav communal leadership widened. Meanwhile, the Yugoslav government pressed for the refugees' departure. In addition, the Danube was beginning to thaw and the boat company demanded the return of its riverboats. The Mossad was left without the means to reenter negotiations for ships, and April passed without any progress. Pressure on Jews to leave the Reich continued to escalate, but the Mossad had nothing to suggest to further its plans for the other groups either.

Agami went to Kladovo in April, burdened with a sense of responsibility for the group's situation. He found it difficult to present the situation to the refugees in stark objective terms. Life on the riverboats, which they believed had been at its conclusion, had grown grimmer than ever. Agami promised to do everything possible to find them a ship and money to maintain them in the meantime.[33]

The Darien

The next stage of the Kladovo story begins in May 1940 in Athens. There Tsameret and Agami came across a ship, registered in Panama and owned by a retired sea captain who wished to sell it and buy a home for his wife and himself. The price for the ship (soon to become the *Darien*) was set at $60,000. Although the Mossad was receiving small installments from Istanbul, the $42,000 paid for the *Wetan* could not be recovered all at once, and the Mossad opened negotiations to buy the *Darien* through its Greek agent, Pandelis.

Tsameret and Yehieli began a campaign for funds with the sole intention of transporting the Kladovo group, though this would require more than one voyage. In mid-May and early June the Mossad sent cables to New York, Geneva, and Jerusalem expressing grave concerns that lack of funds might ruin the prospective deal and spell the end of efforts to rescue the Kladovo group.[34]

Raising the money was difficult nevertheless. The Mossad's capabilities had fallen into disrepute. The JDC hoped that another party could be found to take responsibility and rescue the refugees. It was also pressing Storfer to aid the group and had made further aid to the Yugoslavian communities contingent on their purchase of a ship, in an effort to prompt them to act.[35] To the Mossad, it seemed as if the situation conspired to set a cruel trap—a ship was within its grasp, but by the time its purchase was arranged there might be no chance of sailing it. The likelihood of a successful transport was clouded by Italy's preparations to enter the war; it was uncertain whether the Mediterranean would remain open.

Yehieli, enraged by the JDC's maneuverings, demanded to meet with their representatives in Geneva. A meeting was held on 28 May. Yehieli bitterly criticized the JDC's refusal to expend the $45,000 necessary to secure the *Darien* and threatened to renounce all responsibility for the affair (as did

Golomb in a cable to the Zionist organizations in New York).[36] The JDC agreed to cooperate on the condition that the Jewish Agency and the Zionist Organization in America give half of the money required. The next day, Agami contacted Yehieli from Athens with word that negotiations for the *Darien* had been concluded and that $30,000 was required. On 1 June, Yehieli sent the funds he had received from the Jewish Agency and the JDC to Tsameret in Athens, after a quick consultation with Jerusalem about political difficulties. Italy's preparations to join the war and open a new front in the Mediterranean were alarming. Nevertheless, the ship was acquired and registered in Tsameret's name. (Tsameret, an American citizen, could own the ship personally, since the United States was not at war at this time.) Thus, by the beginning of June 1940, the purchase of the *Darien* was complete and it was ready to be refitted for a voyage.[37]

The Suspension of Aliyah bet and the Transfer of the Darien

On 10 June 1940, Italy entered the war, generating alarm and confusion among the ranks of the Mossad. Yehieli, in Geneva, tried to contact Agami in Athens, but without success. He was able to communicate with Spitzer the next day, but Spitzer was unable to assess the implications of the news. Yehieli and Spitzer decided to wait a few days while developments took shape and to receive word from Jerusalem.

Agami and Tsameret believed that there would be enough time to bring the Kladovo refugees out before the sea-lanes became impassable. Yehieli was not quite sure. News came from Hungary and Bulgaria of continuing aliyah activity. Storfer, too, continued to make plans for Jewish emigration. Klueger Aliav reported from Rumania in mid-June that the Mediterranean remained open.

In Palestine, a hurried meeting of those involved in aliyah bet planning was called in response to an urgent cable from Mossad emissaries.[38] A decision on whether to continue the preparation for the *Darien* voyage had to be made. It was decided to discontinue plans for the Kladovo group's voyage in light of the new dangers posed to shipping and to halt all other aliyah bet activity. Although Agami and Tsameret cabled strenuous objections from Athens, Golomb proceeded to suspend operations and instructed the Zionist office in New York to send no additional funds to Athens until further notice.[39]

Agami, determined to resist the new orders, returned in mid-June to Palestine to lobby for the continuation of operations. Tsameret remained in Athens, and Yehieli informed Spitzer of the decision. Spitzer was incensed. He called into question the Mossad's sincerity of purpose in trying to rescue the Kladovo group and pointed out that other groups were still continuing with illegal aliyah plans. He demanded that the refugees be transferred to Rumania, but the Mossad members refused, arguing that the refugees were likely to be safer in Yugoslavia than in anti-Semitic Rumania.[40]

At some point in July, the *Darien*, the ship that had been assigned to take the Kladovo refugees to Palestine, passed from Mossad control to Yehuda

Arazi, one of the Haganah's liaison group for planning cooperation with the British war effort.[41] The timing of the two events raises the question of whether the *Darien*'s transfer to Arazi was included in the June decision to discontinue plans for the Kladovo group, and whether these in fact formed two parts of a single strategic decision. Clarifying this issue may illuminate the stances of the Mossad, Haganah, and Yishuv leaders toward aliyah bet in the face of the ongoing difficulties encountered and the challenge posed to support for aliyah bet by the political option of cooperation with Great Britain.

Why was the *Darien* transferred to Arazi? One answer was given by Agami and Klueger Aliav. They have contended that it was never the Mossad's intention to give up the *Darien* entirely.[42] Although the ship was indeed transferred and the Mossad received payment for it, they claim that it was a sort of ruse whereby the British would pay the Mossad, while the Mossad would still be able to put the ship to its own purposes. Another answer was proposed by Arazi and David Hacohen (a leading member of the liaison group), both proponents of a cooperative strategy with the British.[43] In their view, the Mossad had no idea whether it could continue its operations. It transferred the *Darien* because of important plans for cooperation with the British—plans that would serve to strengthen the Zionist political position. In addition, the sale enabled the Mossad to erase a deficit it had been carrying throughout 1940.

Ze'ev Shind provides yet a third version, stating that the sale was the beginning of a new strategy combining aliyah bet work and cooperation with the British.[44] As members of the Haganah, the Mossad's people could function in both areas and work toward the success of both. However, in weighing the two goals, "saving Jews came first," should there be any conflict. Berl Katznelson had put forth this formulation in a meeting attended by Golomb and Dov Hoz (one of the most influential Haganah leaders), Mossad representatives Braginsky and Shind, and representatives of the Jewish Agency's political committee, Shertok and Reuven Shiloach. Braginsky voiced objections, but was outvoted. After the meeting, Shind, Shertok, and Shiloach left for Egypt to set concrete plans in motion.

The transfer of the *Darien* to the liaison section was a source of bitter controversy. The topic arouses explosive emotional responses to this day. Proponents and opponents each saw the dire necessity of their stances. On the one hand, the Mossad's agents were reluctant to relinquish, for the sake of long-term plans, even a slim chance of rescuing the Kladovo refugees, to whom they felt personally obligated. For them the *Darien* was not just another ship; they held a personal stake in it. The ship embodied the frustrations of the Mossad's past disastrous failures and represented the salvation of a group that had borne far too much hardship and suffering—by now many of them had been encamped on riverboats for seven months. On the other hand, the proponents of a cooperative strategy with the British saw the acquisition of the *Darien* as a long-term investment, one that might later be applied to rescue work.

The development of the war since spring of 1940 coalesced to make this a strategic time to offer assistance to the British: France had been invaded and vanquished, Italy had entered the war and expanded the fronts of hostilities into the Mediterranean, and there were fears of an invasion of England itself. The Zionist leadership expected to implement a range of cooperative activities in summer 1940: intelligence work, sabotage aimed at enemy transportation arteries and in the Balkans, parachute drops to aid partisan warfare, and more. Apparently, few results came of these plans.[45]

For exactly what purpose Arazi and Hacohen needed the ship remains unclear. Again there are several different accounts. Arazi's first account was that the ship was to be fitted with torpedoes and disguised as a cargo ship; it would sink oil tankers going from Bakau, Rumania, to Varna. In another account, however, Arazi described a plan to use the *Darien* to transport commandos from Palestine to lay the groundwork for a British invasion force.[46] The *Darien*'s background in illegal aliyah was to come into play here. Arazi was to organize an illegal immigrant voyage on board the *Darien*. The refugees were to be transferred at sea to another ship on which the commandos would be waiting to board the *Darien,* and on which the immigrants would continue on in secret to Palestine. The commandos were to land in Istanbul, ostensibly as illegal immigrants who had tried to reach Palestine on the *Darien* but were forced to turn back, either because of mechanical trouble or British patrols. The idea was to camouflage sabotage work with illegal immigration. Arazi contended that this plan received the approval of the British command in Egypt and was ready to be carried out. There is no documentary proof of this.[47]

David Hacohen did not indicate in his own version what specific plans were considered when the *Darien* was purchased. He mentioned only that the liaison group and the British were discussing a number of sabotage actions in Rumania and on the Danube that called for the use of a boat. One idea, apparently, was to block the Danube to German shipping by sinking a boat in the river's "Iron Gate" (the narrow passage of the river as it crosses from Rumania to Bulgaria). Other ideas involved blowing up boats along the Danube or attacking the oil refineries in Rumania that were supplying the Germans. Ze'ev Shind knew of a plan to place a mine in the Danube, set to explode after the mine-laying ship had made good its escape.[48]

To implement so many plans required a number of boats, and Hacohen's group had begun a search for vessels in May 1940 through the Nahshon (later to become the Ayalon) Company. The liaison group faced all of the same difficulties in procuring boats as had the Mossad. At about the same time, in spring of 1940, Arazi had asked Shmarya Tsameret in Athens to find a vessel, and Arazi traveled to Greece to investigate the matter himself soon thereafter. In April and May, Tsameret provided Arazi with several contacts among Greek seamen and shipping agents that might lead to a vessel, but all these were rejected by the liaison group.[49]

Thus, in June 1940, as the Mossad's sources of funds were drying up, Italy had entered the war—lowering the prospects for aliyah bet and raising the hopes for cooperation—and as the liaison group was having difficulties finding suitable vessels, the sale of the *Darien* seemed to offer a better way for Shertok, Katznelson, and the Haganah heads to make political headway than did aliyah bet. This was the background for the decision to interrupt immigration work, given the new security situation, and to offer the use of the *Darien* to the British. According to Agami, the decision was reached at the home of Moshe Shertok. "We were all there," he reports without naming the participants, "and we received the money."[50]

The reasons for placing hard-won resources at the disposal of the British war effort would appear to have been extraordinarily important to those involved. All knew how difficult it was to obtain a ship. We must keep in mind Tsameret's contention that despite Italy's entry into the war, it was still possible to go on with illegal sailings, and other groups had continued to operate in Europe. The JDC was prepared to go on, and the Zionist organizations in New York demanded that the Kladovo group be taken out or the money returned.

Eliyahu Golomb, as head of the Haganah, was responsible both for aliyah bet and for cooperation with the British war effort. Thus, two different and opposing strategies were carried out under the same institutional framework, and the sale of the *Darien* exposed the areas in which the two strategies were most in conflict with each other. Was it indeed possible to carry out both sets of goals, which served such opposing interests? Can we conclude that Yehuda Arazi and Zvi Yehieli were working against each other in pressing for their respective priorities? It would seem that the use of the ships for military purposes endangered the refugees, endangered the ships themselves—so difficult to acquire—and could result in German termination of Jewish emigration.

According to the testimony of former Mossad members, they were aware of these dilemmas; nevertheless, they chose the path of a dual strategy. The principle that guided them in approaching any conflict between the two policies was the one Katznelson had formulated: to give priority to rescue of Jews.[51] But did this principle in fact guide the decision to sell the *Darien* to the British in July 1940? Or should we ask the question already about the decision to halt the emigration of the Kladovo group? The events may lead to a conclusion that the awareness of the dual strategy was clearly formulated at a later stage, when Mossad members had to explain to themselves why they were ready to give up the *Darien*.

The ship changed hands sometime in July. On July 15, Shind wrote to Tsameret: "The arrangements to transfer the ship here [to Alexandria] are complete. We have been given the funds. Await further details and the name of the ship's agent. Continue [further] contacts with 'Ovdim'—Yehuda Arazi."[52] This cable was the final authorization that completed the transfer of the *Darien* to the liaison group—to Yehuda Arazi. Tsameret wanted to pay off the debts remaining from the previous arrangements for the *Darien*, which consisted of money owed to their agent Victor Meyer and to the Jewish community members in Athens who had supported the aliyah bet activity from the start. He was informed by Shind that a representative of the Atid

Company would arrive to take charge of the *Darien* and that he would be empowered to clear up the debts to Meyer. Thereafter, the Atid Company would be responsible for operating the ship.[53]

The *Darien*'s transfer in effect marked the end of another stage in the Kladovo affair. In June, Spitzer obtained the permission of the Yugoslavian government to land the refugees who were still on board the riverboats in a tent camp in Kladovo. This permission was granted based on the commitment by the Jewish Agency to bring the refugees to Palestine as legal immigrants. Until such time, the JDC was prepared to pay for their upkeep.

The Jewish Agency, the Yugoslavian Communities, and the JDC Search for a Solution

The Jewish Agency pursued two different paths to aid the Kladovo group. It attempted to obtain immigrant certificates for the refugees to give them legal status, and it approached the Zionist organizations to provide funds for the refugees' maintenance. The Agency encountered an inflexible attitude among the British authorities on the subject of authorization for the immigrants. The pretext for the British refusal to admit the group was that it contained fifth columnists. The agency's immigration people and Moshe Shertok had un-successfully applied to the Mandatory administration for permits for a part of the group during the winter of 1940 when it became clear that they would have to spend the winter on the river. Appeals to London brought no result. In May and June, Eliezer Kaplan, who had always opposed aliyah bet, backed the plan to buy the *Darien* and proposed to help pay for it out of Jewish Agency funds to match those given by the JDC.

In June, Shertok reported that there was still no agreement in London to permit the refugees to enter the country. The Agency sent an official letter to Spitzer guaranteeing eventual entry to the Kladovo group, but there was no British confirmation of this.[54] Shertok and Golomb pressed their people in London to make a most urgent plea on behalf of the refugees.[55]

During the summer of 1940 a few certificates were issued, primarily due to efforts of relatives of individuals in the Kladovo group in Palestine. In March 1941, four groups of 111 children and 96 adults were allowed to enter the country under the Youth Aliyah framework and with other certificates. They traveled via Bulgaria, Turkey, and Syria. These were the sole survivors of the Kladovo group. The Jewish Agency was unable to bring the rest of them to Palestine legally. It failed to keep up a relentless campaign on their behalf, and appealed to the British authorities only intermittently, whenever the Mossad encountered setbacks in its own attempts to bring the group out. In effect, the Agency relied upon illegal immigration to solve the Kladovo problem.

The Yugoslavian communities and the JDC, by providing funding, made it possible for the group to remain in Yugoslavia. Yugoslavia was one of the major way stations for Jewish refugees en route to Palestine, and the Yugoslavian Jewish communities bore the brunt of the effort to assist them. In this, they demonstrated commendable solidarity with their fellow Jews. The government, in response to British pressure, continued to demand that the refugees leave the country; but at the same time, the authorities were sensitive to the fate of the refugees and to the position of Yugoslavian Jewry.[56] Spitzer himself was tireless in his efforts to obtain assistance for the refugees.

Concern for the Kladovo group was especially great because of the living conditions they had to endure. Inadequate hygienic conditions led to disease both in the cold winter months and during the hot summer. The situation improved somewhat after July 1940, when the refugees were permitted to set up camp on shore. In September, they were transferred to the town of Sabac on the Sava river, 250 kilometers northwest of Kladovo, and farther away from the Black Sea ports. There the refugees lived in solid buildings and were able to organize a more orderly social and cultural life. Funds were scarce, and in reports to the JDC Spitzer noted that the Jewish community had spent 12.5 million dinars ($625,000) from January to December 1940 to maintain the refugee group. Aid for all the refugees in Yugoslavia totaled 30 million dinars, half of which had been raised locally. Spitzer wrote to the JDC:

> We will need $55,000 per month. We leave it to you to determine how much a small community can raise on its own for these purposes. In Yugoslavia there are 70,000 Jews. If we assume that we can raise half of the amount locally, that means that each family must contribute five dollars a month. This is a very large sum.[57]

The JDC, the prime source of funds for maintenance of the group, demonstrated a certain ambivalence.[58] Formally, the JDC was opposed to illegal immigration, but in some sense it was forced to take such a position. It was an official organization recognized by the United States government, and it wished to cooperate with the British in refugee aid committees. During the course of 1939, the attitude of the JDC to aliyah bet developed and led to direct support of it as a way to save thousands of Jews from the Reich. At first, the JDC assisted the refugees only through the agency of the Jewish communities where they found shelter. When the war started, the JDC received an ever-growing number of appeals for assistance from groups unable to continue their journey. The host communities wanted the refugees to leave as soon as possible, for they were a drain on local resources and their prolonged stay was likely to have adverse effects on the attitude of the governments concerned.

In this situation, the JDC was called upon to relieve the budgetary and other pressures on the communities by granting assistance both to the refugee groups on their way to Palestine and to the aliyah bet organizers. It helped in the acquisition of ships, and gave aid to the Mossad, the Revisionists, as well as to Storfer. The JDC determined the level of aid to be given to each of these groups according to its judgment of the soundness of each one. That was the instruction it gave to its European representatives, Morris Tropper and Joseph Schwartz, in early 1940. They were asked to follow up and determine whether the JDC's funds were indeed being used for their stated purpose and whether departures of refugee groups were in fact taking place.

In 1940, the JDC was having a difficult time raising funds, and it had to tighten its already inadequate budget. It was forced to borrow on the strength of future income in order to maintain essential aid programs. As the costs involved in maintaining the Kladovo group continued to rise, the JDC was asked to increase its share. Sima Spitzer asked the JDC to commit itself to supplying a certain sum per person for as long as the group stayed in Yugoslavia. This the JDC refused to do, believing that this would weaken the motivation to get the group out of the country.[59]

The JDC took part in the purchasing efforts aimed at transporting the refugees and thus became one of the bodies pressuring the Mossad to bring the job to a swift conclusion. Without the help of Mr. Sally Mayer (the JDC's representative in Switzerland) and Tropper, it would have been impossible to maintain the group and to purchase the *Darien*. The Mossad agents appreciated the efforts of the JDC, even while keeping some distance from it as an organization that was anti-Zionist in orientation. Despite arguments that took place over various aspects of the work, the Mossad and the JDC managed to cooperate with each other. The JDC in fact preferred working with the Mossad to working with the Revisionists, Storfer, or with unaffiliated individuals, but was wary of what it saw as the Mossad's particularistic outlook. It therefore continued to work with the others as well.[60]

The *Darien*—An Immigrant Ship Again

In September 1940, two months after passing over into Yehuda Arazi's recognizance for work in the war effort, the *Darien* was again placed at the disposal of the Mossad. Plans to bring out the Kladovo refugees went into high gear. The explanation for this about-face is not a simple one.

Throughout the period from July to September, it had remained unclear just what the *Darien* was to be used for. At the end of August, the ship had sailed from Piraeus to Alexandria, and a month later, from Alexandria to Istanbul. While the ship had remained in Piraeus to be inspected by the agent of the Atid Company as arranged, very little was actually accomplished. The agent seemed lazy and negligent, and did nothing either to reach a compensation settlement with the Greek agents or to send the ship on its way, despite its readiness.[61] The agent's behavior prompted Tsameret to wonder whether the decision to transfer the *Darien* to war work had been final. The immigrant ship *Libertad*, sent in July by Konfino from Bulgaria, had arrived safely in Palestine, and Storfer was going ahead with his plans. These continuing operations gave him further cause to speculate that perhaps his colleagues in Palestine were changing their minds. He cabled to Shind on August 7: "Ship has not yet sailed. Atid Company doing nothing. Wire whether ship is leased to Atid or to Spitzer Company. Must know next step." But Tsameret's hopes were groundless. Shind sent him an unequivocal reply: "The deal with Atid stands. We are attempting to renew contacts with Spitzer."[62]

Tsameret, who was intimately acquainted with the shipping market, knew that without the *Darien* there was virtually no possibility of bringing out the Kladovo group. On August 11, he repeated his arguments, this time to Arazi.[63] On August 16, he was directed by Shind to dispatch the *Darien* to Alexandria as quickly as possible. Tsameret complied, and the *Darien* left for Alexandria after about ten days.[64]

But at precisely the same time as the *Darien* was making its way to Alexandria, a decision was made to resume the Kladovo work. Eliyahu Golomb summoned Yehuda Braginsky, who had headed the Mossad in Paris until the outbreak of the war, and asked him to lead the Mossad team in Istanbul and solve the Kladovo quandary. Golomb informed Braginsky that the *Darien* had again been designated to convey the Kladovo group and that funds to prepare the ship for its voyage were forthcoming from the Zionist movements in the United States.[65]

The sources suggest that the reasons for this decision had to do with the blow to the prestige of the Zionist leadership in Palestine arising from the mishandling of the Kladovo case thus far—already it was considered a major failure of the Mossad and of the Zionist movement. An overriding sense of obligation to take action to resolve the matter had resulted. No less important, it would seem, was the fact that there were others who continued to engage in secret aliyah work.[66]

One thing that emerges quite clearly from the course of events in the summer of 1940 is that the *Darien* was not assigned to any specific task in connection with the war effort, although various ideas had been put forward. Sending the *Darien* from Alexandria to Istanbul had to be coordinated with the liaison group,[67] but to judge from the way the plans involving its use were rejected, the British apparently were not interested in the ship. When the ship reached Mossad hands once more, it was in the same physical condition as it had been at the end of June: its hull had been reinforced by a steel frame, but it had not yet been outfitted for carrying passengers. These alterations were to be performed in Constantsa. It now appeared as if the rest of the mission would be fairly simple and that the Kladovo refugees would finally be rescued. In fact, however, when the *Darien* reached Sulina in December, the refugees were unable to get there. Why were the events unfolding this way?

Braginsky's task upon arriving in Istanbul on September 26 was to assure the completion of the job (including transfer of the refugees to the Black Sea) within two months. By December, the Danube might be frozen and impassable. Braginsky first had to purchase fuel for the boat, which proved problematic. Coal had to be paid for in foreign currency. Braginsky and Klueger Aliav (now in Istanbul and working alongside Braginsky) lacked the necessary $4,000. Golomb, in informing the American offices of the Zionist Organization that the Kladovo plan was once more operational, had requested the funds to pay for it.[68] But the Zionist organizations demanded to know where the funds sent previously had gone and contended that sufficient money had already been sent for the supply and refitting of the boat. Further funds were unavailable.[69]

Securing additional funding at this point required the active cooperation of Spitzer. But he, too, was disinclined to place much trust in the Mossad. The Mossad had, after all, made several promises that had gone unfulfilled. The fact that Spitzer was hesitant to cooperate with the Mossad was known in Jerusalem, and Braginsky was directed to meet with him right away to work out a satisfactory plan of action.[70] Braginsky was unable to succeed in this task. Spitzer was unable to obtain a visa to enter Turkey, and Braginsky could not get one for either Yugoslavia or Bulgaria.[71] Another meeting planned for mid-October between Barpal and Spitzer also never took place. After some time, Spitzer did appeal to the Zionist Organization and to the JDC to send funds to Braginsky, which Spitzer was willing to have deducted from the Kladovo aid budget.[72] The money finally arrived at the end of October, and the *Darien* sailed to Constantsa on 2 November.

Meanwhile, the war drew closer. Fighting in Greece grew heavy, and with the Italian army experiencing difficulties it was likely that the Germans would step in to assist. In Greece and Bulgaria, there was a very palpable fear of a German invasion. Thus, once again, the question arose of what to do with the *Darien*. Braginsky and his colleagues felt uneasy about leaving it for extensive refitting in Constantsa. They decided to take on board 160 legal immigrants (who paid full fare) for passage to Istanbul, where they transferred to the Palestinian boat *Hannah* for the voyage to Palestine.[73] This delayed work on the *Darien* by a week. It sailed back to Constantsa only on 9 November. Two more weeks of work were needed to prepare the *Darien* to receive the Kladovo group: two critical weeks, considering the danger of an early frost as had occurred the previous year.[74] It is therefore even more critical to consider why the group did not sail to Sulina during the month of November.

Spitzer had been ready and able to send the refugees on to Sulina during November, but would do so only on the condition that the ship was in dock, ready and waiting to receive them. We know that the refugees were ready to leave between 9 and 11 November. They had said good-bye to people in Sabac and had packed their bags. Groups had been formed and group captains assigned to make their departure more orderly. They were to travel down the Danube on Yugoslavian boats—the same riverboats on which they had lived in Kladovo—and were to reach Sulina within six days.

The trip was postponed by ten days and set for 20 November, and then put off for yet another two or three days. No one unpacked; all were ready. On 29 November they had still not left, however, and no departure date had been set. They knew that the ship waiting for them was "illegal," and that they would be joined by other illegal immigrants in Rumania. But, other than rumor, they had no information as to why they had not left yet.[75]

The only possible explanation permitted by the sources we have is that every time Spitzer received word that the *Darien* would not be ready by the set deadline, he delayed the refugees' departure from Sabac. Undoubtedly, he felt that past experience warranted such a course. Spitzer had no idea how advanced the work on the *Darien* was at that point, and he suspected that in reality more time was being "wasted" on transporting legal immigrants. How could he justify sending the refugees to Sulina under those circumstances?[76] It is possible that had Spitzer been able to meet with Braginsky or Barpal he might have been assured of their intentions and plans and have felt that he could trust the Mossad.

At the end of November, the *Darien* sailed for Sulina ready for its voyage and carrying 160 immigrants who had forced their way on board (including refugees from Poland, people from Rumania, and twenty Hehalutz members).[77] Upon arrival, it appeared that the Kladovo group was not there yet.

The Kladovo group had set December 2 as the embarkation day when the Yugoslavian shipping company began a series of postponements that ended with the cancellation of the contract. Two other plans for a combined journey, via train to Bulgaria and by a Rumanian barge to Sulina, could not meet the scheduled dates and were delayed until 16 December. Spitzer's confidence was further undermined by the news of the *Patria* tragedy in Palestine and of the sinking of the *Salvador* (an emigrant boat organized by Konfino from Bulgaria that had sunk in a storm). He concluded that the refugees were safer in Yugoslavia than on board the *Darien*, whose safe entry into Palestine was not assured.[78] The *Darien* waited for the Kladovo emigrants until 29 December, but when still they failed to arrive it departed Sulina amid a new storm of controversy, as we shall see.

The Kladovo refugees were crushed, and some appealed for help to Storfer and to the leadership of the Jewish communities, but to no avail. Storfer could offer no help; the Mossad discontinued its activity. Unable to leave Yugoslavia, the refugees waited for spring to come, and with it, they hoped, some solution to their predicament.[79]

The Nazi invasion of Yugoslavia began in the spring of 1941, on 6 April. In June, the refugees were put in a camp. In October, the men were murdered by the Germans, who claimed it to have been an act of reprisal for a partisan operation that had taken place in an area south of Belgrade. The women and children were gassed in May 1942. The Kladovo men were the first group of Jews to be killed by the Nazis in Yugoslavia. They came to symbolize for the rest of the Jewish community the failure of the Mossad to carry out its stated goals.[80]

Whose Ship Was the Darien?

In the darkest days of December 1940, as the *Darien* waited in Sulina for the riverboats that never arrived, the argument over who controlled the ship erupted afresh. Yehuda Arazi and David Hacohen demanded that the *Darien* be returned to them. It was not the property of the Mossad, they claimed, and was now required for war work. The Mossad emissaries in Istanbul challenged the right of Arazi's group to hand over to the British a ship that was needed to transport immigrants regardless of formalities. The conflict, seemingly a struggle between two distinct groups, actually involved people who were active in both refugee work and war work. Ze'ev Shind, Yosef Barpal, and Ruth Klueger Aliav, for example, were all active in both efforts at this point. For them, the conflict became one that each had to wage in his or her own conscience.

In order to understand the debate and its result, it is important to understand exactly why and for what purpose the *Darien* was needed at just this time, in December 1940 and January 1941. During July to September 1940, when the *Darien* was at the disposal of the liaison group for work in the war effort, it was not used for this purpose. Yehuda Arazi then agreed to transfer the ship to the Mossad in order to rescue the Kladovo refugees. We find no hint of any objection throughout October and November to the *Darien*'s being used for ferrying legal immigrants or for its preparations to pick up the Kladovo group.[81] Arazi and Hacohen consented to this because it was in their interest that the ship be used in this manner and because they had no other mission for it in that period. However, they considered it a loan, to be called in on demand, and rejected the contention that for the period in which Braginsky had refitted and used the *Darien* for the Mossad's purposes the status of the ship had changed.

However, Arazi and Hacohen were at this point ready with a sabotage plan in the Danube River for which they needed the *Darien*. Although both pushed for the plan's implementation, the British intelligence service was not yet ready to begin, though it demanded that all preparations be made.[82] British intelligence had followed the course of the *Darien* and expressed dissatisfaction about it to Arazi. The link between foreign policy and the intelligence services proved a factor here. British diplomatic personnel often worked for the intelligence services; Major Whitehall, for example, was both a consular official in Istanbul and an intelligence agent. Thus, in the very same months as Britain's unyielding policy on Jewish immigration and the reverberations of the *Patria* and *Salvador* incidents were provoking waves of criticism, arrangements were underway to bring the illegal Kladovo refugees to Palestine aboard a British boat!

The consequences of such an absurdity would have been clear to those in the intelligence services with Foreign Office connections, and it is a reasonable assumption that they quickly made them clear to the liaison group. The liaison group, alarmed at the prospect of seeing all plans for cooperative war work collapse, would have raised a hue and cry within the Zionist leadership. Despite the many disappointments in the late fall of 1940, the leadership still set great store in a policy of cooperation with England.[83] Yehuda Arazi and David Hacohen were personally involved in the *Darien* matter, and they would be directly implicated by any action it became involved in. Thus, the *Darien* became the focus of a political conflict between the Mossad agents and the war liaison group. Theoretically, Katznelson's formula giving priority to aliyah bet missions was designed to resolve such conflicts, but in practice it proved difficult to apply.

Arazi arrived in Istanbul in mid-December, and told Braginsky that his refusal to hand over the *Darien* would cause irreparable damage to the Zionist cause. Hacohen recruited Golomb's aid, and Golomb wired the following to Braginsky on 27 December: "*Darien* sold absolutely every delay in transmitting to buyers is not only unfair but endangering good name and position. See the cable David [Hacohen] Yehuda [Arazi] and act accordingly."[84] On 29 December Braginsky replied: "Due difficulties liberation obligations do not see possible fulfillment of your request in accordance your cable. Discuss matter again with Kadmon [Barpal]."[85] Now there began a struggle between Braginsky on the one hand and Arazi, Hacohen, and the Mossad leaders in Palestine on the other. Ze'ev Shind, Ruth Klueger Aliav, and Shmarya Tsameret were caught in between, grappling with an agonizing choice.

Although at first the Mossad agents believed that the Kladovo refugees might still arrive, by 27 December it was clear they would not and that the ship's passengers would be other refugees from Rumania.

A more difficult phase began when Barpal, followed by Hacohen, rushed to Istanbul to convince their colleagues to give up. This raised for the Mossad agents the question of authority and discipline alongside the question of relative priority between aliyah bet and war work. Where did the chain of command lead? To Braginsky in Istanbul, or to the Haganah (and Mossad) chiefs in Palestine, led by Golomb? We know from Braginsky's testimony and that of Klueger Aliav that the question of discipline was taken very seriously and that they knew a principle was at stake that could not be lightly dismissed. Shmarya Tsameret put it bluntly when he asked, "Who are we to make decisions against those of the leadership?"

What, however, was the alternative? Against the authority of the leadership were pitted the lives of 160 Jews on board the *Darien*. Forcing them to leave the ship meant, in all likelihood, sentencing them to die. And hundreds more were waiting in Varna hoping for a boat—the *Darien*—to take them on.[86]

On 29 December, the *Darien* left Sulina for Constantsa, and Alexander Shapiro, from the Palestine office in Bucharest, took the responsibility of preparing a list of passengers. Nothing seemed to go well for the Mossad agents over the next weeks. The *Darien* ran aground on 30 December, and only heroic efforts saved it from sinking. Nevertheless, it was badly damaged and required repairs.

During this time, pressure on the Mossad agents intensified. They were called to a dramatic confrontation with David Hacohen. He read them cables from Moshe Shertok referring to a letter from Chaim Weizmann that made it clear that all hope for future cooperation with the British rested on putting an end to the *Darien* problem. He demanded that the 160 passengers be put ashore and the ship be handed over to him at once. All but Braginsky gave in. The *Darien* was damaged, and there was no longer any hope of saving the Kladovo refugees. On 5 January, Arazi wired to Palestine:[87]

1. The owners have agreed to hand over the ship.
2. Hope to take possession by end of January.

3. Delay was caused by need to cancel prior commitments and make alternate arrangements for cargo.
4. Owners request my assistance in this and I will remain here until *Darien*'s departure arranged.

Even so, the *Darien* incident did not end. None of the Mossad agents dared tell the refugees on board that they had to disembark. The situation for Jews in Rumania had worsened in January 1941. More than a hundred Jews were killed in pogroms in Bucharest, including Zionist leaders. As Braginksy later wrote: "After three days Ruth [Klueger Aliav] called me and asked me to meet her. She said, 'What is going to happen?' I asked her if she was willing to commit herself to go on working with me and not look back. Ruth said yes, and the voyage continued."[88] The *Darien* was repaired in Constantsa, and plans were made to take on 500 more refugees. On 31 January, Braginsky wired: "The management has decided to continue working without interruption. We also ask that you help make an agreement with Yehuda [Arazi]. If there are problems and further opposition, Kadmon will come to you immediately. It is essential to go on."[89]

Feverish preparations took up the next two weeks. The *Darien* was scheduled to leave Constantsa on 19 February. Shind went to Sofia to organize an additional group of passengers and to make financial and fuel arrangements for the trip. In addition to a group of 300 immigrants to go aboard the *Darien* itself, Shind wanted to hitch on a barge, called the *Struma,* which could hold another 350 passengers. His negotiations were almost concluded when the German invasion of Bulgaria intervened, forcing the *Darien* to leave without the *Struma.*[90] The ship sailed on 27 February 1941, arriving in Istanbul on 2 March, where it remained for a week. Forty survivors of the *Salvador* and a number of refugees from Poland and Czechoslovakia were taken on board; the captain, who quit, was replaced, and coal was loaded for the journey.

All the while, Hacohen had been trying to make other arrangements for the *Darien* refugees, so that he might take control of the ship himself. Several ideas were mentioned, including putting them ashore in Egypt, in Bengazi, in the Greek isles, Athens, and various other places. He hoped to obtain the help of British political authorities in Turkey.[91] Yet, once again, policy decisions were preempted by objective circumstances, and on 10 March the *Darien* departed for Palestine. On 19 March, the ship was intercepted and impounded by the British (who, of course, were actually the owners of the ship). The passengers were interned at Atlit for a year and a half. Thus, the odyssey of the *Darien,* replete with many failures, ended with one success: the rescue of 786 Jewish refugees from Rumania, Poland, and Bulgaria.

The *Darien*'s arrival in Palestine represented the final episode in the dramatic events of 1940. The Mossad, which had been caught unprepared for the war, had managed to recover somewhat and to place its people in various spots to help Jews leave Europe. Aliyah bet had increasingly become a rescue mission, and as such there was less and less selection of immigrants according to the requirements of the Yishuv. However, selectivity was not completely abandoned, partly because of the British fears of a German fifth column planted within refugee groups. The Mossad felt obligated to check each refugee, since the Jewish Agency had committed itself to exert vigilance in this matter.

As 1940 progressed, the Mossad activists developed an attitude toward the situation in Europe that was quite different from those prevailing in Palestine or America. They were in direct contact with the Jewish communities and their leaders, and were able to receive via Switzerland shocking reports of the fate of Jews in the occupied zones. This firsthand knowledge gave them a feeling of mounting urgency in their mission—a sense that seemed to get lost when the same reports were read by those farther removed, in the relative calm of everyday life in Palestine and America. The gap in attitude was evident by the spring of 1940. The fear of losing precious time was not of paramount consideration among the political leadership, as it was among the Mossad activists in the field. Yehieli and Agami began to establish contact with people in Poland and to send funds with agents. Despite failures and setbacks, the Mossad expanded its activity in the first six months of 1940. There was a general feeling that their mistakes could still offer valuable lessons for coming operations.

In June 1940, however, Italy's entry into the war caused a sort of paralysis in the Mossad, returning it to the situation of the first months of the war. The *Darien* was sold and the Kladovo group was all but abandoned; Yehieli left Geneva for Palestine with little reservation about neglecting aliyah work.[92] Agami also departed, leaving Tsameret as the only Mossad member in Athens. The Mossad's activity in Istanbul later that year proved to be brief and ineffective, and the Kladovo *Darien* incident was a critical event in this regard.

Why didn't these men resist more forcefully the decision to halt illegal immigration work? One can understand their helplessness, perhaps, in the face of the war's expansion into the Mediterranean. But, apart from the security problem, it seems that Zionist policy played a role in bringing aliyah bet to a halt at this juncture. From the historical perspective, one can say that the Mossad erred very seriously. For a short period of time the Mossad resumed work in Istanbul, but the Kladovo *Darien* affair caused a new crisis.

4

Revisionist Aliyah

Principles and Working Patterns

In contrast to the ambivalence that plagued the Jewish Agency, the Haganah, and the Mossad, the Revisionist movement unequivocally supported the idea of aliyah bet. Revisionist leaders voiced no qualms about having to resort to unorthodox methods, and the potential damage to Zionist political interests did not worry them. The Revisionist movement was in extreme opposition to the Zionist policy conducted by the labor coalition. Their differences were so profound that in 1935 the Revisionists split from the Zionist movement and formed a separate political party, which they called the New Zionist Organization (NZO). The Revisionists saw the creation of a Jewish state in the entire land of Israel as an ultimate and immediate goal. Their dispute with labor was not limited to political considerations alone; it also extended to social policy and labor's Socialist vision of a new Jewish society.

Ze'ev Jabotinsky, the leader of the Revisionist movement, formulated the Revisionist view publicly on at least two occasions. In a speech in Warsaw as early as 1932, he advocated illegal entry to Palestine as a form of preferred Zionist "adventurism" that might bend or break laws to a positive result. In his 1939 article "The National Sport,"[1] illegal aliyah was assigned a pivotal role: simultaneously shaping the individual Zionist character, contributing toward the reality of statehood, and elevating the status of the Revisionists within the Zionist movement. According to Jabotinsky, participation in secret aliyah rendered the individual an independent-minded militant who asserted control over his own destiny, while illegal aliyah itself was an effective tool in achieving statehood. Insofar as the Revisionist movement's status was considered, steadfast and unequivocal support for aliyah bet would demonstrate its superiority to mainstream Zionism both morally and politically—in the concern it demonstrated for the fate of all Jews and in its unqualified pursuit of a national home.

So strong was the Revisionist leader's avowal of the aliyah bet that he refused to refer to it as "illegal aliyah," with the implicit denial it carried of the right of every Jew to immigrate to Palestine. Instead he argued that it was Britain's restrictions that contravened natural law,[2] and he sought to

69

convince the Rumanian and Polish governments on these grounds. On several occasions he urged them to challenge British immigration policy, either directly or through the League of Nations.

Thus, by virtue of Jabotinsky's leadership the Revisionist movement considered secret aliyah as an imperative. However, each of the movement's three wings had its own views regarding its practice and implications. The underground militant faction Irgun (IZL) saw aliyah bet as a means of gaining new recruits. For its purposes, careful selection and training of immigrants—and secrecy—were required.

The Revisionist youth organization Betar pressed for an aliyah of young people—and in large numbers. Betar argued that youth were of greatest service to the Revisionists, both as proponents of its ideals and as a force attracting Jewish youth in general to join the Revisionists. The NZO, the political party espousing the Revisionist view, sought to expand its influence within the Jewish communities as a whole and in Palestine. This required establishing a strong institutional base in Palestine through immigration of party activists. Aliyah was viewed as a means of augmenting the movement's political strength and advancing its effort to gain political strength within the Yishuv and the Zionist movement.

Moreover, differences arose over the selection of immigrants. Quantity or quality—which should take priority? This was a significant debate because it revealed the underlying humanitarian and political motivations for promoting aliyah. Was aliyah bet primarily a rescue effort, aimed at saving persecuted Jews, or was it meant to serve the ends of a particular political group? If the emphasis of aliyah was rescue, then it was immaterial who organized aliyah efforts, how they were organized, and who was sent to Palestine. The ideas proposed tended to be contradictory, and no clear answers were formulated. Jabotinsky's basic concept was an aliyah "for all who need it"—that is, a nonselective effort, unlimited by any sort of political criteria. The circumstances under which aliyah bet was carried out made it difficult to approach the problem theoretically or rationally. In most cases, these were operations that arose out of a bitter struggle for survival. On one side the German threat loomed menacingly, while on the other, British immigration policy choked off the most obvious avenue of escape.

In addition, efforts to organize secret aliyah were affected by local conditions and problems. Poland in 1938–39 was bursting with Betar youth seeking any and every exit route. Vienna, Prague, and Bratislava were, at the same period, like volcanoes about to erupt, prompting desperate thousands with nowhere to go to respond eagerly to anyone who seemed to offer a chance at escape. Necessity and practical realities were the anvil on which methods, planning, and ideology were forged. While ideology and social class certainly played a role in determining how Revisionists approached aliyah planning, the most decisive factors undoubtedly were the specific circumstances of each locality and the personalities of those involved.

Revisionist Attempts at Centralizing Aliyah

The first Revisionist efforts at secret aliyah were made in Austria and Poland in 1937 and 1938. These were the work of individuals and of the Revisionist sympathizer Moshe Galili. (See Chapter 1.) Aliyah bet work tended to attract those with a streak of daring, a talent for improvisation, and contacts in the business world (to gain access to credit and to the authorities). Because of its unpredictability and riskiness, aliyah activities also required a pronounced single-mindedness, and the organizers tended to compete with each other and work at cross-purposes. In late 1938 and early 1939, while the dimensions and urgency of the problem grew, conflicts among the organizers and public criticism of them were also mounting. In addition, the divergent interests of the movement's wings became more pronounced, adding to frictions. Irgun sought more potential members, while Betar pressed for its own constituency. Most of its members could not afford to pay for tickets but could no longer bear the anguish of being left behind. The NZO wanted to save those who had been faithful to the party, and these people generally possessed the necessary funds as well.[3]

The central leadership felt that a more formal arrangement was called for and that the movement's role in aliyah activities should be defined. Allegations that Revisionist aliyah organizers had abused their positions and misused funds reached the central Revisionist office in London, and initial attempts at an accord on organization of aliyah from Poland had been made by Eri Jabotinsky (Ze'ev Jabotinsky's son), the leader of Betar in Palestine, and Hillel Kook of the Irgun.[4]

Ze'ev Jabotinsky used the opportunity of a major meeting called in Paris in February 1939 to coordinate the work of the Irgun and Revisionists in Palestine as a venue to address the question of the movement's role in aliyah. Aliyah activists from various countries and Irgun, Betar, and NZO representatives took part. Disputes among the parties were strident, and only by virtue of Ze'ev Jabotinsky's moral sway was a compromise reached.

It was agreed that all aliyah work would be centralized under an agency called the Center for Aliyah in Paris. It would supervise operations to be carried out by the three wings: Eri Jabotinsky (Betar) was responsible for overland transportation; Yitzhak Rozin (Irgun) for sea transportation and clandestine landing; and Yosef Katznelson (NZO) for financial transactions. Financial accounts were to be monitored by the NZO. Shlomo Yaakobi (Yankelewitz), a lawyer, was assigned the task of exercising overall control and arbitrating disputes. It was agreed that the interests of the movement as a whole were to guide the selection of candidates for immigration. A percentage was set aside for Betar members, and Irgun requirements for trainees were to be met.

Following the meeting in Paris, efforts to centralize Revisionist aliyah continued. However, in the wake of the St. James Conference (the final British attempt at negotiating a solution between Arabs and the Yishuv) and the 1939 White Paper, the emphasis of aliyah efforts shifted somewhat to one of political struggle against Britain. The Revisionist leadership adopted two additional plans regarding secret immigration. First, immigrant ships were to be supplied with weapons in order resist British coastal patrols, and second, a strategy should be developed to inundate Palestine with thousands of illegals to arrive simultaneously aboard a flotilla of vessels. Both decisions reflected the basic Revisionist commitment to inflammatory protest and militant struggle.

It is interesting to note that at this time, Ben-Gurion, too, advocated illegal aliyah as a show of rebellion against the White Paper. However, he received little support from the Zionist Organization and soon abandoned the idea. The Revisionists took several concrete steps toward realizing such a plan, but at some point their efforts failed. They launched a massive fund-raising campaign in the United States and South Africa and set up an aliyah bank. They also dispatched a team of envoys to collect funds and to stir up activity. Nothing came of these efforts, however. The Center for Aliyah and the Aliyah Bank were unable to arrange the transport even of those groups that were already organized and awaiting departure.

The NZO office in London did make contacts with several chartering and brokerage firms.[5] During the summer of 1939, negotiations began for three ships: *Naomi Julia, Parita,* and *St. Bruek.* Nevertheless, even after great preparation, only two ships were organized in a centralized, coordinated fashion: the *Parita* and the *Naomi Julia.* These arrived in Palestine in August and September 1939. The *Parita* and the *Naomi Julia*'s voyages were the exception to the rule; the other Revisionist vessels, by far the major part, were arranged privately by individual Revisionists without coordination with the Aliyah center.

There are two reasons why the Revisionists were unable to implement a centrally organized arrangement: the mounting pressure against Jews in German-ruled territories and the large size of the network of individual Revisionist aliyah agents already at work in Warsaw, Vienna, Prague, and Bucharest. These agents were under pressure to arrange transport for the growing numbers wishing to leave Europe. They saw the decisions of the central office regarding who would be chosen to leave, how much the refugees could be asked to pay, and how the operation would be supervised at the local level as irrelevant given the reality of the situation. Conflicts between the central office and those established organizers in the field were ongoing. An examination of prewar Revisionist aliyah shows that the central office attempted to impose order and accountability on the quasiprivate organizers, but to little avail.

The Problem of the Independent Revisionist Aliyah Activists

Following the Anschluss (March 1938), Vienna became the center of operations, though a large percentage of those leaving continued to come from Poland. Betar continued to insist on a larger allocation of places in aliyah vessels for its Polish members. But the proportion of youth movement members among the emigrants decreased over time, and the illegal immigration came to consist of those who were better able to pay the expenses of such ventures. The Center for Aliyah in Paris received many complaints of poor organization, abuses of power, diversion of public funds for personal use, and intolerable shipboard conditions. The central offices relayed these criticisms to the activists in the field, but rather than prompt improvements in operations, these only served to fuel hostilities.

One example of this was the case of Wilhelm (Willi) Perl, a Vienna lawyer and former Betar activist.[6] Perl apparently began his independent aliyah operations following a meeting of prominent Revisionists and other leaders of the community called by Eichmann in May 1938. Eichmann demanded that a large-scale Jewish emigration be organized from Austria. Previously, Perl had worked closely with Galili, and though he objected to the Vienna NZO's decision to suspend cooperation with Galili in 1937, he continued organizing aliyah missions.[7] Working in cooperation with Paul Haller and Hermann Flesch (members of a Revisionist activist group known as Action), Perl planned the voyages of two ships, *Daraga I* and *Daraga II*. These reached Palestine in October and December 1938, respectively. (The *Daraga II* was the first vessel to sail down the Danube, proving that this route could be used as an alternative to overland travel across Europe.)

Perl, Haller, and Flesch arranged several other voyages in the months that followed: *Ely* and *Geppo I* and *II* (January–February 1939); *Sandu* and *Ageus Nicolaus* (March 1939); *Aghia Dezioni* and *Astia* (April 1939); and *Niko* (July 1939). Together, the three were responsible for the escape of 3,758 people. This was accomplished without supervision or aid from the offices of the movement. Nevertheless, accusations of fraud were lodged against the group and registered with the NZO. Though they acted independently, the public and the passengers perceived them as representatives of the Revisionist movement and demanded accountability from the NZO.[8]

The individual Revisionist agents involved in emigration work were so numerous and well-established that they were quite capable of achieving adequate results independent of the central office. They were able to finance the operations out of passenger fares and did not in general require the movement's structure, guidance, and support.[9] The movement expelled some members on the grounds of operating independent aliyah networks and on charges of corruption. Those who were expelled, however, felt they had been unfairly judged since in their belief they had proceeded according to the movement's own principles.

In response to the proliferation of agents, the central offices in Paris and London attempted to take control and denounced private aliyah work for damaging the reputation and credibility of the movement. Yehuda Benari, the general counsel of the movement, sent letters to Revisionist leaders in Austria, Czechoslovakia, and Rumania demanding that disciplinary measures be taken against private operators and other activists, along with threat of expulsion.

Haller and Flesch were eventually expelled, and even Perl, a major figure in independent aliyah and among the first people to engage in such work,

Jewish refugees on a boat in the Mediterranean, summer 1939.

The *Astia*, spring 1939.

Two refugees from the *Asimi*, after arrival in Palestine, summer 1939.

Jewish refugees crowded on a boat in the Mediterranean, summer 1939.

was for a period suspended from the NZO until charges against him were cleared. On 5 June 1939, Benari wrote to Jabotinsky saying that he had tried to investigate the nature of Perl's work and charges of his improper accounting practices for some time:

> As I have already touched upon one unpleasant topic, allow me to mention yet another—the matter of Dr. Perl. At his request I have granted him four extensions of the deadline for transferring certain documents to me. The last extension lapsed on 17 May, and at that point I suspended his membership. . . .
>
> I felt obliged to inform Dr. Perl that unless he desists from the private venture that he has started, I shall be forced to take the same steps against him as I took with regard to Haller and Flesch, etc. In response he sent me a wire, in addition to a letter, in which he expressed his willingness to submit to my demand and end his venture. Thus, only [the question of Perl's financial accountability] remains to be resolved.[10]

Benari's files contain much information that attests to Center for Aliyah efforts to centralize and exercise control over the work being carried out in cities across Europe. Yet the lack of agreement among the Revisionists over the nature of aliyah—and whether the movement had a right to attempt to direct it—extended even to those offices that kept close and steady ties with the Center for Aliyah in Paris and London. A dispute that arose among activists in the NZO/Betar office in Prague is one such example.[11]

The office had conducted a very successful immigration operation, and at its head were two eminent Revisionist members, Oscar Rabinowitz, a prominent member of the NZO in Prague, and Eliyahu Glazer, head of Betar in Czechoslovakia. The two clashed over a matter related to financial accountability, and the dispute extended to the role of the Center for Aliyah in the operation of the office. Rabinowitz, though a steadfast Revisionist supporter, held that the NZO and the Center for Aliyah had no role and no authority in aliyah bet from Czechoslovakia. The operation had been developed locally, and his own involvement in it, Rabinowitz asserted, was as a private individual and not as a party member. Glazer thoroughly disagreed and called Rabinowitz before the NZO court in London. The war intervened, however, and the matter was never settled.[12]

In the case of an operation organized by Avraham Stavsky in Greece, movement control seemed to disintegrate over time. Stavsky began his work in close cooperation with the Center for Aliyah and enlisted the services of Jacques Aron, a private entrepreneur with rather questionable business practices. Working together, Stavsky and Aron brought five vessels carrying some 3,000 people to Palestine in the summer of 1939. As their operations progressed, however, Stavsky found himself working with Aron in a private capacity and independently of the Center.[13]

Thus, the Center for Aliyah and the Revisionist movement were quite unsuccessful in controlling the communities where movement members continued to work simultaneously as private individuals and as movement representatives. Aliyah operations from Rumania, an important center of immigration for the NZO, are a good example of this mounting problem.

The Effort to Coordinate Aliyah through Rumania

For geographical and political reasons, Rumania became the chief point of embarkation for illegal ships in 1939. The route out of Rumania, via the ports of Constantsa and Sulina, obviated the need for transit visas for the Southern European and Balkan countries (the way to the Italian and Greek ports previously used). Of equal importance, however, was the Rumanian regime's permissive attitude toward Jewish emigration. Throughout the previous year, the local Jewish organizations had endeavored to encourage this attitude.[14] Revisionists in Rumania likewise sought to meet with the king, government ministers, and lesser officials in order to cultivate their favorable leanings.

Ze'ev Jabotinsky was received by the Rumanian king on two occasions: in London in summer 1938 and in October 1938 in Bucharest.[15] In these meetings, an agreement was reached regarding transit visas and assistance for Jews en route to Palestine. Jabotinsky also hoped to convince the Rumanian government to press the British regarding their policies in Palestine, and in particular those dealing with Jewish immigration. Jan Kostin, the NZO's political representative in Rumania, met with the minister of internal affairs, the prime minister, and other high officials to seek provisions to facilitate aliyah bet from Rumania.

By late 1938, the Rumanian government had taken many cooperative measures. It consented to the passage of refugees through its territory and instructed its consuls in Eastern and Central Europe to issue the necessary visas without the usual red tape. The government also agreed to permit local organization of aid to the refugees, purchases of provisions for the trip to Palestine, and entry of aliyah organizers into the country. However, in the spring of 1939, the government attached a proviso to its free-transit policy for refugees, allowing entry to further refugees only if a vessel awaited them in port.

The Rumanian attitude greatly facilitated logistics. In January 1939, Glazer, Haller, and Perl obtained transit documents for groups of up to 400 and 600 people from the Rumanian consuls in Austria and Czechoslovakia. The refugees were able to travel directly to Constantsa and embark on their sea voyage.[16] Further evidence of the government's cooperation are found in an NZO report of 1 November 1939.

1. Internal affairs ministry has approved entry for our transports from Germany, Czechoslovakia and Poland. The foreign ministry has issued instructions [to permit the groups' entry] to its consuls in Vienna, Prague and Warsaw.
2. Our representatives Propes, Glazer and Haller have obtained an extraordinary permit to receive an unlimited number of transit passes, without the usual formalities.
3. Despite prior difficulties, transit visas have been granted to Eri Jabotinsky and to Yosef Katznelson.[17]

In Rumania, a serious attempt was made to centralize activity, separate functions and delegate tasks, both before the Paris conference in February 1939 and after. The three wings of the Revisionist movement—Betar, Irgun, and the NZO—agreed to a joint leadership team, yet coordination problems and disagreements over the goals of aliyah operations continued to beset the movement.

The leading Revisionist figures in the country held prominent positions in economic and public life. Jan Kostin was a senator in the Rumanian parliament, and Edward Kenner was a well-known businessman. The two men took responsibility for approaching government officials in the internal affairs ministry, the police, and the security police (the Siguaranza). Jacob Schiber, Eugene Meisner, and other Betar members took charge of organizing and supplying the emigrant groups throughout their stays in Rumania. Michael Goren (Gorenstein), a member of NZO, was an engineer with numerous contacts. He supervised fund-raising and dealings with lesser government

officials and members of the security police. A lawyer by the name of Theodore Dankner, an NZO member who headed the local Palestine Office of
the Jewish Agency, arranged official bribes necessary to secure visas, passports, and the like.[18] Irgun members were sent from Palestine to escort the
immigrant ships.

The existence of a firm established for Jewish emigration, "Rompalia,"
is indicated in certain documents, although none of the Revisionist activists
have confirmed this. Rompalia's legal papers[19] give its purpose as facilitating
the emigration of Jews from Rumania to Palestine and other countries. In
addition, the papers state that it was "to be a vehicle for all of our activity
that cannot be directly undertaken in the name of the NZO and Betar."
Kenner's home address is listed as the temporary headquarters of the
company.

Because of the lack of independent corroboration, it is difficult to judge
how long this cooperative effort was in place. The documents referring to the
company are dated January 1939. We know that high-level contacts were
made in October 1938 (Jabotinsky's and Kostin's talks with the king, the
prime minister, and other senior officials). It is possible that not until October
were agreements in principle on the passage of Jewish refugees through Rumania framed.[20] Thus, only in the wake of these was Rompalia established.
In any event, the central bodies of the movement soon divested themselves
of the company. Ownership was transferred to local movement members who
operated on a private basis.

The documents pertaining to Rompalia date from the period before the
Paris conference—showing that the effort at coordination emerged locally.
Despite the sophisticated attempts made to cooperate, the voyages that were
organized during this period (and for which Jabotinsky and others sought
arrangements with government) were all sponsored on a semi-private basis:
the *Ely* and *Geppo* by Haller and Perl, and the *Katina* and *Geppo II* by Glazer
and Rabinowitz's Czech offices.[21]

On the eve of the war, the Center for Aliyah succeeded in organizing two
ships: the *Parita,* which reached the shores of Palestine in August 1939 and
was seized by the British, and the *Naomi Julia.* Problems of a different sort
arose in these voyages—those involved in coordinating the various facets of
a centrally organized venture. The ships were acquired through a French
company at the instruction of Eri Jabotinsky and Glazer (who had left Prague
in March 1939). Betar in Poland assembled the groups who were to sail aboard
the vessels, while a Greek shipping agent prepared the craft for the voyage.
However, the emigrants from Poland failed to arrive in Constantsa as scheduled; they were held back at the Polish frontier, unable to obtain permission
to cross.[22]

The *Naomi Julia* was kept waiting idly for them in port. At the same time,
two other groups from Austria and Slovakia were waiting on boats in the
Danube for clearance to enter Rumania. These groups had been arranged
through the independent efforts of two members of the Revisionist movement.

The groups were threatened with deportation back to the Reich, and the Revisionist aliyah office in Bucharest agreed to substitute them for the original passengers of the *Naomi Julia*.

The ship sailed on 25 August but was seized off the shores of Palestine. The tugboat *Catherine* was to have met the immigrants outside the territorial limit but failed to appear for the rendezvous. The vessel was confiscated and its crew arrested. (According to the terms of its lease, the *Naomi Julia* was not to have entered Palestinian waters.)

Thus, despite the planning that had gone into the *Naomi Julia* transport, the voyage that actually materialized came about through a combination of independent work and coordinated activity. With the numerous seizures of vessels and the outbreak of war, the cost of hiring vessels soared.[23] Thus, as the war began, aliyah bet entered a different era, under vastly changed conditions.

The *Sakariya* Affair[24]

As war broke out at the end of August 1939, Revisionist Aliyah organizers were in the midst of solving the problem of transport for two groups that had been organized long before. One group of 400 people had been assembled by Naftali Paltin, Betar's leader in Prague, as early as March 1939, but the German invasion had barred its departure from Czechoslovakia. Another group of 350 had been formed by Yehoshua Citron (Halevi), head of Betar in Bratislava. Attempts were made to reschedule their departure, and the two groups kept in close communication with each other and with London and Paris. Both groups consisted of a varied population, including Betar youth, older Revisionist movement members, and unaffiliated Jews.

The Bucharest office, headed at the time by Eri Jabotinsky and Eugene Meisner, took charge of arranging travel down the Danube and sea passage to Palestine.[25] After months of negotiations, the two acquired the *St. Bruek*. They were aided in negotiations and financing by Reuven Hecht, an activist engaged in a broad range of activities linked to aliyah bet who was based in Switzerland.

The *St. Bruek* was acquired on behalf of the Bratislava group. A lease was signed on 21 July 1939, stipulating length of the journey, cost, additional charges for delays, and port of embarkation. It also contained a provision allowing for the addition of other passengers along its route. The ship's owner tried to alter the contract in his favor in August, and on 26 September, after war had broken out, he decided to cancel the lease.[26]

The immediate departure for the Prague and Bratislava groups was now out of the question. Funds had become extremely scarce, and the Bucharest office proved unable to recover the losses incurred in the *St. Bruek* venture. It requested assistance from the NZO executive in London, and Shlomo Yaakobi tried to collect on debts owed by the movement's partners in the

Naomi Julia transport. They carried on a lengthy correspondence through the end of the year, but without result.[27]

Meisner and Eri Jabotinsky worked at a fever pitch, negotiating simultaneously over several vessels. They opened discussions with Jacques Aron over the *Varko*[28] and with the agent Davara. There was also competition in the market: Perl was at the time seeking transport through Davara for a group of 400 he had organized in Vienna with Storfer's assistance. Yet Jabotinsky remained hopeful. In a letter to the NZO executive of 4 October, he averred that within ten days a large convoy would be ready for departure. It would include the Bratislava and Prague groups, a contingent of Polish Jews waiting in Hungary, and a number of Rumanians. Jabotinsky believed that Betar would make up about 40 percent of the entire lot.

His optimism proved ill-founded, however. Negotiations with Davara fell through; the *Varko* proved to be too expensive, and in the months that followed prices rose tremendously. Meanwhile, the financial resources of the Center for Aliyah plummeted, virtually ruling out any further activity in the very weeks that were so crucial to the Jews in Reich territory. All realized the need to leave as quickly as possible, given the threats, violence, and steps taken toward a mass expulsion of Jews to Lublin.

Paltin and the group in Prague realized they had to leave regardless of whether a ship awaited them in Rumania. The expense of maintaining the group had grown steadily, and Paltin had already been forced to spend money paid for ship's passage on provisions. By early October, Paltin had resolved to set out. He realized that as long as he was able to fund the trip from Prague to Rumania, he had a slight amount of leverage. Once his money ran out, he would have no choice at all, and would be entirely dependent on decisions made in London and Bucharest. He sent a blistering letter to the NZO executive on 10 October, declaring that by the time the letter had reached its destination, he and his people would already be on their way.[29] He also warned Bucharest, since leaders there had not responded to his complaints and requests. He proceeded to lease Yugoslavian riverboats to take his group to a Rumanian port. The fate of the group was now up to Bucharest.

Those in Bucharest—especially Michael Goren and Meisner—urged Paltin to remain, but it was too late. The group arrived in Rumania in the first week of November. The Bucharest office hired a barge, the *Spyroula,* to ferry the refugees to Sulina. The group boarded at Moldava Vysha on 9 November 1939, and arrived in Sulina on 22 November.

Another period of waiting and uncertainty now began that was to last two months.[30] For most of the period, the passengers remained on board the *Spyroula.* Conditions were barely tolerable. The barge consisted of two large compartments divided into areas for men and women, with one space designated for families. The only enclosed cabin on board became the dispensary, and it was staffed by doctors from among the refugees. A strict daily regimen was instituted, and the passengers were divided into groups and assigned leaders from among the Betar members. The group leaders, instructed by those in charge, dealt with the allocation of space, rationing of food, contacts with the outside world, and social events. Many of those on board the *Spyroula* had been inmates of concentration camps. Despite difficult circumstances, a remarkable degree of cooperation was achieved on the cramped barge.

Every effort was made to relieve the tedium and the hardship, and the birth of two infants cheered the refugees somewhat. But winter came early and conditions grew more bleak. The boat was not equipped with heat, and the cold was bitter. The local Jewish communities sent warm clothing and blankets in response to the urgent requests of Wilhelm Filderman, head of the Refugee Aid Committee in Rumania and a representative of the JDC.[31] This was little more than a palliative, however. Supplying the group with food proved costly, and the Revisionist movement had no money to pay for expenses despite its repeated appeals to the JDC and local communities. Some money was supplied by the movement's overseas branches, but it was not nearly sufficient. In the meantime, the worsening cold made it necessary to move some of the women and children onto a riverboat, the *Stefanu*. While not fit for travel, it at least had heat. Eri Jabotinsky, who was burdened with the task of ensuring the day-to-day survival of the group, was simultaneously engaged in a desperate search for funds with which to acquire a ship.

Willi Perl's Last Transport

In October 1939, Willi Perl had one last opportunity to organize the passage of a group of Palestine-bound émigrés. He did this with the help of Storfer and Robert Mendler (who became Storfer's representative in Prague). After the war began, Eichmann centralized all emigration activity under Storfer's direction, at first shrinking and then eliminating the private organizers' range of maneuver.

Perl hired a German riverboat, the *Saturnus,* to take 200 Jews from Vienna and 600 from Prague to Sulina. They embarked on 1 November and arrived twelve days later. Perl had paid for the river journey in deutsche marks, using funds from the local Jewish communities, but foreign currency was needed for sea passage. Storfer had the ability to obtain this, but he failed to do so. (Storfer had contacts at the Central Bank in Prague, which at this time still permitted currency transfers for Jewish emigration.) Perl calculated that he had just enough money to pay for the rest of the trip, but when his Greek shipping agent broke their contract, he was left empty-handed.[32]

Perl sought help from Michael Goren in Bucharest, with whom he had a long-standing relationship. Goren, aided by a friend in the "Rumania" company, located and arranged the hire of the *Sakariya*. The 3,500-ton, Turkish-registered vessel was operated by the brothers Avni Oglu[33] and carried coal from Greece to Turkey. The first contract for the vessel contained no mention of the purpose of the imminent journey, stating only that it would require four days' sailing time and that the ship would be carrying 900 passengers. Nevertheless, the ship was leased for a one-month period. The price of £6,750 was to be paid in two installments, the first (£3,000) upon signing of the lease and the balance when the ship sailed.

The *Sakariya* was to have reached Sulina during November, but it was delayed several times. Not until 10 December did it finally arrive. Only then did the ship's Turkish owners and crew learn the nature of their mission. The plight of the refugees on the *Spyroula* and the *Saturnus* had achieved international notoriety. Reports had appeared widely in the press on the refugees' pitiful struggle and alleging that the groups' organizers were exploiting the refugees for profit.[34] The *Sakariya*'s owners were well aware of the consequences of engaging in illegal immigration voyages, and on 12 December they declared they were canceling their agreement with Goren.[35] Goren and the others tried to persuade them otherwise, offering them a much larger sum of money and a guarantee that the passengers would be transferred quietly and secretly to other vessels outside the territorial limit.

Goren could not meet both these conditions on his own, however. First, he required the assistance of Irgun for transfer of passengers at sea. The second problem, that of extra funding, remained open. Goren, representing Perl, concluded an agreement with Eri Jabotinsky for the secret debarkation of the passengers outside Palestinian waters, in exchange for which Goren would take the group on the *Spyroula* aboard the *Sakariya* at no cost.[36] Thus, Perl, acting privately through Goren, presented the Center for Aliyah's office in Bucharest with a chance to solve the problem of Paltin's group. The two groups had been thrown together by fate, even though Perl had worked privately rather than under movement auspices.

Perl was displeased with the arrangement, as it did nothing to resolve the financial question, but he had little other choice than to accept.[37] At this point, the *Sakariya* would be lost without the cooperation of the Revisionists. The deadline for returning the *Saturnus* to its owners rapidly approached, leaving no time for further maneuvers. On 25 December, Perl's group boarded the *Sakariya,* though the ship's refitting had not been completed.

The two groups slated to sail together now totaled 1,350. As a result, the owners raised their price once again and demanded a price fixed per head rather than a lump sum as previously arranged. The organizers tried to procure the necessary funds by further increasing the number of passengers. (Citron's group in Bratislava had no funds to pay for a journey and were therefore left out of plans for the *Sakariya,* though they had been promised a ship months before.)[38] Perl traveled to Budapest and organized a new group of 530 people (226 from Vienna and 304 from Hungary). The group left Budapest on 30 December 1939, aboard the riverboat *Gruenn.* These brought the total passengers for the *Sakariya* to 1,880. In addition, the Rumanian government, according to its agreement with the aliyah organizers, claimed the right to place Jewish refugees already in Rumania on the transport, adding another 20 percent to the total. Thus, the *Sakariya* was finally meant to take on 2,200 Jews.

On 22 January 1940, a new contract was signed between the owners and representatives of all the parties involved.[39] This agreement specified that there would be 2,200 passengers and that the owners would be paid £13,200. The JDC supplied most of the necessary funds within several weeks. The

JDC was the logical source—indeed, the only conceivable source—for the added funds, which amounted to £3,000. The JDC's representatives showed particular concern for the plight of the refugees and had contributed toward their upkeep. Yet they had also entertained grave doubts about the integrity and ability of the organizers.[40] Ironically, their suspicions and hesitations had contributed to the delays in arranging transport, increasing rather than relieving the sufferings imposed on the refugees, and had indirectly contributed to the international attention to and criticism of the episode.

On 1 February, the *Sakariya* left Sulina harbor and made its way to Palestine relatively quickly and easily. Despite extreme crowding on board, the passengers suffered no great discomfort. Betar members served as group leaders and maintained order and discipline. Social and cultural activities and food distribution were all conducted in the style of the most organized of the illegal immigrant ships.[41] At the mouth of the Dardanelles, the ship was met by a British naval vessel and escorted to Palestine. The escort through international waters was in fact in contravention of international law, and on the basis of this the owners argued that the ship had been taken to Palestine by force and prevented from sailing to a purported destination in Latin America. This proved to be a successful legal defense, and the crew members were immediately freed by court order. A short time later, the ship was also released.[42] The passengers were interned at Atlit for a lengthy period and were finally released under an agreement to subtract their number from the quota of admissable immigrants. This brought the *Sakariya* affair to its conclusion.

Shortly before the *Sakariya*'s departure, the Revisionist aliyah operation in Bucharest fell apart. The huge concentrations of refugees and the criticisms leveled by both individuals and agencies[43] undermined the Revisionist organizers' confidence and ability to function. Further cooperation with private operators proved to be impossible as well. Eri Jabotinsky, Glazer, and Paltin—all central figures in the Revisionist aliyah operation—sailed aboard the *Sakariya*. Yaakobi died in November 1939 and thus did not live to see the successful conclusion of the saga. His death deprived the movement of its only hope of ever untangling the financial and organizational relationships between private organizers and movement representatives, as well as among Irgun, Betar, and the NZO. Although the Irgun succeeded in making contacts in Poland (with the intention of smuggling Jews into Rumania), the Irgun agents sent to Rumania (Rafaeli and Schwartzmann) decided to set up an independent operation. They wanted no part of the debts of the now-defunct Bucharest office, and they were convinced that they could be much more effective on their own.[44]

The policies the NZO formulated at this time show a trend toward reducing the scope of secret aliyah until practical solutions were found for those groups already assembled and prepared to leave. The NZO closed the aliyah office in Greece, in the interests of economy.[45] The NZO was determined to solve the plight of the Citron group, even though no financial arrangements had yet been concluded between the private figures involved and the movement. The Center for Aliyah sent Eliyahu Bidner (Ben-Horin) (who was active in

Betar and Irgun in Palestine) to Rumania, where he located a Jewish banker who was willing to provide the necessary credit.[46] Having established a basis for a cooperative venture, Ben-Horin promptly left Rumania for the United States in order to raise funds for aliyah work and for the movement. He was not on the scene, therefore, when plans went awry.

Friction continued to plague relations among Irgun, the NZO, and Betar because of Irgun's independent efforts to smuggle Jews out of Poland. Ben-Horin's attempt to create an office representing only the NZO and Betar did not come to fruition. The Irgun people were raising their own funds and engaging in their own search for vessels, highlighting the lack of organization within the Revisionist movement.

One should bear in mind that the distinction among the three Revisionist wings was more apparent to those inside than to those outside the movement. Uncoordinated activities were perceived as symptoms of weakness and disorganization, and this negatively influenced the public confidence in Revisionist operations. The *Sakariya* affair had certainly weakened the Center for Aliyah in this regard. The internal rifts in the movement and its diminished reputation are factors that may help us understand the failures of the Center in the *Pencho* affair and its inability to cope with the problems that arose once that ship had put to sea.

The Voyage of the *Pencho*

The Citron group, which was left waiting in Bratislava and refused transport on the *Sakariya,* was organized early in 1939 by Yehoshua Citron (Halevi), the leader of Betar in Slovakia.[47] Like Paltin's group, its plans were interrupted by the German invasion of Czechoslovakia. Neither group managed to leave the country between April and September 1939, when there had presumably been a chance to do so and when there was considerable traffic in illegal immigrant ships, both private and Revisionist. We have no information as to why this was so.

Citron forwarded funds to the NZO to pay for transport, and these were apparently paid for the lease of the *St. Bruek* (which fell through). The group was left with neither vessel nor money. Lack of funds prevented them from joining the *Sakariya* transport. No alternative solution was found at that time, even though those in Bucharest and London were well aware of the danger threatening the group should it be deported back to the Reich.[48] Every delay jeopardized these people's lives.

In Bucharest (February 1940), Eugene Meisner and Jacob Schiber decided to recondition the *Stefanu* (the riverboat that had housed some of Paltin's group) as a means of transport for the group. To make the *Stefanu* seaworthy required a new engine as well as structural modifications. Lengthy repairs were begun but remained uncompleted. The Citron group grew ever more alarmed. In the first months of 1940, a few Betar members as well as some others had left the group, and the police continued to threaten them with

The *Pencho* on the Danube River, summer 1940.

deportation. Citron dispatched impassioned and furious letters to the executive, charging Bucharest with gross mismanagement. London demanded that Meisner "resolve the affair quickly" and that he "exhibit greater understanding for the group and its leaders."[49]

Financial difficulties and the disintegration of the Bucharest office continued to prevent the final preparation of the *Stefanu*. Only after about a hundred freed Buchenwald inmates joined the Citron group and added money to the budget was Citron able to arrange for their departure. (The inmates had been released through the efforts of Recha Freier, a German Jewess who was among the founders of Youth Aliyah and who rescued many Jews from concentration camps by getting them entry visas to different countries.) The repairs to the *Stefanu* were completed, the boat was registered in Bulgaria under a new name, *Pencho*, and it proceeded upriver to Bratislava in March.[50]

A letter sent on 3 April 1940, to prospective passengers provided some details about the forthcoming voyage. No hint was given that they were undertaking anything illegal; indeed, from the European end all arrangements were quite legal and aboveboard. There was also no mention of the difficult physical conditions that might be expected. The boat on which they would sail was not described in terms of its size or passenger accommodations. The letter focused on what constituted permissible baggage, with a list of recommended items, including medications, pocket money, and various food products. The letter further noted that a few spaces were still available and that it was still possible to purchase a ticket. The full fare was to be paid by all passengers, without exception; but the amount of the fare was not specified.

It was stressed, however, that the boat would sail as scheduled, whether or not it was completely filled.[51]

Conditions during the voyage itself are reflected in some of the orders of the day that have been preserved. Overcrowding and the elements of uncertainty necessitated strict discipline in washing and sleeping arrangements, use of the deck, and lights-out time. A duty roster for cleaning and other tasks was also organized. Infractions of rules were to result in specified penalties.

The voyage lasted far longer than anticipated. After leaving Bratislava, the Rumanian authorities refused to allow the *Pencho* to reenter Rumanian territory, fearing a recurrence of an episode like the *Spyroula* or *Saturnus*. The *Pencho*, which did not appear to be seaworthy, was driven from port to port seeking permission to take on food and water. In July, the boat was forced to sail upriver again as far as Yugoslavia. The Yugoslavian authorities halted the boat near the village of Dobra, but the Rumanians would not permit it to leave via the Iron Gate. Thus, the boat remained at anchor off Dobra from 26 July until 16 August.

Once again, orders of the day provide an insight into conditions on board during that period, including the state of food supplies and the mood among the passengers. A report sent to the Jewish community of Belgrade, which apparently contributed toward the maintenance of the refugees, pointedly stated that the group was on the verge of starvation. Food, in fact, was provided by the JDC. The relief agency also leased a Yugoslavian barge to relieve some of the overcrowding while the *Pencho* remained at Dobra. But it was impossible to prevent tensions among the passengers. The survivors from Buchenwald, most of them German Jews, did not get along well with the rest of the group, who were mostly Czech nationals. There was also friction between Betar and Revisionist members and the nonaffiliated Jews. Many people believed that the journey had little chance of success and wished to remain in Yugoslavia with the Kladovo camp. However, they were not permitted to do so.

Throughout these weeks, there was hope that a second boat might be found as an alternative to the *Pencho*, but as the waiting period lengthened, the Yugoslavian authorities decided to take action. They towed the *Pencho* out of Yugoslavian territory and through the narrow Iron Gate, the straits that led to the Rumanian section of the Danube. For the next three weeks, the boat drifted in international waters between Bulgaria and Rumania, unable to put into port. Fuel, food, and water supplies grew dangerously low. Only on 11 September 1940, five months after leaving Bratislava, was the boat allowed by the Rumanian authorities to take on fuel and proceed down the Danube to the Black Sea.

Because of the long delay, the boat's Bulgarian registry had lapsed, and the harbor authorities at Varna refused to renew it. The *Pencho* therefore set sail without any flag of registry. An Italian warship intercepted the refugee boat, but once having established the identity of the boat and its passengers, allowed it to proceed.

The following day, however, the engines malfunctioned and no one was able to repair them. The boat was left stranded on the open seas, near the Dodkan Islands. Unable to navigate, the *Pencho* ran aground, tearing a gaping hole in its hull. The boat began to sink, and only through feverish efforts were the passengers able to rescue themselves and part of their food supply. They landed on one of the nearby deserted islands, where they remained for ten days. A group of five young people set out in a lifeboat to try to spot a ship at sea but did not return.[52] It was not until October 18 that an Italian warship picked up an SOS signal and steamed toward the island. Two hundred passengers were taken aboard and landed at Rhodes. A few days later, the rest of the refugees were transferred there as well.

The Italian authorities sought to deport the refugees back to the Reich and to Slovakia, on the grounds that some were former German citizens and some held valid passports. The Slovak Foreign Ministry agreed to accept those from Slovakia on condition that the German authorities do the same.[53] The Germans refused, citing various legal technicalities. In January 1942, the refugees were transferred to southern Italy, where they remained for the duration of the war.

The *Pencho* was the last transport arranged by the Revisionist aliyah office. The episode was doubtless a serious blow to the Bucharest office, which apparently lacked the connections in government and shipping circles that might have ameliorated the group's plight. For five months they suffered from hunger, loneliness, isolation, feelings that the whole world had turned against them and internecine quarrels.

The aliyah office in Rumania ceased to function, even though it was the last Revisionist aliyah center operating in Europe. With the closing of this office, movement-sponsored aliyah from Rumania ended. A few of the organizers continued working to organize a transport of immigrants for the *Struma,* but then disaster struck. From then on, Revisionist aliyah activists would work under the aegis of the Mossad and the Yishuv-sponsored Rescue Committee.

5

Private Aliyah: Konfino and Aliyah bet from Bulgaria, 1939 to 1940

Why Private Work?

Private initiative in illegal aliyah organization was not entirely financially motivated. True, thousands of Jews were saved by businessmen, seamen, and adventurers who found an opportunity to reap a profit in the Jews' desperation to leave Europe by any means. In addition, a number of individuals associated with Zionist movements were also involved in the phenomenon of private aliyah. For these organizers, aliyah activities, while at times generating a financial return, primarily constituted a Jewish Zionist response that was aimed at rescuing Jews.

Yet the official Zionist bodies—the Jewish Agency, Hehalutz, and others—opposed free-lancers, in part because their activities were not coordinated with official policies and at times seemed to work against them. From this angle, private aliyah was open to criticism in a number of respects, including degree of organization, organizers' attitudes toward the immigrants, and the manner of selecting immigrants. Private aliyah organizers opted for those who could pay the fare rather than those with appropriate skills and preparation. Far outweighing these considerations in their view, however, was the appearance that private aliyah was motivated by desire for material gain. This damned private aliyah in their eyes; its organizers seemed to be exploiting the Jewish tragedy. Thus, they considered all privately sponsored aliyah reprehensible behavior; they recognized no distinction between those motivated by financial gain and those with the interests of the Jews and the nation in mind.

The Revisionist leadership, whose aliyah work to a large extent depended on individuals acting in a private capacity, did not find these activities wholly objectionable. They, too, criticized the methods and the profit basis of private aliyah, but at the same time they refused to reject private aliyah per se. Such work, even with its many shortcomings, could not be considered immoral given the desperate circumstances that prevailed. Furthermore, the Revisionists claimed, the ongoing existence of a private aliyah network constituted an indictment of the low level of activity on the part of the Zionists.

There were indeed private organizers who believed in aliyah bet as a political and moral imperative and wholeheartedly identified with it as a cause. At the same time, however, they completely disregarded the one element of the clandestine immigration effort that both the Revisionists and the Mossad sought to implement: the selection of immigrants on the basis of the needs of the developing state and their degree of preparation. The private organizers claimed that the need for rescue was their overriding concern and, in principle, felt that the opportunity of escape ought to be offered to all Jews on an equal basis. In practice, however, this principle meant all Jews who could afford it.

Finally, in contrast with the brokers, agents, and smugglers who were organizing emigration to the Americas and to the Far East and who were independent of any Jewish organizations, a significant portion of the aliyah bet organizers were affiliated in some way with the Zionist movements and were relatively inexperienced in shipping matters.

Moshe Galili, Willi Perl, Paul Haller, and Baruch Konfino all belonged to Zionist movements. Some of them began their aliyah work within a movement framework and only later ventured forth on their own. The private organizers claimed that their decisions to set out on their own had nothing to do with a desire for personal gain but instead owed to the superior effectiveness of independent work—to the suitability of such activities to a flexible independent operator rather than to a centralized, bureaucratic movement.

Perl and Konfino[1] have stated this most forcefully. Private aliyah, they argued, was a superior solution because from the very first steps the path of the aliyah bet organizer was strewn with illegalities. Not only did clandestine aliyah activities violate British laws governing immigration, they often entailed infringements of standing laws in the countries of embarkation as well as in transit countries. Neither the local Zionist organizations nor the local Palestine agencies could afford to brazenly flout authority, and this militated against their open participation in aliyah bet work and hampered them in the cases in which they were directly involved.

Moreover, the nature of the work called for a great flexibility in decision-making and a talent for improvisation. Imaginative, unconventional habits of mind as well as a daring, even reckless, quality were virtually required traits of the aliyah organizer. These were not the attributes that typified the "organization men" in the Zionist establishment, and, consequently, aliyah organizers seldom came from among their ranks.

Likewise, the nature of the activity was ill-suited to the movements' typical way of functioning, which was democratic and hierarchical. Indeed, the wide latitude required for rapidly reaching and implementing decisions was one reason that separate channels and centers, the Mossad and the Center for Aliyah, had been established—to maintain a separation from the Zionist organizations' normal working routines. The major elements in preparing clandestine voyages had to remain confidential and could not be openly debated in policy discussions. Not surprisingly, the independent organizers often produced better results than did the official Zionist organs.

Dr. Baruch Konfino was an ophthalmologist in Sofia and a prominent Zionist who was affiliated with General Zionist party and was head of the Zionist Theodore Herzl club in Sofia. In the early 1930s, he had been involved in helping German Jews who had reached Bulgaria to leave Europe, in cooperation with Recha Freier. Being alert to the political situation, and having seen firsthand the numerous problems involved in finding passage for German Jews, Konfino became more radical in the search for solutions. He reached the conclusion that an independent effort would fare better than one coordinated with a movement after the difficulties encountered with the *Ageus Nicolaus* in March 1939. The arrangements for the voyage had been coordinated by the Sofia Theodore Herzl club and the Mossad in Palestine. As final preparations were being made for the voyage—the refugees were assembled and waiting, and the Bulgarian port and police offcials in Varna had been bribed to look the other way—the Mossad informed Konfino that he had to postpone the ship's sailing since it could not ensure debarkation arrangements in Palestine. As a result, the Herzl club withdrew its sponsorship of the trip.

The refugees (and no less the Bulgarian authorities) were incredulous that the trip could be canceled on the basis of what seemed a technicality. To Konfino, these actions confirmed the disparate evaluations of those on the scene and the decision-makers in Sofia and in Palestine. The higher-ups failed to comprehend that, given the dynamics of preparing a ship and a group of refugees, at the point they had reached there was no choice but to sail. Given the psychological investments of those directly involved, to turn back at such a time was impossible.

Despite orders to the contrary, Konfino instructed the ship to proceed on its journey. His fellow members in the Herzl club advised against it, and he was supported by only a handful of colleagues. The *Ageus Nicolaus* finally arrived in Palestine after several delays, its journey fraught with tension throughout. The arrival of the ship was unexpected by the Mossad, and the refugees were arrested by the British authorities. Not until much later were they allowed to go free. In the aftermath of the voyage, Konfino was widely criticized by members of the Mossad in Palestine and by fellow Zionists in Sofia for having acted irresponsibly and out of greed.

Konfino claims that it was this episode that caused him to reconsider the entire complex of difficulties surrounding the organization and supervision of aliyah. He concluded that the central issues were equally intractable in both frameworks—centralized and private. Centrally organized efforts had proved unable to offer conclusive answers to questions arising in the selection of immigrants, prices to be charged, fiscal accountability, and disembarkation. In Konfino's opinion, private aliyah could not be said to aggravate any of these. Given the desperate circumstances and the vulnerability of the refugees, the only insurance of fair treatment and sincerity of purpose in both cases lay in the dedication of those who took the tasks of practical implementation upon themselves. Konfino has maintained that aliyah organizers such as himself, even when acting in a private capacity, remained Zionists first and foremost. As such, they adhered fully to the movement's purposes and ideals and retained an abiding sense of responsibility. Their identification with the Zionist cause constituted the moral restraint that prevented corruption, misuse of funds, and exploitation of the refugees' vulnerability.[2]

Private organizers tended to work outside official channels—avoiding shipping companies and official involvement—and in this way they reduced the number of factors that might impede their success. The main difficulties for the private aliyah organizer lay in financing—in procuring funds for initial investments and for daily operating costs—and in choosing the refugees who were to comprise each transport.

In theory, the sale of tickets was meant to finance private aliyah operations; but, in practice, hiring and refitting vessels required funds before fares could begin to be collected. Procuring these capital outlays did not merely entail short-term credit. Volatile prices and the indefinite length of time required for refitting vessels forced private organizers to seek access to public funds.

The absence of any financial margin is illustrated in a problem Konfino had in compensating a group of Jewish refugees whose voyage had to be canceled. The group had traveled down the Danube in March 1940 to board the *Rudnitchar* and sail to Palestine. The authorities barred the ship's departure, and the refugees were left stranded in the harbor. Konfino was unable to refund the money paid for their passage, since those funds had been spent on refitting the vessel and hiring the crew. In order to compensate the refugees, therefore, Konfino had to find other sources of funding.[3] (Some of these refugees were taken on board the *Rudnitchar* in June 1940.) It is true that all aliyah bet operations faced financing problems; but the Mossad and the Revisionists at least had an address to turn to—the Jewish Agency or the Histadrut in Palestine, Zionist organizations in England and the United States, or the JDC. In most instances, there was but a slight chance of obtaining sufficient funds from these sources. Nevertheless, this chance was something the private organizers lacked entirely.

Another dilemma that the private organizers faced was the matter of the makeup of the immigrant groups. In the case of the privately organized ships, the composition of the passenger lists was haphazard and was in general the product of circumstance—the concentration of refugees at any given moment in a particular point of embarkation. The resulting groups lacked organization and leadership, whereas the Mossad and Revisionist transports generally contained a nucleus of people capable of taking the lead during the voyage. These people worked to create an atmosphere of mutual responsibility and helped ease the difficulties of life at close quarters.

Konfino was well aware that the social dynamics on board ship had an important influence on the quality of the passengers' lives at sea. Indeed, many of the criticisms and accusations lodged against him came from those on transports he arranged, and this tended to damage his public image. However, Konfino did not consider this criticism a valid reason to slow down or halt his work, since he recognized how difficult it was for the passengers to make allowances for the problems involved in organizing illegal aliyah.[4]

Despite all the attendant problems of private aliyah, most of which lay in the supervision of all operations by a single individual, Konfino felt that there was simply no better alternative available. The centralizing of decision-making, planning, refugee selection, and financing in the same hands raised problems and questions at every step of the way, but given the circumstances, private efforts did hold out an equivalent chance of success. This was the decisive point.[5]

Konfino displayed tremendous energy throughout the period in which he was active in organizing aliyah (February 1939 to December 1940). Through his efforts, 3,683 people reached Palestine on eight separate transports. He searched tirelessly for new means to translate his ideas into action. He sought and found help from colleagues and friends in the Zionist movement in Hungary and from the Hehalutz emissary from the Yishuv, Shlomo Tamir. These contacts directed refugees to his boats. He was also in touch with the Mossad, meeting several times over the winter and spring of 1940 with Zvi Yehieli and Ze'ev Shind. He investigated alternative routes to Palestine, in one instance pursuing the possibility of using an Italian shipping line from Trieste to take refugees to Libya, whence they would proceed to Palestine. His search for vessels was not limited to the local market in the Black Sea region; it extended to Italy and Greece as well. Konfino was also instrumental in finding vessels and arranging provisions and fuel for the groups that Storfer was organizing out of Vienna.[6] He also offered assistance when sudden problems developed, such as in the sinking of the *Pencho*.[7]

Despite the commitment he displayed, a dark cloud shadowed Konfino's work from the summer of 1940 on. The botched refitting arrangements for one vessel (the *Libertad,* which sailed to Palestine in June 1940) and the sinking of another (the *Salvador,* in December 1940) ultimately ruined Konfino's reputation, and with it any hopes he may have had for further rescue efforts.

The *Libertad* and *Salvador*

The *Libertad* and *Salvador* are part of a group of boats whose departures were arranged under wartime conditions. As such they comprise a distinct episode in the account of Konfino's aliyah work. (The *Rudnitchar* sailed three times in the fall of 1939).

In early 1940, several months into the war, the Bulgarian authorities prohibited Konfino from again using the *Rudnitchar*, a vessel that had already made four trips to Palestine. The *Rudnitchar* had been well-suited to Konfino's operations: it was quite seaworthy, and additionally, it could be used for travel upriver on the Danube. It is not clear precisely why the Bulgarian authorities decided to stop the scheduled departure of the *Rudnitchar* and to forbid Konfino to continue his work. Konfino believed that the Germans had demanded use of the ship for espionage purposes (a member of the crew, it turned out, was a German spy). However, it is more likely that the Bulgarian decision was the result of British pressure on the Balkan countries to put a halt to the flow of Jewish illegals from their shores.[8]

The Bulgarian order to Konfino to cease his activities came in March 1940 when the *Rudnitchar* was preparing to take on a new transport of refugees and sail down the Danube. The refugees were left with no alternate means of passage. Some of them returned to Hungary, while others managed to reach Bulgaria, where they waited in the hope that a new transport would be arranged. Konfino commenced a feverish search for another vessel but found the market very limited; his strained financial situation also made it difficult for him to make an attractive offer. After a fruitless search, he decided to acquire an old sailing boat with an auxiliary motor, called the *Chipka,* which he had refurbished and renamed the *Libertad.*[9]

Konfino intended the boat for between 700 and 800 passengers. But many in the Jewish community (among them Konfino's supporters) expressed doubts that the craft was truly fit for travel. The Jewish Consistory in Sofia (the leading organ of Bulgarian Jewry) and the communities of Burgas and Varna appealed to him not to expose passengers to what they regarded as a patent safety risk. At the same time, however, the refugees stranded in Varna entreated him to find a solution to their worsening situation. As foreign nationals without permits to remain in Bulgaria, the refugees were liable to deportation. Some even threatened Konfino and his agents with bodily harm unless a transport was arranged for them.[10]

In the face of conflicting pressures, Konfino decided to proceed with the plan to use the *Libertad.* Shortly before its scheduled departure, however, the boat's engine was tampered with, rendering it useless. Konfino charged his opponents in the Jewish community with sabotaging the boat in order to prevent it from leaving. The Bulgarian police refused to extend the boat's stay in port so that repairs could be made and in the first week of June towed it out into open waters. There it was left to make its way under sail to Palestine as best it could.

The voyage of the *Libertad* was plagued by misfortune. Though it was to take on provisions in Istanbul and the Greek isles, its slowed sailing time rendered stocks on board inadequate and the passengers suffered from hunger and dehydration. On the voyage the boat sat in doldrums for days at a time, unable to proceed. It finally reached the Palestine coast in July 1940, with an escort of British vessels (picked up near Cyprus) following close behind. Once in Haifa, the *Libertad* was seized and confiscated.[11]

Konfino's next (and final) attempt at a transport proved disastrous. In his later account of these events, Konfino claimed he had decided to abandon aliyah bet activity even before the completion of *Libertad*'s voyage because of the problems it caused. This contention is not corroborated by other evidence, and in fact Konfino continued activities even after the *Libertad* episode. Between June and December 1940 (the period between the voyages of the *Libertad* and the *Salvador*), he aided Storfer in organizing his three ships and maintained his contacts with the Mossad and with Sima Spitzer concerning the Kladovo group. He chartered a river barge in Bratislava to take refugees down the Danube and proceeded with plans to send a transport of immigrants to Palestine aboard a frail and ancient craft, the *Struma* (which was later to set forth from Constantsa on a tragic journey).[12]

It is also clear that in the fall of 1940, when the opportunity arose to acquire a small sailing boat, the *Tsar Krum* (which became the *Salvador*), Konfino's network was still active. For this transport, Konfino decided to work through a public committee made up of Zionists from Sofia and Varna. Konfino found his friends in the movement willing to work with him on this venture and eager to avail themselves of his knowledge and experience.[13]

The preparations for the *Salvador* transport began after a summer with no aliyah activity and in the wake of Italy's entry into the war. Storfer's three ships were already en route to Palestine. Mossad agents in Istanbul and Constantsa were preparing for the departure of the *Darien*, which was intended to rescue the Kladovo group. The *Salvador* therefore formed part of a renewed offensive in the illegal aliyah campaign.

The *Tsar Krum* was a very old boat and lacked an engine. It was also quite small, measuring approximately twenty meters by five meters and weighing but a hundred tons. Konfino bought it from Angel Paskeliv, one of his most valued contacts in the shipping business.[14] The boat was in extremely poor condition, but plans were drawn up for extensive repairs and refitting. The hull was to be repaired, an engine installed, and the craft made generally seaworthy. For a variety of reasons, however, these plans were not carried out. Nevertheless, passengers were put aboard and promised that a tugboat would be provided to substitute for a motor. The boat would be towed to Istanbul, and there, the group was assured, another tugboat would take them to the Mediterranean.

These promises were never kept. Moreover, the size of the group was not kept within agreed limits. When the committee had initially negotiated the purchase of the boat, it was decided that no more than 250 people would go aboard. In fact, the boat sailed with 350 passengers and was also meant to pick up fifty of the survivors of the *Pencho* wreck who still remained on Rhodes. This would have brought the total to 400 passengers. The boat was overcrowded; its lifeboats were unusable, and there were not enough life preservers. Furthermore, it had neither compass nor charts.

The boat was towed from Varna on 3 December 1940, and reached Istanbul under sail, where Bulgarian Jews and Konfino's agents provided the passengers with food and water. The *Salvador* left Istanbul on 11 December.[15] In the sea of Marmara it hit a storm, split in two, and sank. Most of those on board drowned. (It should be pointed out that the storm also claimed two other boats, one British and one Turkish.)

Before the *Salvador* sailed, the leaders of the Bulgarian Jewish consistory had reminded Konfino and the committee members of what had happened to the *Libertad*. Three days before the departure of the ill-fated craft, they cabled to Konfino a warning not to put to sea given the boat's perilous state of disrepair. The *Salvador* was sent on its way, however, with neither an engine nor a tugboat. None of the members of the public committee who worked with Konfino on the project had themselves inspected the condition of the boat, relying implicitly on Konfino's judgment. Just what the actual purpose of this committee was remains unclear, although the treasurer of the group appears to have drawn a salary for his work. The bombastic reply to the Consistory's cable read as follows: "Only weaklings fail to fulfill the ideal . . . to which we are committed for Zion's sake. . . . Your instructions will not halt our plan even for a minute. Long live the doers!"[16]

The sinking of the *Salvador* caused utter dismay and aroused a storm of indignation. The Bulgarian consistory set up a commission of inquiry to identify those responsible for the disaster. The commission found Konfino and Davidov, the committee's treasurer, directly responsible and charged the rest of the committee with negligence. It denounced "the unacceptable conditions [of the craft], the lack of basic safety measures, the failure to provide a tugboat and the unreflecting, puffed-up phrases used in reply to warnings received from various sources prior to the boat's departure."[17]

This severe and unequivocal censure had no precedent among criticisms leveled at other aliyah bet organizers. The public furor over the episode was so great that it found its way even into the headlines of non-Jewish newspapers.[18] Sofia synagogues said special memorial prayers for the victims of the *Salvador*. So deep was the outrage expressed against Konfino that he felt he might have to cease his activities. The Bulgarian government was also alarmed by the tragedy. Under international law, responsibility for allowing the craft to set to sea fell on it. Indeed, in diplomatic correspondence and in official statements, the British took the Bulgarian authorities to task for their failure prevent the boat's departure. The Bulgarian authorities ordered Konfino out of Sofia until further notice. Konfino's opponents claimed that it was only his temporary expulsion that saved him from the hands of the Jewish community.

Konfino's reaction to the tragedy and the public outrage that followed are recorded in two letters he wrote to Storfer in December 1940.[19] The first was written in response to a letter from Storfer, in which Storfer expressed sorrow over the fate of the *Salvador*. In his letter, Konfino spoke of the *Patria* tragedy, which had claimed the lives of Bulgarian Jews among others (see Chapter 2). He expressed grief over the *Salvador* tragedy, but also complained of what he felt were unwarranted accusations. He continued, noting that although he had succeeded in bringing several thousand refugees to Palestine, for which he had received not a word of thanks from anyone, after one tragic occurrence, all were quick to denounce him. Despite the attendant risks, he argued, it was necessary to go on with illegal aliyah for the sake of those thousands who could not otherwise be rescued. The sea would always claim its victims, he stated, but this alone was not reason enough to cease operations. He added that despite his family's objections he was prepared to offer his assistance to Storfer and inquired as to his immediate plans.

The second letter, dated 29 December, was written once again in reply to a letter from Storfer, this time regarding the British policy of expelling illegal immigrants from Palestine, Konfino stated his conviction that this, too, was insufficient reason for the aliyah effort to cease. "I am convinced that this aliyah is necessary, because we have no other avenue."[20]

Konfino planned to resume his activities in this period (late 1940 and early 1941), this time with a new and daring concept in mind. He suggested using small sailboats and motorboats in order to counter British efforts to expel the illegals once they reached Palestine. Since larger passenger ships were in short supply even for the British government, the British would have no means of transporting the illegals to distant colonies; the small craft they would seize could hardly be used for this purpose. In this connection, he advised Storfer to use his river barge at Bratislava to take refugees out to the Black Sea. However, in March 1941 the Germans entered Bulgaria and his activity ended until after the war.

Konfino's two letters to Storfer document the firm belief Konfino held in the vital importance of aliyah bet. Although his position within the Jewish community was now very vulnerable indeed (he would soon be sent by the Bulgarian authorities to a camp outside Sofia), Konfino was at this stage prepared to do all in his power to aid Storfer, now the central figure in aliyah work. The letters to Storfer seem to corroborate Yehieli's own assessment of Konfino's character: "a somewhat naive person, to some degree an idealist, with idealistic aspirations, who because of the circumstances surrounding his work came to concentrate heavily on the mercenary side of things."[21]

It may well be the case that despite his pragmatism and worldliness, and despite his deep involvement in financial maneuverings to fund his operations, Konfino retained a degree of pure idealism, and this committed him to aliyah bet no matter what the cost. Konfino was undoubtedly a fighter, convinced of the righteousness of his cause. He willingly risked his own reputation and his position in the community for the sake of that cause. In this, perhaps, we may discern one of the basic differences between him and Storfer, whom we will discuss at length. This degree of commitment nevertheless does not ex-onerate Konfino from the personal responsibility he bore for the *Salvador* tragedy. Nor does it absolve him from blame in the reckless way in which he was prepared to endanger people's lives at sea. Neither naiveté nor a fighting spirit, not even sincere belief in a principle, can justify these failings.

6

Nazi Expulsion Policy:
Berthold Storfer and the Immigration

Policy and Principles

During late 1938 and 1939, a consensus emerged among the various Nazi agencies regarding the Jews residing within the borders of the Reich: the Nazis determined that these Jews should be forcibly expelled rather than quarantined internally or deported to Reich-held territories. The policy of forced emigration was part of the Reich's overall strategy in preparation for war. Forcing the Jews from Germany, Austria, and the Czech Protectorate was part of the new order at home, a precondition for the successful war of expansion. As such, it demonstrated the link between racial policy, foreign policy, and the war of expansion. After the war had begun, the Nazis still allowed "their Jews" (in contrast to the Jews of occupied Poland) to emigrate, and not until the idea of the Final Solution was shaped and prepared for implementation did the Nazis prohibit Jewish emigration. This is the general framework within which one should examine Nazi attitudes toward illegal immigration.

Jewish emigration was a source of friction among the various agencies. Disagreement centered on where and how Jews should emigrate, and the question was bitterly debated between the Foreign Office and the S.S. (guard echelon—*Schutzstaffel*). The security service of the S.S., the Sicherheitsdienst (S.D.), which had been assigned responsibility for Jewish matters, was most prominent in this debate.[1]

The S.D.'s central concern was that the Jews' be forced out. Their ultimate destination mattered little: the S.D. equally favored emigration to the United States, to Shanghai, and to Palestine. On some occasions, the S.D. even rendered assistance in organizing the exodus, allowing Jews in certain instances to take property and foreign currency out of the country. The S.D. even condoned Zionist illegal immigration activities to an extent, as long as these held out the possibility of transporting Jews from Germany. Arrangements for such emigration were formulated in quite detailed fashion by Adolf Eichmann in Austria.

In contrast, to the proponents of emigration in the Foreign Office the

Jews' final destination was of foremost importance. The Foreign Office had feared that Jewish emigration from the Reich might contribute to the creation of a large and possibly strong center of Jewish population, particularly in Palestine. The Foreign Office approach to the Palestine question was couched in a combination of diplomatic considerations—the Arab factor and British policy, as well as fears deriving from the myths of anti-Semitism. Palestine, it was held, might evolve into a kind of Jewish Vatican, the source of venomous anti-German propaganda as well as the headquarters of the purported Jewish world conspiracy to conquer the world.[2] The Foreign Office enunciated its position in a circular to all German diplomatic posts, dated 25 January 1939.

It is to be hoped that the friends of the Jews in the world, especially those in Western democracies who dispose over so much space on all continents, will allot the Jews a territory outside of Palestine *not in order to establish a Jewish state but instead, a Jewish reservation*. Germany has a major interest in seeing that the Jews continue to be dispersed [emphasis in the original].[3]

In addition to the debate over the ultimate destination of the Jews, the means of bringing about their expulsion was also a source of contention. According to the principle of the Aryanization of Jewish property, Jewish wealth could not be allowed to leave the country, and furthermore, that the state should contribute toward the exit of penniless Jews was anathema. It was Eichmann who finally arrived at a means of arranging rapid and large-scale Jewish emigration that required no outlay of foreign currency by the German treasury. Eichmann had been placed in charge of "solving the Jewish question" in the Danube basin after the annexation of Austria in March 1938.

Eichmann's plan consisted of three components. First, "Jewish policy" was to be concentrated in the hands of a single German agency, thus simplifying official procedures. Second, the expenses of those Jews who lacked means of their own (savings, foreign currency) were to be paid by foreign Jewish organizations. And finally, Jewish efforts to organize and unify emigration activity were to be encouraged. At the same time, Eichmann waged a campaign of violence and terror against Austrian Jewry, particularly wealthier and prominent individuals. To speed their exit from the Reich, Eichmann even offered to release Jews arrested in Vienna who could produce entry documents for other countries in exchange for payments, and was prepared to do the same for others interned in concentration camps. He also was ready to facilitate arrangements so that shipping and travel agents could procure entry permits for emigrants, even by paying large bribes to consular officials (although he insisted this be done in secret so as not to involve the Reich in newspaper scandals).

To further facilitate emigration, Eichmann permitted the Jewish community organizations to reopen their offices and to direct their efforts toward making Jewish emigration more "efficient." (The offices had been closed following the German annexation.) Eichmann's final step toward centralizing Jewish emigration was the creation of the Zentralstelle fuer juedische Auswanderung (Central Office for Jewish Emigration) in August 1938. According to Eichmann, he took this step in response to requests to alleviate the complex bureaucracy surrounding emigration that Jewish community leaders Joseph Loewenhertz and R. Orenstein had made of him.[4]

Within the Zentralstelle, a system was established whereby, in order to receive an exit permit, a Jew had to prove that his expenses abroad would be paid either by relatives or by Jewish organizations. The Jewish community, and chiefly the JDC, was in charge of supplying these funds.[5] Jews who were unable to pay their way out of the country were subsidized by money confiscated from other Jews. Without a doubt, the system was a marvel of German efficiency and saved the Reich from having to pay for organizing Jewish emigration.

So effective in meeting the goals of the S.D. was Eichmann's system that it was proposed as a model for the Reich by S.S. Gruppenfuhrer Reinhard Heydrich, head of the S.D. and second in command to Heinrich Himmler (head of the S.S. and German Police). As a result, in January 1939 a central bureau for Jewish emigration was established in Berlin. In an address to the committee responsible for creating the bureau, Heydrich was reported by one of those present as saying,[6]

> . . . We should continue to promote emigration by all available means. . . . First the Jews themselves should be approached. On the basis of their international connections they are in the best position to find opportunities for entry into other countries and to obtain the necessary foreign exchange. The proof of such a strategy is best shown in Vienna, and the establishment there of the *Zentralstelle* as early as August 1938.

In short, Heydrich favored Jewish emigration in any form and would even assist Jewish organizations to achieve this end. In this same vein, he referred specifically to illegal immigration to Palestine and expressed explicit support for it. At the same meeting, Heydrich was reported to have said,

> . . . In theory, illegal immigration was something that should be opposed, but in the case of Palestine it was undeniable that groups were making their way there from many countries in Europe in this manner. . . . Germany should also, at least unofficially, take advantage of the opportunity.

Heydrich's position was accepted by the entire committee, including the representatives of the Foreign Office. This commitment clarifies the attitude of the S.S. toward illegal immigration and toward those who were involved in organizing it.

Pino Ginsburg, who had been sent to Germany in January 1939 as a Hehalutz and Mossad emissary, accurately observed that "they wanted to get most of the Jews out of the areas under their control regardless of their destination, and they were concerned that the Palestine route would be taken over by Jews from other countries."[7] Ginsburg later described the practical effect that the S.S. policy had on his work. He and his colleague, Max Zimmels, a member of kibbutz Ayelet Hashahar, had originally arrived in Germany on one-week passes after having difficulty obtaining entry permits at all. The Jewish Reichsvertretung (an umbrella organization of the Jewish community formed in 1933 to consolidate Jewish actions vis-à-vis government policy) was quite uneasy about the emissaries' status. On their second day in the country, Ginsburg and Zimmels went to the Gestapo offices in Berlin in an effort to obtain a visa for an extended stay. They were informed that Germany was not interested in increasing the number of its Jews by permitting Palestinian emissaries to stay; the only reason for which Jews would be permitted to enter was to organize Jewish emigration. Ginsburg and Zimmels explained that indeed this was part of their task. Even before the two had made their way back to the Jewish community's office, Otto Hirsch, chairman of the Reichsvertretung, received a phone call saying that the two had been granted permission to remain.

Several weeks later, Ginsburg and Zimmels were contacted through the Office of the Jewish Community by a German named Alexander von Hoepfner, who offered to assist them and spoke of travel companies with which they could work. Von Hoepfner, it turned out, had several contacts in the S.S. whom he made use of to aid the aliyah bet activists and the Berlin community. Although Ginsburg never found out whether von Hoepfner held an official post in the S.S., the party, or the civil service, von Hoepfner made it clear that his assistance was not rendered as a private citizen, but that he represented higher authority. Through von Hoepfner, Ginsburg was put in touch with an individual who was knowledgeable about all matters pertaining to Jewish emigration and who was capable of having concentration-camp inmates released so that they might leave for Palestine. This person, too, was linked in some way to the Gestapo.

Immigration activists in Vienna and Prague discovered that a similar situation obtained there as well.[8] It is clear that in the months preceding the war, the Mossad's and other Zionist (and non-Zionist) groups' successes in arranging the emigration of German, Austrian, and Czech Jews was to a certain extent the result of the S.S. stance.

Illegal aliyah planning in Germany in summer 1939 took on a new dimension as a result of the initial successes scored by refugee ships and because of pressure and indirect aid from the German government. According to Ginsburg, the Reichsvereinigung (which had replaced the the Reichsvertretung in June 1939) had offered to budget an enormous sum (some ten million marks) for a large-scale plan to send 10,000 German Jews out of the country aboard German vessels departing from either Emden or Hamburg. Through von Hoepfner's intervention and Gestapo support, the German Hamburg Line agreed to cooperate with the Mossad. According to Ginsburg, details of the plan were in place by August 1939, and the operation was meant to take place in the fall. However, the war put a stop to the plan.[9] Ginsburg left Germany, but attempted to resuscitate the plan from Holland. The plan was abandoned finally, since it was impossible to sail to Palestine from the

North Sea (via the Atlantic and the Straits of Gibraltar) on ships flying the German flag.

German attitudes to Jewish emigration did not alter appreciably during the first few months of the war. The S.D. continued to press for Jewish emigration, and German as well as Jewish sources indicate that the system created during 1939 continued to be used. At the same time, the Germans began to look for alternative routes (the sea-lanes had been closed to them).

One attempt to find alternate routes involved von Hoepfner in November 1939. Von Hoepfner had traveled to the Mediterranean countries and approached the German embassy in Rome in an attempt to obtain Italian transit visas for Jews lacking entry permits to a final destination. In a letter dated 17 November,[10] the German ambassador asked the Foreign Office to instruct him on the proper response to give von Hoepfner's request. The ambassador's letter stated that von Hoepfner claimed to have acquired two Greek ships for the purpose of transporting Jews and that he worked for Kurt Lischka, acting head of the Zentralstelle and deputy to Heinrich Mueller of the Main Office for Reich Security (Reichssicherheitshauptamt).

The Foreign Office showed no urgency in replying to its ambassador, and after a week had gone by von Hoepfner contacted Berlin. Two days later, Lischka sent a letter to the Foreign Office to which von Hoepfner's report on his activities (dated 1 December) was appended. In his letter, Lischka confirmed von Hoepfner's trustworthiness and stated that von Hoepfner's trip to Italy and Greece had been condoned by the S.S. and the S.D. in order to explore possibilities for Jewish emigration, especially under wartime conditions. Lischka ended by saying, "It is of utmost importance to explain to the Italians that passage through their country is the only way for German Jews to immigrate, and since it is in the German interest, they should do everything to facilitate it—even for those who do not have certificates to Palestine."[11]

The correspondence very likely reflects the different attitudes toward procedure that held between the Foreign Office and the S.S. where matters regarding illegal Jewish immigration to Palestine were concerned. Guarding sensitive relations with other countries was a foremost responsibility of the Foreign Offices, and this naturally gave rise to considerations of legality and protocol.

The Italians, for their part, were not eager to allow illegal immigration activities to be organized in their country after the outbreak of war, even though Italian ports had served as a primary staging area for illegal refugee ships previously. (The Mossad, Revisionists, and private organizers had all made use of Italian ports.) The Italians were successful in their quest to discourage operations. Except for five groups of legal immigrants (totaling 5,851) who left for Palestine from Trieste in November–December 1939, no other refugees ships sailed from Italy at that time, despite attempts made by the Mossad, Konfino, and Storfer.[12]

From a memorandum of the Reichsvereinigung, dated 1 February 1940, it would appear that real expectations were attached to plans to go ahead with illegal aliyah through the Hamburg America Line.[13] In the Zentralstelle in Berlin, the obstacle presented by the Italians was viewed with grave concern. In May 1940, the Italians instructed their consuls in Germany to cease issuing visas, and thus closed the only alternative route for this plan. Mueller, head of the Gestapo and of the Jewish Emigration Office, sent a sharply worded note to the consular section of the Italian embassy in Berlin.

Mueller's attitude toward "the Reich's Jews" differed sharply from the one the regime had adopted toward Jews in countries occupied or annexed by Germany, and even toward Jews in German-allied states. Germany refused to allow foreign Jews transit through its territory. In the eyes of Nazis dealing with Jewish immigration, each "foreign" Jew traveling through the Reich was virtually depriving a German Jew of his chance for emigration.[14] Mossad agents attempted to organize emigration from Poland through German territory, but their efforts were blocked on these grounds.[15]

As late as the summer of 1940, there was still talk of large-scale plans for the emigration of Jews from Germany. Such plans were most likely limited to the idea for a Jewish reservation on Madagascar.[16] For a certain period this idea seemed viable, since French colonial control of the island had passed to Germany. There is some indication that emigration to Palestine was still an option being discussed. During June and July of 1940, the German general staff was still contemplating an invasion of England, and with its anticipated conquest would come control over the Middle East and the British colonies.

It is possible that such a consideration lay behind a meeting held by Eichmann with Lischka and representatives of the Reichsvereinigung on 3 July 1940. Jewish communal representatives from Austria and Prague were present at the meeting and were ordered to present within twenty-four hours a draft plan for the mass removal of all Jews from the Reich.[17] Eichmann stressed that what was envisioned was total emigration.

After Eichmann left the meeting, the Jews argued with Lischka, saying that no such plan could be formulated in one day. Lischka informed them that it would be sufficient to produce a very general plan that could later be elaborated. The Jewish representatives replied that such a plan could be applied only to Palestine. Within the Jewish community, illegal immigration continued to be discussed even after the departure of the three ships organized by Storfer in late summer 1940. In a meeting of 17 October 1940, the Reichsvereinigung tabled a proposal to acquire ships for illegal aliyah.

The change in German attitude to Jewish emigration came in early 1941. At that time, during the invasion and war on the Soviet Union (the Barbarossa Campaign), the decision was made to exterminate the Jews of Europe, ending any hope that German Jews might reach Palestine as illegal immigrants.

Berthold Storfer and Emigration
from the Reich in 1940

Nazi efforts to implement a policy of expulsion after the start of the war centered on Berthold Storfer, an Austrian Jew widely involved in the business affairs of his country. Storfer, while working beneath the Zentralstelle in

Vienna, successfully arranged the transport of 3,500 Jews out of the Reich to Palestine aboard three ships—the *Milos*, the *Pacific*, and the *Atlantic*—in the fall of 1940. This accomplishment establishes his stature among illegal aliyah activists. Such a feat, given wartime conditions, was extraordinary.

Nevertheless, Storfer is not generally recognized as an important figure in the illegal aliyah story. Indeed, Storfer's actions and motives have been depicted in a manner far from complimentary in the accounts of ex-Mossad agents such as Braginsky and Avriel (Ueberall), Revisionist aliyah organizers, and even people associated with the JDC. Some have gone so far as to brand him a Nazi agent and Eichmann's right-hand man.[18] Others have described him as an individual who thirsted for power over the lives of others during a time of immense tragedy and as a man basically driven by greed who saw in the plight of his brethren an opportunity to be exploited.[19] Yet still others have praised him. The Vienna Archives contain many letters extolling Storfer's work. Dr. Joseph Loewenherz (head of the Vienna Jewish community), leaders of the Reichsvereinigung in Germany, members of the Danzig Jewish community, and individuals whose lives Storfer saved all have expressed appreciation and gratitude for his efforts.[20]

To this day, the views of those who took part in the events diverge considerably. Storfer remains a controversial figure, though most admit that in retrospect his behavior can be cast in a different light, especially since he shared the fate of most European Jews.[21] What really did prompt Storfer to involve himself in illegal aliyah work? Storfer's own answer—his official answer, at any rate—was that the regime chose him on Loewenherz's recommendation.[22] Certainly there were deeper reasons.

Storfer was born in the Bukovina region in 1882. He began his career as a lumber merchant and worked in various aspects of the industry for many years in Budapest. During the First World War, Storfer was in charge of supplying the Russian-Rumanian front, for which he was twice decorated. Following the war, he served as financial adviser to the Czechoslovakian and Austrian governments and as consultant to several large firms in Hungary and Austria. He became an expert in bank credit transactions and in maritime transport. In 1936, Storfer became president of the firm Rudolf Reichert and Sons. Thus, his social and financial standings were quite solid.

In the summer of 1938, Storfer was invited by Loewenherz to attend the Evian Conference, convened at the initiative of President Roosevelt to find a solution to the political refugee situation. Storfer was part of the delegation unofficially representing the views of Austrian Jewry. Contemporary records give no clue as to why Storfer was selected for this purpose. There is no indication of any public activity on his part in the Jewish community prior to this, and he was neither a public figure nor a man with an international reputation.

In July 1938, Austrian Jewry was already in the grip of a desperate search for refuge, and mass flight had begun. Some 80,000 Jews left Austria in the year preceding the war. The Evian Conference did not produce an adequate response to Austrian Jewry's plight. The pressures to leave

only intensified; the situation for those trying to get out was utterly cha-
otic. Agents and intermediaries of various kinds abounded, who, often for
exorbitant fees, offered their services in navigating the bureaucratic laby-
rinth surrounding the emigration process. So desperate was the situation
that the leaders of the Jewish community (and Storfer among them) actually approached Eichmann with a request to centralize the emigration
bureaucracy. This meshed with Eichmann's own plan to bring all Jewish
affairs under his direct control and resulted in the establishment of the
Zentralstelle in August 1938.

From August 1938 to the outbreak of war in September 1939, Storfer's
involvement in illegal aliyah grew. In the first months, he participated only
indirectly. From early 1939 on, however, Storfer became increasingly influential in Jewish emigration matters. In March 1939, at a meeting held at the
Zentralstelle, Eichmann reacted to international press criticism of "irresponsible" immigration activities undertaken by a firm called "Zentrum," by observing that Storfer's new responsibility for emigration would prevent the
repetition of such occurrences.[23] During these months, Ginsburg, Braginsky,
and Ueberall reported on discussions held with Storfer concerning the *Atrato*
and other vessels.[24]

With the outbreak of war, Storfer's importance and activity spread, and
in March 1940 Eichmann named him sole agent in charge of emigration
arrangements. Storfer was placed in charge of supervising and approving plans
initiated by other groups, and his position enabled him to reject, aid, or
subvert these. His former opponents were forced to turn to him for help.
Ehud Ueberall, the Hehalutz emissary, in the fall of 1939 needed to arrange
financial assistance for a group that had grown larger than anticipated. (These
were the refugees who became to be known as the Kladovo group.) With
Hehalutz itself in difficult financial straits, Ueberall had no choice but to
appeal to Storfer.[25]

In all his activities Storfer employed a Greek shipping agent, Sokrates
Avgerinos, who located and negotiated for vessels and made contacts with
other travel and shipping firms on Storfer's behalf. Avgerinos also hired
crews, had ships outfitted for passenger transport, and established links to
consular officials in order to negotiate for registries and transfers of
ownership.

Several of Storfer's family members represented him in the Balkan
countries. His brother Joseph was sent to Bucharest, and his brother-in-
law Goldner served as a roving agent in Slovakia, Hungary, and elsewhere. Storfer also established ties with emigration activists in various
Jewish communities—with Robert Mendler (who worked with Willi Perl)
and Baruch Konfino in Bulgaria, for example. Storfer himself made numerous trips to Greece, Rumania, Slovakia, and Hungary to secure bank
guarantees and short-term loans, and he personally conducted negotiations
with the national Danube shipping companies of those countries and other
non-Jewish bodies. Storfer became the main link in the transit route from
the Danube to the seaports.

Storfer and the Central Office for Jewish Emigration

Nevertheless, Storfer's activities were possible only because of the thrust of Nazi policy, which forced Jews to emigrate and emphasized that they should make the arrangements themselves. Yet because of their single-minded focus on the exit of the Jews, considerations such as passenger safety, the dangers of travel close to battle zones, and the cost of travel were immaterial to the S.S. members who controlled Storfer's work. The S.S. steadily pressured the Jewish leadership to speed emigration; Eichmann would sometimes summon the heads of the Jewish community organizations, berate them for what he considered the slow pace of emigration, and make fresh demands of them. At one such meeting, Eichmann insisted that all Jews be out of Vienna by February 1940.[26]

In his relations with Storfer, however, Eichmann did not simply make demands; he and his men continuously monitored Storfer's office and required copies of all correspondence and reports on all meetings and decisions. Zentralstelle officials conducted surprise inspections, often confiscating his ledgers and files.[27] They were able to quote from his telephone conversations and were thoroughly conversant with all the details of his relations with the Jewish organizations abroad and in the Reich.

The Zentralstelle interfered in the selection of Jews for emigration through Storfer. Almost all emigrant groups were formed according to lists drawn up by a committee of the Jewish community on which Storfer's agency was represented, and Storfer had the power to alter the lists at the behest of the Zentralstelle.[28] Storfer himself claimed that he attempted to compile the emigrant lists with the needs of Hehalutz and the Yishuv in mind.[29]

The Zentralstelle also determined in which regions Storfer operated. He was not allowed to help the refugees of Kladovo, for example. Storfer exhibited some concern over the Kladovo group, since quite a few of them were Viennese Jews. (In doing so, he was also trying to improve his tenuous relations with the JDC.) When his efforts became known to the S.S., Storfer was forbidden to deal with the matter. The Zentralstelle was interested only in removing Jews from Reich territory; the fate of refugees in Yugoslavia was none of its concern. It seems clear that this case was not an isolated incident of S.S. restrictions on Storfer's scope of operations.[30]

The Zentralstelle supervised Storfer's finances, too. His transactions required large sums in foreign currency, and the rate of exchange and the transfer of money had to be ratified first by the Nazis and then by the Jewish community.[31] The JDC (which supplied the community's funds) often pressured the communal body to obtain a more favorable rate of exchange from the Zentralstelle by delaying payment. Whenever this occurred, Storfer's emigration activities had to be postponed. He had virtually no other source of foreign currency.

Storfer was also limited by Eichmann's order that he work only with the national Danube companies and with the German Hapag Line. The shipping companies were well aware of Storfer and the tenuous Jewish position and they sought to exploit this. Storfer encountered many difficulties in trying to reach agreements over prices and sailing dates.[32] He did not hesitate to complain to the Zentralstelle, explicitly accusing the companies of using their monopoly in order to extract higher prices, and even asked Eichmann to intercede. After all, Storfer wrote (putting it in the Germans' own terminology and logic), it was in the interest of everyone dealing with the Jewish question. Why should the companies be permitted to put a wrench in the works?

Some of Storfer's communications with the Zentralstelle display a remarkable degree of self-assurance, even brashness. He often got what he wanted. The shipping companies were obliged to compromise with him. He tried as far as possible to place most of his business in the German Danube Line, because he was able to exert more pressure on it through the Zentralstelle than on foreign companies. He therefore preferred that emigrants sail from Vienna rather than Bratislava. Eichmann opposed this in early 1940, but by the time of the sailing of the three ships (September 1940), he had agreed.[33]

From the available evidence, it appears Storfer received no special aid from the Germans in dealing with the Balkan countries. He apparently had difficult dealings with the Rumanian regime, the municipal authorities in Tulcea, and the Greek government.[34] Storfer had little advantage over the Mossad and Revisionists arranging illegal aliyah in these countries: he, too, had to resort to bribes in order to curry favor with consulates and local police. Storfer complained of English interference with the Balkan governments and of their attempts to make crew members shy away from illegal aliyah work.[35] British pressure on Panama to restrict ship registration forced Storfer to seek other solutions (in Spain, for instance).

In his direct dealings with German officials in transit countries, consulates, and embassies, Storfer received such aid as extension of passports and exchange of foreign currency.[36] In general, however, German officialdom was unresponsive to Storfer. The Germans appeared responsive only in comparison with their attitude toward other aliyah organizers.

The Mossad, the JDC, and Storfer

Storfer failed to establish close working relations with Jewish organizations outside Germany. Neither the JDC nor the Mossad was disposed to trust him, and he was viewed as a Nazi collaborator or an opportunist. From outside the Reich, it was difficult to grasp the severity of local conditions; some Zionist leaders even criticized the Jewish communal leadership in Vienna for, in their view, allowing fear to make them overly hasty in carrying out German instructions.[37]

The foreign Jewish organizations tended to place their trust in those closest to them politically or in those who had been well-known as public figures before the Nazis came to power. Storfer was neither of these, and furthermore, he was not in a position to establish the kind of routine relations with foreign organizations that might have diminished their distrust of him. The local Jewish community was in charge of such contacts.

Storfer's difficulties with the Patronka group illustrate the JDC's considerable mistrust of him. Moreover, the Mossad's intervention at the late stages of Storfer's attempted transport introduce another aspect of failed cooperation—a standoff between the Mossad and Storfer from which both parties were to suffer.

In December 1939, when the *Sakariya*, *Hilda*, and Kladovo groups had been organized, Storfer had also organized a group of some 600 refugees in Bratislava. He arranged for them to sail on a ship called the *Astria*, but it sank in a storm on its way to pick them up.[38] The refugees found themselves stranded in their temporary camp. (They came to be known as the Patronka group, after their camp.) As the early-winter frost was already hard upon them, Storfer began to contemplate a spring departure on a ship large enough to hold over a thousand passengers. By February 1940, Storfer had expanded his plan and was considering two ships, the *Sirus* and *Popi*, to carry 1,400 to 1,600 people, which included a group in Vienna. Avgerinos made the necessary preparations to acquire the ships, and Storfer was to take up his option on them by the end of March. Through Loewenherz, he asked the JDC to pay for the purchase.[39]

The JDC's representatives, Mrs. Van Teijn in Holland and Sally Mayer in Switzerland, were uncertain how to act. The purchase required allocating $55,000 to the Vienna community, and though an agreement had been reached with Loewenherz in January, they delayed transfer of the funds. Nevertheless, Storfer believed that the deal had a good chance to succeed, and he was optimistic that Loewenherz would reach an understanding with the JDC. He continued preparations, establishing a timetable and organizing crews and the terms of the voyage. He arranged with the German Danube Line to take the refugees as far as Sulina, and used the influence of the Zentralstelle to overcome difficulties the company introduced.[40] All the preparation seemed to augur success, and he was convinced that this transport would be among the most organized.

However, by 17 March Storfer had begun to have doubts. He wrote to Loewenherz: "The money must be wired at once to the Greek Commercial Bank in Piraeus. The situation is delicate, and if action is not taken swiftly and decisively, we may lose the ships."[41] Two weeks later, though, when the transfer had still not been made, Storfer grew anxious and wrote to Loewenherz again, describing worsening business conditions and demanding immediate assistance.[42]

The misgivings of the JDC held sway despite positive reports from the Vienna community regarding Storfer's plan, and the money was never transferred. From the available evidence, it would appear that the ships were in fact ready to put to sea, and the trip might have taken place on 22 or 23 April, just as Storfer had forecast.[43]

What caused the JDC sufficient concern to hold up the $55,000? The Mossad had intervened at this stage and, through Chaim Weizmann (who met with JDC representatives in Geneva), it convinced the JDC that the Mossad ought to exercise a degree of supervision over Storfer by controlling the flow of funds to him. The Mossad had argued that Storfer might well submit to German pressure to place agents among the refugees.[44] Yet far more was involved. To understand what took place, we will need to examine the entire web of relations between Storfer, in the Reich, and the Mossad, dispersed throughout bases in the Balkans.

The problems of acquiring, registering, outfitting, and supplying ships plagued Storfer as much as they did the Mossad and Revisionists, and all bid for the same ships in the Balkan countries and Turkey. The Mossad had also been interested in hiring the *Sirus* and the *Popi*. Yet Mossad agents saw little or no possiblity of cooperating with Storfer. To them, he was a loathsome figure whose approach was completely alien to the socialistic pioneering spirit of Palestine. The Mossad, first of all, objected to Storfer's unselective approach to aliyah. Furthermore, Storfer supported private aliyah operators, whom the Mossad regarded as no better than vultures.

The Mossad had been forced to depend on Storfer until early 1940, and thereafter found itself entirely under the control of the Nazi-aided Storfer. For Mossad agents like Moshe Agami, operating alongside Lischka, von Hoepfner and the S.S., and Gestapo men in Vienna and Berlin had been difficult indeed. Yet working with them seemed justifiable, a tactical exploitation of the enemy for the sake of a noble cause.[45] In contrast, Storfer was viewed as a collaborator and traitor. To work with him, and furthermore to take orders from him, was unthinkable. The Mossad's distrust of and aversion to Storfer, combined with communications received from Hehalutz comrades in Berlin and Prague, led it to challenge Storfer's authority in emigration matters within the Reich.

Although the Mossad agents had left German territory in September 1939, they maintained communication with Hehalutz comrades there in order to continue operations. Their colleagues Jacob Edelstein of Prague and Paul Epstein in Berlin were their main sources of information. Edelstein and Epstein assessed the situation as possibly offering a foothold to the Mossad, believing that cooperation with the Germans was necessary but that the Germans were indifferent to which party carried out aliyah operations. Therefore, they believed that if the Mossad could demonstrate its capacity to effectively arrange operations, it might be able to resume activities in the Reich and break Storfer's grip on Jewish emigration work.

Edelstein and Epstein shared Mossad doubts about Storfer; they had no confidence in him as a representative of Jewish interests. The Mossad adopted their point of view, but, in fact, this led the Mossad to act in a way that actually made rescue work more difficult. The attitude not only brought about operational failures such as the *Wetan*, but also contributed to the failure of Storfer's planned transport in April 1940.

The Mossad thus sought to avoid contact with Storfer as much as possible, and in cases where contact was unavoidable, to meet him on its own terms. Two meetings that took place between Storfer and Zvi Yehieli in 1940 illustrate the ever-widening rift between the two parties and the irreconcilable positions they held. The first of these meetings took place in Bucharest in February 1940, and the second in Geneva in May of that year.[46]

On the first of these occasions, Yehieli was heavily influenced by the substance of Edelstein's report to Geneva several weeks earlier. Edelstein had castigated the Viennese leadership for what he regarded as its abject acquiescence to Nazi demands and warned of dire consequences should Storfer take control of aliyah operations in the Reich, including Czechoslovakia.[47] He warned the Mossad that there was good reason to fear that refugee groups might be infiltrated by German spies, since Storfer was incapable of standing up to the Gestapo.

Edelstein also described deteriorating circumstances that lent themselves to a takeover by Storfer. He spoke of an impending plan to prevent those of working age from leaving the country and permitting only the aged and children to emigrate. Yet, within the Czech community, the role of the Zionist Palestine Office in Prague had been undermined because of its inability to organize aliyah. Moreover, the Kladovo group had not left Yugoslavia, and large groups already organized in Bratislava and Prague were still waiting. Edelstein demanded that the Mossad take responsibility for getting these groups out and that it resist any attempt by Storfer to broaden his authority.

The meeting between Yehieli and Storfer took place at the same time as the Prague community was preparing to transfer £44,000 to the Mossad for the purchase of a ship (the *Wetan*), on which the Mossad intended to transport 1,500 Hehalutz members and older Zionists from Prague. The Mossad hoped that this ship would also provide a solution to the Kladovo problem.[48]

This was the background for Yehieli and Storfer's first meeting. It was arranged at Storfer's insistence, and Yehieli opposed the meeting.[49] The two men met at the Hotel Athens in Bucharest in February 1940. According to Yehieli, Storfer made an effort to be cordial, explaining the nature of his work and expressing his desire to cooperate with the Mossad. The gist of Storfer's message (again, according to Yehieli) was that emigration was absolutely essential given the threat of mass expulsion to Lublin, but that "irresponsible" aliyah operations, as in the case of the Kladovo group, had endangered all efforts. Storfer contended that since he had been authorized by the Nazis to organize Jewish emigration, he was responsible for ensuring that aliyah activities were properly carried out and past errors corrected. For this purpose he required not only that all aliyah operations be coordinated, but that he supervise the initial stages of each one as well. He expressed the desire that this could be done in cooperation with Yehieli and his group.

To Yehieli, Storfer's bid to cooperate with the Mossad was a ploy to facilitate his work within the Reich—to legitimate his refugee selection process, to ease his relations with the JDC, and to secure disembarkation arrangements in Palestine. Today, however, Storfer's proposal comes across as a sincere effort to establish dialogue. From the information available, it would appear that in February 1940 Storfer himself was not certain that he could control all emigration activity alone, although he was in the process of taking specific measures toward this end.[50] His position was still somewhat insecure, and he needed a link with the Mossad to reinforce it.

It is unlikely that Yehieli was capable of viewing Storfer in this light when the two men met on 25 February 1940. From Yehieli's account of their conversation, it is clear that the exchange served only to heighten the level of misunderstanding, hostility, and mistrust between them. The discussion degenerated into an acrimonious barrage, with Storfer condemning Ehud Ueberall over the Kladovo affair, berating Edelstein for blocking cooperation with him, and accusing Yehieli of undermining the aliyah effort.[51] Storfer warned Yehieli not to engage in any activity that had not first been cleared with his office. He informed Yehieli that the money promised by Edelstein for acquiring the *Wetan* would not be forthcoming unless Yehieli agreed to cooperate. (Storfer, though not yet officially in charge of arranging all Jewish emigration from the Reich, did have a link to all currency transactions arranged by the Jewish communities.)

Yehieli, in anger, threatened to reveal the details of their discussion to the community in Prague and to halt Mossad operations there if the Hehalutz and Zionist refugees came to any harm. Storfer feared having this information exposed to the Germans, as it would portray him as subverting emigration activity. Storfer ameliorated his demands somewhat, yet the meeting ended inconclusively. We have no documentation of Storfer's reaction to the discussion.

Storfer's threat to delay the Czech funds, and the entire exchange, deeply disturbed Yehieli and his colleagues. They decided they ought not to sever contact with Storfer for fear of endangering their comrades inside the Reich. Through Agami, they contacted Edelstein in an attempt to clarify the extent of Storfer's actual power. Agami wired them that "We received reassurances from Edelstein . . . [who] promised once again that the money would be put at our disposal as soon as required, and also stated that they were prepared to transfer the sum we would require in Turkish currency in Istanbul from the Czech National Bank."[52] Assured by this message, Yehieli, Klueger-Aliav, and Agami continued on their way to Istanbul to negotiate for the *Wetan*. Yet the funds indeed failed to be relayed, and the ship was lost. Evidence points to the intervention of Storfer here, though there is no conclusive documentation of it.

The setting for the second meeting between Storfer and Yehieli four months later was even more complex than that for the first, and in this case it was the Mossad who was eager to meet. Storfer had been appointed to oversee emigration from the Reich some two months earlier, and he was confident that no activity could be organized without him.

The Mossad remained extremely hostile to Storfer, despite the consequences of having refused to cooperate with him previously—the loss of the *Wetan*. The Mossad held Storfer responsible for having deliberately sabotaged the arrangement. Storfer, for his part, denied that his delay of the funds transfer had stopped the deal; he held that it was the intervention of the Turkish government that had terminated the negotiations.[53]

Following the loss of the *Wetan* and the failure to rescue the Kladovo and Prague groups, the Mossad came under intense pressure from the Jewish communities and was severely criticized by the American Zionists and the JDC. The Mossad wished to pressure Storfer to take their people from Kladovo, Prague, and Berlin in place of the Patronka group and additional groups from Vienna and Danzig.

To this end, the Mossad did all it could to persuade the JDC to grant it power of approval over funds transfers to Storfer. In early April, Yehieli met with JDC representative Sally Mayer and Chaim Weizmann (who happened to be in Geneva). Yehieli's description of the danger of allowing Storfer total control suggested possible infiltration of refugee groups, and it sounded an alarm in both men. Consequently, the JDC ceded the Mossad a degree of control over funding channeled to Storfer: funds would be released only with a signed authorization from Shmarya Tsameret, the Mossad agent in Athens.

Thus, the Mossad gained a temporary tactical advantage with which to challenge Storfer. The question was, would he submit to Tsameret's authority—and the Mossad's—by agreeing to Mossad inspection of his ship? Or would he, like the false mother in the Solomonic judgment, declare "neither you nor I will have one," and scuttle the plans of all involved? Nevertheless, the Mossad's position was actually rather weak. The JDC would not be able to hold out very long under pressure from the communities to transfer the funds to Storfer. Even Hehalutz representatives in the various German-controlled territories had begun to report that the situation had passed tolerable limits and that cooperation with Storfer was imperative.

Furthermore, the future of illegal aliyah was in question in spring 1940. Not only did those who had all along opposed aliyah bet express doubts about it, but even longtime supporters such as Nahum Goldmann of the World Jewish Congress, a man who had raised large sums for it, now wavered. All questioned the dubious results and growing risks of illegal immigration. Opinion in Palestine had become sharply divided once the war had broken out, and by April 1940, opposition was strong. It was an extremely inauspicious time to engage Storfer in a struggle for control. Ironically, in choosing to challenge Storfer, the Mossad was taking on the one man most involved in organizing Jewish emigration and implementing the policy that was most likely to save Jewish lives.

Following his meeting with Mayer and Weizmann in Geneva, Yehieli traveled to London to consult with the Zionist leadership (including Ben-Gurion and Kaplan) to receive endorsement for illegal aliyah operations. One of the most important topics of the discussion was the problem of Storfer and his selection of emigrants. In faraway London, fears of fifth columnists loomed large and selection of candidates according to Zionist criteria seemed feasible. So adamant was the Zionist leadership about the need to shut out Storfer that Yehieli was compelled to urge a degree of moderation. Yehieli also reported that Storfer had made an opening to meet with the Mossad, and that the Mossad ought not refuse. Nahum Goldmann also supported this view. It was therefore concluded that cooperation with Storfer should continue, but that the Mossad should turn over no facet of the operation to him outside the Reich.[54]

Armed with this decision, Yehieli arrived in Geneva on 11 May 1940, to meet Storfer. (Two days earlier, the Germans had launched the war on the western front.) Leon Hermann, the Berlin representative of the Zionist Palestine Office, was also in Geneva, and he informed Yehieli of the latest developments and Storfer's status. According to Yehieli:

> [Hermann] didn't really tell us anything new about the situation of the Jews or the movement. The only news was about the assignment of exclusive responsibility for Jewish emigration work to the "counselor" [Storfer]. He related to me what the responsible bodies in Berlin thought of [Storfer], which was thoroughly negative. They treated him with great distrust and agreed that he had to be approached with extreme caution. But they also recognized a need for a modus vivendi with him; otherwise there was no way to continue working inside the Reich. I asked Leon if he meant cooperation at any cost and under any conditions, and his response was negative. Our comrades and the responsible bodies are hoping for some form of compromise. It was clearly their understanding that complete and open cooperation, in the sense of maintaining a joint organization, was out of the question.[55]

At their second meeting, Storfer presented Yehieli with his plan to take 3,100 Jews out of the Reich.[56] He stated that the lists had been approved by the Palestine Office, and he demanded Yehieli's support in arranging transit documents for Rumania and disembarkation in Palestine, and in getting Shmarya Tsameret to release the JDC's funds.

Yehieli objected to the proposed lists on two grounds. First, the Prague Hehalutz group, which contained one thousand people and was already organized for departure, was not included. Furthermore, Storfer proposed that five hundred Jews from Vienna should go aboard, while the Kladovo group was still marooned in Yugoslavia.

Storfer told Yehieli that he would deal with these two issues at a later time. The Prague group, he argued, had refused to work with him earlier in the year. He had therefore undertaken other commitments. Storfer also maintained that the Kladovo group was not his responsibility. He expressed a willingness to make a small contribution on their behalf, though the Vienna community remained opposed to cutting its own allotment to help them.

In sum, Storfer had nothing new to offer. Yehieli heard nothing to persuade him to change his attitude, and he refused the terms Storfer offered. To Yehieli's demand that Prague Hehalutz be placed on the next transport, Storfer had replied that the Mossad must suspend all independent operations first and put itself under his authority. He wanted the Mossad to make the disembarkation arrangements in Palestine and acquire the transit documents in Rumania, yet he was unwilling to transfer the sea leg of the Palestine journey—the Black Sea and the Mediterranean—to Mossad control.

Cooperation under such conditions did not fall within the terms of the instructions Yehieli had been given in London. To agree to Storfer's terms would have implied the Mossad's failure, spelling the end of its independent operations and undoubtedly tipping the scales against official Zionist support of aliyah bet. Yehieli, in all likelihood, realized that Storfer would eventually carry out his plans with or without the Mossad. Storfer had enlisted the support of community figures in Czechoslovakia and elsewhere who were pressing for the refugees' departure. The JDC (and Tsameret) would sooner or later have to accede to the demands to transfer needed funds. Yehieli saw that it would be better for the Mossad to stay unentangled with Storfer. Storfer, for his part, left the meeting angry, disillusioned, and bent on retaliating. Not only had he failed in his bid to gather all power and authority around himself, but the immediate problem of disembarkation remained unsolved.[57]

It may be argued that Storfer's offer represented an opportunity to join in a national rescue effort of the highest priority, and that the Mossad deliberately failed to do so. In the same vein, one could speculate that cooperation with Storfer at that stage would have been a catalyst to aliyah work, joining the forces inside and outside the Reich, and this in turn might have compelled the JDC to be more forthcoming with financial support. It might have been possible to do more to get comrades of the Zionist movement out of the Reich by cooperating with Storfer than by working against him or without him. Yet, Mossad's fears regarding cooperation with Storfer were genuine, and these apprehensions prevented them from assessing his work in a different light. In noncooperation with Storfer they saw the best chances of proceeding with their work. The two failures of the spring—the *Wetan* and Storfer's ships for the Patronka group—were not taken as an ominous warning.

Undoubtedly, personal considerations were involved in Yehieli's decision to continue to operate independently of Storfer, but the most important single factor was the inability of the Mossad to see in Storfer anything but the representative of a perverse set of values. The basic worldview of the Mossad agents continued to dominate their thinking, even after it had been made obsolete by the reality imposed by the Nazi regime. Even Leon Hermann of the Palestine Office supported Yehieli's position,[58] though he had been the one who conveyed the Hehalutz members' desire for a compromise with Storfer. Support of this kind from their colleagues inside the Reich gave Yehieli and his comrades the moral justification for the position they adopted.

The failed opportunity for dialogue brought disaster in its wake. The first casualty was the Kladovo group. The Mossad failed to rescue the Kladovo group partly because it had no agent in Belgrade to inspire confidence in Sima Spitzer to send the group on its way. Had a combined effort been undertaken, Storfer might have been able to persuade Spitzer to overcome his misgivings, and the rescue might have succeeded. The second casualty of the failed dialogue was the Prague Hehalutz group. The group was not able to emigrate and was first deported to Theresienstadt and then gassed at Auschwitz.

Likewise, it proved impossible to organize groups inside the Reich without going through Storfer. This became clear to those in Berlin after Leon Hermann returned at the end of May 1940, and the Berlin comrades reported as much to Geneva. At that point, however, it was already too late to alter the situation. The Mossad itself soon discovered that it could do nothing for the Zionists in Berlin. After six weeks, Pino Ginsburg informed Otto Hirsch, Leon Hermann, and Erich Frank that the Mossad was no longer able to promise to bring them to Palestine and advised them to try to leave on Storfer's transport.[59]

At this time as well, the JDC came to a realization that full cooperation with Storfer was necessary regardless of Mossad objections.[60] The lengthy delay in its transfer of funds to Storfer had been the result of a struggle not of its own making. The leaders of the JDC now accepted that Storfer's ships represented the only hope for Kladovo, Bratislava, Danzig, Berlin, and Vienna.

Although Storfer was angry and felt wrongfully distrusted, he nevertheless recognized that he was dependent on the JDC, and he began to seek a way of winning favor with it.[61] An occasion presented itself when Loewenherz was called to Budapest to meet with Storfer and the representatives of the JDC. Storfer wished to attend, understanding full well the importance of it, but in a letter of 3 June, he indicated that he wanted Loewenherz to raise the issue of support for emigration. No actual record of the meeting in Budapest exists, but according to Yehieli's reports, Storfer was present. Apparently, he joined Loewenherz there after a few days. At the meeting, a compromise on Kladovo was reached: Vienna was to contribute toward the upkeep of the group in Yugoslavia, while the JDC was to pay for the rest of their journey. This was satisfactory to Storfer. Storfer also convincingly presented the conflict between himself and the Mossad as a difference among two Zionist positions whose relative merits the JDC was not in a position to judge. Palestine did not belong to any one Jewish or Zionist group, he contended.[62]

After the meeting, tensions between Storfer and the JDC temporarily subsided, only to be intensified again in the wake of Italy's entry into the war in late June. The JDC sought an assurance from Storfer that if it transferred funds to him through Greece they would not be confiscated by the government following the opening of the Italian front (as had occurred in the Netherlands). In the absence of such a guarantee, the JDC proposed that the £13,800 that had been delayed by Tsameret and was about to be transferred to Storfer be returned to the United States.

Storfer had meanwhile proceeded to arrange his transport and was incensed by this threatened setback. He sent a sharply worded letter to the Vienna communal leadership vehemently objecting to the JDC's administrative interference. He stated that no further guarantees were possible. In the same letter, Storfer detailed the preparations he had made for the acquisition of three ships.

At this time, the JDC also came to question the safety of sea travel. On 10 July Storfer reported a joint decision by the communities of Berlin, Vienna, and Prague to proceed with emigration arrangements.[63] He stressed that this decision was made only after an exhaustive effort to ascertain the safety of sailing conditions on the Mediterranean. In stressing safety, Storfer showed his sensitivity toward Morris Tropper's concerns and hesitations (prompted in part by Hehalutz) over the new risks involved in undertaking a sea journey. Storfer made a point of the care being taken by his men in seeing to every detail in advance in order to maximize security and guarantee a smooth journey for the refugees, despite the expanded war front. Nothing was left to chance. He concluded by saying: "We could do no more under the circumstances, and one who looks for weaknesses will find them everywhere. The pessimist has an easier time of it than those of us who try."[64] To cast the most favorable light on the responsible attitude he was taking, Storfer compared his own operation with the faulty work being done by others. Storfer finally succeeded in stabilizing his relations with the JDC, and he received the required funds for the transport.

The persistence and depth of the doubt held by Storfer's contemporaries is notable in the ambivalent attitude of the Berlin Jewish community. When writing to him officially or when engaged in negotiations with him, the leaders of Berlin Jewry took great care to stress Storfer's public position. They wanted to clarify that they turned to him only in his official capacity, not as the owner of a private office or business.

Thus, for example, they acceded to Storfer's stipulation that each emigrant sign a waiver declaring his awareness of the potential dangers of the journey and accepting full personal responsibility. This waiver was a pure formality of course, as they knew full well that there was no alternative.

Interestingly, a full-blown discussion of the waiver of liability was actually held. The meeting was attended by Storfer, Loewenherz, and representatives of the entire community.[65] The decision to require the declaration applied not only to Vienna, but to Prague and Berlin as well. In response to this decision, and in light of the growing risks of sea travel in the newly widened theater of war, Erich Frank and Georg Israel wrote to Loewenherz and Storfer and declared that, the waiver notwithstanding, the moral responsibility remained with the organizers of the transports.[66] (In Berlin, this was the Reichsvereinigung.) The emigrants, the letter stressed, continued to view those in charge of emigration arrangements as a *responsible Jewish public body, not as private individuals*. It was the obligation of Storfer and of the others involved to observe this trust painstakingly. In the final analysis, they wrote, the moral responsibility rested entirely on the organizers. The Reichsvereinigung wrote to Storfer in a similar vein in early 1940, when it invited him to Berlin for talks about emigration affairs.[67]

Dr. Mermelstein, a leader in the Vienna community, in a long memorandum regarding the JDC and Storfer's request for further allocations, emphasized his view that the emigration effort was a rescue operation and not a profit-making venture. Such reminders by community figures demonstrate that they were more than a little dubious of Storfer and the nature of his operation.

It was against this background of uncertainty and distrust, and after the failures of April 1940, that Storfer succeeded in sending the largest-ever group of refugees to Palestine. In turning now to consider the history of these three ships—the *Milos*, the *Pacific*, and the *Atlantic*—the conditions under which Storfer worked and the standards to which he committed himself in terms of both the safety of the refugees and his own integrity should be borne in mind.

The Voyage of the Three Ships

Storfer acquired the three ships—the *Emily* (*Atlantic*), the *Betty* (*Pacific*), and the *Kenisbey* (*Milos*)—through Avgerinos toward the end of summer 1940. Along with these, he also acquired the *Rosita,* which was destined never to set sail for Palestine. By July 1940, the ships were in the registration process in Spain and were equipped as dual-purpose (cargo and passenger) vessels.[68] According to Storfer's plan, the *Atlantic* was to carry some 1,800 passengers, the *Pacific* about 1,000, and the *Milos* about 700, bringing the total to approximately 3,500. The *Rosita* was to carry a group of 1,200 at a later time. It was registered in Panama, rather than in Spain. At this time also, Storfer reported that preparations were already being made to accommodate passengers: sleeping bunks, kitchens, toilets, and so forth.

The ships were to sail from Piraeus to Tulcea, Rumania (located on the Black Sea at the mouth of the Danube), where the refugees were to arrive via German Danube Line rivercraft. The Rumanian government as well as the German Danube Line stipulated that the refugees were to embark on their journey down the Danube only when the three ships were safely in Tulcea, awaiting their arrival. According to the original plan, the journey was to have taken place in August. Difficulties in obtaining Spanish registry and in currency transfers to the Rumanian bank delayed the arrival of the ships. At this juncture, the German Foreign Office instructed its commercial attaché in Bucharest to assist Storfer with the foreign-currency transactions. Meanwhile, registry of the ships remained unresolved, and at the last minute Panamanian registry was obtained with the help of a bribe to the Spanish and Panamanian representatives in Bucharest.[69]

August passed, and the ships remained in Piraeus. Meanwhile, another problem cropped up that threatened to abort the voyage. The German Danube Line rivercraft had been scheduled to begin repatriating ethnic Germans from the Balkans to the Reich by 10 September. This demanded a close coordination of the two operations. The director of the German Danube Line, Schutz, met with Storfer at the end of August, but was neither patient nor flexible, in contrast to his earlier attitude. By the end of the month, when the trip had not taken place, Schutz began to doubt Storfer's ability to bring off the operation, and he used the opportunity to pose new conditions. His manner was obstinate and unpleasant. The weeks that followed were tense, and during this time the large group of refugees from Berlin gathered in Vienna. Storfer—with Eichmann's help—reached an agreement with the German Danube Line. The refugees would sail on 2 September and 4 September.

The Slovakian police and foreign ministry also created difficulties for Storfer. The refugees in Bratislava, who had remained there since November 1939, were given until 8 or 9 August to leave or else be deported back to the Reich. Storfer was well acquainted with this sort of maneuver, and knew that the only solution was the payment of a considerable sum to the heads of the Slovakian police. He assigned this task to Rotenstreich, his local representative.[70]

During the last month, difficulties arose all along the intended route. It was indeed possible that a combination of relatively small obstacles could have forced Storfer to cancel the operation even at that late stage. The new Rumanian government (under Antonescu, who assumed power in September 1940) was less disposed to deal favorably with Storfer than its predecessor. In August, as plans were finalized, pressures mounted over the composition of the passenger groups. Various groups in Vienna, Berlin, Prague, and Slovakia demanded that the numbers of their own groups in the transport be increased. Dannecker, Eichmann's representative, also scrutinized the proposed lists to ensure that Nazi priorities were adhered to.[71]

Despite these pressures, Storfer explained to all who approached him that the following considerations guided his selection of passengers: 1) long-standing commitments to certain people, such as the Patronka group; 2) a past record of prompt payment, as in the case of the Danzig community; 3) an organized and disciplined Zionist pioneer element that could help a great deal in organizing the passengers throughout the journey, such as existed in the Berlin group; and 4) the preferences of the German authorities regarding emigration from specific communities.[72]

The community leaders were under intense pressure. The twelve-day interval planned between the departure of the first group and the second was itself a source of tension. All wished to be included among the first 2,700 rather than among the last 1,500.[73] From testimony gathered afterward, it appears that right up to departure, people paid Storfer enormous sums of money to get into the transport. These were as high as £300 per person, over ten times the official fare of £20–30.[74] Storfer absolutely denied ever receiving such payments, though he admitted that many people pressed him to be added to the lists. It is clear that he had the power to do so even after the selections committee—composed of community representatives and his own men—had made its decision. There are some indications that Storfer used his power to pressure those whom he suspected of acting against him or who had criticized him and his operations.

The Danube voyage lasted two weeks.[75] The first group left from Bratislava, but because the Slovakian police forced several dozen more refugees onto the boats, Storfer received permission to have the next group embark in Vienna. The Danube boats were overcrowded, and food was in short supply. The group from Slovakia suffered from particularly poor conditions. The passengers arrived in Tulcea between 15 and 18 September, but the ships on which they were to set sail had not yet arrived. The refugees had to wait three more weeks before they departed for Palestine.[76]

The Preparation and the Voyage

The arrival of 3,500 people in Tulcea, a small town of a few thousand people, brought about drastic changes in the life of the town. Food and water consumption doubled, demand for goods rose, and prices soared. Lumber and other materials for outfitting the ships were especially sought after. In such a market, prices knew no bounds: It was the chance of a lifetime for the locals to rake in huge profits.[77]

The first contingent of 2,700 to arrive went aboard the *Atlantic* and the *Pacific*. Despite previous reassurances, neither ship was quite ready. Berths, kitchens, and toilets were still being installed, and food supplies for the trip had not yet been loaded. Furthermore, the crews that had signed on in Piraeus for one month had to be let go once the ships reached the Black Sea. The British consulate in Bucharest successfully exerted pressure on crew members to convince them not to sail. Recruiting new crews in September 1940 was no simple matter, and prospective crewmen demanded outrageous wages.[78]

For the entire three-week period of preparation, the passengers were forbidden to go ashore. Their only means of communicating with land was through the harbor authority. Nevertheless, the passengers engaged in a brisk trade with the townspeople, especially in foodstuffs, which were in short supply on board.

The Atlantic

The *Atlantic* had 1,829 passengers. Among these were 329 people who had been in Bratislava and who were members of Maccabi and of Hehalutz in Prague, 189 people from Bratislava who had been staying in Vienna, 761 Austrian Jews, 25 from Berlin, and 525 from Danzig. More than 500 passengers were over age 65, and there were more than 100 children under ten years of age. There was no organized youth movement among the passengers, and partly because of this, social relations were disorganized and difficult. Storfer described the social conditions from the first as "each for himself and very few for all."[79] There were also quite a number of freed inmates from the Buchenwald and Dachau concentration camps, and their physical and emotional states were particularly fragile. Crowding on the ship was unbearable. The combination of poor physical conditions, the haphazard composition of the group, and the absence of a core group within it militated against formation of close bonds or a sense of common purpose that might have assuaged tensions. In Storfer's view, life aboard the *Atlantic* would have been considerably easier had the passengers achieved a better rapport and established routines and internal discipline. Storfer seemed unaware that this was not for lack of desire to do so but that it resulted from the social makeup of the group and the physical conditions on board the ship.

Crowding was exacerbated by the excess luggage passengers had brought on board. They rejected outright Avgerinos's proposal to forward the extra baggage by rail, and some suggested instead that their group should be divided between the two other ships. Storfer rejected this idea, since it required negotiating with the Rumanian authorities, who were already hostile, fearing that any change might lead to the creation of a refugee camp in Tulcea. Storfer also turned down the passengers' request that some of them should go aboard the *Rosita*. (That ship was not yet outfitted for sea, and it was intended for other groups entirely.) In an attempt to bypass Storfer, the passengers turned to the Rumanian authorities. Yet their appeal only compounded the suspicions of the already hostile Rumanian authorities. According to Storfer, the increasing ill will the request created made it imperative to move the refugees as quickly as possible, in whatever state of readiness.[80]

Having no alternative, the passengers finally adjusted to their situation, and the *Atlantic* sailed on 7 October. It ran aground in the harbor, and though it was undamaged, a delay of two days ensued while a tugboat was sent from Sulina. Once safely in Istanbul, provisions were brought on board. The ship proceeded to Crete, where it loaded coal, but the fuel proved insufficient. When the supply ran out, the boilers were stoked with wood—including bunks, chairs, and cabin partitions (according to the captain's report to Bucharest of 14 November). The ship was gradually turned into a vast shell, and living conditions became intolerable. As it approached Cyprus, the *Atlantic* was seized by the British navy.

Storfer anxiously reported the plight of the *Atlantic* to the Vienna community and the JDC. On 20 October all contact with the ship was lost. He knew only that coal supplies had run out and that the crew was demanding additional payment. In the meantime, Italy had declared war on Greece (29 October 1940), making the seas more dangerous than ever. Despite his uncertainty and worry, Storfer did not spare the *Atlantic*'s passengers his criticism.[81]

On Cyprus supplies were replenished, and the British decided to escort the ship to Haifa. The passengers greeted the announcement with wild rejoicing. (Mr. Cavaghan of the Royal Navy was put in command.)[82] In the report of the British commander, which was substantive and relatively restrained, Cavaghan expressed deep shock over the hygiene, safety, and organization of the passengers, as well as the poor condition of the ship. He also wondered how the ship had reached Cyprus at all. The hold of the ship contained several hundred people, and in order to breathe they had cut air holes through the hull close to the waterline. Cavaghan noted also that the ship had neither lifeboats nor life jackets.

The British commander put the English speakers on board in charge of maintaining order, and instituted a strict regime of rewards and punishments, including threats of the death penalty for certain offenses. Escorted by several British ships and sailing on calm seas, the refugees finally arrived in Haifa on 24 November. Luck had even smiled upon them—at one stage an Italian warplane had circled above but had not recognized them as British vessels. In Palestine, they found a country in mourning. Although the *Atlantic* had been the first of the three ships to set forth, the *Pacific* and the *Milos,* to which we shall now turn, had reached Palestine ahead of it.

The Pacific

The *Pacific* was not ready for its voyage when the refugees were placed aboard in Tulcea. However, the eager refugees went to work building the required installations and organizing shipboard routines. Letters written at the time spoke of sharp arguments with Goldner (Storfer's brother-in-law) over building supplies and food. Since Storfer and Avgerinos wanted to save as much food and water as possible for the actual voyage, the refugees drank river water. This was often used by the townspeople when no better supply was available, but it caused intestinal disorders during the first days.

The social dynamics on the *Pacific* were quite different from those aboard the *Atlantic*. First of all, though the ship was crowded, living conditions were somewhat more comfortable. A total of 1,061 were placed on board the *Pacific*. These included 470 Hehalutz and other Zionist movement members from Berlin, 432 people from Bratislava (some of whom were from Hehalutz), 84 from Vienna, and another 75 who boarded in Bulgaria.[83] But the main factors that shaped the way life developed on the *Pacific* were the Berlin Hehalutz members' organizing skills and their emotional preparedness for the trip to Palestine.

The Berlin group took charge of the entire ship. Erich Frank of Hehalutz and Hans Raubel of the Zionist movement formed a "high command." The passengers were divided into three groups, headed by "captains." Each group was given a daily assignment, performing maintenance chores or organizing cultural activities. Study groups were arranged in the Hebrew language, Judaism, and agriculture. All requests and complaints were routed through the group captains, who formed an advisory council, and a committee for order and safety was formed as well. Money in the passengers' possession was pooled for emergency use, and pocket money was distributed from this common purse. Each passenger had to consent in writing to obey the instructions of the group captains. This chain of command made life on board considerably easier than on the *Atlantic*.

The ship's passengers very quickly coalesced into a unified group and adopted an attitude of collective responsibility. The ideology of the Hehalutz group provided positive reinforcement: going to Palestine constituted the individual's contribution to the Zionist ideal; the journey was a test of one's mettle and the skills that would soon be needed. Conditions on the *Pacific* were little better, yet the letters of Frank and his comrades reveal tangible differences in the lives of the passengers aboard the two ships. The personal and collective discipline turned problems into challenges; to them, overcoming difficulties became a source of satisfaction. The Hehalutz group served to bolster individual strength and resolve in the face of the pressures and uncertainties that abounded. Setting foot on the fragile and crowded *Pacific* was already seen as a transition to freedom, as Erich Frank wrote: "Through this self-organization we participated after a long period of oppression in a self controlled and free 'society' with self esteem. In some respect we could again find a room for ourselves."[84]

The *Pacific* sailed from Tulcea on 11 October 1940, but it was immediately realized that neither the dynamo nor compass was working. Furthermore, the ship's engineer (who had arrived on board only hours before sailing time) was unfamiliar with the boiler and could not operate it. The ship was put into port in Varna, Bulgaria, for repairs to its instruments. More coal had to be procured and the engineer had to be replaced; the delay proved longer than anticipated. The local Jewish community agreed to pay for the repairs and part of the extra food and water in return for passage for eight Jewish refugees who had been staying in Varna. The passengers' leaders turned to Storfer for the remainder of the expenses. Storfer, however, was unable to send the money immediately and advised them to contact Baruch Konfino. (Konfino had offered to cover the added expenses in exchange for passage for twenty Hehalutz members.) Konfino and the ship's leaders negotiated a detailed agreement, but, according to Raubel and Frank, Konfino broke his word. Instead, forty additional passengers were forced aboard with the active and violent assistance of the local police, and food rations were diminished even further.[85]

On 17 October the *Pacific* sailed for Crete, arriving five days later. Both engine oil and water supplies had run out. The ship's leaders attempted to contact Avgerinos, but they were unable to reach him at the given address. The leaders appealed to the Jewish community in Athens, and the Jewish Refugee Aid Committee there supplied them generously. Thus, the voyage was allowed to continue.

The ship arrived undetected off the coast of Palestine, near Rosh Hanikra. However, no provision had been made for landing, and apparently neither the Haganah nor Irgun expected it. The *Pacific* therefore proceeded to Haifa, arriving on 15 November, and surrendered to the British authorities.

The Milos

The smallest of the three ships (and the best, by the passengers' account) was the *Milos*. Of its 702 passengers, 652 were Czech Jews (220 from Brno, 250 sent by Mendler from Prague and Slovakia, and 182 Betar members from various parts of the Protectorate). The other 50 were from Vienna.

The passengers sailed down the Danube under particularly crowded conditions, and upon arrival in Tulcea the same circumstances as had greeted the other two groups awaited them. As with the *Pacific*, it fell to the passengers to finish the work of outfitting the ship. Ernst Braun of Brno and Alfred Kornfeld, a Betar member, were chosen as leaders of the *Milos*. The two instituted a very strict regime among the passengers, and it was enforced all the way to Palestine.[86]

One problem among the *Milos* passengers was an ideological friction that developed between the Zionists and certain Czech Jews on board who did not consider themselves Jews, let alone Zionists. For them the transport was a way of escaping the Reich, and they planned to join the Czech forces being formed by the government-in-exile. Despite a degree of antagonism caused by their presence, a cooperative spirit prevailed on the *Milos* as on the *Pacific*. Similarly, this ameliorated the hardships of the journey.

The *Milos* was delayed in Tulcea a rather long time, but its departure was hurried and sudden, leaving little time to stock sufficient supplies of water and engine oil. Storfer transmitted a message to the ship saying he would await the ship in Piraeus and gave an address through which he could be reached in case of emergency. The Black Sea was calm, but a severe storm arose on the Sea of Marmara. Neither food nor fuel was to be had in any of the ports along the way, and attempts to contact Storfer were fruitless. The passengers appealed to the Jewish community of Athens in desperation. Once more the Athens Jewry came to the rescue, but in no uncertain terms they charged Storfer with willful neglect—leaving the transport undersupplied in order to increase his profits.[87] The ship proceeded to Haifa and arrived on 17 November.

The ordeal was not yet over. Those aboard the *Milos* and *Pacific* were scheduled for deportation to Mauritius by the British. (See Chapter 2.) They awaited the arrival of the *Atlantic* aboard the *Patria*.[88] The plan to damage the *Patria* to keep it from sailing ended disastrously; the ship sank, and 267 drowned. The survivors were allowed to stay on in Palestine. The *Atlantic* arrived after these events had transpired, and its passengers were first interned at Atlit, then deported to Mauritius, according to British orders. (Most remained there for the duration of the war and legally immigrated to Palestine afterward.) Thus ended the saga of the three illegal ships, the last organized transport out of the Reich to Palestine.

Storfer: Serving the Public Good or in Business for Himself?

Precisely when and why Storfer's activities ceased is unclear. From the available information regarding the desire of refugees to leave, the opportunities to emigrate, and so on, it does seem that the end of emigration efforts owed less to British deportation policy and withering Zionist support for aliyah bet than to changes in German policy. German arrangements for promoting Jewish emigration from the Reich were canceled as plans for the invasion of Russia began to take shape. Legal and organized emigration was completely suspended with the expansion of the war into southern and eastern Europe. However, instances of individual departures from the Reich (though not from German-occupied territories) took place until October 1941.

In March 1941, Storfer apparently still believed he could continue emigration efforts, and so proceeded with his plans. The fourth ship, the *Rosita,* was still at his disposal,[89] but he was unable to use it. The Germans had projected their power into Yugoslavia and Bulgaria and were directly influencing events in Rumania. Although these circumstances might have improved

Storfer's situation, the S.D. apparently no longer put faith in a plan for mass Jewish emigration. As the war of expansion continued, the number of Jews under Nazi rule increased, and the proportionate impact of forced emigration came to be insignificant. At that point, the Nazi regime turned to the Final Solution. Storfer nevertheless continued to work on arrangements for emigration to Spain, Lisbon, and Shanghai, apparently until October 1941.[90]

How should we assess Storfer's activities? The charges leveled against him by his contemporaries include the following: that he worked for Eichmann and was thus an S.D. and Gestapo collaborator, that he selected candidates for transports not out of Zionist considerations but according to German pressures, and, finally, that he exploited his position for financial gain. In addition, we should ask: To what extent did he deal justly with others engaged in organizing or supporting aliyah? How did he view his responsibility? What standards did he set for himself in consequence of this view? A fair assessment of the man and his work might emerge if we could say something conclusive about each of these points.

With regard to the charge of collaboration, we have to bear in mind that Storfer's association with Eichmann took place in a context wherein political authority over Austrian Jewry was S.S.-controlled. In this situation, practically any community activity that took place could, strictly speaking, be construed as an act of collaboration; every Jewish leader in Berlin, Vienna, and Prague who had dealings with the Germans could be said to have collaborated with the Nazi regime and the S.S. Furthermore, we need to bear in mind that this collaboration, as it were, took place before the Final Solution became the policy of the S.S. or of the Reich. Storfer operated during a period when forced emigration was policy, a context in which every act directed at getting Jews out of the Reich was an act of rescue. It was not yet the case that each place on the transports was "bought" at the price of another Jew's life. Therefore, to describe Storfer's activities as collaboration with the Germans seems unjustified. A more accurate description is as a Jewish rescue effort that fit into the plans of Nazi policymakers. At that time, any aliyah work, including that of the Revisionists and of the Mossad, might be considered in the same light: Even if these groups based themselves outside the Reich, they still required the cooperation of German authorities.

At the same time, it is noteworthy that Jewish leaders were aware of the moral implications of the position they were in and that they debated the question of the right posture to assume in dealings with the Germans. The correctness of the calculated distinctions that they made and the relative weight to assign to such criteria are very difficult to judge or to determine fairly. At what point did reporting to the Nazi authorities go beyond the necessary minimum? In dealing with the Nazis, what constituted standing up for Jewish dignity and what indicated its opposite? When did cooperation proceed only from the force of circumstance, and when did it flow from a dynamic of compliance that blurred the awareness that one was facing the enemy?

There were those, like Jacob Edelstein and Ehud Ueberall, who were convinced that Storfer had overstepped the fine line dividing necessary co-operation from collaboration in each of these areas. They accused Storfer (and the rest of the Viennese Jewish leadership) of failing to offer any resistance to the regime. Nevertheless, other figures in similar situations, including Erich Frank (Hehalutz leader on the *Pacific*), Otto Hirsch (leader of the Berlin Reichsvertretung) and Paul Epstein, assessed Storfer's role quite differently.

For our part, we can only pose these questions and note that even at that time there were no generally accepted and clear-cut standards. Those who were actively involved in the events relied on intuition and emotion and weighed particular circumstances from a specific ideological vantage point. Those outside the Reich were perhaps less able to make conclusive judgments. The evidence shows that the range of options open to Storfer was strictly limited. The officials of the Zentralstelle closely monitored his actions. He was understandably wary and afraid of arousing their ire, but he was none-theless able to use their official backing to further the cause of aliyah. The same might equally be said of the Jewish leadership in Berlin and of the aliyah activists there, who were no more independent of the regime than was Storfer.[91]

Storfer's role in the selection of refugees for emigration must also be judged in the framework just outlined. It is quite true that Storfer applied criteria other than Zionist ones in compiling his lists. However, this constitutes a criticism only from the Zionist point of view, and it does not necessarily stand in terms of Jewish or humanitarian values. It should be remembered that the reverse of such criticism was applied to the Mossad and the Zionist movement in general. Both the Mossad and the Revisionists preferred their younger comrades, but in order to cover some of the costs involved, both groups compromised by also selecting older Zionists who could pay their way. Storfer, too, compromised with economic and political realities. The process of dismantling the Danzig community and evacuating its members was com-pleted by Storfer, but it had been begun before the war by the Revisionists.[92] Those released from concentration camps had a high priority on Mossad lists too. If there were those who left under S.S. pressure, there is no doubt that they did not include Nazi agents (in spite of what the British Foreign Office maintained). Storfer was faithful to the commitments he made to Zionist groups that organized themselves, and he clearly appreciated the leadership skills of the Hehalutz groups from Berlin and Prague.

We are unable to determine the truth of the allegation that Storfer abused his position for private gain. We know that his accounts were meticulously checked by the Zentralstelle, especially foreign-currency transactions, and the Jewish community closely supervised transactions in German currency. Storfer certainly handled huge sums of money, and he did not live in desperate poverty; he had no intention of doing so.

In considering such a charge, we should bear in mind that this was a stock accusation leveled at all aliyah organizers. Even in the Mossad and in the American Zionist movement, there were similar charges of misuse of funds (though not for private gain). Storfer operated in a business context, not as a Jewish public servant directing a nonprofit organization. This cast a different light on his work than what might be said of the Mossad, for example. Before the war, there were Revisionist aliyah organizers who also ran their operations on a business basis; some even saw this as the most efficient way of doing things.

We do not have accurate information about the nature of Storfer's relationship with Avgerinos. Was he owed a share of the profits as Storfer's partner, or was he simply engaged as Storfer's agent? We have no indication of what profits there were, if any. The budget statements included in the records show only the average fare charged per person and do not give a breakdown of costs. We do know that there were many refugees who paid much more than the average rate, but this cannot be measured precisely to show whether tens of thousands of the JDC's and of the passengers' funds went into Storfer's own coffers.

The question of whether Storfer dealt fairly with other aliyah organizers is particularly weighty. On numerous occasions, Storfer actively sought to discredit and impugn the reputations of his competitors and of others involved in aliyah work. He acted in such a way toward the Mossad, the Revisionists, Konfino, and others. He had an interest in proving that only he was capable of making reliable arrangements, and did this not only by pointing to his own positive record but also by stressing the failures and irresponsible behavior of others. One can readily understand his hostility toward the Mossad in light of the relationship that developed between them. Less comprehensible, though, is why he found it necessary to act in this way toward Konfino, who had established a fairly close relationship with him. The two men met on a number of occasions, and Konfino was prepared to assist Storfer when necessary. In the same vein, it is unclear why he went out of his way to stress the failings of the Revisionists in the *Sakariya* affair when he had maintained a close link with those involved, including Robert Mendler, one of his closest associates.[93]

Storfer never spoke of any broad common purpose linking him with others active in the aliyah effort or of the similar objective circumstances in which they were all forced to work. The contrary was true, and thus Storfer cannot be said to have displayed any collegial solidarity, as it were. He also showed no inclination to assist refugee groups that had run into difficulties. When he felt himself to be on the defensive, as happened when the Relief Committee in Athens came to the aid of the *Milos* and the *Pacific,* he responded in very strong language and imputed highly improper intentions to the Committee. He seemed incapable of viewing its action as arising from genuine dedication and a sense of obligation; all he saw was that his reputation was at stake.[94]

It is likely that an understanding of Storfer's own view of his role would give us a better sense of how he ought to be evaluated. In none of his letters and in none of his known statements do we find any indication that he saw himself as a leader with responsibility to a community. He presented himself, rather, as an honest businessman called upon to carry out a certain task and determined to do so to the best of his ability. He was very protective of his reputation and sensitive about what people said about him.[95] In defending his good name, in no instance did he take the apologetic stance that, after all, he was working for the sake of the people, for the rescue of the people, or for a broader national cause.

In sum, it is fair to say that Storfer began his activity as a figure from the business world, called upon by Loewenherz to represent the Jewish community at Evian, and he never really ceased being a businessman. His work did not present itself to him in larger terms. He remained true to what he had always been. It seems that he did appreciate the extent of his power, but this did not confer on him any wider public obligation as far as he was concerned. His practical and moral responsibility began and ended within the narrow framework of an agent executing a given task.

Perhaps modesty prompted Storfer to ask of Loewenherz, in a hurt tone but with a hint of criticism, "How did I come to be mixed up with such company?"[96] Or perhaps it was only the expression of a pettiness of character—one that prevented him from rising to the challenge that fate had thrust upon him.

7

The White Paper and
the Fate of European Jewry

The Tenets Shaping British Policy

British policy was among the most influential factors shaping aliyah bet, and at the same time, the British stance weighed heavily on the positions the Zionists adopted toward illegal aliyah. In seeking to understand British policy, several questions arise. How clear and consistent was British policy? How accurately did Zionist leaders assess the importance of the immigration issue to British policymakers—or the value of illegal aliyah for Zionist interests?

Essentially, British policy on Palestine was but one aspect of a broader approach to imperial interests. The government determined the overall thrust of its policy in the Middle East, its attitude to the Islamic world, and its relations with its allies within this context. Authority on questions pertaining to Jewish immigration to Palestine belonged primarily to the Colonial Office and the Foreign Office. The high commissioner of Palestine, the chief administrator, reported directly to the colonial secretary (a cabinet-level post). The Colonial Office for the most part held sway during the 1920s and early 1930s, and the Foreign Office played a minor role in this period. However, by the eve of the Second World War (and during the war itself) Foreign Office involvement in policy grew ever more pronounced.

The British government had undertaken a major reassessment of its Palestine policy during 1938 in light of changing conditions in the Middle East and Britain's strategic-economic position in a world that teetered on the brink of war. (The possibility of war actually strengthened the arguments of those who sought a new policy.) Britain concluded that the goals embodied in the Balfour Declaration were unrealistic and could not be carried out, while the goal of a establishing a Jewish national home had been adequately fulfilled. The result was the White Paper of 1939, which imposed an absolute quota on Jewish immigration. To the Zionists, it constituted an abandonment of the British commitment to build a Jewish national home.[1] Yet, throughout the war period, Britain upheld the immigration restrictions set forth in the White Paper.

Embodied in the White Paper restrictions were several assumptions, first and foremost that immigration to Palestine (and the creation of a Jewish national home) was to be considered a separate issue, unrelated to the plight of Jewish refugees seeking to leave Europe. Such a stance had been manifest as early as the first Mandate immigration regulations, and it was implicit in the economic quotas that came to be established as well. During the 1930s, pressure from the Zionists and others had mounted, and it had become increasingly difficult to maintain this distinction. Yet the government adamantly held forth, and even made its participation in the Evian Conference on the disposition of European refugees in July 1938 conditional upon the acceptance of this principle. Even in the most pressing circumstances, such as those facing the *Sakariya* and the Kladovo groups, the British persistently maintained this strict distinction between refugee policy and immigration policy.[2] This view is the key to understanding British attitudes toward illegal aliyah.

This position justified Britain in nullifying immigration certificates granted to the Jews of the Reich before the war. Once the war began, these people became enemy aliens and potential security risks.[3] Therefore, they were no longer eligible to immigrate to British-held colonies. The British steadfastly held to this position despite the adverse public reaction it caused, since any admission of a connection between the validity of certificates issued and the plight of refugees would have automatically undercut its interest in controlling immigration.

To the British, illegal immigration was a tactic designed to further the goals of the Zionist movement. This is best seen in a Foreign Office report of 17 January 1940 analyzing the factors behind illegal aliyah. The report ascribed largely political goals to it, and offered the considerable expansion of activity in the wake of the 1939 White Paper as proof. The report stated that "Illegal immigration into Palestine is not primarily a refugee movement.... [T]he traffic has attained its present dimensions only since the White Paper limits Jewish immigration."[4] The report acknowledged that there had been a small but steady flow of illegal immigrants even before the White Paper; but this was deemed a separate phenomenon (whose humanitarian appeal was being exploited by politically minded organizers).

The Foreign Office report also assessed aliyah bet as serving the partisan political ends of Zionist groups. It identified Revisionist involvement in illegal immigration as a means of organizing an eventual takeover in Palestine. This was clear, the report continued, from the composition of their transports: "The illegal immigrants whom the New Zionists [Revisionists] transport to Palestine are carefully picked and trained young men of military age and young women, and not old men and women or children, [as in] a true refugee movement." Assuming the basic dynamic of aliyah bet to be political, and having decided to maintain a strict separation between the refugee and immigration issues, the British were able to frame their opposition to aliyah bet as a contest pitting two morally symmetrical forces: British imperial interests versus Zionist national aspirations. Conceived in these terms, British policy seemed to be quite defensible.

Apparently, the British failed to appreciate the extent to which German policies drove Jews to seek escape to Palestine. Instead, they chose to believe that Zionist groups controlled the flow. Thus, punitive measures against the Zionists, such as reducing quotas, were expected to decrease or even eliminate illegal immigration. The British also hoped to take advantage of the rift between the mainstream Zionists and the Revisionists. They believed they could persuade the Jewish Agency that Revisionist activity, and illegal aliyah generally, served to weaken the Jewish Agency's position by robbing it of control over immigrant selection.[5]

After the war began, another consideration surfaced, especially in Colonial Office circles: that the Germans were supporting illegal immigration in order to subvert British interests. The Germans, it was argued, sought to drive a wedge between Britain and the Arab and Islamic world by inflaming the most vulnerable spot in British-Arab relations. Continued illegal aliyah would serve to demonstrate Britain's ongoing betrayal of Arab interests. Of less importance, but related, was the British fear that German infiltrators and fifth columnists would be sent to the Middle East under cover of refugee groups. The Germans might either plant non-Jewish Germans aboard the immigrant boats or coerce Jewish refugees to cooperate with German intelligence by threatening relatives left behind in the Reich. Lastly, the British thought it possible that the Germans would take advantage of illegal immigration to rid themselves of undesirable Jews.[6]

These arguments formed the basis of British opposition to illegal immigration. Guided by these, the Foreign and Colonial Offices, the main policy actors, endeavored to work in close cooperation, but a degree of friction arising from basic differences in orientation was inevitable. The Colonial Office gave most weight to the view of aliyah bet as a major test of Britain's credibility in the Middle East. Some officials even regarded the cessation of aliyah bet as Britain's foremost priority in Palestine.[7]

In comparison, the Foreign Office viewed the problem in a broader context. It staunchly defended the White Paper, but tended to see the issue not only in terms of Middle East policy, but also in the context of wider foreign-policy ramifications. Various sectors within the Foreign Office—the Refugees and Near Eastern Departments and the British Embassy in Washington—tended to see the issues from different perspectives. In cases where it seemed that the political costs of unyielding opposition were too great, the Foreign Office tended to favor expedient compromise. For instance, it was sensitive to the United States government's stance taken in response to Jewish appeals. The propensity of the Foreign Office to grant favorable treatment to the appeals of friendly governments in certain circumstances was based on the consideration that flexibility would win greater support for British immigration policy generally. In this sense, the Foreign Office served as an important counterweight to British thinking on the issue in general.

Tactics of Prevention

The overall strategy the British employed to halt aliyah bet was to make financial, political, and personal costs prohibitive. The Foreign and Colonial

Refugees from the *Ageus Nicolaus* in the Atlit Detention Camp, summer 1939. Their fingerprints are being taken by British police.

Refugees from the *Ageus Nicolaus* in Atlit, 1939.

The *Tiger Hill* off the shore of Tel Aviv, September 1939.

The *Patria* intercepted off the shore of Tel Aviv by British soldiers, August 1939.

Offices each acted in its respective domain to achieve this—in the immigrants' countries of origin, in transit corridors, and in Palestine and its coastal waters. The British authorities also interfered with Jewish organizations and individuals active in illegal immigration through legal and diplomatic means. The tactics the British used to disrupt illegal aliyah included intimidation of the activists (particularly at sea) and imposition of stiff penalties: confiscation of vessels, imprisonment of captains and crews, and onerous fines. As we have seen, news of these penalties spread throughout the maritime trade and was quite effective. The number of those willing to take part in illegal ventures dwindled.[8]

The simplest solution for the British would have been to reach an agreement with the European states to prohibit Jews from leaving for Palestine without proper documents. This proved impossible because most of the emigrants came from the Reich, where Jewish emigration was arranged legally. It was difficult to interfere even in the next link in the chain—in the countries lying along the route down the Danube to the Black Sea, or between the Reich and Italy—since the refugees here traveled by conventional means, via the national transportation services.

Once the refugees reached the Black Sea, the governments concerned could not help but wish to speed the refugees on their way; all wished to avoid costly refugee encampments. The British asked the countries of the Danube basin—Rumania, Bulgaria, Hungary, and Yugoslavia—to bar Jewish refugee transports from entering their territorial waterways.[9] Rumania, whose ports were among the most extensively used, responded to this British heavy-handedness by citing the principle of free navigation on the Danube. Halting Jewish transports, the Rumanians argued, would have wide implications for travel on this major route, and Rumania refused to be involved in this. Protracted British efforts ultimately won from the Rumanian government a promise to halt convoys of Jewish refugees traveling by land, which was particularly damaging to aliyah bet organizers in Poland. The British viewed this as but a partial victory at best. Britain sought to have Turkey bar illegal immigrant vessels from the Bosporus and the Dardanelles, but failed. The Turkish authorities argued, like the Rumanians, that the resulting damage to the principle of free navigation would have wide ramifications that would be difficult to control.[10]

Having failed in this area, the British sought to have the Black Sea countries prevent their flags of registry from being used by the Jewish illegals, and to have these governments specifically bar their citizens from serving as crew members. The British met with great success on paper. Bulgaria, Rumania, Turkey, and Greece all enacted regulations to this effect.[11] In practice, however, these regulations were difficult to enforce, and the vessels, seamen, and ports of those countries continued to be involved in aliyah bet.

On several occasions, the Colonial Office upbraided the Foreign Office over this lack of enforcement. One instance is a memorandum from the head of the Near East Department of the Colonial Office, Harold Downie, to the head of the Refugees Department in the Foreign Office, J. E. Carvell. Downie wrote concerning the refusal of the Turkish government to make involvement in illegal Jewish immigration a punishable offense. The Turks would go no further than to issue stern admonitions. Downie felt this was insufficient and asked the Foreign Office to exert maximum pressure on the Turks and not limit itself to polite requests. In his reply, Carvell pointed out that although many of the Turks' excuses were weak, their unwillingness to violate freedom of commerce was in fact well-grounded. Carvell underscored that Turkey was under no obligation to aid Britain in its fight against illegal Jewish immigration. While the Colonial Office was apt to take a less charitable view, it is clear that Foreign Office officials could sometimes appreciate and even sympathize with the reluctance of the transit countries to enact special legislation affecting their citizens or to forsake principles of free commerce.[12]

British attempts to seek cooperation from the transit countries was complicated further because some governments in the Balkans, particularly Rumania and Yugoslavia, tried to maneuver between opposing forces, trying not to annoy the British while hoping to avoid a clash with the Germans. Like the Germans, they were also eager to be rid of Jewish refugees and Jewish nationals of their own.

Gaining the cooperation of other governments proved equally problematic. One ruse the aliyah organizers employed to evade the Greek governmental ban on the use of Greek boats for aliyah bet was to transfer the boats to Panamanian, Uruguayan, or other such registry. After making several representations to the government of Panama, the British finally elicited a promise to forbid the use of a Panamanian flag of convenience by aliyah bet vessels and to withdraw Panamanian registry from several boats known to be involved in that work.

The British authorities also asked Liberia and Paraguay to take disciplinary measures against certain of their consuls who made a practice of issuing fictitious visas for Jewish refugees.[13] It was clear, however, that even when British requests met with the assent of the governments they approached, their enforcement was perfunctory at best. There was no inclination among the states concerned to take stringent measures against violators. Thus, although Panama withdrew its registry from a number of vessels that the British had intercepted prior to September 1939 (the *Atrato, Colorado,* and *Liesl*), Panamanian registry was subsequently obtained for the *Pacific, Milos,* and *Atlantic,* as well as the *Darien.* Neither could it be said that the governments concerned were always in full control of their own bureaucracies. Consuls in smaller cities continued to issue fictitious visas in return for handsome fees. Local officials at various levels continued to take bribes for various permits and licenses, and continued to help the refugees.[14]

British efforts went even further, to extremely legalistic procedures. At one point, the British requested that the Yugoslavian authorities check the passports of Jewish refugees from the Reich to see that they were properly stamped with the letter *J* (for "Jude"). British intelligence reports suggested that the Germans might be departing from their standard procedure and issuing passports lacking the *J* designation in order to speed the Jews' exit. The British suggested to the Yugoslavian authorities that they might bar these potential illegal immigrants from entering Yugoslavia on this pretense. The British also warned Belgrade that Jewish refugee populations in Yugoslavia could grow to "dangerous" levels as a result of Rumanian restrictions on refugee transit.[15] The Yugoslavians consented to these procedures.

The Colonial Office felt such diplomatic measures lacked efficacy, and it suspected the Foreign Office of letting extraneous concerns impede the struggle against illegal immigration. For its part, the Foreign Office complained that neither the Mandatory administration in Palestine (that is, the Colonial Office) nor the Navy had given it their full cooperation: illegal vessels continued to reach Palestine, and those aboard were allowed remain in Palestine. When the Foreign Office approached the Balkan and other governments requesting that they enact strict regulations, these facts were raised, and they served to undermine the credibility of Britain's resolve to halt illegal aliyah. Indeed, when the Jews appealed to the governments of the transit countries to facilitate the flow of refugees, they referred to these same facts as evidence that the issue was indeed not so serious to the British.

The Colonial Office was fully cognizant of this situation, yet it, too, felt bound by international convention. The Palestine administration and the Admiralty would not pursue immigrant vessels outside of territorial waters, and they were thus sometimes unable to apprehend the boats or their crews. The immigrants were transferred just outside the territorial limit to small craft. The British might capture these, but this had no deterrent effect; it simply raised the costs of aliyah operations somewhat. The British could not countenance seizing ships in international waters; it was too flagrant a violation of international law. Such a course was rendered even less tenable because of the ships' cargo—refugees seeking asylum. It was hard to imagine anything more damaging to the international standing of Britain's Palestine policy.

Furthermore, if the naval authorities intercepted the ships on the high seas, what could be done with the refugees? (The idea of establishing refugee camps for the Jews somewhere outside of Palestine was first proposed in March 1940, but it was at the time rejected.[16]) It was impossible to send the refugees back to their home countries, since most came from the Reich, which refused to accept them. The Hungarian, Rumanian, and Bulgarian governments also barred refugees from returning. In one instance, the British attempted to repatriate some 150 Hungarian Jews who had sailed on board the *Sakariya*.[17] Yet by March 1940, after several months of negotiations, the British had managed to repatriate a total of two Jews to Hungary.[18] This protracted and ultimately fruitless effort may have influenced the decision of the Colonial Office to seek the aid of the Navy Contraband Control Service in seizing illegal immigrant ships in international waters (despite the objections of the Foreign Office and the Navy, and in particular, of Winston Churchill, at this time first lord of the Admiralty).

The Colonial Office had long searched for a legal pretext to intercept aliyah vessels on the high seas. Its only legal recourse had been to arrest and try the crews of confiscated vessels under the security provisions of emergency powers enacted in the early 1930s to cope with the Arab riots. This course no longer seemed justified in the relative domestic calm of 1939. Thus, the high commissioner sought to make it a punishable offense to violate the immigration laws of Palestine.[19] This proposal was abandoned, however, after lengthy consideration. Expert legal opinion held that crews could be arrested for violating immigration laws only if caught inside Palestine territorial waters.

The key to the justification the high commissioner sought came in the form of the suspicion that the Germans were infiltrating the Jewish refugee groups (a claim often made but never substantiated). This was the only argument the government was ever able to muster for engaging in a campaign that amounted to piracy in seizing ships in international waters. Implementation of such a policy was problematic, however. The commander of the Mediterranean fleet, though in agreement with the policy, felt that constant monitoring of shipping in the area would prove too burdensome for a navy at war.[20] In December 1939, the naval command finally agreed to make an example of one boat as an experiment. Despite his openly stated reluctance, Churchill (still first lord of the Admiralty in January 1940) also agreed to this plan, on the condition that such a course not become a routine affair.[21]

The first attempt to seize an illegal transport at sea was made against the *Rudnitchar* (Konfino's boat), which had been a frequent blockade runner. The boat eluded patrols in this case as well, despite the state of alert. The Navy and Colonial Office were bitterly disappointed. The intercept plan was activated a second time, and this time the *Sakariya,* with more than 2,000 people aboard, was captured. (The *Hilda* was also intercepted by a routine patrol.) The crew had to be arrested on security charges, because the Mandate administration had proved unable to enact a legal mechanism to prosecute the crewmen for violating immigration laws.

The Colonial Office requested that the Contraband Control Service be directed to seize illegal vessels on an ongoing basis, and as justification it cited the likelihood of capturing German agents. The naval authorities did not consider the threat of infiltrators to be serious enough to warrant changing the orders of the already burdened Mediterranean fleet. The Navy thus ordered that illegal immigrant ships be captured, but stipulated that no special patrols would be added to search for them.[22] Nevertheless, the Navy proved very successful in blockading the Palestine coast. Only two ships, the *Libertad* and *Milos,* managed to penetrate the territorial limit. Yet the policy of intercepting refugee boats at sea failed to create the deterrent effect the British had hoped for. Aliyah bet organizers came to assume that the refugees and their boats would fall into British hands and made little or no effort to evade British patrols.

An excellent illustration of the elements of British policy and of the extreme lengths to which the British were prepared to go in pursuit of their goals is provided by the campaign to thwart the transport from Bulgaria arranged by Baruch Konfino in March 1940. The British learned of this plan, which once again involved the *Rudnitchar*, in the middle of March. The British authorities immediately began deploying all of their diplomatic resources in the hope of preventing the boat from sailing. The intensity of activity gave the appearance that the entire British future in the Mediterranean depended on stopping this one refugee boat.

Ambassador Rendel, the British envoy in Sofia, contacted the Bulgarian foreign ministry on 20 March 1940, and in the strongest terms asked that the departure of the *Rudnitchar* be stopped. He detailed the new policy on seizing refugee ships on the high seas, emphasizing that crews would be arrested, vessels confiscated, and owners fined. A week later, however, he learned that the *Rudnitchar* had left Sulina and had gone upriver. The passengers who were to go aboard were then in Rustchok, Bulgaria.[23]

While Rendel continued to seek Bulgarian cooperation, the British ambassador in Bucharest asked the Rumanians to stop the *Rudnitchar*'s progress up the Danube. In London, Carvell alerted the Admiralty to the pending departure of the *Rudnitchar,* and instructed British consular posts around the Black Sea and the Mediterranean—in Malta, Cyprus, and Palestine—to report the ship's movements to the Navy. Downie, well aware of Rendel's activity and Carvell's concern, was pessimistic, for he knew that the Navy was not prepared to take any but routine measures.

The British had engaged in a massive diplomatic offensive. Deputy Under Secretary of State for the Colonies John Shuckburgh felt that, "In the circumstances it seems that all possible action has been taken."[24] In the end, however, the Navy was not called upon to capture the *Rudnitchar* at sea. The Bulgarian government forbade its departure at the last minute and ordered Konfino to desist from using the vessel as an immigrant transport.[25]

This episode concluded the stage in British policy that aimed at preventing boats from leaving the Balkan countries and deterring future aliyah bet operations. Neither the deportation of refugees back to their countries of origin nor their internment in another country was yet contemplated.[26] It was in March 1940 that a sharply worded memorandum sent to John Bennett in the Colonial Office proposed the establishment of internment camps for the Jewish "illegals" somewhere outside Palestine. (The memo stipulated that the costs of such an operation were to be borne by the Yishuv in Palestine.) The memo argued that the immigrants, their leaders, and the organizers had to be stopped once and for all. The kid gloves had to be removed. Yet the idea received little support at the time in Colonial Office circles.[27] Marginal notes added to the proposal show that it was not regarded as a worthwhile contribution and that it reflected an insufficient grasp of the complexities of the problem.

The Palestine high commissioner's cables of 18 and 23 March 1940, reflect the prevailing thinking in the Colonial Office.[28] The high commissioner was opposed to an expulsion policy, he said, because it might lead to violent reactions by the immigrants and by the Jewish population in Palestine. The administration had no desire to engage the Jews in open conflict, which would necessitate the use of force. The latter course would mean reinforcing the British armed presence, which could hardly be thought beneficial for Britain.

Moreover, the Colonial Office had no place to suggest as a location for a refugee internment camp, as no agreement existed with any of the British colonies regarding the acceptance of such a population. In some of the colonies, conditions were considered inhospitable to those used to a European climate; in others, such as Cyprus, the objections were political and strategic. Yet the expulsion and internment plan resurfaced some six months later, By this time, fall 1940, it was offered as the only solution to the illegal immigration problem.[29]

The Deportation Policy: Development and Implementation

The British intelligence services kept the government abreast of the plans and preparations of the aliyah bet organizers throughout the spring of 1940. They were aware, for example, of Storfer's activities, and his contacts and negotiations with the Greeks and the Turks.[30] The British also knew of the Kladovo group and the reasons why it had been unable to leave for Palestine. It was, indeed, quite clear that the group would not long be able to remain in Yugoslavia.[31]

A flood of information regarding aliyah bet plans—some of it accurate, some not—reached the British authorities in April and May of 1940. The news from Yugoslavia was that the Kladovo group would make an attempt to reach the Black Sea via a land route. Diplomatic action was taken to forestall any such development. A report received on 19 May 1940, indicated that aliyah bet work was being organized again from Budapest, in the wake of German pressure to step up Jewish emigration. Naval intelligence sent word on 25 May that three boats carrying a total of 3,000 people had sailed from Constantsa. This report was unconfirmed by other sources, but a search was undertaken during the next seven days. A boat called the *Pizet* was reported to have sunk in the Black Sea on its way to Constantsa to pick up illegal immigrants.[32]

These reports, coupled with the expansion of the war to the western front, tended to confirm the British view that aliyah bet was being used by the Germans as a tactic against Britain. The degree of German involvement in organizing Jewish emigration seemed to offer no other explanation.[33] British officials also concluded that the German influence over Rumania, Bulgaria, and Hungary was instrumental to the emigration activities organized in those countries and that they formed part of the German plan to destabilize the British position in the Middle East.[34] The need to reevaluate deterrents to immigration became ever more urgent.

In June 1940, the British received news that the *Libertad* organized by Konfino had set sail, and this sparked yet another round of diplomatic activity. These efforts proved fruitless, however. As he left the Bulgarian foreign ministry after one final attempt to halt the transport, Ambassador Rendel discovered that the *Libertad* was at that very moment already on its way to Istanbul.[35] The British issued an alert on 25 June to all its diplomatic posts in the Mediterranean notifying them of the *Libertad*'s sailing. Despite requests made to Greece, where the boat stopped for two weeks for repairs and provisions (on the island of Sikri), the Greek authorities refused to deny aid to the boat or to prevent its departure. For the British, failure followed upon failure, and the boat slipped through their patrols and reached Haifa unescorted on 18 July 1940, ending a four-week odyssey. The Colonial Office knew well enough that confiscation of the boat would hurt no one, as the owners had already been paid several times over the boat's not very considerable value.[36]

Downie, who had urged the Foreign Office to protest to the Bulgarian and Greek governments, knew that this was in any case a futile gesture. In Palestine, the passengers of the *Hilda* and the *Sakariya* had to be released from internment in order to make room for those who had arrived on the *Libertad*. At this point, however, Downie concluded that the policy of deterrence had reached a crucial turning. He believed that the the flow of illegal immigration would not increase now that Italy had entered the war, but he could not be sure of that.

In September, as Storfer's three ships set sail, the vague proposals and rough ideas began to crystallize into a tough new British policy: expulsion. High Commissioner MacMichael demanded that illegal immigrants be deported to Australia.[37] The Australian government had agreed to accept 2,000 German nationals from Palestine for the duration of the war, and MacMichael suggested that the illegal refugees might be added to this number. He again stressed the importance of seizing the immigrant boats in international waters to avoid physically deporting the Jews from Palestine, which was bound to provoke the local population.

The proposal to send the refugees to Australia was not accepted, and Mauritius was chosen instead.[38] The suggestion that the refugees not be allowed to enter Palestinian territory was found to be impracticable, even though all agreed that deportation from Palestine was bound to anger the Yishuv and set off a political storm among Jews elsewhere. Nevertheless, the British decided to force a confrontation on the issue and carry out a deportation.

British determination to go through with this step was undoubtedly reinforced by the realization that the expansion of the war and the heightened German influence in the Balkans had effectively neutralized diplomatic options. A total of 120,000 refugees were said to be planning to leave for Palestine from Rumania, with German help.[39] Even the Greek government, which was certainly not suspected of sympathizing with Germany or its satellites, did nothing to prevent the transfer of Greek boats to Storfer. Thus, even Greece, which until this time had been the most cooperative of the Mediterranean and Balkan governments, had become a tacit supporter of the new wave of illegal immigration.[40] In this situation, British officials felt they could hesitate no longer. Britain's entire Middle East policy—the White Paper and relations with the Arab and Islamic world—hung in the balance. Seen in this light, the possible resistance by the Yishuv, the main difficulty with a deportation policy, became a secondary consideration.[41]

High Commissioner MacMichael was instructed to announce the new policy of the government, which stated that illegal immigrants would spend the duration of the war in camps outside Palestine and only afterward would their final disposition be decided.[42] In his statement, however, MacMichael exceeded his instructions, and stated absolutely that the refugees would never be allowed to enter Palestine. MacMichael's adamant position owed to his apprehension that Jewish pressure on the government might persuade it to be more lenient. In addition, like many others in the Colonial Office, he had less than perfect confidence in his Foreign Office colleagues' ability to withstand American and public pressure. In order to forestall and neutralize the effect of that pressure, MacMichael and others argued, a firm and unambiguous policy was called for—one that would be harder to retract.

MacMichael urged that the Zionist leaders be prevented from reporting to the Americans on the events surrounding the illegal deportations, and he also argued against entering into negotiations with Weizmann over the new policy. He had no wish to ask the help of the Zionist leader in restraining the Palestinian community and thus, as he put it, to be "beholden" to Weizmann.[43] MacMichael sensed that the Zionist leaders were reluctant to enter into a confrontation with the government at that time, and understood that some members of the Jewish Agency were uneasy about aliyah bet. The high commissioner correctly assessed the Zionist leadership's dismay over the German role in organizing Jewish emigration. In correspondence with the colonial secretary, MacMichael emphasized that even among the more extreme Revisionists one could detect a certain understanding for the British position.[44] Weizmann himself, as we have seen, proposed that the refugee boats be intercepted at sea and sent to another colony in order to prevent the deportation of Jews from Palestine itself. This approach, consistent with Weizmann's misgivings about illegal activities and with his great faith in the value of a cooperative relationship with England, coincided with the high commissioner's viewpoint.[45]

MacMichael also accurately discerned the Foreign Office's sensitivity to American reactions to a deportation order. This was borne out when the embassy and the American government duly warned London of the angry mood of the American Jewish public. Stephen Wise, head of the American Zionist Organization, cabled a strongly worded message to the British embassy in Washington: "It would be hell if this happens. . . . The Jews of the U.S.A. will feel it an outrage."[46]

The Foreign Office persisted in questioning the wisdom of the course the Colonial Office urged. Ironically, Foreign Office skepticism was aroused precisely because it agreed with the assessment of the Colonial Office of the direct causes of illegal immigration—both in terms of the German role and of the difficulties encountered in dealings with the Balkan States. Given these factors, the Foreign Office failed to see how interning the refugees in another British colony would deter the Germans from organizing Jewish emigration. Whether they planted their agents and unloaded their Jews in Palestine or elsewhere in the Empire was immaterial to the Germans.[47]

Similarly, the deportation policy aroused a degree of opposition in the Foreign Office Refugees Department. Officials there pointed out that it was no punishment to send the violators of British law to live in a British colony. Instead, the Jews would be taking up space that might have provided a haven for non-Jewish refugees. Even if the deportation scheme could be justified since it upheld the White Paper, it nevertheless posed a threat to other principles of policy relating to refugees and the interests of the Empire. At the same time, some of the comments made about the deportation plan contained barely concealed anti-Semitic innuendo: "It will be hell for Mauritius. The Jews should be glad that they are to be sent to such a lovely place."[48]

The various officials and ministerial offices did share the idea that the government ought to take a firm stance with the Jews. The colonial and foreign secretaries and their subordinates held forth against Jewish pressure to rescind the deportation order. MacMichael felt he had correctly judged prevailing public opinion in Palestine and was confident in his ability to manage the transfer of the refugees from the *Milos* and the *Pacific* to the *Patria*, the ship that was to transport them to Mauritius. When it was learned that the *Atlantic* had been seized off the coast of Cyprus and that the local authorities were unwilling to keep the refugees, the *Patria*'s departure was delayed so that the *Atlantic* passengers could also be put aboard. In the meantime, MacMichael

announced the new policy, deportation, and was fully prepared to face resistance and a general strike on the part of the Yishuv. The *Patria*'s tragic
sinking came as a shock both to the high commissioner and to policymakers
in London. An unprecedented amount of political activity against the deportation order ensued, and the sinking shattered the self-assurance of many
British officials. The subject was discussed in the War Cabinet on 27 November 1940. Against the wishes of the colonial secretary, but with the support
of Churchill, now prime minister, the *Patria* survivors were allowed to remain
in Palestine.[49]

Nevertheless, this action was an exception, and deportation of illegal immigrants remained official policy. The main reasons Britain offered for maintaining the policy and for standing behind MacMichael's announcement were
the expected reaction of the Arab world and the conviction that the White Paper must under all circumstances be upheld. It was feared that unless the principles of governmental policy were affirmed, the entire episode might appear to
have been manufactured as a way to allow the British to give in to the Zionists.
Deportation was indeed carried out against the refugees on the *Atlantic*.[50]

There were but two people who steadfastly held that the *Patria* survivors
ought not to be allowed to remain in Palestine: MacMichael and General
Archibald Wavell, the commander in chief of British forces in the Middle
East. Wavell wrote to the war secretary on 30 November asking that the
Cabinet reverse the decision of 27 November that allowed the *Patria* survivors
to remain. Wavell warned that "From the military point of view it is disastrous.
It will be spread all over the Arab world that the Jews have again successfully
challenged a decision of the British government. . . . It will again be spread
abroad that only violence pays in dealing with the British . . . [The] certain
result will be a great increase of anti-British feeling."[51] The issue of the *Patria*
survivors was raised again in the Cabinet on 2 December. MacMichael's
arguments (presented by the colonial secretary) provided reinforcement to
Wavell's statement of the dire consequences of proceeding with the decision.
Churchill, however, was firm in his commitment to the decision of 27 November, and the refugees were allowed to remain.[52]

Having failed in the case of the *Patria,* MacMichael saw to it that the deportation of the *Atlantic* passengers was carried out as planned, despite all the efforts of Weizmann and the other Zionist leaders to prevent it. The massive
resistance the British had feared failed to materialize, but the deportation
nevertheless had repercussions. Public opinion and the press were aroused,
both in England and in the United States.[53] The criticism was unprecedented.

The Rift between the Foreign Office and the Colonial Office

The outcry prompted second thoughts and soul-searching in the Foreign Office, particularly in the Refugees Department, since it was the longtime op-
ponent of the Colonial Office policy on illegal immigration. Foreign Office
officials saw that the American and British publics were less than satisfied

with the current stubborn and severe policy toward Jewish refugees. Public support had been strained for a policy that kept refugees aboard crowded boats for months at a time, languishing in subhuman conditions in the dead of winter (as in the case of the *Sakariya* and Kladovo groups). While the government had no desire to enter into a public debate over this issue, Carvell pointed out, it could hardly avoid responding to those who were only too ready to challenge the government, regardless of whether these arose out of sincere humanitarian convictions or out of partisan considerations.

Moreover, the Foreign Office counseled, the indiscriminate use of the argument that German spies were probably infiltrating the ranks of refugee groups (the main argument offered to the United States in justifying the expulsion policy) was insufficient and an injudicious rationale on which to base policy. The Foreign Office felt, therefore, that the argument ought only to be used when there was concrete proof of agents having been found among the refugees. One senior Foreign Office official, Thomas Snow (formerly ambassador to Finland), wrote,

> I cannot help feeling that we have been sailing a little close to the wind. . . .
> If it is really the case that neither the authorities in Palestine or here know
> definitely that a single enemy agent has arrived in this way, we would suggest
> that there is reason for caution in including this argument in our propaganda.[54]

In order to address the situation, Richard T. Latham, now head of the Foreign Office Refugees Department, and other officials in the department undertook a careful reexamination of the factors behind the illegal immigration phenomenon.[55] In a memorandum under the heading "The prospect of repressing illegal immigration to Palestine," submitted by Latham on 28 December 1940, he stressed in particular that it was incorrect to view illegal immigration solely as a means of adding new Jewish citizens to the ranks of the Yishuv. He argued that it was equally the consequence of the Jews' sense of mutual responsibility and their desire to rescue their fellows from Hitler. Indeed, the primary Jewish concern was for the safety of the refugees, and deportation to another crown colony—even where all hope of entering Palestine was lost—was not an effective deterrent. In fact, deportation might encourage illegal immigration, since in effect it assured the Jews of ocean transport to a safe haven. Latham saw the willingness of Weizmann and others to see the refugee boats intercepted and transferred elsewhere *before* reaching Palestine as corroborating his view.

The memorandum concluded, "Our prospects of putting a stop to the illegal immigration traffic *within the four corners of the White Paper policy are poor*" [emphasis added].[56] Britain might be able to reduce this traffic, but it could not eliminate it altogether. Yet Latham knew that a mere reduction would hardly satisfy the Colonial Office, deeply concerned as it was about Arab reactions. The Foreign Office thus concluded that a new policy initiative was necessary. What had worked between February and September 1940 could no longer be expected to produce the desired results.

The friction between the two ministries increased, fueled by the public outcry in the United States and the requests from the British embassy in Washington for guidance in trying to defend British policy. In the midst of this controversy, the Foreign Office Refugees Department, together with the Near Eastern Department, set out to revive an earlier proposal to settle Jewish refugees in British Guiana.[57] This idea had first been broached before the war and had been considered again in April 1940. On both occasions the proposal had been rejected, but now the two Foreign Office departments favored the idea and they based their support on an evolving understanding of the illegal immigration problem. The problem, they felt, was not a short-term political issue that affected one geographic area alone, but a larger and very serious matter that had wide ramifications not only for the war effort but for the aftermath of the war as well. Although both departments accepted the White Paper policy with regard to Palestine, their thinking now leaned toward the establishment of a *second* Jewish national home as a haven for refugees, as proposed by Carvell and Baggally in April 1940.[58]

Officials in the Refugees Department and the Near East Department considered the proposal as having several advantages. First, it provided a challenge for the Zionist movement, since it involved them in a solution to the plight of the refugees. Second, it relieved the pressure on those British colonies that had been asked to shoulder some of the burden of the refugee and illegal immigrant population. It also alleviated the need to budget funds for the internment of the refugees for the duration of the war. (American funds were to be solicited for the project.) Finally, it resolved the postwar Jewish refugee problem, since it would no doubt prove impossible to repatriate all the refugees to Europe, and they could in this way be directed elsewhere than to Palestine, where they would only complicate British Middle Eastern interests.

The proposal to establish a second Jewish national home in British Guiana was discussed from the fall of 1940 through the winter and spring of 1941. During this period, the *Darien* arrived in Palestine and the government decided to deport its passengers. This decision was not carried out, however, since no suitable vessel could be found to take the deportees to Mauritius.[59] In the meantime, fears of a wave of illegal immigrants 120,000 strong dissipated. Indeed, illegal immigration activity entered a lull after the *Darien*'s arrival.

The Foreign Office considered this falling off to be a result of the spread of the war to Southern Europe and the Balkans. One Foreign Office official (the signature is unclear) wrote on 7 April 1941: "Now that the Germans are everywhere the problem is solved by itself. Unless the traffic breaks out in a new form, I think this can go by."[60] The comment was unwittingly prescient. The Germans first restricted and then forbade the emigration of Jews from all territories under their control. The Jewish Question in Nazi policy entered the phase of the Final Solution—genocide. Yet the issue of illegal immigration did not cease to plague the British—this time with the case of the *Struma,* to which we now turn.

II

ALIYAH, RESCUE, AND THE FINAL SOLUTION, 1942 TO 1944

8

The *Struma*

The *Struma* and Its Passengers

Although the security of the Jews in Rumania was already in doubt, the inauguration of the Fascist-leaning Ion Antonescu dictatorship in September 1940 marked a new deterioration in their situation. Street violence and anti-Semitic looting reached new heights in the pogrom that swept Bucharest during the Iron Guard (a paramilitary Fascist organization) putsch of January 1941.

The Soviet-German war erupted in June, with serious ramifications in all territories either occupied by the Germans or under German sway, including Rumania. At Jassy, four thousand Jews were massacred by Rumanian troops and thousands more died in deportation trains sent westward from the front. In the Bukovina region and in Bessarabia, areas evacuated by the Soviets and recaptured by Rumanian forces, the Rumanians took savage "revenge" for alleged Jewish perfidy and pro-Soviet sympathies. With the army's collaboration, local authorities carried out a bloody series of anti-Jewish outrages that killed tens of thousands. Thousands more were expelled to what was then German-held territory in Transnistria and across the River Bug where, it could be assumed, German execution squads would deal with them.[1]

Racist legislation, already passed in August 1940, was stepped up after June 1941. Jews were required to wear the yellow badge,[2] to remain indoors at certain hours, and forgo traveling by train. In the summer and fall of 1940 a series of economic sanctions was introduced, barring Jews from owning businesses or apartment houses. In May 1941, forced labor was imposed on Jews of the Regat area who were not "doing their share" of military duty. Social, economic, and political pressures mounted as law and order were eroded. Jewish refugees from Poland and elsewhere in Europe fared even worse. In the spring and summer of 1941, many of them were stripped of their temporary-residence permits. Although the government still favored emigration as a solution to the "Jewish Question," it began to entertain other options, such as deportation, starvation, and mass killings.[3]

Leaving Rumania became much more difficult. There were very few avenues left for legal emigration: overland routes were blocked, and the rail link between Bulgaria and Turkey was severed with the German advance into

Bulgaria in March 1941. The only other alternative was to sail to Turkey across the Black Sea and from there to continue to Palestine either by land or sea. This option was extremely hazardous. Not only was there a dearth of boats, but the few available had less freedom of movement as the number of countries at war increased. Rumanian ships ceased to sail into the Mediterranean for fear of British naval action. (Rumania broke off diplomatic relations with Britain on 7 December 1941.) The Black Sea became a war zone, patrolled by Soviet and German gunboats and submarines.

As the situation worsened, the Zionist leadership in Palestine appealed to Britain to display compassion for the plight of Rumanian Jews and accept a greater number of immigrants from that country. Repeated requests were sent to the British high commissioner in Palestine and to the Colonial Office, beginning in December 1940.[4] Weizmann also appealed directly to Churchill on 5 December 1941. He described the "inhuman" situation in Rumania and asked that Britain help find some way to relieve the suffering of Jews there, lest the issue cloud future relations between Britain and the Jewish people.

In December 1941, after diplomatic relations between Rumania and England were cut, Jewish Agency leaders asked that unused immigration certificates issued to Rumanian Jews continue to be honored. This, of course, was a partial solution that could help only a very limited number of people. A notable appeal for looser immigration standards was lodged by the Rumanian Immigrants Association in Palestine. This appeal emphasized the important contribution to the war effort that new arrivals from Rumania could make.[5] Despite all of these efforts, however, immigration quotas were not relaxed.

The Zionist leaders in Palestine and in Rumania were wary of encouraging aliyah bet at this stage. Their resolve had been weakened by the traumatic *Patria* affair, the deportation of the *Atlantic* group, and the vexed *Darien* episode that ended with passengers interned at Atlit. The Mossad no longer had agents in Rumania or Constantinople and seemed to have been paralyzed by the *Darien* experience.[6] In addition, the ranks of aliyah bet supporters had been depleted. Several leading Rumanian Zionists were killed in the Iron Guard pogrom at Bucharest in January 1941, including the head of the Palestine Office. As we have seen, the NZO was also unsuccessful in organizing aliyah bet in the wake of the ill-fated *Sakariya* and the *Pencho* episodes.[7]

The events of the winter and spring of 1941 profoundly shocked the Jewish community in Rumania and spurred it to search more energetically for avenues of escape. To some, aliyah bet was not the worst choice by far, even if it meant deportation to Mauritius. Indeed, once the British had declared their new policy of deportation, the British ambassador in Bucharest received many requests from would-be deportees.[8]

Resourceful young people willing to take extraordinary risks tried to get across the Black Sea on small motorboats.[9] Three such crafts made the crossing in the summer of 1941. The first, called the *Hainarul,* with nineteen people aboard, reached the coast of Alexandretta but later sank in a Mediterranean storm. The passengers were rescued and, after detention in Aleppo, reached Palestine. In August, the *Cari Nou* made it as far as Cyprus, with twelve passengers aboard. In October, twenty-one passengers of the third boat were captured off the Anatolian coast and imprisoned in Turkey until March 1942. A number of similar boats were purchased by groups of Jews and prepared for the journey, but not all of them actually succeeded in leaving Rumania. In short, Rumanian Jews demonstrated signal courage and determination in attempting to escape the country against all odds.

Such was the situation when the *Struma,* candidate for an aliyah bet voyage since 1940, was once again proposed for a voyage. The ship was known to be very old, and it was hardly thought fit for the purpose, as it was not equipped with a motor powerful enough for sea travel.[10] It bore a first registry date of 1830, had been under Greek ownership (under the name *Macedonia*), and flew the Panamanian flag. It measured 53 by 20 feet, weighed 180 tons, and was being used as a cattle barge on the Danube.[11] Ze'ev Shind later explained that the Mossad had intended to lash the boat to the *Darien* and tow it, thus enabling 250 more passengers to sail. However, the German entry into Bulgaria forced the Mossad to abandon the plan. As a result, the *Struma* remained behind in the hands of Pandelis, the owner.

Pandelis, eager to make some new arrangement, contacted Revisionist figures in Rumania and proposed that they organize a group of emigrants while he refitted the boat. In the NZO office, where details of the *Struma* were known at least as early as April 1941, arguments ensued between NZO and Betar members over who would sail and how they would be chosen.[12] As repairs to the vessel dragged on, the bickering intensified. The NZO aliyah office, headed by Eugene Meisner, finally announced that it would no longer help organize the transport. An unsuccessful search was mounted for other boats.

Meanwhile, the Rumanian press carried daily advertisements for passage on the *Struma* in September 1941. These were placed by a private firm, Touristime Mordia, directed by two Jews apparently close to the NZO aliyah office.[13] The price of a ticket from Rumania to Palestine direct was set at 200,000 lei per adult; children under twelve sailed for half-price. Those who wished to sail in more spacious cabins were offered tickets at 350,000 lei. Prospective passengers were offered photographs of the ship's new diesel engine, six-bed cabins, and merchant marine license that certified it was fit for travel.[14] All passengers were assured of getting three meals a day and some sort of berth. Upon arrival in Palestine, they would present entry permits issued in Istanbul. These were said to be certificates that had not been used because of the war. Pandelis was to travel to Istanbul by train once the ship left harbor; there he would see to the matter of certificates. Thus, the passengers had reason to believe that this was not to be an illegal voyage.

Nevertheless, dismal descriptions of the ship's condition also appeared in the Rumanian press. It was reported that it was not seaworthy and alleged that the government was granting the ship a license only in order to bring harm to its Jewish passengers.[15] The prospective passengers then hired a Rumanian ship's officer, Tinigaru, to inspect the *Struma* and verify the claims of Pandelis and his associates. Tinigaru reported that Pandelis had in fact spoken the truth and that the ship was indeed safe. After this, there was no problem in filling the passenger list. Most of the people who signed up were those who had already been registered with the NZO aliyah office for quite some time, including sixty Betar youth.

Most of the others were paying passengers drawn from the upper middle class. Some had relatives in Palestine and many had forwarded their savings. All had had professional training and many were university graduates. Pandelis continued adding names to the passenger list until the very last moment. The only passenger to survive the sinking of the ship, David Ben-Yaakov Stoliar, testified to the British police (on May 3, 1942) that he himself had signed up only fourteen days before the departure date.

The passengers boarded a special train in Bucharest that would take them to Constantsa on Sunday, 7 December 1941. The inspection of passengers and the actual boarding process lasted until Friday the twelfth. The *Struma* left Constantsa that day at two in the afternoon, headed for Istanbul. It was on the ship that the significant gap between the true situation and Pandelis's descriptions became apparent.

The *Struma* was in extremely poor condition. Its engine, far from being the spanking new diesel in the photograph, was antiquated and faulty. Facilities on board were woefully inadequate to serve the 769 passengers. There was no kitchen and not nearly enough food. There was one toilet. The berths bore no resemblance to the cabins in the photographs. It was obvious that Pandelis had paid off the Rumanian officer and that the gloomy press reports had been accurate. Bulgarian crewmen arrived only a day before sailing time and even then did not seem to know their business. The ship's mechanic, in particular, was unfit for his job. For the passengers, there was no turning back. Once aboard, they had to proceed, despite the hazards.

The passengers separated into groups, which were headed by Betar members. One of them, Yaakov Berkowitz, was made boat leader, and the other young people led the small groups. Food and water rationing was organized as the trip to Istanbul got under way. Normally, such a voyage took hours. The engine failed at the outset, as did the generator. Unable to proceed, the ship remained immobile. For an entire day, it slowly drifted with the wind. On Saturday the thirteenth, the *Struma* found itself at Tulisa on the Rumanian coast. A Rumanian ship responded to its distress signal, and the captain agreed to repair the engine and to see the boat safely out of Rumanian waters. In return he demanded three million lei, which the passengers paid in jewelry, watches, and dollars.

The engine was patched up but continued to fail sporadically, and the *Struma* limped to the Bosporus. On Sunday, 14 December, as the engine once again failed, the ship neared the edge of a minefield. On Monday, it was towed by a Turkish vessel to Istanbul and anchored in quarantine. No one was allowed to go ashore or communicate with anyone onshore.[16]

The first phase of the *Struma* saga drew to a close. The passengers were relieved, because although they had been outrageously defrauded by Pandelis and his associates, they had finally reached Istanbul. The trip, they hoped, would now continue more smoothly. Many actually believed they would be given immigration certificates. They could not imagine that Britain and its allies would abandon 769 Jews who had saved themselves from certain doom in Rumania.

Ten Weeks at Istanbul[17]

The *Struma,* as noted, was placed under strict quarantine in Istanbul's harbor. Even repeated offers of bribe money failed to move the Turkish authorities. The ship was carefully guarded to prevent it from establishing contact with the outside world. Finally, after ten days, the authorities permitted the JDC's spokesman in Turkey, Shimon Brod (a Polish-born Turkish citizen), to communicate with the passengers. Brod, a businessman whose main occupation was to coordinate refugee aid, tried to bring a minimal amount of food onto the ship, hardly enough to satisfy the requirements of the group. This was permitted once every seven days. Otherwise, passengers remained incommunicado, a society of strangers with a collective fate.

Because of the shortage of provisions, meals were served once a day. The makeshift kitchen, constructed by the passengers themselves, served a hot meal weekly. Sanitary conditions grew ever worse: dysentery was soon added to the refugees' other problems, and this kept the ship's twenty doctors busy round the clock. Medication was dispensed with extreme frugality. Surprisingly, no one on board died, perhaps because of the cool weather. Only a single person was hospitalized in Istanbul.

Those in transit tried to fill the empty days with various cultural activities. Hebrew classes were organized, as were study groups in Jewish history and Hebrew literature; other ideas were proposed but could not be implemented under the prisonlike conditions. Social intercourse became increasingly difficult. Hunger, loneliness, idleness, and, above all, the terrible psychological strain took their toll. There was a great uncertainty about the future: contradictory rumors flew about the ship. The worst fate that anyone could imagine was repatriation to Rumania.

Illustrating the common feeling of hopelessness is the story about one of the older men, an engineer, who was so desperate for food that he plotted to break into the food bin. By carefully observing the changes of the guards, he succeeded one night in stealing an orange. He was caught and severely punished.

Another man stole the orange of a sleeping child. The thief was caught red-handed and, amid cries of "Hang him!" from distraught onlookers, was placed before a disciplinary tribunal. His sentence was to be deprived of oranges until the ship reached Palestine.

A child tried to take a herring while the scarce food was being transferred from a Turkish launch. This incident, too, resulted in formal disciplinary proceedings and a severe punishment. On another occasion, there was an attempted "mutiny" against the ship's committee: a member was accused of unethically eating a whole herring by himself. These pathetic episodes reveal the dimensions of the calamity and the deep despair that tormented those aboard the ill-fated ship.

It was at this time that Britain and Bulgaria declared war against each other and Panama joined the Allies. The captain of the *Struma*, a Bulgarian national, refused to proceed southward to the Dardanelles, because he feared he might be subject to arrest there by the British as an enemy alien. Repairs on the engine proceeded at a snail's pace and, even then, with little apparent result.[18]

The passengers had not entirely given up hope that they might be allowed to disembark at Istanbul and proceed to Palestine by rail. Letters and accounts of those days reflect the high pitch of fear and tension that gripped the refugees. They could not believe that their plight was properly understood, for surely if it was, a solution would be found for them. All they needed to do, they thought, was to make their situation clear or continue explaining it until someone appreciated what was happening and responded. Though this was not to be, the ship's committee did try to approach the problem rationally and take effective action. They sought to communicate with people who might have political influence in Turkey, in Palestine, and in the United States, and they sent out names and addresses of useful contacts. They tried to reach journalists who could publicize the crisis. This, they hoped, would exert pressure on the British to alter their position. They also drew up plans for the rest of their trip in the Mediterranean. Negotiations over this actually reached an advanced stage. They proposed shortening the sea voyage by traveling to Alexandretta by rail, where they would again board the *Struma*.[19]

The ship's committee was in an especially painful position. Its members were the inevitable targets of passenger frustration, hostility, and violent outbursts. The committee seemed to be a link to the world outside, but such contact was limited to the weekly food shipment, and members had only fragmentary and unverifiable information at their disposal. Their authority was openly questioned, and threats of violence were aimed at them.

The committee appealed for immediate aid to the ship. If only the food-supply difficulties could be properly dealt with, they argued, the *Struma*'s problems could be addressed more calmly. They asked for better-quality food to achieve at least a subsistence level.[20]

At the end of ten weeks, at dawn on 23 February 1942, a Turkish coast guard vessel approached and ordered the captain of the *Struma* to leave the harbor and sail toward the Black Sea. The captain refused, and a loud protest broke out among the passengers who lined the decks.[21] They hung out bed-sheets on which "S.O.S." had been painted, appealing to the harbor authorities and inhabitants. Over the sides of the ship they hung signs in French reading "Jewish immigrants" and "Save us!" The coast guard patrol drew back at first, but returned with armed reinforcements. One hundred and fifty police boarded the *Struma* and began beating the passengers. A struggle broke out, but the police soon overpowered the "troublemakers" and forced them belowdecks. The *Struma* was then towed from the harbor, despite the fact that it had no provisions for a trip of any kind: no water, no food, no fuel, and no motor oil.

Just before morning, there was a loud explosion and the *Struma* sank ten kilometers from shore. Those on deck could see land, but no one was watching them, and no one came to their assistance. It took twenty-four hours for Turkish boats to arrive on the scene. There they found one man still alive.

Reports of the sinking spread during the night of the twenty-fourth, but the Turkish authorities refused to deny or confirm them. Jews who inquired were told that the government wished to keep the matter quiet. David Stoliar, the sole survivor, was sent to a military hospital and kept in isolation, and after release from the hospital he was imprisoned. Jewish community representatives were not allowed to contact him. Two months later, Stoliar received permission to immigrate to Palestine.

Who sank the *Struma*? And how? These questions have been exhaustively examined,[22] and the known facts point to a mistaken attack by a Soviet submarine. Still, the question we must raise is: why was the ship forced to leave Istanbul harbor and why was no haven found for its passengers?

Zionist Policy: To Conform or Innovate?

Records of the Jewish Agency executive and the political department in the *Struma* affair aptly illustrate the weakness of Zionist diplomatic strategy with relation to Britain. During the first few weeks of the *Struma*'s stay in Istanbul, the Agency failed to take any political measures to aid the refugees, even though the ship's departure from Rumania had been reported in Palestine and was the subject of discussion at an Agency meeting on 14 December 1941.[23] The political department took action only three weeks after the *Struma* had reached Istanbul, when a few released passengers revealed the extent of the suffering aboard ship.

The Agency wanted to find a way to bring the refugees to Palestine without turning the issue into a major confrontation with the British. Shertok, who did not seriously expect the British to agree to concessions for special cases, nevertheless hoped that the *Struma* problem might be subsumed within a broader context of arrangements under negotiation between the political department and the authorities. This was his underlying assumption over the next five weeks. But at the beginning of February, he realized that such hopes were in vain.

There were three main issues between the Agency and the Colonial and Foreign Offices at the time: first, an argument over the principle that enemy nationals could be permitted into Palestine. This now applied to Rumanians as well, so no country remained in the German sphere of influence from which Jews could be admitted. Second, the special request that the not inconsiderable number of immigration certificates issued to Rumanian Jews, but not used before the declaration of war, be utilized. And finally, discussion of the possibility of bringing Jewish children from the Balkans to Palestine under the Youth Aliyah program. In addition, a new immigration schedule was expected for the first half of 1942.

Shertok sought to deal with the *Struma* in this framework. Hence his initial response to letters regarding the *Struma* sent from the Agency's office in London was to suggest that political efforts be focused on lifting the immigration ban against nationals of hostile states.[24]

Shertok met with John McPherson, director-general of the British government offices in Palestine, on 19 January. Raising once again the unresolved questions of the certificates issued to Rumanian Jews and Youth Aliyah permits for children from the Balkans, Shertok asked McPherson to issue several hundred immigration permits to *Struma* passengers. In presenting the case that way, Shertok hoped to avoid a direct confrontation with the British over aliyah bet, on which the British were known to be extremely sensitive and determined not to budge. The authorities consistently refused, for example, to entertain proposals to free the *Darien* group, which had spent the past ten months in detention at Atlit.

McPherson did not reject Shertok's request out of hand, and he promised to look into the matter. Perhaps this explains Shertok's overly optimistic assessment. At the end of January, he sent McPherson a long and detailed memorandum in which he linked the *Struma* issue to that of the *Darien* group and to the Rumanian certificate holders who still lived in the hope that London would permit them to immigrate.[25]

Shertok's optimism was unfounded, however. On 8 February he received a positive reply on the admission of children from the Balkans, but this was accompanied by a categorical refusal to include children from the *Struma* within that framework: the first stage in Shertok's strategy had collapsed. The second stage was to follow eight days later, when a new immigration schedule offered admission to 3,000 Jews. Shertok's request that those aboard the *Struma* be included by the new schedule was denied.[26]

Shertok soon realized that his approach was not working. Meanwhile, time was passing and, aboard the *Struma,* the suffering was growing more intense. Pressure on the Agency mounted from the Histadrut, the JDC, and the Rumanian Immigrants Association. At the Agency executive meeting of 8 February, there was direct criticism of the line pursued by the political department. Demands were made for direct and unilateral action to free the *Struma.*[27]

Faced with this new situation, and in anticipation of his next meeting with McPherson, set for 14 February, Shertok sent him another lengthy and closely argued memorandum. In it, he repeated the traditional arguments justifying aliyah bet in humanitarian and moral terms, placing the problem in the context of the dangers facing the refugees and their suffering, while rejecting the substance of British objections. The document detailed the circumstances that prompted the *Struma* passengers to set sail on such a dubious vessel, the inhuman living conditions on board, and the isolation, hunger, and disease. It also pointed out that the information came from those fortunate few who had obtained immigration certificates and were permitted to leave the ship.

But, in addition, Shertok for the first time took explicit issue with the British refusal to grant certificates to the *Struma* group on the grounds of the "illegal" status of its members. There was no foundation, he also claimed, to the British fear of enemy plants within the refugee groups. There had never been such agents before, nor had any evidence been produced that the Germans had ever exerted pressure on departing Jews to serve as spies. He emphasized that the Agency was quite willing to undertake security checks on the immigrants and stressed that Britain's primary duty at this stage was to save lives.

That same day, the chief rabbis appeared before the high commissioner to plead the case of the *Struma*. The rabbinical deputation left empty-handed, as had a delegation from the Rumanian Immigrants Association two days earlier after a meeting with McPherson.[28]

Shertok reported to London on the failure of his efforts and asked that greater pressure be applied. Berl Locker (who headed the JA London office) and Lewis Namier (of its main staff) accordingly appealed once more to the Foreign and Colonial Offices, but to no avail. Weizmann's letter of 18 February to Lord Moyne, the colonial secretary, was not even granted the courtesy of a reply.[29]

McPherson, in his meeting with Shertok, stressed that the government had no intention of changing its position on illegal immigration and that this pertained to the *Struma* case as well. There was nothing new, he pointed out, in Shertok's arguments. There was no chance even for the children on the *Struma* to be granted entry under Youth Aliyah.[30]

Shertok fell back upon conventional Zionist tactics and asked his colleagues in London to try one more direct appeal to the government, at least for the children. The following day, McPherson offered a significant compromise when he informed Shertok that the children on the *Struma* aged eleven to sixteen would receive immigration certificates. This willingness to make an exception for the children, in response to pressure from London and Jerusalem, was accompanied by an equal measure of obduracy as to the fate of the other *Struma* passengers. Shertok thought further leverage ought to be applied. He instructed Arthur Luria, secretary of the Zionist Organization's American section, to request the JDC to approach the American administration. It was hoped that the Americans could manage to get the Turkish authorities to permit the *Struma* access to a transit camp, with expenses paid by Jewish organizations, but the JDC had already made a similar proposal to no avail.[31]

On 18 February Shertok received word from Constantinople that Turkey planned to tow the *Struma* out to sea. He turned to McPherson and explained in earnest that even the children had not yet been allowed to disembark.

What else could have been done? Public opinion in England and the United States could have been aroused if certain steps were taken. This had not been the Agency practice in the past, nor was it seriously considered now. Possibly, once all attempts to free the group had failed, it was assumed the incident would develop as had others: the ship would reach the Mediterranean, the British would seize it, and passengers would be interned either in Palestine or Mauritius. It was equally possible, however, as the ship's captain pointed out, that the *Struma* was to be returned to the Black Sea, which would seal the fate of those on board.[32] Was there no way that the Mossad, set up to bring Jews into Palestine illegally, could act directly to save the group?

The Mossad and the Struma *Affair*

The *Struma* affair is hardly mentioned in the records of the Mossad. Shaul Avigur, who was then the head of the organization, would later be surprised by his inability to recall what steps had been taken to save the people from the doomed vessel.[33] Yet the Mossad did not entirely ignore the plight of the *Struma*.

In the summer of 1941 it planned to return its operatives to Constantinople, where they might help save Rumanian Jews from the ravages of the pogroms that accompanied Operation Barbarossa. Zvi Yehieli and Ze'ev Shind arrived there in September and October, respectively, of that year. Yehieli immediately set in motion a search for a ship; by November 6, he had acquired a small yacht with a powerful motor from the Danish envoy in Turkey. The boat was renamed the *Lilly-Ayala*,[34] and would have suited the purposes of the Mossad if a neutral flag of registry could have been obtained. It seemed that this problem could be resolved with the help of the Portuguese consul in Turkey, who was of Jewish descent and who had served as go-between in the purchase of the *Lilly*. But this hope was dashed when the Portuguese government refused permission. Similar attempts to obtain registry in Spain and Argentina also failed. It was during those weeks that the *Struma* arrived in Istanbul.

Throughout the period from December to February while the *Struma* remained in Istanbul, a boat in Mossad's possession was anchored in the same port—a boat that could have accommodated a significant number of *Struma* refugees if only a flag of registry had been found for it. Shind later stated that he and Yehieli tried to help those aboard the *Struma* repair their ship so that it could continue toward Palestine. It was in such poor condition, however, that this proved impossible.[35]

Many questions remain. How energetically did the Mossad agents try to transfer the *Struma* refugees once they discovered that the vessel could not be made seaworthy? Did they seek help from British intelligence (with whom they were in contact), with Turkish harbor authorities, or with shipping agents like Pandelis, with whom they had worked, in order to find a flag of registry for the *Lilly*? Did they step up their activities significantly in early February, when Shertok realized that his political tactics had failed? Shind himself has stated that primarily they endeavored to get Turkish permission for the refugees to disembark and proceed to Palestine by rail.

Some of Shind's remarks on the *Lilly* and the failure to solve the *Struma* dilemma deserve to be cited here:

> We had the *Lilly*, but it was useless. It no longer flew the Danish flag, and there seemed to be no country in the world willing to place the boat under its protection. In Palestine people could not understand why we did not transfer at least part of the *Struma* passengers to the *Lilly*. From far away, without on-the-scene knowledge of the particulars, this seemed a legitimate complaint. In actual fact, though, it was impossible. We simply did not have the means to accomplish it. Given the condition of the *Struma,* there was only one power that might have helped—the power of the Allies and of the English in particular.[36]

Returning to the question raised before—could the Jewish Agency political department have instructed the Mossad to save the *Struma* refugees?—we must conclude that in February 1942 this was simply not a viable option. Among the reasons was that such a step had not been planned to occur during December or January, when it was thought that political action would suffice. Zionist policy proved unable to save the lives of 769 passengers.

British Policy

Since the incident of the three boats and the *Darien,* the British had not been called upon to confront the illegal aliyah question. The *Darien* case was handled in accordance with the high commissioner's instructions and the Cabinet decision of late 1940. With the war expanding, German control spreading across Southern Europe, and German influence strongly felt in the Balkans, the British could reasonably conclude that illegal immigration was no longer a serious problem. The *Darien* passengers, interned so long at Atlit, did not concern Britain. Requests by the Jewish Agency for release of the group were routinely turned down. The *Darien* refugees languished until a ship should become available to carry them off to Mauritius. In January 1941, the camp at Mauritius was capable of absorbing six thousand Jewish refugees, but only two thousand had been sent there. Meanwhile, even during the quiet period between March 1941 and the outbreak of the *Struma* affair, the British authorities followed the movements of Jewish refugees and kept up to date on boats that might be used for aliyah bet. Developments in the Balkans were reported by British consuls and naval attachés in Turkey.[37]

From Constantinople came the report on 19 September 1941, that the Rumanian press had announced the *Struma* voyage, and that the boat was registered in Panama. Further word, this time from Harold MacMichael, Palestine high commissioner, arrived at the Colonial Office on 9 October, saying that the *Struma* was scheduled to depart from Constantsa the previous day and asking that it be barred from passing through the Dardanelles. Should this prove impossible, MacMichael continued, the ship ought to be intercepted and sent back. He emphasized that the Axis powers were stepping up their anti-British propaganda campaign, partly intended to inundate Palestine with Jewish refugees.[38]

The colonial secretary responded two days later. He reminded Mac-Michael that the ship's passage through the Dardanelles could not be blocked, owing to Turkish objections to interference with international shipping in the straits. He asked MacMichael to clarify the proposal that the ship be turned around. MacMichael replied by suggesting that Turkey be persuaded to bar passage through the Dardanelles on a legal pretext: that the ship's unsanitary, overcrowded conditions violated the agreement of the Monterey Convention. If this failed, he suggested, the ship ought to be intercepted and forced to go back.[39]

MacMichael's main worry was that the Navy was too preoccupied with military tasks to intercept the *Struma* if it reached open waters in the Mediterranean, and that it would be caught only upon approaching Palestine. This eventuality he wished to prevent at all costs. He hoped to convince the colonial secretary of the need for force in order to reroute the *Struma* at the mouth of the straits. He referred to the precedent of a French ship, suspected of carrying arms for the Vichy government, that was intercepted and inspected by British naval forces in Turkish waters. MacMichael's cable was forwarded to the British ambassador at Ankara, Hugh Knatchbull-Hugessen, who responded negatively on 15 October.

Five days after the ship reached Istanbul, the deputy director-general of the Turkish Foreign Ministry reported its arrival to the British ambassador.[40] The Turkish official expressed irritation over the burden of decision-making shifted onto Turkey from the Danube countries. He declared himself quite ready to see the ship and its passengers return from whence they came. The Monterey Convention obliged the Turkish government to permit the ship to continue on its way, but the Turkish authorities thought the ship might sink in Turkish waters and rescued passengers would remain in Turkey. However, the deputy director-general of the Turkish Foreign Ministry noted, if the British assented to the refugees' entry into Palestine, the Turkish government would be happy to help them reach their destination.

The Turkish representative clearly believed that the British ambassador would welcome this proposal. Yet Knatchbull-Hugessen's reply was ambiguous. He told his interlocutor that

> His Majesty's Government did not want these people in Palestine; they have no permission to go there, but that from the humanitarian point of view I did not like his proposal to send the ship back into the Black Sea. If the Turkish Government must interfere with the ship on the ground that they could not keep the distressed Jews in Turkey, let her rather go towards the Dardanelles. It might be that if they reached Palestine, they might, despite their illegality, receive humane treatment.[41]

This dispatch aroused the wrath of the Foreign and Colonial Offices and the Palestine high commissioner. MacMichael cabled back at once to the Colonial Office, asking that a "most immediate" message be sent to the ambassador in Turkey:

> It is most important both from policy and security points of view that these illegal immigrants should be prevented from coming to Palestine.

MacMichael further stressed that the Turkish Foreign Ministry was most likely justified in its anxiety over the possibility that the *Struma* would sink in the Sea of Marmara, as the ship's weight was excessive.[42]

The high commissioner hoped to foster growing Turkish displeasure with aliyah bet through-traffic. The British government had in the past sought just this kind of cooperation, but without success. Now, finally, the Turks were beginning to find illegal immigration irksome.[43]

The next day, Edmond Boyd of the Colonial Office drafted a brusque letter to the Foreign Office over the behavior of its ambassador. Instead of feeling relieved that the Turks had finally come around to the British point of view, Boyd complained, the ambassador was conveying the erroneous impression that Britain had altered its policy. The ambassador had absolutely no grounds for implying this and should be instructed at once to explain it to the Turks. Moreover, he should support their proposal to send the ship back to the Black Sea. Boyd contemptuously rejected the idea that it was somehow "humane" to send a boatload of people to Palestine aboard a limping, overcrowded, and inadequately stocked vessel.[44]

The harshest response came from Lord Moyne, the colonial secretary. He seemed to have the strongest reaction to Hugessen's words:

> I have just seen Knatchbull-Hugessen's telegram No. 2460 informing the Foreign Office that he has advised the Turkish Government to send on illegal Jewish immigrants to Palestine and that the Turks had been prepared to turn them back to the Black Sea port from which they have come . . .

After Britain had painstakingly explained all this to the Turks, the secretary asserted, their leaders ultimately came to accept the British policy. Was this success now to be completely undermined by the overindulgent attitude of the British ambassador? A tolerant attitude would crown the voyage of the *Struma* with success, he argued. It would reach Palestine and in its wake would come a wave of Jewish refugees from the Balkans to inundate the country. As for the ambassador's "humanitarian" motives, Moyne sarcastically noted, one might as well extend these to the tens of thousands of Jewish refugees left behind who would be more than happy to join those aboard the *Struma*. He concluded his letter in undisguised anger:

> I find it difficult to write with moderation about this occurrence, which is in flat contradiction of established Government policy, and I should be very glad

if you could perhaps even now do something to retrieve the position and to *urge* that the Turkish authorities should be asked to send the ship back to the Black Sea as they originally proposed [emphasis added].[45]

The Foreign Office, having been on the receiving end of these severe reprimands on account of its envoy in Ankara, sent him a dispatch on 24 December. He was instructed to return to the Turkish Foreign Ministry and explain there had been no change in British immigration policy. The refugees would not receive permission to remain. There was thus no reason why the Turkish authorities should refrain from executing the plan that they themselves had proposed: returning the *Struma* to the Black Sea. The tone of the reply to Knatchbull-Hugessen was milder than that of Lord Moyne's letter. Although it expressed the substance of the colonial secretary's view, it did not actually demand that Knatchbull-Hugessen "urge" the Turks to send the ship back, stipulating merely that he hasten to correct any misapprehension that British policy had changed.[46]

The reasons for this toned-down reply become clear if we look at the Foreign Office response to Lord Moyne, written by Thomas Snow on 29 December.[47] Snow explained the difference between the Foreign Office communication to Knatchbull-Hugessen and the colonial secretary's letter, which did not derive from a basic disagreement with the points Moyne had made. Rather, it reflected a wider consideration of the factors involved, such as American opinion, given the moral aspects of the problem. Should disaster strike the ship on its way back to the Black Sea, Snow maintained, Britain would be held responsible. The Turks would be quick to point out that the ship was sent away at British behest, and this in turn would cause untold damage to British interests in the United States. While he fully appreciated the difficulties occasioned in Palestine and the Middle East by the arrival of illegal immigrant ships, he had to see it in a wider context. Moreover, he maintained, it was more than likely that these were the considerations that prompted Knatchbull-Hugessen to voice his "humanitarian" concern. After all, a significant portion of the people on the ship were refugees fleeing from Nazi terror.

It was quite apparent that the British were well aware of the *Struma*'s state of disrepair. They correctly assessed its chances of reaching any port as dim. Their chief concern, however, was that Britain would be blamed for the disaster and that the refugees would thus end up causing a problem that the British government would be obliged to solve.

On 29 December, Knatchbull-Hugessen reported that he had done as instructed.[48] This ended one phase in the development of British policy in the *Struma* affair, in which the attempt by a British official to temper policy with a humane attitude was swiftly quashed.

During January 1942, British activity concerning the *Struma* was centered in Palestine—around MacMichael and McPherson—rather than in London. Although the ship's continued presence in Istanbul, where repairs dragged on at a snail's pace, grew more burdensome, high-level discussions were not resumed until early February. The British, for obvious reasons, were not eager to involve themselves in settling the fate of the ship.

The second stage of the affair began on 5 February, after the Turkish authorities agreed to permit the *Struma*'s engine to be repaired. They obviously wished to be rid of a distressing problem. Meanwhile, pressure from Palestine on the British government had been steadily mounting.[49] On 4 February, British intelligence sent a cable that assessed the ship's poor present condition, predicting that the Turks would turn the ship out of Istanbul harbor and indicating that the passengers were determined to continue on their way to Palestine. Many among them, the report stated, were planning to join the Allied forces and fight against the Nazis.

On 9 February, Knatchbull-Hugessen reported that the Turkish foreign minister had once again raised the *Struma* issue. The minister stated that he would have to send the ship back to its point of embarkation since no solution had yet been offered. This time, Knatchbull-Hugessen adhered punctiliously to his instructions and to his government's policy: to encourage the return of the ship to Rumania without explicitly recommending or pressing for a decision. Knatchbull-Hugessen concluded from his talk with the foreign minister that the Turkish government would order the *Struma* to leave on 16 February, and he reported this to London. Yet Knatchbull-Hugessen himself had no doubt that his government bore responsibility for the Turks' decision and said as much in his cable to the foreign secretary.[50]

Now the British came under increasing pressure to alter their position. Efforts begun earlier by the Jewish Agency went into high gear, with help sought in both London and Washington. There were appeals from the JDC and its supporters. These activities did have some impact on the Colonial and Foreign Offices.

Knatchbull-Hugessen's dispatch was passed around among senior officials, who commented on it. While they differed somewhat in opinion, all officials agreed that sending the *Struma* out to sea was tantamount to signing a death warrant for those on board. The ship could not be expected to weather another trip on the Black Sea; the danger of its sinking was considerable. And if by some chance the ship should succeed in reaching a Balkan country, there was every possibility that the Nazi-influenced governments there would have the passengers killed. Indeed, the Rumanians were explicit about their intention to do just that.[51]

There were those officials who continued to argue for the hard-line position, even if it would cost lives. But there were others who called for moderation and compromise, and still others who were undecided. It may have been Snow who wrote the note on Knatchbull-Hugessen's cable that began, "This is a terrible dilemma." And, he asked, "Can nothing be done for these unfortunate refugees? Must they take such an inhuman decision? If they go back they will all get killed."[52] Another official, who supported the sympathy of the prime minister for the refugees, wrote: "I understand, however, that the Prime Minister's heart had also been stirred by these latest telegrams."[53]

Yet this group within the Foreign Office, the so-called "moderates," found themselves unable to produce a credible response to the weighty claims made by the Colonial Office and the Palestine high commissioner. They kept introducing new arguments to influence the final decision. These included moral and tactical points such as the impact on public opinion in the United States, in England, and in the German-occupied areas. They proposed that rather than send the ship back to Rumania, where the passengers' lives were in certain danger, they be detained on Cyprus, assuming the ship managed to get that far. They sought to prove that such a step was worthwhile, despite the objections of the governor of the island. Rendel proposed that Foreign Secretary Eden meet with Lord Moyne to find a more humane solution.

The hard-liners in the Foreign Office repeated and fully identified with the arguments raised by the Colonial Office, adding comments of their own to the Knatchbull-Hugessen dispatch. Charles Baxter, a typical member of this group, noted: "These are illegal immigrants who may include Nazis."[54] In this view, there was no justification for seeking to change the stated governmental policy, which absolutely ruled out the entry into Palestine of illegal refugees. Neither did they consider it fair to ask Cyprus to provide some other solution. The consequence of such a compromise, they pointed out, was likely to be a stream of other illegal transports that would follow in the wake of the *Struma*. There were those who would have liked more time to consider the matter, but Knatchbull-Hugessen had stressed that time was running out.[55]

In the face of growing internal criticism, concern and public pressure, MacMichael partially relented and agreed to accept children in the eleven to sixteen age group. Several days later, he extended this to include all the *Struma* children, seventy in all. MacMichael made it clear to the colonial secretary how very great a concession this would be and how dangerous it would be to British interests in Palestine if all the *Struma* refugees were permitted to enter the country. He stated that he had received explicit information that there were German agents on the ship, and added:

> Palestine cannot afford to increase the unproductive element in the population, and reports indicate that the *Struma* passengers are largely of the professional class. Supply position is already stringent, and as you know we are faced with the threat of locust invasion.[56]

MacMichael's offer was transmitted to Knatchbull-Hugessen in Ankara so that he might inform the Turkish Foreign Ministry. This gesture would seem to have given the policymakers in London the additional time they felt they needed. Rendel was able to arrange a meeting between Eden and Lord Moyne. The upshot of their discussion was that the arguments of the colonial secretary convinced Eden, who wrote a memorandum to that effect to the prime minister in advance of the Cabinet meeting scheduled for February 18.[57]

The *Struma* situation was not dealt with on the eighteenth, but it nonetheless affected the substance of the discussion. The agenda included a proposal to release the *Darien* group (after nearly an entire year in detention). Churchill supported the idea, stressing that the decision to arrest and deport illegal immigrants had been taken at the end of November 1940, when it was feared that Palestine was threatened by a wave of illegal immigration. When it became obvious that this was not to happen, it was possible to release the detainees under existing security guidelines. The colonial secretary, on the other hand, adamantly objected to Churchill's reasoning. Using the *Struma* as a prime example, he argued that illegal immigration had not ceased. On the contrary, intelligence reports indicated that a new wave of thousands of refugees might be expected.

The proposal to release the *Darien* group was rejected, the decisive argument being the same one behind the original deportation order. This had the additional effect of lending indirect Cabinet support to the Colonial Office's hard-line position on the *Struma*. For different reasons, both Lord Moyne and Foreign Minister Anthony Eden had preferred to deal with the ship in a general context, rather than have to discuss the specific fate of the people on board or the appeals made on their behalf.

This sealed the fate of the *Struma*. Turkey would not allow children to disembark, and was unwilling to negotiate with Britain over this question. A week passed from the time they received the British request to the day on which the *Struma* was forced out of Istanbul. On 22 February, the passport service of the consulate in Istanbul reported that Turkish authorities had begun preparations to tow the *Struma*.[58] The same day, an urgent message arrived from the Foreign Office asking that action be delayed until the children were removed. On 23 February, the Turkish government informed the British that they would carry out the deportation that very day, as indeed they did.

To conclude, one must stress that British policymakers knew full well that by their acts of commission and omission they had condemned the *Struma* passengers to die. What they could not know was just what form death would take—whether at sea or on land, at German hands or Rumanian. The moderates in the Foreign Office had been unable to alter the position that the Colonial Office and the Palestine high commissioner clung to, refusing to remove even one jot of the policy they had framed.

The Turkish Point of View[59]

Given its geographic location and its neutral status in the war, it was natural that Turkey should have become the initial destination of large numbers of Jewish refugees and the scene of much aliyah bet activity. For most refugees, this was but one more station along a long and arduous route; but for some, their temporary stay in Turkey proved longer than expected. The Turks hoped to prevent this situation from continuing, and they developed a policy that combined a willingness to make some concessions with a desire to remain in control of refugee traffic.

On 12 February 1941, the Turkish parliament enacted a law that granted right of passage through Turkey to Jewish victims of persecution in Germany and neighboring countries. This was granted to those who either held valid entry documents for a country into which they could enter immediately upon leaving Turkish territory, or else legal entry visas for their final destination. Administrative guidelines, sometimes rather severe, regulated the implementation of this law, but overall Turkish policy was a major step in favor of Jewish refugees on their way to Palestine. Many Jews, either individually or in groups, did in fact arrive in Palestine via Turkey at this time.[60]

Conversely, the Turkish authorities tended to be quite strict with arriving refugees. Those who lacked entry documents for their final destination were deported or detained for lengthy periods. The Turkish government cooperated with Britain in its efforts to stem illegal traffic to Palestine. Turkish law forbade the use of Turkish-registered vessels for this purpose and threatened shipowners and seamen with punishment for taking part in such activities. Moreover, the authorities saw to it that these laws were enforced. While many illegal ships traversed Turkish waters en route to Palestine, they did not always get the provisions or assistance they required.

Siding with Britain over the issue meant crossing the Germans, however, and it is possible that Berlin's position influenced Turkish calculations. Ankara did not interfere with the local Jewish community or with Jewish organizations when they lent aid and support to Jewish refugees and refugee ships reaching Turkey.[61] The irony was that Jews, having been turned into refugees by German policies, were dependent on third parties who either did not want to clash openly with the Germans or else were active supporters of those policies—Turkey, as an example of the first case, and Rumania, of the second.

The sinking of the *Salvador* in the Sea of Marmara off the Turkish coast in December 1940 distressed the Turks, not least because some actually blamed Turkey. The Bulgarian government, for example, responding to British protest that held Sofia responsible, vigorously rejected that contention, claiming that the sinking took place within Turkish jurisdiction. How could Ankara have allowed the frail vessel to be put to sea unescorted? The harbor authorities at Varna had provided an escort up to the Turkish territorial boundary, but Turkish authorities had failed to follow suit.[62] In the British press of the day there was criticism of Turkey's stance, despite government efforts to muffle this criticism. The sixty survivors of the *Salvador* remained in Turkey until they could join the *Darien* group. Britain refused to grant them entry documents for Palestine, and the refugees refused to return to Bulgaria.[63]

Turkey wanted to prevent a similar future occurrence. This was, in the opinion of the British ambassador, why they provided coal and water to the *Darien*. Small boats carrying Jewish refugees from Rumania and Bulgaria also reached Istanbul and were detained there waiting for a fateful decision. The positive Rumanian attitude to Jewish emigration, combined with the escalation of anti-Jewish measures there, produced a steady stream of refugees heading for Turkey. Ankara took this as an indication of disaster ahead unless some way was found to regulate the flow of Jews in transit across their country.[64]

These were the concerns of Turkey when the *Struma* affair confronted the authorities with a new crisis. The ship was detoured to Istanbul when it appeared to be heading into a minefield, but at the same time it was guarded and placed under strict quarantine. This action was meant to signal that Turkey did not intend to take responsibility for resolving the *Struma* problem. The ship may have been in a Turkish harbor, but it was preparing to continue on its journey. This explains, as well, the authorities' stubborn refusal to permit any sort of communication with the ship during its first two weeks at Istanbul. Afterward, provisions were sent to the ship under controlled conditions and only to the most limited extent.

Several days after the ship's arrival, Turkey called in the British ambassador to determine his plan of action regarding the *Struma*. At that stage, apparently, the Turks believed that it would take days before the ship's engine was repaired. They hoped Britain would deal effectively with the refugee problem. In the time between Knatchbull-Hugessen's two answers to Ankara, the Constantinople harbor authorities received a note from the Bulgarian captain of the *Struma,* warning that the ship would not be in shape to continue its journey.[65] Even if the engine were repaired, the structure of the vessel would not withstand further stress. The captain contended that the only solution was to find a replacement ship. The Turks saw that the situation was not as clear-cut as they had at first thought, and it raised grave policy questions. They grew wary of the refugees' intentions and tended to suspect them of having deliberately sabotaged the ship.[66] This opinion was also expressed by the ship's agent: he believed the refugees' desire to disembark and continue by rail motivated their stubborn refusal to resume the voyage. The Turkish government, confident that this was so, ordered the harbor authorities to repair the ship at the expense of the local Jewish community.

On 10 January, about a month after the ship's arrival in Istanbul, the captain asserted in yet another letter that the *Struma* could not put to sea again.[67] Moreover, political conditions dictated that either the crew be replaced by Turkish seamen, that the Turks provide an escort as far as Syria, or that the authorities permit the passengers to disembark and continue overland. The captain stated his own preference for the second option. The Turks would not agree to any of the three proposals. They felt the ship ought to return to Rumania, but they were still unwilling to take that step. The Rumanian government refused to take the refugees back. The Rumanians contended that since the Jews had emigrated illegally, they could not now be readmitted.[68]

In mid-January, the Turks faced a dilemma. The *Struma* affair was viewed with grave concern. Why not send the ship away in January? Repairs were completed that month, albeit much later than anticipated. As more time elapsed without a resolution, the Turks came under increasing pressure. Every agonizing hour the refugees spent waiting in the harbor increased their hardship and magnified the cruelty of deportation. After a month-long pursuit of a political solution failed to produce results, it was unclear what other option the Turks could exercise.

Perhaps the Turks had already decided to send the ship back to the Black Sea. Nonetheless, they approached the British for the last time. That apparently explained why permission was granted to those few refugees to disembark and tell the world their story. The Turkish Foreign Minister personally took up the matter in order to make it perfectly clear to London what further steps would be taken and what was at risk. But his discussion with the British ambassador failed to produce a more favorable response.[69] At that point, the foreign minister informed Knatchbull-Hugessen that the ship would be expelled on February 16. Both men understood quite well that in the Turkish view the onus of this decision lay with the British.

About a week later, MacMichael agreed to accept the children of the *Struma*. This decision was quickly transmitted by Knatchbull-Hugessen to the Turkish authorities. Ankara refused to allow any passengers to disembark. This surprised the British, as well as Zionist leaders. The six passengers who previously had been allowed to leave the ship received immigration certificates for Palestine. Why, then, the refusal to permit the children to land?

Perhaps the Turks took MacMichael's offer not as a sign of compromise but as an indication that the rest of the passengers had no hope of being offered asylum. The Turks had no interest in affording Britain the chance to appear magnanimous for so small a price. They accordingly rejected Jewish appeals for the children to be permitted to land, demanding instead that the British find a way to transfer them to another vessel.[70] This was, of course, no more than a pretext, but these political considerations closed the door on the children's last chance.

Throughout the episode, Turkey's position had been that the entire matter was British responsibility. True, last-minute British appeals caused a delay in the deportation order, but in the week between 16 and 23 February neither side would budge from its stated position. The Red Cross appealed to the Turks to reconsider, as did the Zionist and Jewish organizations. None of this helped as long as the British were unwilling to offer an alternative for the passengers as a group. The deportation was enacted on the twenty-third, after Turkey had informed Britain of its decision. The 769 Jews on board the *Struma* were doomed.[71]

The controversy aroused by the ship's arrival in Istanbul and its lengthy stay in the harbor were but a prelude to the shock and wave of protest that its sinking evoked. In the aftermath, both Zionist leaders and British policymakers had to reformulate their policies.

9

After the Sinking of the *Struma*

Small Boats on the Seas

The *Struma* disaster did not stop Jews from trying to leave Rumania. The same forces that motivated desperate Jewish escape measures in 1941 were still evident in 1942. The British indeed hoped that the *Struma*'s fate would deter other Jews from taking such a course, but that was not to be. As long as the Rumanians allowed Jews to depart, Jews sought every available escape route.

Between March and August 1942, seven small boats left Rumania carrying some 200 refugees. It was a slow but steady trickle, several dozen people leaving at a time. There is little information available on those voyages, but enough material exists to allow a partial reconstruction.[1]

Many of the people on these boats were former employees of foreign consulates, or representatives of British and American companies. They acted independently, without assistance from Jewish organizations. The sailboats they acquired were small enough to obviate the need for strict registration procedures and insurance requirements. The passengers learned to operate and navigate the boats on their own, and were thus independent of non-Jewish crewmen. Acquisition and preparation of the boats were costly, but the refugees came from middle- and upper-class backgrounds and managed to afford these expenses. They were also able to "purchase" travel documents for Latin American countries. The overall cost per person ranged from 600,000 to 700,000 lei (about $1,000), which included bribes paid to bureaucrats and government offices. These boats were entirely legal from the Rumanian point of view, and harbor authorities provided escorts through the coastal mine-fields.

Exit permission was granted despite German opposition. The passengers knew this; they were also well aware of other dangers that attended their voyage. It was uncertain that they would reach Palestine or gain entry visas for Palestine upon reaching Turkey. Only two of the boats (*Michai* and *Mirchea*) survived the journey: most were wrecked off the Turkish coast. The fact that such escapes were attempted despite the risks testifies to the refugees' desperate determination for survival. The course they took resulted from the new German policy to interdict Jewish emigration, the sinking of the *Struma*, and the withdrawal of Yishuv-linked bodies and other organizations from the support of aliyah bet.

The story of the *Mirchea*,[2] which sailed from Tulcea on April 10, 1942 and reached Palestine on 20 May, after a tortuous passage, illustrates numerous common features in the saga of the small boats. Forty people sailed aboard this boat. They had learned of the sinking of the *Struma* several weeks before departure, but preferred to believe the account circulated by Pandelis and the Rumanian authorities, who claimed that the passengers had been rescued and had continued by rail to Palestine.[3] Preparations for departure of the group began as early as January 1942. The most difficult obstacle was acquisition of a boat. Having achieved this, the group obtained necessary permits by bribing various officials. The captain and crew were entirely made up of Jews. Paraguayan visas were arranged for a tidy sum through intermediaries in the "Merkozen" travel company.

The passengers were given special rail passes for the trip from Bucharest to Tulcea, where they set sail on April 10, feeling quite hopeful. Clearing customs and passport control was not difficult. Displaying the Rumanian flag, the *Mirchea* was guided by a police boat past harbor defenses at Sulina.

The first mishap of the journey occurred at Constantsa, where a Rumanian naval vessel fired upon the *Mirchea*, which had sailed too close to shore. Once it established its identity to officials, the ship was permitted to go on. Later, the compass malfunctioned, but the captain was able to find the Bosporus after four days at sea. Thus, on 20 April, only four months after the *Struma* had sailed into Istanbul, another boat full of Jewish refugees dropped anchor.

Turkey, seeking to avoid further complications, refused the *Mirchea* permission to remain. After passing through the Dardanelles, the boat encountered heavy seas, but it was not permitted to take shelter in ports along the coast. Warning shots were fired on two occasions as the ship approached the shoreline. Near Izmir, engine trouble and leakage developed. Word was sent to one of the Turkish Jewish leaders, who organized relief supplies and engine repair. The authorities prohibited passengers from contacting the British consul, and they intercepted a memorandum sent to him.

The *Mirchea* eventually continued the journey, remaining close to the Turkish coast. Near Castellorizzo, which was Italian-controlled, several shots sailed across her bow, slightly wounding the captain. The *Mirchea* halted and surrendered to the Italians, who treated the passengers with compassion. The captain received medical attention, and two days later the group proceeded.

The next stop was at Mersin, on 1 May, to address engine trouble. The Turks dispatched a mechanic to rectify the problem. This time the passengers were permitted to contact the British authorities, and the consul in Istanbul had food supplies sent to the boat before it sailed again.

Near Tyre, the *Mirchea* was met by a British vessel and instructed to sail to Haifa. Ten miles out of Acre, a coastal patrol intercepted the passengers and escorted them into Haifa Bay forty days after leaving Constantsa. On 20 May, the *Mirchea* was interned in Atlit.

Michai reached Haifa a few days before the *Mirchea*. The other boats did not fare so well, sinking or colliding along the Turkish coast. The Turks increasingly lost patience as more and more refugees washed up on their shores expecting to be allowed to proceed overland.[4] The Turkish government threatened to send the refugees back to the Black Sea, but the British feared that such a move would lead to another disaster. Ze'ev Shind commented: "The tragic spectacle of refugees setting out in small sailboats, driven only by the power of their desperation, is unfolding graphically along the shores of the Bosporus and the Golden Horn. It is not something that can remain hidden; [the attempt] before our eyes, like lepers confined in their boats, with their aged, their women and their children; dependent on the good will of rulers, with the assistance of the Jews of Constantinople and the selfless dedication of a number of individuals who supply them with food and water."[5]

In November 1942, Rumania ordered a halt to the emigration of Jews aboard Rumanian vessels. This was probably issued at Germany's behest, though Bucharest considered the loss of a large number of boats.[6]

Britain: Politics of Frustration

The sinking of the *Struma* challenged British policy and discredited its unyielding stance toward Jewish refugees. Criticism in Parliament and public opinion was scathing. The American press took a similarly critical line. Before long, the Foreign Office and its U.S. staff felt pressured to take some action.[7]

The colonial secretary was called upon to explain his posture before Parliament in the House of Lords and in meetings with Jewish representatives. Although he adhered faithfully to the official position, the Colonial Office began to consider a new approach. This coincided with personnel changes in the department that took place in late February 1942. Lord Moyne, who was in command during the *Struma* episode, was replaced by Lord Cranborne, who favored more flexibility toward illegal immigration provided there was no violation in principle of the White Paper. Lord Cranborne was determined to avoid another sea disaster.

According to Cranborne, it was necessary to return to a policy of subtracting illegal arrivals from legal immigration quotas, rather than expelling them, so that refugee boats leaving Europe would be able to complete their journeys. The flight of the small boats from Rumania, while involving a handful of people, was an added factor leading Cranborne to this conclusion. He found it difficult, however, to convince his Cabinet colleagues.

The debate between Cranborne and the Foreign Office hinged on the advisability of an entirely new policy, as against ad hoc concessions. The Foreign Office warned that a new official policy would advertise the fact that refugees arriving illegally in Palestine would be legalized. That, in turn, would encourage others to attempt illegal immigration. On the other hand, a strategy of ad hoc concessions, the implementation of modified guidelines only as the need arose, would uphold a measure of uncertainty as to the ultimate disposition of the illegals. That was preferable, it was argued, if the aim was to avoid inundation of Palestine by illegal immigrants.

Cranborne's opening volley in this debate came in the form of a memorandum to the Cabinet, where he called into question a number of the assumptions underlying general governmental policy in Palestine, and its stand on illegal immigration in particular.[8] It was an illusion, he suggested, to believe that the Arabs and the Jews would eventually come to terms with the White Paper. The Zionists, he stressed, had already evinced radical opposition to the White Paper, and there was no reason to believe they would alter their point of view. Therefore, Britain should be prepared to face a difficult decision on the matter, even though "for the time being . . . the White Paper must stand." The problem ought nevertheless to be addressed, Cranborne argued, in terms of the critical, post-*Struma* state of affairs. The White Paper, he continued, did not require the expulsion of refugees arriving illegally in Palestine. It was thus possible to count their number against the total immigration envisaged in 1939. The principles guiding British policy ought to be reviewed, given the important new factors that affected the position of the Jews and physically impeded the flow of immigration. In his opinion, considerations linked to the Arab reaction were now balanced by humanitarian considerations. Both the security issue and the closely related "fifth column question" might be resolved through cooperation with the Jewish Agency. Cranborne sought to impose three limitations on refugee immigration:

First, the number must not exceed the legal ceiling set by the Mandate administration. Second, refugees must be acceptable to the security services in Palestine. And third, refugees must fit the economic criteria of the country.

Such a policy, Cranborne suggested, would effectively respond to current criticism of the government and would best address its problems.

Cranborne had few Cabinet supporters. In a preliminary discussion of his memorandum, only the American Department at the Foreign Office voiced approval of his scheme.[9] They undoubtedly had in mind the plight of the *Darien* refugees, held for so long in detention, who were also the focus of a great deal of anti-British criticism in the United States. The American desk felt that a new policy would be justified on the basis of the *Darien* case alone. On the other hand, the Middle Eastern section argued against upsetting the Arabs, adjudging the Jews in any case to be committed to the Allied cause.[10]

Lord Cranborne was opposed by the War Office, as well, and by the Palestine high commissioner. They countered his reasoning with all the shopworn arguments: security, the fifth column threat, the absorptive capacity of the country, and, above all, the flood of Jewish refugees that a clear change of policy would allegedly release. After several months of unrestricted immigration, it was argued, when the legal quota was exhausted, how would the government then deal with a new *Struma*?[11]

Cranborne's proposal was defeated, and the government repeated its standing position. Yet some faint indication of Cranborne's input may be read in the following line from the government's statement: "Any illegal Jewish immigrants reaching Palestine should be treated with humanity. . . . "[12]

Cranborne was routinely invited to resubmit his proposal for late discussion, concluding what may be called the first attempt to introduce a basic change in British policy. In his role as colonial secretary, Cranborne could not effect such change, so the War Cabinet chose instead a policy of "wait and react."

The issue did not long remain dormant. Responding to interpellations in the House of Lords and in the Commons, Lord Cranborne and Harold Macmillan (secretary of state for Parliamentary affairs) declared that the Colonial Office would do all in its power to prevent a second *Struma*.[13]

Contingency plans were drawn up in the Colonial Office for the future arrival of a refugee boat.[14] The Foreign Office was requested to instruct its ambassador in Ankara to report such an event without delay and indicate Turkey's intentions. Similarly, the British naval command in the Mediterranean was to be kept informed of the movement of such vessels, in order to avoid mistaken attacks against refugee boats flying enemy colors. The British fleet was to provide an escort for such boats, bypassing Haifa, to the Suez Canal.

The next act of the drama advanced on 19 March 1942, when intelligence provided by the Palestine high commissioner's office reported that the *Michai* was approaching Istanbul, carrying some 1,400 refugees.[15] The news threw Lord Cranborne, who feared a disaster worse than the *Struma*, into a panic. He sent a personal message to the foreign secretary (through Randall, at the time head of the refugee desk at the Foreign Office), requesting that nothing be said to intimate to the Turks a desire on the part of Britain to see the boat turned back.[16] Foreign Office officials remarked that Cranborne was asking the ambassador in Turkey to overreach a governmental decision. Cranborne proceeded to compose a more moderate cable to the ambassador, retaining a sense of urgency: "Please ascertain at once what are the intentions of the Turkish authorities. . . . If they intend to turn the ship back as they did in *Struma* case *please press them urgently to suspend any such action*" [emphasis in the original].

Cranborne also asked the War Office about the possibility of transferring the refugees to transit camps in either Egypt or Syria, or perhaps Cyprus. At the same time he cabled the high commissioner in Palestine that it would be necessary to permit the refugees into Palestine following a period of detention for security purposes at Atlit. The number of arrivals would be counted against the total that was legal under the White Paper. Such a course would indicate the direction of the government's policy, Cranborne noted, and would free his department from the problems of *ad hoc* decision-making. The high commissioner was requested to reply by the following day. MacMichael, who did not share the fears of the colonial secretary or his sense of urgency, stated his opposition to the plan. He proposed that the refugee boat be escorted to Mauritius, where the refugees might be interned.[17]

A direct confrontation between the two men was avoided at that stage, because two days later word came that there were only fourteen refugees on the *Michai*—not, as had been reported, fourteen hundred. The sigh of relief at the Colonial Office was almost audible as a new round of communications and notes were sent out. Lord Cranborne instructed MacMichael to intern the refugees temporarily at Atlit, where the *Darien* group had been held. Word was sent to the ambassador in Ankara, so that he might inform the Turks.[18] At that time, too, the *Euxine* reached Constantinople with thirteen people aboard. The British proposed to deal with this on the same basis as the *Michai* group.[19]

A short respite followed, though reports were constantly received about Jews planning to leave from Rumania. Cranborne therefore continued to design his next move. The Jewish Agency pressed the Colonial Office to issue Palestine visas upon refugee arrival in Turkey. Such visas would ostensibly simplify arrangements for rail passage to Palestine, thus avoiding the problems and fears associated with sea transport. The idea met with stiff opposition from the Foreign Office.[20]

Meanwhile, the *Mirchea* was commencing its difficult journey. As noted, the British did not have clear instructions on how to respond to *Mirchea*'s plans. Should they request permission from the Turkish government for the boat and its passengers to remain in Turkish ports? Or should they pass in silence over Turkish orders to move the boat from one port to another?

Cranborne was determined to achieve a clear and stated policy. Talks were held with the Foreign and War Offices over possible places of refuge, such as Eritrea, Ethiopia, and Cyprus. The proximity of such locations to the Mediterranean was Cranborne's chief criterion, as this would enable the boats to reach their destination safely and under their own steam, with British naval escorts.[21] The round of discussions on the matter forced Cranborne to the conclusion that he would have to return to the ideas outlined in his memorandum of 5 March, and to attempt once again to win support among the various government offices. In an attempt to cut the Gordian knot once and for all, MacMichael was summoned to London in late April to take part personally in the discussions, which were punctiliously prepared by the secretary's staff.[22]

Cranborne and MacMichael reached agreement over the policy changes to be sought, based on the earlier memorandum to the Cabinet and the cable that the secretary had sent to Jerusalem on 19 March. They decided to call upon the Cabinet to reopen the issue—under the government's provision for renewed discussion of 5 March—and circulated a draft of their proposed plan. The Foreign Office, in response, noted its preference for a one-time concession (release of the *Darien* group from detention) rather than a full-fledged policy change. Cranborne was opposed: such a course had already proved incapable of preventing disasters at sea. To win over the Foreign Office, Cranborne cited MacMichael's support for his position. He particularly emphasized the high commissioner's fear of possible violence in the Yishuv if the government failed to provide safe transit for the refugees.[23]

Cranborne also sought to allay Foreign Office fears of hostile Arab reactions, citing MacMichael's opinion that such meetings could be handled without much difficulty. Cranborne's basic argument was that there could be no hope for orderly, legal Jewish immigration to Palestine for the immediate future, and therefore "illegal immigration" ought to be reclassified. Otherwise, he pointed out, Britain would in effect be punishing the Jews and preventing them from immigrating at all.

As a result of his preliminary consultations with the Foreign and War Offices, Cranborne submitted a modified plan for Cabinet approval. The changes were semantic and stylistic, indicating the seriousness with which the other departments approached the matter. Nevertheless, the new plan departed to a significant degree from the March memorandum.[24]

Cranborne introduced a distinction between refugees on their way to Palestine and those already there, reserving the government's largesse for those who successfully reached Palestine. This group would qualify as legal immigrants, following a precautionary security review, provided that they met the neccessary criteria. This decision would not be publicized; knowledge of it would be restricted, as far as possible, to official circles. As for refugees en route to Palestine, there was to be no compromise: illegal immigration was to be adamantly fought.

The new provisions in this decision not only represented a concession to those who had opposed the March proposal. They also resolved the long-standing *Darien* question and offered generous terms to the *Michai* and *Mirchea* groups, as well as to those on other boats that would shortly arrive in Palestine. The policy was not framed to guarantee prevention of a second *Struma* misfortune, since the refugees would have to make their way in their own frail boats, and there was no provision for obtaining the release of Jewish refugees held in Turkish detention. What, indeed, would be the fate of refugees who arrived in Turkey but whom the Turkish authorities would order deported?

The Cabinet voted on 20 May in favor of the proposal, ending the first phase of the policy debate, and the colonial secretary reserved once again the right to reopen the issue if the number of refugees exceed the legal yearly immigration quota. Almost immediately, however, the government was impelled to modify its decision, granting permission to enter Cyprus after the *Dordeval* and *Euxine* had been wrecked off the Istanbul shore. The ill-fated passengers were rescued and assisted by the Turks, who termed their response a "one-time" act of mercy.

The constant traffic of small refugee boats, and the information obtained about the preparation of many more, increased the difficulties of securing permission for Jewish refugees to remain in Turkey. The British consulates and the embassy in Ankara were forced to devote a great deal of time negotiating with the Turks.[25] Moreover, the decision to charge the Jewish Agency or refugees themselves for passage to Cyprus engaged the British in difficult bargaining with the Jewish Agency.[26]

By September 1942, the British embassy in Ankara found itself—against its wishes and despite the new government's new policy—preoccupied with Jewish refugee matters. The Turks were fed up with the seemingly endless stream of Jews arriving in their country with nowhere to go. They warned the Rumanian authorities that anyone arriving without documentation for a further destination would be turned back.[27] London should have been satisfied with this step: Turkey was doing what Britain could not do, and was helping to stem illegal Jewish immigration. In fact, the Turkish message to Rumania deeply troubled the British ambassador, the Foreign Office, and, above all, the Colonial Office.[28]

The Foreign Office instructed Knatchbull-Hugessen, the ambassador, to voice British support for Turkish discouragement of illegal Jewish immigration, but to convey unequivocally that Britain expected to be informed of impending deportations, so as to be able to declare its position. Thus, the British government sent conflicting signals to the Turkish authorities. The Colonial Office was aware of this, but realized that this was inevitable, given the inner contradiction in the policy adopted by the government. The moral responsibility of Britain on the one hand, and its seeming inability to come to the refugees' aid while they were still en route on the other, increased tensions for British representatives in Ankara.[29]

The British ambassador in Ankara had the unenviable task of dealing with the Turks every time another refugee boat arrived. He was prevented from openly declaring that Britain would take responsibility for the arrivals, but he was similarly barred from agreeing to their deportation. Nevertheless, he was required to ask the Turks to give prior notice of their intentions, so that his government might adopt a position on a case-by-case basis. This further strained the relations between the two countries, already complicated by disagreements over the transit camp for Greek refugees at Izmir, which was run with British support.[30]

At this point, the second phase in the major policy debate began. The ambassador felt that he had lost control over the situation and questioned whether he could continue implementing a badly conceived policy. He dispatched an irate cable to the Foreign Office when it became necessary to guarantee that refugees from the *Vitorul* would not be deported: "I feel our attitude toward irregular traffic should be clearly defined and published and we should publicly disclaim all responsibility for the consequences, if traffickers continue in their present way."[31]

Uncertainty born of inconsistency, the ambassador felt, was the crux of his predicament. British protection and internment of refugees on Cyprus meant that the government was encouraging illegal immigration in practice, while declaring its opposition in principle. The chief beneficiaries of this state of affairs were the shipping agents: a gang of adventurers, scoundrels and profiteers who raked in huge sums from desperate Jews. And the main victims of the policy were the refugees themselves.[32]

The Colonial Office would not agree to a public disclaimer of responsibility for the refugees. Cranborne and his staff sympathized with the ambassador, but they understood that any British declaration would have to include assumption of full responsibility for the refugees, coordination with the Ankara government, and explicit procedures for transferring the refugees to British colonies. Not even the Colonial Office was prepared to go that far; instead, they felt obliged to opt for a lack of clarity.

Ambassador Knatchbull-Hugessen refused to relinquish the matter. On 16 October he sent a long, detailed letter to the Foreign Office in which he set out his argument for an unambiguous policy. He expressed the contention that the existing situation could not be permitted to continue much longer.[33]

This led to a meeting of representatives from the Foreign and Colonial Offices to resolve their differences. Held on 17 November, the caucus produced a joint response that was then forwarded to Ankara. Upon receiving word of the arrival of Jewish refugees in Turkey, the ambassador was to provide assurances to the Turkish government that the refugees would be received in some British colony. Such transfer would be effected as soon as possible.[34]

The decision sparked an interesting reaction from the embassy in Ankara: "From the local point of view we should welcome adoption of these proposals. There are however certain wider objections which I think you should take into account before reaching final decision."[35]

Knatchbull-Hugessen spelled out these new considerations in a subsequent letter. The Rumanians were proposing to permit the emigration of seventy thousand Jews for ransom. The proposal to which he referred was that of Radu Lecca, in charge of Jewish affairs in the Rumanian government, who had recently arrived in Turkey to negotiate over the Jews being held in Transnistria, later known as the "Transnistria Plan." Were the British indeed prepared to accept responsibility for a group this size?[36]

Knatchbull-Hugessen's reply and reaction demonstrates once again how British policy was inadequate to confront the problems at hand. It attempted to cope with past but not with present contingencies, and policy review was painfully slow. The government's decision of November 1940 to expel the illegal immigrants may have been applicable for the next half-year. Yet it continued until May 1942. Although the circumstances during that year had changed, it took the government until November 1942 to reach a new decision. By December of that year, however, the government again confronted a contingency for which no provision had been made—the appeal to rescue tens of thousands of Jews.

Indeed, during the fall and winter of 1942, as the details of the Final Solution became public knowledge, the focus of debate would shift. It would no longer be possible to separate the question of illegal flight from the fate of European Jewry. Britain would not only face demands to provide refuge to those able to escape, but would also be asked to render active assistance in saving Jews from annihilation.

Zionism: Politics of Helplessness

The *Struma* disaster clearly illustrated the inadequacies of Zionist policy in the face of British obstinacy. The Hebrew press in Palestine quoted Shertok's statement: "*Struma* revealed the abysmal poverty and frailty of our position, our utter helplessness and our lack of [political] standing as a Jewish nation."[37]

This sense of impotence was accompanied by feelings of rage against Britain, vented in statements by Yishuv leaders as well as in letters to the press and editorials. Headlines hurled the accusation, "Murderer!" at the high commissioner—a sentiment that articulated the turmoil in the ranks of the Haganah and prompted the incensed to seek vengeance.[38] After an interval of intense discussion among the leadership and in the press, public interest seemed to diminish. The case of the *Struma* left less of a lasting impression than the sinking of the *Patria* had fifteen months earlier.

In the following year, it was the Mossad that most clearly reflected the shake-up produced by the *Struma* affair. The failed efforts of the Mossad to come to the aid of the *Struma* refugees and the trend toward seeking greater tactical cooperation with the British in the war effort led the Mossad to look to its British contacts for ways to implement further illegal immigration. Indeed, this line of thinking had already been evident in the *Darien* episode, and had introduced problems of conflict of interest.

Britain was increasingly dependent on others for intelligence from the Balkan countries, for the rescue of downed pilots, and related military tasks. Similar factors led them to lend support to the Greeks and Poles, who provided discreet conduits for information and supplies and the means to rescue Allied personnel. In the summer of 1942, Shind and Yehieli reported to the Mossad that the Greeks had developed an excellent communications network using sailboats between the Greek islands. Flying the swastika alongside the Greek flag, these boats passed freely between Turkey and the Black Sea, bringing in food and clothing and smuggling out young Greeks. In addition, the Greeks were secretly hoping to evacuate 2,000 Greek refugees interned in a Turkish camp.

The Poles, too, were using Constantinople as a base from which emissaries were sent back into Poland. Shind and Yehieli noted that the Poles, like the Greeks, enjoyed British support, which was a distinct political and logistical advantage. Envoys of Free French, Yugoslavia, and Czechoslovakia also transmitted information and anti-Nazi propaganda to their countries, under the British diplomatic umbrella.[39]

The question asked by the Mossad was how to adopt similar methods and so turn Constantinople into a base for obtaining information and providing relief and rescue. Shind exhausted the services of Eliyahu Epstein (Elath), who was in Constantinople for the political department of the Jewish Agency to advance cooperation with British intelligence and other agents and to open talks with British and American intelligence. These discussions enabled Shind to send a proposal back to Palestine, calling for the use of Jewish refugees from the Balkans as a source of information. If the British could specify the kind of information they required, the Mossad would gather it through its local contacts. In exchange, the British would be expected to help the Mossad bring these Jews out of the Balkans and to Palestine. British assistance would include logistical support pertaining to sea transport to and travel through Turkey, while the Mossad, together with the political department of the Jewish Agency, would debrief the refugees and transmit their information to the British. This way the British would continually upgrade their information.

This proposal was aired at a meeting of the Mapai (Labor party) executive on 24 June 1942 and in a meeting, held a week later, of the supervisory committee of the Mossad.[40] At the time Shind and Yehieli were both in Palestine, and a number of Mossad decisions clearly reveal the influence of their thinking. The proposal was accepted, along with the idea that the Mossad should keep a permanent representative in Constantinople. Yehieli was to proceed there first, and Shind would follow on 21 October.

The following guidelines were established for the work done there: the Mossad would try to coordinate and cooperate with Diaspora Jewish bodies such as the JDC; it would work closely with other intelligence agencies, who would benefit from the information supplied by the refugees in Istanbul and then in Palestine; the refugees would be routed to Palestine through the port of Mersin, which had been turned into a British naval facility. The refugees would get to Mersin on Rumanian boats, but the British would allow them to come and go freely. From there, the Mossad would ensure the refugees' safe passage to Haifa aboard a craft manned by Mossad crews. For example, the *Lilly,* a Mossad-owned boat, would serve this purpose (and transfer some of the refugees to Cyprus). Other boats could be acquired in Egypt through Ruth Klueger-Aliav. Meanwhile, new recruits to the naval wing of the Haganah (the Palyam) would be trained.[41] The Mossad would strive as far as possible to facilitate the immigration of young Zionist "pioneers" from Europe, whose passage had to be funded by Jewish organizations abroad.

The Mossad thus sought a well-thought-out and orderly system, hoping to avoid fly-by-night operations run by a constantly shifting group of travel agents and emissaries, operative since the *Darien* affair of early 1941. In this fashion, the Mossad tried to prepare for both the potential and the pitfalls involved in such a venture.

Given the approach of the Mossad, it is possible to assume that the executive of the Jewish Agency would have properly assessed the new realities and the need to assist European Jews. Despite the patent failure of Zionist policy over the *Struma* incident, sharp criticism was not voiced within the Agency executive or in the press. Did Jewish leaders believe it was mainly the job of the British and Turks to save the ship and its passengers, or did this reflect a certain distance from the plight of European Jews? There can be no doubt that the Yishuv keenly felt a loss and fully appreciated the grief of the stricken families whose relatives went down on the ship. The National Committee (Va'ad Leumi) declared a general strike, the youth movements organized protest meetings, and the Association of Immigrants from Rumania published open letters to the British high commissioner and to the British government, holding them directly responsible for the tragedy. Many other private individuals did likewise.

At the Agency executive meeting of 26 February 1942, as the first news arrived of the sunken ship, tentative opinions surfaced regarding the political tactics to be employed. There was an undeniable need for more time and more information in order to properly absorb and assess the significance of what had occurred. It was considered whether to charge the British and Turks with moral culpability and leave it at that, or seek to benefit other refugee groups still in Turkey by renewing demands for the release of the *Darien* group. Eliezer Kaplan claimed:

> We cannot submit a claim for new immigrant permits in compensation—there can be no compensation for this tragedy. Even the release of the detainees at Atlit [i.e., the *Darien* group] will not compensate for the *Struma* disaster. We dare not diminish the elemental human anguish. Some seven hundred men, women, old people and children, innocent of any crime, have been drowned. Any demand we make now will weaken the force of that feeling.[42]

The scale of the disaster, Kaplan argued, required a nonpolitical reaction that would emphasize the human and ethical dimensions. Eliyahu Dobkin, the deputy head of the aliyah department, felt instead that despite the tragedy they would be remiss in not attempting to exact from the British new permits for refugees.[43]

Between March and October 1942, the Jewish leadership in Palestine was preoccupied with aliyah—but not illegal aliyah. The emigration of Jewish Polish refugees from Russia was on the agenda, with discussions of their possible transport overland via Iran. In addition, there was concern for the release of internees on Mauritius, as well as for the question of getting certificate recipients from the Balkans (and children from those countries) to Palestine.

The most urgent item at hand, however, was the *Darien* group, still interned at Atlit. Difficult camp conditions there and vocal dissatisfaction from the detainees with Agency handling of the matter put Yishuv leaders under considerable pressure. With the replacement of Lord Moyne by Lord Cranborne, they made a fresh attempt to persuade the Colonial Office to release the group. Public opinion and the climate in Parliament seemed favorable because of the *Struma* disaster.

The Zionist leaders used two arguments to justify the release of the *Darien* group: the potential contribution these immigrants would make to the Allied war effort and to the Yishuv; and the humanitarian claim that could justly be made on behalf of Jews who had saved themselves from Nazi-occupied Europe. The allegedly negative and suspicious attitude widely taken toward Jewish refugees, in contrast to the way non-Jewish Poles and Greeks were treated, was deeply resented, Zionists said. This so-called double standard, traceable to political considerations, was at the core of the Yishuv approach to the British. With the economy of Palestine improving and military requirements burgeoning, Shertok called upon the government to permit expansion of the labor force by releasing the detainees from Atlit and returning the refugees from Mauritius to Palestine.[44]

Discussions among Zionist leaders included a consideration of tactics. They sought to use one concession as a springboard for further requests and demands. Each time word came of a refugee boat on the Black Sea, such as the *Michai* or the *Mirchea,* Jewish leaders lodged a new appeal with the Foreign and Colonial Offices. Most of their activity centered around London.[45]

Although the problem of refugee boats cropped up again and again, no new approach was adopted. The desperate flight of the "boat people" from Rumania was not heard as a plea for rescue. The political leaders did not view aliyah bet as a lever to induce Britain to change its policy. The idea that hordes of refugees and likely future sea disasters could be used to force a more flexible British position does not seem to have been a factor in political discussions. Facilitating aliyah bet in 1942 was simply not central to Zionist thinking or diplomacy.

The decision of the British Cabinet on 20 May 1942, to free the *Darien, Mirchea,* and *Michai* refugees and accept them as legal immigrants was applauded in Jerusalem and considered a political victory, but the accompanying decision to transfer Jews stranded in Turkey to detention centers on Cyprus elicited negative reactions.[46] Though Shertok believed that the British decision not to expel Jews arriving in Palestine meant a policy change, he did not propose to exploit this to launch a campaign for a much larger immigration. At the same time, he viewed the decision from London not to divulge the terms of its new guidelines as a positive step. Until then, the British had refused to adopt secret decisions regarding Palestine, based on the fear that these would leak at an inopportune moment. The May decision therefore departed from the previous norm, and Shertok hoped this might become precedent, enabling the Yishuv to win other immigration concessions more easily. Thus, the new policy was kept secret and did not play the galvanizing role in prompting aliyah that it might have under less restrictive conditions.

Zionist demands on immigration took into account wartime restrictions on travel. In June 1942, Shertok asked for an immigration quota of 5,000 for the next six months, explaining it in the following way:

> Several days ago we sent to the government a letter on the immigration quota. We had a disagreement over this with the aliyah department. They suggested ten thousand as the number we should demand. But in our letter to the government we demanded only five thousand. Our labor bureau demonstrated a need for fifteen thousand new workers. In our memorandum to the government we proved that if twenty thousand workers were to arrive in the country now they would be absorbed in the economy immediately. *But it would be absurd to demand so large a number at this time, when transport and travel conditions are so difficult. Although in normal times we demand the full amount of certificates according to the state of the economy, we are now in wartime conditions and therefore we felt we had to settle for a figure of five thousand* [emphasis added].[47]

Perhaps this tendency to limit immigration worked to keep the small boats on the margins of Agency deliberations, though the British agreed to admit certificate-holders from Rumania and Bulgaria. Bucharest's willingness to allow Jews to emigrate, at the height of the anti-Jewish violence there, seems not to have prompted anyone in Jerusalem to reconsider.

Indeed, Zionist leaders hesitated to take responsibility for unconventional operations that departed too much from what was considered safe. This may be regarded as a failure to adjust to the prevailing climate.

Thus, in the Agency executive meeting of 26 April 1942, in a discussion of the emigration of Jewish children from Rumania (with British approval), the question of safe-transit guarantees arose. Dobkin proposed that the *Lilly,* for which a neutral flag of registry was unsuccessfully solicited, be registered in Rumania for the purpose of transport to Palestine. He favored asking the International Red Cross to place the ship under its protection. Shertok believed the Soviets would not explicitly guarantee not to attack a ship flying enemy colors (safe conduct); he therefore suggested they take the chance of simply informing the Soviets of the ship's departure without obtaining a formal guarantee. To this Rabbi Yehuda Leib Fishman, the representative of Mizrahi Religous Zionism, objected, arguing that the Agency could not be held responsible for the children's lives. Dobkin explained the complexities to him, but ended by agreeing that a guarantee of safe conduct was desirable. Therefore, he suggested two conditions for carrying out the operation: first, that the children's parents and the Palestine Office in Rumania take full responsibility; and second, that the Soviets explicitly guarantee not to attack the ship.

Yitzhak Gruenbaum, who chaired the meeting, at first sounded somewhat vague, but finally he supported Shertok:

> We should continue our efforts to persuade the Swiss government to lend its flag for the purpose of transporting the children, and to persuade the Bulgarians to allow the children to pass through to Turkey. We should also ask the Red Cross to seek a promise from Russia and from other governments not to harm the ship, even if it sails under the Rumanian flag. If we do not succeed in this, we will have to inform the children's parents that they alone must bear responsibility, though we will do all we can to arrange passage for the children.[48]

The plight of European Jewry was still seen in the context of the overall problems of the war. Disparate reports of pogroms, massacres, and expulsions did not yet present a coherent picture of an unprecedented, coordinated German policy of genocide. There was not yet a conviction, therefore, of the need to reorient Zionist policy along mass-rescue lines. At that point, the Yishuv itself was still coping with the threat of enemy invasion of Palestine and the need to mount a defense against anticipated Arab attacks should Rommel's advance reach as far as Palestine.[49]

During the summer of 1942, cumulative reports of mass murder occurring on an unprecedented scale reached Palestine from Europe and were published in the Hebrew press. On 27 and 30 August Richard Lichtheim (the Jewish Agency's delegate to the League of Nations in Geneva, and one of the Zionists' most important sources of information on developments in Europe) dispatched two letters that factually far exceeded previous accounts of Nazi atrocities. These letters, which took a month to reach Palestine, contained trustworthy testimony about the secret plan of Hitler and Germany's top leadership to systematically destroy European Jewry in death camps across Eastern Europe.[50] But the full import of these letters was not yet appreciated.

In September 1942, the Agency executive was treating the European Jewish problem in much the same way as they had two years earlier. The desire of the Hehalutz movement activists to set up a forward base in Istanbul, from which they might keep in touch with comrades in occupied lands, was not acted upon favorably. Political leaders in Jerusalem thought that Haim Barlas, as representative of the immigration department in Istanbul, and Dr. Joseph Goldin, chairman of the Palestine Office there, were quite capable of dealing with such organizational arms. Their tasks, however, usually boiled down to little more than keeping up with correspondence and cables to and from Geneva.

In this atmosphere, a proposal raised at a Jewish Agency executive session on 16 October elicited somewhat greater interest.[51] The idea was to make Palestinian entry permits available to Jewish refugees reaching Turkey. A tenuous parallel existed between the refugees already in Istanbul and refugees from Germany at the outbreak of the war, who had traveled to Trieste, it was argued. Should not the British now treat the refugees in Turkey as they had treated the earlier group?

The arrangement proposed was said to be highly unrealistic, however. There was no free travel provided for Jews between Rumania and Turkey, as there had been between Germany and Trieste. In order for Jews to reach Turkey, it was first necessary to assure their emigration. Otherwise, only limited numbers of individuals would get out, such as those who sailed on the small boats.

As late as 25 October, at a meeting of the executive, Moshe Shapira questioned the factual basis of the fears that chairman Gruenbaum had expressed about the survival of European Jewry:

> All sorts of rumors are reaching us about the murder of Jews by the Nazis. He [Gruenbaum] cabled to all sorts of places, and the replies all say the same thing: that Jews are being sent to labor camps and are disappearing. The situation in the Warsaw ghetto is worsening. The Jewish police there has been abolished and the ghetto committee dismantled. Instead a German commissar has been appointed, with a police force composed of Ukrainians and Latvians.

To all the rumors, Shapira replied: "It seems to me that they all contain a measure of exaggeration. . . ."[52]

Gruenbaum, on the other hand, wanted to mobilize international Jewish communities immediately to inform and warn the world. His colleagues on the executive were skeptical about the ability of the Yishuv to press Jewish and non-Jewish organizations abroad into action on behalf of European Jewry. For that reason, the organization decided to allocate funds for cabling institutions, governments, and Jewish as well as non-Jewish organizations abroad, to urge help for the Jews of Europe. Gruenbaum, who asked for the sum of one hundred pounds, received only fifty.

Several days later, executive committee members were shocked when a group of Jewish civilians who had lived in Palestine before the war arrived in the country from occupied Europe. Through an exchange plan of German nationals and British subjects, these people reached Palestine in the midst of the war. What they had to relate began a turn in the approach of the Yishuv to the plight of European Jewry.

10

Nazi Policy from Deportation to Genocide: Closing the Gates to Jewish Emigration, 1943 to 1944

In 1941, Jewish policy of Germany entered its most radical phase—that of the Final Solution. From that point on, the trend toward giving precedence to ideological considerations above all others became more pronounced. The S.S., the dominant force in anti-Jewish policy since 1939, became virtually the sole executive authority in this area as it took on the task of coordinating the various official bodies operating in countries under German occupation and in Germany, to implement the Final Solution. Approaches to the issue that offered alternatives to genocide were nullified. This was made official by Reichsfuehrer S.S. Heinrich Himmler in the order of 23 October 1941: Jewish emigration from the Reich was henceforth forbidden.[1]

The desire to impose the Final Solution on all the Jews of Europe necessitated coordination and cooperation between Germany and its allies. Apart from Italy, most supported the anti-Semitic policy of Germany. Nevertheless, not all were prepared to go along with the extreme step of annihilation that was now proposed. This reluctance became more significant as the prospects of a German victory gradually faded and the war became ever more costly. In the fall of 1942, after Fieldmarshal Rommel lost the El-Alamein battle in North Africa and the German army was defeated in Leningrad, the allies of Germany were constantly aware of changes in the strategic positions. The course followed by these allied countries may be traced schematically from collaboration to dissociation from German policies, including the anti-Jewish policy. From this period on, skepticism and reserve toward anti-Jewish Nazi policy demonstrated some measure of independence from Germany.

These developments had a decisive impact on Jewish emigration to Palestine. The British policy to bar Palestine to Jewish "enemy aliens" was thus compounded in effect by the German policy of barring Jewish emigration altogether. Aliyah activities were now illegal both at the point of departure and entry. On the other hand, the growing reluctance of the Balkan States to follow Nazi demands became for the Jews in the West a potential political pressure to help their brothers.

Attempts to Close Rumanian Ports to Jewish Emigrants

Himmler's order of October 1941 was transmitted to German embassies abroad and to the special attachés of the RSHA appointed to the diplomatic missions to supervise Jewish matters.[2]

In Bucharest, the German embassy arranged a conference on the subject between its adviser on Jewish affairs, Gustav Richter, and Rumanian vice-premier Mihai Antonescu. This was meant to lead to Rumanian legislation to reinforce Himmler's order. During November and December 1941, while plans for the voyage of the *Struma* proceeded, the two men met twice in order to discuss Germany's new policy.[3] Richter focused on its political, economic, and military aspects. Politically, he argued, the policy was justified for two reasons: first, because Jewish refugees were conducting anti-German propaganda in the Allied countries, and second, because Germany's support of the Arabs precluded providing additional manpower for the Yishuv. Militarily, Richter argued, the policy would halt the flow of Jewish refugees into the British army. The economic factor was linked to the wealth taken out of the Axis countries by Jewish refugees, thereby weakening the Axis and strengthening the Allies.

It is difficult to accept that these arguments alone explained the decision of Germany to cut off Jewish emigration, since the Final Solution was, at this time, being implemented at a furious pace. Richter presented only the a posteriori "rationalizations" with which Germany sought to mask the truly irrational nature of Nazi ideology. This was the purport, too, of the structure and the substance of the discussions between Richter and Mihai Antonescu. Richter raised the issue of legislation in terms of a requirement Germany was making of all its allies—France and Hungary, for example—for their entry into Europe's "new order." Freeing the country from the Jews (the term used was *Evakuierung*) was one of the pillars of this "new order."[4] For that reason, Richter contended, Rumania had to set up legal guidelines to define the Jewish population, conduct a meticulous registration of all those defined as Jews, abolish the existing association of Jewish communities (led by Wilhelm Filderman), and establish a Judenzentrale appointed by the regime and responsible for carrying out the state's directives. The Germans realized that ending emigration would be especially difficult in Rumania, where many officials directly benefited from their role of facilitating Jewish emigration.

Richter was indeed satisfied with the results of his talks with Antonescu, but a close examination of Rumania's implementation of the emigration and deportation policy—two sides of one coin, as far as Germany was concerned—will reveal Rumania's ambivalence on the entire problem.

On 23 January 1942, Eichmann received a further report from Richter on discussions of the emigration question, this time with Marshal Ion Antonescu himself rather than his deputy. The discussion took place under a cloud: the departure of the *Struma* despite German demands and the promises given by the Rumanians. Richter was at pains to point out that Antonescu had apologized for the incident and promised it would not be repeated. The departure took place because certain orders were not carried out by the head of the secret police (the Siguaranza). The officer in charged had been dismissed for his act of insubordination. Ion Antonescu, for his part, fully subscribed to Germany's policy of prohibiting Jewish emigration, Richter added, and Rumania would strictly enforce it. Antonescu pointed, as proof of his determination to stand by this policy, to the fact that Rumanian newspapers were now forbidden to print travel or shipping notices likely to help Jews looking to escape the country.[5]

A survey of Rumanian policy in 1942 shows that many obstacles were placed in the path of those trying to leave, but not to the extent implied by Marshal Ion Antonescu to Richter. The report of their talk raises several questions: how, for instance, would there even be a question of shipping and travel notices for Jews if Jewish emigration was legally forbidden? Then, too, one suspects that Richter's report of the sacking of Rumania's secret police chief was based not on what he was directly told by the head of the Rumanian state himself, but from information about Rumanian affairs gleaned elsewhere. As noted, a small but steady trickle of Jewish refugees continued to leave Rumania on yachts and small vessels throughout 1942, without assistance from Jewish organizations.[6] The boats evaded German naval patrols active in the port of Constantsa and the Bulgarian coast. The refugees were aided by various officials and bureaucrats who had a direct financial interest in helping the boats get away. The Germans employed a network of informers to gauge emigration and interfere in it as much as possible. But with the exception of one vessel, the *Paskarush*, from which refugees were actually removed through German intervention, such boats generally did sail unhindered.[7] It is true, of course, that German countermeasures and the unfortunate case of the *Paskarush* deterred many. This was particularly true of the Jewish leadership, about which more will be said.

Plans to Deport Rumanian Jewry

In conjunction with these events, the RSHA drew up plans to deport Rumania's Jews. On 28 July 1942, Eichmann informed all the agencies involved that deportations to Lublin would begin in September, and that these would be coordinated with Rumania. In August, Radu Lecca, the Rumanian official in charge of Jewish affairs, went to Berlin to finalize details of the operation.[8] The deportations were to be implemented upon his return at the end of the month. Yet some difficulties arose. Apparently, the combined pressure of the RSHA and the German Foreign Office failed to persuade Bucharest to act. The Rumanian official meant to coordinate the operation with a committee set up by Eichmann did not arrive in Germany as scheduled in September. The German railways official who went to Bucharest to arrange for a daily train to the destination point in the east (then the concentration camp at Belzec) found an unwillingness to formulate, let alone finalize, an arrangement to reserve a train for this purpose. He returned to Berlin empty-handed. Just then, Ion Antonescu, who was in Berlin to coordinate the movements of Rumanian troops, agreed to carry out the deportation plan; but he did not go beyond a verbal commitment. Manfred Killinger, the ambassador to Rumania, and Richter approached Mihai Antonescu with a demand for a specific timetable, but he put them off with a vague and ironic response: How was it, he wondered, that Germany, which had only last year opposed the Rumanian-assisted transfer of Jews to Transnistria, now demanded such a deportation?[9]

The Germans could not comprehend the change in Rumania's attitude. It was clear to Killinger that a decision on Marshal Antonescu's part must have been responsible—that is, the change was actually a matter of policy. He believed, however, that the failure to implement plans already made during the summer had its roots in the deteriorating relationship between certain Rumanian and German officials. This applied first of all to the poor reception given to Radu Lecca during his visit to the German Foreign Office in August, and secondly to Richter's aggressive and tactless manner of handling the authorities in Bucharest. Killinger demanded Richter's removal. In December, he wrote to Berlin reporting that Marshal Ion Antonescu was willing to deport Bolshevik Jews but would refuse to carry out extreme measures against the Jews as a whole.[10]

Himmler apparently realized by January 1943 that no general deportation of Rumanian Jews would take place unless the Bucharest regime was changed.[11]

But the explanation for Rumania's position rests neither on Lecca's hurt sensibilities nor on Richter's clumsy handling of his assignment. Richter understood that more substantive considerations were involved, chiefly the growing skepticism in Rumania's leadership about the wisdom of an all-out pro-German strategy. Germany suffered particularly serious defeats on its eastern front in the fall of 1942. Rumania lost many of its forces at Stalingrad, and Marshal Ion Antonescu blamed the German command's cavalier attitude about the excessive loss of lives of Rumanian troops. This attitude, the Rumanians believed, was responsible for a heavy casualty rate.[12]

Jewish leaders in Rumania kept up a constant protest against Rumania's Jewish policy, exploiting all available arguments. Wilhelm Filderman[13] pointed out in his petitions to Marshal Ion Antonescu that official steps against Jews were not only illegal and immoral, but also detracted from the national honor of Rumania, making the country Germany's lackey. Thus, he argued, Rumania had deported Jews to Transnistria, unlike Hungary and Italy, which had opted not to deport their Jews. Filderman's contention that the Transnistria deportations were carried out in response to German demands is not, in fact, supported by the evidence, but his argument did apply to existing plans for deportation to the east. Ion Antonescu was sensitive on this point, and his national pride was pricked, which probably added to his disinclination to comply with German plans. Although an unashamed anti-Semite, Ion

Antonescu held himself responsible for the Jews of the Regat, who had been part of old Rumania since its establishment in 1878, as opposed to those of Bukovina and Bessarabia, who, in his opinion, had betrayed Rumania to the Soviets in 1940.

A cluster of factors, therefore, led Rumania to modify its position on the Jewish issue. This new stance would crystallize—with certain variations—as the war progressed. We may conclude that in the fall of 1942 the Rumanians believed they could radically alter their Jewish policy, but the Germans made it clear that, though they might not be able to carry out deportations without Rumania's cooperation, they would not permit the Rumanians to deviate from what the Germans considered the minimal requirements of their political interests.

The Transnistria Plan[14]

Transnistria is a region situated between the rivers Bug and Dniestr, and although not annexed to Rumania, it came under Rumanian administration following its conquest from the Soviets. About 150,000 Jews were exiled to Transnistria, mainly from Bukowina and parts of Bessarabia retaken by Rumania in the summer of 1941. A year later, only half the Jews remained alive. Transnistria was one huge death camp where the exiled died of starvation, disease, and epidemics as well as physical abuse. Their plight aroused the concern of Jewish and non-Jewish organizations, and the Jewish leadership of Rumania desperately sought ways to help the Transnistria prisoners.

On 9 October 1942, Filderman was invited to meet with two Rumanian businessmen, former owners of the Conrad Star shipping company (since transferred to German ownership). The two had continued to work for the firm and maintained close relations with its German owners as well as other German figures. They proposed that Filderman pay for a Jewish emigration operation that they would organize. His reaction was positive, but he insisted that safe conduct be guaranteed for the emigrants. This clearly implied an assurance from the German authorities. Filderman also insisted that Jews in Transnistria be the first to emigrate, and that, in preparation for their departure, they be returned to Rumania. The two Rumanian businessmen, Burstyn and Tester, promised to transmit Filderman's requests to the proper authorities and bring back an answer. Shortly after, Radu Lecca made a similar proposal to the Judenzentrale, which fell under his responsibility.

Through Ion Antonescu's personal physician, a reliable source, Filderman soon learned that this proposal had not originated with Burstyn and Tester but with the government. The Rumanian authorities were interested in a ransom-for-emigration deal, to involve the exchange of 70,000 Transnistria prisoners for 200,000 Rumanian lei per person (then about $500). The refugees were to embark from the port of Constantsa and would travel to Palestine.

Throughout, the Rumanians continuously affirmed that the Germans had given their consent to the plan, and even hinted that Killinger, the German ambassador, was one of its initiators. There is, however, no evidence to support such a claim.[15]

The first mention of the scheme in German documents occurs on December 12, about two months after it was first raised.[16] Killinger reported the proposal to Berlin in terms that support Lecca's representations to the Judenzentrale. Killinger spoke of 70,000 Jews and suggested the sum of 200,000 lei per person. He noted that the information was given to him by Lecca, who was privy to all aspects of the plan, and who reported that both Marshal Ion Antonescu and Mihai Antonescu supported the idea. According to him, the refugees were destined for Iran, Syria, and Palestine. The technical details, including transport, had yet to be worked out. Killinger told Lecca verbally that there was no chance of the plan's receiving German approval, given the political, economic, and military interests that Germany wished to protect. Killinger inferred from this that although Ion Antonescu was eager to be rid of Jews, he would no longer cooperate in carrying out radical measures. He asked the Foreign Office to instruct him on the desired response. It was a serious matter, involving an apparent shift in Rumania's policy. Germany needed to exercise caution, given the already strained relations between the two countries.

On 9 January 1943, almost a month after the ambassador in Bucharest had sent his message, the Foreign Office sent its reply.[17] The plan was unequivocally rejected, and Killinger was instructed to make every effort to prevent its implementation. The cable pointed out that emigration ran counter to the Nazi principle of a "comprehensive European solution of the Jewish problem." The reply's phrasing makes it clear that the Rumanian offer was not primarily perceived as an overture to the Jews as such, but as a signal to the Allies that Rumania was altering its political orientation. It was unlikely that the Allies would treat Rumania any differently, but they were liable to interpret the Rumanian step as a sign of faltering Axis unity. The cable concluded with a commitment to help Rumania solve its Jewish problem, namely by deportation of Jews to the east.

Germany's position slammed the door on the Transnistria plan. Jewish organizations in Rumania and outside it, unaware of this, continued to discuss the matter. But their initial caution turned to skepticism as the negotiations dragged on. On 2 January, before the Foreign Office reply to Killinger, Filderman proposed a more modest plan to transfer 5,000 orphans from Transnistria to Rumania while travel onward for them was explored.[18] Rumania seemed to approve the idea. Richter learned of it, and quickly informed Lecca that he must urge the Rumanian government to reject the plan. He reported this to Eichmann, enclosing a translation of Filderman's memorandum.[19] Thus, the limited proposal to rescue the children was temporarily blocked. In the spring of 1943, however, the proposal once again became a priority of the German-Rumanian agenda. Discussions on the matter continued over two years, and will be referred to later.

The Nazi Blockade of Jewish Emigration from the Balkans, 1943

Those in charge of Jewish affairs at the German Foreign Office and the RSHA believed that the prohibition against Jewish emigration from Europe was on the verge of breaking down. That was the impression created both by informants and public statements regarding the evacuation of Jewish children from the Balkans to Palestine. Because various sources reported on the selfsame plan, it appeared that a number of similar initiatives were afoot, so that the emigration plans took on bloated proportions.

Thus, Filderman's request for the transfer of 5,000 children from Transnistria was linked with a better-known plan under which Britain, early in 1942, had approved the immigration of 270 children from Bulgaria to Palestine (through the Youth Aliyah program). The Germans received information in December 1942, subsequently confirmed by a statement from the British colonial secretary, Oliver Stanley, that 4,500 children and 500 adult escorts would be allowed to emigrate. Stanley's statement of 3 February 1943, regarding the designation of 29,000 entry certificates still available under the terms of the 1939 White Paper therefore struck the Germans as yet another stage in a Jewish emigration campaign.[20] "These plans must be strenuously opposed," the German Foreign Office and the RSHA made clear. In order to sabotage such operations, they used an array of informants, agents, and representatives of the RSHA, the Wehrmacht, and the Navy to watch any movements by Jews and anyone likely to aid them. These sources sent detailed instructions to Berlin on the steps necessary to block emigration attempts.

On 4 February, Eberhard von Thadden, the deputy Foreign Office official in charge of Jewish matters, wrote to the German ambassador in Rumania instructing him to demand that Bucharest retract any decision permitting the emigration of Jews.[21] A similar instruction was sent to the embassy in Sofia. The reasons cited were, again, linked to military considerations, propaganda, and the Arab position. Most important, however, was the "comprehensive European plan" to solve the Jewish question. Another letter was sent on 1 March to Bucharest, this time signed by Karl Rademacher (the late head of the Jewish and the German national desk).[22] The letter expressed deep concern about the progress made in January and February toward carrying out the plan for a "youth emigration." Two groups of children had already set out from Hungary and had arrived in Constantinople.

Rademacher stressed that Axis disunity on the emigration issue might endanger agreements in other areas of endeavor as well. The Allies would be sure to exploit such fissures if they were apparent. The Foreign Office particularly feared contacts between German allies and the Western powers— a possibility that Killinger had hinted at in a reply to Luther at the Foreign Office, referring to the Transnistria plan. Rumania hoped for more generous treatment by the Allies, Killinger indicated, without entering into specifics. Rademacher in his letter generalized the issue and made it more urgent. The determination of Germany to prevent Jews from escaping via the Balkans stemmed first of all from its dedication to the Final Solution, but was reinforced by considerations of Axis solidarity. The ideological aspects and the pragmatic ones were complementary here. The Foreign Office was fully aware that the Allies stood ready to capitalize on any evidence of disunity among Axis countries and wanted to use the Jewish refugee issue as a lever.

Yet the Germans were unable to prevent the departure of children's contingents from Rumania. In response, Germans stationed at the Bulgarian border town of Sviligrad were unusually brutal in inspecting a group, consisting of seventy-four children, that was about to cross into Turkey. Two children, Polish nationals, were even removed from the train and sent to the east.[23] These terror tactics had their intended effect, and the Rumania travel company that arranged passage for children's groups was forced to ask the German embassy in Bucharest for clearance to send another group on 6 April 1943. This gave the Germans the opportunity to state their position clearly and prevent the departure. In discussing this with a Rumania travel company representative, a German embassy official explained that the Final Solution would include Jewish children as well. If Rumanian agencies tried to circumvent German prohibitions, Jewish escapees would be stopped in Bulgaria and sent elsewhere. The reference to Poland was only slightly veiled.[24] That very day, Killinger instructed Radu Lecca to notify Dr. Gingold, head of the Judenzentrale, that the seventy-four children would be arrested. Accordingly, the organizers, including the chairman of the Zionist Organization in Rumania, Misho Benvenisti, decided to cancel the departure.

Still the German Foreign Office was not satisfied. Information arrived from Constantinople about a thousand transit visas to be granted by Turkey to children and their escorts and about negotiations between the Turks and Jewish organizations regarding Jewish refugee or transit camps to be set up in Turkey.[25] Other informants reported that the Hungarian and Rumanian governments had signaled their approval of such an emigration. This greatly troubled the RSHA and the Foreign Office. The German ambassador in Bulgaria was instructed to press Sofia to deny transit documents to Jewish children. The Bulgarians reportedly hesitated, apparently for humanitarian reasons, but mounting German pressure caused them to cancel permits already granted.[26] Police in the town of Russe were instructed to stop a group if it nevertheless reached Bulgaria. The German ambassador was also informed that this policy would apply to future cases.

Eichmann was not backed up by the cables received from Bucharest and Sofia on 12 April, however.[27] Five days earlier, he had received a disturbing report that Bulgaria and Rumania were duplicitous in their avowed adherence to Hitler's Jewish policy. Their pledges to prevent emigration were apparently not being fulfilled; indeed, they even showed signs of relaxing some laws on Jewish legal status and property ownership. Britain was in fact pressuring the Bulgarians to permit 4,500 Jewish children and their guardians to leave for Palestine.

Still more alarming was a report that reached Eichmann on 3 May 1943, to the effect that a Greek ship, the *Smyrni,* flying the Greek flag, and a second ship with a Bulgarian registration were preparing to transport Jews.[28] There

Youth Aliyah group members from Hungary and Rumania in Atlit detention Camp, March 1943.

was, it seemed, a secret plan to take 1,500 people out of Bulgaria and others out of the Bukovina and Bessarabia regions. Other reports indicated that Rumania had still not utterly abandoned the Transnistria plan and that discussions with Jews were ongoing regarding the exit of 5,000 orphans to Palestine. The Germans learned, too, that the Jewish Agency tried to obtain British permission to use two Rumanian ships, the *Bessarabia* and the *Transylvania,* captured by the British in 1941 in Istanbul, to transport the Transnistria orphans.[29] Official Rumanian sources claimed that the Fuehrer himself had assented to the plan when Marshal Antonescu met him in Germany in April 1943.[30]

The German navy in the Black Sea, asked to prevent and deter emigration, informed Bucharest that Jewish emigrants on Rumanian vessels ought to be forbidden to embark, as the British would confiscate ships nearing Istanbul and important Axis shipping materiel would be lost. Furthermore, the German navy announced that it would not grant safe conduct to vessels bearing Jews.[31] This effectively prevented the use of such small craft for emigration, even though they would have sailed under Red Cross protection, according to terms agreed by Jewish and non-Jewish organizers in Rumania and by Marshal Ion Antonescu at a meeting in Bucharest on 24 May 1943.[32] But the Red Cross protection could be granted only if there was safe conduct.

Certain German officials tended to favor even more drastic measures to stop emigration. On 27 May, Admiral Fricke, commander of the Black Sea fleets, issued a top secret order regarding "renewed preparations for Jewish emigration from Rumania via Turkey." The order stated that since this defied German orders and Bucharest had taken an equivocal position, Germany would act unilaterally to prevent Jewish emigration. They would act outside Rumanian territorial waters, capture the vessels, escort them to the Crimea, and there mete out "proper treatment." If for any reason it proved impossible to effect a capture and escort, then the ships were to be sunk. Such actions were taken unbeknownst to the Rumanians, in order to avoid "political complications." General Doenitz, navy commander in chief, objected to Fricke's order and canceled it for the time being.[33]

During the summer of 1943, the Germans were unable to put Fricke's radical proposal to the test—and not only because of opposition in the German naval command. Although a number of ships were available to the Jewish organizations, they were unable to use even one during those months.[34] Nevertheless, the Germans felt concern. It was at this time that the Swiss envoy in Berlin, Pelcher, approached the German authorities on behalf of the British government with the request to authorize the emigration of 5,000 Jewish children from Eastern Europe to Palestine. A second British request was similarly transmitted: that safe conduct be granted to a ship bringing Jewish children from Bulgaria to Palestine.[35] The British requests were part of a group of similar proposals accepted by the Allies in May and June of 1943, and referred to in German documents as "*action juif.*" These included the transfer of 500 children from Holland to Sweden, the emigration of 2,000 children from France, 500 from Belgium, and 500 to be sent from Holland via Portugal to Palestine. Argentina had offered to accept 1,000 children. Even Hungary and Slovakia were prepared to permit Jewish children to leave under the aegis of the Red Cross.[36]

Over the summer of 1943, various German agencies considered formulating a response that would stop such "actions" without harming German interests. Their intention was to strangle the requests yet somehow avoid making them a major issue. To that end, Himmler met with von Ribbentrop, and a conference was then held between the various department heads of the Foreign Ministry, the governmental secretary, and representatives of the RSHA, including Eichmann. The conference essentially affirmed that all such requests were to be turned down as part of a unified Axis policy.[37] The decision was framed rather adamantly, confirming the German principle that no Jewish emigration could be considered, certainly not to Palestine, a country that Germany had promised to the Mufti (the central leader of the Arab national movement in Palestine, who was expelled by the British in 1938). Where the emigration to other countries was concerned, this might take place in the form of an exchange for German prisoners or other Axis nationals, on a one-to-four or one-to-ten basis. If Britain wanted to arrange for Jewish children to emigrate, the British Cabinet would have to declare that their destination was Britain itself, and for the 5,000 children, 20,000 Germans or Axis nationals under forty years of age would be exchanged. Safe conduct was to be denied to neutral or Red Cross ships bearing Jewish refugees.

It was also decided to inform the Rumanian government that, contrary to the Rumanians' understanding, the German foreign minister had not lent approval to the emigration of 7,000 Jewish children, but only agreed to consider the request. Finally, it was decided that the German government would retain the option of responding favorably to such requests when and if this could be useful for German propaganda.

A comment by Eichmann during preparations for that conference aptly illustrates the German virulence regarding the fate of the Jews at that juncture. Eichmann told von Thadden that if a policy of "population exchange" were accepted, it ought to be done very quickly, as it would soon be impossible "from the technical point of view" to effect such a policy, given the way anti-Jewish laws were being implemented.[38] Notwithstanding that interministerial discussions were being held to prevent the survival of several thousand children and their guardians, what is so striking about Eichmann's comment is that it reflects the terrible degree to which the Germans' Final Solution had succeeded. The entire discussion of emigration was a side issue in the context of a genocide taking place so rapidly it would have been extremely difficult to interrupt.

The German position on Jewish emigration in 1943 was an unqualified no. Correspondence between the Foreign Ministry and the RSHA returned frequently to efforts being made to sabotage each attempt to rescue Jews from German-controlled and Axis territory. But in 1944, Germany's allies seemed increasingly determined to renounce Germany's Jewish policy. The Balkan States believed the Allies would go easier on any country that improved the status of its Jews, and attempted to sidestep their obligations to Germany. But Berlin did not alter its policy on Jewish emigration throughout this period, not even when it became apparent that its satellites were unprepared to implement that policy. Germany continued to oppose Jewish emigration even when, as we shall see, German patrol boats were guiding refugee boats through Black Sea minefields off the Bulgarian and Rumanian coasts.[39] At every juncture, when German agencies had to choose between permitting or preventing the emigration of Jews, they consistently chose to bar it. A clear example is their handling of the Turkish ship *Tari*.

The Tari *Episode*[40]

The *Tari* was able to accommodate about 1,500 passengers, and its owners had proposals from both Jews and non-Jews regarding Jewish emigration from the Balkans to Turkey. They considered sending the vessel as far as Palestine. For such a voyage, an official Turkish permit was necessary. It was procured in the spring of 1944 when the special U.S. representative, Ira Hirschmann, arrived in Turkey.[41] The Turks agreed to allow the ship to make one trip to Rumania to take on a group of children if Germany would grant the ship safe conduct and guarantee Red Cross protection. The Red Cross approved, and asked the German ambassador in Turkey, Franz von Papen, to forward to Berlin its request for safe conduct.

This took place on 25 March 1944. Von Thadden immediately rejected the request. But von Papen, who anticipated a deeply negative reception, was reluctant to transmit Berlin's response. Several days later, the Turkish foreign minister went in person to von Papen with the same request, which compounded the German ambassador's quandary.[42] The Turkish minister urged von Papen to present himself to von Ribbentrop—an even more delicate task.

In the interim, the German Foreign Office received the same requests through its ambassadors in Rumania and Switzerland and from Red Cross headquarters in Geneva. All expressed humanitarian concerns, and von Ribbentrop, the German foreign minister and a great supporter of radical anti-Jewish policy, had to consider his response carefully. On 4 April, about ten days after he had first transmitted the Turkish inquiry to Berlin, von Papen cabled yet again to explain the significance of the joint effort being made to persuade Germany to react positively this time.[43]

Three weeks later, von Ribbentrop advised von Papen that the request for safe conduct would be approved. He stressed that this was not to be made a precedent, nor did it represent a change in Germany's policy against Jewish emigration. Yet, just after the cable was sent to Ankara, von Ribbentrop telephoned the head of the Jewish Department at the Foreign Office with the urgent message to cancel the previous communication and await another. The reasons for this change of course remain unclear, but as late as 7 July—two months later—when further queries about safe conduct for the *Tari* were received, the Foreign Office again responded that it needed another month before an answer could be given.[44] Clearly, no answer was tantamount to a refusal.

During those weeks of waiting for a reply from Berlin, some 1,000 Jews were going from Constantsa to Istanbul aboard five converted cargo ships, without the benefit of German safe conduct but with the firm knowledge that German naval forces patrolled the Black Sea. These five ships carried roughly the equivalent number of passengers planned for the *Tari*, yet Germany allowed them to push off, at a time when Admiral Fricke had his earlier proposal to sink Jewish refugee boats. The explanation undoubtedly lies in the strict orders to Rumanian harbor authorities in January and March from Marshal Antonescu that refugee boats were to be permitted to embark without interference from German patrol boats. General Doenitz, for his part, countermanded Fricke's plan, possibly because of Antonescu's unequivocal position.[45]

At any rate, German coastal patrols led the Jewish refugee ships safely through the minefields to open sea. German ambassador Killinger tried personally to appeal to Antonescu to enforce the prohibition on Jewish emigration, but he was refused an appointment with the marshal in July 1944 and the appeal was snappily rejected. From a discussion he held with Mihai Antonescu, Killinger understood that there was no chance of altering the marshal's position.[46]

Did the Germans indeed abandon their strenuous attempts to prevent Jewish emigration, as suggested by Fricke? This question may partially be answered by examining the case of the *Mefkura,* a refugee ship sunk in the Black Sea.

The Sinking of the Mefkura[47]

On the night of 3 August 1944, three Turkish ships departed from Constantsa. Arranged by the Mossad's agents in Turkey and the Zionist Organization in Rumania, the vessels were carrying about 1,000 Jews destined for Palestine. The boats were called the *Bulbul,* the *Morina,* and the *Mefkura*, and they were a "flotilla" bringing Jews out of Europe without official permission.[48] The *Bulbul* took the lead and the slower *Mefkura* could be found at the rear, as Germany's naval command transmitted to the captains the coordinates of the mine-free channel. Both German and Rumanian patrol boats escorted the ships out of the harbor.

The first day of the journey was relatively uneventful. A minor repair to the *Mefkura*'s engine was made quickly. On the night of 4 August, flares lit up the ship's deck and it was ordered to halt. Subsequent events are hazy, owing to discrepancies between two versions of events given by the captain of the ship and the survivors. The captain initially claimed the boat was fired upon before he was able to make out warning signals or respond to them. Later, however, he stated that he was ordered to halt the ship and he instructed the passengers to put on life jackets, explaining what the signals meant. Before the passengers were able to follow his instructions, he said, the boat was fired upon by an unknown attacker. The captain added that the firing came from a black object in the water that appeared to be an approaching submarine. Some of the survivors have testified that there were indeed flares but that the captain took no precautionary steps. Instead, they claimed, he blacked out the ship's lights and attempted to flee, after which the firing commenced.

The *Mefkura* was hit dead center by the third shell fired, and amid a tremendous explosion, more firing was directed at the sinking ship. Most of the passengers, who had been asleep, were caught in the ship's hold and drowned. Several dozen jumped overboard in a panic without life jackets, while the captain and his crew took the ship's only lifeboat. Firing continued even after the *Mefkura* disappeared beneath the waves, aimed apparently at helpless survivors in the water. Toward morning, five of the 320 passengers, after hours in the cold sea, were rescued by those aboard the *Bulbul,* which had been stopped by several patrol boats before the *Mefkura* was hit. According to witnesses, these were similar to the craft that had given escort from Constantsa. But after establishing its credentials, the *Bulbul* had been allowed to continue on its way.

Who attacked and sank the *Mefkura*? Was this a German action conforming to plans since May 1943, to deal with refugee ships that the Germans were unable to prevent from sailing? Was this an act of violent deterrence, reminiscent of what had been done at Sviligrad in March 1943 to the children en route to Palestine, which successfully put a stop to overland emigration attempts? There is no simple or ready answer.

Undoubtedly, it was thought that the Germans deliberately sank the ship. The survivors' testimony and the logic of the events themselves indicated this. Eyewitnesses stated that three patrol boats of the type used by the German coastal patrol in Constantsa had been the attackers. This was corroborated by passengers and the captain of the *Bulbul* in testimony about the boats that stopped that ship and demanded a show of identification. Some survivors also claimed to have heard shouting in German from the direction of the attacking boats after the *Mefkura* sank. Yet the *Mefkura*'s captain insisted that he was waylaid by a submarine, and that he saw it coming near the scene of the wreck once he was safely in the lifeboat.

An investigating committee established in Constantinople, assisted by the British naval attaché in Ankara, accepted the captain's version featuring the submarine and thus rejected the testimony of survivors on this point. Their final report found it impossible to determine the identity of the attacker with certainty, or decide whether the attack had been deliberate or not. Nevertheless, the villainous British press depicted the sinking of the *Mefkura* by a German submarine, and this was generally accepted at the time.

After the war, the incident was reexamined by a German investigator, Jurgen Rohwer, who was instructed by the German courts to probe thoroughly and determine exactly who did it. Reopening of the case took place when survivors petitioned for compensation. Rohwer found that the vessel was indeed attacked by a submarine, but that it was not German but Soviet, and it was likely to have launched the attack by mistake. Rohwer's investigation brought to light that the Germans had removed their submarines from the area following a period of high tension with Ankara over the erroneous sinking of two Turkish boats. Soviet submarines were active in the area, however. One reported by radio the sinking of a Turkish vessel carrying 200 soldiers. The report also mentioned that a small boat was seen near the wreck. The place, time, and details of the report convinced Rohwer that it in fact referred to the *Mefkura*.

The survivors' stories about German patrol boats did not, in Rohwer's opinion, negate his conclusion. He believed that the captain, as an old seaman, would have been better able to identify the attacker than his inexperienced and panicked passengers. The latter were convinced that the Germans wanted to attack them, and were thus disposed to view the patrol boats as the culprits. Their claim to have heard the attackers shouting in German was incredible, given the din of the firing and the distance away of the assault boat. It should be noted that Rohwer did not relate in his report the interception of the *Bulbul*, and he therefore does not raise the possibility of a link between the patrol boats that stopped the *Bulbul* and those that allegedly attacked the *Mefkura*.[49]

If we assume that the Germans allowed the three ships to embark but sank only the *Mefkura*, then we must come up with an explanation. Those involved in arranging the voyage from Rumania focused on the identity of those aboard the *Mefkura*. According to them, Rumanian counterintelligence had informed the Germans—a contention later proven false—that aboard the *Mefkura* were officers from General Tadeusz Bor-Komorowski's Polish (London-directed underground) Home Army. That is why, it was charged, the Germans wanted to sink the ship. This thesis is supported by an unsigned communiqué sent on 8 August from Section 2 of the German Naval High Command:

> The Jews are continuing to send Polish and Serbo-Croatian partisans for the Allied forces in the Near East through their emigration offices, placing them on boats used for transporting emigrants. We have identified those listed below as passengers on the *Mefkura* when it left Rumania, who boarded the ship with false papers supplied by the Jewish partisan movements in the various emigration organizations . . . [here a list of persons appears]... we allowed the ships to depart in order not to draw the suspects' attention, and informed the counterintelligence department of the navy so that it might take the necessary steps. The above-mentioned did not reach their destination.[50]

The document does not give accurate information, nor did its authors demonstrate knowledge of the Polish army at that time. How did it fall into the hands of Jews involved in rescue work, and who would have had an interest in passing such information along? It is impossible to ascertain from oral testimony how and why this might have occurred, and the entire episode must remain an open question.

In the context of German policy prior to and during August 1944, the deliberate sinking of a refugee boat is not entirely implausible. On 17 August 1944, the idea of intercepting such ships was raised yet again among German military and political figures in Rumania, though in somewhat different form. After the three ships had sailed, and before other plans were canceled in response to the sinking of the *Mefkura,* the German embassy learned of a major effort being planned for the emigration of 4,000 Jews aboard the *Smyrni* and other vessels. Killinger again tried to exert pressure on Antonescu to put a stop to the plan, in meetings between the ambassador and the Rumanian vice-premier (12 and 14 August), but he was again rebuffed.[51] Then the naval authorities were directed to intercept the boats. This time, however, the word *Versenkung* (sinking) was not used. If we take into account that the proposal came during the German retreat from Transnistria, barely a week before Rumania surrendered to the Allies, it is possible to understand the significance of the plan.

These facts provide the setting for the rescue attempts that were made by Jewish and non-Jewish organizations, including efforts to organize the rescue of European Jews through illegal immigration to Palestine, to which we now return our attention.

11

The Evolution of
Zionist Rescue Policy

Facing a New Reality

The dilemmas of illegal immigration brought Zionist leaders to an impasse by 1942. Although the political strategy that was to have saved the *Struma* demonstrably failed, there was no far-reaching critique of overall Zionist policy. Instead, as in 1941, the leadership banked on passivity. Spontaneous attempts to reach Palestine were even hailed, but this was a far cry from leaders taking the initiative in planning immigration operations. Zionists derived satisfaction from Lord Cranborne's announcement that Jews who reached Palestine on their own could receive the necessary certificates, which would be subtracted from the standing quota, but they did not capitalize on this by expanding the activities of illegal aliyah.

Both the British and the Zionists were largely reactive and passive at the time. Britain, having enunciated a new policy, remained troubled by the plausible prospect of large numbers of refugees leaving the Balkans and stamping toward Palestine. The Zionists, for their part, complacently anticipated the arrival of such refugees who would probably be permitted to remain in Palestine and thus put British policy to the test.

The Germans, however, and the Jews (as much as they were able) were far from passive during 1942. The Germans were implementing their Final Solution against the Jews of Europe. The Jews, for their part, though trapped in Nazi-controlled Europe, kept up a desperate search for avenues of escape. But when asked to report on the current situation, Rabbi Dov Weismandl, an Orthodox leader from Slovakia, wrote to the representatives of Palestine Jewry that "No prisoner can release himself."[1] In Palestine, however, the leadership had not yet hit upon the idea that if they were to do anything to help the Jews of Europe, they would have to pour all their energies into the task and resort to unconventional tactics.

*

In retrospect, the fall of 1942 stands as a turning point in the Yishuv's perception of the fate of European Jewry. It was then that the position of the Yishuv improved, with the threat of a German invasion lessening and war-long economic recession easing in Palestine. Market conditions improved, and there was a new demand for labor. The Mandatory administration accordingly agreed to permit the immigration quota to rise.[2] Taking advantage of this development, the Jewish Agency's immigration department requested entry certificates for Polish Jewish refugees who had fled to the Soviet Union and now sought to escape, in line with a recent Polish-Soviet accord. Some difficulty was encountered in determining the number of Jews who were to be included in the total Polish refugee category. As relatively few Polish Jews managed to reach Palestine in this manner, Agency officials—loath to see certificates unused—proposed to allocate entry permits to Jews from Middle Eastern countries who had long sought to immigrate.

Toward the end of 1942, as the Yishuv geared up for economic and social revitalization, a group of seventy-two men, women, and children arrived from Nazi-occupied Europe. These were Palestine residents who were traveling or visiting family in Europe when the war broke out and had been trapped until the belligerents arranged a transfer of civilian nationals. The Jewish Agency appealed to the British government. When German nationals had been caught in similar situations, Berlin had been willing to accede to an exchange. After lengthy negotiations, three such groups were released, the largest containing seventy-two. Another, released early in 1941, had been spared the Germans' harshest treatment. Others, by contrast, had experienced ghettoization, starvation, deportations, and labor camps. They had beheld the machinery of genocide and described in detail what they knew, including the use of gas for extermination in the death camps. The full horror of the Jewish tragedy was starkly revealed.

European Jewry and the Yishuv now stood divided. For the one, the future held only death and destruction; for the other, having lived through a period of relative hardship and danger, tomorrow signified new achievements and development. Such sharp contrasts might well have created a certain distance between the two communities. In reality, in the consciousness of the Jews of Palestine, their fate and that of European Jewry were inseparable. Over half the Jewish population of Palestine had immigrated to the country after 1933, and the overwhelming majority still had family in Europe. To them, the Nazi exterminators had an immediate and personal significance. This much can readily be seen in letters to newspapers, appeals to community leaders, and personal correspondence, as well as in offers to undertake dangerous missions to aid victims and bring relief to the ghettos.[3]

Private reactions found their echo in public responses. There were public statements by political figures, editorials in the press, and contributions by leading writers and intellectuals. These typically combined agony and profound grief over the destruction of entire communities with an indelible sense of isolation and guilt. There was guilt for the fact that those living in Palestine were not with the victims in their extremity, and for the fact that while the mass murderers were claiming their victims unopposed in Europe, there had been little clear awareness in Palestine of the full import of what was happening. The tide of outrage swept over those who knew but did nothing, those who wished not to know, the murderers themselves, and in some sense, perhaps, over the victims, too. Guilt and outrage were compounded by shame—shame for mankind and for the Jews—and a desire to identify those responsible: responsible for failing to realize the truth or even suppressing it; responsible for preventing, by their indifference, help from reaching those in need; responsible for the tragic sense of impotence that gripped the Jewish people of the free world.[4]

Side by side with the overwhelming shock that struck the Yishuv, however, came a searing sobriety manifested at two levels: on the one hand a revulsion for, hatred, and fear of what the Nazi regime had set out to do to the Jews; and on the other, a deep traumatization from what seemed so unbelievable and so unprecedented.

The first-level response was reinforced as the war dragged on and further information about Nazi barbarism was published in the Jewish and international press. Associated with this first, "rational" response was a dawning realization: while the brutality of the Nazis indeed exceeded any past atrocities, the fact was that in a war so total the very worst was to be expected and the numbers of Jewish victims might be expected to swell accordingly. Although the Yishuv leaders, in particular, realized that the Nazi excesses went beyond any persecution the Jews had experienced in their history, and although such men as Weizmann and Ben-Gurion pointed out early on that to the Nazis, Jews represented the first-rank enemy, still, they tended to think of Nazi persecution as part of one long continuum with acts of Jew hatred in the past and as essential to the experience of Exile itself.[5] Perhaps because of this, it was difficult for them to piece together the individual items of unspeakable horror to form a coherent picture of something new and unprecedented. Thus, it may have been their perception of Jewish history as precisely a history of persecution that made it more difficult for them to realize that this time means and ends had been joined to make the death of the Jews an absolute goal: the Final Solution. The diabolically systematic way in which the Nazis pursued their goal, and their strict adherence to what had been defined as a major war aim of the Third Reich, were elements that only gradually filtered through to some of the leading minds of the Yishuv. Only then was there a response at the "irrational" level, where no historical explanation could possibly come to grips with what was so incredible, so shockingly new.[6]

These considerations may help to explain why Shertok, arriving in England in late November 1942, after the Jewish Agency's first public reaction to accounts from exchanged civilians, was quite sure the information on him was something as yet unknown and unexpected. Upon arrival, however, he was shocked to discover that the facts of the Final Solution had been known in England in some detail for some time.[7]

Formulation of a new policy demanded sober reevalutation of everything that had taken place since 1933 and an assessment of what might be expected in the years to come. In late 1942 and early 1943, this was particularly difficult to achieve. Different Zionist leaders arrived at often opposed conclusions. For example, Richard Lichtheim, the Agency's representative in Geneva, was in constant communication with Jewish communities in Europe and formed a different opinion from Yitzhak Gruenbaum, who received Lichtheim's reports.

In September 1942, Lichtheim had sent his good friend Nahum Goldmann, then in the United States, an extremely pessimistic letter. In it he stated his view that the Jewish people and Zionism itself no longer had any future. The Jews of Eastern Europe were no more: those who had not yet fallen victim to the Nazis were unlikely to escape. A very few might survive, especially Jews in Western Europe hidden by Gentiles. When the war ended, there would be no one left to care about fulfilling the Zionist mission. In the West, where most surviving Jews would be, they would no doubt return to their former homes, rebuild their lives, and resume assimilation. Only the Jews of the Islamic world would remain, but it was not for these that Zionism had sought a solution.

Gruenbaum, on the other hand, reached a diametrically opposed conclusion. As he saw it, the remnant Zionist movement in Palestine now bore the entire burden of responsibility for the future of the Jewish people. Only the Yishuv could provide the nucleus for renewal of the nation. Therefore, he argued, the Yishuv was charged with a "mission of redemption," and it must wage a "struggle for redemption." It dare not deviate from that task, regardless of the difficult days ahead, despite grief over the great destruction and tragedy overtaking Jewry.

It should be remembered that Gruenbaum was one of the outstanding leaders of Polish Jewry. Indeed, in the eyes of many in the Yishuv and among its leaders, Gruenbaum personified Polish Jewry. He had immigrated to Palestine in the mid-thirties, following long years of service to the Zionist cause and as a Jewish representative in the Polish Sejm. He had led the Rescue Committee for Polish Jewry—known as the "Committee of the Four"—from the outset of the war. This was the man who now spoke of the necessity to maintain Zionist enterprise and struggle for redemption.

Most of the Yishuv's leaders agreed more with Gruenbaum's grim determination than with Lichtheim's utter despondency. But they still faced the question: what could be done to aid those Jews still alive in Europe? How could they be rescued? The only large populations that had as yet escaped decimation were in the Balkans, satellites of Nazi Germany. There, too, the Jews faced a worsening situation and a heightened vulnerability. Even though the German advance had been halted, an end to the war was not imminent. Any attempt to rescue Jews required immediate action.

The Yishuv leadership was guided by the accurate supposition that, even had the Allies made rescue one of their war aims, their ability to affect German policy was extremely limited in the fall of 1942. Given the exigencies that ruled out negotiating with Germany, that prohibited contributing to the German economy or transferring foreign currency to occupied areas, there was little the Allies were able to do. Nevertheless, many Zionist leaders sensed that the Final Solution was a central ideological principle for the Nazis. This understanding prompted the Zionists to demand immediate rescue action by the Allies. Without a concerted effort from the Allies, there was no hope of slowing down or stopping the Final Solution. Yet, under the circumstances, the Zionists recognized that the Allies had to fight the war on many fronts under terms already set, which the Zionists also accepted. This somehow undercut the force of Zionist demands that such rescues be assigned top priority.

The Yishuv had no leverage over the Allies in seeking rescue activity. The Jews of Palestine were just as dependent on the British and the Americans as were other peoples, both great and small. The governments-in-exile of such nations as Poland, Czechoslovakia, and the Netherlands were hardly able to act as they saw fit. Each step they took required prior Allied approval. The Yishuv, by comparison, was in a much weaker position. Unlike the governments-in-exile, it had little to offer in terms of organizing resistance movements, and had even less international stature. In that sense, the Yishuv was quite similar to other Jewish communities in the free world. It could take up traditional Jewish responses, such as hunger strikes, special prayers, and fast days, in a sad attempt to move world public opinion and the Jewish public at large to press the Allies on the rescue issue. Indeed, the mobilization of world opinion for active rescue was practically the only weapon the Yishuv could wield. But here the Yishuv leaders had to face the determination of the Allies to pursue the war according to their own lights. Humanitarian concerns were held secondary to military interests.

This predicament—utter dependence on the Allies on the one hand, and inability to do much else on the other—represented all that Zionist ideology and political development had tried to negate. Ironically, the Zionists had always sought to act independently if possible, using all available forces to their best advantage and with maximum maneuverability. Zionist strategy placed a premium on pragmatism and action. Yet here the Yishuv found itself hemmed in, unable to act, deprived of any significant recourse or response to the destruction of European Jewry.

Zionist leaders adopted different positions in the face of the new situation. Golda Myerson Meir, who was a central figure in the Histadrut (Labor Union), addressed the executive committee, saying: "There can be no Zionism now other than the rescue of Jews."[8] Gruenbaum, in a meeting at the Zionist executive in Jerusalem, supported the opposite view: "Zionism supercedes everything—this is what has to be proclaimed whenever great disaster threatens to divert us from the struggle for our redemption in the land of Zion. . . . Especially now, we must preserve the priority of the fight for redemption."[9]

Every Zionist leader had to come to deal with the likely costs and benefits of whatever course was advocated, weighing the chances and risks of rescue work and the future ability of the Zionist enterprise to withstand the test of survival.

Those who viewed rescue as the only possible priority tended to come from the second-echelon leadership of the labor Mapai party, chiefly active in the Histadrut. These included Avraham Hapt, Golda Myerson Meir, Anshel Reis, and Melech Neustadt. They argued that unless the Zionist movement addressed itself primarily to rescue, the future of the entire Yishuv would be jeopardized. There could be no strengthening of the Yishuv without first taking action to save the Jews who remained in Europe. Only the Diaspora could ever ensure its success.[10]

They did not demand that all activity and development in Palestine itself be suspended, only that the order of priorities be changed. The necessity of rescue was primary, and they sought to rock the Yishuv out of its routine. In order to test the various proposals being made, they claimed vast sums of money had to be raised with unstinting effort. There could be no cold calculus of what was feasible or not. Rather, the psychology of going all out had to be adopted, even if it proved possible to save only thousands, or hundreds, or even some dozens of Jews. Success would be measured only in those terms: "The greatest enemy of rescue is the despair of ever rescuing anyone."

As David Remez, the Histadrut general secretary, said in his opening remarks to the Mapai conference on 10 February 1943:

> For the first time we are being forced to decide to waste money. We are facing a challenge for which there is just no guarantee that we will succeed, no guarantee that the funds will not have been spent in vain. But we have no choice but to spend them, because we are talking about saving lives.[11]

Between these two extreme positions, however, a third, position was taking shape. It was championed by the top Mapai leaders in the Jewish Agency executive: Ben-Gurion, Kaplan, and Shertok. They were unwilling to restrict themselves to a cost-benefit analysis—that is, weighing too carefully the chance of success of each rescue plan. Rather, they argued that any plan offering reasonable possibilities had to be tried, even if it meant spending unusually large amounts of money. However, they were not ready for a major change in priorities.

Thus, they felt that to bribe officials, shipowners, or government ministers was perfectly justified if this would help save people. Other funds ought to be allocated for purchasing boats when a chance to bring refugees to Palestine presented itself. In the cause of rescue, they were willing to take the risk of being defrauded by shipowners. Caution could not be allowed to prevent persecuted Jews from escaping Europe. Paying ransom money, or an emigration fee, seemed acceptable to them so long as this aided escape. One might characterize this approach as one that supported action within the range of the possible—with no preconceived limit of what was possible.

Ben-Gurion did not support proposals that offered solely an opportunity to vent Jewish outrage or assuage Jewish guilt feelings. He backed ideas that were properly planned with real potential, and that the Yishuv could actually carry out. Both he and Shertok felt success was to be measured against what was achievable, however small, and not against the dimension of the destruction. Shertok argued that the rescue of 30,000 children, although pathetically small in absolute terms, would be an important achievement in relative terms. The fact that help could not be extended to millions should not be allowed to sour ideas of whatever could reasonably be done.

As Ben-Gurion said, "Rescue of the Jews of Europe has a moral as well as a financial aspect. This is now one of the central issues. It is not only helping the Jews of Europe, it is also the chance for Eretz Israel to raise itself up. . . . The fact that the Jews of Eretz Israel have stood in the forefront of rescue work will redound to the credit of Zionism."[12]

This position, seemingly so logical, had this weakness: there was no objective standard by which to determine which plan had the greatest chance of success and which was hopeless. Decisions like this counted on the balance between the daring and recklessness of planners and the caution of policymakers.

Those taking this position were aware of the objective limitations to any action the Yishuv might undertake on its own, but also cognizant that opportunities did exist for meaningful action. The responsibility for carrying out such rescue activities had to be directed to the Jewish people, who also needed to raise funds and exert pressure on the Allies to adopt a better rescue policy. That required a sensitive reading of what was possible. At times, those who advocated such a course overestimated the readiness of the Allied governments—for whom the Jewish issue was never paramount—to sanction Jewish rescue activities. On most occasions, however, Zionist leaders were more realistic in their expectations. Their stance resembled that of a government, charged with representing Jewish interests; they were unwilling to accept what was happening in Europe as the death knell for Jews. The Yishuv had a responsibility to frame a policy of rescue that was commensurate with the political limitations of the situation.

It was precisely this deliberateness and sense of balance that drew fire from those who took the more extreme positions. Hapt, for example, criticized Ben-Gurion at the Mapai central committee, declaring that "a sense of proportion and rationality" was inappropriate, and that such thinking disregarded the enormity of the tragedy and the manner in which it was carried out. Only the terrible events in Europe ought to guide the policy of the Yishuv.[13]

Despite such differences, however, there was no one in any of the three camps who fundamentally disagreed—as Lichtheim seemed to—with the proposition that Jewish existence would henceforth depend on the implementation of a new Zionist program. All were committed to the idea that the destruction of the Diaspora communities necessitated an even greater obligation to ensure the survival of Zionism. In this hour of crisis, they fully identified it with the survival of the Jewish people. For that reason, even Ben-Gurion's critics within Mapai and the Histadrut supported his attempt to find a path of compromise between rescue and the continued development of the Yishuv. The scarce resources available had to support both goals, and therefore a separate fund was established for rescue work. Funds from the Jewish National Fund and the Keren Hayesod, allocated to development programs, were not diverted to rescue. The special fund was also to be used to aid the families of men fighting in the British army, and was therefore called the "Mobilization and Rescue Fund." Rescue efforts were thus seen as part of the Yishuv's overall war against Nazism.

In the context of the Holocaust, rescue, and the role of Zionism, the importance of immigration—legal and illegal—was reevaluated. Ben-Gurion considered the primary function of the Yishuv to absorb the surviving remnant of the Jewish people after the war, and that meant preparing the country to receive all Jews, including those who were not brought up on Zionist ideology and those who had no preparation for a pioneering life. Concluding that after the war there could no longer be a secure future for Jews in the Diaspora, Ben-Gurion included the Jews of Turkey, Yemen, and other Middle Eastern countries among those he imagined would require resettlement in Palestine. Accordingly, he believed it was vital to go on with work that, in retrospect, may seem rather petty in the face of the Holocaust, such as maintaining a supply of labor to the kibbutzim, putting up new settlements, and trusting that the Labor party would be the dominant political power. Through all of this, the Yishuv may ultimately attain its goals.

The distinction between legal and illegal aliyah became blurred during that time. Even when the British authorities granted entry certificates, there were stages of aliyah work that remained illegal: the foremost concern of Jews was escaping from Nazi-occupied Europe. In their determination to do so, Jews demonstrated their fierce and heroic desire to live and resisted the Final Solution. In its various forms, aliyah work demanded calculated, rational planning, daring, and sometimes a disregard of all established rules. Organizing such operations answered the palpable need to take action, in keeping with the essential Zionist ethos of the time.

Organizing this required reestablishing communications with European Jewish leaders and laying down guidelines for cooperation. New and resourceful methods were indeed found to make such networks possible, which in turn led to greater understanding for and identification with the Diaspora on the part of Yishuv emissaries. This helped broaden the concept of rescue to include assistance to the communities themselves. The result was a greater degree of cooperation between those who were directly involved in aliyah and those who organized relief work, including joint political activities in Britain, the United States, and elsewhere.

Aliyah and Rescue

Zionist approaches to rescue and aliyah developed in stages. Two main directions for further activity were decided in meetings of the Jewish Agency executive during November 1942: the first one directed at the international community and the other at the Yishuv itself. The international phase of the Agency's rescue program had three targets. The Agency called upon the Allies to publicly announce measures to be taken in retaliation for German acts of genocide, including bombing German cities, punishment of German nationals held by the Allies, and prosecution of German war criminals after the war. Such statements of intent, the Agency felt, would be fully consistent with other declarations already made by the Allies.[14] The Agency also called upon the Allies to permit the transfer of funds to individuals and communities for humanitarian purposes, along with supplies of food and medicine to Jews in ghettos and concentration camps. In making these demands, the Yishuv pointed to the precedent of Allied relief to the victims of hunger in German-occupied Greece.

The Jewish leaders hoped as well to take advantage of the hardships of Germany's satellites and to hold over them the growing threat of retribution after the war. This, it was hoped, would detach them from the machinery of the Final Solution.

The neutral countries were asked to open their doors to Jewish refugees. They were assured that the Allies, supported by Jewish organizations, would try to provide the refugees with food and maintenance. Similarly, the Agency hoped to assure the neutrals that a permanent home would be found for each refugee at the end of the war.

Meanwhile, the Yishuv planned to take unilateral action—first, by reestablishing contact with the European Jewish communities through Palestine-based organizational structures. Accordingly, a "Jewish Agency Rescue Committee" was formed in March 1943, in which all public groups active in Palestine took part, including the non-Zionist, Orthodox Agudat Israel, and the New Zionist Revisionists (neither of which were represented in the Jewish Agency itself). The committee was directed by Yitzhak Gruenbaum and Eliyahu Dobkin, two of the leading members of the Committee to Rescue Polish Jewry. Actual decision-making power regarding both policy and implementation remained in the hands of the Agency executive.[15]

Since the beginning of the war, communication posts had been maintained in Constantinople and Geneva. Through these posts news of the European communities had been transmitted. Geneva was the base for several important organizations, including the World Jewish Congress, represented by Moshe Silberschein; Agudat Israel; Hehalutz, represented by Nathan Schwalb and Henny Bornstein; and the Jewish Agency, represented by Richard Lichtheim and Moshe Pazner. Constantinople was originally the smaller center. Most activities there were carried on by the Palestine Office, which had organized the aliyah of about 2,000 refugees from Vilna in January 1940.[16]

During 1942, the Constantinople base grew, with the addition of agents of the Mossad and delegates of the kibbutzim. The Rescue Committee, eager to establish sound operating procedures, sought to profit from the experience of both the Geneva and the Constantinople networks as well as that of the prewar Zionists. One of the Committee's first goals was to communicate with surviving Jews, to let them know that they had not been forgotten and that efforts were being made to find a way to help them. Information brought out from German-occupied or controlled areas helped in planning the campaign of agitation that the Committee wished to carry out, both internationally and on the home front. Other plans involved the establishment of other centers for communication and rescue work, in Spain and Sweden, although this much-discussed idea was never adopted.[17]

In late 1942, and even in January 1943, the feeling that no one in the Allied governments was receptive to Jewish demands had not yet taken hold. British opinion was aroused and lent moral force to Jewish demands for rescue activity, as expressed by such prominent figures as the Archbishop of Canterbury and Cardinal Hinsley, as well as many members of Parliament. The foreign secretary, at a special session of Parliament on 17 December, read the joint Allied declaration that stated the intention to prosecute war criminals, and explicitly mentioned the persecution of Jews for the first time. In an extraordinary gesture, the House rose to honor the memory of countless murdered Jewish victims.[18] President Roosevelt repeated this declaration. Thus, there seemed reason to hope that, this time, the Allies would surge beyond mere lip service.

As Ben-Gurion and Moshe Shertok saw it, the Jews of the Yishuv, who had first grasped the terrible implications of the tragedy, had the duty not only to initiate and keep up pressure for rescue activity, but also to educate the greater public about the situation.[19] In retrospect, their trust in the power of an informed world opinion appears to have been exaggerated, perhaps even naive; but at the time, there seemed to be a basis for optimism. Under the circumstances, Zionist leaders were willing to overlook certain ideological tenets in order to allow the favorable climate of opinion to have maximum effect. Recall the proposal, accepted in principle by Shertok, that the British government try to bring Jews out of Nazi Europe while Zionist leaders would relax the demand to send them on to Palestine. The idea was put forward by members of the British Parliament, a rescue lobby led by Mrs. Eleanor Rathbone (MP), who hoped to facilitate rescue work by separating it from the Palestine question. Shertok's attitude was also approved by the London office of the Agency.[20]

Shertok's assent to a formula implying that Zionist political demands constituted a practical obstacle to greater rescue efforts deserves close attention. The Zionist movement had throughout the 1930s insisted on viewing the fate of Jews as inseparable from the Palestine question. Shertok's position demonstrated his laudable sensitivity to these extraordinary circumstances, in which normal procedure had to be overruled.

It also demonstrated his magnificently firm confidence that Zionism, as the ideal political solution for the Jews, would eventually see vindication. We may, therefore, conceive of him as a faithful advocate of what we have described as the realist approach within the Zionist leadership. He was willing to exploit any opportunity to facilitate rescue, which unavoidably meant cooperating with the British. He suffered no anxiety that alternative sites for refugee shelters might someday pose a serious challenge to Zionism. Moreover, past experience had shown that it was quite difficult to find such sites. Indeed, Shertok was certain that Britain would have to turn to Palestine as a solution should a large-scale exit of Jewish refugees from Europe become possible, as it had when it approved the entry of 4,500 children with 500 adult escorts, and as had occurred again when the colonial secretary announced a policy of unrestricted utilization by Balkan Jews of 29,000 available immigrant certificates. Shertok was opposed by Dobkin and Gruenbaum, who distrusted the British so strongly that they denied even a tactical distinction between the fate of the Jewish people and the Palestine question. For them, only an unswerving devotion to the Zionist cause and a firm demand to abolish restrictions on immigration could lead to the true salvation of the Jews.[21]

The Bermuda Conference was convened by the Allies in April 1943 to discuss the "refugee problem," largely in response to American and British public pressure. Nothing of practical import resulted, indicating that the optimism of Shertok and his supporters was unfounded after all. The Bermuda Conference did succeed in pacifying, for quite some time, the non-Jews who had called for rescue action. The gap between the Allies' readiness to help save Jews and the unabated pace of the Nazi onslaught was thrown into sharp relief by the coincidence of the Bermuda Conference and the Warsaw Ghetto's last stand. It had proven beyond the power of the Jews of the free world and of the Yishuv to impress upon the Allies the urgency of rescue action over the spring and summer of 1943.

It was during this time that the Palestinian rescue mission in Constantinople drew up its plans and established contact with European Jewish communities. Funds from the Yishuv began reaching Jewish communities in Slovakia, Rumania, and Bulgaria. Money was passed to Jews in Poland via Zionist groups in Hungary. The activity of the center in Geneva was also stepped up. Despite frequent and counterproductive quarrels among the various organizations, highly important contacts were maintained with Jews in Western and Central Europe.

Both offices stressed that a great deal could be done to help the Jews in the German satellite countries, and they noted that even in Poland there were Jews who had survived in hiding and desperately needed help from the Yishuv. Any contact with Jews, individuals or groups, was to be considered rescue or aid activity. They argued that prolonging Jewish life, even if only by a few hours, was essential; that it was vital to keep hope alive, even if there was no guarantee of deliverance; that the message that the Yishuv cared meant that Jews were not abandoning their brothers and sisters under German occupation to their fate. Most important, however, were actual efforts to get Jews out of Europe.[22]

In the jargon of the time, relief work organized by the Palestinian rescue missions was referred to as "minor projects." "Major projects," on the other hand, included the Transnistria Plan (see Chapter 10), which sought to ransom 70,000 Jews, or the Europa Plan, in which Jewish leaders offered huge sums to Dieter Wisliceny, who supervised the deportation of Jews from Slovakia. These were broadly conceived rescue plans requiring the Allies' serious cooperation.[23]

During 1943–44, some of the "minor projects" carried out depended on the Yishuv and required the exclusive expenditure of Jewish resources. Many leading figures reached the painful conclusion that only limited rescue operations were possible. Deep despair posed the most serious threat to the morale of those masterminding the rescue missions, and it was their solemn task to fight it.

*

The year 1944 brought growing uncertainty about the future. The end of the war was in sight, but its effects on political calculations were less clear than at the outset. British policy had not changed, despite the substantial contributions of the Yishuv to the war effort. Zionists would once again have to engage in a primeval struggle to achieve their goals. The inconceivability of Zionism without the Jews of Eastern Europe caused palpable unease and confusion. Imponderable questions were raised about the prospects of Zionism in a world deserted by potential immigrants. What effect was this likely to have on the Zionist movement—on the attitude of the survivors to Zionism, for example? How would it weigh on the workaday and long-range thinking of governments and politicians who had supported (or opposed) Zionism before the war?

Ze'ev Shind, the Mossad agent in Constantinople, did not believe that the Holocaust would make Zionists of the majority of survivors (most of whom had not been Zionist sympathizers before the war). It was an illusion, he declared, to count on their support. He pointed out that the survivors would want to know straight out what the Yishuv had done to save Jews from destruction. Only a direct answer, one that could point to concrete action, had any chance of winning over survivors and creating a basis for dialogue with them. Otherwise, he warned, "their accusation will rankle so poisonously that the Yishuv will never be able to free itself of it."[24]

During the first part of 1944, therefore, he urged massive efforts to improve the rescue campaign. Only this, he insisted, would prevent a postwar moral crisis between the Yishuv and the remains of the Jewish world. In any event, the Zionist movement would have to conduct a wide-ranging postwar effort to win Jewish support. Shind expected that most of the survivors would be too exhausted to begin their lives anew or rebuild their once-proud Jewish identity. He believed they would prefer simply to go back to their old homes. Some were liable to conclude that it would be wiser to cut all ties with the Jewish people, to escape the frightful taint attendant upon being called a Jew.

Quite a few Yishuv emissaries agreed with this assessment. This only reinforced their view that, while the war prevented them from speaking face-to-face with the Jews of Europe, all energies had to be channeled into rescue work. It was therefore incumbent upon the Yishuv to support requests for assistance and funds from Constantinople and Geneva. The rescue emissaries also appealed for the permanent posting to Constantinople of one of the Yishuv's leading figures, in order to facilitate the decision-making process. This leads to a detailed consideration of the work conducted in Constantinople and the factors that governed relations in the rescue mission there.

The Yishuv Delegation in Constantinople–Istanbul

The status of the aliyah center in Constantinople changed dramatically once the Rescue Committee decided it was the hub of rescue and relief activity. Constantinople was chosen for a variety of reasons, including Turkey's neutrality, its proximity to the Balkans, and the presence there of envoys from European governments-in-exile and the Allies. Representatives of the Yishuv—especially those of the Mossad—were already established, but there was another advantage. As noted before, the Mossad was searching for new openings for illegal aliyah activity.[25]

In Constantinople in December 1942 were Haim Barlas, director of the Palestine Office, and his assistant, Dr. Joseph Goldin. There was also Venya Pomerantz, sent by the Kibbutz Meuhad movement to establish contact with members in Europe. A month later, Menahem Bader arrived to undertake the same task for the Kibbutz Artzi movement. These two, together with Ze'ev Shind of the Mossad, constituted what they called the "Histadrut Rescue and Relief Committee," through which they hoped to solicit a larger share of Histadrut funds for relief and rescue work.[26] Others joined them in the course of 1943, as the various movements represented on the Rescue Committee sent their own members to Constantinople: Yaakov Grifil of Agudat Israel, Yosef Klarman of the Revisionists, David Zimend of the General Zionists, and Akiva Levinsky of Youth Aliyah. Throughout the tenure of the Constantinople mission, it was constantly augmented by representatives of other public and private bodies from Palestine, and by lawyers who tried to use the contacts established by the Office to help individual Jews escape Nazi clutches. This tended to complicate the work of the mission, whose legal status was ambiguous. Only Barlas had official standing as a Jewish Agency representative, and he was recognized as such by the Turkish and British authorities. All the others in Turkey took the guise of private businessmen and were constantly apprehensive that their activities—much of them illegal—would prompt the authorities to expel them.[27]

We may say, then, that there were two stages in organizing the rescue mission: the formation of the Histadrut committee, and the expanded group formed subsequently. This created a distinction between a "core" group and a "periphery" that proved to be problematic. The distinguished Histadrut members had "seniority" and were better acquainted with the communications network. They also benefited from special allocations from the Histadrut and the kibbutz movements.[28] Thus, when the mission first required the formation of subcommittees, it was natural that Bader, the eldest and most experienced in financial matters, be selected as treasurer. (Bader had been involved in negotiating the *Haavarah* (transfer) agreement on behalf of his kibbutz movement in the thirties.) Venya Pomerantz, who had established the first contacts with Hungary via couriers, took over communications. The subcommittee on aliyah was chaired by Shind.

Finances and communications were the two central functions in the mission, and the Histadrut representatives clearly dominated the group. This caused a good deal of suspicion that some were serving their own movements rather than the general Jewish public. On one occasion Zimend and Levinsky, representing Zionist Youth, accused Pomerantz and Bader not only of reporting inaccurately on the role of youth movement members in relief, rescue, and resistance activities in the ghettos and concentration camps, but also of falsifying the signatures on letters received from Europe, in order to portray those affiliated as associated with leading rescue and resistance efforts.[29] Further evidence of the simmering tensions within the mission emerges from the frequent meetings devoted to organizing and reorganizing the mission's work. Thus, it was only in November 1943, after most of the Yishuv emissaries had arrived, that it was decided to establish an extended forum of eight to enable those who were not part of the original labor delegation to participate in daily considerations and decision making. Pressure to keep the number of key officers rather small derived from the dire need to keep contacts with agents and couriers—many from the roguish underworld—shrouded in the darkest secrecy.

During the summer of 1944, when the aliyah organizers began to enjoy a modicum of success, some movements came to resemble special interest groups. There was almost unbearable tension around the selection of refugees for places on the transports as well as strenuous jockeying for position in an ignoble effort to appear to have done the most for the survivors. In the prevailing atmosphere, Agudat Israel and the Revisionists, for example, embarked on independent fund-raising efforts and aliyah arrangements.

This tendency was sharply condemned by the Jewish Agency and Mossad representatives on the Rescue Committee. It was the Committee, representing the entire Yishuv, that had authorized the mission's work in the first place. In Palestine, care was taken not to split up the Committee, and the Constantinople mission was instructed to try to do likewise. In July 1944, after eighteen months of activity, there were further discussions, in which delegates of the JDC and other relief agencies also participated. This reestablished crucial procedures for an equitable division of funds and immigration certificates.[30]

Another set of problems that beset the rescue mission involved the attitude of many toward their chairman, Haim Barlas. He was a senior member of the Agency's immigration bureau and as such had been involved in innumerable problems of refugee immigration since the war began. To his credit, he had successfully arranged for the immigration, via Trieste, of certificate-holders from Germany, as well as more complicated deals for the immigration of Lithuanian Jews in January 1941 via Soviet Russia and Turkey. Barlas had also lobbied to effect with the Turkish Council of Ministers for free passage for Jews with Palestine immigration certificates.[31]

Nonetheless, there was some feeling in the mission that, if rescue was a top priority of the Yishuv, rescue ought to be entrusted to a leading public figure and not merely to a machinelike bureaucrat. Only one who counted himself among the most important of policymakers, the argument ran, would have the glib self-assurance required to approve maverick, daring operations. Haim Barlas clearly, they argued, did not fit the bill. He was a dedicated, energetic, and loyal civil servant who would find it unthinkable to break standard regulations and violate time-honored norms, which he was morally bound to uphold as the Agency's official representative in Ankara.

This became a frequent subject of discussion in the Agency executive as well as in the Mossad, the Histadrut, and Mapai. The mission members' appeals for the assignment to Constantinople of one of the Yishuv's ranking leaders did not meet opposition. Indeed, there were occasions in which approval was readily granted. Such resolutions were never implemented, however. Instead, leading figures such as Kaplan and Shertok made brief visits to Constantinople either for the purpose of conducting high-level discussions or to resolve breakpoint tensions in the rescue mission itself. Other visitors included Chief Rabbi Isaac Herzog and Hebrew University president Judah Magnes (who represented the JDC in Palestine). This arrangement did not, of course, answer the basic demand of mission members: to replace Haim Barlas. Only Shaul Avigur, head of the Mossad, remained in Constantinople for a significant period during 1944, when he conducted aliyah operations there. It is hard to escape the conclusion that the handling of this issue somehow revealed the way the political leadership viewed the work of the rescue mission that constituted the main effort of the Yishuv in relief and rescue work.

Despite all this, the rescue mission did manage to achieve the modicum of cooperation needed to plan its activities. It kept open reliable lines of communication to Rumania, Hungary, Slovakia and Greece. Contact was further advanced through the mail, telephone, political agents, businesspeople, and diplomats. Couriers were sent by the mission from Slovakia and Hungary into Poland and Austria, as well as the Theresienstadt camp. On the other hand, communications with Bulgaria proved difficult to maintain, despite geographical proximity.

In the rescue mission's files are letters from the European communities and replies from Palestine; reports on rescue operations; descriptions of planned activities; reports on the various countries and the prevailing realities there; and reports on Palestine and the Jewish free world. Letters from occupied Europe include, of course, requests for financial assistance, sent in various ways: sometimes the plea was for cash (American or Swiss currency), which was then greatly in demand but extremely risky. Deals were also made to unlock assets in Europe in return for payment in dollars, francs, or pounds after the war.

The complex system of communicating with the European communities and transferring relief funds to them was first developed in Geneva, where it held sway until 1943. Constantinople offered certain advantages, however, mainly its proximity to Palestine. Correspondence to and from the Yishuv moved much more swiftly there. Constantinople soon became a major transfer point for personal mail, newspapers, and Zionist movement newsletters from Palestine. Zionists and other Jewish community figures in Europe emphasized repeatedly how important these links with the Yishuv were.

The visits to Constantinople by major Yishuv leaders and the letters they sent to Europe also served to narrow the great psychological distance between the besieged communities and the Yishuv, bringing home to the Jews in Europe the fact that the Zionist leaders were directly involved in relief and rescue work. While the instructions and requests sent to European community leaders lacked official authority, they were of course received with the utmost seriousness.

At the same time, visitors from Palestine emerged with a better under-standing of the needs of the Jews of Europe, motivating them in turn to increase their own involvement in relief and rescue work. Receiving in hand a letter brought out of Europe by a courier left a lasting impression and could lead to an even more dynamic policy. Visits by Kaplan, Shertok, Magnes, and others were followed by larger allocations to rescue budgets and by a greater degree of risk-taking in planning.[32]

Special Difficulties in Planning Aliyah

During 1943 and 1944, planning and executing aliyah seemed feasible not only because the attitude of the Yishuv leaders altered, but since the political circumstances in the Balkans changed. At that juncture in the war, there were a number of countries—Rumania, Hungary, and even Bulgaria and Slovakia—that hinted at their interest in ridding themselves of their Jews in some way other than "deportation to the east," as the Nazis euphemistically called the death-camp transports. This satisfied those governments as a means of expressing independence vis-à-vis the Germans.[33] Planning for aliyah served as a negotiating point that Jewish community leaders in Europe exploited in talks with their governments.

Aliyah made it possible to expand the scope of illegal border crossings from Poland, and then from Hungary, into the Balkans. Smuggling refugees from Poland and the Ukraine into Slovakia, Hungary, and Rumania became possible only after tremendous odds were overcome and permission was se-cured for the refugees to stay in the transit countries for a while. It was easier to persuade those governments to grant such permission when local Jewish leaders could demonstrate that the refugees would soon be on their way to Palestine. Staff at the Palestine Office in Budapest later testified that official Hungarian attitudes toward the refugees improved considerably after the departure for Palestine of several groups of refugee children in January and February 1943.

An entry certificate for Palestine did not alone ensure that a Jew could leave Europe. An individual certificate-holder might have the privilege of transit through Turkey, which was indeed of major importance. However, he or she still had to arrange for additional means of transport: usually a seat on the single-car train that ran between Turkey and Bulgaria weekly. This was no solution at all for large groups of adults or children.

There remained two major and interrelated obstacles. One was the objective difficulty of arranging transportation in wartime, and the second was the policies of England and Nazi Germany, on which the question of rescuing the surviving Jews depended most. These two nations controlled travel on the Black Sea and the Mediterranean.

Members of the rescue mission in Constantinople formulated an aliyah policy that took full advantage of the positive intent of the British colonial secretary, Oliver Stanley. He declared in Parliament in February 1943 his government's consent to the entry into Palestine of 4,500 Jewish children from the Balkans with 500 adult escorts, and to unrestricted use of the 29,000 certificates remaining from the total allocated under the terms of the White Paper.

When the Mossad began to reorganize itself in summer 1942, it was able to take into account all the difficulties it had experienced in past attempts to organize aliyah bet. The renewed activity, which took place against the background of the Rescue Committee's Istanbul mission, was planned to take advantage of every resource and opportunity. In the Mossad, the thrust was toward creating a bona fide master plan. Not all of the details were worked out, nor did the Mossad find it necessary, as did the political echelon, to concern itself over the possibility of a British refusal to accept such a plan.

Mossad in particular sought to broaden the area of cooperation with the British. Indeed, in 1942 it had reached a decision to seek the cooperation of British intelligence services in planning aliyah operations, and it was implemented, as noted, in the services given to the British at the Information Center for Investigation in Haifa. [34] Another major plan that the Mossad was involved with and wanted to capitalize on was the "Parachutists Plan." This plan was one of the most important efforts in cooperating with the British in the war. Parachutists from the Yishuv jumped beyond enemy lines to contact British pilots hit and captured in mission. [35] In the context of aliyah work, the nine parachutists who reached Rumania were of utmost importance. They became the direct link between the delegation in Constantinople and the Jewish community in Rumania.

As long as Britain was ready to allow legal immigration, why not test the limits of the permissible by transporting more than the 4,500 children and their escorts? Why not, in other words, combine legal with illegal immigration? The Transnistria Plan and the British agreement to accept large numbers of Bulgarian Jewish children seemed to indicate that this was the proper direction to pursue. The Transnistria Plan was perceived by the Mossad foremost as ample evidence that Rumania once again encouraged Jewish emigration. In correspondence with the Yishuv leadership, the Mossad did not dwell on the ransom or on other particulars. Instead, such letters emphasized the importance of Rumania's avowed change of heart. [36]

The Mossad's appraisal was based on reports that the Rumanian government was willing to provide ships for Jewish emigrants if only the British would agree not to seize the vessels in the Mediterranean. The source of this information also intimated that Rumania would see in the safe voyage of one refugee transport a sign that subsequent ships could pass on. Rumanian shipping companies were willing to offer a variety of ships for this purpose.[37] British approval was needed in order to secure a Soviet guarantee of safe passage in the Black Sea. (Sea voyage became even riskier after 1942, owing to Soviet-German naval battles that claimed many neutral vessels.) Had the Rumanian ships actually been made available, it would have been possible to transport the 5,000 orphans of Transnistria whom the Rumanian government had first offered to release, even when the plan as a whole ran into some difficulties.[38] Such a step might have served as precedent for all future rescue activity, including immigration from Bulgaria.

The ability to arrange aliyah from Rumania with the help of Rumanian ships would also have solved the terror of sea transport that affected Jews in Bulgaria and other Balkan countries, well aware as they were of the disasters of the *Salvador* and the *Struma*. Some were convinced that the only way out was to pressure the governments involved to provide a safe overland route, such as by rail from Rumania via Bulgaria and Turkey to Palestine. There were several groups of children from Hungary whose exit was planned exactly this way.[39] One group indeed completed its journey in January 1943. Yet, as noted, the number of immigrants that could be accommodated overland was severely limited. Rail transport in Turkey was so heavily taxed that freight and military supplies were kept waiting for weeks in harbors and depots. Thus, despite all the dangers of sea travel, it was an indispensable element in any plan that involved large numbers of emigrants. This made it seem worthwhile to maximize the security of shipping arrangements and allay the fears and suspicions of the various governments. Britain's participation, if only indirect, would have impressed upon all concerned, including local Jewish leaders, the gravity of the commitments behind the plan and the measure of safety required for the sea journey.

Fear of untoward wartime developments interfered with carrying out plans that seemed, on paper, well thought out. Speedy implementation was of the utmost importance. During this period, Turkey came under increasing pressure from both sides to enter the war. It was difficult to know just how long Turkey would maintain its neutrality, on which so much of the rescue activity depended.

Throughout this period, many contended that the type of approach being proposed was unfeasible. Legal and illegal operations, they argued, must remain separate, since cooperation with Haim Barlas, who was responsible for handling immigration for the Jewish Agency, would lead the Mossad to lose some freedom of maneuvering by going through formal channels, both British and Zionist. They argued that any cooperation with the British would end in a failure, as was the case in the Kladovo *Darien* incident.[40]

Nevertheless, in early 1943 the advantages of combining legal and illegal immigration still seemed to outweigh the disadvantages, particularly since this seemed to offer a solution to two main problems: securing transportation and protecting the immigrants at sea.

We will be able to assess to what extent these assumptions stood the test of reality by examining the first project that was attempted: the aliyah of one thousand Jews from Bulgaria.

12

Aliyah and Rescue:
The Case of Bulgarian Jewry, 1943

The "Grand Plan" for 29,000 Immigrant Children

In December 1942, when extermination of the Jews became public knowledge and when the British foreign secretary took the floor in the House of Commons to condemn Nazi genocide, about half of the Palestine immigration certificates allotted to Jews under the White Paper of 1939 had not yet been utilized. British immigration policy, wartime conditions, and the Final Solution had combined to create a situation in which 34,000 certificates were still available fifteen months before the end of the five-year limit.[1] British policy on Jewish immigration resulted from three assumptions: that the Holocaust was not related to the issue of Palestine immigration; that enemy aliens were not permitted to enter Palestine; and that anyone entering the country under conditions other than those stipulated by law was considered an illegal.

Over the course of 1942, each of these assumptions was somewhat undermined. The *Struma* incident highlighted the inhumanity and arbitrariness of the first one. The January 1942 agreement to permit the immigration of 270 Hungarian and Rumanian children—both countries then at war with Britain—violated the bar against enemy aliens. And fear of another sinking and the steady trickle of small boats that continued to reach Palestine weakened the third assumption. Public outcry against the fate meted out to the Jews of Europe, and pressure on the government by members of Parliament to do something constructive about Jewish rescue, made it impossible to adhere strictly to the prior position. In December 1942, therefore, the Cabinet voted to permit 4,500 children and 500 adult escorts to emigrate from Bulgaria to Palestine. This step, taken over the protest of the British high commissioner in Palestine, had the heartfelt support of the prime minister, and effectively negated the rule against the entry of enemy aliens. Colonial Secretary Oliver Stanley announced on 3 February 1943, that the certificates remaining were to be used to rescue Jewish children from southeastern Europe. Aliyah was thus directly linked to rescue, rather than to the absorptive capacity or the labor needs of Palestine, or to Arab reaction. On 2 July 1943, the British

Cabinet approved the proposal of the colonial secretary, which stated that any Jewish refugee who reached a neutral country in transit would receive clearance for Palestine. In this manner, all immigrants were given legal standing.

These radical changes in British policy were the result of the mounting tension about the perceived priorities of the war effort, British interests in the Middle East (including its Palestine policy), and the demand to aid in the rescue of European Jews.

Ironically, it was the White Paper, so criticized by Jews, that enabled the British government to propose a special rescue program. While rescue was seen as subordinate to the war effort and as properly constituting a multi-national—not an exclusively British—concern, a plan of rescue based on the White Paper's provisions could be fairly large-scale without being too radical. It could also demonstrate that Britain was indeed sensitive to humanitarian demands.[2] British politicians came to realize in 1943, however, that declarations of intent were insufficient: political structure and the progress of the war made it imperative that sound programs be diligently implemented and perhaps adapted to unconventional methods. This meant greater resistance to the Jewish policy of Germany, its satellites, and the neutrals, and more rescue activities. In this British statesmen and officials could not avoid exploring the means of rescue efforts, however modest.

Changing policy in the field of immigration was a slow process. Adjusting to the idea that unconventional methods were required in order to enable Jews to emigrate took even longer. Bureaucratism and inflexibility were indeed responsible for the failure of some rescue plans adopted basically in good faith (although with an eye to political benefits) by the Foreign Office and the Colonial Office.

This chapter will follow these developments in British policy as they unfolded from 1943 to 1944, in the context of Mossad efforts to emigrate a thousand Bulgarian Jews.

*

In December 1942, Britain was faced with a double challenge. Reports indicated Rumanian interest in exchanging 70,000 deported Jews in Transnistria for a sum of 200,000 lei per person ($400 in the official rate of exchange).[3] At the same time, the Jewish Agency requested a special permit for the aliyah of Jews from Bulgaria in light of the growing oppressiveness of that country's Jewish legislation and fears of deportations. There was a rather small Jewish community in Bulgaria of 70,000. Jewish Agency officials in London suggested that Britain allow Bulgarian and Transnistria Jews to find any safe haven—even Mauritius—to avoid complicating their emigration by freeing it from Palestine policy considerations.[4]

The Transnistria plan could be dismissed as extortion, as an attempt to divide the Allies and thus neutralize the rescue aspect of the plan.[5] The Jewish Agency proposal with regard to Bulgaria, however, could not be dismissed in the same way. On the contrary, the numbers involved were limited, and

Sofia, unlike Bucharest, was not anti-Semitic and favored Jewish emigration, believing that would relieve Bulgaria of German pressure to deport its Jews.

On 23 November 1942, Oliver Stanley replaced Lord Cranborne as colonial secretary. His appointment was accompanied by discussions in the Colonial Office on the Jewish refugee issue. The point was raised that a British initiative to bring large numbers of Bulgarian Jews to Palestine might silence pressure groups demanding an end to British inaction and thus benefit the government. This proposition seemed to combine mild daring with stodgy adherence to the White Paper, yet it would be accepted with alacrity by the Zionists and their supporters.[6] The plan was supported in the Cabinet Committee on the Refugees, which was established on 23 December in the wake of Eden's declaration on the plight of European Jewry and the punishment of Nazis after the war ended for their criminal acts. The high commissioner, who early in December had opposed the entry of enemy aliens, was instructed to act in accordance with the secretary's orders. Winston Churchill enthusiastically welcomed the proposal, and it was approved by the Cabinet on 14 December 1942.[7] Two days later, the Foreign Office asked the Swiss government, representing British interests in Bulgaria, to transmit the British request to Sofia. On 14 January, exactly one month from the British Cabinet's decision, the Bulgarian government approved the plan. Both adults and children would be allowed to emigrate, and the British were urged to act swiftly, despite "technical" difficulties. The nature of such problems was not explicitly stated, but the Swiss envoy explained that the Bulgarians were eager to forestall a German plan to deport Jews.[8]

The Foreign and Colonial Offices did not, however, take sufficient notice of the stress on urgency. Instead, they embarked on routine procedures to draw up the lists of children, with their names and addresses. This was done in conjunction with the Jewish Agency in Jerusalem and its representatives in Sofia, the immigration office of the Mandatory administration in Palestine, the Passport Control Office of the British consulate in Istanbul (PCO), the Swiss envoy in Sofia, and the government of Bulgaria.

This procedure usually lasted about nine weeks; in wartime, considerably longer. The Jewish Agency immediately lodged a request to simplify the procedure by granting a priori approval to the lists to be submitted by the Swiss envoy in Sofia.[9] The Agency's request, however, was itself put through channels, though it was not answered by the end of March.

The original plan was to transport the children by train from Sofia to Istanbul, and then by sea to Palestine.[10] The British ambassador in Ankara, Knatchbull-Hugessen, was therefore instructed to appeal to the Turkish authorities for cooperation. The colonial secretary intended to announce the rescue plan in Parliament after Bulgarian approval was granted, but he had to wait for Turkish consent. Impatient, he instructed the Ankara ambassador to press the Turks and emphasize that London and Washington wanted help given to Jewish refugees and might be expected to show appreciation.[11] The Turkish answer was a qualified yes. Thus, by the beginning of February, the colonial secretary believed that all those who brought the plan to fruition had reached an understanding of full cooperation.

As public pressure in favor of a rescue effort increased, Stanley arranged to announce in Parliament the Bulgarian plan and the allocation of 29,000 certificates to refugee children.[12] Stanley's statement drew favorable response both in Parliament and in the press, and raised people's expectations. The British government was deluged by proposals for ways to broaden and carry out rescue schemes. One of the most active public committees (The Rescue from Nazi Terror) was led by Eleanor Rathbone, a member of Parliament, who saw Stanley's announcement as an opening to persuade the government to aid rescue work on a large scale. A vital area was the proper organization of transportation from Bulgaria to Palestine, including arrangements for safety and security throughout the journey. Miss Rathbone and her colleagues demanded that England pressure the neutral countries to establish transit camps for Jewish refugees. They further demanded that Britain and the Allies issue an explicit warning to Axis satellites against any cooperation with the Germans.[13] Such demands were also raised by the Jewish Agency, which sought to extend the rescue program to all of southeastern Europe. The Agency also asked that the exchange program be expanded to include Zionist veretans and other Jewish leaders.[14] All of these ideas reflected the perception that the Bulgarian plan was but the thin edge of a wedge in a multinational rescue. However, this was not Stanley's or the British government's intention. They did not pretend to lead a general rescue policy, which had to be discussed jointly by the Allies and in any case subordinated to the war effort. Prior to Stanley's announcement in Parliament, the colonial secretary was warned by officials from the refugee division at the Foreign Office, as well as by members of his own office, against excessive optimism and exaggeration of the significance of his announcement. Britain, they stressed, must take care lest it arouse hopes of mass rescue that would not be fulfilled. The frustration and anger would then be directed at Britain and cause unmitigated harm.[15]

The colonial secretary met Jewish Agency representatives on February 5, 1943, presenting the Bulgarian plan with careful emphasis and trying to prevent unrealistic expectations. Stanley stated that this was a response to the Agency's request "to save at least the children of Europe," but that it did not grant the right of entry to Palestine to any refugee. The British government would refuse to permit the "irregular [*sic*] immigration of adults" to take the places allocated to children and to interfere otherwise with the plan.[16]

But the following weeks showed the colonial secretary that it was not the waves of illegal immigrants streaming toward Turkey that impeded the plan, but the inflexibility of his own government. The British ambassador in Ankara, who viewed the entire matter through the lens of wartime British-Turkish relations, was skeptical and hesitant about such an ambitious program. If it hinged on rail transport through Turkey, Knatchbull-Hugessen thought it was bound to fail, as transport in general was overloaded, owing mainly to the extraordinary demands placed on the rail system supplying the British army.

Knatchbull-Hugessen thought it unrealistic to ask the Turks to make a further effort for Jewish refugees. Thus, he suggested on 6 March that the plan be abandoned.[17]

The Ministries of War Economy and War Transport had their own perspective on the issue. They felt Britain did not have shipping to spare for such purposes. They also objected to the request put up by Jewish Agency of leasing or buying two Rumanian ships, the *Bessarabia* and the *Transylvania,* captured in 1941 and lying unused in Istanbul Harbor. Their opposition was based on wartime boycott regulations and on the profit in foreign currency the Germans might derive from Rumania's payment for the ships. The high commissioner in Palestine, for his part, also refused to simplify the bureaucratic procedures for identifying the children and granting them entry permits.[18]

The Foreign Office and Colonial Office realized that they had to engage in an immediate effort to convey to their officials in Ankara, in Palestine, and at the War Office the urgency of the matter. In an internal communication in mid-March, Boyd Randel wrote:

> It seems to me that we are here not for the first time up against the compelling demands of military and refugee—that is political—interests, but that in the present instance the political interests might be judged to have a high priority. On this we may have to seek a decision from higher authority . . . I am sending a copy of this letter to Marshall (Admiralty) and J. N. Wood (Ministry of War Transport).[19]

The men of the Foreign and Colonial Offices apparently agreed that this plan went beyond purely humanitarian refugee aid involving "political interests." Ironically, this interest was keeping the White Paper policy. Completion of the operation took on such importance that Boyd called it the most significant so far for the Jewish rescue. The British public shared that view, Boyd argued, and this made it all the more imperative to overcome the resistance of British officials. Letters and cables were sent to the high commissioner, the minister in Cairo, and the ambassador in Ankara. Knatchbull-Hugessen, in particular, was asked to cope with any difficulties the Turks might raise and to ask their assistance in sea and land transport.[20]

The Bulgarian Government and the Emigration Plan

This correspondence took place two months after Bulgaria had granted approval to the emigration plan. In the interim, matters had fermented, and by mid-March the Swiss reported that the Bulgarians were more hesitant, less confident, and now demanded to know precise details of the transport arrangements Britain was making, as a precondition to approval of final refugee lists. The Bulgarians did state that they would allow 450 children to leave weekly, and that twice a week two railway coaches would be reserved for Istanbul.[21]

Jewish sources in Istanbul began to report a hardening of official Bulgarian behavior toward the Jews. Such reports coincided with news of a further wave of deportations in other parts of Europe.[22]

The Germans stepped up their pressure on Bulgaria and its neighbors to stop the flight of refugees. In January 1943, RSHA representative Theodore Dannecker arrived in Bulgaria to begin the process of deporting Bulgaria's Jews. The Bulgarian minister for internal affairs, Peter Gabrowski, reached an agreement with Dannecker that called for deporting 40,000 Jews from the annexed areas of Thrace and Macedonia. The Jewish commissar, Alexander Belev, was prepared to add 6,000 Jewish leaders. On 22 February, Dannecker and Belev signed an agreement stipulating the deportation of 6,000 Jews from Thrace, 8,000 from Macedonia, and 6,000 from the old territory of Bulgaria. The Bulgarian government confirmed the agreement on 2 March 1943, and several days later Jews were expelled from Thrace and Macedonia, and important Jewish figures in Plovochiv, Varna, Russe, and Kyustendil were arrested. (These last were later released, however.) The deportations were suspended after pressure was exerted by the opposition, and the 20,000-person level stipulated in the Belev-Dannecker agreement was not reached. During the April visit of King Boris to Berlin, von Ribbentrop complained that the deportations had not been completed. The king replied that the Jews were neccessary for his labor force and he was not prepared to do without them. Von Ribbentrop stressed that Germany's aim was a radical "final solution" to the "Jewish question." In April and May, the Germans increased their pressure on the Bulgarians, and Belev, as the official responsible for Jewish matters, presented the king with two alternative plans: one involving handing the Jews over to the Germans and their "deportation east," and the other involving their expulsion to the countryside. The king ordered the Jews expelled to the countryside on May 25.

In view of the Nazi attitude, permitting Jews to leave was a dire violation of Axis unity and seen as such by Britain and its allies.[23] Bulgarian Jews and the delegates of the neutral countries had a full picture of the political situation. Nevertheless, indications of a general expulsion of Jews from Bulgaria were contained in letters reaching Constantinople from Sofia, Varna, Plovdiv, and elsewhere. The Jews tried, with the few resources at their disposal, to oppose this policy and pleaded for transportation to Palestine in their letters to Constantinople.[24] Refugees who had smuggled themselves out of Bulgaria by taking enormous risks and paying huge sums reported that the border was now effectively closed and that children with immigration certificates had been turned back from the Bulgarian-Turkish frontier.

The refugee desk at the British Foreign Office feared that Germany might smash the plan completely, and sent messages to the Bulgarians through the Swiss legation in Sofia warning against deporting Jews of Sofia. As two months passed without any active steps to implement the rescue plan, Jewish and other public pressure in Britain began to mount. Palestine had not even approved procedures for compiling evacuation lists of children, and no one was able to say how they would be transported from Istanbul to Palestine.

Various organizations proposed rescue operations, based on word that some countries were prepared to allow Jews to leave. Slovakia was reportedly willing to sanction the exit of 1,000 minors by special train to the Turkish border or even to Istanbul. Reports from Rumania indicated that the authorities would permit the remaining Transnistria orphans to leave. In France, there was said to be a plan to transfer hidden Jewish children to Spain in order to prevent their deportation. On the eve of the Bermuda Conference on Refugees (April 1943), public critcism of rescue inactivity grew more severe. The failure of the "grand plan"—the trans-Bulgarian rescue plan— was seen by critics as a failure of the British government.[25]

Stanley's New Initiative

Oliver Stanley grew increasingly concerned. On 14 April 1943, he sent an extraordinary letter to the foreign secretary regarding the Bulgarian emigration plan:[26]

> Dear Anthony,
> I am getting very worried about the proposed transfer of Jewish children from Bulgaria to Palestine. Although I made a statement on His Majesty's Government's policy in this respect several months ago, no progress is being made with the practical arrangements. The trouble is that a number of interests have to be consulted about the various proposals; these interests include both Departments here and also authorities in the Middle East. Theoretically, of course it is my responsibility to try push the thing through but practically, it is almost impossible to exert any real pressure at this distance.

Stanley concluded that drastic measures should be taken. He proposed that the minister resident in Cairo, Lord Moyne, be assigned to see that the government's stated policy be carried out. A special assistant ought to be appointed, with the power to act swiftly and decisively to bring about whatever was necessary.

Stanley hoped for Eden's support in a detailed Cabinet-level discussion of the refugee matter. Stanley had a clear understanding of the obstacles encountered by those attempting to implement the plan, and tended to favor a compromise between the bureaucrats and refugee-aid organizations. The latter argued that a special body be appointed in order to blast though normal channels. It ought to have the power to issue entry permits, to send material assistance to refugees in enemy countries, and to contact neutrals to arrange refugee aid.[27] Stanley would not agree to a special body, but acknowledged that there was some truth to the arguments of the refugee-aid organizations. Routine procedures, as followed until then, had not resulted in the implementation of declared government policy. He therefore raised his own proposal.

Anthony Eden, on 20 April, expressed reservations held by officials in his ministry. Though he agreed with Stanley's assessment and quite understood his motivations, he could not see his way clear to allowing the minister in Cairo to meddle in Foreign Office matters. After all, a great deal of the necessary preparations had to go through Ankara, and that meant using the ambassador—an F.O. man.[28]

Knatchbull-Hugessen, in answer to Eden, treated Stanley's proposal as a mere technical rearrangement: the latter urged appointment of a coordinator in Turkey once the refugees began to arrive in a steady stream. The ambassador also expressed the view that the Jewish issue was but one of quite a few matters being discussed between Britain and Turkey. Therefore, it seemed ill-advised to separate this from the field of the embassy's activity. The Turkish government was being quite helpful in aiding the Jews, the letter continued, and was acting in full cooperation with Jewish organizations as well as with the American embassy. Transfer of these dealings to the resident minister in Cairo could hardly be expected to produce better results.[29] The embassy's unwillingness to see the Bulgarian emigration plan placed in the hands of an outsider effectively blocked Stanley's proposal.

All that Oliver Stanley had wanted was that one official deal exclusively with the Turks in all matters related to transport for the refugees. This, he thought, would be a more forceful approach. Anthony Eden's reply, therefore, dashed Stanley's expectations. In the meantime, another month had passed, and British politicians again faced the unpleasant fact that they were not determining the course of events. On 25 May, the Bulgarian minister of internal affairs announced that the Jews of Sofia would have to move to provincial towns. The Turkish frontier was absolutely closed to Jews. Swiss representatives in Bulgaria reported that this step came in after mounting German pressure, which became more effective as the emigration plan failed to be implemented. Nonetheless, the Swiss emphasized, Sofia had not canceled the plan; rather, they stated that they were not in a position to say when it may begin.[30]

During those first dismal weeks of May, the Foreign Office and Colonial Office continued to deal with arrangements for the journey as if nothing untoward had occurred in Bulgaria. A more urgent tone in messages to the high commissioner had produced results: MacMichael was prepared to approve lists submitted by the Bulgarians on condition that these were prepared with full cooperation from Jewish figures known to the Jewish Agency. The Navy, too, agreed to provide safe conduct to a large neutral vessel, properly identified, that would make a specified number of trips to transport Jewish refugees. The Navy was willing, as well, to assist in finding ships, normally used for bringing food supplies to Greece, that might be available for single trips to carry refugees.[31]

Despite the apparent progress made, Jews were unlikely to leave Bulgaria or any other Balkan country in the coming weeks. Stanley, eager for the emigration plans to move forward, urged the colleagues in his office and the Foreign Office to press on, but he was forced to tell Parliament why, in the half-year since the government's decision, not a single Jewish child had been saved.[32] The government tried to prevent these questions from reaching the floor by engaging individual MPs in private discussions. Stanley, for his part, took the view that the government could save itself from a messy wave of criticism only by taking further action in favor of the refugees. He shared this with both the high commissioner in Palestine and the resident minister in Cairo. The closing of the Bulgarian-Turkish frontier to Jewish refugees when in fact the German policy was to refuse any Jews to leave, he claimed, necessitated an immediate reconsideration of the immigration policy.[33]

Stanley explained that legal immigration was practically blocked off. Illegal immigrants reaching Palestine had been sent to Cyprus by Britain. In light of that, Stanley proposed doing away with distinctions between legal and illegal immigrants. Any refugee reaching Turkey or another neutral who was unable to remain indefinitely ought to receive entry to Palestine under White Paper allocations. This policy could last as long as there remained unused immigrant certificates. If radical political changes in the Balkans created tens of thousands of emigrants, the policy would be reviewed. Despite the passage of time, this proposal very closely resembled Lord Cranborne's of the previous year, when it had been decided to grant immigrant status to refugees who reached Palestine, though the distinction between legal and illegal immigrants was retained.

Oliver Stanley had digested the information he had received from MacMichael regarding turmoil in the Yishuv over what he called "the democracies' incapacity to help the Jews." The Yishuv, MacMichael reported, was organizing itself to confront the British. The Zionist leadership was taking a more aggressive position, and its political demands were becoming more extreme.

Ambassador Halifax reported from America that the Zionists were winning widespread public support there. There was general agreement of the need for a Jewish state in Palestine, in particular to save the Jews from the Nazis. There was also no denying that after the war there might be thousands of refugees desiring to enter Palestine, Halifax maintained, urging Cabinet action.

In the spring and summer of 1943, it was most difficult to continue to preserve an absolute separation between the question of Palestine and what many believed was necessary in light of the Nazi genocide. It was equally impossible to divorce the Palestine question from Middle East policy as a whole. More than ever, it was apparent that the White Paper had run its muddling course. A new solution was needed for the deepening conflict between the Yishuv in Palestine, driven by the horrifying fate of the Jews of Europe, and the government's nonpolicy. Lord Cranborne expressed this conflict when he proposed that the White Paper be declared the basis of long-range policy but that immigration would be permitted even after the end of the stipulated five-year period (March 1944).[34]

General Jan Smuts was the only British political figure to connect the Palestine issue directly and unequivocally to the Holocaust, but possibly the Cabinet acknowledged as much when it decided on 26 June to establish a committee for Palestine.[35] At that meeting, too, Stanley urged examination of his proposed change of immigration policy—a change that received Cabinet approval a week later, on 2 July. Neither the government nor Stanley viewed the change really as "anything out of the ordinary." But it afforded a chance of entry to Palestine for escapees from Nazi Europe.

Stanley communicated the news to the Jewish Agency on 7 July.[36] He asked that the decision be kept confidential, ostensibly for the sake of the refugees themselves. Some claimed, Stanley confided, that it had been his public announcement in Parliament in February that made the rescue plan fail, as it prompted the Germans to crack down harder. During the coming months, other reasons were cited for keeping the decision secret: hostile Arab reaction, for example (to be discussed further). Several days after this meeting, the Jewish Agency put the Cabinet decision to the test. To understand it, we shall turn to follow Mossad and Jewish Agency activities to rescue Bulgarian Jews.

The Mossad and the Emigration of the "One Thousand"

Early in 1943, the Mossad began a coordinated campaign to win cooperation of the British, Turkish, and American authorities in organizing large-scale aliyah. The plan was to transport Jews from both Rumania and Bulgaria. Mossad's representatives asked that a high-ranking Zionist leader come personally to Turkey to conduct negotiations with Ankara (with the help of the British embassy) over the acquisition of shipping. Such a step, it was hoped, would heighten diplomatic pressure on Turkey as well as take the fullest advantage of what was perceived as a favorable British posture.

Jerusalem accepted the Mossad proposal relying on the new British Policy as expressed by the colonial secretary. In March 1943 Eliezer Kaplan, treasurer of the Jewish Agency, and Eliyahu Epstein (Elath) of the political committee, who in 1941–42 had coordinated activities between the Yishuv and British intelligence, arrived in Constantinople. Epstein had established close contacts within the British foreign service and assorted Turkish ministries. He was also acquainted with officials of European governments-in-exile stationed in Turkey, who were able to facilitate communications between the Yishuv and the Jews of Europe. The men of the Mossad felt that the presence in Turkey of the well-connected Epstein and the highly placed Kaplan—in conjunction with the work of the Agency's people in London—improved their chances of persuading the British to honor the pledge made in Parliament by the colonial secretary.

Kaplan and Epstein met British embassy and consular staff as well as Turkish officials. They asked Britain to support their request to the Turks to permit local shipowners to engage in Jewish emigration work. Anatolian shipping agents had offered Barlas and his colleagues three craft; Turkish Interior Ministry officials asked the British to request their use. Such vessels were preferred over ships registered in the Balkans, as they did not require German or Soviet guarantees of free passage. The British agreed, and Kaplan and Epstein departed from Constantinople several weeks later feeling that the nagging problem of transportation from the Balkans to Turkey could indeed be resolved. In fact, they believed that moving the immigrants from Turkey to Palestine would prove the more difficult problem.[37]

That optimism was soon dashed, however. Barlas's negotiations with the Turks reached a dead end. The British, expected by Kaplan and Epstein to lend a helping hand, failed to do so.

Ze'ev Shind, who supported the policy of blending legal and illegal activities, had serious doubts about the chances of obtaining ships through official channels. He therefore renewed his search for disused older vessels—a market that he and his associates had successfully exploited in the past. Shind was aware that such boats tended to be rickety and did not usually meet government safety criteria. Nevertheless, he believed that by using such vessels with officially licensed craft it would be possible to bring out a larger number of young people, with or without certificates. Upon arriving in Turkey, Shind therefore sought to reestablish the contacts he had made during 1940–41, and concentrated on finding a suitable ship and crew. He was hoping to find an experienced Bulgarian seaman with close ties to harbor authorities and the police.

Amazingly, Shind located just such a ship within a few weeks: the *Maritsa,* a Turkish freighter that could be refitted to carry about 250. Since the Turks might be expected to withhold a passenger-carrying license, Shind shrewdly sought to change the ship's registration. His efforts in the past to find a new registration for the *Lilly,* in Mossad hands since December 1941, had proved unsuccessful; he therefore sought someone who'd take the matter in hand for him. When he met Jordan Spasov, a down-on-his-luck Bulgarian seaman who hoped to rebuild his seafaring fortune, Shind was delighted.[38] Moreover, Spasov had relatives in the Bulgarian police and the internal affairs ministry. He therefore assured Shind that he would have no trouble securing both a Bulgarian registry for the ship and a permit to transport Jewish emigrants.

Shind's contact with Spasov was facilitated by an Italian salt in Turkey who, through Pandelis, had had dealings with the Mossad before and during the initial phases of the war. The Italian, Dandria, vouched for Spasov's reliability, stressing that the Bulgar could be expected to repay the Mossad with loyalty in return for its help in obtaining a new ship. The Mossad planned to transfer the *Maritsa* to Spasov after two voyages, but in fact the ship formally passed to his name when Bulgarian papers were obtained for the vessel. Under the circumstances, whether or not Spasov would stick by his agreement, the Mossad would depend on his own integrity. He was in a position to defraud the agency if he wished.

This situation made both Shind and Teddy Kollek (in Constantinople on mission of the Agency's political department) uneasy about signing the agreement. Sporadic talks with Spasov ensued for two months. He remained in Bulgaria, making contact with him difficult. Dandria sometimes served as go-between. Shind and Kollek therefore resolved to invite Spasov to Constantinople to "work on him," as they put it. For ten days they wined and dined him, attempting to "read" the man; but he still failed to inspire sufficient confidence. He did not seem particularly bright or resourceful, but he did appear honest enough and touchingly willing to work to get his ship. In a May 1943 letter, Shind and Kollek let it be known that they had decided to close the deal with Spasov: "There is no other choice."[39] Thus, with a certain amount of trepidation, Shind and his colleagues proceeded to acquire the ship (for £6,500) and refit it for the voyage. It was transferred to Spasov's ownership and duly registered in Bulgaria.

The Jews in Bulgaria were aware of Colonial Secretary Stanley's statement in Parliament authorizing transport of children and their escorts. Dr. Izidor Baruch, formerly of the Palestine Office, prepared lists of travelers in line with instructions sent from Constantinople. The list did not include members of Zionist youth movements, for two reasons: they were too old to fit the British requirement that immigrants be children, and the Germans told their allies that aliyah was calculated to supply soldiers to the Allies. The Bulgarians, with other Balkan governments, argued that the emigration of children was a humanitarian gesture that could not be refused;[40] by the same token, they forbade the emigration of young people sixteen and over.

The Zionist youth movements interpreted the Palestine Office list as an act of overt discrimination, despite their patchy knowledge of the underlying considerations. Indeed, they went so far as to make accusations of nepotism. They appealed to the rescue mission in Constantinople to instruct Dr. Baruch to add young pioneers to those on the emigration list.[41] But the hands of the mission were tied, as were those of Dr. Baruch. Shind and his colleagues hoped that the *Maritsa* would provide a new cause for young Zionists, under camouflage of a legal transport.

In April, it was learned that Bulgarian border guards turned away numerous children, which effectively stopped the plan to rescue 270 certificate-holders from the Balkans. It was feared that the Bulgarians might also abrogate the promise to let Bulgarian Jews emigrate.[42] Increasingly, the news from Bulgaria was most disturbing: many prominent Jews had been imprisoned. Dr. Baruch was removed from his post and replaced by the head of the Jewish Consistory (the formal organization of Bulgarian Jewish communities).

Communication between Bulgaria and Constantinople grew worse in May. Shind and Barlas found that their couriers were not reaching their destinations.[43] No word came from the Zionist movements—even from those members who had until then been in frequent touch. Shind and his friends could not help but fret about the fate of the Jews in Bulgaria and on the *Maritsa*.

The rescue mission in Constantinople tried to restore communications with Zionist groups in Bulgaria through Jordan Spasov, with whom the Mossad had finalized an agreement calling for two refugee voyages. Spasov and his brother succeeded in transmitting funds and letters to Zionists in the areas of Plovdiv and Varna,[44] which was how word of the planned illegal transport reached them. The involvement of Spasov aroused contradictory reactions.

Some felt (as stated in their letters) that the plan was a hopeful sign, and that they were prepared to trust Spasov to carry it. Others were convinced that working with Spasov was a major error.[45]

At that point, Spasov announced that he had wrung from the Bulgarian authorities a license to transport up to 1,000 people under age sixteen and over age thirty by the end of July. The *Maritsa* had to be made ready, other vessels obtained, and the passengers organized within a month. Barlas and Shind immediately decided to utilize the license to bring out the Jews on the list submitted to the British, in line with London's offer to accept 5,000 people. To this list they wished to add Zionist youth and young pioneer trainees.[46]

Naturally, time was of the essence. It was preferable to take the entire group out at once, but this would require a rather large group of boats. The *Maritsa* could hold 250, but the Red Cross was unlikely to grant protection to a boat so old and decrepit, an advantage that larger and shaplier ships would enjoy. The Mossad therefore needed to find better vessels, as well as assign passengers to the various boats. Here, the Mossad would require the unstinting cooperation of Jewish organizations in Bulgaria.

Spasov was handed a list of 1,800 people by Shind and Barlas. He was then asked to transmit it to the head of the Zionist movement in Bulgaria, Dr. A. Romano. Spasov indeed went to Bulgaria and handed the list to Romano, who was to select a thousand transportees. The lists from Constantinople were meant to establish Spasov's bona fides as an authorized representative for the Mossad and the Jewish Agency. But the meeting with Romano did not go well: Romano was not favorably impressed by Spasov's character. He doubted that he was a man to be trusted with the lives of a thousand people. In reporting as much to Constantinopole, he asked some contacts in the Internal Affairs Ministry and the Sofia police for background on Spasov and for a confirmation that the transfer license had in fact been issued.

As Spasov had not obtained it through official and legal channels, Romano was unable to obtain a satisfactory answer. This only confirmed his worst fears as far as his distrust of Spasov, with whom he now refused to cooperate.[47] Shind and Barlas tried in vain to change his mind. But the telephone line from Constantinople to Sofia was poor and discussion was repeatedly interrupted; they failed to make themselves understood.

Barlas and Shind did not give up: they decided to try a different tack. They would approach the British with the license obtained by Spasov and, on the strength of it, appeal for London's help in obtaining other boats. Given the time limit, Shind and Barlas asked again that the British pressure the Turkish authorities to permit use of three Turkish ships, whose owners had already agreed to assist aliyah.

If all could be settled, Shind and Barlas would notify Romano that the ships and their passengers would sail under Red Cross protection—which would probably ease his suspiciousness of Spasov. The ships obtained from the Turks would provide the needed transportation from Istanbul to Palestine (the part of the journey that Bulgarian ships should not make). This solution would also serve to legalize Spasov's activity under British aegis, and bring to Palestine a number of young Zionists.

But a surprise lay in wait for Barlas and his colleagues when they turned to the British embassy.

Barlas, the British Embassy in Ankara, and the Immigration Plan

On 4 July Barlas went to the British embassy in Ankara with a photocopy of the permit issued by Spasov 19 June in the name of the Bulgarian Ministry of Internal Affairs and an exit permit issued by the Bulgarian police. Barlas asked that John Bennett, the ambassador's chief assistant, open immediate negotiations with the Turks to allow three Turkish-owned vessels—the *Akbal*, the *Nazim*, and the *Nekat*—to carry Jewish refugees from Varna to Istanbul before more time was wasted.[48] Knatchbull-Hugessen voiced objection to the small size of the craft, as the Admiralty preferred larger and more identifiable ships. The three boats in question were also outfitted to carry coal, not passengers. John Bennett did not deny that help had been promised in obtaining Turkish boats for aliyah. He did, however, insist on clearing the matter with London and on checking the Bulgarian permit for the thousand émigrés through the Swiss embassy in Sofia. Only after this was done, Bennett stated, would an approach be made to the Turkish authorities.[49]

The British diplomats knew, of course, how Spasov's license had been obtained and that the Bulgarians were bound to deny official knowledge of it. The British could accomplish little through this maneuver, and precious time would meanwhile be wasted. The members of the rescue mission took this as an act of deliberate obstructionism, which they set out to counter.

In London, Foreign Office reaction was more favorable. It transmitted the question of the permit's validity to the Swiss, but simultaneously took steps required for obtaining safe-conduct guarantees from the Italians and the Germans for the hospital ship *Sontay*, intended for Jewish refugees.[50] Joseph Linton, the Jewish Agency representative in London, was told that the preliminary steps had already been taken. Sir Lewis Namier, the British historian and Zionist member of the Jewish Agency Political Department in London, concerned about the passage of time and the chance that the exit permit might lapse, was told at the Foreign Office on 15 July about the *Sontay*, and asked to retain confidentiality.[51] The ambassador at Ankara was instructed to disregard his own misgivings and make every effort to secure Turkish consent for the Jewish Agency's request. The communication from London stressed that Britain had an interest in leaving no doubt that all possibilities had been thoroughly explored.[52] On 16 July, London reported that the Swiss were still unable to confirm the validity of the exit permit. The matter was within the authority of the foreign secretary, and as he was away at the moment, it was deemed best to wait a few days. On the basis of this response, Bennett and Ambassador Knatchbull-Hugessen decided once again to delay an appeal to the Turkish authorities. In light of all this, Randall suggested to the Colonial Office that the high commissioner meet with Shertok to give him the same assurances that had been given to Namier, and to transmit to him the information regarding the *Sontay*.[53]

In London, Stanley was anxious for the plan to be carried out. But in order to prepare the *Sontay* to transport immigrants from Istanbul to Haifa, it was necessary to obtain a firm Bulgarian confirmation. The Office for Sea Transport was instructed to refrain from reassigning the *Sontay*, but she could not remain idle for very long. The British drew Bulgaria's attention to this fact, and warned that they would make the matter public if Sofia's consent was withdrawn.[54]

On 21 July a report arrived from Bern revealing that the Swiss ambassador had consulted the Bulgarian foreign minister and the latter had emphatically denied authorizing an exit permit.[55] This report angered the British ambassador in Ankara, who made his feelings clear to Barlas. Bennett summoned Barlas on 29 July for a formal dressing down.[56] Barlas, who knew of the permit's origin, was in an uncomfortable postion but defended his staff.

Moshe Shertok, invited to talk to first secretary of the Palestine administration, John McPherson, did not hesitate to confirm that the permit had been obtained through bribery, and that it was therefore understandable that the Bulgarian foreign minister had "overlooked" it. Nevertheless, Shertok maintained, the permit existed and it might be used to save 1,000 Jews. The journey from Varna to Istanbul could be accomplished with two ships sailing under the Bulgarian flag. (Shertok was referring to the *Milca* and the *Maritsa*.) The British were asked only to help ensure the next leg, from Istanbul to Palestine.[57]

It was here that the true difference in approach between the British authorities on the one hand and the Jewish Agency on the other was revealed. The first secretary upbraided Shertok: Britain could not permit itself to act thus or approve an illegal maneuver. It would be impossible to conceal the illegality indefinitely, and the children would suffer in the long run. (Britain was concerned, as McPherson said, with the 4,500 children rather than with the one thousand). All the British officials agreed with the first secretary.[58] The Ankara embassy took an even stronger line. In its view Barlas not only gave false information, but he was also unscrupulous. His report on the Turkish boats and their owners' supposed agreement to carry Jewish passengers was incorrect, it was said, and he was generally unreliable.[59]

It once again fell to London to urge Knatchbull-Hugessen to be more flexible and moderate, and to instruct him to assist Shertok, who was to arrive in Turkey in early August to deal with the Turks concerning ships.[60] London knew through Bern that the exit permit had been issued by parties who wished it to be valid.[61]

Shind, who had not entirely depended on Barlas's British contacts, had gone ahead and acquired a second boat, the *Milca*, similar to the *Maritsa*, that he transferred to the ownership of Spasov's partner. The Mossad was now in a position to transport half of the thousand Jews. Negotiations were also begun with a Swedish shipowner, with the intent of increasing that number should the British-Turkish avenue prove fruitless.[62]

The license obtained by Spasov was due to lapse at the end of July. Since British help failed to arrive, the Mossad was willing to go ahead with the first 500, without the British and without Red Cross protection. It was assumed that once the refugees were on board the two boats, a way would be found to clear the rest of the way for them between Istanbul and Palestine. The chance that the *Maritsa* and the *Milca* would not be able to proceed through the Mediterranean led the Mossad to consider a more complicated alternative. One possibility was a midjourney transfer at sea to the *Lilly,* which flew a Palestine flag and had been available since the *Struma* episode. The *Lilly,* manned by a Haganah crew, would provide a relatively safe means of travel to Palestine, as long as the vessel sailed close to the coast. Though such a transfer did require the assent of British intelligence officials, Shind believed that this could be accomplished.[63]

The plan was endangered, however, by the attitude of the Zionist leaders in Bulgaria. They were reluctant to send people to sea aboard frail boats under the guidance of a man whom they did not trust. No doubt their attitude stemmed in part from the sad experience of the *Salvador,* which had sunk in December 1940. In part, too, there were initial signs that anti-Jewish actions were coming to an end, thus lifting the threat of deportation to Poland.[64]

Despite the setback that they had suffered, Zionist youth in Bulgaria did not express bitterness or anger toward the rescue-mission members. The slight amelioration of their circumstances, the realization that the Bulgarians had stood up to the Germans as to general deportation, and perhaps also the uncertainties surrounding the Spasov project all played a role in reconciling them somewhat to the sorry situation. One member of the Hashomer Hatsair youth movement, a refugee in Bulgaria, put it this way: "We hoped for aliyah and we did not achieve it. We appreciate all your efforts to get us out of here, and it is not your fault that they did not succeed. We are grateful for all your attempts to come to our aid and relieve our suffering. If you were unable to do so, we do not wish to blame you."[65] Indeed, the Zionist youth sought to maintain contact with Constantinople, seeking money and communications from Palestine. Their letters sometimes expressed the idea that only the end of the war would provide a solution for their plight.

What lessons could be derived from the "Bulgarian thousand" experience? The availability of a ship, an exit permit, and a willing group of émigrés was apparently not enough to effect a plan for aliyah. "The Jews are not helping the sea transport," Shind wrote. "Romano and Baruch are not assisting us enough."[66] The local Jewish community lacked the kind of leadership that would coordinate efforts with the Mossad. There was no chance for success without agents from Palestine and a cadre of pioneer youth or responsible veterans willing to risk aliyah bet even under questionable circumstances. These conclusions affected the debate when dissatisfaction within the Mossad was heightened by the Bulgarian episode.

Ze'ev Shind was keenly disappointed. Half a year had gone by since aliyah work had entered into its new phase, yet no concrete results had been obtained. Though he was well aware of all the steps that had been taken, having participated in all the decisions, he felt that something was obviously amiss: appeals to the British had not been forceful enough, perhaps, and too much consideration may have been paid to the needs and concerns of local Jewish leaders in Europe. The lack of Mossad agents in the field able to direct aliyah organization on the scene, and the Mossad's dependence on the British for obtaining large ships in good condition, made the combined legal-illegal strategy seem to be the only viable option at that stage of the war.

The rescue mission in Constantinople appealed to Jerusalem to send them a central figure in the Yishuv's leadership—if not on a permanent basis, then at least for a while. Shertok arrived for a visit in August with startling news of a change in British immigration policy. This could potentially revolutionize the work of the Mossad in Constantinople. The way from Turkey to Palestine now stood open, possibly to thousands of Jews. Turkey had approved the right of passage for Jews en route to Palestine in 1941, on condition they held valid entry permits for their destination. The new British policy, they hoped, amounted to what Ehud Ueberall Avriel, who replaced Teddy Kollek, dubbed "the Balfour Declaration for aliyah bet." The chance to massively broaden their efforts, with the cooperation of British intelligence, now seemed quite realistic. The difficult part of the refugees' journey would be limited to the trip across the Black Sea to Turkey, which ought to reassure European Jewish leaders who hesitated to organize seagoing groups.

Shertok and the Mossad activists assumed that this decision had been kept secret for the same reason that Lord Cranborne's decision of 1942 to "legalize" all Jewish refugees arriving in Palestine had been: fear of provoking a negative Arab response. However, as noted, British behavior during the ensuing months proved that they were wrong.

In August, the British appealed to the Turkish authorities to supply a ship transporting Jews from Bulgaria, in accordance with the request of Barlas and Shind. But Spasov proved unable to renew the previous permits, despite repeated attempts. Until October, efforts continued to bring Jews out of Bulgaria on available ships. When it appeared finally that this would be impossible, plans to organize a departure were focused on Rumania.[67]

In the Histadrut executive council, Yehuda Braginsky, a veteran Mossad activist, demanded to know why the Mossad was not conducting a critical review of the *modus operandi* of its representatives in Constantinople. He blamed the crisis in the Bulgarian case on the confusion of the task of the Mossad with that of the Jewish Agency.[68] Nevertheless, a full-dress discussion was not held over this issue, despite what was apparently a major strategic failure.

Efforts to organize aliyah were shifted to Rumania. It could be expected, though, that in Rumania, too, problems would be encountered in dealing with local Zionist leaders who were on record as opposing sea transport. However, at the end of May the British were prepared to give their assent to emigration from Rumania. The Navy and the War Shipping Office altered their former position, agreeing now to lease Rumanian ships *Bessarabia* and *Transylvania* through the good offices of Turkey, and requested the Turks to arrange it. The Rumanians voiced their agreement both to the emigration and to the lease of the vessels, but it was still necessary to obtain German approval.[69] The Jewish Agency and the Mossad were willing to view it as an encouraging signal to renew emigration from Rumania, to which we shall return shortly.

British Policy: Back to "Tradition"

The discussion and correspondence over the Bulgarian plan continued into August, though concentrated efforts fell off somewhat. During the month, the *Sontay* remained available for Jewish immigrants, though the Foreign Office warned that this would not hold very much longer. If and when a ship was needed to transport children, the Navy would see that a suitable vessel was found within a reasonable time.[70]

There was no apparent way to overcome Berlin's refusal to permit the children to leave. But the the procedures used by the British to execute their plan were less than adequate. They were slow to move forward in wartime, and did not react to developments as they occurred. Over two months passed before London appreciated that Bulgaria's plea back in January was serious. In that interval, the Germans successfully exerted pressure on Sofia to close the Turkish frontier. Two more months passed while the colonial secretary tried to expedite procedural routine, until he gave up and instead proposed an outright change in policy. Meanwhile, Jews had been expelled from Sofia and Jewish emigration was prohibited.

Even when British policy changed, there was no willingness to take extraordinary—and if need be, illegal—measures. British military authorities did not hesitate to do so when British pilots were shot down over enemy territory, but in the matter of Jewish child refugees, the authorities stood behind the high commissioner's view that illegal means were undesirable as they would sooner or later be discovered by the Germans and the Bulgarians.

After August 1943, even Oliver Stanley lost some of the determination that had characterized his previous efforts to save Jews, within the parameters of Britain's Palestine policy. The view that the best way to rescue Jews was to bring the war to a swift conclusion once again held sway. British policy returned to its former duality: the government declared itself in favor of rescue but in practice did nothing about it. The public outcry of the winter and spring of 1943 faded to fatigue by summer. Replies to the inexorable memoranda submitted by committees for Jewish refugees and victims of Nazi persecution were repetitive summaries of British efforts and pointed out that the Germans strictly refused to allow Jews to leave. The memoranda writers were undoubtedly right in demanding that the authorities stop the inertia of routine thinking and routine action: good intentions of some of the ministries were insufficient against the apathy or impotence of lesser officials who lacked the ability to carry out initiatives; and the government, in seeking to steer a clear political course, could not alter its policy slightly; it had to overhaul the entire system.[71]

A clear example of Britain's failure to speak with one voice is the manner in which the government informed the various parties concerned of its decision of 2 July establishing the new immigration policy for Jewish refugees reaching neutral countries.

As already noted, the colonial secretary wished to avoid publication of the decision, for the good of the refugees themselves. Jewish Agency officials, prepared to accept this reasoning, were nonetheless shocked to discover, roughly a month after the decision, that even the Turkish government had not been informed. What, they wondered, was the sense of such a move, if the decision remained a closely guarded secret even from governments that might respond constructively? The Agency's representatives in London and Jerusalem appealed to the government and high commissioner to transmit the information at least to those likely to be concretely involved: chiefly the Turkish and Swiss and their envoys in the Balkans. This request was not granted.

During August and September, news continued to arrive that Hungary and Rumania were willing to allow Jews to leave, both as individuals and in groups. Such emigrants were required to present Turkish transit visas, but the Turkish consuls were not cooperative. Bureaucratic procedures stretched into many weeks and finally blocked prospective emigrants from leaving. Complaints about this reached Jewish organizations in various countries and strengthened criticism leveled at Britain by U.S. groups. In mid-August, even the British ambassador in America, Lord Halifax, began to wonder what had become of the decision taken on 2 July. The Americans apparently knew nothing of the new policy. Informing them of it was likely to soften much of the anti-British criticism, Halifax wrote.[72] Circles close to the Intergovernmental Committee on Refugees, reorganized following the Bermuda Conference, took Britain to task for not making use of available means to save Jews from the Balkans. Halifax was instructed to ask the Americans to keep it secret so that rescue might not be harmed by publicity. U.S. officials, missing the logic behind this request, objected to it.

Over the next several months, another aspect of the British position was revealed. It was not so much concern for the refugees that lay behind the decision not to publicize the new policy, but rather the opposite: the fear that a massive wave of refugees from the Balkans, including non-Jews, might pour into Palestine. Harold MacMichael expressed this in response to a further request by Moshe Shertok that Britain inform Ankara in the interests of rescuing possibly large numbers of European Jews. The purpose, MacMichael wrote to the colonial secretary, was not to encourage more Jews to flee the Balkans, but to improve the situation for those who had already left.[73] Furthermore, it was in Britain's interest that some immigration certificates remain available after the end of the five-year period of the White Paper, until the end of the war. The resident in Cairo and the ambassador in Ankara supported this position, as did Oliver Stanley. At the end of November, the British government remained determined not to inform Ankara of its decision in July.[74] Only in March 1944 did the British ambassador to Turkey transmit the information, following changes in U.S. rescue policy.

It seemed as if Britain had returned in the fall of 1943 to the position it had taken a year before. The desire to help Jewish refugees, as expressed in the plan for Bulgaria's Jewish children, fell victim to caution and suspicion aimed at preserving the balance between refugee policy and the White Paper.[75] However, a number of trends surfaced that ruled out the balance approach the British were seeking.

During the first eight months of 1943 the colonial secretary and certain elements in the Foreign Office had advocated a more flexible approach to the White Paper to bolster rescue efforts. This was designed to strengthen Britain's two roles as defender and ruler of Palestine, on the one hand, and as a democracy required to respond to the Holocaust, on the other.

But this outlook concerning the war and the Holocaust, which had permitted Britain to turn the chance to save 29,000 into a "grand plan," also led to its failure. What had been lacking from the start was an appreciation of the need to make an accurate assessment of the relationship between the war and the Holocaust—in other words, to evaluate the amount of effort required to make rescue a wartime priority. Therefore, policy lacked the agility and adaptability necessary to adapt procedures to the rapidly changing conditions of the times. The emigration plan encountered significant difficulties because it meant taking irregular and daring action to achieve goals not defined as priority war aims. For that reason, even minor changes in bureaucratic convention or in methods of obtaining transport were taken as transgressions. When modifications were finally implemented, after debate, it was no longer possible to put them to effective use. Eventually, the special conditions that had for a time prompted the British to view the war, the Holocaust, and Palestine in one context came to be conceived as no longer prevailing. Final victory appeared close at hand, the Arab Middle East was mobilizing once again and realigning itself with Britain, and Britain in 1944 insisted on separating the fate of the Jewish people and the future of Palestine. Still, before 1944 ended, the Mossad and the rescue mission in Istanbul had managed to adjust to the changing political circumstances and succeeded in organizing immigration from Rumania.

13

Rescue at Work: The Mossad and Aliyah bet from Rumania

The Debate Over Immigration via Sea Routes

By 1943, the Jewish leaders of Rumania were cognizant of the political struggle against their government's Jewish policy. Led by Wilhelm Filderman, they demonstrated an acute sensitivity to the changing concerns and vulnerabilities of the Rumanian regime. To prevent Rumania's total capitulation to German demands on "the Jewish issue," Jewish leaders used an approach that combined appeals to legality and constitutionalism with arguments related to Rumanian national pride and national interests. Their central aims were to prevent a mass "deportation to the east," to stop the Transnistria deportations, to return Jewish deportees, and to aid Jewish refugees.

Methodically, if without early successes, Filderman and his associates focused on preventing deportations (begun in late 1942). This seemed to coincide with efforts of Mihai Antonescu, the deputy prime minister, who sought an approach to the Allies in the hope of improving Rumania's postwar political position. As we have seen, the Germans were aware of these attempts and did all they could to oppose them, including clamoring for Antonescu's resignation. The German intervention failed to change Rumania's political leadership, although it did succeed in barring Jewish emigration or effecting a significant alteration in Rumania's Jewish policy during 1943.

The situation improved somewhat toward the end of 1943, but the press was filled with anti-Jewish hate propaganda following massive defeats at the front. It was difficult to judge whether this government-approved campaign presaged new policy decisions. In the summer of 1943, Filderman had been deported to Transnistria, while the German-language press of Bucharest carried vicious slander of him. Expectations of war's end were accompanied by anxiety: What price would the Germans exact in their retreat from Transnistria and Rumania, and how would they treat the helpless population?

The German occupation of Hungary in March 1944 augmented this anxiety with the realization that Rumania's turn might be next. The trend toward seeking an understanding with the Western Allies therefore made headway during that period, becoming an almost desperate attempt to rule out a Soviet invasion. Marshal Ion Antonescu did nothing to prevent his deputy's attempts to signal Rumania's intentions to the Allies. One consequence of these activities was the replacement of the Rumanian envoy in Turkey in December 1943 by a man who favored the idea of feeling out the Allies. His appointment was meant to convey the growing political strength of those in Rumania who shared his views.[1] These maneuverings held a risk, of course, since they could propel the Germans toward a decision to occupy Rumania, as had occurred in Hungary. Berlin was especially concerned that its allies would abandon Germany, as had the Italians. Rumania's leaders, therefore, had to tread very lightly in formulating and establishing a policy that would simultaneously avert the danger of a German occupation and win favorable surrender terms in the event of an Allied invasion of Southern Europe or a Soviet invasion via Transnistria.

In 1943 and 1944, the Jewish leadership in Rumania viewed emigration as an option that could both save Jewish lives and offer the regime an avenue for protecting the Rumanian national interest. Behind this idea was an attempt to exploit the exaggerated assumptions of the Rumanian government with regard to the influence of world Jewry on the policies of the Allies. These assumptions, albeit founded on anti-Semitic mythology, were believed by Jews to offer leverage in official dealings. As the Allies were opposed to the Axis countries' Jewish policy, a change in that policy could be portrayed as the sign of a more general reassessment. This was the message Jewish leaders gave to various Rumanian officials. Moreover, the Jews saw that the authorities were well aware of their ongoing communication with Geneva and Constantinople, cities that could serve as conduits to the Allies. The Jews detected in Rumania's willingness—however inconsistent—to allow Jewish refugees to pass through the country, and to permit the departure of Rumanian Jews, confirmation of Bucharest's desire to keep open such channels to the Allies. From their informants within the government, the Jews learned of Germany's constant efforts to reverse decisions of this kind. They concluded that there was a struggle between Germany and Rumania that focused on the Jewish emigration issue: a struggle with important implications for the independence of Rumania and for the coordination of policy between the two countries.

But while Jewish leaders were in agreement on the importance of emigration, it was deeply split over the desired means of managing it. Had it been possible to transport Jewish emigrants in large, oceangoing craft, under Red Cross protection, then only one matter would have been the subject of disagreement: who, among the many who wished to exit, would. It became clear, however, that while most of the political forces with a stake in the issue favored Jewish emigration (except the Germans), they were unable to reach a common decision in principle, and thus Jewish emigrants had to resort to small cargo ships. It was highly doubtful that the Red Cross would recognize and grant protection to such transports.

With the *Struma* tragedy so clearly etched in their minds, fear of sea transports was a constant factor for the Rumanian and Bulgarian Jewish leadership. They were still mulling over the *Paskarush* incident (discussed earlier), in which passengers had had to stay on board for weeks under very harsh conditions, and then got nowhere. The Jewish communities of Bucharest and Czernowitz were then required to care for the hapless refugees for many months.

Among the Zionists, only Shmuel Enzer, head of the Palestine Office, was prepared to agree to any type of emigration, as long as it was organized by representatives of the Yishuv. Opposition to aliyah bet organized by the Mossad was nothing new for Rumanian Jews. Although Rumania had been a major staging area for illegal immigration before the war, the Zionist leaders there had not been involved in its direction, and had aided only minimally in organizing it.

Aliyah bet in Rumania was organized by two Mossad emissaries, Yosef Barpel and Ruth Klueger-Aliav, who were uneasy about directly involving leaders of the Jewish community in the organizational aspects of their activities. Moshe Oruchowski, who headed the Palestine Office until his murder in the pogroms of January 1941, was considered by the Mossad as having been good to deal with by virtue of his noninterference in their activities. Only in the *Darien* episode had a member of the Palestine Office staff been directly involved, and in that case the Yishuv emissaries themselves were no longer in Rumania.

Along with the considerable hesitancy of Rumanian Jewish leaders regarding sea transports, it should also be noted that Rumanian Jews had organized the extraordinary and dangerous flight of small craft during 1941 and 1942. These were the factors that the Mossad and the rescue mission in Constantinople needed to take into account when they began to plan aliyah from Rumania.

To all of this, however, another factor has to be added: the troubled relations among the various Jewish leaders in Rumania. There were acrimonious arguments among them, including accusations of dishonesty and abuse of privilege. A good deal has to be related to a lack of trust and a secrecy that affected all public activity. It must be remembered that official Zionist activity had been outlawed since the summer of 1941, so that any activity carried on was done so illegally and hidden from not only the bulk of the membership, but also from many leading figures as well. Contacts with the Zionist movement abroad, in Geneva and Istanbul, were maintained only by a very limited circle of people and through methods that dictated a high degree of caution and discretion. There was fear of denouncement either by the secret police or other hostile forces.

Zionists had cultivated contacts with Rumanian officials at various levels. Filderman's contacts with Marshal Antonescu, effected through the marshal's optician, are very well known, as are the contacts between the chief rabbi, Shafran, and the royal family, and between the Zionist leader A. L. Zissu and Antonescu. Apart from these contacts with the highest echelon of Rumanians, Jews maintained contact with officials at lower levels: with the chief of police, the deputy minister for internal affairs, the secret police, and various other officials. Bribery was freely accepted. As far as we can tell from the evidence we have, there was no one who refused to accept "dirty" money.

Thus, it is hardly surprising that in this atmosphere charges of profiting from the public purse should have been made. Jewish communal welfare and relief were handled by agencies, some voluntarily chosen, some appointed from above; rescue and emigration were the province of both legal and underground bodies. This produced a highly complex and problematic set of relationships among Jewish leaders, who sometimes came into conflict even as they pursued similar goals of safeguarding the Jewish community and preventing further anti-Jewish legislation. Mutual distrust certainly played a role in such conflicts alongside personal rivalries and antipathies. The Rumanians were also involved in encouraging this divisiveness in order to weaken the position of Jewish leaders.[2] Correspondence from Rumania to Geneva and Constantinople of that period shows a lot of disunity among the Jewish leadership.

Dov Berger, who parachuted into Rumania in August 1944, reported:

> The level of internal life [among the Jews] and personal relations does not meet even minimum standards. Everyone accuses everyone else of all sorts of charges, first of all the abuse of trust. It is a catastrophe that since Oruchowski's death no one has succeeded in running the Palestine Office without being accused of stealing, and therefore escaping to Palestine. [Public] business here has never been run in the most satisfactory manner, and the affairs of state have themselves set the tone for this. During wartime and in the absence of public control, things have become much worse.[3]

Things had reached such a crisis, he explained, because the Zionist movement had been prevented for several years from operating openly and democratically. Underground conditions being what they were, Zionists required the guidance of delegates' conventions to set policy and elect officials to carry it out. There were sincere and committed people who voluntarily took leadership and represented the movement's interests; but there were also various usurpers who took advantage of the situation for personal gain. Thus, the Jewish leadership had both types and—even worse—it was not always easy to distinguish between them. This, indeed, was the assessment of the rescue mission for quite some time. Haim Barlas, Eliezer Kaplan, Shaul Avigur, and others frequently lectured their Rumanian Zionist contacts on the need to overcome their internal divisions.[4]

Yet other differences spoiled the relations between the Zionist youth movements and elder Zionists. The former were natural allies of the rescue mission in Constantinople and had in the past formed the backbone of aliyah bet networks. They also provided information regarding Jewish affairs and advised on the choice of a *modus operandi* within the community. They were the first ones to offer cooperation, to set up communication with those in the labor camps, and to send couriers into Transnistria. But the youth movements had been particularly hard hit by the deportations, and many members were in labor camps or in hiding.

The youth movement members complained that they were not involved in decisions but were then asked to carry them out. This applied to relief funds sent from Palestine for distribution among the deportees in Transnistria and labor-camp inmates; and the complaints dwelt on the drawing up of priority rosters for emigration. The youth movements demanded a significant proportion of places aboard immigrant boats, since they had spent long years in training for life in Palestine and had proven their loyalty. They would, they argued, render the greatest of advantages to the Yishuv. Furthermore, they contended, the Rumanian authorities had blocked their legal exit from the country, so that illegal immigration remained their sole hope for escape. (Their view of the illegal nature of aliyah bet was thus focused on the act of emigration rather than on illegal entry to Palestine.) Lastly, they faced the greatest amount of danger from the authorities. They thought they were the ones who ran the greatest risk by virtue of their involvement in illegal relief activities; therefore, they should be among the first candidates for emigration.

It hurt the youth to see places on immigrant boats sold to clods with financial means, and they accused the arbiters of reaping personal profit from these funds. In part, they blamed the Yishuv's rescue mission, which, after all, was acting as a conduit for relief funds and was putting the wrong sort in charge of emigration work:

> You ask us why we are not more active, why we don't show more initiative, but you take from us all our capacity for activism, you hand over all the formal powers and the funds to the likes of Enzer and Egosi ? a central figure in the Palestine office. In whose name and to what purpose?[5] Your letters absolutely astounded us. How can you tell us that we lack an understanding of the movement? . . . This is no ordinary matter of partisan disputes . . . and we cannot sit silently by [when] they betray our most basic needs, such as aliyah bet. . . . Everything is fraudulent and deceitful, and you, through your ignorance, have helped them. We, two hundred young pioneers from Bucharest and one hundred other movement members, appeal to you for aliyah bet. In this matter criminal behavior has taken place. Status-seekers are leaving, while trainees with two and three years of hard work behind them, and our people in Transnistria and in the concentration camps are waiting in vain.[6]

These and other letters express the young Zionists' sense of betrayal and neglect.

In fact, the Mossad learned by debriefing immigrants arriving at Haifa on the Milca, the Maritsa, and the Kazbek (to be discussed below) that places on the Mossad boats had been raffled off, to the dire disadvantage of refugees and young pioneers. In several cases, young Zionists who had been included in the passenger lists were left behind. Such was the anger and bitterness among the Zionist youth that in some of their letters they complained.[7] A further cause for friction between the youth movements and the established Zionist leadership was the matter of refugees being smuggled across the border from Hungary after the German occupation. An underground received the refugees, hid them and supplied them with forged papers, and sent them on to Bucharest, and from there to Istanbul. These refugees were given priority in assigned places aboard immigrant boats, as per the instructions of the rescue mission in Istanbul. The expenses were borne by the rescue mission directly.

Youth movement members focused the organization of this underground railway on two border locations: Torda and Timisoara. The significant funds required were funneled chiefly through the relief committee in Bucharest. But adult functionaries were suspected of being apathetic to the plight of the refugees and skimping on the funds forwarded for this purpose. Otherwise, more Jews might have been smuggled over the border, and refugees caught by the police and the border patrols were not ransomed when they might have been.[8]

The rescue mission found it difficult to determine which charges were well-founded. Moreover, among the various youth movements there were frictions and personal conflicts. These often derived less from ideological zeal than from narrow partisanship. Each movement angled for a greater allocation of transport berths, and to this end the movements sometimes reported the existence of activities and branches that did not always correspond to reality. Letters arrived from Rumania with this type of statement: "Members of Betar and of Agudat Israel should not be given places in illegal transports." Or, "The orphans of Transnistria ought to be transported in a few larger ships, so that they do not take up the places meant for young pioneers on the smaller boats."[9]

This raises an interesting question: What was behind this purported "egoism" in the matter of aliyah? How was it that dedicated youngsters who risked their lives to maintain the link with the Jews in Transnistria and offer them assistance, and who sent back anguished reports on the situation of the children there, demanding that no effort be spared to rescue them, how was it that they, too, fell prey to the partisan particularism of their elders?

The answer is complex and difficult. One facet of the problem is expressed in a letter by Eli Shayau, a member of Dror (Zionist Socialist Youth Movement) in Hungary, in which he spoke of the infamous "darker instincts" that seemed to rule his comrades whenever the question of leaving for Palestine rose. In the face of what seemed imminent escape, all other values, responsibilities, and feelings of mutual sympathy dissolved.[10] Another facet was the perception of having been deeply wronged by those who were turning aliyah bet into a cross market for the highest bidders. Without means of their own, the young people were in effect shut out.

Yet another problem was the way aliyah bet was seen by the youth in 1944. To many of them, it retained the same purpose and elan that it had possessed before the war, intended for the young pioneers who could not wait for immigration quotas. Indeed, the act of illegal aliyah came to represent the crowning of a career of Zionist activism and years of training for settlement in Palestine. It was too unbearable that now they were to be denied this chance. As one of them put it in October 1943, "Find a way for us to immigrate . . . find a solution for the pioneering movement . . . send us a boat, do something concrete. We are waiting for you to come up with the solution that will save us."[11]

This, then, was the complex psychological, social, and political situation that faced the rescue mission as it set out from Rumania. They were the target of many mutually contradictory messages about Zionist leaders, and about specific activities and organizations. At the same time, they realized that although the Jews of Rumania stood a better chance than anyone of leaving Europe and thereby saving their lives, there was actually very little that the rescue mission could do to effect change in Rumania. Many of the difficulties facing the mission were bound up with forces at work within Rumania, both in the Jewish community and outside it, and ultimately determined by the course of the war and the anti-Jewish policies of the regime.

In 1943 and 1944, it was not possible to choose one's partners as scrupulously as one might wish, as it was also hard to tell, from a distance, who was right and who was wrong. There was no time to undertake full-scale inquiries, and it was likely that many of the charges leveled at public figures could be refuted. In 1944, there was no choice but to accept that the Rumanian secret police stood able to add certain people to the passenger lists; hence the rumors that Jews who had served as Siguaranza informants were being granted places on Mossad boats. Even the charge that Zionist leaders were selling sea passage at exorbitant rates, perhaps even raking something off the top, lost something of its shock value,[12] since there was scant choice but to go on working with these people. The view in Constantinople was that there appeared to be little hope that a better alternative could be found. Although so many norms and standards of behavior had been abandoned in the stark reality of occupied Europe, there was one value that the rescue mission needed to uphold above and against all others: the goal of rescue.

The Mossad had come a long way since 1940, when cooperation with Berthold Storfer—who had at Eichmann's behest organized the voyages of the *Milos,* the *Pacific,* and the *Atlantic*—had seemed out of the question. How differently would Zvi Yehieli have reacted to his encounters with Storfer in Bucharest and Geneva if they had taken place in 1944? Such speculation need not have troubled Yehieli and Shind as they helped organize aliyah in 1943 and 1944, for it would be inaccurate to say that the two situations were analogous.

The question that faced the Mossad and its rescue mission was how to implement aliyah despite the seemingly irreconcilable differences and conflicts, despite the lack of a modicum of cooperation, among the Rumanian Zionists. The answer, which the Mossad proposed, had three components: a) It would attempt to cajole the various groups into a more cooperative relationship; b) it would mix legal and illegal activities, as in Bulgaria, but, it was hoped, with greater finesse; and c) it would try to set up a separate network of maximum independence from the Zionist organizations, which would answer to Constantinople and thus form parallel leadership.

Contested Authority: Bucharest and the Yishuv's Delegation

The optimistic assessment of Kaplan and others in the beginning of 1943 that organizing transport from the Balkans to Constantinople would prove relatively simple, and that Turkish boats would be made available, turned out to be groundless. Despite a report by Misho Benvenisti, chairman of the Zionist Organization in Rumania (confirmed by the Red Cross in Bucharest), that Ion Antonescu had requested and received Berlin's permission for the shipping out of 8,000 children, no boats were available in Rumania.[13] The rescue mission in Constantinople urged the Rumanian Jewish leaders to acquire vessels on the local market, but precious little was achieved.

Yet it was the belief of the Mossad that Rumania—even more than Bulgaria—was a fertile field for the strong strategy of combined legal and illegal operations. It was difficult to distinguish between substantive objections to sea transport and objections deriving basically from personal antipathies. Shind and his colleagues therefore sought to mobilize both Enzer and Benvenisti—who respectively supported and opposed aliyah bet—for combined legal and illegal transports. This *modus operandi* also seemed to fit the Rumanian context, where so much already depended upon bribe-taking and other illegal activities.

In the summer of 1943, Enzer had been offered a chance to purchase a Greek-registered barge, the *Smyrni,* that could be refitted for use on the open sea. The aliyah committee of the Rumanian Zionist Organization had no reason to believe, however, that Rumania would permit a transport to sail under a Greek flag. In addition, the price being asked for the vessel was steep. It was necessary in any case to consult Constantinople over the advisability of buying it. It was decided to send a delegation of committee members—Benvenisti, Enzer, and Moritz Geiger—to Braila to inspect the boat. Their hope was that, if the *Smyrni* could indeed be made seaworthy, an exit permit could be obtained for it. That would make the transport more or less legal.

In late August or September, Constantinople sent word recommending the purchase, with Shind's promise to provide the necessary funds. He and the other mission members misread the joint action that was taken to inspect the boat as a sign that Enzer and Benvenisti had resolved their costly dispute over sea transport. They believed that one successful transport would open the way to others.

In the fall of 1943, it seemed that conditions were once again favorable for aliyah bet, but plans fell afoul of political exigencies. Both the Rumanians and the British were willing to allow children onto the transports, with accompanying adults. This stipulation revived internal struggles over the composition of the passenger lists. Shaul Avigur, who arrived in Constantinople in October to help coordinate operations, dispatched a stern message to the Jewish leaders in Rumania demanding greater cooperation and unity. He lectured them about the responsibility they bore and appealed to their historical sense by reminding them of the collapse of the ancient Jewish revolt against Rome and the sacking of Jerusalem's temple after internecine fighting.[14] Avigur had no formal authority over the Zionist leaders, but his position in the Yishuv and the Mossad lent weight to what he had to say.

Such attempts elicited mixed reactions. Some admitted that the exhortations from Constantinople had struck a chord and agreed wholeheartedly that the paramount need was for unity; others angrily denounced what they saw as the Palestinians' lack of understanding for local matters, because of which they appeared to belittle serious issues. And some even advocated severing contact with Constantinople.[15]

The Pandelis Controversy, Fall 1943

The intermediary for the sale of the *Smyrni* was Pandelis, also eager to receive the commission to refit the boat as a passenger carrier.

Sometimes referred to as "the fat one," Pandelis has played an intriguing role in our story, having been involved in aliyah bet since 1939. His involvement produced a new round of acrimonious arguments among the Rumanian Jewish leaders, in which every vexed aspect of the issue of sea transports was rehashed.[16]

It was also well known that Pandelis had excellent contacts among the lower port officials at Constantsa and Braila as well as with various police. He was therefore regarded as able to persuade his contacts to take desired steps. Under the dire conditions at the time, these connections were absolutely vital. Pandelis's connections, his freedom to maneuver, his ability to grease palms and arrange all sorts of shady deals were behind the fraud he perpetrated on the *Struma* passengers and organizers. Everyone had believed it when he lied that the ship was in sound—even excellent—condition. When the Rumanian press reported otherwise, Pandelis bought off the officer sent by the Jews to inspect the ship.

Was it proper, then, to turn once again to this cheat and pirate? Benvenisti absolutely refused to entrust to Pandelis the job of refitting the *Smyrni*. He went so far as to ask the youth movements not to deal with Pandelis at all. But from the reports reaching Constantinople, it seemed to the rescue emissaries that the entire debate had been reopened; for it was not only to Pandelis that Benvenisti objected, but to the general proposition of travel on boats like the *Smyrni*.[17] Moreover, this time doubts were expressed among Enzer's circle, as well. Though they supported aliyah bet, they objected to assigning the refitting to shifty Pandelis. They believed a way could be found to legalize the trip and obtain Red Cross protection if someone more trustworthy was retained.[18]

It turned out, however, that the Red Cross could not grant recognition and protection to a ship flying the flag of a belligerent. It would be necessary to transfer the *Smyrni* from Greek to neutral ownership. This proved untenable.[19]

As these details were being worked out, Shind and his colleagues informed the aliyah committee in Bucharest that the *Milca* and *Maritsa,* which could not be used in Bulgaria, would be assigned for use in Rumania. Pandelis would oversee the transfer and the preparations for a departure from Constantsa.[20]

By this act, Shind and the other emissaries were announcing their trust in Pandelis, hoping to put an end to a controversy that they viewed as obstructive. Those who opposed Pandelis refused to accept the decision handed down from Constantinople. Benvenisti, in particular, strongly opposed sea transports, alleging Mihai Antonescu had warned him that no exit permits would be granted to boats carrying Jews, for fear that Soviet submarines would sink them. Mihai Antonescu was unprepared to accept that responsibility on Rumania's behalf.[21] Benvenisti argued that the situation for Jews in Rumania in the fall of 1943 did not justify such desperate sea voyages.

Enzer and his supporters, however, decided to go ahead with preparations regardless, and to use connections in the Rumanian government to obtain permits. Work on the *Smyrni* went on at a slow pace, and in Constantinople, it was decided to put the *Milca* and *Maritsa* into service first.[22]

Shind and his colleagues had two considerations behind that decision. The *Milca* and *Maritsa* were ready and could be transferred quickly to Constantsa through Pandelis. There was no chance of Red Cross protection for them, but at least their Bulgarian flag would save them from Soviet or German naval attacks. The sole concern was with possible German action against the boats in Constantsa. If Enzer could obtain the exit permit, however, the Germans would not likely prevent the ships from sailing.

The Mossad men were willing to take this admittedly large risk, at least partly because of their own frustration at having nothing to show for almost a full year's work. They were worried that, as in Bulgaria, the lack of coordination between the mission and the leaders on the scene would scuttle plans for Rumania. They did not want to dictate to the Rumanian Zionists on internal matters, but they did want to make it clear that aliyah operations had to take precedence over other considerations. Shind was firmly convinced that after one successful voyage, the Rumanian Zionists would all fall into line behind aliyah bet.[23] Thus, he and his colleagues felt justified in setting up a semi-independent operation, independent of the local leadership and instructed directly from Constantinople. This was how the ORAT (Official Rumania Expeditini Transportoi Bucoresti Colea) was established in December 1943.

ORAT was not intended to be Pandelis's private bureau, but rather a front organization for the Rumanian authorities, which the Mossad would operate from Constantinople. Apart from Pandelis, ORAT was staffed by youth movement members who would work hand in hand with the Palestine Office. The latter organized passenger groups and took care of their paperwork. Pandelis was to oversee the technical aspects of the operation and obtain exit permits from the police and harbor authorities. Thus, ORAT was meant to give the Mossad added flexibility without negating approaches being made to the Rumanian government at higher levels.

Yet this step elicited strong objections. Even members of the Palestine

Office—Enzer, Geiger, and Nussbaum—were unhappy with the arrangement, which obliged them to work in close daily contact with Pandelis. They worried that prices would be driven up and that the office would only strengthen Pandelis's position, giving him the chance to intervene directly in the organization of aliyah operations. Benvenisti and his supporters decided to withdraw entirely from such work directed by the Mossad.[24] Against this backdrop, another brouhaha erupted between the Palestine Office in Bucharest and Haim Barlas's attempt to facilitate Jewish emigration from Rumania.

The Bela-Chita Incident

Barlas was trying to expedite the emigration of children from Rumania with certificates as well as Turkish transit visas. He was unable to secure a Turkish vessel for this purpose, and therefore decided to use a boat obtained by the Mossad from the same agent who had sold it the *Milca* and the *Maritsa*. This new one, called the *Bela-Chita,* flew a Bulgarian flag of registry and was in exceptionally good condition. Barlas therefore believed he could convince the Red Cross to place the boat under its protection. Because the children's emigration permits had originally been negotiated by Benvenisti, Barlas disregarded the current conflict between Benvenisti and the Mossad and sought to involve him in a project with which he was already identified. Knowing that Benvenisti would have no truck with Pandelis, Barlas sought another to work with Benvenisti and oversee operations. Barlas found a Jew named Z. Becker, a Zionist who was not a member of the aliyah committee, but had in the past worked as a shipping agent and got on good with Benvenisti, Filderman, and the Rumanian representatives of the Red Cross.

The Rumanian Red Cross, headed by Dani Britianu, were involved in relief work for the Jews in Transnistria. In October 1943, a dynamic new Red Cross representative arrived in Rumania, Charles Kolb, and he offered to facilitate Jewish emigration. Like Britianu, Kolb was involved in the transfer and distribution of funds from Geneva to Rumania. He established good relations with the Jewish leadership and stated his willingness to help arrange Red Cross protection for the planned transport.

It was Kolb, too, who worked to bring deported Jewish children back to Rumania from Transnistria in anticipation of their departure for Palestine— as Filderman had demanded. Kolb was aware that, after the Bulgarian plan had failed, the British were interested in seeing a group of children leave Rumania.

All of these factors tended to reinforce the organizers' confidence that a common push would this time produce results. Becker, who was involved in the planning, sought from Barlas an official letter from the Jewish Agency stating that the children would receive proper entry documents for Palestine. This, he felt, would aid in obtaining an exit permit from the Rumanian authorities. Barlas sent him the required letter.

Lack of coordination with the aliyah committee in Bucharest introduced an element of confusion at this point, because both Becker and the committee were approaching the same government officials with similar requests, the committee seeking exit permits for the *Milca* and the *Maritsa*. In the absence of an official stamp of this kind, Enzer and Geiger asked Shind to persuade the Rumanians to issue an exit permit. His letter was to suggest that every emigrant who reached Turkey would receive a transit visa there. This would prove to the Rumanians that the passengers had a bona fide destination.

Shind received this request during Barlas's temporary absence from Constantinople. Unable to consult him, Shind sent the following declaration:[25]

> On the basis of the agreement of all the governments concerned, we confirm that every Jew arriving in Istanbul from any Rumanian port whatsoever will definitely receive all necessary documents and will continue his journey at our expense. Given that assurance, we can affirm that any vessel carrying Jewish emigrants will be unloaded here and will be able to immediately return to its port of embarkation.

Though Shind lacked the formal authority to issue such a letter, what he wrote did in fact have a basis. As noted, in July 1943 Britain decided to permit any Jewish refugee reaching Turkey to enter Palestine. This guaranteed a Turkish transit visa, according to the Ankara policy that dated from 1941.[26]

The two letters from Barlas and Shind, arriving at a time of high tension among Rumanian Zionists, stirred up intense conflict and equally intense scrutiny by a variety of persons. Becker, supported by Filderman and Benvenisti, hurried to utilize the Barlas letter and declared that he, Becker, was the sole representative of the Jewish Agency authorized to organize aliyah. The second letter, Becker charged, was nothing but a forgery by Pandelis, whose unsavory reputation was, allegedly, widely known. Becker stressed that no one but Barlas was authorized to sign a commitment on behalf of the Jewish Agency—a fact that other local figures confirmed.

At that point, the controversy engulfed the rescue mission itself. Barlas, who was still in Ankara when Kolb's inquiry for clarification arrived, knew nothing of Shind's letter, so that when Simonds, the representative of the Red Cross in Ankara, contacted him and asked who was authorized to sign for the Agency, he innocently replied that he was the only one with the authority to do so. When asked further whether Shind could have sent such a letter to Bucharest, Barlas confidently answered that Shind could not have. This was reported to Kolb, who in turn reported that the letter was a forgery, and Becker thus informed the Rumanian authorities.[27]

Enzer and the Bucharest aliyah committee were devastated. They raised a furor over the incident, complaining of the lack of coordination between Barlas and Shind. They also protested against the direct arrangements made with Benvenisti and Filderman "behind their backs," while they, to their chagrin, had been forced to work with Pandelis. This mishandled affair strengthened the hand of those who opposed aliyah bet, had put the committee in a bad light with the authorities—and with the Jewish public at large, which had already been fairly critical.[28]

In Constantinople, too, the affair did not pass quietly. Barlas took a dim view of Shind's action, which, he felt, had upset the delicate relations built up with the Turks. Barlas recalled his own unfortunate experience with Spasov's permit, which the British refused to treat as bona fide.[29] He was adamant that he alone was to approach the various governments concerned. Shind, on the other hand, felt that Barlas was overzealous in protecting his own status and that he showed a lack of imagination. As a result, he thought another opportunity had been lost. However, Shind's strictures against Barlas would have been of little significance of themselves had it not been for Barlas's unpopularity among the rescue mission generally.[30]

It has remained unclear why Barlas did not wish to involve the Bucharest committee in his dealings with Becker. The evidence does not allow us to answer satisfactorily. Perhaps Barlas thought that had he succeeded, as hoped, in obtaining an official permit and Red Cross protection, it may have opened the field to smaller craft transports. This would have furthered the attempts to make use of the *Milca* and the *Maritsa,* which were only slightly different from the *Bela-Chita.* Perhaps they, too, might have received the desired permits.

It should be noted that the *Bela-Chita* sailed in April 1944, with Red Cross protection, carrying 150 children from Transnistria. The *Milca* and the *Maritsa* preceded her, though they did not have the Red Cross's recognition, as shall be seen later.

Aliyah bet Voyages in the Spring of 1944

The first year of the Mossad's activity within the rescue mission ended in 1943, with no concrete achievements. Shind and his colleagues decided it was time to take a major risk: to arrange and effect a transport without official permits. This required Pandelis's know-how and connections, as well as the full cooperation of the prospective passengers, particularly in the youth movement. A successful attempt would further independent actions of this kind.

This decision implied some recklessness: even if the Rumanians did nothing, the Germans had to be reckoned with. There was also the danger of an accidental attack by the Soviets. "We need heaven's help," Shind wrote to his friends in Palestine.[31]

The Zionists in Rumania were dealt a setback in January 1944 when the *Maritsa,* having evaded the Germans at Varna, sailed for Constantsa, only to be confiscated by German patrol boats. Thus, without having carried out one rescue mission, the *Maritsa* seemed lost. It was in this difficult situation that Pandelis demonstrated his particular skills. Through intensive lobbying with the Rumanian authorities, who were bought off handsomely, the boat was returned after several weeks.

The Germans were determined to interfere. For months they had been receiving copies of correspondence between the rescue center in Geneva and Bucharest, as well as some from Constantinople. Hans Volti, who ran between Bucharest and Geneva for Swiss intelligence, provided the Germans with these papers for photocopying. Germany's embassy was fully apprised of Zionist plans, Zionist contacts, and the help Zionists got from Jewish organizations.

All this was transmitted to Rumania as evidence of the "crimes" Jews were plotting against the regime, purportedly to overthrow it. In January, the heads of the youth movements and the Zionist organization were arrested, including Benvenisti, Enzer, and Nussbaum. Incriminating evidence was found in the possession of a member of the Dror youth organization: a letter from Lova Gokovsky, a Palestinian Jew who had parachuted into Rumania a month before the arrests took place. Forged identity papers for refugees crossing the border and foreign currency sent by Jewish organizations were seized. The men were charged with helping refugees cross the border illegally, conspiring with foreign agencies, and plotting a revolt. The Jews felt indignation and fear. After five to six weeks, most of the adult arrestees were released, but quite a number of the young were incarcerated for months.[32]

The rescue mission in Constantinople was shocked. There was grave concern for the Rumanian comrades and worry about the information that the Germans might obtain, especially regarding Gokovsky. The reports to Palestine were gloomy indeed. A chance for success had been snatched away, and in its place stood a disaster that virtually nullified the efforts of an entire year. The grim determination of the Mossad agents to stick it out came to the fore. There was to be no admission of defeat. During those very days a new contract was signed for a boat called the *Firin,* a Bulgarian vessel obtained through a friend of Pandelis. This brought the number of boats at the Mossad's disposal to four.

At that point, port authorities in Varna ordered the *Milca, Firin,* and *Bela-Chita* to quit the harbor. It was difficult to know just why the order was given and what it implied. It was thought likely that the Germans were behind it. Nevertheless, Shind and his colleagues decided to move the boats to Constantsa, where German influence was also palpable. However, without a permit, the boats could not be transferred to Turkey, and had no means to obtain a permit. They hoped that, with Pandelis's help in Rumania, they could keep the crafts from falling into German hands.

This was how things stood in February 1944: Jewish and youth movement leaders in Rumania were under arrest, charged with serious crimes against the state. *Maritsa,* in Rumania to take on refugees, had been seized by the Germans (though Pandelis pledged its release). And a small flotilla of Mossad boats was forced to leave Varna, with nowhere to go but Constantsa. What might their fate be once they arrived? Would they ever again assist aliyah operations?

In the history of aliyah bet crucial decisions were made at crisis points, which added to the considerable tensions of this work. Shind instructed Pandelis, then in Bucharest, to begin registering passengers for the three boats. He believed this would motivate Pandelis to be zealous in protecting the boats when they arrived. Indeed, Pandelis showed his mettle in this regard, and the earlier decision to establish ORAT also proved its worth at this juncture, despite controversy. Pandelis used ORAT as a base for Jewish leaders at large, including Geiger, aliyah committee members, and youth movement fellows, who proceeded to make plans for the transports.[33]

Preparing the *Milca* and *Maritsa* for a sea voyage went ahead at a furious pace. The ORAT office was besieged by hundreds desiring to be assigned places on the boats. Into the void created by the January arrests stepped Pandelis, able now to assert greater power in the selection of passengers to his personal profit. The Mossad emissaries in Constantinople were interested in one thing: seeing the boats put to sea. Nothing else mattered, including selection of immigrants and methods used to secure places. It was felt that only a supreme effort would save the aliyah bet mission from a final flagrant failure.

In mid-March 1944, when Benvenisti and Enzer were released, the *Milca* was ready for departure. The decision was made to send her on with or without Red Cross protection. On 19 March a permit for the voyage was granted by Rumania, and the ship left Constantsa on March 23 with 203 immigrants aboard—most of whom had paid substantial sums.[34]

It was now up to the Istanbul mission (Constantinople) to arrange the next stage: transit through Turkey for travelers without Turkish visas. The rescue mission used its political connections to obtain Turkish permission for the passengers to disembark in Istanbul and proceed by rail to Palestine. In this the mission received essential help from the American embassy and particularly from Ira Hirschmann of the new War Refugee Board.[35] Barlas also received a letter of confirmation from the Colonial Office that authorized the passengers' entry into Palestine. The *Milca* arrived in Constantinople on 1 April, and after several hours the passengers were on a train to Palestine. Time did not even permit the debriefing of the immigrants by the rescue mission.

The tone of reports to Palestine from Constantinople during April was reassuringly optimistic and encouraging. They spoke of ferrying 2,600 immigrants to Istanbul in five boats, including a newly purchased Bulgarian vessel, the *Vita,* practically ready. It seemed that the tactics used by the Mossad on Rumanian Jewish leaders were beginning to pay off. The *Milca*'s voyage was a breakthrough that, it was projected, could open the way for many more boats.[36]

During the next six weeks, 1,400 Jews sailed off: the *Bela-Chita* and *Maritsa* left in April, followed early in May by a second trip by the *Milca* and another by the *Maritsa*. The two other boats did not sail, however.

Problems arose, related to Pandelis's operating style, among other things. As noted, his involvement in arrangements in Bucharest was far greater than anticipated, because of the arrest of the chief Zionist leaders earlier in the year. His conduct aroused a great deal of resentment among Jews. They lamented that the emigration operation was becoming the private business of a seemingly predatory adventurer. This only reinforced the views of Benvenisti and Filderman, who remained opposed to Mossad-style sea transport.

They, like others, passed their critical assessment of ORAT to Kolb, who during May was involved in arrangements regarding a transport of children from Transnistria aboard the Turkish boat *Tari*.[37] Kolb had just purchased food and life jackets, arranged through Benvenisti and Filderman. The trip seemed all but assured, lacking just a German promise of safe conduct. Kolb was convinced that Pandelis's arrangements were being made independently of most Jewish leaders. Undoubtedly, Kolb still recalled the troublesome Shind letter, which had convinced him that Pandelis was ringleader of a forgery and bribery scheme. However, there is reason to believe that Kolb acted out of sincere concern for victimized Jews, a desire that emigration be as safe as possible. He did ask the Rumanian authorities to forbid the departure of boats that were not recognized by the Red Cross.[38]

Independently, A.L. Zissu—since January, head of the aliyah committee—sought to have Pandelis slapped down, again out of fundamentally positive motives. During the course of his work with Pandelis, Zissu had formed ideas of his own for aliyah operations, and he was preparing to put them into effect in the spring and summer of 1944. These developments created a situation that the rescue mission could not have foreseen: the most cooperative people in Rumania were impeding the operation.

The Leadership of A. L. Zissu, Summer 1944

A.L. Zissu was a well-known figure in the Zionist movement in Rumania. He was a writer and journalist who had long fought anti-Semitism. Before the war, Zissu battled with the non-Zionist Filderman, criticizing his views in his newspaper, *Our Rebirth*. Zissu's opinion of Filderman had not changed during the war, despite Filderman's tremendous efforts on behalf of Rumanian Jewry. Zissu himself had since become less active in Zionist affairs, and with the discontinuation of his paper, he was no longer heard from in public. Nevertheless, he continued to follow developments in the community and in the Zionist movement closely.

Early in 1943, he helped to form an alternative Zionist leadership, which viewed itself as an underground organization. Zissu would not allow himself to be used as a government tool in actions taken against Filderman (though his opinion of the Jewish leader had not altered). He, like Filderman, viewed the "Jewish Center" with abhorrence.

Zissu supported sea transports for Jewish emigration, but he refused to work with Enzer, whose personal integrity he doubted. As the controversy of the aliyah boats heated up, Zissu became more directly involved. He retained amicable relations with Mihai Antonescu, the chief Rumanian proponent of disengagement from Germany, whose position steadily improved as the notion of an Axis victory faded.

The arrests in January 1944 prompted Zissu to join the aliyah committee, pushing him to the fore of Zionist activity once again. Another thing he thought of was the German occupation of Hungary, which placed upon Rumanian Jews the responsibility of helping Hungarian Jews cross the border.[39]

Aliyah was for Zissu both an integral part of Zionist work and a way to help the refugees from Hungary escape annihilation. In order to make the border-smuggling operation a success, it was necessary to demonstrate to Rumania that the refugees would finally leave the country. Zissu hoped to turn the "hikes" (as the border crossings were called) into a mass movement, with a new and more daring approach to emigration. He projected plans for large-scale departures aboard large, safe vessels. The trips of the Bulgarian boats in the spring of 1944, in which he took an active part, appeared a necessary first step toward bigger operations.

Zissu gauged as best he could the political atmosphere. Rumanian policy toward the Jews, which had grown more liberal as the Allies gained momentum, had by the spring of 1944 gotten harsher. In anticipation of an Allied invasion of Southern Europe, the Rumanians had had to change their Jewish policy. Ira Hirschmann maintained close contact with the new Rumanian envoy in Turkey, Alexander Cretzianu, with a view to facilitating Jewish emigration from Rumania.[40] Hirschmann's role in initiating Red Cross efforts to arrange a transfer of 1,500 orphans from Transnistria indicated to Zissu that Jewish emigration had indeed become an important item on the international agenda.

This he sought to impress upon the Rumanian authorities, demanding that they do their share—that they in fact make Jewish emigration an official policy. The time was past for secret deals, ambiguous declarations and camouflaged approval for the departure of Jews; what was required now was large Rumanian ships. While other Jews thought along similar lines, Zissu expressed himself better.

His work on the aliyah committee was taken by many Jews as a positive sign. Indeed, many attributed to him the successful sailings of *Milca* and *Maritsa* between March and May 1944 and did not associate him with the attendant corruption. The youth movements viewed him as their champ and believed him to be responsible for longer passenger lists following the *Milca*'s first trip. In April Enzer left Rumania, a move that satisfied the youth movements, which had accused him of improper conduct. In their letters, the young Zionists talked of a fresh beginning for aliyah work.[41]

There was certainly a need for reorganization of aliyah activity. Pandelis had acquired tremendous power.[42] The exorbitant price of a ship's passage to Istanbul was a scandal in the community. Pandelis was paid in foreign currency by the rescue mission, but he also pocketed millions in Rumanian lei from private passengers. He sought to limit the number of nonpaying emigrants and went as far as to send falsified reports to Constantinople regarding the passenger lists. All this was discovered later when immigrants reached either Palestine or Constantinople and were interviewed by Mossad emissaries.

Zissu was determined, therefore, to get rid of Pandelis. He had been willing to go along with him during the spring, when there seemed to be no alternative. But Zissu looked into other options that would restore aliyah as a means of getting to Palestine.[43]

It was not only Pandelis who profited from questionable operations; so did Radu Lecca, who supervised all Jewish-related matters for the Rumanian government. Enzer had, through Lecca, obtained permits for the Palestine Office and, in return, had paid Lecca handsomely. Enzer's later departure and the passing in turn of control to Pandelis and Zissu jeopardized an important source of income for Lecca.

He therefore approached Pandelis and asked that twenty (according to some sources, 200) places on the next transport be set aside. Pandelis's lukewarm reply aroused grave doubts about the security of Lecca's interests, and he resolved to transfer emigration work to the Jewish Center, over which he held sway. This provoked a sharp reaction by Zissu, who regarded the Center as a front for collaborationists. He believed that Lecca would try to place on board the transports numerous informants and miscreants who had helped in his actions against Rumanian Jewry. The time was ripe, Zissu felt, to use his official contacts, especially with Mihai Antonescu, to block Lecca's machinations.[44]

But Lecca himself appealed to Marshal Ion Antonescu and pointed out the "illogical" in Jewish emigration: Pandelis had become chief beneficiary of these activities, deriving tremendous profits from ORAT, while the reputation of the Rumanian government suffered. It was noted that, if anyone was to profit from Jewish emigration, it should be the government itself. The marshal seemed to accept Lecca's point, and on 30 May 1944, he ordered a temporary halt to Jewish emigration. A government committee was set up to discuss the matter and suggest alternate means of organizing transports.[45] The committee was composed of Ion Antonescu and Mihai Antonescu, senior ministers and Lecca, the under secretaries for foreign affairs and the Navy, and the chief of police. The composition of the committee indicated the seriousness with which the government viewed the subject. Zissu saw the committee's establishment as a positive sign. He himself was called to appear before the group in the first week of June. He hoped that it would approve his own ideas about Jewish emigration, leaving Lecca, the Jewish Center, and Pandelis out of the picture entirely.

The committee decision on 10 June did not completely satisfy Zissu, but the government showed itself to be fully informed of the details of Rumanian aliyah work. It identified the Jewish Agency as the final authority in matters of Jewish immigration and therefore demanded that its representative in Rumania supervise Jewish emigration. The government apparently believed that the Jewish Agency was part of a world Jewish network that had key influence on the Allies. Therefore, the government took pains to point out the distinction between the anti-Jewish policy of it and Germany, relating the instances in which Bucharest had rejected German proposals that Rumania's Jews be part of the Final Solution. Rumania had always sought to solve its "Jewish Question" through emigration. At the same time, the government knew of the organizational problems of emigration activity and of abuses, about which it had received numerous complaints. The government was interested in preventing unscrupulous people from exploiting the emigrants. It would not permit damage of the good name of Rumania or a taint on governmental desire to help the Jews.

To Zissu's chagrin, Lecca remained involved to some degree in Jewish emigration affairs, but the government's decision offered a reasonable chance to oust Pandelis. Zissu was named to head an emigration bureau with sole authority to compose passenger lists. The Rumanian government undertook to provide ships, the passenger price to be set by the Rumanian Marine Company (S.M.R.). In the meantime, permission was granted for the departure of four ready ORAT boats—*Kazbek, Morina, Bulbul,* and *Mefkura.*

A special tax was levied on emigrating Jews, half to go to the Rumanian government and half to the Jewish Center, ostensibly to help pay for services provided by the Jewish community.[46] Thus, Radu Lecca retained inroads into the Jewish community and a source of revenue. He submitted lists of emigrants for approval of the Internal Affairs Ministry, and the portion of the tax allocated to the Jewish Center passed through his office. Pandelis was not entirely forced out of the picture, either, though after the four boats had departed, his role would be minimal. Nevertheless, Zissu took the new developments as a major step toward legal and large-scale emigration. Did the Rumanian decision actually help emigration? To answer this, one has to turn once again to Constantinople.

Between Constantinople and Bucharest

In May, after intense activity that brought 1,200 Jews out of Rumania, the rescue mission was again in turmoil. Germany confiscated Bulgarian vessels in Varna, grounding the entire Mossad flotilla. The *Firin* and *Vita* had not made even one trip; the *Milca* had made only two trips; and the *Bela-Chita,* one. Only the *Maritsa,* in Constantinople, was saved. Despite the severe setback, plans were afoot for the acquisition of replacements from Turkish sources. These were berthed in Burgos, in Bulgaria, and had no permits for Rumania. The Mossad wished to preserve the transports' momentum, so Zissu and Pandelis were asked to prepare the *Smyrni* for departure.

Shind waited three weeks, until 20 May, in the vain hope of obtaining a permit for all the Turkish boats to sail to Constantsa. It was then decided to launch the largest of the boats, the *Kazbek.* Perhaps while the preparations were made, the license would arrive. The *Kazbek* reached Rumania on 23 May, at the height of the emigration controversy.[47]

The rescue mission was apparently unaware of the new problems. On June 5, before Bucharest's decision on Jewish emigration, Zissu reported to Constantinople to supervise emigration arrangements. That would now, he stressed, take a more legal route, without the need for subterfuge or the like. ORAT could continue only if the Jewish Agency would announce approval of the organization and its methods.[48]

Shind clearly did not understand it all. His main consideration was that time was passing without a departure being made from Constantsa. Contradictory reports came from Pandelis and Zissu, each demanding that the other be removed. A confidential letter also arrived from Meir Rubin, director of the Palestine Office and of ORAT, which helped the Mossad in dealings with Zissu.[49]

No one in the Mossad doubted the significance of the political concessions that Zissu had won for Jewish emigration, but they felt that, in the short term, his actions were more harmful than helpful. Zissu had cleared away many obstacles to emigration at the highest government levels, but he had damaged the positions of those who had benefited from the "ancien regime." These people were in a position to create daily difficulties through bureaucratic foot-dragging and other forms of interference that nullified the gains Zissu had won in principle and—more important—blocked actual aliyah operations.

The delay of transports, the Mossad felt, was tantamount to putting a stop to them. In this situation, Shind's inclination was to replace Zissu with Rubin. Barlas opposed such a move in recognition of Zissu's important overall contribution to the Zionist cause in Rumania. He had some influence on the Rumanians and had reestablished for the movement a credible leadership. Would the Mossad imperil all that on the basis of Pandelis's complaints? It could well be, he contended, that Pandelis himself had delayed the departures of the Mossad's boats for self-gain.

These were weighty considerations, as was the information that Zissu got legal status in Rumania for refugees from Hungary. He and a veteran Zionist from Hungary, Dr. Arno Marton, were both engaged in a major effort to transport refugees.[50] Moreover, Zissu reported to Constantinople on the availability of two Rumanian vessels, the *Alba Julia* and *Or de Mara*.[51] The course seemed, then, to persuade Zissu and Pandelis to cooperate more with each other and get the ships to sea. A June 24 letter from the Constantinople mission to Palestine indicated progress in this direction. Rubin was facilitating communication between the two men. The *Kazbek* was slated to leave Constantsa the following week, after which four others would depart.[52]

The Bulgarians announced in late June that they were willing to release the Bulgarian boats of the Mossad. That meant that the Mossad's Turkish "fleet" could be joined by the *Milca*, *Firin*, and *Vita*. So the picture grew brighter. Earlier in the month, two additional parachutists from the Yishuv had landed in Rumania: Shaike Dan (Yeshayhu Trachtenberg) and Yitzhak Ben-Efraim. With their entry on the scene, it was hoped that the strained relations between Zissu, Rubin, and Pandelis would improve. As Mossad representatives, the two parachutists could be expected to infuse a degree of discipline regarding instructions received from Constantinople.

The *Kazbek* reached Constantinople on 8 July, with 750 people aboard. From discussions with the passengers, the Mossad got a clearer understanding of what had occurred in Rumania. In particular, the agency was impressed by Zissu's stature among immigrants, deriving chiefly from their admiration for his successes with the regime. The immigrants blamed Pandelis for the delays, saying that at the instigation of Lecca he added the names of suspected Nazi collaborators to the passenger lists.

The Mossad expected immigrant boats to continue arriving at the rate of one each week, which would bring some 3,000 Jews to Turkey during July. Intervening delays occurred again, however. Internal squabbling in Bucharest worsened; this time, Pandelis accused Zissu of preventing the passenger lists from being finalized. The first report to arrive from the parachutists, dated July 2, was also discouraging, noting the breakdown of cooperation between aliyah groups and chaos in all money-related matters.[53]

Eliezer Kaplan and Shaul Avigur arrived in Constantinople during the second week of July and sent several letters to Zissu and Rubin, Zionist movement members, and the parachutists.[54] All the letters struck the same note: internal divisions on the Rumanian side had damaged the ability of the Rumanian Jews to help themselves and others. Reestablishing unity was imperative. Monumental rescue efforts by the Yishuv and Zionists in Rumania were being squandered. Planning was not accompanied by action. In addition, past experience had shown that the Rumanian government needed cooperation from lower echelons of the administration, harbor authorities, shipping firms, and so on. Problems of implementation served to nullify government declarations.

In the Mossad it was clear that Pandelis, if he felt wronged, would lash out in revenge. As for Zissu, it was thought his sense of public responsibility would outweigh any sense of injury. Nevertheless, Avigur and the others decided to proceed with caution. Zissu would not be edged out completely: instead, Filderman was to be asked to function alongside Zissu in selecting immigrants for the transports. The choice of Filderman was calculated to placate the non-Zionists in the Rumanian community who complained that Zissu was overpartial to Zionists in the passenger lists. The JDC, a major source of funds for the transports, was particularly sensitive to such charges. Kaplan and Avigur thus hoped to please everyone and steer Zissu into a more compliant position.

In their calculations, however, they surprisingly overlooked the extremely poor relations between Filderman and Zissu. The latter understood the new order as yet another attempt to hem him in. Writing to Lichtheim on June 29,[55] Zissu described his political convictions, his motivations for becoming publicly active once again, and his present difficulties. He had criticized Filderman so severely, it ruled out that the two might work together. He took a principled stand against Filderman's non-Zionist assimilationism as well as against Filderman's legal stance in official negotiations regarding Rumanian Jewry. The fact that Kaplan, Avigur, and Shind could conceive of this proposal as a means of nudging him, Zissu, into a more moderate position simply demonstrated their alleged ignorance of Filderman's character and of the political facts of life. Thus, Zissu rejected the idea, stating he would cooperate with Pandelis only if the latter's influence were strictly limited to transporting immigrants from Constantsa to Constantinople.

On 19 and 20 July Pandelis sent two cables[56] informing the mission in Constantinople that he had been granted permission by the Rumanian authorities to operate an emigration bureau and use boats berthed in Constantsa and elsewhere. He explained that Rubin would compose the passenger lists and payment would meet Constantinople's stipulations. Thirteen percent of the passengers would pay more and come from the more affluent classes, in order to defray expenses as well as cover the government emigration tax. Payment of the tax would actually be handled by ORAT, under government supervision. Pandelis requested an official letter guaranteeing that passengers would disembark at Constantinople and would continue their journey from there, as Shind requested in November 1943. Rubin confirmed the new arrangements at ORAT.

This turn of events strengthened Shind's resolve either to force Zissu out or to set up an alternative emigration center under Pandelis and Rubin that would handle illegal immigration.[57] On July 27, Ira Hirschmann transmitted to Shind the text of Mihai Antonescu's announcement of the past May regarding Jewish emigration, which Hirschmann had obtained from Cretzianu in Ankara. The announcement granted Rumania's permission for Jewish transports aboard medium-size craft of Turkish registry or aboard Rumanian ships to be leased by the Rumanian Marine Company for this purpose.[58]

This information seemed to break the Mossad's patience with Zissu, for the declaration was (mistakenly) interpreted to mean that there had been no official opposition in May to the departure of emigrants on the four Turkish boats at Constantsa, as Zissu had reported. The Mossad believed that Zissu had sent a false report urging them to break with Pandelis. The Mossad also received trustworthy reports that denied Zissu's claim that two Rumanian boats—the *Alba Julia* and *Or de Mara*—would be placed at his disposal.

The Mossad concluded that "Zissu's desire for independence and his unreasoning hostility to ORAT has led him up blind alleys."[59] It was therefore decided not to await a full report from Dan and Ben-Efraim and to demand Zissu's immediate resignation. Barlas was obliged to send a cable to Zissu relieving him of his post as the Jewish Agency's representative. In a compromise formula, Zissu was asked to "concentrate his energies on bringing large numbers of Jews out of Hungary and sending them on through Rumania en route to Constantinople, rather than involve [himself] in the petty details that were holding up transports."[60] Passenger lists, Zissu was told, would now be drawn up according to instructions that Constantinople would forward to Rubin. The immigrants' passage would be arranged by ORAT, in consultation with the aliyah committee of the Zionist movement.

In one thing particularly, the Mossad had been correct. Zissu received this cable and, while he planned eventually to take drastic countermeasures, he actually did nothing to delay the departure of the *Bulbul, Morina,* and *Mefkura.* All three left before dawn on 5 August, a week after the cable was sent from Constantinople. Afterward, Zissu sent an ultimatum to Barlas, demanding that he reverse his decision by the fifteenth of August or else the entire Zionist executive in Rumania would resign.[61]

Opposition to the decision to separate Zissu from all aliyah activity came from an unexpected quarter: the two former parachutists. They had had several weeks in which to observe the local scene and, under pressure of the events, reached a conclusion different from the Mossad's. They sided with Zissu, believing that Pandelis had tried to undermine him from ulterior motives and that Rubin, who was meant to represent committee interests, had lost his judgment and was little more than putty in Pandelis's hands. They believed that the decision in Constantinople had been based on incorrect reports submitted by Rubin and Pandelis, or by Pandelis alone, who had forged Rubin's signature. They recommended that the letter of recognition sent to Rubin be canceled and that Pandelis be told that Zissu would henceforth represent the Jewish Agency in Rumania.[62]

In consequence, Zissu and the aliyah committee resigned, but the emigration bureau that he headed continued to operate and the *Alba Julia* was indeed being refitted. In this intolerable situation, the parachutists, sans approval from Constantinople, decided to fine Rubin, to restrict the field of Pandelis's authority and return to aliyah planning through Zissu's bureau. The full significance of this step becomes clear in connection with the fate of the *Bulbul, Morina,* and *Mefkura.*

The Three Boats: Bulbul, Morina, Mefkura

The departure of the three Turkish boats from Constantsa in August 1944 took place at a critical juncture. Relations between Germany and Turkey were tense in July, and Berlin sought to avoid exacerbating those tensions. After many boats had been sunk in the Black Sea, the Germans withdrew their submarines from the mouth of the Bosporus.[63]

But on 1 August Turkey broke diplomatic relations with Germany. It was thought possible that Germany might respond by restructuring Turkish shipping in the Black Sea. This would have endangered the Mossad's three Turkish boats. Until a few days before, the Turkish flag had been an advantage for the Mossad boats. Indeed, the Mossad had tried for years to use Turkish-registered vessels. Now that they had in fact succeeded, the rug was being pulled out from under them. Perhaps more than anything else, what pained the Mossad was that the boats reportedly might have sailed during the past weeks, and had not because of the internal dispute. There was now reason to think they would never take off or sail.

In Bucharest, all were ready for the long-awaited voyage. A thousand immigrants, including 300 Transnistria orphans, were already in Palestine in their dreams. The conflicts over places on the boats now were over. A large amount of money had been required to refit the boats, purchase food, and pay various middlemen from the lowliest port workers to the under secretaries of the government. Would the trip, after all that, be canceled?

Mihai Antonescu and Charles Kolb, who supported Zissu and of course emigration, advised against a sailing. Several passengers, having parted with

Two orphan sisters from Transnistria in Atlit Detention Camp, summer 1944.

their life savings to book passage, canceled. There were others, however, who eagerly took their places, undaunted by the dangers, desperate to go at any cost.

To sail or not to sail? This was undoubtedly one of the most difficult decisions faced by the aliyah committee in Bucharest, and the departure of the boats was delayed until the committee voiced its opinion. On 4 August Ben-Efraim wrote to Shind: "The three small boats are leaving tomorrow. All the people are at the harbor. There were hesitations about sending them under the new conditions. But today we decided in favor. The *Salah-a-din* and the *Smyrni* are being prepared—the passenger lists are ready."[64]

In a more detailed letter of August 8, the parachutists wrote:

Orphans from Transnistria in Atlit Detention Camp, July 1944.

The last group of boats left in an atmosphere of tension. . . . We opposed delaying the trip. There were quite a few of the more affluent passengers who cancelled at the last minute. On the other hand, there were 1,500 more people in the port than there were places on the boats, all of whom had to go home. The boats left despite the disapproval of the government (the prime minister), which demanded a guarantee from the Turkish authorities. The Turkish envoy in Bucharest protested against this.[65]

The parachutists, with Zissu's backing, threw the weight of their moral conviction behind a decision to sail. Zissu then declared to the committee that this complied with desires of the Yishuv.[66] "The decision to sail looks today somewhat overhasty: did eagerness for a launch overpower prudent

Jews from Rumania in Atlit Detention Camp, summer 1944.

concerns for safety?" A balanced examination would indicate that it did not.

All the transports that sailed in 1944 were obviously undertaken at great risk. The Germans would not guarantee safe passage, but they did not molest the boats, either in the ports that they controlled or on the open sea. The rescue mission and the emigration organizers in Bucharest concluded from this that the Germans had defaulted to Rumania on the question of Jewish emigration. This, indeed, is borne out by German documents. Berlin had tried to prevent the granting of exit permits and the preparation of vessels. There was no indication that they would do in August 1944 what they had not done up to then—attack civilian vessels displaying the Red Cross symbol, whose departure they had assented to—simply because they flew the Turkish flag. The risky decision to send the boats on their way on 4 August was consistent with past Mossad policy.

The boats sailed close together, with the *Mefkura*—in worse condition than the others—taking up the rear. The German navy had provided the boats' captains with escort and signal flags facilitating departure from the harbor and the mined area around it.[67] That night, the sea was calm. A temporary engine failure on the *Mefkura* was repaired while the boat was towed out of the minefield by German and Rumanian coastal patrols.

Just after midnight, the *Mefkura* was illuminated by flares signaling her to halt. The captain failed to respond and carried on. Several minutes later, the boat was fired upon and began to burn. It split in two and sank. At that point, machine-gun fire was directed against passengers in the water. The captain and crew abandoned ship immediately, using their lifeboat. Out of 350 passengers, only five survived.

The other two boats safely reached their destination. The *Bulbul* had also been ordered to halt (apparently by the same vessel that fired upon the *Mefkura*), but after having halted and identified itself, the boat was allowed to proceed. Upon entering the Bosporus, a sudden storm hit that prevented it from sailing on to Istanbul. Instead, it dropped anchor at Igneada, where the travelers disembarked and continued overland. Several weeks later, the passengers of both the *Bulbul* and *Morina* were in Palestine.

The Aftermath of the *Mefkura* Sinking[68]

The rescue mission had kept a worried vigil the night the *Morina* sailed alone into the harbor at Istanbul. The next day, when it was learned that the *Bulbul* had taken shelter at Igneada, it was hoped that the *Mefkura*, too, had taken shelter. But that was not the case.

Several hours later, word of the *Mefkura*'s sinking arrived, initially believed to have been caused by the sea storm. The German radio service in Rumania announced the wreck of the *Mefkura* on 5 August and the BBC carried confirmations the following day. So many rumors circulated about the anatomy of the disaster that it was impossible to distinguish truth from fiction. Ten days later, the truth emerged from five survivors now safely in Istanbul. This did not end speculation, for the captain and crew reached Istanbul somewhat later and gave a different version of events.

Finally, an investigating committee was appointed, made up of Barlas, Avigur, and Reuven Resnick, the JDC representative in Istanbul. The committee also received a promise from the British naval attaché that expert investigators would be called in. It appeared, at any rate, that quite some time would pass before a clear conclusion could be reached.[69] In the meantime, decisions had to be made about further transports. Immigrants were waiting in Constantsa, including 1,500 children from Transnistria waiting to leave on the *Smyrni*. The Mossad and the rescue mission decided that the transports must continue.

During those weeks, Yishuv leaders were determined to take the fullest possible advantage of Admiral Horthy's announcement of 19 July ending the deportation of Hungarian Jews and enabling those with certificates to leave for Palestine. The rescue mission wanted this implemented through the port of Constantsa, since the Rumanians had already stated willingness to permit Jews to travel through their territory. In addition, there were already large numbers of refugees in Rumania for whom transport had to be arranged. These factors assured the need for future aliyah work, whatever the hazards.

Avigur was well aware of the likely public outcry following the *Mefkura* disaster. However, he thought that aliyah was the only way to rescue the Jews. Therefore, he believed that Mossad decisiveness and faith in the essential justice of its cause could overcome all obstacles. He himself believed passionately in what he called "the historical truth of aliyah bet," and with equal passion he presented these ideas before his colleagues and superiors. He agreed wholeheartedly with the Hebrew writer Joseph Haim Brenner, who wrote: "Leave the dead to their rest and let the living go on working."[70]

On 13 August, about a week after the tragedy, letters were sent to the key people involved in Rumania: Zissu, the parachutists, youth movement members, Rubin, and Pandelis. The letters conveyed the rescue mission's decision to go on, explaining the various considerations that had been taken into account, both for and against future aliyah operations.

> The reasons [that force us to continue] are the facts rooted in the situation itself, which has not changed because of the disaster. Saving Jews, especially those from Hungary, is imperative, and building Palestine through immigration is also imperative. Under present conditions, we have no alternative but sea transports. No matter what the reasons for the disaster were, *it is our firm opinion that immigration by sea transport must continue no matter what*... [emphasis in the original]. Independent immigration is an unconditional obligation.[71]

The letters expressed the extent to which aliyah bet had come to be seen as an integral aspect of the Jewish national struggle, one of whose major aims was rescuing the Jews of Europe.

The letters to Rumania also detailed the preparations to be made before the first group sailed. This would be a fairly small group of determined Zionists from the pioneer movements. The best safety equipment was to be used, and the passengers were to be trained to handle it properly. This time, unlike in the past, the boat would take the shortest route, avoiding the coastline. Latest intelligence sources indicated that German submarines were not at sea but that German coastal patrols were still active near Rumanian and Bulgarian ports. The Mossad would directly fund the transport itself. In short, all possible precautions would be taken. As Avigur wrote, this was the kind of safety consciousness needed—not a preoccupation with safety so single-minded as to stop all aliyah attempts.[72] If the first transport got through safely, others would surely follow, especially that of the Transnistria group.

It was in this spirit that Avigur and his colleagues set out to resolve the still-open question of authority in the organization of Jewish emigration. They asked the former parachutists in Bucharest, who had disagreed with the decision to oust Zissu, to render their opinion on how to proceed. The considerations guiding their discussions in early July were reviewed. This time, it was decided to leave the solution to representatives on the scene. There were now four Palestinians in Rumania, following two more human parachute drops. As a group, they were now in a position to play a key role in the aliyah operation. As noted, the original parachutists agreed with Zissu's assessment of Pandelis and Rubin. Ultimately, Zissu himself took over direction of the aliyah bureau and placed heavy responsibility in the hands of the parachutists.[73]

Zissu and the younger Zionist leaders were in full accord with Constantinople over the need to go on with the transports. The nine successful journeys up to that point gave them confidence. Despite the distress caused by the *Mefkura* incident, they urged the rescue mission to step up its activity, for the front was drawing closer to the Rumanian frontier and the future was unpredictable.

They confronted the concerns of the veteran Jewish leaders in Rumania, who were heavily influenced by the *Mefkura* sinking and disgusted by the obstructionist tactics of Radu Lecca, who had sought to prevent the sailing of the pioneer group. The transport was prepared under unbelievable tension and pressures. The debate within the Jewish community, the political uncertainty, the German retreat and the Soviet advance—all this added to the very somber atmosphere. After several delays (some due to steps taken by Lecca and the German ambassador, Killinger), 23 August was set for the transport to sail.

All was ready when, once again, the schedule was disrupted. It was on 23 August that Rumania surrendered and the government resigned. There was no choice under the circumstances but to delay the departure once again, even though there was no telling when—or if—aliyah from Rumania would resume.

14

Rescue at Work: The War Refugee Board, Ira Hirschmann, Britain, and Aliyah Activities in Istanbul, 1944

Approaching 1944: Rescue Politics in Transition in Britain and the United States

The Rumanian government, as recounted, had repeated its readiness to allow Jews to leave the country. In the past, such declarations had not produced far-reaching results. But in the fall of 1943, the announcement was linked to a new plan. A year after the Allies had rejected the ransom of the Transnistria Jews, a new threat hung over the Jews of southeastern Europe. As Soviet forces advanced, the Germans began to plan their retreat, and it was feared that this would include the mass murder of the remaining Jews.

Rumanian Jewish leaders appealed to the Antonescu regime to transfer Transnistria refugees to Rumania proper, and appealed to the Jews of the world to pay for this transfer and to provide for the survivors. The American Jewish Congress and the JDC asked the U.S. government once again for permission to transfer funds to Rumania, despite wartime boycott regulations. This request had fallen on deaf ears in early 1943. Now there seemed to be a greater sensitivity and sympathy among Treasury Department officials, who appeared willing to authorize the transfer despite British objections.

An intense debate over the rescue issue, both in the press and in Congress, lasted through the fall months of 1943. The Emergency Committee, headed by Peter Bergson (Hillel Kook), waged an energetic campaign on behalf of a vigorous U. S. rescue policy. The group, established by members of the Irgun delegation in the United States and local Revisionists after the failure of the Bermuda Conference, was vocal in seeking support from the media, and among political figures, church leaders, and intellectuals. During the fall of 1943, it pushed for a congressional resolution in favor of an official rescue policy—the so-called "Rescue Resolution." Public discussion and congressional review of rescue tarnished the image of the government as a bearer of humanitarian ideals.

This bolstered internal pressure on Treasury Secretary Henry Morgenthau, Jr., who already had grave doubts over his government policy toward European Jewry. Officials at the Treasury Department formerly involved in refugee policy—Roswell McClelland, Josiah E. Dubois, and John Pehle—not only criticized the State Department, proving how it had been actively hostile to rescue and refugee aid and had deliberately misled the public, but also pointed out the serious consequences of a failure to implement a suitable rescue program. Their unyielding pressure led Morgenthau to approach Roosevelt with the proposal to establish a special government agency to deal with rescue matters.[1]

The American ambassador in Ankara, Laurence A. Steinhardt, also sent messages expressing the will and opportunity to do something for the Jews. The newly arrived Rumanian representative in Turkey, Alexander Cretzianu, belonged to the group that favored a rapprochement with the Allies. Steinhardt advised him to urge Bucharest to help transfer Jews back from Transnistria. Word of this changed American stance was communicated to London by Lord Halifax in Washington. More Americans were demanding a more dynamic policy, Halifax wrote, tipping the balance in favor of the Jewish organizations and their supporters. In the past, Britain had found, the tension between such groups and their opponents had tended to reinforce British-American cooperation on refugee policy. Other factors now mattered, however. Among these were the approaching presidential elections, and the increasing political impact of Jewish demands in the shadow of the meager results of rescue efforts in 1943, which appeared even more distressing in light of the news from Europe.

London understood well enough that the Anglo-American consensus and cooperation exhibited at the Bermuda Conference had experienced a sizable setback. The Americans were acting unilaterally and creating the impression of spearheading rescue efforts. This placed the British in a delicate situation: should they oppose American initiatives and thereby present Britain as a force working against humanitarian action? Or should they allow events to determine British policy, and thereby run the risk of upsetting the fragile balance between rescue and the White Paper? In November, acting under American pressure, the British announced that they had decided to extend the time limit of the White Paper, allowing immigration to continue beyond the March 1944 deadline, until all allotted ceritificates were used up.

Thus, by the end of 1943, it was clear that Britain was no longer a leader in determining rescue policy. Preparations in Washington for the establishment of a special body to aid European Jewry—the future War Refugee Board (WRB)—were in full swing. It was known that President Roosevelt was about to issue a statement condemning Nazi genocide and threatening to punish any who cooperated in it.

These steps corresponded to the demands that the so-called "refugee enthusiasts" (as described in Foreign Office records)— Lady Rathbone and

Lord Perth, for example—had been voicing throughout 1943. They untiringly bombarded the Foreign Office and the Colonial Ofice with memoranda analyzing and evaluating the performance of the government in rescue matters and proposing an alternative policy.[2] They advocated the establishment of an independent office with the authority to set and execute rescue policy. They believed that such an office would effectively force the ministries to accede to irregular procedures, if necessary. Such a body, they argued, ought to be headed by dynamic, imaginative, enthusiastic people. These oft-repeated proposals were never adopted. Instead, pains were taken to convince the refugee enthusiasts that their criticism was baseless and that there was therefore no need to raise the issue in Parliament. The similarity of the American actions to the proposals of the British refugee enthusiasts seemed to indicate a degree of identification with the critics of British policy.

Roosevelt finally announced the establishment of the WRB on 22 January 1944, in a special presidential order. The Board included representatives of the Departments of State, War, and Treasury, and it had a wide degree of latitude. It was empowered to engage in any action likely to advance the cause of rescuing Jews from German-occupied and German-dominated countries. Thus, contacts with Axis satellites such as Rumania and Bulgaria and transfer of aid parcels and funds to Jews in Nazi concentration camps were within its purview. Representatives were to carry out their activities with the help of American diplomats abroad, including friendly foreign embassies in enemy countries. A memorandum about the WRB was sent to American diplomatic posts, indicating the role they were to play.[3]

The British Foreign and Colonial Offices were, however, displeased. They felt the move indicated a lack of solidarity with Britain, and appeared to conflict with the decisions reached at Bermuda that assigned chief responsibility for rescue work to the Intergovernmental Committee on Refugees. The goals of the WRB, as formulated by its acting chairman, John Pehle, were even more disturbing to Whitehall. The Board, Pehle wrote, was to act to put a stop to the barbarism against the Jews in the territories directly or indirectly under German control. Until then, the democracies had chiefly discussed aid to refugees already in neutral territory. Now the WRB proposed to call upon all citizens of occupied Europe to save Jews from the death camps and labor camps, to hide them, and to render assistance. The WRB declared its readiness to fund such efforts despite the boycott regulations.

Such developments raised fundamental questions at the Refugee Desk of the British Foreign Office: what did rescue in wartime entail, Randall asked, and were the objectives of the rescue effort as important as other war objectives? This was the same man who, ten months earlier, had depicted emigration plans as a British political interest. How could huge sums be raised to buy food for starving Jews, he asked, without affecting the boycott?[4]

Britain tried to evaluate the shift in American policy. This was by no means a useless exercise, but of far greater significance was the question of how the American policy would affect Britain, and what steps Britain ought to take in response. Should Britain conform to America's position, or could it continue to adhere to its own established policy? Opinion was divided on this question. There was a general consensus that the establishment of the WRB, with the energetic Pehle at its head, had confronted Britain with a serious problem. How would it be possible, as Ambassador Halifax put it, to "teach Pehle the facts of life?"[5]

The authority of the WRB caused great anxiety for the State Department representative on the Board, who appreciated the wide powers it had been granted. State Department officials ought to maintain a distinction between activities directly related to American interests and the war effort, on the one hand, and rescue work on the other. The latter did not strictly come under the definition of "political" work, but should rather be considered "humanitarian." In a guidance letter to the ambassador in Ankara, Assistant Secretary of State Stettinius wrote:

> You will realize, however, that these negotiations (concerning Jewish refugees) are on an entirely different level than those relative to Turkey's position in the war; and that this Government is simply addressing a humanitarian appeal to the Turkish Government, as to other governments, rather than a request that they take certain action favorable to us at some sacrifice to them.[6]

This distinction characterized the American approach to rescue, which, even after the creation of the WRB, continued to be viewed as marginal. This approach would become increasingly evident.

War Refugee Board Representative in Turkey

The WRB prepared to send a field representative to Turkey, one of the most convenient bases for establishing contacts with countries under Axis control. Prior to that, the agency requested a report on local conditions from American ambassador Laurence Steinhardt. Steinhardt was asked specifically about the feasibility of opening transit camps in Turkey and about the transport that Turkey might provide for Jews traveling from the Balkans. Finally, he was queried about possible obstacles or restrictions imposed on the passage of refugees.[7]

Steinhardt did not answer these questions directly. Instead, he composed a lengthy memorandum explaining why so few Jews were able to reach Turkey. This was not, he argued, attributable to Turkish policy, but rather to the ban against Jewish emigration that Germany had imposed on the Balkan countries, and also to the extremely difficult land transport situation and the dangers involved in sea travel. Thus, although Turkey was officially opposed to an influx of refugees, it still offered more in refugee aid than could practically be implemented. It was not the case, he argued, that, as some critics of Turkish policy charged, the reluctance of Turkish consuls in the Balkans to issue transit visas was primarily responsible for blocking the exit of Jews. It would be possible to ask Turkey to provide a ship for Balkan Jewish refugees, but only if the Allies guaranteed to replace the ships in case of sinking. In sum, the ambassador held out little hope for large-scale Jewish emigration from the Balkans, and therefore felt that pressure on the Turks to relax their own position was unwarranted.

Despite his preference for a general response to the questions put to him, however, Steinhardt consistently refrained from dealing with the shift in the posture of the Balkan countries toward Germany, and their desire to demonstrate this, among other things, through their Jewish policy. Thus, he did not elaborate on the opening this presented for pushing rescue to the fore (although he encouraged the State Department in the fall to pursue the Rumanians on their Jewish policy). His position was in fact consistent with the attitude of a diplomatic officer whose responsibility, as he saw it, was to prevent new friction from developing in interstate relations. From this point of view, rescue initiatives might well be seen as the source of just such friction, even though the newly created WRB signaled a change in national policy. Steinhardt nevertheless saw fit to point out that he was on friendly terms with figures active in rescue work and had in the past been instrumental in facilitating their activities.

The tone of Steinhardt's message was not encouraging with respect to the policy initiative upon which the WRB meant to embark. It seemed to warn of a deterioration in delicate U.S.-Turkish relations. It is quite possible, too, that the State Department's instructions to its ambassador, stressing the distinction between political and humanitarian aspects of U. S. policy, was responsible for the line Steinhardt took.

This was the situation when Ira Hirschmann arrived on the WRB assignment of saving Jewish lives. A prominent Jewish businessman, Hirschmann was also a close associate of Pehle, chairman of the WRB. As a member of the U. S. delegation to the Evian Conference (1938), Hirschmann had already had some experience in the refugee field. He had been involved in the Revisionist Emergency Committee and was proposed by it, as early as September 1943, to aid Jewish rescue work in Turkey. At the time, however, Ambassador Steinhardt insisted that it was unnecessary for him to go to Turkey, as many Jewish organizations were already represented there; one more would hardly be beneficial, in his view.[8] Thus, Hirschmann's departure for Turkey was delayed until after the formation of the WRB. Even then, he left the United States as a private individual, receiving his official credentials only en route. His stay in Turkey consisted of the initial six weeks he spent there: from 26 February to 8 April 1944, and then from June to September.

En route to Turkey, Hirschmann stopped for a few days in Palestine to meet with the heads of the Jewish Agency and the Rescue Committee. In Cairo, he was informed by British officials on the rescue situation and on British policy. Once in Istanbul, he was briefed by the American diplomatic corps and Jewish representatives from Palestine and Jewish organizations. He also talked with news correspondents who, through many years of experience had acquired knowledge both of the Turkish elite and the Jews in the Balkan countries. Hirschmann formed an especially close working relationship with Joe Schwartz, a *New York Times* correspondent in Ankara who became his principal adviser.

Shortly after his arrival, Hirschmann forwarded a lengthy report to Washington, detailing rescue-related matters.[9] This illustrates just where he differed from Ambassador Steinhardt; as Hirschmann clearly felt no obligation to preserve previous American policies, neither was he concerned about Turkish sensitivities. He tended to be far more critical than Steinhardt of the Turkish government. He was, in fact, convinced that Ankara would not be won over by humanitarian arguments, given the rather harsh Turkish attitude to minorities in their country—Jews included. It would therefore be best to present rescue as part of the American *political* interest in achieving its war aims. This, in turn, would mean that rescue and refugee immigration would be perceived as falling in the context of Turkey's own political interests. Hirschmann, unlike Steinhardt, felt that Turkish resistance to granting transit visas had played a significant role in halting the emigration of Jews with valid certificates for Palestine. It was intolerable that processing a transit visa took fourteen to seventeen weeks, during which the applicants often lost the chance to emigrate. In addition, the Turks were far from flexible even with regard to their permission for nine Jewish families per week to enter the country en route to Palestine. The permits were granted on condition that the families leave Turkey within twenty-four hours.[10]

Hirschmann assumed that it was possible to maneuver with the Balkan countries because they sought a new tactical position. He believed that his duties should include establishing contact with various political forces inside the Balkan countries with a view toward expanding rescue work (about which more will be discussed shortly). But, in addition, Hirschmann felt that it was up to the Allies to provide transportation facilities and to declare their intention to allow large numbers of refugees to enter their countries for a defined period. Such a step, even if impractical, would have propaganda value in neutral states like Turkey, whose rescue aid was crucial.[11] Exit from Europe and arrangements for entry to safe havens had to be coordinated, and therefore the two problems had to be dealt with simultaneously, in order to assure success.

These two problems—opening discussions with representatives of the Balkan countries and arranging for transportation with the help of Britain and the United States—formed the focal points of Hirschmann's activity during his first stint in Turkey. He proved to be only partially successful in both areas.

The Tari Affair

Hirschmann's arrival in Turkey coincided with that of two new representatives from the Yishuv, whose aim was to advance the cause of rescue. The party from Palestine consisted of Chief Rabbi Yitzhak Herzog and a lawyer, Mordekhai Eliash, known as an able organizer and skillful mediator. High on their agenda was the acquisition of Turkish boats for Jewish refugees. Hirschmann met with them, as he had with other members of the Yishuv delegation, to hear their assessment of the situation. From Barlas he had learned of a number of Turkish boats that might be suitable for refugee travel. These were the *Wetan,* the *Nazim,* and the *Akbal.* As noted, Barlas's negotiating with their owners reached a fairly advanced stage, but it still remained to obtain approval from the Turkish government.

Barlas and the other Yishuv representatives were unsuccessful in their requests to high-level officials. Similar British approaches to the Ankara authorities during the previous year had led nowhere. Hirschmann decided to take up the challenge of persuading the Turks to change their position.

He sought to establish contact through Steinhardt, who, in addition to his position as American ambassador, was a close friend of Turkish Foreign Minister A. Neumann. This in itself was a new departure. Until then, negotiations over visas or transport for refugees had been conducted at the middle and lower echelons of Turkish officialdom, not at the level of ambassadors and ministers. The personal intervention of the American ambassador and the special envoy of the U.S. gave the talks impetus.

Turkey's foreign minister rejected the request for the three boats, but offered instead a better ship, a passenger vessel called the *Tari.*[12] This was to be a one-time offer, given in consideration of the ambassador's personal interest in the matter. Nevertheless, this was a significant departure from the established pattern of Turkish refusals to such requests. Hirschmann and Steinhardt believed it would be possible, after the first successful voyage, to arrange others.

The Turks set several additional conditions on their offer of the *Tari.* The first was the demand that a safe-conduct guarantee be obtained from the belligerents. The second was that the United States commit itself to replacing the *Tari* with a ship of similar quality should the Turkish vessel come to any harm. Hirschmann and Steinhardt agreed and proceeded to bring the negotiations to a conclusion.

At that point, difficulties were raised unexpectedly. Both the American and the British navies objected to the replacement guarantee. A lengthy and heated correspondence developed among Hirschmann, Steinhardt, and the WRB heads, on the one hand, and the joint Anglo-American naval command in the Mediterranean. The exchange illustrated the reluctance of the naval authorities to join in rescue work and exposed the limitations of the WRB's authority over the military. Steinhardt was sharply critical of the hypocrisy of those in the naval command who demanded that Turkey and other neutrals provide ships and other resources for rescue operations but were themselves unprepared to make an effort to implement work that the President himself had declared of paramount importance.[13] It took long weeks of arduous negotiation for Steinhardt and Hirschmann to obtain the needed guarantee of a replacement. But by this time they had run into other obstacles—this time from the Turkish side.[14]

The speculative owners of the *Tari,* realizing that the United States government was involved in making the arrangements, began to demand ridiculous prices for the lease. Hirschmann believed that Jewish representatives had in the past been prepared, out of desperation, to agree to any price so long as a ship was obtained, and had thus made his own job much more difficult. After a harrowing bargaining, during which Hirschmann complained to the Turkish foreign minister about the shipowners' dishonesty, an agreement was finally reached. The Red Cross and Jewish organizations in Rumania were to prepare groups of refugees for the trip. At the end of March and early April, they were informed that the voyage would take place in a few days. Provisions were bought by Charles Kolb of the Red Cross, and lists of refugees were compiled by the Palestine Office.[15]

But the first condition that the Turks had set and to which the Americans had not objected—a safe-conduct guarantee by all sides—turned out to be the factor that doomed the plan's success. This should not have been such a surprise, after all. Germany was still opposed to Jewish emigration and tried to stop it, whether individuals or groups were involved. Hirschmann himself wrote to the WRB that the destruction of the Jews was a central aim for the Germans, the only war aim that they were likely to achieve. Why, then, did he believe the Red Cross representative in Ankara, Simonds, when he told him that the Germans would agree to permit safe passage for the ship? Simonds apparently thought that there were new circumstances in the spring of 1944 that would convince the Germans, if only on a one-time basis. He did not, however, explain this in detail, and Hirschmann, who was so eager to see the plan succeed, tended to take what Simonds told him uncritically.[16]

When German consent failed to arrive, Hirschmann asked Steinhardt to approach Turkey's foreign minister and request an application to the Germans for safe conduct. The minister put the request to the German ambassador. He explained that the ship would carry Jewish refugees, and that this was of humanitarian concern. Despite the evident importance the Turkish government attached to this request, and despite the efforts of German ambassador von Papen to obtain his government's consent, it was all to no avail. Simonds was annoyed that the Americans had intervened through the Turks, and felt that the Turkish request had brought political calculations into play that led to its failure. German sources we have cited do not bear this out, however. Hirschmann and Steinhardt then tried to exert pressure on Germany through other neutral countries: Sweden, Portugal, and Switzerland. They even turned to the Vatican's representative in Turkey. As the Swedish foreign minister had pointed out to the WRB's representative some two months earlier, however: "You simply do not understand. The reason for the German refusal is quite simple—*Hitler's plan to destroy the Jews* [italics added]. Before their defeat they will try to murder and exterminate every Jew under their control."[17]

Tari thus did not sail in April, or in the following months. The Americans continued to believe for a time that the absence of a German response left room for a positive answer at a later stage. They therefore retained the ship for a long period, paying huge sums to its owners. In the summer it was agreed that the *Tari* would make short trips along the Turkish coast, from where it could easily and quickly return if needed should the Germans send the hoped-for guarantee.[18] In the meantime, ways of using the ship without safe-conduct status were discussed. One proposal was that the *Tari* sail from Bulgaria under the Bulgarian flag. Another was that the ship serve as a sort of "floating hotel" for refugees reaching Turkey illegally aboard small boats. Once 1,500 passengers had been collected in this manner, the *Tari* would proceed to Palestine. None of these plans ever came to fruition however, for they involved risk, daring, and unorthodox methods that were not appropriate to the operations Hirschmann and the WRB were able to pursue.[19]

Each of the alternatives discussed (including one that involved neutral shipping) foundered on the German refusal to permit Jewish refugee ships to sail safely. Even as Germany's position among its allies became weaker, and even as its ties with Turkey became taxed until they finally broke in August of 1944, it continued to refuse Jews permission to leave. The democracies had to decide whether to put refugees to sea in craft without a protective umbrella, as the Jewish organizations were doing. This question was raised more frequently as Mossad boats kept reaching Turkish shores. Before turning to this aspect of the problem, we should examine the steps Hirschmann took in pursuing the cause of Jewish emigration with Balkan representatives.

Negotiations with the Balkan Countries

As the WRB representative, Hirschmann was authorized to meet with nationals of enemy countries. This authorization was given because it was clear to the policymakers that rescue efforts would fail, given the wartime circumstances, unless there could be direct contact with enemy governments on this score. Nevertheless, the State Department was extremely wary of such contacts. At this stage of the war, as noted, contacts and negotiations with Balkan governments had already taken place. It was therefore very important that positions staked out with great care in the past, and with careful coordination with the other Allies, not be upset through the misinterpretation of promises made at this new stage. The State Department therefore instructed Hirschmann to keep strictly to the Jewish issue, defined as a humanitarian concern, in any discussions he held. The Department was more worried, however, that the Balkan governments would try to broaden the scope of any negotiations to include postwar arrangements in Europe.

As early as March, Hirschmann informed the ambassador and the State Department of his intention to meet with the Rumanian envoy in Turkey, Alexander Cretzianu, to explore the possibilities of Jewish emigration. Hirschmann planned this meeting because of the political posture taken by Cretzianu and the latter's close association with Mihai Antonescu, who favored leaving the Axis and appeasing the Allies. In addition, disturbing reports had begun to arrive of the arrest of Zionist leaders in Rumania and of German efforts to block emigration plans. Hirschmann's letter to the State Department reveals that he was sensitive to the Department's concerns about contacts with the enemy, and he stressed his own intention to observe the limits imposed on any discussions he might have with Cretzianu. He would not, he stated, stray into political matters of any kind.[20]

Having received Steinhardt's blessing and the State Department's warning, Hirschmann set himself a defined and, he believed, achievable goal. He wanted Rumania to facilitate the departure of Jewish refugees, in particular the 5,000 orphans and other survivors from Transnistria. The Rumanians could certainly be asked to arrange for their transfer to Rumania and for more relief to prospective emigrants prior to departure. This was to be the first priority with the Rumanian envoy—an important item both because of the danger facing the Jews in Transnistria and because their transfer to Rumania had already begun in December 1943 under pressure from Filderman and other Jewish leaders (it was later slowed under German pressure). In Hirschmann's judgment, on the basis of reports he received from the Red Cross and from Jewish organizations, starting the process again had the potential both of eliciting Rumanian cooperation and of actually saving some Jewish lives.

With these thoughts in mind, Hirschmann met Cretzianu on March 11, 1944, through the good offices (and at the home) of Simonds, the Red Cross representative in Turkey. Cretzianu received his points in a positive manner, promising sympathetic consideration from his government and a prompt reply. Cretzianu appeared to appreciate the parameters of Hirschmann's brief, with their essentially humanitarian thrust, and asked why the Americans had not previously indicated how vitally important the issue was to them.[21] He sought to emphasize, too, that his government, even though it had always opposed the Germans' Jewish policy, was now prepared to make far-reaching changes in its policy.

Hirschmann emerged from the encounter with a feeling of satisfaction and even excitement. In his diary he wrote: "It was highly successful. I talked well and incisively bringing out the same in him, and I carried it off as it should have been."[22]

On 18 March the two met once again. Cretzianu read Hirschmann a cable sent by Marshal Ion Antonescu, in which the Rumanian leader promised to release the Jews in Transnistria and transfer them to Constantsa, in groups arranged as per Hirschmann's stipulations. Hirschmann was overjoyed by this success, and he wrote: "This is a monumental achievement, I can hardly believe it myself."[23]

Several days after this meeting, the Red Cross confirmed from Bucharest that refugees from Transnistria had already begun going to Rumania. The pace of the transfer was so rapid that during March some 48,000 persons had already been moved. The numbers involved indicate that the transfer must have actually begun long before Hirschmann's meeting with Cretzianu, although their talks certainly helped facilitate the process.[24] It should be remembered that it was in late March that the Mossad boats shipped out. We cannot be sure to what extent Hirschmann's intervention influenced Rumania to allow the boats to sail, after having held up such activity for so long and for so many reasons. After the occupation of Hungary, Hirschmann and Steinhardt warned the Rumanian government, through Cretzianu, not to reverse their newly relaxed Jewish policy and in particular not to halt the transfer of refugees from Transnistria. The Rumanian response was of course immediate, and indicated that as long as Antonescu remained in charge there would be no hardening of Rumania's Jewish policy.

Because of this success, Steinhardt and the State Department consented to enlarge the range of contacts to include the Bulgarian envoy in Turkey, A. Balabanov. Bulgaria was especially concerned that the Allies might bomb Sofia, and was anxious to prevent it. There were very few pro-German elements left in Sofia in the spring of 1944, and the regime hoped that by the war's end it would have distanced itself considerably from Germany.

The meeting with Balabanov was arranged, once again, by Simonds, and took place about a week after Hirschmann's first discussion with Cretzianu. In this, it is not clear what specific goal Hirschmann had in mind. His demands referred in general terms to improving the status of the Jews, restoring their confiscated property, and closing down the labor camps. Yet he did not raise the important issue of the ban against Jewish travel through Bulgaria to Turkey, or indeed the official prohibition of Jewish emigration from Bulgaria.[25]

Hirschmann was much more formal at this first meeting with Balabanov. He used a strong, even belligerent tone when warning the Bulgarian at the outset that "[I]t would be a deliberate distortion of [my] intent and of the truth were Balabanov to read anything more into this than a humanitarian discussion regarding the Jews and persecuted minorities."[26] Balabanov replied favorably to Hirschmann's demands, and in particular stressed that Bulgaria's new government was no longer sympathetic to Germany. He hoped that the Allies would appreciate that. He further pointed out that, throughout the war, Bulgaria had pursued a Jewish policy that might be called helpful and positive.

Hirschmann's first six-week stint in Turkey may, in sum, be characterized as dynamic, possessed of momentum and crowned with success. There was a change in Turkey's position on supplying a ship for refugees, and better conditions were created for organizing emigration from Rumania.[27] The rescue of Jews from the Balkans no longer solely concerned Jewish organizations. It had become a matter discussed by ambassadors and ministers, and dealt with at the highest government levels. There was a general feeling that a turning point had been reached.

The single most important factor behind this feeling, however, were the refugees themselves, who now began to reach Turkish shores. True, they did not come on the *Tari* and other ships that Hirschmann tried to acquire, but in small vessels traveling without safe-conduct protection—boats acquired by the Palestinian emissaries led by the Mossad. Hirschmann's work also contributed to the success of the Mossad's efforts, as noted, but in order to fully appreciate his position we need to examine the change in his perception on illegal aliyah.

From Opposition to Support

Aliyah bet was a well-known phenomenon to the acting personalities in 1944. Steinhardt knew of past Mossad efforts to organize a Jewish exodus from the Balkans. In early 1944, he submitted a detailed report to the State Department on current efforts by the Yishuv delegation to get the Jews out of Bulgaria and Rumania. His report makes clear that he did not consider these efforts to be of much value as a means of saving Jews, and depicted them as the work of ideological parties in the Yishuv on behalf of members trapped under Nazi control.[28]

Hirschmann, arriving in Turkey, began to learn about the "illegal immigration" operations from aliyah operatives like Ehud Ueberall Avriel (with whom he spoke and whom he hoped to recruit for his own work) and from American and British diplomats. Among his close associates, Joe Schwartz (the *New York Times* correspondent) was especially knowledgeable about the efforts being made in Istanbul and in the Balkans.

In a letter to the WRB in Washington, Hirschmann explained the distinction he saw between legal and illegal immigration. The letter, written after the first Mossad boats arrived from Rumania, was sent 19 April. The letter is therefore not merely a theoretical consideration of the issue, but a studied response related to what was until that point the only tangible success in Jewish rescue work. As Hirschmann correctly defined illegal aliyah in 1944, it involved Jews who had not obtained official permits to leave their country or legal entry papers for their destination, and who traveled in boats without Red Cross protection or safe-conduct guarantees from the belligerents: in short, all components that were applicable to the *Milca* and the *Maritsa* voyages.[29]

Just as Hirschmann's first impression of Ueberall Avriel was lukewarm, his impression of aliyah bet was that it could not be the basis of his own work, nor was it the kind of endeavor in which he could exert his influence and authority as the official representative of the U. S. government. In this he agreed with Steinhardt, and was even more critical than the ambassador in regarding aliyah bet as less than serious. "This way is not my way," he wrote, "and I cannot support it." He observed in his diary that he could not pursue legal and illegal activities simultaneously.[30]

It is difficult to determine exactly what caused Hirschmann to be so negative about aliyah bet at the outset of his mission. His diary reveals a mixture of formal considerations and insufficient confidence in aliyah bet activists, together with a determination to go beyond small and limited operations (which was how he understood the illegal refugee work) in order to save people in much larger numbers. It is also likely that Turkey's fears of a sea disaster like that of the *Struma* caused Hirschmann to view illegal activities as endangering all aid to refugee operations. This concerned both Hirschmann and Steinhardt, who did not believe that the small craft acquired by the Mossad were at all seaworthy. Their view was only reinforced when the Red Cross representative reported to them on the split within the Jewish leadership over the wisdom of putting to sea without permits or Red Cross protection. The Red Cross in Rumania, it will be remembered, backed those who opposed such trips.

The Jewish political aspects of the illegal operations, as they surfaced on the Istanbul scene, also elicited negative reactions from the two American officials. Various Jewish organizational spokesmen—both those, like the Revisionists and the Agudah, who were represented on the Rescue Committee and those not part of the Palestinian delegation—complained to Steinhardt and Hirschmann that the Mossad and the Jewish Agency accorded preferential treatment to Zionists, particularly to movement members in allocating Palestine certificates or places on refugee boats. Steinhardt and Hirschmann were both meticulous in their determination not to be perceived as mere tools of Zionist politicians, and the fragmentation of aliyah operations among so many groups made it all the more difficult to judge the situation accurately.[31] Still, it is understandable that in February 1944, when Mossad efforts undertaken months before had not yet produced tangible results, there was little confidence. Yet there was every hope of acquiring the *Tari* and transporting 1,500 people at one time.

Reality, however, was to turn the tables on this situation. While negotiations over the *Tari* and the Swedish ship *Bardalanda* were becoming intractable, and efforts to obtain a safe conduct guarantee were shunted onto a diplomatic merry-go-round, the Mossad's first boat, the *Milca*, arrived. The *Maritsa* followed, and only then did the *Bela-Chita,* with its legal permit and Red Cross status.

Despite their objections to aliyah bet, Steinhardt and Hirschmann found themselves intervening with Ankara to permit the refugees to land even without valid documents. It was unthinkable that Jewish refugees would be turned back and returned to Nazi Europe after escaping. Such a step would have damaged not only the prestige of the American president but also his government's credibility, now that rescue work was a declared policy of the United States.

Steinhardt and Hirschmann turned to Turkish foreign minister Neumann, and in addition solicited the aid of the British embassy and of the consular official to expedite the transfer of the refugees to the special train bound for Palestine.[32] This operation, as already observed, came off smoothly and efficiently. In early April, Hirschmann was ready to return to the United States. In his summary report to Steinhardt, he wrote: "I suspect that during the spring and fall months there will be an increase in this illegal immigration activity, and you had best be prepared for it."[33]

During the same period, the embassy was asked by the WRB to confirm reports that the Germans, while refusing explicitly to grant conduct, were standing aside and allowing refugee boats to cross the Black Sea. If these reports were true, as the successes of several small boats seemed to demonstrate, then rescue planning ought to begin shifting to such operations, the Board argued. If that were the case, the ambassador was instructed to ask the Turks to furnish other small boats. The Board further suggested that

Steinhardt check to coordinate these steps with the British embassy. London was about to extend the lease of five small boats, known as the Adana boats, placed at the disposal of the Turks since the early days of the war. The Board proposed that the extension be made conditional on the provision of several Turkish-registered boats for use in Jewish rescue work.[34]

Steinhardt displayed a certain ambivalence. As noted, the agreement between England and Turkey to extend the lease was finalized without reference to the WRB. On the other hand, it became obvious that whether or not he favored the Mossad operations, Steinhardt would have to intervene in moving the refugees to the train, because they lacked Turkish entry permits. He was concerned that the trickle of such illegal refugees might become a sizable stream, upsetting the Turkish authorities. The latter were prepared, he believed, to accept a volume of some 500 refugees per week. As he was already involved somewhat in Mossad activities, he might as well maintain regular contact with the Mossad and thus keep apprised of new developments.[35]

Steinhardt therefore combined the WRB's query with Barlas's request to obtain consent for Turkish-registered craft to ferry refugees from the Black Sea ports. The shipowners themselves were willing to do so, and insisted only on receiving official government consent.

After the trips of the *Milca* and the *Maritsa*, and after the arrival of the *Bela-Chita,* it will be recalled, there was an interruption in the sailings and the *Maritsa* sank on its way back from Istanbul to Constantsa. It was in this period, too, late May to June 1944, that the Bulgarian government barred its boats from transporting Jewish refugees from Rumania. Thus, the Mossad was liable to find itself without any boats at all. The need for Turkish-registered vessels was therefore all the more urgent. With Steinhardt's assistance, the Turkish government did give its hoped-for consent, and thus the Mossad could proceed to acquire boats that were in much better condition than the *Kazbek, Morina, Bulbul,* and *Mefkura.*[36]

Nonetheless, Steinhardt did not, as the Board suggested, publicize in the Balkans the Turkish and British agreement to permit individuals and groups reaching Turkey to continue through to Palestine. Thus, he took the same position as the British in adamantly refusing to release policy details, for fear of multiplying the influx of refugees beyond what they considered optimum.[37]

Hirschmann returned to Istanbul in mid-June, after a two-month absence. While in the States, he spoke to a Jewish and non-Jewish audience about the refugee operation in terms of a tragic human drama, and painted the American ambassador's role in glowing terms. He called for a "bridge of ships" to freedom, from Constantsa to Istanbul. This elicited a favorable reaction from the WRB and was very well received by Americans generally. Several weeks after Hirschmann's campaign across America, Steinhardt arrived on home leave to bask in the favorable publicity. The climate of public opinion, the personal satisfaction the two men felt, and also the stark reality that there did not seem to be any alternative to the Mossad's *modus operandi,* combined to change their minds about aliyah bet. These men became fervent supporters of a program that they themselves had only a short time ago declined to condone.

During the summer of 1944, both Steinhardt and Hirschmann were intimately involved in planning aliyah and relief activities. The meetings they attended included discussions of the difficulties of Jewish emigration from Rumania—which stemmed partly from the internal divisions in the Rumanian Jewish organizations and partly from basic problems of transportation and politics. The two officials at times actually chaired sessions of such Jewish organizational conferences in Turkey and played an active role in deliberating on aliyah bet and other illegal activities—notably, illegal border crossings, which often preceded the seaborne leg of the journey and had become the norm of rescue operations.

During July and August 1944, Hirschmann met again with the Rumanian and Bulgarian governments to confirm their support for the Jewish-organized emigration work and to forestall any German countermoves. Hirschmann succeeded in removing the Bulgarian ban on transport of refugees aboard boats flying the Bulgarian flag. This permitted the return to active service of the *Vita,* the *Firin,* and the *Milca.*[38]

The one area in which the change of attitude on the part of Steinhardt and Hirschmann was most evident was their support of Mossad refugee-boat operations following the *Mefkura* episode. Hirschmann and Steinhardt backed up Shaul Avigur in the expanded meeting of the Yishuv delegation and the Jewish delegates held after news of the sinking was received. In contrast to their position, the Joint's representative, Reuven Resnick, hesitated to support further such operations, and Eri Jabotinsky, representing the American Revisionists' Emergency Committee, actually opposed continuation.[39] The position taken by Steinhardt and Hirschmann was heavily influenced by the dismal fate of Hungarian Jewry, the indecision and controversy with which the democracies responded to the challenge of Horthy's cessation of the deportations and the permission to emigrate to Palestine, on which we will elaborate below. If it was going to prove impossible to save hundreds of thousands, at least they could save several thousand. That was better than nothing, Hirschmann wrote to Washington in his reports to the WRB.[40]

British Reaction to War Refugee Board Work in Istanbul

The British were forced to reassess rescue policy in the context of war priorities and the Palestine immigration. It was harder to justify the policy in the face of mounting public pressure and in the light of the WRB's activities. After the German invasion of Hungary and while the movement of Jewish refugees from Rumania was advancing (April and May 1944), the British were compelled to follow the WRB policy in spite of great resentment.

From the British perspective, Pehle and the rest of the people in the WRB were not ready "to learn the facts of life." In February 1944, Pehle and his colleagues were pushing the President to declare heavy punishments for Nazis and their collaborators involved directly or indirectly in the extermination of the Jews.[41]

The formulation of such a declaration had begun in late 1943. The British did not believe that, apart from propaganda value, it would achieve anything tangible. Some felt that such a pronouncement might even have adverse effects, and they pointed to the precedent of December 1942, which had certainly not prevented the escalation of anti-Jewish persecution. Britain also knew that the Soviets would not sign a declaration that singled out the Jewish issue and that had not been coordinated beforehand with them.[42] While London pondered such weighty questions, however, Lord Halifax transmitted the text of the declaration as drafted by the WRB. This gave British officials the opportunity to amend the text, focusing the declaration on the conduct of the Axis satellites and presenting victimization of the Jews as just another example of Nazi tyranny.

While such ideas continued to simmer in London, however, Roosevelt at last issued his long-awaited declaration on 22 March. This was three days after the invasion of Hungary, an event that aroused the Jews' worst fears.[43]

Knatchbull-Hugessen in Ankara was also pushed into action by Ira Hirschmann, the WRB's representaive in Turkey. The British embassy's displeasure both with Hirschmann and with the support he received from the American ambassador, Laurence Steinhardt, emerges plainly from dispatches forwarded to London. Embassy officials angrily complained that the Americans took credit for every concession won from the Turks, without acknowledging British efforts. The *Milca* passengers, in Istanbul on March 31, would have been deported back to Rumania, the British embassy contended, had the consulate there not issued them visas for Palestine. Without those, Steinhardt would have pleaded in vain with the Turks to allow the refugees to stay in Istanbul. The mutual backslapping of Hirschmann and Steinhardt in the American press was typical of the American one-sidedness and self-satisfaction.[44]

Yet the Refugee Desk at the Foreign Office could not hide its displeasure that in two months' time four refugee boats bearing 1,200 Jewish refugees had left Rumania without any British help.[45] There was renewed apprehension that the ceiling on Palestine certificates issued might be reached before the war ended, when Britain would still be obliged to cooperate in rescuing Jews. Plans for transit camps in Tripolitania, Cyprus, Egypt and elsewhere were once again put on the agenda. It was decided not to grant entry to Palestine to Jews who were not in immediate danger. This applied to Jews in Turkey and Yemen, and to Jewish refugees in Italy and Mauritius.[46]

British misgivings reached their peak in the second part of July 1944, after Admiral Horthy, the Hungarian dictator, proclaimed an end to the deportations and allowed Jews with certificates to emigrate to Palestine and holders of foreign passports to depart for other countries. This announcment was transmitted to the Allies through the Red Cross. The Hungarian envoy in Constantinople himself delivered the message to the representatives of Palestine Jewry there, Haim Barlas and Eliezer Kaplan.

The United States greeted this announcement enthusiastically and was prepared to provide refuge for those fleeing Hungary. Britain was asked to make the same commitment. The Red Cross reported from Hungary that those eligible to go under the new terms totaled approximately 41,000.[47]

Horthy's emigration idea was particularly threatening to Britain because it was phrased in terms to which Britain had previously agreed: those to be granted permission to leave actually held immigration certificates for Palestine, recognized by British authorities. Horthy put a stop to deportations and did not demand anything in return. The logistics of the emigration appeared feasible, since the Balkan countries were prepared to cooperate, as were the Red Cross and neutral countries, provided the United States and Britain would take the lead. But the estimated number of refugees seemed to the Foreign and Colonial Offices too large to permit smooth absorption by Palestine, and the Hungarian figure did not include the other groups of refugees that, it was believed, were about to set out from Rumania and Constantsa to Istanbul. (These were groups on the *Kazbek, Bulbul, Morina, Mefkura, Firin, Vita,* and *Salah-a-Din.*) The high commissioner reported that Palestine could accommodate only 4,000 immigrants within the White Paper limits. The British government had now to establish a clear policy in response to the Hungarians, largely in order to reply to Washington.

On 4 August in London, the Cabinet Committee for Refugee Affairs (set up in January 1943) met to discuss the Horthy announcement. The colonial secretary stated, "It is impossible to reject the proposal because this would gravely harm Britain in domestic and American opinion; to accept is also impossible, because its implementation would lead to civil war in Palestine and to an Arab reaction to the stream of immigration."[48] Stanley painted for the Committee a daunting picture of 800,000 to a million refugees clamoring to enter Palestine. How, he asked, could Britain expect to cope with that? Until now it had done all it could to avoid the problem during wartime. The sense of the Committee was that Britain ought not commit itself to America's program unless Britain's obligations under the plan were thoroughly delineated. The Committee decided to recommend a full government discussion of the issue.

On 9 August the matter was thus considered, and it became clear that the White Paper could no longer serve as the basis of rescue policy. The colonial secretary stated his reservations, citing at length the opinion of the high commissioner, and he received strong support from the resident minister in Cairo, Lord Moyne. Their view of the problem took only its Middle East aspects into account. From that vantage point, it was impossible to find a solution that bridged the gap between the proposed size of the immigration and the likely reaction of the Arabs.

Britain was unable to withstand American pressure, however, and on 16 August the two Allies issued a joint statement responding favorably to Horthy's declaration. Temporary refuge was assured to those leaving Hungary. The British told the Americans that the number of refugees Britain could accommodate was strictly limited, a position that the Americans accepted. But once again, Germany came to Britain's assistance and vetoed the plan.

Approaching the Fall of 1944

Rumania's surrender to the Soviets in August 1944 and the entry of Soviet forces into Bulgaria altered the Jewish situation, of course. Hirschmann felt there was no longer much danger to Jews, and, he thought, a new period had begun in which the main issue was not emigration but relief and rehabilitation. The abolition of anti-Jewish laws, the return of Jewish property confiscated by the Fascists, and the reintegration of the Jews in the economic life of their countries were what Hirschmann considered the new political goals of the WRB and the other relief organizations. There was, he believed, no further purpose in using frail boats that put Jewish lives at risk, or in smuggling Jews across frontiers and moving them to Palestine against the Mandatory government's laws. This was now, once again, illegal activity that he could not accept. A substantive disagreement appeared to develop among Hirschmann, the Mossad, and the Palestinian delegation. This was the division between Hirschmann and the Yishuv mission in Istanbul (whose activity in the fall of 1944 will be discussed later), which ended the large cooperation that had developed during the spring and summer of that year.[49] As far as the Yishuv delegation was concerned—and the Mossad agents in particular—the uniting of rescue activity under the coordination of Hirschmann and the Board was acceptable as long as their own goals carried considerable weight, as in the summer of 1944. Yet the goals of the Mossad and Yishuv were not fulfilled with the liberation of Rumania from the Nazis and Antonescu.

The British reacted in much the same way as the Americans, after Soviet forces had occupied Rumania. During the fall of 1944, they hoped to return to the official procedures predating the rules adopted in July 1943 and in the spring of 1944. The Colonial Office welcomed a proposal from Shertok and Eliyahu Dobkin to restore the usual immigration procedures. The British viewed the plan of accepting 1,500 immigrants a month until a total of 10,300 was reached as a return to the White Paper policy. This scheme was meant to remove the tension that had arisen over the previous ten months between rescue needs and the policy of limited entry. In December, Britain informed the Turkish government that it was no longer prepared to guarantee entry to Palestine to every refugee reaching Turkey. In the British view, refugees arriving in November and December were no longer fleeing mortal danger, but simply Zionists trying to immigrate. Those in actual danger, as in Hungary, were not believed able to leave. British policy had come full circle: political considerations that had guided prewar and early-war decisions—predicated on a distinction between the Jewish question in Europe and the future of Palestine—once again held sway by the fall of 1944.

*

What was the contribution of the War Refugee Board to rescue and aliyah work between the founding of the agency and the liberation of the Balkans? It would appear that American involvement, and in particular the activity of Hirschmann and Steinhardt, had a significant impact on the Turkish Foreign Ministry and the Balkan governments. In the latter case, those elements supporting a policy of rapprochement with the West combined with a relaxation of anti-Jewish measures enjoyed a greater measure of influence and credibility, because they pointed to tangible results like direct contact with American representatives. Even when it was stressed (by Washington) that these contacts were directed only to the humanitarian aspects of the Jewish situation, and were not to be considered political, it was difficult for Balkan statesmen to accept this at face value.

A mutual dependence developed between the success of Yishuv operations and the interests of the WRB envoy. The rescue mission required the latter's intervention with the Turkish authorities, without which it would have been virtually impossible to carry out the transport of refugees, for the WRB wanted tangible proof of the successful rescue of Jews from the Nazi grip. It reaped the benefit of what the Mossad had been planning for long before the Board and its representative reached Istanbul.

It must be asked, however, whether these achievements were what the leaders of the WRB, and all those who rejoiced at what was to have been a decisive change in the dimensions of rescue work, had hoped for. Ambitious and far-reaching projects—free ports, refugee camps in neutral countries, the assignment of large American and British ships to the transportation of survivors, and a decisive attack against the German satellite countries to liberate the Jews—were never implemented. These projects lay outside the range of the Board's activity in Turkey, which was the result of the placement of the WRB and its effectiveness within the overall policy framework in Washington.

Rescue operations on a large scale might have been put into effect had the policy of rescue moved from the realm of intent and declaration to the plane of practical implementation. In March 1944, Reuven Resnick of the JDC wrote from Istanbul to his colleagues in the United States: "Over a very brief period the Allies were able to move 20,000 Yugoslavs from southern Italy to Egypt. They used two troop ships for this. There are ways to move people for non-military reasons if there is truly a desire to do so. This ought to serve us as an example."[50] Such a thing did not occur. Despite the sincere dedication of Hirschmann in Istanbul and of other WRB representatives, this kind of approach to the rescue of Jews did not have the chance to develop. Hirschmann's hope—"turning a window in the Balkans into a huge gate through which masses will pass,"as he expressed it while in the United States in the spring of 1944—was never realized.[51]

15

A Time of Transition:
Aliyah bet, Fall 1944

Aliyah and the Political Debate

Autumn of 1944 is the final segment of our story. Although many of the features that characterized the aliyah effort throughout the war continued to shape events in late 1944, several important new factors appeared. The changes they introduced make it necessary to devote a separate examination to this brief period of several months. Apart from the interest that their impact on aliyah and rescue work may have for us, these changes also indicate a transition process that led to postwar illegal immigration, starting one year later.

November 1944 saw the departure from Rumania of the immigrant boat *Salah-a-Din,* with 370 aboard. This next month, the *Taurus* followed, carrying 950. In addition, refugee convoys totaling over a thousand arrived in Bulgaria overland from Rumania, and then to Palestine.[1]

The war was over in Rumania and Bulgaria, though it raged on elsewhere in Europe, including Hungary and Yugoslavia. This situation determined how the aliyah workers planned their next moves. They worked under the assumption that conditions were inherently unstable, that any day might bring a significant deterioration, and that therefore any and every opportunity had to be fully exploited. The boats from Constantsa in the fall of 1944 went only as far as Istanbul, where the passengers disembarked and continued by rail (as others had earlier that year). The transports were organized through immigration bodies established in Rumania in late 1943, in coordination with ORAT, in which Pandelis continued to be involved. The social composition of the immigrant groups remained similar.

Yet in late 1944, aliyah bet carried elements that would become dominant during 1946–47. Thus, political conflict with the British became more pronounced as an aspect of illegal immigration work. In addition, the Holocaust survivor population became a prime consideration of Zionist leaders.

Another consideration was the relation of the great powers to the Zionist program: Would the United States be as supportive as was anticipated? How would the vagueness of the Soviet position resolve itself? De facto control of the Balkans gave the Russians the power to dictate whether or not aliyah would proceed. Would the Soviets take an ideological, anti-Zionist view of aliyah, or would they see the Zionists as a factor in Middle East affairs that provided greater potential for their own political and diplomatic maneuverability? Similarly, it remained to be seen whether the Soviets would extend their ban on emigration to all East European Jews under their control, or limit that restriction to the Soviet population per se.[2]

Eminent Yishuv figures who had been conducting missions abroad during the summer of 1944 returned to Palestine at this time. They were Eliyahu Dobkin, who had been in Western Europe for some time, where he had met with refugees and survivors in Spain and southern France; Moshe Shertok, who returned from London in the wake of the Joel Brand Affair; and Shaul Avigur, returning from the rescue mission in Constantinople. Their reports renewed a wide-ranging political debate, part of a process of policy reevaluation intended to set the leadership's long-range and intermediate goals.[3] Discussed were the relations between the Yishuv and Britain and the chances of reaching some accord regarding the fate of the survivors; the desired pace of implementation for the Zionist program; and time constraints. Alongside these issues—basically continuations of previous discussions—questions also reemerged about planning for immigration and settlement. Would prospective postwar immigrants be asked to go through a lengthy process of preliminary training before embarking for Palestine, to prepare them and to equip them for the economic and social needs of the Yishuv? This had been examined before the war and now had to be addressed again in view of a decimated, post-Holocaust Jewry.

Those who returned from missions abroad were asked to report on the attitudes among survivors and refugees toward Zionism and Palestine. Similarly, they were asked to derive lessons from the rescue work. This information would be used to guide work in Jewish communities in liberated Europe. Most involved in these discussions were convinced that as many Jews as possible would have to be brought to Palestine quickly; the Zionist movement might not have this opportunity again. Dobkin and Avigur agreed on the importance of this interim period before proper governments, with their own interests and agendas regarding the Jewish population, were reestablished.

In his summation to the Jewish Agency executive, the Histadrut executive committee, and the Mapai central committee, Dobkin asked: Who would work in the communities abroad, alongside the emissaries from Palestine, to reorganize Zionist activity in postwar Europe? He was clearly influenced by his talks with survivors, from whom he had heard many views concerning the reconstruction of their lives.

Some survivors had found refuge in neutral countries, where they had received material support from the JDC. Many wished to go on in this manner, lacking the strength to begin life over again. Some hoped to return to their former homes and erase the memory of the war years and, indeed, their own Jewish identities. But others emerged with a strong desire to rebuild their lives within a Jewish social framework and to punish the Nazis and their fellow travelers. This nefarious group Dobkin identified as the Zionist movement's prime target.[4]

He was particularly impressed by a group of youngsters in Toulouse who called themselves the Armee Juive. During the war, they had smuggled Jews into Spain and Portugal over the Pyrenees.[5] Their activist stance represented for Dobkin a strength for Zionism as a whole, and for them he foresaw an essential role in Zionist activity abroad. He wanted to see their determination, loyalty, and energy channeled into Zionist work on behalf of survivors and for free immigration to Palestine. They themselves had told him, he stated, that struggle was *the* authentic form of Zionist work for the immediate postwar period. They would prefer illegal to legal immigration for the very reason that it entailed this element of struggle.[6] A group such as that, Dobkin thought, could certainly be the standard-bearer for many who might lack organization but shared the same vision of the future. With their help, the number of potential immigrants could significantly increase.

Also emergent were surviving members of Zionist youth movements, who had gone underground during the war. These were people who had forged close ties with the Yishuv. Even in the maelstrom of the Holocaust, they had preserved the identity of their group and their own ideological commitments. Many of them remained in touch with the latest developments and topics of public debate in Palestine, aided by Zionist emissaries in Europe. The youth movement members expected to be the first ones to be brought to Palestine once immigration was renewed. But Dobkin—along with several others, such as Avigur—believed that the young Zionists ought to serve as a leadership group in rebuilding Zionist activity abroad before immigrating. At the same time, the immigration of some of these movement members could serve as an example to others, who could later join movement ranks themselves.[7]

Dobkin advocated rapid immigration on a large scale, seeing this as the only means both to secure for the Zionist movement a central role among the survivors and to ensure the future of the Yishuv. He thus agreed with Ben-Gurion's declaration of June 1944 calling for the immigration of a million Jews. For Ben-Gurion, the success of the Zionist venture depended on just such an influx. It was apparent that this could take place only if the prewar selectivity in immigration was abandoned. Indeed, the selective approach had already broken down just prior to the war, even if it was not yet fully rejected. Certainly, by 1942 all thought was directed toward the urgent need for rescue, without regard to selective standards, such as economic or social fitness, to build Palestine.

Nevertheless, immigrant certificates were distributed to the youth movements proportionally, as determined in Palestine. In the fall of 1944, there were some Zionists (including Dobkin) who proposed a return to the old selective criteria. "We have to consider the good of the country and what will afford the best conditions for the integration of immigrants," Ben-Gurion stated. "The priorities must be as follows: pioneer-settlers, youth, people of means and professionals."[8] Rabbi Fishman, speaking on the same issue, proposed that any Jew willing and able to come be given the means to do so, but he was outvoted. Gruenbaum stated explicitly: "Aliyah must be according to Zionist criteria, not just according to rescue needs."[9] This debate expressed the tension between the obligation that was felt toward all the survivors and the preference for an elite group of younger people, trained and ready to undertake national goals.

Ben-Gurion's solution was twofold: First, he called for training in Palestine itself, to the greater benefit of survivor-immigrants. Second, he considerably expanded the concept of "survivor" to embrace all Jews of the Diaspora—not only those who had lived under Nazi occupation. Every Jew could now be considered a survivor, he argued, and as such had an essential contribution to make to the future of the nation. Ben-Gurion was expressing a wider definition of Zionism, which included almost any form of collective Jewish activity. "Zionist concerns" and "Jewish concerns" were equivalents in his lexicon, just as the "Zionist political interest" was, in his view, identical with the "Jewish political interest." His definition extended to all Jewish people, including those who had not taken part in building the Yishuv and who, perhaps, were not aware of the role they were to play in Zionism.

His concept was a product of adaptation to new conditions, and it highlighted the need for swift action. This meant abandoning the prewar agenda for gradual national development of the country. It also meant preparing to accept all survivors while seeking to retain a certain order of priorities regarding immigration and settlement. This changed approach was incorporated into actual planning. It was decided, for example, to place the highest priority on relocating children and young people; parents could come afterward. Similarly, any solution that was non-Zionist—be it liberal, Communist, or something else—was to be opposed because it would automatically mean a loss for the Jewish national cause, a loss that could no longer be afforded in the wake of the Holocaust.[10]

In a sense, the debate over aliyah in the fall of 1944 echoes what took place before the war. Political and economic considerations came once again to the fore. In turn, these were linked to perceptions of the status of Zionism within world Jewry and of conditions in Palestine. Once again, there was controversy between Gruenbaum and others over the nature of the relationship between the Yishuv and the Diaspora. Ben-Gurion denied the possibility of a conceptual distinction between the two (as indeed he had throughout the war). Such a division would have been incompatible with his view of the Jewish people as a nation of survivors, a remnant of a people upon whose shoulders rested the task of building the national homeland.[11]

Aliyah was also a central concern in political discussions about the Zionist stance toward Britain. When Shertok, Ben-Gurion, and others spoke of large-scale immigration, they were well aware that this would require British cooperation. Yet mass immigration was discussed in the context of the coming confrontation with the Mandatory regime. Talk of aliyah "by any means" did not indicate that the Zionists expected illegal action to bring in waves of immigrants. Ben-Gurion, particularly, took a political approach in which mass immigration signified a goal and an essential Zionist value as well as a weapon for political struggle. What he had in mind was not an "aliyah revolt" along 1939 lines, but a tremendous demonstration of Jewish pressure in liberated

Europe, in the democracies and in Palestine, that would produce an Anglo-American effort to resolve the issue.

> Given the fact that there are Jews [who need a home]; to the extent that there exists a world conscience; to the extent that Roosevelt and Churchill (and we must not rule out the Russians) have no interest in seeing the Jews merely rot, our central demand must be that they let us bring to Palestine those Jews who wish to come. Let us bring them here in an organized fashion, in a manner befitting enlightened governments; not in an unstoppable elemental drive, but organized and directed according to a plan and with the aid of England and America. This is not out of the realm of possibility, and it must be done as soon and as quickly as possible.[12]

Shertok, who supported this position, felt that Zionist policy should focus on freer immigration and should divorce this issue from demands touching on Palestine's future status. This had been his position since 1943, when he had asked that Jews be evacuated from Europe. At that time, he had said, "It was not possible to implement a mass immigration to Palestine, and so it was not worth entering into a major conflict with the [British] government." In 1944, he added:

> The main point is not how to break the White Paper. The point is Jewish immigration. This will have the same effect . . . We will achieve greater success in our arguments to the authorities in England and in America and before world opinion if we concentrate on the liberation of these people rather than on nullifying the White Paper. Let the cancellation . . . come as a byproduct of this effort.[13]

Chaim Weizmann, for his part, indicated his general agreement with this approach during discussions in Palestine in December 1944. But he believed that the assassination of Lord Moyne by Revisionist extremists had made the moment less than opportune for stepping up the conflict between the Yishuv and Britain. Thus, his position was far more modest in tone than that of Ben-Gurion or Shertok. He spoke of the arrival of 300,000 immigrant in Palestine over two years. This was attainable, he believed, both in terms of economic absorption and in gaining Churchill's support.

Despite such differences in approach, Zionists stood united on many fronts. All agreed that rescue and relocation had to be the central concerns of the Yishuv and of Zionism. They urged a new political strategy whose goal was Jewish independence in Palestine.

Utilization of Legal Immigration Certificates

With political thinking in the Yishuv focused on expanding immigration, Dobkin and Shertok turned to utilizing legal immigration permits, which had been allocated in 1943. These included about half of the 34,000 permits available under the White Paper, which Britain had agreed to issue to seriously endangered children. A strange situation had developed: Jews in newly lib-erated areas of Rumania and Bulgaria wished to emigrate to Palestine but were barred from using available certificates, while Jews still under Nazi occupation were entitled to such certificates but could not leave.

The Jewish Agency had to decide whether to challenge the British openly on this issue. If they succeeded in obtaining new permits for the Balkan Jews, thus breaking a White Paper quota, this might clear the way to a different immigration policy. Alternatively, some temporary solution might be nego-tiated, perhaps awarding available certificates to some survivors. Because it considered immediate aliyah to be of supreme importance over the short term, the Agency decided to try to reach an agreement with Britain.

Talks with the Colonial Office in September 1944 resulted in an agreement in principle. Three thousand certificates would be reserved for refugees who might succeed in fleeing the occupied zones, while the rest would be made available to Jews in the liberated zones.

Discussions with the Palestine high commissioner entailed another round of arguments over the total number of certificates remaining. MacMichael contended that the Colonial Office erred when it stated that there were as many as 13,700. Part of the difficulty in establishing the correct figure was that letters had been sent to Jews in Nazi-occupied areas guaranteeing places on the roster in order to help them avoid deportation. MacMichael counted these letters as certificates already issued, though they had not been used. He contended that those with letters could demand the right to immigrate at any time. The Agency vehemently objected and refused to reduce the number of certificates. There was also disagreement over the number of immigrants who had entered the country illegally during the war and the number already deducted from the total quota. MacMichael was interested in reducing the total of eligible immigrants. After lengthy negotiations, he and Shertok reached a compromise figure of 10,300, of which the Agency was free to assign 7,300. Immigration was not to exceed 1,500 per month, and it was to be terminated completely by April 1945.[14]

The Zionists considered this ceiling far from satisfactory. Even the most pessimistic realized that the figures did not meet the minimum emigration requirements of survivors. Moshe Agami, the Mossad emissary in Bucharest, and Venya Pomerantz in Bulgaria feared that publication of this paltry quota would cause potential immigrants to lose heart completely, and therefore kept the news to themselves.

Shaul Avigur was particularly effective in detailing the place of aliyah in the postwar rehabilitation of survivors. He made no distinction in this regard between legal and illegal immigration, speaking instead of "aliyah by any means."

In selecting prospective immigrants, he took a very broad view. He was influenced by what he knew of the harsh conditions for survivors in liberated parts of Europe. Jews attempting to recover property discovered that those who had benefited from confiscation ("Aryanization") policies were now loath to part with what they had gained. Returned Jews were finding strangers in their homes, shops, and businesses. Jewish claims for restitution went un-heeded. Anti-Jewish feeling had been cultivated during the war and was especially evident, Avigur explained, among those who had benefited from the deportations. Anti-Semitic incitement was continuing, sometimes bursting into violence against returning survivors. This was reported by Jews in Poland, Rumania, and Bulgaria.

Once again, Jewish survival was at stake. Avigur stressed that it was imperative to make clear and swift decisions about the extent of the Yishuv's involvement in survivor affairs. There were large areas of Europe with which the Yishuv had been out of touch during the war. As a result, some Zionists in Europe felt neglected and even betrayed. There were young people who had come of age without any contact with Zionism. The time had come, Avigur argued, for the Zionist movement to demonstrate, through the words and deeds of its emissaries abroad, its commitment to rebuilding a future for survivors. The movement had to put itself at the center of Jewish life, and the essence of the Zionist message was aliyah. Transitional stages in the journey to Palestine had to be cut short as much as possible, partly because there would be other groups offering to rehabilitate survivors, such as the anti-Zionist Agudat Israel, the JDC, and the Communist parties (many of whose members were Jewish).[15] In keeping with this approach, Avigur pressed for aliyah "by all means available," beginning with the most natural candidates for this: surviving members of Zionist pioneer youth movements. They would serve as the trailblazers and prompt masses to follow. But time was a vital factor. Within a year or two of the liberation, Zionism had to cement a popular movement that would bring a million Jews to Palestine.[16]

The decisions of the Histadrut executive committee in early October sprang, therefore, from a policy that viewed aliya bet as integral to postwar Zionist efforts. It was decided to establish several aliyah centers in Europe, staffed by Yishuv emissaries. They would see to the resumption of Zionist organizational and youth movement work and would create focal points for aliyah activity.[17] The official certificates would be quickly used up, but ever-greater numbers would reach Palestine illegally. In turn, the "illegals" would demonstrate that the established quota was woefully inadequate. The new situation would place growing pressure on Britain to change its policy. Aliyah bet would thus serve as both a justification and a tool for promoting British policy reassessment.

Reorganizing the Rescue Mission in Constantinople

Throughout its tenure, rescue mission members in Constantinople feared that they might be stopped at any moment by political consequences of the war, attitudes of Ankara, or the Allies' position. The mission had or-ganized transport for 1,900 people aboard four boats. An acceptable sys-tem had been established for coordination within the mission itself, and between it and the various agencies working closely with it. Activity in the summer of 1944 was comparable to that of the summer of 1939, when the Mossad and the Revisionist Aliyah Center had boats at their disposal and opportunities to acquire others. Although there was not real symmetry between the two situations, in 1944 as in 1939, circumstances intervened to halt activity.

The first blow to the Mossad was the *Mefkura* incident, already discussed. Horthy's declaration of July 19, in which he stated Hungary's willingness to permit Jewish emigration, led to a decision to continue aliyah activities regardless, and to proceed without delay with the sailing of the *Salah-a-Din,* scheduled to depart August 23. On that day, however, Antonescu was deposed in Rumania and the new regime surrendered to the Soviets. Young Zionists ready to set sail had to postpone their departure, as developments in the Balkans were followed closely in Constantinople.

A wide-ranging discussion took place in a series of meetings of the rescue mission committee with representatives of the JDC and of the WRB.[18] It was decided to maintain the existing office in Turkey, where constant contact was possible with Allied embassies, with European governments-in-exile, and with Western Jewish organizations. Similarly, it was decided to keep open the transit route leading by sea to Constantinople and from there by rail to Palestine. At the same time, operations were to shift to the Balkans. It was hoped that a presence there would facilitate contacts with Jews in Hungary and with survivors throughout Eastern Europe. This would entail the transfer of a group of aliyah workers to Bulgaria and Rumania, where they would continue to represent the Yishuv (though they had no official business in the region). Emissaries were instructed to work within existing structures and with the greatest possible speed, as there was no telling how new developments might affect the chances for Jewish emigration. They were also asked to design long-range plans and to draw together all factions able to assist locally in rescue and aliyah.

Without waiting for confirmation from Palestine, the emissaries set to work, although formal accreditation procedures via the Palestine authorities might have given them access to the Balkan countries as official Yishuv representatives. Instead, they used the only other official avenue of entry: posing as personnel attached to Allied missions. These missions were arriving in the liberated zones with large staffs and many journalists in tow. Seizing this opportunity, Venya Pomerantz entered Bulgaria as a correspondent for the Jewish Telegraphic Agency (JTA) in mid-September. Yosef Klarman, of the Revisionist movement, used the same pretext to enter Rumania in early October. Moshe Agami, representing the Mossad, and responsible for smuggling out Greek Jews with the Resistance, went to Rumania as correspondent for the New York Yiddish daily, *Forverts* (*Forward*). David Zimend, representing the Noar Zioni youth movement, arrived there on behalf of the Tel Aviv Hebrew daily, *Davar*. Thus, a few weeks after the German retreat from Rumania and Bulgaria, the rescue committee and the Mossad joined local Jewish leaders and the Palestinian parachutists on the scene, who were prepared to organize postwar Jewish communal life, Zionist activities, and aliyah.[19]

Renewed Efforts in Bulgaria and Rumania

In Bulgaria and Rumania, Jews received different treatment during the war. Those in Bulgaria had not suffered directly from a full-scale anti-Semitic assault, even under a Fascist regime. Deportations from Bulgaria affected the Jews from newly annexed areas in Thrace and Macedonia. Labor camps to which Jews were sent in Bulgaria were less severe than those elsewhere. Jewish inmates were permitted an internal organization that distributed relief funds and other forms of assistance. At the same time, Jews suffered from their expulsion to the provinces—notwithstanding that this saved them from deportation. With the cessation of hostilities, many Jews found themselves penniless and helpless. Their property remained confiscated.

Bulgaria had not declared war against Soviet Russia, but the Soviets, in preparation for their occupation of the country, declared war against Bulgaria on 5 September 1944. Four days later, Bulgaria surrendered. On 16 September the Red Army entered Sofia. A coalition government was installed in which Communist elements wielded the decisive influence.

Generally speaking, Jews viewed the Soviet Union mainly as a force against fascism. They therefore tended to welcome the new regime, although with reservations about communism. In that context, the biggest challenge facing traditional Bulgarian Jewry was how to come to terms with the new-found power of Jewish Communists, dubbed "collaborators" in contemporary parlance.[20] The Zionist movement, too, had to define its new role within the Jewish community and vis-à-vis the Communists. This entailed fateful organizational and ideological maneuvering. Recruiting the youth was high priority for both Zionists and Communists. Young Jews had compromised their education during the war, and certainly had had no exposure to Zionist youth movements. Many to whom the war had brought personal tragedy were now ambivalent about their Jewishness. The fact that liberation had come at Soviet hands was a key factor that, along with the zeal of local Communists, cast an aura of legitimacy over Soviet ideology and the Red Army. Moscow's universalist message, professing an attractive answer to the "Jewish problem," was a serious challenge to Zionist ideology. Young Jews, unused to jousting intellectually with the Left, were liable to be carried along by the pro-Communist momentum. That is how the situation appeared to the Yishuv's emissaries, and their decision to gear their activities in Bulgaria to the leftist challenge was fully supported in Palestine.[21]

One of Venya Pomerantz's first steps was to seek a channel of communication with the Jewish community at large, to announce his arrival and broadcast the Yishuv message he bore. He secured permission for a weekly radio program in Hebrew, which enabled him not only to demonstrate the Zionist presence in the country but also to underscore the role of Palestine in rebuilding postwar Jewry. The broadcasts enabled the Zionists to conduct important educational work in the community.

Pomerantz also worked to establish the Zionist movement as a legal organization and to formulate new kinds of activity for both adults and youth.[22]

His letters home emphasized the importance of expanding the role of the movement rather than limiting it to aliyah and Palestine alone. He sought to make the Zionist movement an active partner in the national Jewish Consistory and—through the creation of a Jewish bank that would raise capital abroad and support small business locally—to have the movement play a role in revitaling the community. He also wanted to see the Zionists involved in reestablishing a network of Jewish schools, and even called for activity in local politics: He advocated joining the leftist "Fatherland Front" coalition in order to avoid the Zionist movement's being branded as reactionary. This broad program was calculated to communicate the Zionist-Socialist message to large numbers of young Jews.

Pomerantz and his colleagues were well aware that Moscow would determine whether Bulgarian Jews would be permitted to participate in building the Yishuv. This problem applied to all the areas dominated by Soviet forces throughout Southern and Eastern Europe. The Zionists' chief worry was that the Soviets would impose their own solution to the "Jewish Question." It was also unclear how the Soviet authorities would define the Jews' civil status in areas under Soviet control for only part of the war—for example, Bukovina and Bessarabia. Would they be made Soviet citizens, and if so, would the emigration laws of the U.S.S.R. apply?

These and other questions were raised among Jewish, Zionist, and Soviet representatives in London. The talks exposed a distinctly ambivalent Soviet attitude toward Zionism and Zionist aims. Although the Soviets seemed somewhat satisfied with the Zionist program, they also agreed with the Arab critique of Zionism and supported Arab claims in Palestine. In any event, Soviet spokesmen stressed throughout that Marxist criteria alone defined the Soviet approach to Zionism and to Jewish peoplehood. The Jews of the U.S.S.R. were Soviet citizens and could not be regarded as having any role to play in fulfilling the Zionist program.[23]

Communism was thus a dual challenge to the Zionists: on the external political plane as well as within the Jewish community. Most of the Zionist leaders viewed it as a serious threat that, if successful, might lead to the virtual extinction of the Jews in Eastern Europe—a fate not very different from the Nazis' plan. Despite the substantive differences between the German and Soviet ideologies, and between their respective attitudes toward the Jews, a Communist victory would isolate parts of world Jewry and impede efforts to ensure collective Jewish survival.

In Rumania, too, Jewish Communists competed with the Zionists to win over the younger generation. But in the first few months following the Soviet occupation, they did not make their influence as rapidly or as strongly felt as in Bulgaria. This was due to the general standing of the Communist party in Rumania, Rumanian attitudes to the U.S.S.R., and the manner in which the Jewish community had been organized during the war.

The first steps toward extricating Rumania from the war were taken in March 1944, when Bucharest, with the backing of the king and the blessings of the opposition, sent a representative (Barbu Strilei) to Cairo to negotiate with the Allies.[24] The point was to seek beneficial terms for Rumania's with-drawal from the war and to save Rumania from the Soviet thrust toward Southern Europe. By 14 April Bucharest had drafted an agreement in prin-ciple for a cease-fire with the Soviets, which the Allies approved in June. Soviet confirmation was delayed, however, while Soviet troops continued to press through Transnistria toward Rumania proper.

When Ion Antonescu was deposed and he and his entourage arrested, a new government was installed under General Constantine Sanatescu. The new government included traditional Rumanian political parties and one Communist representative, Lucreziu Patrascanu. In reprisal, the Germans shelled Bucharest. The government, which had planned to allow the Germans to withdraw without hindrance, mounted a counterattack to push the German army beyond the frontier. Before dawn on 31 August, Red Army troops reached Bucharest, one day after a Rumanian delegation went to Moscow to sign the cease-fire agreement. The Soviet troops behaved as an army of occupation. The depredations of the departing Germans were still fresh in Rumanians' minds, so that excesses by Red Army troops rankled all the more. The formal signing of the Soviet-Rumanian cease-fire did not take place until 12 September.

There was great popular hostility toward the occupying Russians, inten-sified by military commandeering of food and other supplies and by the removal of machinery and entire factories to the Soviet Union. The govern-ment had little choice but to accede to all Soviet demands regarding economic, political, military, and security matters. The democratic constitution of 1923 was reintroduced, guaranteeing equality to all citizens. Political parties began to reorganize and to publish their affiliated newspapers. Political prisoners were released, and the government agreed to pay restitution to groups who had suffered the loss of rights or property under the Fascists—including the Jews. The government was subject to supervision by a committee of the Allied powers, chaired by a high-ranking Soviet officer.

Soviet economic demands only escalated the inflationary pressures in Ru-mania, further exacerbating the difficult conditions of everyday life and con-tributing to shortages of food and clothing. Moreover, thousands of refugees requiring immediate shelter and assistance poured in from areas close to the fighting front. The Rumanian Communist party and the Social Democratic party—both marginal in prewar Rumanian politics—chose this moment to launch a political campaign.

Zionist youth movements printed leaflets to express their gratitude to the Soviet liberators, while simultaneously affirming their own Zionist convictions about a Jewish state in Palestine and free immigration there. The youth claimed to be the vanguard of the future Jewish state.[25]

Among the Rumanian Communists—both veteran and newly recruited—there was a disproportion of Jews. But the community's leaders, who for the most part had remained entrenched in their positions during the war, were anti-Communist. (Among these, for example, were Filderman, the non-Zionist, and Zionists such as Zissu.) Rumania's Jewish population was the largest among the survivor groups, more than a quarter of a million strong. Over 90,000 refugees had returned from labor camps and deportation to Transnistria. Many others continually arrived from Poland, Slovakia, and Hungary.

Returning Jews, as well as many of the Regat itself, congregated in major cities. Some Bucharest Jews had even succeeded in retaining prewar property despite confiscation laws. Nevertheless, the vast majority were penniless. Starvation, which threatened all of the population, was particularly severe in their case. The Rumanian Jewish leadership had sufficiently overcome its internal divisions and personal animosities to form an effective relief and support system for deportees, labor-camp internees, and families without breadwinners. Large sums and much organizational energy had gone toward the support and rehabilitation of orphans sent to Bucharest from Transnistria during 1944. We might say that the organizational structure of the community had been strengthened as a result of the war. Ironically, the anti-Jewish laws had helped in this by forcing the Jews to depend on their own resources. Similarly, close ties with Jewish relief agencies abroad had promoted the organizational development of Rumanian Jewry. Contact with the rescue centers in Geneva and Constantinople and with the Red Cross, as well as activities related to aliyah, had aided in the crystallization of a strong, centralized Rumanian Jewish leadership. Thus, it was easier to deal with the Communist factor in Rumania than in Bulgaria.

The Parachutists in Rumania

During the first weeks after the Soviet occupation, the parachutists from Palestine played a pivotal organizing role in Jewish activity in Rumania. The group numbered nine by then, including four who were captured and imprisoned for some months during 1944 and released when Rumania surrendered. Four others had arrived in the summer of 1944—Yeshayhu Trachtenberg ("Dan" or "Shaike Dan") and Yitzhak Ben-Ephraim ("Theo") in June, Baruch Kaminker and Dov Berger in August. Uriel Kenner had arrived in September, after the cease-fire.[26] Upon liberation, they dropped their cover and declared themselves a Palestinian delegation.

Areas of responsibility were divided between them as follows: Dov Berger was to organize training farms (*hachsharot*); Shaike Dan was responsible for aliyah; Ben-Ephraim was treasurer and liaison with the adult Zionist leaders; and Baruch Kaminker was in charge of relief distribution. They hoped to gather together all the Zionist pioneer youth under a single umbrella group, the "Labor Youth Front."[27] The fact that the parachutists were not the emissaries of particular movements seemed to them an advantageous circumstance. They hoped to foster a new national identity and avoid partisan divisions among the youth, without directly challenging the movements as such. In this, they believed they were accurately echoing the mood and aspirations of the young people themselves. This provided the basis for united activity, taking precedence over the variety of prewar youth organizations and the different backgrounds of the parachutists themselves.[28]

The group concentrated on what was most natural to the youth movement: training farms and youth activities. Even in Rumania, where some limited Zionist activity had continued during the war, the young people did not exceed a thousand. There was therefore an opportunity to reorganize the youth, recruit new members, and train them to lead youth in newly established clubs. New programming material had to be designed to take into account the social needs of the war generation, to incorporate more recent developments in the Yishuv and in the Jewish world, and to bear the message of Zionism.

Dov Berger arranged educational seminars and Hebrew lessons for youth group leaders. He also initiated a project to translate key Zionist writings into Rumanian.[29] The educational materials being developed also had to transmit information of contemporary concern, such as major political decisions and Zionist efforts to rescue Jews. Pamphlets were printed describing the extermination of Polish Jewry. In addition, materials were produced in Hungarian for use among Hungarian Jewish refugees. The overall aim was to produce a sizable collection of educational and program materials.[30]

The first group leaders' seminar took place in September and was deemed successful. In its wake, a plan developed to stage a three-week national seminar for youth leaders. Several dozen new clubs were opened, and youth movement membership climbed rapidly to ten thousand. Training-farm facilities were expanded, as was the pool of candidates for aliyah.

A second focus of activity was the network of Jewish schools, in which the parachutists sought to play a major role. The Jewish school system had expanded after the expulsion of Jewish pupils from Rumanian schools during the war. Although Zionists erected new schools under the aegis of the Jewish Central Organization, their curriculum did not reflect a Zionist agenda. When the liberation came, Jewish Communists sought to penetrate and take control of the system. The Palestinian parachutists felt that they ought to try to prevent this through their own active involvement in education. However, a lack of adequate personnel prevented their plans from being implemented. In any case, the Jewish schools soon lost their central role in educating Jewish pupils, as the laws of the new regime restored the pupils' right to attend public schools and universities, which was the preference of most Jewish parents.

The parachutists did not agree with the local veteran Zionists on how to deal with the Communist challenge. The former were inclined to seek a modus vivendi rather than a head-on confrontation, believing that Zionism would be ill-served if portrayed to the younger generation as a reactionary movement allied with traditional parties. Advocating a policy of cooperation, they wanted the movement to be involved chiefly in aid and rehabilitation programs. The Zionists would then be conspicuous in service to returning deportees, in finding homes in the Regat for Jews from Bukovina and Bessarabia before these areas were annexed again by the Soviets. The parachutists also believed that it was vital to transfer Jews to the Regat from Transnistria before Soviet citizenship could be imposed.

On Communist initiative, a "general Jewish council" convened at the end of September, including representatives of various organizations and parties.[31] The Jewish parties—Zionists among them—viewed this as an attempt to establish communist control in Jewish affairs. After much hesitation, Filderman (who led the Rumanian Jewish party and represented the Union of Jewish Communities) decided to participate in the meetings of the council. A. L. Zissu, leader of the Zionist movement, refused to do so, in part because he and Filderman had failed to reach a consensus.

The parachutists, on the other hand, thought it opportune to participate in the council rather than shun the new body.[32] A deep rift developed over this. Zissu wanted all Zionist energies and activities to be directed toward one goal only: aliyah. There was no justification, in his view, for any official dealings with the authorities except over Jewish emigration. Moreover, he sought to reapply strict criteria for aliyah certificates, believing that only those active in the Zionist movement deserved this privilege.

He believed that he was engaged in a fight for ethical norms in the movement, and he continued his attempts to oust Pandelis through the summer of 1944. Zissu's stand had been supported by the parachutists. Now, after liberation, the situation changed. They came to believe that Zissu did not fully grasp the nature of aliyah work among the Jewish and general public. They were dismayed, too, at his continuing feud with Filderman, which no longer seemed to possess rhyme or reason and which was, in fact, detrimental. Filderman had won the confidence of the JDC and the Red Cross, with whom the parachutists had to cooperate. Playing along with Zissu had therefore become a liability, quite apart from the fact that he was incapable of taking instructions. Tensions increased once it was understood that Zissu's plans for aliyah were not to be implemented after all.

The *Salah-a-Din* had been set to depart from Rumania, with a group of 300 young Zionists aboard, on the date of the surrender. The boat remained in the possession of Pandelis and ORAT, which he and the Palestine Office continued to operate jointly. The new Rumanian regime granted permission for the boat to depart; no objection was raised by the Soviets, either. The government mandated that the Red Cross supervise all arrangements, but the local Red Cross representative worked closely with Pandelis. This reopened the unresolved conflict with Zissu, and once again it seemed that progress was being blocked for no good reason.

Since September, direct mail contact with Constantinople had been interrupted, which made both Zissu and Shaike Dan hesitant to give the *Salah-a-Din* a go-ahead. Other members of the team, however, were of the opinion that this was but a pretext for Zissu to avoid collaborating with Pandelis. Shaike Dan was of a mind to travel to Constantinople to clarify the matter, but was afraid of not being allowed back into the country, as he had no legal status in Rumania. Aliyah operations therefore ground to a halt again.

The arrival of Yosef Klarman, Moshe Agami, and David Zimend in early October brought a welcome end to this. Important work had been done by the parachutists to revitalize the Zionist movement, but their status in the country was only temporary. Indeed, they were technically under British military command and under orders to return from Rumania as of September. Efforts were made to delay their departure, but these proved unavailing. Two members of the team left by the end of September, and three more were to leave by early November. Two remained until the following month. Dov Berger alone was able to stay on in Rumania, but a good deal of his time was devoted to the British delegation.[33]

Agami and the Voyages of the Salah-a-Din and the Taurus

Moshe Agami was one of the most experienced among the aliyah bet workers. Until 1940, he had been active in Geneva, and in 1942 and 1943 in organizing overland clandestine routes from Persia to Palestine. In 1944, he began to work with the Greek resistance and British and American intelligence in organizing the flight of Greek Jews. His experience made him a logical choice for taking over operations in Rumania, where he faced numerous challenges, like that of bringing some order into work in Rumania. He also had to finalize accounts with Pandelis and other elements involved in aliyah operations, such as the Rumanian and International Red Cross.

Agami set out early in his Rumanian mission to determine whether and at what price it was possible to dispense with Pandelis and his services. While he generally agreed with his colleagues in Constantinople, who believed that the successes of aliyah bet in the Balkans owed something to Pandelis's involvement, he also believed that the Mossad had grown overly dependent upon its Greek agent and that his conflict with Zissu had stymied operations for too long. It was Agami's belief that Pandelis no longer wielded as much influence with the Rumanians now that the regime had changed. For the same reason, Pandelis's anger was no longer to be feared much.

Yet, as Agami discovered soon enough, Pandelis was still indispensable to the implementation of aliyah plans.[34] Pandelis retained the backing of the Rumanian Red Cross, the body named by the government to deal with Jewish emigration. Moreover, despite the change in regime, many of the middle- and lower-level bureaucrats and officials in the state administration had remained the same, and their influence on the procedures affecting aliyah was crucial. In this sphere Pandelis was the expert, and he was rapidly demonstrating his rapport with a new set of officials: Soviet ones.[35] Therefore, Agami decided it was prudent to go on working with Pandelis, reach an agreement regarding debts to him, and entrust Zissu with the responsibility for overland transportation (which they now thought capable of providing a solution for large numbers of Jews). This proved untenable, however, because Zissu adamantly maintained his objection to Pandelis's role in ORAT. Agami was forced to conclude that it was less dangerous to break with Zissu than with Pandelis. Not everyone would have agreed, but once made, Agami's decision was supported.

Pandelis still held the Mossad to account for some £80,000, a sum that Agami was unable to reduce through negotiation. He suspected Pandelis of inflating his costs and wasting large sums, though the accounts appeared to have been carefully kept and bills had been countersigned by Rubin. Agami hoped to use this to his advantage and speed the departure of immigrant boats by promising payment to Pandelis only after the acquired vessels set sail.

Three weeks after Agami's arrival, the *Salah-a-Din* left port carrying 370 immigrants, mostly young pioneers and the remainder refugees. The Mossad and the Jewish Agency paid for the trip. The high proportion of *halutzim* (youth movement trainees) among the passengers was due to Agami's and his colleagues assessment that the trip itself was rather risky. The boat had been ready for two months, but there was no official Soviet permit for its departure. The trip was therefore something of a test case—the first immigrant voyage since the change of regime. It was felt that the movement members would be more likely to accept the consequences should Soviet intervention stop the departure at the last minute. The *Salah-a-Din* reached Constantinople safely, having made the crossing without a hitch. The passengers received Turkish transit visas and entry documents for Palestine.

Agami had been guided by two main considerations: the strong desire of Jews to emigrate to Palestine, and the likelihood that success would have a positive effect on others apprehensive about a sea journey. The safe arrival of the *Salah-a-Din* seemed to bear this out, as the number of applicants for passage to Palestine increased tenfold. The tragic memory of the *Mefkura* would appear to have given way to hope that safe sea travel was once again possible.

Agami and his colleagues hoped to keep preparation for the next voyage to an absolute minimum. Places on board would have to be assigned according to predetermined criteria, partly because passengers with means would be defraying some of the trip's expenses, and partly because growing demand necessitated some procedure for selection.

The Shipping Market and Boat-Purchasing Policy

The optimism in Rumania, Istanbul, and Palestine in the wake of the *Salah-a-Din* affair prompted an effort to assemble "a significant fleet" for aliyah. Conditions in the shipping market had eased somewhat. More boats were available, and fewer restrictions were placed on civilian use of shipping. Shipowners were eager to find clients, and a contract for aliyah work was becoming a more attractive proposition, as the success of the *Salah-a-Din* encouraged shipowners, including some who had worked with the Mossad in the past, to seek out organizers. The owners of the Bulgarian-registered *Firin* and *Milca,* for example, as well as the owners of the Turkish *Morina* and *Bulbul,* offered their services.

The Mossad had to consider whether it was more worthwhile to purchase boats or continue chartering. Purchase was certainly more expensive in the short term, but it also allowed for greater control and flexibility. Nor was it clear what kind of boat was the best with respect to utility. If the boats were

Members of the *Gordonia* youth movement in the streets of Bucharest, September 1944. On the back of the photograph, which was mailed to Palestine, a participant wrote: "Our members marching in the streets of Bucharest. Our white and blue flag waving proudly together with the red flag under once-hostile skies. Hundreds of our members are singing songs of Zion and of the 'Hehalutz' movement. Jews, weeping for joy and embracing in the streets, are congratulating one another with the traditional blessing: that we have lived to see this day. Movement members in the hundreds shout: Aliyah aliyah, in spite of everything."

to continue making the crossing only as far as Constantinople, with the remainder of the trip made overland, smaller and somewhat less comfortable craft were sufficient. Less food supplies would be required, and no clandestine disembarkations on the Palestine coast need be arranged. On the other hand, should it become impossible to keep open the transfer route through Constantinople, boats would have to sail the entire distance to Palestine, and smaller vessels would hardly be adequate. Yet larger boats would be more vulnerable to Soviet seizure, as the Russians were looking to carry their wounded down the Danube. They had already commandeered the *Smyrni*, largest of the Mossad's vessels.[36]

Yosef Barpal was dispatched from Palestine to deal with these questions, which entailed policy as well as budgetary decisions. It was finally decided not to adopt any one policy, but rather to assemble a group of boats of different sizes under various terms: charter as well as purchase. During November, Agami negotiated over twenty small boats built for the Rumanian army but never actually used.[37] In Constantinople, negotiations were conducted to purchase a medium-size freighter, the *Asia*, as well as two other

New arrivals at Atlit Detention Camp, fall 1944.

The *Smyrni*, arriving in Palestine in 1946 under the name *Kibbutz-Galuiot* (Gathering the Exiles).

boats, *Vici* ("The Big One") and *Anastasia* ("The Saint"). Agami purchased the freighter in Rumania; the others were chartered in Constantinople. All three sailed to dry dock in Constantsa for refitting. An additional larger boat was chartered in January 1945. Thus, as 1944 ended, the Mossad could not say that a lack of ships prevented aliyah operations from proceeding.

However, questions of efficiency and policy in ship acquisition could not be allowed to cause any delay in operations as the Turkish government had begun to display a growing reluctance to open Turkish ports to Palestine-bound immigrants. This change in attitude took place after the British announced they would no longer grant all refugees reaching Turkey free entry to Palestine. Instead, the British were willing only to seek a safe haven for them. The Turkish authorities also called upon the Allied representation in Rumania to scrutinize the documents of Jewish emigrants thoroughly in order to prevent "illegals" from taking passage to Turkey.[38] The Rumanian authorities, for their part, announced that small boats would no longer receive permits to embark during the winter months, because of the dangers attending Black Sea crossings under storm conditions.

The Rumanian action took Agami and his colleagues by surprise. They detected a cooler attitude from the Soviets, who were refusing to release the *Smyrni* (despite earlier promises) and were detaining three refugee convoys attempting an overland route through Bulgaria. Jewish Communists began to wield greater influence and, as a consequence, made more of a point of their opposition to aliyah. Under the circumstances, Agami and his colleagues decided to organize a transport aboard the *Taurus,* a Greek-registered boat in Pandelis's possession. It reached Constantsa on 25 November and was ready to load a week later. The passengers totaled 950, and the plan was to disembark at Constantinople; nevertheless, the boat was sufficiently supplied for Palestine, should that become necessary.

The transport included survivors of the Vilna ghetto, Rozhka Korczak and Avraham Lidovsky, who were leading efforts to organize the survivor population. They had crossed several borders illegally to establish contact with the Palestinian team in Rumania. They were put aboard the *Taurus* because Agami realized what impact their arrival and their account of their experiences would have in Palestine.[39] Agami's great fear was that the Turks would order the boat towed into the Black Sea for a return to Rumania, and he implored his friends in Constantinople to prevent this. But the boat reached port safely, the passengers were permitted to disembark, and the British granted entry permits to each and every one.[40]

Despite all the worrisome developments, then, a new wave of optimism followed the arrival of the *Taurus.* The Vilna ghetto fighters and partisans produced a sensation in Palestine, as expected. Agami was instructed to spare no effort or expense to maintain the pace of aliyah. Avigur demanded that the ceiling of 1,500 per month be broken, and that talks be opened with the Soviets and with Jewish Communists to persuade them to give political support.[41] This was deemed important, as British patience was wearing thin (the concession to the *Taurus* group notwithstanding). In Turkey, political conditions continued to grow less benign for the rescue mission, particularly once the WRB representative left Constantinople. (Indeed, Hirschmann no longer saw the need for illegal immigration, since the Balkan countries had been liberated.) The instructions from Palestine were to continue as before, to seek continued Turkish cooperation, but to prepare the boats for a Mediterranean crossing just in case: in other words, "aliyah by any means."[42]

By December 1944, the Palestine Zionists were interested in a return to the methods of 1939, though on a grander scale and with better support. A struggle for free aliyah was the policy of the Agency, the Histadrut, and the Mossad. This meant not only a political struggle as such, but the physical organization of aliyah operations through a joint mobilization of the immigrants themselves and the Jewish public in Palestine. Aliyah bet became a factor of consensus and unity among Zionists. The total immigration figure for the period from October to December was slim, however. Only 3,317 certificates were utilized—less than the legally allowable 1,500 per month. About half the total figure was represented by the *Salah-a-Din* and *Taurus* groups. The supporters of aliyah bet claimed that, with the proper backing, it could be the most effective means of bringing Jews into the country. But Agami complained in December and January of insufficient funds and of a cutback in the amount of credit available to him, the result of his failure to repay debts.[43]

The first months of 1945 were extremely cold in Rumania, and basic necessities were scarcer than ever. Widespread starvation threatened the population. Meanwhile, refugees crossing into Rumania from Hungary and Poland related details of anti-Semitic violence being committed against Jewish survivors attempting to return to their former homes. They appealed to Agami and Zimend to become involved in *bricha*: helping Jews to escape from Eastern Europe.[44] Agami agreed, believing that the growth of the Jewish refugee population in Rumania would create greater pressure on the authorities. He demanded greater funding from Palestine, as well as the assignment of new emissaries to help him handle the expanding Rumanian operation.

In spite of all his efforts, however, Agami could not overcome the mounting difficulties: confiscation of boats, denial of permission to dock, new fees demanded for the use of dry-dock facilities, orders forbidding the registration of immigration applicants, and more. There was little doubt that Soviet opposition lay behind all of this.[45] As the *bricha* turned from a trickle to a stream, it was decided to direct the refugees toward Yugoslavia and Italy.

The Stara-Zagora Affair

The rescue mission sought to renew overland routes via Bulgaria to Turkey, and finally by rail to Palestine. Two groups of children had used this route in January and March 1943. During 1944, nine families a week took this route, as did other families and individuals who obtained travel documents by various means. The cessation of area hostilities led aliyah workers to consider using this method once again. The overland route had advantages over sea travel, as it was not associated in anyone's mind with past tragedies. David Zimend, put in charge of this, was to work together with the reopened Palestine Office. Venya Pomerantz carefully sounded out the Bulgarian authorities and reported that they were indeed prepared to grant transit permits. Many of the arriving refugees had immigration permits for Palestine, which they had received earlier, as a means of saving them from deportation and from the death camps. These permits had been distributed by Swiss diplomats to people whose names the Jewish Agency had supplied to the British authorities. The Agency and the British had agreed, however, that these permits would not be regarded as valid immigration certificates in themselves.[46] The refugees, on the other hand, fully believed that the documents entitled them to entry into Palestine. The Yishuv's representatives in Bulgaria and Rumania refrained from informing them otherwise.

Several hundred refugees in Bucharest were formed into groups for overland travel in November 1944. Of these, some held the type of permit described. Rail transport to Bulgaria was arranged in Bucharest, and Venya Pomerantz was told to expect the group and arrange for the next leg of the journey.

The first group, numbering 153, was stopped for an inspection of papers at the Stara-Zagora rail station, where the stationmaster decided to seek verification from Sofia. The delay seemed to be nothing more than a bureaucratic hurdle, so the next two groups, each with 400 people, were instructed to proceed. The Sofia authorities, however, were unable to supply a clear reason for the delay, but they did not pass an order that would let the people move on. Following strenuous efforts to obtain information, it was finally declared that the affair was out of the hands of the Bulgarian authorities, being handled by the Soviet delegate to the Allied council. No response was forthcoming, other than advice to wait patiently.

The refugees were in the meantime confined to their cars. The sanitary facilities on the train and in the station, not intended for heavy and extended use, soon became inadequate. People began to fall ill, and the supply of drugs was exhausted. The threat of contagious infection, even of epidemic, mounted. Bulgaria was prey to severe shortages that winter, and supplies at the small town, far from urban centers, could not sustain the hundreds of people who had suddenly descended on it. The Jewish community leaders in Sofia tried to help in whatever way they could, including publicizing the plight of refugees in the press. The Mossad emissaries smelled a repetition of Kladovo—an experience they would not soon forget. The entire plan for overland aliyah was at stake.[47]

David Ben-Gurion arrived in Bulgaria about three weeks after the first group had been stopped. As chairman of the Jewish Agency executive, he was asked to deal with the "Stara-Zagora refugees," which totaled about a thousand. Ben-Gurion met the Soviet representative to the Allied council but could not obtain a satisfactory answer to the problem. It seemed that a solution was not yet in the offing. Ben-Gurion was given two reasons: The Soviets claimed to be concerned about the possible presence of Red Army deserters and Soviet citizens, and secondly, the Poles in the group would have to obtain emigration permits from the new Polish government in Lublin. The refugees would have to be inspected and the proper documents obtained before the group could continue.

Both Ben-Gurion and the aliyah activists were skeptical but were unable to speed up the process. Accordingly, they decided to appeal to the British and American representatives in Sofia.[48] The British envoy relayed the call for assistance, and American Ambassador Steinhardt in Ankara asked the State Department to exert pressure on the Soviets.[49] Washington agreed, but two more weeks would pass before any change in the Soviet position came about.

During that time, the group at Stara-Zagora was joined by other groups, part of a steady stream traveling toward the Black Sea and Turkey with the idea of reaching Palestine. Another group of 360 refugees was detained near the city of Russe, as was a group of 300 at Skoplia. The problem seemed to have gotten out of control, and the Soviet replies recalled statements about the fate of stranded Jewish refugees that were made before the war by the British and other governments, as if nothing had happened in the meantime.[50]

During the last days of December, the Russians announced that the refugees had been granted permission to proceed. The groups soon arrived at the Turkish frontier, where they had to wait another week until the British government decided to grant the members of the group entry certificates out of the January quota. Finally, they were allowed to enter Turkey.

Thus, the aliyah issue had returned in January 1945 to the fall of 1939. There was tremendous pressure to leave Europe and large groups of refugees were congregating in the Balkan countries, but opportunities to travel to Palestine were becoming fewer. The British exerted political pressure to allow only those Jews with valid British documents to leave.[51] The Soviets were using their bureaucracy to impede aliyah at every turn. Travel from Rumania to Bulgaria had been effectively halted, as had the crossing from Bulgaria to Turkey. So even the minimal number of certificates allocated to Jews in Rumania could not be fully utilized. Had it not been for this, Shaike Dan contended upon his return to Palestine, it would have been possible to transport thousands from Poland and elsewhere.

That is why the refugees were instructed to move toward Yugoslavia and Italy. A half a year would pass before the first aliyah boat would depart Italy. By the end of 1945, the Balkan countries had ceased being the focus of aliyah work. Soviet control posed a serious obstacle to the flow of Holocaust survivors. Under the new political conditions, aliyah workers lost the maneuverability they had once enjoyed when it had been possible to pay off the proper officials to obtain valid or forged permits.

Ben-Gurion Visits Bulgaria

Emissaries in Rumania and Bulgaria appealed in October, 1944, to the Yishuv political leaders to send a major figure to meet with the newly liberated Jewish communities. In the past, when the rescue mission in Constantinople had persistently asked that a top-ranking leader be sent on a permanent basis, it proved unobtainable. As noted, prominent leaders did go to Istanbul for short visits. Balkan emissaries were therefore surprised that their request had been accepted by the Agency, even more that Ben-Gurion himself would visit Bulgaria and Rumania. No doubt this reflected the commitment of Ben-Gurion himself to establishing an immediate and close relationship with the surviving Jews of Europe.

Ben-Gurion wanted to encounter these Jews himself, in order to get a sense of their willingness to become part of the Zionist struggle. He viewed them as primary candidates for large-scale aliyah, and he viewed aliyah as the primary pressure the Zionists could exert. In addition, he hoped to gauge, at least indirectly, Soviet intentions regarding Jewish emigration to Palestine. Ben-Gurion had a deep distrust of the Russians, believing them capable of maintaining their former anti-Zionist policies and extending them to Southern and Eastern Europe. This would constitute, as he saw it, a disaster second only to the Holocaust itself. These were among his considerations in coming to the Balkans when the aliyah issue was once more dividing political opinion in Palestine with respect to relations with the British.[52]

The visit had had to be postponed twice while permits were sought, particularly for Rumania, with its 400,000 Jews, which was Ben-Gurion's primary destination. Upon arrival in Constantinople, however, he stood little chance of being admitted to Rumania. He therefore proceeded to Bulgaria, where he hoped to be able to complete further arrangements. In Sofia, where he discussed the matter with the Soviet representative, he realized that the Soviets would not permit him to visit Rumania.

Nevertheless, Ben-Gurion returned from Bulgaria with the sense that his visit had been of the greatest importance. In Bulgaria he had been treated as political representative of the Jewish community, almost on a diplomatic level. The local Jews had received him enthusiastically as their national leader. The mass gatherings were marked by intense feelings of excitement, outpourings of affection, and expressions of respect, all of which made a tremendous impression on him. His diary reveals that it was a truly moving experience for him.[53]

Ben-Gurion spent seven days in Bulgaria. He met with Bulgarian politicians from various parties, to whom he expressed gratitude for help during the war and for the positive attitudes shown to the Jews by Bulgaria. He dwelt on this especially in conversations with the Church and the Metropolitan, who had acted persistently to prevent the expulsion of Jews from Sofia in March 1943. These talks were given a political character as well, as he spoke not only of the past but also of the future: of the need to find a solution in a Jewish state in Palestine. His constant refrain was that free aliyah was the only way to achieve that goal. In his talks, he played down the differences between the Yishuv and the British government, pointing out that the Jewish Agency worked together with the British authorities. He was therefore seeking the cooperation of Bulgaria in assisting Jews to leave the country under easier conditions, including the right to take some property with them.

An interesting aspect of Ben-Gurion's talks with non-Communist Bulgarian leaders was his criticism of the authorities for assisting Jewish Communists to take over the Jewish Consistory and thus to control much of the Jewish community, though they were not supported by the majority. He spoke of the Jewish Communists as opportunists and lackeys not motivated by ideology. He gave vent to fears regarding communism and echoed the assessment of the Yishuv's emissaries. He met Jewish Communists face-to-face and rebuked them for taking "unfair advantage" of the plight of the people.

In meetings with the American and British representatives to the Allied council, he refrained from confrontations over the White Paper. Instead, he spoke of practical issues—in particular, the thousand refugees stranded at Stara-Zagora and elsewhere—and asked them to use their influence as best they could with the Bulgarians and with the Soviets.

He spent most of his time at meetings with the Jewish community, for whom he showed deep empathy. He saw in these people a group that had been robbed by the war of its self-confidence and its economic base, and spoke to them as the potential builders of the Zionist dream. The visit showed Ben-Gurion's ability to think like a statesman, searching constantly for a way to turn this most difficult hour into an historic opportunity, to make suffering and weakness fuel the drive to regain strength and energy. He spoke of the friends and allies of Bulgarian Jewry, of the need to repair and strengthen Jewish organs so that they might impart consciousness and vision to the young. At the same time, he sympathized with the plight of individuals and sought, not as a political leader but as a human being, to offer some form of comfort. These two qualities made themselves felt and left a profound impression.

During those seven days, Ben-Gurion also sought to take a direct hand in coping with the difficulties facing the aliyah effort. He listened to Jews tell of their apprehensiveness over sea travel. He attempted to provide answers and reassurances. He dealt with the legal problems related to the recovery of confiscated property, and tried to assess the impact on the Jews' desire to emigrate of the government's decision to require emigrants to leave all property behind. He discussed approaching the Bulgarian regime with a proposal to allow Jewish emigrants to transfer property to Palestine.

Equal to these concerns was his interest in Jewish education. He visited schools and formed an impression of the extent of Communist influence there. He demanded changing the curriculum to make Hebrew an integral part of Jewish education, along with Jewish history and the Bible. To stress the importance of the language of the Zionist movement, he spoke Hebrew throughout these visits (with one exception, when he spoke in Yiddish), and his words were translated. He devoted serious discussion, too, to the Yishuv's emissaries, and he agreed with their appeal for reinforcements.

The one incident that, he claimed, moved and shocked him more than anything else was his visit to the Jewish poor of Sofia. There he met Jews who had been destitute even before the war and who were left, after their expulsion to the countryside, completely bereft. Nor had they been able to recover what had been theirs when they returned to Sofia. They were given shelter in public buildings no longer in use, many people packed into each room, with no furniture, no heat, and not even the minimal sanitary facilities. Among the inmates were many children, barefoot and practically naked, despite the December temperatures. The mothers, left without husbands, had given up in despair and were unable to struggle anymore. Neglect and helplessness reigned.

Ben-Gurion was unable to shake the idea that in these pitiful creatures he had met not just a group of poor, downtrodden Jews from Bulgaria, but the thousands of Jewish survivors in liberated Europe. He wrote in his diary that he felt their anguish, and that his responsibility—the moral obligation of the Yishuv as a whole—was to work to bring these people back to life. More than anything else, he remembered the grim sight of the children whose innocent suffering was too much to bear. These were the ones, he felt, who must be rescued at once, who must be brought to Palestine. Their parents would follow. He had shown a special concern for the children during the war, and this came to the fore during his visit to Bulgaria. The emotional character of his encounter there is reflected in the stanza of Hannah Senesh's poem, "Blessed Is the Match," which he copied into his diary. His immediate response to the barefoot children of Sofia was to raise funds for shoes, for "the thousands of bare feet on the cold stone floors" of postwar Jewish Sofia.[54]

His visit to Bulgaria changed him, just as direct encounters with survivors changed all the Palestinian emissaries. Even the best reports could not adequately express what one saw in face-to-face contact. Far away in Palestine, one read a report with one eye on all the complex problems in Palestine. In Bulgaria, Ben-Gurion had the chance not only to think about the plight of the Jews, but to witness it himself. And so the Jews of Bulgaria became for him all the Jews alive after the Holocaust. They were the last remnant of the people, and also the only hope for the future. They were the hope of Zionism and the reason for Zionism.

But apart from their weakness, perhaps their most visible aspect, he also sensed a profound Jewish strength. Their experience justified to him the demand that he had made in the summer of 1944: that the Zionist cause be given concrete expression through the aliyah of a million Jews within several years' time. It is true that he still harbored the hope that this wish might be realized through an agreement with the British, perhaps even through the help of the great powers. But if that was not to be, the Zionist movement had another option, a tried and tested option that would have to be put into effect on an unprecedented scale: aliyah bet.

Conclusion

We have described the aliyah bet movement during the Second World War from the combined perspective of the Yishuv, Zionist policies, and the history of the Holocaust. The war years separate the high point in illegal aliyah of 1938–39 from the peak years of 1946–47.

Although illegal immigration accompanied Zionist settlement in Palestine throughout the prestatehood decades, leaders of the Zionist movement did not regard this as the high road to fulfillment of the national mission. Yet, under the impact of the Holocaust, it moved from a marginal to a central position in Zionist activity. And many thousands of lives were thereby saved.

Since the days of Theodor Herzl, the Zionist movement had sought to operate within the limits of international legality and recognition. In the wake of the Balfour Declaration, it did not appear that there would be any cause to deviate from that path. When immigration to Palestine took place outside legal bounds, this was, as a rule, a part of a political struggle, at times internal. Within the movement, there were conflicts between the executive and its administrative bodies, on the one hand, and demands made by various dissatisfied groups on the other, who refused to accept either the guidelines or the method of their implementation. This was the case in 1934 with the illegal aliyah organized by the Hehalutz and the Betar youth movements. At other times, the struggle was external, directed against the Mandatory administration, which imposed strict limits on immigration quotas, especially after 1937.

Efforts to organize aliyah bet were preceded by what we may describe as a bottleneck. The forces creating the bottleneck were the economic and political pressures exerted against Jews in Europe, which considerably increased the pool of people seeking to emigrate. Jewish community leaders in Europe— and afterward at the national level—faced a growing demand for bigger emigration, even if that meant contravening regulations.

One can observe this dynamic as early as the first years of the British Mandate, between 1918 and 1920, but it was in the latter half of the 1930s that emigration truly became a necessity. The power of the factors that fueled the emigration movement found expression in the degree of risk regarded as acceptable. In the same vein, visas for countries that had exerted a lesser attraction suddenly came to be very much in demand in the light of the threat to Jewish existence. A gap opened between supply and demand, between opportunities for immigration and the number seeking to emigrate. In that situation, some sought extralegal solutions.

Unlike the stream of legal emigration to various target countries, illegal aliyah depended on objective "push factors" and an organizational and support structure provided by the various Zionist bodies. The ideological impetus and message that aliyah bet bore were the features that gave it its distinctive character, over and above a regular emigration or escape movement of the European Jews. Illegal aliyah incorporated elements of the Zionist idea—the return of the Jewish nation to the land of Israel—together with a struggle to achieve Jewish national independence.

There would have been no aliyah bet had there not been a Jewish population already in Palestine, capable of organizing independent action. By the end of the 1930s, aliyah bet had become a popular movement rather than an activity of select groups. Jews from all age groups, all walks of life, and all political creeds were involved: Communists and Bundists (Socialist non-Zionists that wanted to keep Jewish cultural identity) alongside supporters of the Orthodox Agudat Israel, Revisionist Zionists, Mizrahi religious Zionists, and labor Zionists. After it became a mass movement that lasted over a significant period of time, it also became part of the national consciousness of the Jewish people.

Moreover, aliyah bet became a force on the international scene. It dramatized the refugee problem and underlined the people's heroic and desperate attempt—without the benefit of meaningful political support—to find a positive solution to tremendous difficulties. The eventual public outcry over the Jewish plight in Nazi-dominated Europe influenced governments, such as that of the United States.

From the Zionist point of view, this illustrated how many problems remained unresolved in the relationship of the modern, Christian West to the Jewish people, despite long decades of Jewish emancipation. The demand that the democracies accept responsibility for finding a solution for the Jews from Nazi Germany or in semi-Fascist states such as Poland and Rumania was a cornerstone of Zionist policy in the international arena in the 1930s.

The advantage of aliyah bet over wandering the seas or filling refugee camps in European countries was that it provided a national solution to the "Jewish problem" that removed some of the responsibility from Europe, while drawing attention to the plight of victims. Despite the very real difficulties involved in realizing the Zionist goal during the thirties, aliyah bet expressed the commitment of people who offered a practical solution to the Jewish refugee problem. While one might also find fault with the Zionist solution, especially in light of the vociferous Arab opposition, it was hard to ignore the arguments marshaled by Zionist leaders.

These arguments carried weight with intellectual and political figures in England and the United States who were willing to countenance illegal aliyah as a means of pressuring England to alter its immigration policy. Governments, too, such as those of Poland and Rumania, were interested in supporting aliyah bet and allowed refugees to travel through their territory despite British objections.

Zionist politicians like Ben-Gurion and Jabotinsky sought to capitalize. Their attitude to the illegal immigration movement was ambivalent, but in the final analysis it was determined by political considerations. They discerned in this both an external and an internal aspect. Jabotinsky was full of admiration for the "independent" immigration, as he called it, because he felt it created a positive role model for the Jewish people. For him, aliyah bet could mobilize youth and teach them to express unapologetically and constructively their refusal to comply with the conditions imposed on them. Independent aliyah would save Jews from the dangers that awaited them in Europe. Revisionism also had explicit political reasons to back this aliyah: its opposition to the main-line Zionist Organization from which it had seceded in the mid-thirties, and the opportunity to reinforce the New Zionist (Revisionist) ranks in Palestine.

Ben-Gurion, too, was sympathetic to aliyah bet as an expression of Zionist protest against the immigration situation. However, in 1937, when he took a position against further aliyah bet activity, he was in fact ambivalent. Apart from tactical considerations that impelled him to oppose it, he did not lose his basic admiration for the activist approach that aliyah bet reflected. By 1939, he again supported this activity, not only because it represented a useful political tool, but also because of the example that it set. He felt that the struggle would lead people along the path to a "fighting Zionism," which he regarded as an essential process.

Both Jabotinsky and Ben-Gurion, however, acted primarily in the political arena. They understandably wanted the aliyah movement organized according to political criteria. Their approach was challenged at a fundamental level by the entire enterprise of illegal immigration, whose exponents took the phenomenon to be inexorable and therefore not completely subject to political controls.

The Yishuv leaders could hardly oppose aliyah bet, even without an immediate danger to physical survival as such. Opposition to secret aliyah was regarded by many as basically immoral, while others pointed out that such opposition hardly served the Yishuv's interest in expanding the Jewish population.

Around this issue a conflict developed within the Zionist leadership. On the one hand, those like Berl Katznelson would allow aliyah bet to "point the way." For them, it was a historical, elemental force that would determine Zionist policy. On the other hand, there were those who sought to harness aliyah bet as a tool whenever it might further the political interests of the Yishuv.

The issue brought into sharp focus the two elements that guided Zionist policy: the Yishuv in Palestine and the Jews of the Diaspora. It also illuminated the areas in which the two might come to a conflict of interest. Thus, in 1938, when the Zionist leaders had not yet given up hope for early establishment of a Jewish state in part of Palestine, aliyah bet made a confrontation with Britain inevitable.

In 1938–39, the Zionist leaders came to appreciate what aliyah bet represented and the potential force it embodied. Their support increased as a result, but so did their desire to place it firmly under their control. It was possible to do so in part through expanding the organization of aliyah bet under the executive aegis of the national bodies. This is what led them to establish the Mossad Le'aliyah in 1939 as an arm of the Haganah. At its head they placed Shaul Avigur, an experienced and prominent labor Zionist who was not one of the "founding fathers."

Yet the establishment of the Mossad did not automatically defuse the tensions that we have described; indeed, in a certain sense these tensions were magnified. There now existed an official and legitimate body, supervised by the executive, responsible for promoting aliyah bet. The Mossad, in effect, represented a special interest within the leadership, which was constrained to take that interest into account. The establishment of the Mossad reinforced among its members the self-image of a group dedicated to rescuing the Jewish people and therefore striving to uphold the priority of aliyah in the national agenda.

Moreover, the problem of control over aliyah bet could not be resolved entirely by co-opting labor Zionist activists into an established agency, for the Revisionist movement was also adopting more centralized procedures. In addition, there was large-scale aliyah activity organized by individuals in a private capacity. Neither of these was under Jewish Agency control. Rather, they provided a challenge to the Agency; the Revisionists, indeed, openly flouted its authority.

Who, then, did the aliyah activists represent? Did they represent their superiors in the political establishment, or the immigrants in whose name their activity was undertaken? This was not an abstract question, as became apparent as early as the end of 1938 in the confrontation between Ben-Gurion—who wanted to bend illegal aliyah into an instrument of mass political protest ("an aliyah revolt")—and the activists, who sought to preserve its clandestine character, which, in their view, was the only way to assure success. A more severe confrontation was to occur over the issue of the *Darien,* sold to the British for sabotage work. Aliyah activists retained use of the ship for a time. But when, with a group of immigrants aboard her, they refused to turn the *Darien* over to its proper owners, they found themselves accused of insubordination. This raised quite clearly the question of whether an organization of such independent character could be accommodated within the political system, or whether it constituted a threat to the designated authorities. It was no accident that the Mossad did not resume active operations at sea for two years.

At the same time, the Second World War posed new problems for Jews who wished to emigrate, for aliyah organizers, and for the political leadership—problems that combined to restrict the scope of aliyah operations at the very time when the Jews of Europe needed them most. During the first two years of the war, it was still possible to leave the Reich territories and travel with a modicum of safety in the Mediterranean. Because of the war, emigration organization became an extremely sensitive issue in Nazi Germany, in British policy, and among aliyah organizers. This tended to prevent cooperation among them, and aliyah bet was not given the political or logistical support it required.

The absence of a vigorous aliyah bet during this initial period of the war illustrates the way in which the Yishuv came to stand apart from the Holocaust in the first phase of 1940–42, not just geographically and politically but in a psychological sense as well. That sense of separation was overcome when refugees reached Palestine and related what they knew of developments in Europe. Long before the Final Solution, the refugees who arrived on the *Hilda,* the *Sakariya,* and Storfer's three boats told of the Jews deported to Lublin and Nisko. And long before reports of the Final Solution filtered out to Palestine, the passengers of the *Mircea* and *Mihai* reported what had happened to Jews in Bukowina and Jassy. The helpless confusion of the Zionist leadership and its failure to respond quickly enough to save the *Struma* people indicated that without a relentless struggle, without clear resistance to the British government, no concessions could be wrung for aliyah bet.

The lack of significant aliyah activity during 1941–42 prevented the Yishuv from maintaining direct contact with the Jews of Europe from the beginning of the Final Solution until confirmed reports reached Palestine in November 1942. The full import of this gap is conveyed in the words spoken after the war by Abba Kovner to the Jewish Brigade at Bari:

> Two catastrophes have befallen us. One of them is the catastrophe of the destruction itself, the loss of six million, the severing of the most vital limbs of our people. The second one is that between Europe and Eretz Israel there lies a gray sea which convoys of immigrants had ceased to cross. If during the years of mass murder there had arrived not only sporadic reports but boatload after boatload of thousands fleeing from the death pits, then without any doubt their very presence, their rage, would have been communicated to the Yishuv. I do not know what might have been different had this been the case. I do not know what results such a stream of revulsion would have produced. But I do know this: something would have been different.

This brings us to the end of 1942, when civilian exchange groups arrived in Palestine bearing news of the death camps. Despite the many reports reaching the Yishuv through the press and independent sources, the Jewish public in Palestine and its leaders still apparently could not fully digest the meaning of what had occurred. In the unending search to define Zionist goals and guidelines for action, the Yishuv did not establish the kind of special instruments necessary to meet extraordinary challenges.

Initially, Ben-Gurion had declared that the war would pose new challenges and difficulties beyond the powers of the Yishuv to resolve. He, along with most of the political elite, including the Revisionists, considered the war against Hitler to be the most important contribution that the Yishuv could make. This would, they believed, assure Jews a secure political future in the postwar world. In focusing on the war effort, those who stood at the helm of the Yishuv felt themselves to be fulfilling a leadership function not only for Palestine Jewry but for the entire Jewish people. But these hopes soon dissolved.

The Mossad began to reorganize itself for action during 1942. Ze'ev Shind reported back to Palestine about the desperation and suffering of the refugees who reached Constantinople through independent efforts. The *Lilly* (which the Mossad acquired at the end of 1941 but which could not be used to save the *Struma* refugees) transferred to Cyprus those illegal immigrants who had been interned in Turkey, and thereby helped to find safe haven for them, even if it was outside Palestine.

Mossad members were the first to frame a strategy to establish contacts in the Balkans and organize the Jews there for aliyah. Their approach, which depended on the cooperation of British intelligence (interested in Jews from the Balkans as sources of information), proved ultimately to have been only partially successful. But it also provided a conduit for communication by courier and junior diplomatic officials with the Jews of occupied Europe. (Indeed, this method had already been used by the Mossad in 1941, when the Constantinople representatives of European governments-in-exile performed this function.)

The Mossad also helped to create a rescue organization within the Histadrut, even before the broad-based Rescue Committee was formed by the various parties and agencies. The representatives of the Mossad were called upon to adopt activity which had not previously been acceptable, as well as to seek a combination of legal and illegal activity—as we saw in the case of the immigration of a thousand Jews from Bulgaria. In that instance they were unsuccessful, but the same method was applied in the establishment of ORAT in Rumania, without which the aliyah in 1944 would hardly have taken place.

Aliyah bet furnished the Jews of Europe with a field of activity in which even the most skeptical were willing to invest a great deal of energy because it represented a true avenue for rescue. The funds that were sunk into this far outweighed any other work. This was partly the result of objective factors, such as the high cost of purchasing or leasing boats and hiring crew members. One may say that another factor was the Jews' very willingness to take enormous risks. The principle, as enunciated by Ben-Gurion at the Mapai central committee meeting of August 1943, was that no reasonable rescue opportunity was to be passed up. When such an opportunity presented itself, monetary considerations were not allowed to stand in its way. This is a clear indication of the attitude taken toward aliyah bet at this juncture. As Ben-Gurion saw it, illegal work did bring rescue closer to fruition.

There were rescue operations that the Yishuv undertook without actual help from any of the Allies. In contrast to the gamut of planned activity, these independent operations came to represent a larger share of the Yishuv's rescue work than anticipated. There was no all-out effort to combat the indifference of the Western democracies, even though all were agreed that without their active involvement there could be no large-scale rescue. Perhaps the failure to meet this issue head-on owed something to the fact that the semi-independent operations provided an outlet for frustration and the need to take direct action.

By focusing on the value of independent action it was possible, too, to derive some solace in the face of the awful dissonance between the dimensions of the Holocaust and the numerical results of aliyah bet. In April 1944, after the *Milca* arrived in Istanbul, the Mossad emissaries wrote:

> We shall never forget the proud moment in which the boat, carrying Jews rescued through Jewish efforts, sailed into port—after our "friends" had all said that all that could have been done had already been done. Let the *Milca* testify to the "enlightened" world's criminal failure to act to save the remnants of our people.

This was the feeling among the activists, and they communicated this to the Yishuv at large. Aliyah bet was truly an effort of Jews for Jews.

Thus, we are faced with a dilemma: how to assess aliyah bet if one of its effects was to enable the Yishuv to come to terms with its own impotence and with the pronounced failure to achieve a mass rescue policy. Of course, aliyah did help. But did it not at some level also provide a psychological crutch for those who would rather not have faced the weaknesses of Zionist policy in the face of the terrible crisis? Aliyah bet seemed to offer an avenue of activity, and even scored some successes, albeit small ones. Taken in the wider context, however, did these successes mitigate the overall suffering?

Aliyah bet, in addition to its primary aim, was meant to be the bridge between the Jews of Europe and the Yishuv. There was widespread recognition that the future of the Jewish people and of Zionism depended to a large extent on a massive postwar influx of Jews to Palestine. Only that would underscore the moral and political imperative behind the Zionist mission. The question was: would there remain enough survivors in postwar Europe to carry on such a struggle? These issues were discussed by Yishuv leaders in the Jewish Agency executive, the Histadrut executive council, and other public bodies.

Many viewed aliyah bet as a possible link between the survivors and the realization of Zionist aims—not only by physically bringing the survivors to Palestine, but through the process of mobilizing and organizing rescue during the war and after. Many in the Yishuv doubted whether the war alone would induce the Jews of the Diaspora to adopt a Zionist worldview. Indeed, there were various possible Jewish responses to the Holocaust, including an escape from Jewishness. Effecting the transition from survivor to immigrant therefore seemed essential to keeping the Zionist vision alive and reinvesting it with new meaning. Aliyah was to be both process and goal. The feelings of rage toward Europe and what was perpetrated on the Jewish people had to be harnessed and channeled so that survivors would participate in building a Jewish Palestine. This, in turn, could be accomplished with Zionist emissaries sent to Europe during the war or immediately after its end. Aliyah workers would have to give direction to the inner pressure to leave Europe. They would also have to rely on the help of youth movement elites.

The words of Berl Katznelson, quoted in our introduction, bear repeating in this regard. At the war's end, aliyah was a necessity. This time the leadership understood the "hidden paths of history," and understood that the "surviving remnant," in Katznelson's phrase, was that "historical force" that would have to be followed. Thus, we come full circle, to a situation in which harmony prevailed between the national movement and its organizational bodies. The Zionists had established control over aliyah bet through the Mossad and turned it into a prime instrument of the national struggle.

From September 1939 to May 1945, 50,000 Jews arrived in Palestine, of whom 16,500 were illegal immigrants. Another 1,200 embarked on this journey but never completed it alive. This included those who died on the *Salvador,* the *Struma,* the *Mefkura,* and the small boats.

The number of illegal immigrants in this period is equivalent to the entire figure of illegal immigrants for the twenty years preceding the war. Of the 16,500, there were 5,119 whose preparations for embarkation had been made during the summer of 1939 (particularly those aboard the *Naomi Julia, Rudnitchar II* and *III, Hilda,* and *Sakariya*) and who reached Palestine by February 1940.

During these months, it became clear that aliyah bet had only a limited potential for effecting large-scale rescue and immigration. This weakness did not necessarily negate the historical importance of the movement, which was seen as setting the pace and taking the lead not only in the Yishuv but also in all Jewish communities. Even those who had strongly opposed illegal activities, such as the JDC, came to render vital assistance during the war and funded a large part of its operational costs. Other communities and groups earmarked their contributions for use in aliyah work in all its forms.

At the Twenty-first Zionist Congress, Berl Katznelson declared:

> Illegal aliyah has a special role to play in our struggle. Each idea seeks a sociological base to carry forward its essential message. There was a time when the petty shop keepers were the main support of the love of Zion and who kept the flame burning until the advent of Herzl. After that came the time of the doctors, the lawyers, the students. Many look back on that time as a golden age. After them came a new torchbearer—those "boys" without university degrees and without respectability [who worked] in the orchards of Petah Tikva and the fields of the Galilee. And when I ask myself, "Who in our day are the natural bearers—singled out by their fate—of the Jewish people's struggle for survival? Where are they?" I answer myself: They are afloat on the vast seas, holding aloft the flag of the Jewish plight. They will not tolerate the closing of the Land of Israel to them, they will not allow the world's conscience to relax, they will not permit the implementation of the White Paper. The Jewish refugee is leading this battle and we all are the troops who must fall in line behind him.

Appendixes

APPENDIX A   Total Aliyah from 1939 to 1944

Year	Immigrants	Clandestine Immigrants	Total
Jan–Aug 1939	12,313	6,286	19,139
Sept–Dec 1939	4,092	4,330	8,422
1940	4,547	3,851	8,398
1941	3,647	2,239	5,886
1942	2,194	1,539	3,733
1943	8,507	—*	8,507
1944	14,464	—*	14,464
Total	49,764	18,879	68,549

*There are no clandestine immigrants listed for the years 1943 and 1944 because those immigrants who came to Istanbul without immigration permits received them there and arrived legally in Palestine.

Source: From reports on activities of the Zionist organization for the years 1940–1946 presented at the 24th Zionist Congress, Basel, Kislev, 1947.

APPENDIX B Distribution of Immigration Permits during the War

April 1939	1,200
May–September 1939	7,850
October 1939–March 1940	—
April–September 1940	9,050
October 1940–March 1941	—
April–September 1941	750
October 1941–March 1942	1,250
April–September 1942	2,500
October 1942–March 1943	3,400
January 1943	5,000
February–March 1943	1,000
April–June 1943	12,500
July–September 1943	1,350
October–December 1943	1,350
January–March 1944	900
April–July 1944	600
October 1944	10,300
May 1945	3,000
Total	62,000

APPENDIX C Immigration According to Types of Permits, 1939–1944

Year	Total	Capitalists	Students	Workers	Dependents
1939	16,405	6,179	3,850	2,960	3,416
1940	4,547	2,100	1,144	868	435
1941	3,647	838	1,516	975	318
1942	2,194	265	75	1,724	130
1943	8,507	394	1,639	6,145	329
1944	14,464	459	1,804	11,594	607

APPENDIX D Total Immigration from Passage through Turkey

During 1940–1941	From Rumania, Yugoslavia, and Lithuania	4,411
1942	From Rumania	1,090
1943–1944	Bulgaria	1,681
	Hungary	319
	Rumania	4,488
	Greece	969
	Poland	282
	Turkey	3,234
Total		16,474

APPENDIX E   Sums Transferred by the Jewish Agency or through It during the
Years 1943 and 1944

	Pounds
To Turkey—"Saadia" (code name for Turkey)	197,585
Expenses paid through "The Rescue Agent" (including JC receipts, olim, etc.)	325,962
Total	523,547

In the years 1943 and 1944, 5,253 immigrants came by sea at the average expense of about 93 Palestine pounds per person.

APPENDIX F   Mossad Expenses for Aliyah on Acquisition of Boats and
Departures during the Years 1943 and 1944

Boat	*Pounds*
Milca A	21,497
Milca B	62,739
Maritsa A	14,346
Maritsa B	12,247
Kazbek	55,755
Bulbul	24,889
Morina	16,021
Mefkura	16,496
Combined expenses for three ships	50,745
Salah-a-Din	50,956
Taurus	39,739
Additional broker's fees in Rumania	34,126
Estimated differences	26,744
Transporting passengers from Greece to Palestine by way of Izmir	19,146
Total	445,446

Source: Haganah Archives 14/2217 accounts on entries and withdrawals for the period November 1941 through September 1945, with examination of the Keselman and Keselman account. The numbers round off to the hundreds of thousands.

APPENDIX G   Expenses for Ships That Did *Not* Leave during the Years 1943 and 1944

Ship	Israeli Pounds
Wetan	1,250
Firin	189
Asia	11,183
Anastasia	1,204
Vici	6,430
Other expenses for these ships	21,207
Total	41,463
Total for acquisition and aliyah	486,909

APPENDIX G   Total Aliyah of Jews from Greece through the Efforts of the Aliyah Organization, 1943–1944

1943	273 men, women and children
1944	530. 312 of these were moved in to Izmir on Kayaks.

List of Boats

Boat	Organizers	Port of Departure	Number of Passengers	Land of Origin	Arrival at Designated Port
Velos A	Hehalutz	Piraeus	350	Poland	July 1934
Union	Revisionists		117	Poland	August 1934
Velos B	Hehalutz	Varna	350	Poland	Nov. 1934 expelled by the British
Wanda	Revisionists		50	Poland	Sunk in port in Danzig, passengers rescued
Af al pi	Galili	Piraeus	15	Poland, Hungary, Bratislava, Vienna	April 1937 in the port of Haifa Electric Co.
Af al pi	Galili	Dorado, Albania	54	Poland, Czechoslovakia, 4 from Vienna	October 1937, Tantura
Poseidon A	Hehalutz	Lorion, next to Athens	68	Poland	January 1938
Af al pi	Galili	Fiuma	96	Poland	March 1938
Artemis A	Hehalutz	Piraeus	128	Poland	April 1938
Poseidon B	Hehalutz	Piraeus	65	Poland	May 1938
Artemis B	Hehalutz	Piraeus	157	Poland	July 1938
Af al pi	Galili	Piraeus	156	Poland, Vienna	August 1938
Af al pi	Galili	Piraeus	38	Poland, Vienna	September 1938
Daraga A	Perl (Revisionists)	Sushak	140	Austria, Czechoslovakia	October 1938
Atrato	Hehalutz	Bari	300	Poland	November 1938
Daraga B	Perl	Constantsa	550	Austria, Poland	December 1938
Eli	Haller	Galatz	550	Austria	December 1938
Geppo A	Perl	Tulcea	734	Austria	December 1938
Dalfa	Stavsky (Revisionists)	Constantsa	250	Poland	December 1938

List of Boats (*continued*)

Boat	Organizers	Port of Departure	Number of Passengers	Land of Origin	Arrival at Designated Port
Katina	Rabinowitz, Glazer (Revisionists)	Baltzec	778	Czechoslovakia	January 1939
Atrato B	Hehalutz	Ancona	300	Poland	January 1939
Geppo B	Perl		750	Rumania, Poland, Agudat, Israel, Vienna	Sunk April 16, 1939, people rescued
Atrato C	Hehalutz	Naples	300	Poland	February 1939
Atrato D	Hehalutz	Sushak	400	Germany, Austria	March 1939
Sando	Private company in Rumania		270	Austria, Poland	March 1939 expelled to Rumania
Astia	Flesch, Haller, Perl		699	Vienna	April 1939
Atrato 5 (combined w/the Colorado)	Hehalutz	Sushak	388	Czechoslovakia	April 1939
Atrato 6 (combined w/the Colorado)	Hehalutz	Brindisi	372	Poland, Lithuania, Latvia, Yugoslavia Germany	April 1939
Aghia Dezioni	Perl (Revisionists)	Fiuma	465	Reich	April 1939
Asimi	Zionist Youth with Mizrachi (Hanoar Hatzioni)		470	Reich, Poland and Rumania	April 1939
Atrato 7	Mossad	Constantsa	390	Poland, Austria	May 1939
Ageus Nicolaus A	Konfino	Burgas	800	Reich	May 1939
Karaiza Maria	Konfino		350	Reich	May 1939
Colorado	Mossad	Constantsa	379	Poland	June 1939

Ship	Organizers	Port	Number	Countries of origin	Date
Demetrius	Jacques Aron		244	Germany, Austria, Slovakia, 120 Betar members from Hungary	Captured 3 June 1939
Liesel	Maccabee	Constantsa	921	Reich	June 1939
Colorado	Mossad	Constantsa	388	Poland	July 1939
Aster	Revisionists	Rani (Rumania)	724	Danzig, Rumania, Hungary, Bulgaria	July 1939
Las Perles	Flesch, Haller	Constantsa	370	Danzig, Reich	July 1939
Niko	Perl, Haller	Constantsa	560	Reich, Poland	July 1939
Rudnitchar	Konfino	Varna	305	Reich, Hungary, Bulgaria	August 1939
Dora	Mossad	Flisingen	480	Germany, Hakhsharot & refugees from Holland	August 1939
Rim	Gornstein, Flesch	Constantsa	600	Reich	August 1939
Ageus Nicolaus B	Perl	Constantsa	795	Reich	August 1939
Parita	Revisionists	Constantsa	850	Reich, Poland	August 1939
Osiris	Jacques Aron, Stavsky	Varna	650	Reich	August 1939
Cartova	Jacques Aron, Stavsky	Varna	650	Reich	August 1939
Tripoli	Jacques Aron, Stavsky	Varna	700	Reich	August 1939
Prosula	Jacques Aron, Stavsky	Varna	654	Reich	August 1939
Tiger Hill	Mossad		1,417	Poland	September 1939
Naomi Julia	Revisionists	Constantsa	1,130	Reich	September 1939
Rudnitchar 2	Konfino	Varna	371	Hungary, Reich, Bulgaria	September 1939
Rudnitchar 3	Konfino	Varna	457	Hungary, Reich, Bulgaria	November 1939

List of Boats (*continued*)

Boat	Organizers	Port of Departure	Number of Passengers	Land of Origin	Arrival at Designated Port
Rudnitchar 4	Konfino	Varna	505	Hungary, Reich, Bulgaria	December 1939
Orion	Unknown		502		January 1940
Hilda	Mossad	Baltzec	728	Reich	January 1940
Sakariya	Revisionists	Constantsa	2,228	Reich, Hungary	February 1940
Libertad	Konfino	Varna	355	Hungary, Reich, Bulgaria	July 1940
Pencho	Revisionists	Bratislava	510	Reich	Sunk October 1940
Salvador	Konfino	Varna	320	Reich, Bulgaria	Sunk in Sea of Marmara, 12/1940, 120 perished
Pacific	Storfer	Tulcea	1,062	Reich	November 1940
Milos	Storfer	Tulcea	709	Reich	November 1940
Atlantic	Storfer	Tulcea	1,780	Reich, Danzig	November 1940
Darien B	Mossad	Constantsa	789	Rumania, Bulgaria	March 1941
Struma	Private	Constantsa	769	Rumania	Sunk near port of Istanbul February 1942
Michai	Private		15	Rumania	May 1942
Mirchea	Private		40	Rumania	May 1942
Euxine	Private		11	Rumania	Left in March 1942, sent to Cyprus
Dordeval	Private		20	Rumania	April 1942, sent to Cyprus
Dora	Private			Rumania	Left August 1942
Vitorul	Private		120	Rumania	Left September 1942
Milca A	Mossad	Constantsa	239	Rumania & Refugees	March 1944

Maritsa A	Mossad	Constantsa	Rumania & Refugees	244	April 1944
Bela-Chita	Mossad	Constantsa	Rumania & Refugees	273	April 1944
Milca B	Mossad	Constantsa	Rumania & Refugees	317	April 1944
Maritsa B	Mossad	Constantsa	Rumania & Refugees	318	May 1944
Kazbek	Mossad	Constantsa	Rumania & Refugees	735	July 1944
Morina	Mossad	Constantsa	Rumania & Refugees	308	August 1944
Bulbul	Mossad	Constantsa	Rumania & Refugees	410	August 1944
Mefkura	Mossad	Constantsa	Rumania & Refugees	379	Sunk August 1944
Salah-a-din	Mossad	Constantsa	Rumania & Refugees	547	November 1944
Taurus	Mossad	Constantsa	Rumania & Refugees	958	December 1944
Total	69 Departures		38,542 arrived		
			1,393 Drowned or did not arrive		

Notes

Chapter 1

1. Bracha Habas, *Portzei ha-shearim* (Hebrew), (*The Gatebreakers*), Tel Aviv, 1960 (henceforth Habas 1960), pp. 27–28.

2. Moshe Sikron, *Ha-aliyah leYisrael* (Hebrew), (*Immigration to Israel*), Jerusalem, 1967 (henceforth Sikron 1967), pp. 14–23.

3. During the Mandate period, certain changes were made in the immigrant categories in accordance with various factors. The breakdown presented here is the one defined in 1933, which was not altered substantially during the period apart from the addition of a category for refugees in May 1939.

4. Berl Katznelson, "Meshut betfutsot ha-golah" (Hebrew), ("A Journey Through the Diaspora"), in *Ketavim* (Collected Works), Tel Aviv, 1948 (henceforth Katznelson 1948), vol. 7, pp. 369–383.

5. M. Tabenkin, *Devarim* (Hebrew), (Speeches), Tel Aviv, 1967, pp. 325–326.

6. For further discussion of this point, see Yitzhak Avneri, *Ha-histadrut ha-zionit vehaaliyah ha-bilti legalit leEretz Yisrael mireshit ha-kibush ha-Briti vead Milhemet ha-Olam ha-Shniyah* (Hebrew), (*The Zionist Organization and Illegal Immigration to Palestine From the British Conquest to the Second World War*), dissertation, Tel Aviv University, 1979 (henceforth Avneri 1979).

7. Levi Arie Sarid, *Hehalutz utenu'at ha-noar be Polin 1917–1939* (Hebrew), (*The Hehalutz and Youth Movements in Poland 1917–1939*), Tel Aviv, 1979 (henceforth Sarid 1979). Israel Otiker, *Tenu'at hehalutz be Polin gidolah vehitpathutah 1932–1935* (Hebrew), (*The Hehalutz Movement in Poland: Its Growth and Development, 1932–1935*), Tel Aviv, 1972.

8. A detailed account of the purchase of the *Velos*, its outfitting, and the various problems that arose in the course of the project may be found in Yehuda Braginsky, *Am hoter el hof* (Hebrew), (*A People Striving for the Shore*), Tel Aviv, 1965 (henceforth Braginsky 1965), pp. 19–35.

9. On Revisionist aliya in this period, see Haim Lazan Litai, *Af al pi: sefer aliyah bet* (Hebrew), (*In Spite of All: The Book of Aliya Bet*), Tel Aviv, 1959 (henceforth Litai 1959), pp. 13–65.

10. Jabotinsky's article on "adventurism" was published on 6 March 1932, in the *Morgen Zhurnal* of Warsaw; the Hebrew version appears in his collected works, *bederekh lemedinaha* (Hebrew), (*On the Way to Statehood*), Tel Aviv, 1959, pp. 21–23.

11. From the available literature on the subject, it is difficult to arrive at an exact estimate of the number and frequency of such landings.

12. On conditions for Jews in Poland at the time, see Melzer, *Ma'avak medini bemalkhodet: yehudei Polin 1935–1939* (Hebrew), (*Political Strife in a Blind Alley, Jews in Poland, 1935–1939*), Tel Aviv, 1982.

13. Sarid 1979, p. 568.

14. Braginsky 1965, p. 55 (his conversation with Shertok).

15. Details of "despite-it-all aliya" are found in Litai 1959, pp. 81, 100; and in the lengthy testimony of Moshe Galili-Krivosheyn, the Oral History Documentation Center of the Institute of Contemporary Jewry, the Hebrew University of Jerusalem (henceforth ODC), file 152/55.

16. See Yehuda Bauer, *My Brother's Keeper: A History of the American Jewish Joint Distribution Committee, 1929–1939*, Philadelphia, 1974 (henceforth Bauer 1974), p. 260.

17. Central Zionist Archives (CZA), Minutes of the Jewish Agency, 29, meeting of December 11, 1938 (henceforth Minutes); cf. Avneri, chapters 7, 8 and 9, for a detailed discussion.

18. CZA 528/2651, Lichtheim to Shertok (12 June 1939).

19. Katznelson 1948, vol. 9, pp. 61–82.

20. *Ibid.*, p. 75.

21. *Ibid.*, p. 73, and cf. pp. 75–76.

Chapter 2

1. The Zionist position in favor of full cooperation with Britain is well documented. In the literature on the subject, the matter is discussed in Yehuda Slutsky, *Sefer toledot ha-haganah* (Hebrew), (*History of the Haganah*), Tel Aviv, 1967:1973, vol. 3, book 1 (henceforth Slutsky 1967); Yehuda Bauer, *From Diplomacy to Resistance,* Philadelphia, 1970 (henceforth Bauer 1963); Yosef Heller, *Bema'avak lemedinah* (Hebrew), (*The Struggle for Statehood*), Jerusalem, 1984 (henceforth Heller 1984), pp. 1–70.

2. Beit Berl Archives (henceforth BBA), 39/23 (Mapai political committee). CZA, Minutes, vol. 31 (Jewish Agency meeting, 9/17/39).

3. CZA, Minutes, 31.

4. Nadav Halevi, "The Economic Development of the Jewish Community in Palestine 1917–1947," research paper, Falk Institute of Economic Research in Israel, Jerusalem, 1970, pp. 31–41.

5. BBA 39/23 (Mapai central committee, 11/2/39).

6. *Ibid.*

7. *Ibid.* It seems that these recriminations against the kibbutz movement were actually not grounded in fact. Selectivity and control over the numbers of immigrants were guiding principles of Zionist settlement policy during the 1920s and 1930s. See, for example, Arthur Ruppin, *Three Decades of Palestine*, Westport, Conn., 1975 (henceforth Ruppin), pp. 66-80.

8. BBA 39/23.

9. *Ibid.*

10. *Ibid.* (Shertok to the Mapai central committee, 9/12/39).

11. *Ibid.*

12. CZA, Minutes, 31 (9/30/39).

13. BBA 39/23 (Mapai Central Committee, 9/12/39). Zalman Shazar, Aharon Zisling, and Eliezer Liebenstein held this view.

14. Toward December, Weizmann and Shertok were under the impression, given

the positions of Ironside, Wingate, and Churchill, that the chances for such cooperation were good, and their reports were therefore optimistic. For a detailed discussion of this episode, see Yoav Gelber, *Toledot ha-hitnadvut* (Hebrew), (*The History of Volunteering to the British Army during the Second World War*), Jerusalem, 1979, vol. I (henceforth Gelber I), pp. 149–161. The shifts from optimism to pessimism are crucial for our understanding of the considerations of the Zionist politicians.

15. Evidence for the meeting is found in Sharett (Shertok), *Yoman medini* (Hebrew), (*A Political diary*), Tel Aviv, 1979 (henceforth Sharett 1979), vol. 5, p. 15; Haganah Archive (HA) 14/153 (Yehieli's report, pp. 22, 36); Hakibbutz Hameuhad Archive (henceforth HMA) 4123 II (Israel Idelson's diary, entry for 2/14/40). The exact position of each participant and the relative weights of economic and political considerations cannot be established.

16. HA 14/153 (Yehieli's report, pp. 21–22); cf. Sharet 1979, vol. 5, pp. 15–20.

17. HA 14/153.

18. BBA 39/23 (Mapai central committee meeting, 12/9/39).

19. CZA, Minutes, 31II.

20. Sharett 1979, vol. 5, p. 487; Michael Bar-Zohar, *Ben-Gurion*, Englewood Cliffs, N.J., 1967 (henceforth Bar-Zohar), vol. I, pp. 422-425.

21. Indeed the same argument was used by the British whenever they pressured the Jewish Agency to put a stop to illegal aliya activities. BBA 39/23 (meeting of the political committee, 11/8/40, Shertok's statement).

22. Sharett 1979, vol. 4, pp. 336, 487.

23. On Lichtheim's attitude to aliya bet (he maintained contact with the European Jewish communities by virtue of his position in Geneva), see two of his letters in HA 14/4195I (Shlomo Shamir papers), dated 12/21/39 and 1/24/40.

24. BBA 39/23 (Mapai political committee, 1/9/40, Shertok's statement).

25. HA 14/4195I (Yehieli to Sakharov, 3/25/40 and 4/25/40).

26. Dr. Nahum Goldmann, as representative of the World Jewish Congress, was tied to the policy of the leadership, and was indeed influenced by it; but he also demonstrated a keen sensitivity to the plight of the refugees, and was able to act with a degree of independence. Thus, he was in a position to render assistance and to provide funds for aliya bet operations.

27. Storfer's work, character, and role in organizing emigration are discussed in Chapter 6.

28. CZA, Minutes, 33II (meeting of 11/27/40). The reasons given were unemployment and requests for government economic assistance, as well as the wish to reserve a number of immigrant permits for after the war.

29. CZA, Minutes, 33II. Ben Gurion was out of the country at that time and did not participate in the debates and decisions.

30. *Ibid.*, S25/10582.

31. CZA, Minutes, 33II (11/8/40).

32. BBA 39/23 (11/7/40).

33. *Ibid.*

34. BBA 39/23 (11/21/40).

35. CZA S25/1059: Shertok to Berl Locker, report on these discussions. Cf. BBA 39/23 (his report on the discussions to the political committee of Mapai, 11/21/40).

36. CZA S25/1059, telegrams to London dated November 10, 11, 12, 17, 18, and 19.

37. CZA S25/1716 (12/17/40).

38. *Ibid.*, 11/19/40 and 11/20/40, bearing the signature "Eliyahu." An indication

of the mood at the Zionist offices in London is given by "Baffy" Dugdale in N. A. Rose (ed.), *Baffy, The Diaries of Blanche Dugdale 1936–1947*, London, 1973, p. 178; entry for 11/15/40:

> Awful caboodle at Zionist office about those refugee ships. Lord Lloyd revealed to Chaim [Weizmann] that the ones that have arrived in Haifa are only the forerunners of others now at sea. He thinks that the Gestapo are organizing a vast casting out of Jews from Romanian ports. This of course altered the situation. Chaim is prepared to acquiesce to Mauritius under condition, but will try to get the people on the Haifa ships landed, though he does not think he will succeed. Lewis and I agreed, but this led to painful scene between Chaim and Berl [Locker]. We have cabled to Moshe [Shertok] asking him to keep the Yishuv quiet and to send his suggestions.

39. Munya Mardor, Haganah, New York, 1966, pp. 46–76.

40. Yosef Heller in Heller 1984, p. 38, note 53, attributes the decision to the defense committee of the Yishuv, led by Shertok. This is based on Shertok's letter to M. Mardor, cited Slutsky 1967, p. 1633, after the publication of Mardor's *Shelihut Alumah* (Hebrew), (*Secret Mission*) in 1957.

41. CZA S25/1716 (12/17/40).

42. CZA S25/10582 (25/11/40).

43. *Ibid.*, S25/2648 (12/4/40); cf. the memorandum submitted to the Foreign Office by Weizmann, dated 11/27/40 (published in Leni Yahil, "Selected British Documents on the Illegal Immigration to Palestine 1939–1940," *Yad Vashem Studies* Vol. 10, 1974, pp. 241–276):

> A sharp line must be drawn between Jewish refugees within sight of Palestine and those in boats intercepted and diverted on the high sea. This may not seem logical, but it is human. To turn back such sufferers after they have sighted their Promised Land, and after their nearest relatives have seen the ship which carries them come in, is past human endurance. . . . Should the feeling of His Majesty's Government prove correct, and should the movement develop on a large scale, *the Agency would cooperate with His Majesty's Government in the care* of these immigrants diverted to some British colony [emphasis added].

To the end of the memorandum is appended the following note:

> After relations of confidence and cooperation have been reestablished between the local authorities and the Agency, the future treatment of illegal immigrant ships must be settled by agreement.

44. CZA 25/1716 (Shertok to Weizmann, 12/17/40).

45. CZA S25/2631 (report of constable Haim Caspi, 12/13/40, and that of watchman Poliakov, 12/14/40).

46. *Ibid.* (statement of Berl Katznelson to the Histadrut council, 12/9/40). Katznelson used this forum to voice his opinion because he was in a minority in the Mapai central committee.

47. BBA 39/23.

48. *Ibid.*

49. *Ibid.* The *Asimi* arrived in April 1939 and the *Hilda* in January 1940. The British attempted to prevent them from approaching the Palestine coast, but this produced public demonstrations, rallies, and strikes. These cases, however, were different from the case of the *Atlantic*, since they did not represent any change in principle in British policy on refugees' status in Palestine, as the latter episode did.

50. Despite their impassioned statements of conviction, the militants also recognized the necessity of fighting alongside the British against Hitler. Indeed, at this very

moment, while they were demanding support for aliya bet in Palestine, the militant leaders, lead by Golomb, were instructing the Mossad representatives in Istanbul to forgo the chance of bringing another immigrant ship to Palestine. The ship, the *Darien,* was instead to be offered to the British for intelligence operations, in the hope of winning a greater role in the war effort for the Yishuv. (See Chapter 3.)

51. CZA Minutes, 33II (3/16/41); BBA 41/23, (Mapai central committee, 1/9/41; Mapai secretariat meeting, 3/19/41).

52. BBA 23/41 (Mapai central committee meeting, 1/9/41). It ought to be pointed out that British records bear out the extreme nature of MacMichael's position favoring the White Paper and his firm stand against illegal immigration. Yet, though Mac-Michael consistently chose to apply the strictest possible interpretation of the White Paper, during most of this period, there were no serious differences between MacMichael and the Colonial Office or the government.

53. BBA, 23/41 (3/19/41).

54. *Ibid.* (statement by Sprinzak).

55. See Ben-Gurion's approach ("Paths to a Zionist Policy") in CZA Minutes, 33II (3/22/41).

56. BBA, 23/41 (6/25/41).

57. *Ibid.*

58. CZA, Minutes, 34 (1/18/42).

Chapter 3

1. See Braginsky 1965, p. 246; Agami's statement, HA 3033. For the meeting of 25 August in Geneva, see Labour Archive (henceforth LA), 39m. See also the comments of Eri Jabotinsky about the break in activities in CZA F17/4 (letter to Yaacobi, 4/10/39).

2. ODC, Ginsburg statment.

3. HA 14/4195I (Shamir papers; series of letters from Moshe Agami (Averbuech) dating from October and November 1939, especially his letter of 11/21/39).

4. According to its passengers, the *Hilda*'s engines were damaged through the intentional negligence of the crew (December 1939). The *Darien* ran aground near Constantsa as the result of a deliberate act of the captain, again according to passengers. Similar charges were made regarding other ships as well.

5. See below, on the *Dora* affair. In September 1939, the British intercepted the *Tiger Hill,* the *Parita,* and the *Naomi Julia,* impounded the ships, and arrested their crews. See Chapter 7 on Britain's policy.

6. HA 14/4195 (1/6/40).

7. A Greek shipowner and shipping agent, Pandelis (referred to as "the fat man" in letters and communications), had worked with the Mossad since the time of the *Tiger Hill* and also worked with the Revisionists. Pandelis seemed to use his considerable business sense in overcoming the conflicting interests of both groups of aliyah activists as well as of the various governments involved. Pandelis worked with the Mossad throughout the war years and became indispensable to illegal aliyah activity in this period. Opinions of him varied, but on the whole he was considered to be a man strangely able to combine adventurism and greed with a desire to help the aliyah effort.

8. The list derives from Yehieli's report, HA 14/153; from Agami's account of that period (HA 14/4195); and from papers of the Vienna Archive, including letters from Storfer. Storfer indicates the existence of a 700-person group from Germany,

Austria, Danzig, and Czechoslovakia. I have not found any further documentation regarding such a group. It is possible, of course, that the group broke up, with some of the people later arriving in Yugoslavia and elsewhere in the Balkans. Perhaps, too, there was no separate group, but that there is a confusion in the sources, and that the *Hilda* group is meant. It is worth noting that, of the groups mentioned above, the Mossad managed to accomplish the transport only of the *Hilda* group. Many among the other groups left on Storfer's boats, and others stayed behind.

9. HA 14/153 (Yehieli's report); HA 14/4591I (letter from "Moshe," 1/6/40). Two shipping agents the Mossad worked with were "Tenor" (Victor Meyer, a Jew of German origin) and "Tsaba." Victor Meyer was a prosperous businessman who had lived in Greece for many years. He served as the Greek representative of the Palestine agricultural marketing cooperative, Tnuva, was strongly sympathetic to the Zionist cause, and was ready to lend a hand in order to help Jews. The Haganah had contacted him as early as the *Velos* episode, and he also aided Moshe Galili. "Tsaba" was the collective code name for a Greek family by the name of Vernikos who helped the Mossad arrange for the *Atrato* and the *Colorado* in 1939. This family ran a small "boating company" that, among other things, had dealt in smuggling arms to Spain during the civil war.

10. *Dora* was the vessel that transported members of the German branches of Hehalutz who had been on training farms in Holland, as well as a group from France in August 1939. It had been acquired after much effort, with the help of the Vernikos family.

11. HA 14/153 (Yehieli's report); Jabotinsky Archive (henceforth JA) Kenner collection. Ruth Klueger Aliav and Peggy Mann, *The Last Escape*, New York, 1973 (henceforth Aliav 1973), pp. 220–221.

12. The passengers that eventually boarded the *Sakariya* in January 1940.

13. HA 14/4195 ("Moshe to Eliyahu," 12/14/39).

14. *Ibid.* (1/6/40). In cables and other communications among the Mossad, activists and their contacts were given code names, and various terms were used to conceal the nature of their work: for Yosef Barpal, "Kadmon"; Ze'ev Shind, "Dani"; Yehuda Braginsky, "Yolek"; Shaul Meirov-Avigur, "Ben-Yehuda"; Victor Meyer, "Tenor."

15. On the contact with von Hoepfner, see Ruth Zariz, *Hatzalat Yehudim meGermaniyah beemtzaut ha-girah november 1938–1945* (Hebrew), (*The Rescue of German Jews Through Emigration, November 1938–1945*), Ph.D. dissertation, Hebrew University Jerusalem, 1986 (henceforth Zariz 1987), pp. 256–257.

16. HA 14/153 (Yehieli's report, p. 23).

17. The plan to expel Jews to Lublin was part of a broad plan to concentrate and isolate the Jewish population in a reservation in the Nisko-Lublin area of Poland. The Nazi logic of the plan was that, if isolated, the Jews, as parasites, would lack a healthy body on which to thrive, resulting in their eventual "natural" liquidation. Two groups of deportees were sent from Vienna in 1939, one on 20 October (912 people) and a second on 26 October (672 people). A transport of deportees left Czechoslovakia on October 18 (1,000 people). In Lublin, they found a complete absence of basic living facilities. Leaders of the Prague and Vienna communities who visited Lublin were utterly shocked, and on returning did their utmost to prevent further deportations. The deportations ceased at the end of October, the result of organizational problems on the German side rather than intervention by the Jewish communities.

18. HA 14/153 (letter from Epstein to Zilberschien, 12/9/39), and Zariz 1987, pp. 251–252.

19. The Kladovo group's story is revealed through several main sources:

a) letters sent by members of the group, now in the Central Archives for the History of the Jewish People (henceforth CAHJP), the Vienna Archive (henceforth AW), and the Storfer material (AW/2515); CZA, Geneva files L22; YVA; and JDC Archives;

b) reports sent by the heads of the Jewish community in Yugoslavia, especially to the JDC and to the Jewish Agency, now found in the JDC Archives L6–43 and the CZA, L22 and L15;

c) Storfer's correspondence with the JDC, in AW at CAHJP;

d) Ehud Avriel, *Open the Gates, New York, 1975;* oral testimony in ODC; an interview conducted with him by the author in fall 1979; a letter Ueberall (Avriel) wrote to Storfer regarding financial difficulties arising from the expenses of the group (dated 28 December 1939), now in AW at CAHJP;

e) Agami's account in HA 14/3033;

f) Yehieli report, HA 14/153.

The primary sources do not constitute a narrative account. Only Ehud Avriel, in his book and his oral testimony, attempts to reconstruct the events, but he deals only with the first phase of the episode—from the group's departure from Vienna until its arrival in Kladovo. In describing the fate of the group here, sources are not cited for every detail, except in those cases where the sources conflict. The author assumes all responsibility for the reconstructed account, as well as for any errors that may have emerged regarding some of the details.

20. The *Holm,* a Dutch vessel, was offered to Yehieli by the Vernikos family after it proved difficult to obtain the return of the *Dora.*

21. For a detailed description of the preparations for departure, the fiscal problems, etc., see Hanah Weiner, "Latzet Behol Mehir" (Hebrew), ("To Leave at Any Cost"), in Hanah Weiner and Dalia Ofer, *Parashat Kladovo Sabac* (Hebrew), (*The Kladovo Sabac Story*), Tel Aviv, in progress (henceforth Weiner Latzet).

22. The similarity between Ueberall's and Paltin's difficulties during this period is striking. (See Chapter 4.)

23. HA 3033 (Agami's report); interview with Agami in the summer of 1977; cf. HA 14/153 (Yehieli's report). On the price paid by Spitzer and Ueberall, see CAHJP, AW 2515 (Spitzer to Mentzer in Vienna, 1/23/40; letter to Hehalutz in Prague, 3/18/40, unsigned). The letter to Hehalutz contains a report on the fare collected by the Danube companies.

24. An example of such improvisation was the attempt to acquire a Rumanian river barge that would accommodate the refugees until a ship became available. Negotiations were conducted even before the ship completed its run to Marseilles, a trip that was meant to end in January, whereupon it would return to the Black Sea and tow the barge. While steps were being taken to implement the plan, there was a legal dispute over ownership of the barge between a Greek company and a Rumanian one. Thus, this plan, too, failed.

25. The figure of 10,000 refugees and information on the activity of the Yugoslavian communities on the Kladovo group's behalf are contained in two reports sent to the JDC: JDC Archive 7–15, April 1941. See especially Alexander Klein's report, *Zehn Jahre juedischen Fluechtlingshilfswerks in Jugoslawien, die Donautransporte* (henceforth Klein report), of which section F deals with the Kladovo group, and CAHJP Protocols of the Executive of the Union of the Jewish Communities in Yugoslavia, years 1939, 1940, and 1941 (henceforth Yugoslavia Protocols). On the life of the people during the long stay in Yugoslavia, see Dalia Ofer, *"Mimas'a Aliyah El Hamavet"* ("From Immigration Journey Unto Death") (henceforth Ofer Aliyah) in

Hanah Weiner and Dalia Ofer, *Parashat Kladovo Sabac* (Hebrew), (*The Kladovo Sabac Story*), Tel Aviv, in progress (henceforth Ofer Weiner).

26 HA 14/153 (Yehieli's report, pp. 19, 20, 24). Dr. Baruch Konfino, an eye doctor who was active in Zionist affairs in Bulgaria, organized refugee aliya from Bulgaria on a private basis. See Chapter 5.

27. The most comprehensive source regarding the *Wetan* is Yehieli's report (HA 14/153). It was written about six months after the events and is generally an accurate account. A group of letters written by Agami (HA, Shlomo Shamir file 4195I) to the U.S. Labor Zionist organization that were asked for assistance. The letters date from October to April and present additional though sporadic data on the *Wetan* negotiations. On the matter, also see the references in Storfer's material (CAHJP, AW 2515), especially his self-vindication and his attacks on the Mossad. These occur particularly in his correspondence with the JDC. Comparison of the various sources indicates their relative trustworthiness and provides a fuller understanding of the episode. See also Aliav 1973, pp 350–367. This, however, is a later and somewhat altered account. The account here is based on the three primary sources.

28. CAHJP, AW 2515. Storfer, in a letter of 31 March 1940, reports that Turkish government had stepped in at the last minute to block the sale because of the seizure of the *Sakariya* in Palestine. See PRO CO733/429 (4/4/40). The British consul in Istanbul, Mr. Morgan, quotes in his report the Turkish government regulations issued in March regarding control of Turkish vessels during the war emergency. For further deliberation, see Chapter 7, on British policy.

29. See Chapter 6, on Storfer, for his relations with the Mossad. Storfer himself vehemently denied that his activities had anything to do with the cancellation of the *Wetan* deal. He viewed the charge as gross slander levied by a vindictive Mossad that intended to convince the Joint to cease its support of his aliya activities. Yet the delays in the transfer of funds certainly played a role in the failure of the deal.

30. HA 14/153 (Yehieli's report).

31. HA 14/4195.

32. HA 14/4195. The failure was quite unexpected. We learn this from a note in Storfer's report of 7 April 1940 (CAHJP, AW 2514), according to which the Kladovo people were about to leave for the Black Sea. From this it is clear how certain the Mossad emissaries had been that the *Wetan* deal was about to be concluded, to the point that they had set a date for the group to leave for the Black Sea to meet the ship. This tends to support Yehieli's statement that the cancellation took them completely by surprise. On Storfer's contention that his delay in forwarding payment had nothing to do with the cancellation, see AW 2514, Mitteilung 56, 4/27/40. Also, see Chapter 7.

33. HA 14/3033 and CAHJP AW 2515, Mitteilung 50, 4/15/40, and letters from people in Kladovo quoted by Storfer, 19 and 29 May 1940.

34. HA 4195I, Shlomo Shamir file (Yehieli and Lichtheim to New York, 6/9/40; cables from "Moshe" [Agami] to Meriminsky, 5/22/40 and 5/30/40).

35. Transfer of funds from the JDC to the Mossad was required at the same time that Storfer demanded the transfer of large sums for purchase of his three ships, the *Atlantic, Pacific,* and *Milos*. The JDC hoped that transport for the Kladovo group might be provided with Storfer's help, and pressed him on this. Storfer himself may have been willing to do this, but he was unable to counter the opposition of the Center for Jewish Emigration (controlled by the S.S.), which was interested only in the transport of Jews from the Reich, not from surrounding countries. This was a further

factor in the JDC's reluctance to transfer funds. (For more information, see Chapter 7.)

36. HA 14/153; *ibid.*, Shlomo Shamir 4195I.

37. It is extremely difficult to reconstruct the exact chronology here. The sources are mainly cables, some of which bear no dates and some that are practically illegible. The following reconstruction is a result of cross-checking the various cables to Palestine and to the United States with Yehieli's report (HA 14/153), although the report (written about two months later) may be off by a day or two in places.

38. We have no eyewitness account or minutes of the meeting, but Agami and Yehieli both mention it in their reports.

39. HA 14/4195I (Katznelson to I. Sakharov in New York, 6/14/40).

40. HA 14/153 (Yehieli's report); JDC Archives, Spitzer report.

41. HA 14/209 (cable from "Eliyahu" to Tsameret, 7/17/40).

42. HA 14/3033 (Agami's testimony); interview with Ruth Klueger Aliav at her home, spring 1976.

43. David Hacohen, *'Et Lesaper* (Hebrew), (*Time to Tell*), Tel Aviv, 1974 (henceforth Hacohen 1974). HA 14/2506 (Arazi testimonies, 1949, 1955).

44. HA 14/3031 (Ze'ev Shind's statement, undated and unsigned). The statement appears not to have been edited and is unorganized. He is also mixing dates of plans. The plan he is referring to was apparently December 1940 or January 1941 in its later stages, and was decisive in the debate over the ship at that point. See below.

45. For further information on sabotage plans and other military intelligence plans, see Yoav Gelber, 1983, pp. 133–142.

46. HA 14/209 (cables from Arazi to Tsameret).

47. HA 14/2506 (Arazi's testimonies, 1949, 1955). The agreement to transfer the ship over to Arazi stipulated that it would be contingent upon Arazi's satisfaction that the vessel in fact suited his requirements. In other words, there was an option built into the agreement, which Arazi could choose to exercise or not, and which seemed to imply the need for certain physical specifications. During the period in which Arazi's decision was pending, the ship could not be used for immigration work. Arazi would bear the cost of the *Darien*'s travel from Piraeus to Palestine. In the end, Arazi did confirm his acceptance of the ship and paid £15,000 to the Mossad.

48. Hacohen 1974, and HA 14/3031 (Shind testimony).

49. HA 14/209 (Dani (Shind) to Shmarya, 4/12/40). *Ibid.* (Shmarya offers a ship, 6/17/40). Again, Shmarya offers Arazi a ship named *Ageus Nicolaus*, and *ibid.* (6/16/40, 7/21/40, 9/29/40, the Palestine company Nahshon responds to Shmarya's offers). Use of the Nahshon name in the communications indicates a search for vessels for the war effort rather than for aliyah.

50. HA 14/3033 (Agami's testimony, p. 10). In an interview in the summer of 1977, he did not recall there being any other Mossad activists besides himself at the meeting. At the time, Braginsky and Shind were in the country, but, according to Agami, they were not present.

51. ODC, Yehieli's testimony; HA 3031 (Shind's testimony).

52. HA 14/209.

53. *Ibid.* (7/23/40).

54. CZA L15/324 (Barlas to Spitzer).

55. CZA S25/10582 (Eliyahu to Avi Amos (Ben Gurion) 7/9/40).

56. HA 14/4195I (Dr. Moshe Schweig to Aryeh Tartakower, 1/8/40, 1/26/40). Cf. JDC Archive, Yugoslavia 51, report on refugee activities, undated; Klein report; CZA L22–14 (Spitzer to Geneva, 12/31/39).

57. JDC Archive, Sima Spitzer's report.

58. On the JDC activities, its approach and the development of its position, see Bauer 1974, and Yehuda Bauer, *American Jewry and the Holocaust*, Detroit, 1981 (henceforth Bauer 1981).

59. JDC Archive, 14–19 Yugoslavia, 1/14/40 to 2/22/40.

60. HA 14/153 (Yehieli's report, especially pp. 50–53 and the description of the meeting of 5/20/40).

61. HA 14/209 (Shind to Tsameret, 7/23/40); HA 14/4195I (Tsameret to Arazi, 8/3/40).

62. *Ibid.*, and also 8/8/40.

63. *Ibid.* "Clarify the nature of the link with 'Atid'. I still have the boat. Cable clear instructions." It should be noted that the *Darien* was purchased in Tsameret's name. After its transfer to Arazi, the official ownership documents remained unchanged. This was because of considerations of administrative convenience, even though later interpretations by Mossad activists cited the fact as demonstrating the true intentions for the vessel.

64. The sources do not indicate a specific date for the ship's departure, but by comparing the letters we may say quite definitely that the *Darien* left between 24 and 28 August. It should be noted that David Hacohen contends that the *Darien* was never in Alexandria at all.

65. Braginsky 1974, p. 260. Cf. his letter to Sakharov, 10/16/40, HA 4195I, Shlomo Shamir file.

66. See HA 4195I, Shlomo Shamir file (Braginsky to Sakharov, 10/16/40). In this letter, Braginsky refers to a decision to renew aliya work: "Many reasons have driven us to renew the activity and they are certainly clear to you, but one of the reasons is the prestige of Zionism in America. . . . " This provides clear proof of a process of questioning, discussion and decision related to these matters. If we attempt to narrow down the time of the decision, we can say that it is tied to the announcement of Braginsky's departure to aid Tsameret—i.e., mid-August, as per Shind's letter.

67. It should be noted that David Hacohen, in both his written and oral testimony, contests the ship's presence in Alexandria. He contends that the ship never left Piraeus before it arrived in Istanbul in September 1940. But the documentation we have shows definitely that Hacohen is the victim of faulty memory here. The ship was indeed in Alexandria. This is proved by Shind's cables to Tsameret from Alexandria on 13 and 25 September 1940: HA 14/209, and *ibid.*, Braginsky's letter to Mr. Cohen regarding transfer of the ship to Istanbul from Alexandria, 16 October 1940; see also *ibid.*, 14/4109I (Braginsky to Sakharov). Arazi, too, in his testimony relates that the ship reached Alexandria: HA (Arazi's reports, pp. 49, 55). (Note that there are contradictions in his reports; they should be used with care.)

68. HA 14/4159I (Shlomo Shamir file), (Dalin (Golomb) to Sakharov, 9/23/40, two cables).

69. *Ibid.* (Sakharov to Golomb, 9/25/40).

70. *Ibid.* (Dalin (Golomb) to Ruth Klueger, 9/25/40).

71. *Ibid.* (Braginsky to Sakharov, 10/16/40).

72. CZA L15/122 (Spitzer to Ruth Klueger, 12/7/40, 12/12/40); HA 4195I, Shlomo Shamir (Schwartz to the JDC executive in New York, 10/18/40).

73. This trip is not mentioned by the Mossad workers either in their testimony or in their subsequent books. In interviews conducted with them, they again could not recall it. But it undoubtedly did take place and provided an occasion for Spitzer to criticize the Mossad emissaries for contributing to the delay of the *Darien* voyage.

The trip is mentioned in a summary of aliyah efforts from Rumania from December 1940 to 1944: CZA S25/2493; cf. Spitzer's letter to Ruth Klueger, *ibid.*, 22/14 (12/7/ 40); and *ibid.*, 22/188 (Barlas to the Jewish Agency aliya section, 10/31/40). In this letter, Barlas explains that he was forced to lease the *Darien* because he had obtained Turkish transit visas for 380 refugees, but the rail link from Rumania to Turkey had been interrupted because of the war between Greece and Italy. Similarly, there is a detailed report of the trip by the German consul in Istanbul, who followed the movement of refugee traffic closely (YVA 3141, 11/7/40). This report clearly shows that the trip did take place, but that this trip was one in a series. We are dealing with several trips of this kind that the boat was involved in: legal voyages with legal immigrants on board, bound for Palestine. Reference to Poles among the immigrants is interesting. Apparently, what this refers to is the British plan to provide safe haven in Palestine for Polish war refugees. It is very likely that this trip (or trips) was undertaken only to help pay the expenses incurred in the course of the special situation. But it is also likely that this plan reflects the implementation of those involved in war cooperation projects in order to camouflage the illegal voyage that was planned. The German document demonstrates that they in fact succeeded in this. If this conclusion is correct, then we can point to a far-reaching degree of cooperation between the Mossad and the war-effort team at that point in the events. If the *Darien* indeed made several trips before 4 November 1940, it must have arrived in Constantsa quite some time earlier, perhaps as early as mid-October or at the end of the month. It may also be that the ship was used for trips to Istanbul after 7 November, but that we have no documentation of them.

74. CZA L22/14, Ruth Klueger to Spitzer, 2/13/41.

75. The account here is based on a letter written from the Sabac camp to Vienna on 29 November 1940: CAHJP AW2515. This is one of four letters from the camp, the first one dating from 1 October and two others from December. YVA 0/1 309, letters of Walter Klein, and some other 500 private letters collected by the author.

76. CZA L22/14 (Spitzer to Klueger, 12/7/40).

77. Deutsches Nachrichtsburo (henceforth DNB) in YVA, JM3141 83–24. A report in Bucharest's German press of 9 December 1940 regarding the *Darien* stated there were 300 immigrants from Yugoslavia and 187 from Rumania. This report differs from other data we have, both regarding the number of passengers and their composition, and ought to be questioned. It is interesting, though, that the figure of 500 appears also in a letter from Kladovo dated 29 November 1940. The time of departure appears close to the time indicated by a juxtaposition of other sources available.

78. CZA L22/14 (Spitzer report to Nahum Goldmann); also a summary and translation in English of that report, in the JDC Archive 15–32, 9/1/41.

79. CZA L22/14 (Spitzer to Ruth Klueger, 12/23/40); CAHJP AW 2515, 12/3/40, Z. Herman from Sabac: "My dears, we were already set to leave with all our luggage and things and again we have not left. What can happen now? No one knows. Tomorrow Spitzer is to explain to us what happened. Why didn't the voyage succeed this time? This was my last hope. . . . " It should be remembered that a similar incident occurred in the previous month: see *ibid.*, letter to Mr. Yunes, Danzig, 12/8/40, on behalf of the Danzig group.

80. Hanah Weiner, "The Fate of the Kladovo Group Under the Nazis," in Hanah Weiner and Dalia Ofer, see note 21.

81. See note 73. If my conclusion about the use of the *Darien* for legal immigration is correct, then David Hacohen's and Yehuda Arazi's contention appears to have greater force—namely, that the ship was not transferred to the Mossad, only that it

was enabled to use it. This aspect of the episode suffers, I should stress once again, from insufficient and incomplete source material. There are too many contradictory accounts by various people, and internal contradictions within some of the accounts. As a result, there has been no choice here but to decide between sources based on their apparent accuracy, even though there is no absolute guarantee of this.

82. HA 14/3031 (Shind's testimony); *ibid.* (Arazi testimony, 1949); Hacohen 1974, p. 162. Note that each testimony carries another version of the actual plans for the *Darien*. I tend to accept Shind's account. See also PRO WO193.956 K/L 03107, 9/27/ 40, and CZA S25/3124 (Hacohen to Zaslany (the operational head of all cooperation plans) undated, probably March 1941).

83. Weizmann to Shertok, 1/3/41, in *The Letters and Papers of Chaim Weizmann*, Series A, vol. 20, Jerusalem, 1979, M.J. Cohen (ed.) (henceforth Weizmann Letters 1979), pp. 86–91.

84. HA 14/209.

85. *Ibid.*

86. See Shind's testimony, HA 14/3031, also with regard to the German invasion that was expected in those countries.

87. HA 14/209.

88. Braginsky 1965, p. 282.

89. HA 14/209. The cable is incomplete and it is unclear exactly where it was sent. It was most likely sent to Palestine, though it may have been to New York.

90. HA 14/714 (Shind's report).

91. CZA S25/3124, to Reuven, signed D., undated. The letter expresses keen disappointment over the failures of the *Darien* episode, but finally accepts the reality of the situation. It proved impossible to remove the refugees from the boat. The British intelligence liaison (Major Taylor) was not in Istanbul to help Hacohen. Hacohen was sincerely concerned by the *Darien* affair and believed that it might prevent future cooperation with the British in the war effort. His personal disappointment found expression in the following sentence: "If my hands were not tied and I could speak of the ship as my own project, I might have succeeded in arousing more than a little interest in behalf of Britain's war for human freedom and liberation, but fate decided that I should come here for something quite different. . . . "

92. HA 14/4195 (7/31/40).

Chapter 4

1. "Hasport haleumi" (Hebrew), [Yiddish title "Der natsyonaler sport"] *Der Moment*, April 1939; Hebrew version published in *Hamashkif*, May 5, 1939. Cf. Schechtman, *Zeev Jabotinsky*, Tel Aviv, 1959 (henceforth Schechtman 1959), vol. 3, pp. 197–208; Litai 1959, pp. 21–25, 260–265.

2. See also Eri Jabotinsky, *The Sakariya Expedition: A Story of Extra-Legal Immigration into Palestine*, Johannesburg, 1945 (henceforth Jabotinsky 1945), pp. vii–viii. Cf. Jabotinsky's account of his discussion with the British consul in Bucharest, *ibid.,* p. 27, where he expressed this point of view; and the consul's report on the discussion, PRO CO 733/429.

3. ODC 52 (1), Eri Jabotinsky.

4. See Litai 1959, pp. 154–162.

5. ODC (3, 4, 5) 58, Benari, Glazer, Mordecai Katz. A British firm, Castle, and a French company, Vardouas, apparently offered a number of vessels that were suitable (some after refitting) for aliya purposes.

6. Wilhelm Perl, *The Four-Front War, From the Holocaust to the Promised Land*, New York, 1979 (henceforth Perl 1979). The book describes Perl's operations and analyzes in fine detail the events in which he was involved. It presents an interesting account of his activity in Vienna before the war and during its first few months.

7. See also Eri Jabotinsky's views on Galili and Perl, ODC 52 (12).

8. CZA S6/4289 (a letter to the Zionist executive written on board the *Ageus Nicolaus*, dated 6/9/39); also CZA Z4/10 1096 (a letter from the Jewish community of Salonika regarding the refugees of the *Ageus Nicolaus* and the *Esther*, 5/12/39).

9. This sort of tension between those in the field and a central office was also present in the case of the Mossad, though in that case the friction was not so great as to threaten the network with collapse. One reason for this lay in the socioeconomic background of the Hehalutz aliyah workers. They were not independent figures with established positions in local society. They proved more willing to accept movement discipline imposed by the Mossad. Mossad selection of immigrants according to strict criteria resulted in a higher percentage of immigrants without the means to pay their own way than was the case in the Revisionist aliyah.

10. CZA F17/2.

11. CZA F17/1, F17/2, F17/3, F17/4.

12. CZA F17/2 (4/10/39, signed by Mr. Landman). Benari continued to deal with this matter and appealed for advice to Ze'ev Jabotinsky on 6/6/39 (CZA F17/1). The papers connected to the case of Oscar Rabinowitz are in CZA F17/1 and F17/2. See in particular CZA F17/2, a series of letters dealing with the sale of wood to England and special banking arrangements as ways to reserve funds for aliyah work; CZA F17/1, a memorandum from Rabinowitz from March 1939; protocol of queries and responses between Rabinowitz and Benari, 7/6/39; and a letter from Oskar Rabinowitz to the general counsel (Benari). The date is unclear, but it is certainly after March 1939.

13. Most documents of this matter are in CZA F17/3. Complaints of emigrants on Aron and Stavsky's vessels, CZA S25/2651. See in particular the letter of the Refugee Aid Committee in Beirut to the president of the Alliance Israelite Universelle in Paris, 7/28/39.

14. Theodore Lavi (ed.), *Pinkas kehillot Romaniya* (Hebrew), *Records of Rumanian Communities* A, Jerusalem, 1970; D. Niv, *Bema'arkhot ha-irgun ha-tzvai ha-leumi* (Hebrew), *In the Battles of the Irgun*, Tel Aviv, 1979 (henceforth Niv 1979), Part 2, pp. 117–120; Ephraim Ofir, " 'Aliyah bet miRomaniya," (Hebrew), "Illegal Immigration from Rumania," *Yalkut moreshet* 30, 1981, pp. 38–74.

15. Account given by Schiber to the ODC, 158 (5); and J. Schechtman, *The Life and Times of Vladimir Jabotinsky*, New York, 1961, pp. 115–128.

16. Jabotinsky Archives (JA) 2/36, Kenner collection, documents from Rumania, some of which are unsigned, and including correspondence with the police and the internal affairs ministry. They report on the scheduled entry of refugee groups, the number of people involved.

17. JA, executive files 3: 12 December 1944 (hereafter NZO letter). The events are corroborated by Mossad files. According to Kadmon (Barpal), the Mossad's representative in Rumania, this was generally known in Jewish circles. See his account in the HA 14/343 and Yehieli's report, 14/153.

18. See Schiber's testimony, ODC, 158 (5), and Shapira's testimony, ODC, 158 (6).

19. See Schiber and Goren's testimony, ODC, 158 (5), 158 (4), and JA 6 2/3, (undated, Kenner to the chief of police, sent from 61 Romulis Street, Bucharest).

20. ODC, 158 (4).

21. It should be noted that in oral testimony, Benari related that Haller's traffic in Rumanian transit visas was one factor in the decision to expel him from the NZO. Haller sold the visas at exorbitant rates, to which the movement could not agree. ODC, 52 (3), 158 (1).

22. See Litai 1959, pp. 272–279, on the Shiniatin transport, and pp. 222–250 on the *Parita.* Cf. Aryeh Avneri, *Mivelos 'ad taurus: 'asor rishon laha'apalah, 1939–1944* (Hebrew), (*From Velos to Taurus: The First Decade of Illegal Jewish Immigration to Mandatory Palestine, 1933–1944*), Tel Aviv, 1985 (henceforth Avneri 1985), pp. 229–234. The episode is interesting in its own right. A group of émigrés en route from Poland to Rumania was meant to sail from Constantsa immediately upon their arrival in the port. The group did not receive transit visas, despite arrangements with the Rumanian government similar to those that had been made on numerous occasions in the preceding six months. There are three possible reasons for this: a) the British, knowing of the group's arrival at the border, exerted great pressure on the Rumanian government, and this time succeeded; b) the group arrived before its ship arrived in port, whereas the agreement with the government specified that the ship had to be in port awaiting the refugees' arrival; c) at the mouth of the Danube as well as upriver, awaiting entry to the country, were riverboats loaded with refugees from the Reich who did not have a ship waiting for them—presenting the Rumanians with a problem that they wanted to resolve before allowing the next group in.

23. CZA 17/3 (Eri Jabotinsky, from Bucharest, to Yaakobi, 10/4/39). This is a very detailed account of the episode. It states that "the owners of the ships were aware of the many such ships that were caught [confiscated], on the one hand, and of the 400 to 600 percent rise in the normal prices, on the other. Thus they are asking insane prices or very large bank guarantees."

24. Jabotinsky 1945, on the *Sakariya,* is an important source regarding the affair. The book was published shortly enough after the events to be regarded as a primary source. I have relied upon its account of the general sequence of events. The story of the ship, its crew, and the aftermath of the voyage are amply attested to in British records as well, and a critical comparison of sources might well be undertaken. Perl 1979, pp. 271–340, offers one other lengthy version of these events.

25. It is not entirely clear that this was the case, but a letter from Eri Jabotinsky to Yaakobi seems to imply it. CZA F17/3 (10/4/39).

26. CZA F17/4 (lease contract between Mr. Boya and the emigration office in Zurich, headed by Reuven Hecht, representing the NZO, dated 7/21/39). Interestingly, the contract did not specify the number of passengers. This contract was quite favorable to the NZO because it set an overall sum for the lease, covering a one-month period, with an option to renew for a further three months for another set price. This considerably eased the problem of funding by leaving the maximum number of passengers open-ended. In general, however, and especially after the war began, prices were set according to the number of passengers. Cf. Meisner's cables to Yaakobi of 8/9/39 and 9/26/39.

27. CZA F17/4 (cables from 18, 20, 26, 28, and 29 September, and 4 and 5 October 1939). It is somewhat difficult to understand the precise nature of the negotiations between the movement and the private organizers it worked with. The sources available are limited by and large to cables, which are characteristically terse, their language truncated and elliptical. The tone varies from one of pleading, anger, and explanation to threats of legal action. In any event, they attest to a tense atmosphere burdened by financial pressures and a sense of impending catastrophe among the aliyah activists.

28. CZA F17/4 (Kastel office to NZO, 8/17/39, and letter in French from Eri Jabotinsky to Yaakobi, 12/4/39).

29. CZA F17/3. As early as 26 September 1939, Paltin reported to London that he had only £2,000 remaining from an original total of £12,600. Yaakobi, stunned, cabled Bucharest: "What of Paltin's money? How much does he have?"

30. See Jabotinsky 1945 for details of the story.

31. JDC Archives, 12–4 (12/23/39); 61–42 (12/14/39).

32. Interview with Perl at his home in Virginia, April 1978. His account is borne out by Eri Jabotinsky's letter to Yaakobi of 9/26/39 (CZA F17/3). Perl rejected Revisionist movement involvement at this stage. Cf. HA, Shlomo Shamir file I, (10/16/40, *Milos* transport).

33. Goren's testimony, ODC, 150 (4); interview with Perl, April 1978. Perl asserts in his book that he had already had an option to acquire the *Sakariya* in September 1939, but the evidence indicates otherwise. Cf. JA, *Sakariya* file 2/14/4–6c (the signed contracts with the ship's owners). On the composition of the passenger group, see JA *Sakariya* file 2/12/4–9c (Ludmilla Epstein's report of 5/7/40).

34. HA, Shlomo Shamir file I (undated letters from Braun and Haller from the *Saturnus,* to Mr. Torczyner in Switzerland); *ibid.,* Yehieli, 14/153; CZA L 22/82 (clippings from the *Morgenblatt,* the Yiddish newspaper of Czernowitz, covering developments in December and January).

35. JA 2/14/4–6c.

36. This point is somewhat unclear. Both Eri Jabotinsky and Goren knew full well that a secret debarkation was impossible because there were no coastal craft available. The boat that was to have been used to transfer the passengers from the *Naomi Julia,* the *St. Catherine,* even then was not in working order, and it was the only such boat the Center for Aliyah had. It was sold in order to pay off debts and to acquire the *Stefanu.* For whom was Goren working? He was not a newcomer to aliyah bet activities (despite Eri Jabotinsky's claim to that effect). Was he working for Perl or for the Revisionist office? Or perhaps just for the sake of rescue?

37. Jabotinsky 1945 contains a lengthy account of Perl's objections to the arrangement and of his attempts to change its financial provisions. Goren's version of the events supports this. Perl, however, takes the view today that the cooperation over the *Sakariya* affair symbolizes the harmony between the Revisionists and himself, even when he was acting in a private capacity. He means to show that his private activity was only such in the tactical sense. See Perl 1979, pp. 271–340.

38. That Citron expected at some point that his group might sail aboard the *Sakariya* is borne out by documents in the JDC Archives, 42–6 (report by Ussoskin regarding 600 refugees in Bratislava, 12/14/39).

39. JA 2/14/46c. The representatives were Robert Mendler, in Prague, who worked simultaneously with Perl and Storfer in this period, and Lola Bernstein. Bernstein, as a British subject, was unrestricted in her movements in those countries. She had previously worked together with Perl and Goren. There were some refugees who accused her of seeking to profit from her activities. She was harassed by the British authorities, who invalidated her passport and finally persuaded the Rumanian authorities to have her deported. See the letters of the British ambassador in Rumania, Ronald Hore, to the Foreign Office, PRO CO 733/429, and from Bucharest to Belgrade, 3/30/40.

40. JDC Archives, 14–10 (reports of 12/23/39 and 12/30/39). The JDC was also involved through Filderman in supporting the group. Filderman was head of the Refugee Aid Committee and a prominent figure in Rumania. When Eri Jabotinsky

felt unable to handle the dealings with the Rand Company, he sought Filderman's assistance. Filderman as well as Aaronson, head of the "Rumania" shipping firm, appear to have taken part in the agreement reached on January 22, 1940. Filderman's aid committee funneled JDC assistance to the refugees. The ship was meant to leave on January 26, as stated in the contract of January 22, but at the last minute the owners demanded that a bank guarantee be deposited at a Swiss bank. This, too, was finally arranged by Filderman and Ussoskin, representative of the JDC in Rumania, through the JDC's office in Geneva.

41. See Jabotinsky 1945, chapter 8. For a detailed discussion of life on board ship, see Ofer Aliyah.

42. On the negotiations between the British and the Turkish governments over the release of the ship, and discussions of the matter between the Foreign and the Colonial Offices, see PRO CO 733/455, correspondence among Boyd, Randall, and the ambassador in Ankara, March to June 1940.

43. CZA F17/3 (Ben-Horin to Klinger, 2/16/40; Ben-Horin to Benari, 3/25/40; Meisner to the NZO executive in London and in New York).

44. Niv 1979, Part 2, pp. 192–196.

45. CZA F17/3 (Yaakobi to Shimon Levi, 10/17/39, and Yaakobi to Mr. Siaki and to Nahum Nehemias, same date; letter to Mr. Siaki, 4/17/40, unsigned, apparently by Benari).

46. *Ibid*. (Ben-Horin to Klinger—the executive, 2/16/40). The banker's name was referred to only by the initials A. B., but it is likely that he was Aristideia Blank, a wealthy assimilated Jew with powerful friends in the government and whose services were often called upon by the illegal aliya movement. He was on good terms with Filderman, and he is mentioned by many contemporary sources, such as Schiber, Goren, and Ussoskin. See also PRO CO 733/429/1587, reports from Bucharest on Revisionist activities, and meetings held with Ben-Horin in March 1940. He is mentioned in connection with his help to the aliya effort and his involvement in emigration plans put forward by Jews.

47. Yehoshua Levi, *Habaytah* (Hebrew), (*Homeward*), Tel Aviv, 1950. Levi's book gives an account of the *Pencho* and is the main source for reconstructing the course of events. There are further sources, such as letters by various people and ship's orders of the day, and these corroborate Levi's story. They are for the most part in the Jabotinsky Archives.

48. CZA F17/3 (Kastner to Yaakobi, 10/2/39 and 10/4/39; Yaakobi to Meisner, 10/9/39; Meisner to Kastner, 10/12/39 and 10/21/39.) "The Citron matter is annoying the police, who think the group's departure is being deliberately delayed. . . . We refuse to take on the responsibility, since as representatives of the Bratislava community we would then be answerable to the police for Citron's departure. . . . Cable Lachowitz and myself confirming your agreement, because delay will have irreparable consequences. Kastner" (10/4/39).

49. *Ibid*. On 11 April 1940, Benari wrote (apparently) to Meisner: "Citron's friends wrote to me that their situation is not yet resolved. They have organized themselves on their own, and are greatly dissatisfied with the work in Bucharest." And an unsigned and undated letter (internal evidence indicates that it was written around March-April 1940), Meisner is asked to be patient with the group: "You yourself realize that what we have here is a case of what might be called neurotic mass mentality [*krankenhafte massen psychologie*]. But they have also demonstrated that they are a self-disciplined group full of hope and trust, even when they are sometimes difficult. . . . Keep in mind that Mr. Citron is constantly under pressure from hundreds of people. Each one has

invested in this all that he had, and we owe each one a satisfactory solution, a guarantee."

50. B. Laurence, "Sippura shel *Pencho*, 1940–1942," (Hebrew), *"Story of the Pencho 1940–1942,"* *Yalkut moreshet* 20, 1975 (henceforth Laurence 1975). On the addition of these people, see the discussion in Zariz 1987, pp. 258–260.

51. JA *Pencho* file. This is a unique document, unparalleled in any of the Revisionist, Mossad, and Storfer materials. An uninformed reader of the advertisement would suspect nothing of the real nature of the trip. The orders of the day from the *Pencho* are also unique and directly recount what life on board was like, without the filtering effect of letters or personal recollections.

52. A British ship found them, and they were sent to Cyprus and to Palestine. See Laurence 1975 for further details.

53. YVA, papers of the German Foreign Office, JM 3140–3141, (German embassy in Pressburg (Bratislava) to the Foreign Office in Berlin, 11/2/40, signed by von Kilinger). He asks that the request be looked into, if, as the Italians contended, the transport had been organized by Storfer. On 6 November 1940, Rademacher replied to the embassy in Pressburg: "Storfer was not involved in the transport, and none of the bearers of German passports are to be accepted back." On that same date, 6 November, over the signature of Makanssen [?], the German government informed the Italians that Germany would not accept a single member of the *Pencho* group. On 8 November 1940, the Italians again contacted the German Foreign Office, suggesting that the Americans be approached to provide a neutral ship to transport the refugees to Palestine. The Italian Foreign Office continued to follow up on the matter, and in the summer of 1941 asked Eichmann his opinion regarding the possibility of German assistance in transferring the refugees from Rhodes. Eichmann, however, refused to consider this. In his reply he stated that no German agency had been involved in the transport, and that though there were former German nationals aboard, they had emigrated to Slovakia prior to their departure from that country. He states, "There had been a plan to organize from here a transport of Jews of German nationality to Palestine, but such a transport to Palestine is impossible at the present time."

Chapter 5

1. Interview with Perl, April 1978. Baruch Konfino, *'Aliyah bet mihofei Bulgaria* (Hebrew), (*Illegal Immigration From the Shores of Bulgaria*), Tel Aviv, 1965 (henceforth Konfino 1965), p. 36. We have no way of determining the truth of the contention that private aliyah organizers profited from their refugee work. Those who survived the war, such as Perl and Konfino, deny this.

2. Konfino 1965, p. 36.

3. Konfino 1965, pp. 82–83.

4. Konfino 1965, p. 55; YVA 03/2920 (Emma Weiss's testimony); YVA 03/3255 (Yaakov Toldo's testimony).

5. Konfino 1965, p. 80; YVA 03/3277 (Yeshayahu Haim's testimony).

6. HA 14/153 (Yehieli's report); Konfino 1965, pp. 76–80; JDC Archives 4–19 (testimony of Erich Frank, Hehalutz leader on the *Atlantic*); CAHJP AW2515 (Frank's letters).

7. YVA, 03/2920 (Emma Weiss); CAHJP AW2515 (Konfino to Storfer, 10/20/40).

8. Konfino 1965, pp. 83–84; PRO CO 733/429 (Randall, from Sofia to the Foreign

Office, 1/25/40). Randall, the British ambassador in Sofia, reported that the *Rudnitchar* had returned from a refugee transport, was being readied for another, and that swift action was called for; *ibid.*, 3/26/40, the ambassador in Rumania to the Foreign Office on the same subject; also 3/21/40. These letters reflect the diplomatic pressure brought to bear on the Rumanian and Bulgarian governments. On 30 May 1940, the vice-consul in Varna reported to the Foreign Office that the *Rudnitchar*, formerly used as an illegal refugee ship, was being used to carry lumber from Constantsa to Kalanata, following British pressure on the Bulgarian government in March 1940.

9. *Ibid.*, Randall to the high commissioner in Palestine; Konfino 1965, pp. 78–79. The British claimed the boat was in extreme disrepair and emphasized the danger it posed for passengers. On the contrary, Konfino noted that the boat was fairly sturdy and in good condition.

10. YVA 03/3277 (Yeshayahu Haim).

11. Konfino 1965, p. 84. Mr. Downey to Latham, 8/17/40, PRO CO733/430 W7299, and W7602, 8/24/40, and his reply to Latham. In this correspondence, the Colonial Office upbraids the Foreign Office for having allowed the boat to take on provisions at Sikri, in the Greek isles, rather than forcing it back to sea.

12. YVA 03/3277 (Yeshayahu Haim); YVA 03/3458 (Buku Levi). Corroborating evidence is in British Foreign Office records, PRO FO/371/29160. London asked its ambassador in Sofia in letters dated from October 1940 through January 1941 whether illegal immigrants bound for Palestine on a ship named the *Strotima* or *Struma* were about to depart. In January 1941, Randall reported that two months earlier there had been a plan to send 500 refugees to Palestine, but the plan was aborted after pressure was applied; the boat to have been used was in any case not seaworthy. A CID (Central Intelligence Department) report dated 12/4/40 stated that the boat had been ready for departure in October of that year.

13. Konfino 1965, pp. 85–86. The committee was composed of leading members of the Zionist movement in Bulgaria—Avraham Mashiah, Moshe Kechales, Robert Kechales, Sento Lirasi, David Eladzis, Gershon Yeshayahu, and Davidov (the committee's treasurer).

14. Konfino 1965, p. 56: "In my organization there was one non-Jew, Angel Paskeliv. He was *the most dedicated* among my staff and *my closest advisor*. I turned to him for advice in every matter, without exception. He was *thoroughly dedicated to aliya bet, more so than many pure-blooded Jews*" [emphasis in the original]. He describes their relationship as one of friendship and that it proved helpful for aliyah bet even after the war. He states, "He certainly deserves to be considered one of the 'righteous gentiles.' "

15. YVA, session of the inquiry commission of the Bulgarian Jewish Consistory, 1941 (report in Bulgarian); CZA S25/2601, (testimony of a survivor, 4/7/41).

16. YVA, inquiry commission, p. 9 (original in Bulgarian).

17. YVA, inquiry commission, p. 12.

18. YVA 03/1706 (Albert Michael's testimony); YVA 03/3255 (Yaakov Toledo); Konfino 1965, pp. 88–90.

19. CAHJP AW/2515. One letter is dated 19 December and the second 29 December 1940. These are an important source, since we do not have Konfino's written records from his wartime activity. The first was written in German (Storfer commented on the poor style), and the second was translated into German in Storfer's office, but the original language is not noted.

20. *Ibid.*, 12/29/40.
21. HA 14/153, p. 18.

Chapter 6

1. Detailed discussion of this conflict in the literature on the S.S. and Nazi Jewish policy may be found in: H. Hohne, *The Order of the Death's Head*, London, 1970 (henceforth Hohne 1970), chapters 13 and 14; W. Krausnick, *Anatomy of the S.S. State*, London, 1970, Part I: "The Persecution of the Jews" (henceforth Krausnick 1970); C. Browning, *The Final Solution and the German Foreign Office*, New York, 1978, chapters 1–4; Eliahu Ben-Elissar, *La Diplomatie du IIIe Reich et les Juifs 1933– 1939*, chapters 8–10, Paris, 1969; Francis Nicosia, *The Third Reich and the Palestine Question*, London, 1985 (henceforth Nicosia 1985).

2. David Yisraeli, "The Third Reich and Palestine," in *Middle Eastern Studies*, 7, 1971, "The Third Reich and the Transfer Agreement," *Journal of Contemporary History*, 6, 1972; Nicosia 1985, pp. 29–64, 145–68.

3. See *Documents on German Foreign Policy*, Series D, vol. 5, 1953 (henceforth Documents), pp. 926–933, and Nicosia 1985, pp. 112–140, 168–192.

4. For a broader discussion of the Zentralstelle and its operations, see Herbert Rosenkranz, *Verfolgung und Selbstbehauptung, Die Juden in Osterreich 1938–1945*, Vienna, 1978 (henceforth Rosenkranz 1978), pp. 115–125; and see the testimony of Franz Meyer (Yad Vashem Archives [YVA] 0–1/113) describing his and his colleagues' feelings about being sent by the Gestapo to Vienna in January 1940 to study the work of the Zentralstelle with a view toward establishing a similar office in Berlin.

5. Bauer 1974, pp. 221–301.

6. Documents, pp. 333–336.

7. ODC, Pino Ginsburg's testimony.

8. See Avriel 1975 pp. 41–46, on contacts with Karthaus, a German roads engineer who helped with obtaining legal immigration permits; cf. Braginsky 1975, pp. 151–165.

9. ODC, no. 1521, Ginsburg testimony. Ginsburg speaks of a plan involving far greater numbers than those mentioned by Braginsky or by other aliya activists. Most other sources and immigrant memoirs rely on Braginsky, and we have no outside corroboration for Ginsburg's version, making it difficult to establish which account is correct. See the article by K. Y. Ball-Kaduri, "*Ha-aliya ha-Bilti hukit miGermaniyah ha-nazit leEretz Yisrael*" (Hebrew), "Illegal Immigration from Nazi Germany to Palestine", *Yalkut moreshet* 1963, pp. 127–142. There is some indirect evidence to support Ginsburg's account in YVA JM3140, in a memorandum from von Hoepfner to Lischka, dated 12/1/39, in which he states: "Because of the war, planned Jewish immigration to Palestine from German parts was not taking place . . . ," and he suggests alternatives.

10. YVA JM3140, German embassy in Rome to the Foreign Office.

11. *Ibid.* Perhaps what is hinted at here is that it was no longer possible to sail in German vessels from the North Sea ports, and hence Italy's importance as a point of embarkation. Alexander von Hoepfner met in Italy with Yehieli and with Shind, both of whom sought his assistance. See HA 14/153, Yehieli's report, pp. 24, 26.

12. The legal immigrants came from Berlin, Prague, Vienna, Warsaw, and Bratislava, including Polish refugees there. See Haim Barlas, *Hatzalah beyemei ha-Shoah* (Hebrew), (*Rescue in the Days of Holocaust*), Tel Aviv, 1975, (henceforth Barlas

1975), pp. 20–23. References to the work of Gideon Rufer (Rafael) in Italy at the end of 1939 and to the meetings held by Yehieli and Shind with Konfino in March and April 1940 are found in HA 14/152 (Yehieli's report).

13. CAHJP WA 2515. The German shipping firm Hapag created a subsidiary called Aplah specifically for the job of handling the "special" Jewish emigration (*Sonderauswanderung*), as illegal aliya was called. See also ODC, Ginsburg testimony, and Zariz 1987, pp. 151–153.

14. YVA JM3141, 3/23/40. The signature is unclear.

15. HA 14/153, Yehieli report, pp. 20, 24. See Eichmann's letter, YVA JM3141, 5/10/40.

16. Madagascar, off the African coast, was then under French colonial rule, and had in the past been suggested as a suitable place for mass Jewish immigration. The proposal was raised in the S.D. following the Anschluss. Madagascar came under German control after the occupation of France, making the idea seem far more viable. But scholars are divided over how seriously the proposal was treated outside the S.D. itself. See, for instance, Leni Yahil, "Madagascar: Phantom of a Solution for the Jewish Question," in *Jews and Non-Jews in Eastern Europe, 1918–1945*, Bela Vago and G.L. Mosse (eds.), New York, 1974, pp. 315–334 (henceforth Yahil 1974).

17. Dov Kulka, Azriel Hildesheimer, *Dokumente zur Geschichte der Reichsvereinigung der Juden in Deutschland* (in press).

18. Avriel 1975, p. 77.

19. HA 14/417, report by Kornfeld (a passenger on the *Milos*), 10/16/40. *Ibid.*, report by Braun (who commanded the *Milos*) to the Jewish Refugee Aid Committee in Athens, dated 10/16/40.

20. CAHJP AW/2515, letters dated 11/25/40 by Kurt Rosenberg and Alfred Selbiger.

21. The ODC testimony of Ehud Ueberall, Pino Ginsburg, and Efraim Frank on this point is laden with emotion. Storfer's fate, as related by Eichmann at his trial, is reported in Hannah Arendt, *Eichmann in Jerusalem, A Report on the Banality of Evil*, New York, 1964, pp. 50–52.

22. CAHJP AW/2151, 4/30/40, Mitteilung 40, and letter of Loewenherz from March 1941. Cf. Storfer's résumé as presented to the Vienna police, including details of his professional activities: *ibid.*, AW/655, January 1939.

23. YVA 0–30/5, report of Loewenherz, p. 5 (henceforth, Loewenherz report). The report was collated after the war by Dr. Buenenfeld and is based on the final reports of the Jewish communal institutions before their submission to the German authorities, as required. The report is chronological from May 1938 until October 1942. It is not always accurate, and there are occasional lapses. It was prepared for the trial of the heads of the Zentralstelle in Vienna in 1946.

24. ODC interview with Pino Ginsburg, July 1979. Braginsky 1975, p. 158; Avriel 1979, p. 77. YVA 0–3015, Loewenherz report, p. 21; HA 14/417, Kornfeld report dated November 1940; *ibid.*, Braun report to the Greek Jewish Refugee Aid Committee, November 1940.

25. CAHJP AW/2515, 12/1/39. Ehud Ueberall to Storfer.

26. YVA 0–3015, Loewenherz report, p. 21.

27. CAHJP AW/2515, Mitteilung 70, 5/6/40; *ibid.*, Mitteilung 26, 2/5/40. Storfer reports on a surprise inspection of his office carried out by Alois Brunner and his men. They remained in the office the entire morning and reviewed his account ledgers and copies of his telegrams abroad. He also described a surprise inspection by Dan-

necker during which he examined correspondence between Storfer's office and the Jewish community organization. These were among the top-ranking German officials at the Zentralstelle. YVA, Loewenherz report, p. 19.

28. Occasionally, we find in Storfer's reports that the Zentralstelle added five, fifty, or some other number of persons to the lists (7/18/40, 7/19/40, etc.).

29. *Ibid.*, Mitteilung 61, 4/30/40.

30. CAHJP AW/2515, 6/15/40.

31. CAHJP AW/2515, 3/28/40: Storfer to Loewenherz. *Ibid.*, Mitteilung 38, 1/1/40; cf. letter to the selections committee, 1/28/40; and cf. Mitteilung 47, 4/3/40. *Ibid.*, Mitteilung 90, 7/18/40; cf. YVA, Loewenherz report, p. 20. The rate of five to ten marks to the dollar is mentioned in the context of a special arrangement between Loewenherz and the Joint's secretary in Budapest.

32. *Ibid.*, 1/16/40, Storfer to Cedock Company; 1/17/40, 5/30/40 and 5/21/40: the great dispute with the German Danube Line throughout August over the times arranged to transfer passengers to Tulcea and over the payments to be made; 8/11/40 and 8/24/40, Storfer to the Zentralstelle; the same to Mr. Schutz, of the same date; the Prague report, 9/1/40; Mitteilung 103, 9/12/40, and a letter to the Zentralstelle, 9/17/40.

33. *Ibid.*, 3/18/40, Storfer to the Zentralstelle. Storfer posed this request to Eichmann, and it was denied. In September 1940, however, some of the passengers of the three ships boarded the Danube boats in Vienna. The reasons for Eichmann's refusal and apparent permission remain unclear.

34. *Ibid.*

35. *Ibid*, 9/28/40.

36. YVA JM/3140; the Foreign Office representative in Prague, Zimka, to Berlin, 9/14/40; Storfer's office to the German consul-general in Bratislava, 7/13/40.

37. HA 14/153, pp. 7, 10: testimony of Yaakov Edelstein; cf. Ruth Bondy *Elder of the Jews*, (New York: 1989), chapter 16 (henceforth Bondy 1989). Bauer 1974, p. 229. Bauer makes the point that Morris Tropper, the head of the JDC in Europe, called Loewenherz a "Nazi agent."

38. CAHJP AW/2515, Mitteilung 22, 12/2/39; *ibid.*, *Vertrauliche Aktion Notiz*, 12/25/39. The same storm claimed a British and Rumanian ship as well.

39. YVA, Loewenherz report, p. 20. On the JDC's hesitations, see PRO FO 371/25238/ W6857, telegram from Katzki to Tropper in London, dated 1/8/40, concerning the Loewenherz refugees whose ship was lost. (The wire was transferred to the Colonial Office by the censor, and thus found its way to the Foreign Office.)

40. CAHJP AW/2515, 3/4/40, report on the contract between Avgerinos and Storfer, and *ibid.*, 3/18/40, letter to the Zentralstelle.

41. *Ibid.*, 3/22/40, Storfer to Loewenherz.

42. *Ibid.*, 3/30/40, Mitteilung 45.

43. *Ibid.*, 4/11/40, Loewenherz to an unknown party. Corroboration of this may be found in information transmitted by British intelligence to the Foreign Office and the Colonial Office. They reported quite fully during this period on Storfer and Avgerinos and their negotiations for the *Sirus* and the *Popi*, their talks with the Panamanian consul concerning registry, and on related matters. The reports are dated 3/20/40 and 5/17/40: CO 733/430, W 4712/38/48.

44. HA 14/153. This, of course, was the British line. It is in this period that the British were also pressuring the Joint to stop aiding aliya bet activities. See: PRO FO 371/5238, W 6257, Downey to Caravell, 1/19/40, with notations by Foreign Office officials.

45. ODC, interviews with Ginsburg and Ueberall (Avriel). The testimony of these men bears clear witness to their negative attitude toward Storfer even today. Ginsburg describes Storfer as a slick and power-hungry sycophant, and Ueberall stresses that if the Germans chose Storfer they had their reasons—clearly implying that Storfer was a collaborator.

46. We have only Yehieli's account of these meetings. Storfer mentions his trips to Bucharest and Geneva, but he visited these cities on numerous occasions, and he made no mention of meeting Yehieli. Yehieli presented himself as a potential mediator between the Mossad and Storfer, not as a Mossad agent himself. It should be pointed out that Yehieli is unusually accurate and reliable in his reports. Many details mentioned by him are corroborated by sources in the Vienna Archive (CAHJP AW/2515).

47. On Edelstein's attitude to Storfer, see HA 14/152, Yehieli report, p. 101; also see Bondy 1981, pp. 184–249, on this and on the problems of emigration from the Czech Protectorate.

48. See Chapter 3.

49. HA 14/152 pp. 26–27. Yehieli reported as follows: "On my third day in Bucharest Spitzer called me from Belgrade to let me know that the 'counsellor' [Storfer] had called on him and that he was most insistent upon arranging a meeting with us. I told Spitzer that we had no interest in such a meeting at the moment because E-n [Edelstein] had told me he had full autonomy in carrying out aliyah activities in the Czech Protectorate and that the refugees from Vienna now at Kladovo had no longer any link with the Vienna authorities. That day S-r [Spitzer] called again to say that the 'counsellor' had threatened to interfere in the Czech operation and that in his opinion a meeting was necessary; otherwise, the whole effort to resolve the Kladovo problem might be lost. S-r [Spitzer] told me that the 'counsellor' would arrive by night train and that I might find him at the Athens Palace hotel in Bucharest."

It is worth adding that the Mossad agents were also angry with Loewenherz for having refused to allocate funds for the Kladovo group even though these were Viennese Jews. The Vienna community had allocated £6,500 for a group of 750 people—a meager sum, given prices of the time. Loewenherz even refused to approach the JDC with a request for additional aid for the group, reasoning (accurately) that the JDC would subtract any such amount from the Vienna allocation (*ibid.*, p. 10). The Mossad agents undoubtedly associated Storfer with this approach, which they considered extremely narrow-minded, or, as Yehieli quoted Loewenherz as saying: "My shirt is closer to me than my coat" (*ibid.*, p. 17).

50. CAHJP AW/2515, 2/1/40 and 3/18/40. On this, see also the testimony of Braun and Kornfeld, HA 14/417.

51. Compare the testimony of Kornfeld, HA 14/417. He cites both Storfer and Edelstein on a meeting in Berlin at the Zentralstelle, at which each one tried to argue the case for his own control over emigration activity and to undermine the Revisionists. Of course, Storfer and Edelstein contradict each other on the episode.

52. HA 14/153, p. 29.

53. CAHJP AW/2515, 3/31/40, *Aktion Notiz, ibid.,* 4/27/40, Mitteilung 56.

54. HA 14/153, Yehieli, p. 37. This final point is rather astonishing since the chief point of contention between Storfer and the Mossad, selection of candidates, was the part of the operation that took place entirely *inside* the Reich. Organizational work outside the Reich consisted chiefly of foreign-currency transactions, and this only allowed them to keep closer watch over Storfer's activities. With regard to Yehieli's contention that the meeting was at Storfer's request, the contrary is true. According

to both Yehieli (p. 35) and the records in the Vienna Archive (AW/2515, 4/30/40, Mitteilung 60) it was Yehieli who requested a meeting with Storfer.

55. HA 14/153, p. 39. It is interesting to note that until this point, according to this source, Yehieli did not know about the appointment, although it had been in effect since early March, two months earlier. This raises certain questions about the nature of the contacts between Geneva and the Jewish communities and about the extent to which those in Geneva were truly informed.

56. These were the groups that went aboard the *Milos,* the *Pacific,* and the *Atlantic.*

57. See Storfer's letters for his attitude toward the Mossad: Storfer to Loewenherz, 6/22/40, and Storfer to the JDC, 7/10/40 and December 1940; *ibid.,* on the Kladovo matter. It should be remembered that the chances of an undetected landing were exceedingly slim. British intelligence and naval patrols made it less than likely that a ship could get through. Since September 1939, every ship except the *Rudnitchar* had been caught (as well as many before then).

58. This point is clearly established in Yehieli's report. Erich Frank, interviewed in October 1979, was not surprised by this.

59. CAHJP AW/2515, 7/15/40: Storfer to the Reichsvereinigung. He reports here on a telephone conversation with Erich Frank in which they discussed Ginsburg's letter.

60. HA 14/153, pp. 45–47.

61. CAHJP AW/2515, Mitteilung 61, 4/30/40; *ibid.,* Mitteilung 73, 6/1/40.

62. HA 14/153, p. 46, and CAJHP WA 2515 Storfer to Loewenherz, 7/22/40.

63. *Ibid.,* and see Storfer to Loewenherz, 7/22/40, and Storfer to Tropper, Joint Archive 4–19 (English translation). Cf. Loewenherz to Tropper, 7/8/40.

64. *Ibid.* Storfer to Tropper, 7/10/40.

65. CAHJP AW/2515, 6/17/40, report on discussion of travel conditions at sea.

66. *Ibid.,* 7/17/40.

67. *Ibid.*

68. JDC Archive 4–19, 7/10/40; CAHJP AW/2515, 7/10/40: Yehieli. He maintains that these ships were actually the *Sirus, Popi,* and *Asimi,* which had been offered to him in Athens in late 1939, and which Storfer apparently had acquired for the April transport in 1940. If this is true, it indicates the exceedingly small size of the market.

69. YVA JM/3140, 9/14/40, signed by Zimka and 9/18/40 with the note "passed over for authorization"; and CAHJP AW/2515, 8/28/40; and 8/11/40, Storfer to the Zentralstelle. In this telegram, Storfer mentions a sum of $12,000 to be received by the Spanish consul.

70. *Ibid.,* telegram to Storfer, 8/7/40; and his reply, 8/8/40.

71. *Ibid.,* 8/11/40, Mitteilung 98.

72. *Ibid.*

73. Because of the delays during August, the groups' departures took place after intervals of only two days.

74. HA 14/417, committee of the *Milos* to the Jewish Refugee Aid Committee, Athens, 10/16/40.

75. CAHJP AW/2515, Storfer to Rotenstreich, 8/8/40.

76. There is no explanation of why the journey took so long, but we learn that the deadline of 9/10/40 set by the Danube Line was put off.

77. CAHJP AW/2515, Rundschreiben 14, 10/15/40; *ibid.,* memorandum no. 18, 11/9/40.

78. *Ibid.*

79. *Ibid.*

80. *Ibid.*

81. *Ibid.,* memorandum no. 19, 11/21/40. Another source describing the trip of the *Atlantic* is the letter to Switzerland dated 10/29/40, in which he states that the ship lost its way and only the skill of the captain saved it.

82. P.R.O. FO 371/29160, report by Cavaghan to the Customs Office, 12/13/40.

83. CAHJP AW/2515, Rundschreiben 14, 10/15/40.

84. *Ibid.,* letters from Tulcea; cf. JDC Archives 4–19. A detailed account of the trip by Frank and Raubel, including the composition of the refugee group, its selection, and the way it was organized in Vienna. See also YVA, testimony collected by Ball Kaduri from passengers. On the *Pacific,* see especially the account by Michael Meyer, 02/283, and that of Erich Frank, 01/221.

85. JDC Archives 4–19, letters by Frank, and testimony collected by Kaduri. See also Frank's account, ODC, and the version by Konfino in Konfino 1956, pp. 77–78.

86. CAHJP AW/2515, Braun to the transport leaders, Brno, 10/16/40; and HA 14/417, report to the New Zionist Organization (the Revisionists), 1/24/40, by Alfred Kornfeld.

87. CAHJP AW/2515, Braun to the transport leaders, Brno, 10/16/40, and *ibid.,* to the Aid Committee in Athens from Brown and Kornfeld.

88. The refugees considered the *Patria,* an old French vessel, luxurious in comparison to conditions on Storfer's ships.

89. Mention of the *Rosita* and its movements occurs in FO 371/2916 W233, 2/26/41.

90. A number of documents testify to activity in this direction until October 1941. In the Vienna archive, for example (CAHJP AW/2515), in the Storfer files there is a letter to the Zentralstelle in Berlin about the departure of a group of 140 persons on 11/5/40,; details of their journey to Lisbon dated 11/12/40; and information on their voyage to Honduras from 1/26/41 and again in March 1941.

91. YVA 02/283, testimony of Michael Meyer, describing the unequivocal steps taken by the Gestapo whenever the Palestine Office and the Jewish leadership showed any hesitation in carrying out an emigration plan.

92. On Danzig Jews in aliya bet see the doctoral dissertation of Eliahu Stern, *Korotahem shel yehudei Danzig meaz ha-emancipatsiyah vead ha-girush beyemei ha-shilton ha-nazi* (Hebrew), *The Jews of Danzig, 1840–1943 Integration, Struggle, Rescue,* Tel Aviv, 1983, pp. 459–465.

93. See Chapters 4 and 5.

94. CAHJP AW/2515, 9/4/40, and Rundschreiben 17, *ibid.,* letter to Loewenherz, 11/9/40; letter to Morris Tropper in Lisbon, 11/25/40; letter to Josef Schwartz, 10/29/40.

95. *Ibid.*

96. *Ibid.,* 11/9/40.

Chapter 7

1. See Bauer 1963; M. Cohen 1978; Gavriel Cohen, *Churchill ushealat Eretz Yisrael,* (Hebrew), *Churchill and the Question of Palestine,* Jerusalem, 1976 (henceforth G. Cohen 1976), pp. 15–21; Bernard Wasserstein, *Britain and the Jews of Europe, 1939–1945,* London, 1979 (henceforth Wasserstein 1979). Ronald W. Zweig, *Britain and Palestine During the Second World War,* London, 1986 (henceforth Zweig 1986).

2. This is borne out by a great many comments in official statements, in reports,

and in marginal notes. For instance, Mr. A. Bennett, first secretary in the British Embassy in Cairo, in responding to an appeal to help the refugees on board the *Sakariya,* commented that "So far as Palestine is concerned, H.M.G. deny all responsibility for the plight of these people. It is not quite so easy to say that there are no grounds for intervention . . . since the appeal is *prima facie* on purely humanitarian grounds . . . " (Public Record Office (PRO) CO 733/430/76021/24).

3. Public Record Office (PRO) FO 371/25241 W766/38/48. Memorandum on Illegal Immigration 1/17/40. (All files of the Foreign and Colonial Offices are contained in the Public Record Office.)

4. *Ibid.*

5. CO 733/430/76021/24/10. See also the comment by John Shuckburgh, under secretary for the colonies, dated 1/29/40 to Downie's letter regarding the *Sakariya.* The British regarded the Revisionists as outright enemies, and felt justified in any measures to thwart them. "Whatever may be our obligation towards the orthodox Zionists we certainly owe nothing to Jabotinsky and his associates. They have opposed us from the start and have invariably done their best to make our position in Palestine impossible."

6. CO 733/429/76021/11/40, MacMichael to the colonial secretary, 3/18/1940, regarding the possibility of infiltration through coercion. This contention occurred repeatedly, even when it seemed most unlikely. See FO 371/25241 W2986/38/48, 1/15/40 discussion of Brodetsky, Eban, and Locker from the Zionist office in London, with MacDonald and members of his office. Most pertinent are the remarks of MacDonald, the colonial secretary, to Randall of the Foreign Office, of 2/20/40. "I should not personally have thought that it would be practical for the Germans to introduce very many or very dangerous agents in this way, but obviously we must accept the views on such a subject of the experts who have an intimate acquaintance with it in all its aspects" (FO 371/25240/8150 W2986/38/48).

This attitude did not change even when interrogation of refugees proved the idea to be groundless. Indeed, the British spread rumors that agents were discovered, but when asked to produce them, they were unable to do so. See CO 733/429/76021/1/40, 3/26/40, to Carvell of the Foreign Office refugees section (handwritten comment): "No proof *yet* regarding suspicions sending enemy agents amongst *Sakariya* passengers" [emphasis added].

7. *Ibid.,* 2/1/40.

8. This news was carried particularly over the BBC's service in the Balkan languages. The BBC made use of reports in German news services on actions taken by the British against refugee boats and of Jewish acts of fraud against shipping agents and crews. See CO 733/429/76021/7/40, Carvell to Downie, 1/26/40; and *ibid.,* Downie to Carvell, 2/22/40.

9. *Ibid.,* Ambassador Hoare in Rumania to the Foreign Office, 12/27/39; and notes to Hoare's letter, FO 371/2524 W1934a; 1/21/40; *ibid.,* W7602, Bennett to Carvell, reacting to Hoare's letter, 1/10/40 and Foreign Office to Hoare, *ibid.,* W477/32/78, 1/13/40, a proposal to appeal to the European Danube Committee, to which France and Britain also belonged.

10. See CO 733/400/6578, Foreign Office to the embassy in Sofia, 1/21/40. See *ibid.,* CO 733/429/46021/10 Knatchbull-Hugessen, the ambassador in Turkey, to the Foreign Office, 1/9/40; and *ibid.,* Downie to Bennett, January 10, 1940. See also *ibid.,* FO 371/25239 W2908/77/48, Carvell to Belgrade, 2/29/40.

11. FO 371/25238 W1384/38/48, Hoare in Bucharest to R. Campbell in Belgrade, 1/30/40; *ibid.,* FO 371/25239 W2500/38/48, memorandum to Carvell, 2/5/40.

354 NOTES

12. CO 733/429/2500/38/48, Bennett and Downie to Carvell, 1/10/40; *ibid.*, Knatchbull-Hugessen, 1/9/40, stressing the importance of the strict warning issued by the Turkish government to Turkish seamen in this regard; *ibid.*, Foreign Office to Hoare in Bucharest, 1/11/40 and 1/13/40; *ibid.*, Hoare to Foreign Office, 1/26/40.

13. *Ibid.*, the Panamanian Foreign Office to Dodd, the British ambassador in Panama, 19 December 1939; *ibid.*, FO 371 W76021/11/40, Downie to Carvell, 2/22/40. Downie asked Bolivia, Uruguay, and China to discipline their consuls who had issued visas to the *Sakariya* refugees. See also *ibid.*, 3/18/40, a report of the dismissal of the Paraguayan consul who had issued visas to members of the *Sakariya* group.

14. *Ibid.*, Hoare to the Foreign Office, 2/22/40.

15. *Ibid.*, FO 371/25240 W3207/38/48, Foreign Office to the ambassador in Belgrade, 2/20/40. Attached is the positive reply of the Yugoslav Ministry of Foreign Affairs of 1/13/40.

16. CO 733/429/76021/13/40, Bennett to Mackenzie, 3/21/40, in reply to the general's letter of 3/5/40.

17. Prior to the war, one immigrant ship, *Sandu,* had been sent back to Rumania, and the British referred to this incident on numerous occasions as a "successful" precedent. See CO 733/429/76021/10/40, cable from the colonial secretary to the Palestine high commissioner, 1/18/40, regarding Rumanian nationals aboard the *Hilda,* and Bennett's comments to Carvell regarding Hungarian nationals on the *Sakariya,* 3/19/40 and 3/20/40.

18. *Ibid.*, Downie to Carvell, 2/22/40 and 3/1/40; *ibid.*, Bennett to Carvell, 3/5/40, with handwritten notation by Bennett dated 3/12/40. Here, too, there was some discord between the Foreign and Colonial Offices. The Colonial Office denied that the Hungarian government had to assent to repatriation of the refugees, as the Foreign Office maintained. Downie contended that the refugees should be placed on the next Hungarian vessel leaving from Palestine and sent back, before notifying Budapest. Unfortunately for the Colonial Office, the Hungarian line serving Palestine was not operating at the time, and the plan could not be implemented. See *ibid.*, cable from the high commissioner to the colonial secretary, 3/23/40.

19. *Ibid.*, cables from the high commissioner dated 1/18/40 and 1/19/40.

20. *Ibid.*, CO 733/429/W356/38/48, notation by Bennett to correspondence with Ker, after the *Rudnitchar* managed to evade patrols, 1/11/40.

21. *Ibid.*, handwritten notes, unsigned, 1/4/40.

22. CO 733/429/76021/10/40, from the Admiralty (signature unclear, possibly J. W. Phillips) to the under secretary for the colonies, 3/14/40; and the letter from Downie to Mackenzie noting that the admiralty had agreed to cooperate in intercepting ships as long as this occurred as part of the normal duties of the Navy: CO 733/430/76021/24/30, 3/21/40. Regarding the German agent's comments, see *ibid.*, CO 733/395/75113/2.

23. CO 733/429/76021/10/40; and the note by Mathieson, 3/29/40.

24. *Ibid.*, 4/4/40.

25. FO 371/24097 W76021/19/41. The British Consul in Varna noted that the *Rudnitchar* was not allowed to carry immigrants.

26. CO 733/429/76021/11/40, Downie to Carvell, 2/22/40: "The disposal of the passengers is of course of less importance, from the deterrent point of view, at the present time, than the detention of the master and crew and (if possible) the seizure of the ship." This was written following the capture of the *Sakariya,* when it was thought that 180 Hungarian nationals from the group might be repatriated.

27. *Ibid.*, 3/21/40. The Colonial Office was not yet prepared to adopt a deportation

policy. Bennett wrote in his reply: "The proposal for setting up camps for illegal immigrants outside Palestine is, however, being kept in cold storage and will be brought out again for fresh consideration if the situation seems to warrant it."

28. *Ibid.*, CO 733/429/76021/7.

29. It should be noted that "deportation" refers to two different concepts: both internment in a colony or a refugee camp outside Palestine, and repatriation to the country of origin. Repatriation was the government's official policy, but it could not be implemented. When policy changed, it was in relation to the first option—deportation to a crown colony.

30. CO 733/430 W4717/38/48, reports from naval intelligence dated 3/20/40, discussing Storfer's operation and his ties with Avgerinos, his brother's activities in Bucharest, the support of the Gestapo in Vienna, etc. The *Syrus* and *Popi* are mentioned along with details of the negotiations for their purchase and registration in Panama. Reports from 3/26/40, 4/3/40, 4/17/40, and 5/13/40 detail Storfer's activities in Greece. Storfer is cited as a German agent.

31. *Ibid.*, CO 733/430/76021/19/40, Downie to Carvell, 4/11/40. At that stage, it was thought that the *Rudnitchar* would take the Kladovo group. Indeed, we know of negotiations between Konfino, Yehieli, and Agami in this matter: *ibid.*, and also FO 371/29162 W6030.

32. FO 371/29162 W3060.

33. CO 733/430 W5073/38/48, note by Mathieson, 4/8/40, approved ("O.K.") by Bennett and Downie: "A certain Storfer who was expected in Greece in connection with the purchase of ships for the illegal traffic, is described as 'the head of the Nazi organization for Jew smuggling.' I had to see why the German Government would take pains to organize the traffic if it is only to get Jews out of Germany and into Palestine. This would happen in any case without their efforts, and one can only assume that some members of the transports will actively further German aims in the Middle East."

34. *Ibid.*, note by Locke to the Colonial Office, 7/11/40.

35. *Ibid.*, FO 371/25241 W7899/38/48, Rendel to Halifax, the foreign secretary, 6/13/40.

36. *Ibid.*, see the report on the seizure of the *Libertad*, 7/19/40, note by Downie on the implications, 7/22/40.

37. FO 371/25242 W76021/38/48, 9/21/40.

38. *Ibid.*, 10/15/40.

39. *Ibid.*, FO 371/25242 W11766/38/48, 11/14/40, comments to the letter from the Washington embassy regarding the deportation: handwritten note, signature unclear, 12/2/40, and also the comment by Snow, 12/3/40.

40. CO 733/430/76021/70/40, letter from Plaret, the British envoy in Athens, to the foreign secretary, 11/21/40. A memorandum, apparently written in August 1940, is appended to this and contains numerous details of Storfer's activities. Storfer and his associates are baldly termed agents of the Gestapo.

41. FO 371/25242 W11091, the colonial secretary to the high commissioner, 11/9/40; *ibid.*, the high commissioner to the colonial secretary, 11/18/40.

42. *Ibid.*, 11/9/40. And *ibid*, quoted in the report on the refugees in Haifa port, apparently written by Weizmann, 11/27/40. Weizmann contended that MacMichael's statement turned the refugee deportation question into a major political issue that would determine the postwar status of Palestine. The view of Dexter of the Foreign Office was that the declaration implied "eternal exclusion from Palestine." FO 371/25242 W11766/38/48, 12/2/40.

43. FO 371/25242 W12014, the high commissioner to the colonial secretary, 11/18/40 and 11/23/40. MacMichael believed that it was Weizmann's formal duty to ensure civil peace among the Yishuv. See Zweig 1986, pp. 70–73.

44. *Ibid.*, the high commissioner to the colonial secretary, 11/23/40.

45. FO 371/25242 W72715/38/48, from Berl Locker, head of the Zionist Office in London, to the Foreign Office, 11/9/40.

46. *Ibid.*, 11/14/40, from Butler (Washington) to the Foreign Office.

47. *Ibid.*

48. *Ibid.*, 11/14/40, signature unclear.

49. Cabinet Meeting Summaries (CAB) 65/10, p. 111. The document is found in G. Cohen 1976, pp. 74–76; also FO 371/2542/8159 W12506/38/48, notes by Dexter to the Cabinet decisions, 11/28/40, and by Snow, 11/29/40.

50. The most severe criticism on this matter was that of Latham, in the Foreign Office Refugees Department, 12/28/40 (FO 371/29161 W2714/38/48). Latham attacked both the declaration and the deportation policy as being ineffective as a means of ending illegal immigration: "This is not the place to comment generally upon the arrogant and futile way in which this declaration boldly mortgages the future in order to extricate us from embarrassments due to present timidity or short-sightedness . . . One imagines that the main purpose of this decision was not so much to deter future immigrants as to pacify Arab opinion. . . ." On Latham's suggestions, see below.

51. The document may be found in G. Cohen 1976, p. 177.

52. *Ibid.*, pp. 78–79. Churchill, who opposed the deportation policy, found it necessary to respond to Wavell's message to the war secretary. He disagreed with Wavell's assessment, both with regard to the need to pacify the Arabs and with regard to the violence that would result from the government's actions. His letter to Wavell was quite sharply worded. Wavell, however, was unmoved: *ibid.*, 12/3/40.

53. News clippings from the British press on the *Atlantic* and *Patria* affairs, in CZA S25/2631, and a testimony of a constable at the Atlit detention camp. See also CZA S25/10582, letter from Shertok to Weizmann, 12/2/40, demanding an investigation committee on the behavior of British army and police during the deportation.

54. FO 371/29160 W188, Snow to Downie, 1/14/41. To a request made by Downie, 3/1/41, of McPherson (general secretary of the Palestine administration) to provide evidence for the claim about Nazi agents, McPherson replied (7/8/41): "The police have not been able to find any evidence showing individuals among the illegal immigrants to be enemy agents." CO 733/445/76021/41.

55. FO 371/25242 W12506/38/48, especially Latham's memorandum of 12/28/40, FO 371/29161 W2714 (and see below for further discussion).

56. *Ibid.*

57. See Zweig 1986, pp. 78–82.

58. FO 371/29161 W2714, memorandum of 12/28/40, and notes dating until 4/7/41.

59. CO 733/429/29162, memorandum of the colonial secretary to the Cabinet, 3/28/41, CAB W.P.(41) 74; *ibid.*, memorandum from Downie on this, 3/29/41; *ibid.*, FO 371/29162 W3715/11/48, Foreign Office to the embassy in Washington, 4/3/41.

60. FO 371/29161/9125 W2714. This statement is problematic. The British ought to have feared an even greater wave of refugees once German control was established in the Balkans. They had contended all along that the Germans were forcing the Jews

to leave and that they were supporting illegal immigration to Palestine in order to embarrass the British in their relations with the Arabs. How, then, would the German occupation tend to prevent further illegal aliyah?

Chapter 8

1. For further discussion, see *Pinkas*, pp. 141–177, as well as the introduction to the volume and articles on each of the communities in which the pogroms first took place, such as Jassy, Chernovtsy, and others; cf. HA 14/418, contemporary reports from Rumania.

2. The yellow badge requirement was abolished in August 1941 after an appeal by Wilhelm Filderman, head of the Union of Rumanian Jews, to Ion Antonescu. A month later, however, a new regulation of the same sort was enacted upon the arrival of Gustav Richter, the German embassy's "attaché" for Jewish affairs. Once again, Filderman succeeded in having the order rescinded. For a detailed chronology of anti-Jewish legislation in Rumania, see Pinkas, vol. 1, pp. 128–129.

3. HA 14/418, the appeal by Rumanian Jews to the Jewish Agency on 11/30/41, and Filderman's proposals for Jewish emigration, as submitted to Tozen.

4. PRO FO 371/29168 W9120, Weizmann to Churchill on 2/7/41 and Churchill's reply, 2/12/41.

5. *Ibid.*, 11/20/41. The British reply was a polite no: they had no intention of altering their Palestine policy. *Ibid.*, Downie to Snow, 2/4/41. The British were willing to negotiate, in consultation with the Palestine high commissioner, over the validity of unused immigration certificates issued to Rumanian Jews before diplomatic relations were broken off.

6. See note 4; cf. Weizmann's letter to Churchill. The letter illustrates Weizmann's approach to Zionist policy. He wished to avoid a situation in which aliyah bet would once again constitute the main body of Jewish immigration to Palestine. At that point, it would seem that the Foreign and Colonial Offices were aware that Weizmann and some other Zionist leaders did not favor aliyah bet and would stop it.

7. See Chapter 4 of *The Sakariya Expedition*, "The Voyage of the Pencho."

8. FO 371/29261 W5762, Boyd to Eyers on 5/9/41; CO 733/445, 2/1/41. The Colonial Office memorandum stated that, given the current conditions for Jews in the Balkans, deportation of illegal immigrants to Mauritius would encourage illegal immigration.

9. CZA S25/2193; FO 371/29261 W5095, report on the *Pizet*, which sank without passengers during a return trip from Palestine on 5/16/41; report by the Palestine censor's bureau on immigrant boats in the Mediterranean on 5/13/41.

10. HA 14/721, Shind's report; FO 371/29160 W2506 12/4/40 and 1/1/41. In the British intelligence report, it was stated that ships called *Struma* and *Strotima* were intended for use in aliyah bet, but apparently these are variants of the *Struma*'s name. A cable of 10/19/40 from the ambassador in Sofia reported to Rendel that the *Struma* was intended for transportation of 500 illegal immigrants.

11. CZA S25/2616, Shertok to the director-general, 1/13/42. Wasserstein 1979 (see no. 29, p. 143), reports somewhat different details about the boat. According to his information, it was built at Newcastle in 1867, weighing 204 tons, and first listed with Lloyd's in 1874 under the name *Xanta*. In 1895, it appeared in a list of yachts under the name *Sea Maid*. In 1902, its name was again changed to the *Kasptireus,* and Greek registry replaced the old British registry. In 1934 (the last time it acquired a new

registration), it was christened *Esperos* and registered in Bulgaria. David Ben-Yaakov Stoliar, the sole survivor of its sinking, testified that the boat was owned by Pandelis. This corroborates other information about the course of events as described by Ze'ev Shind (see below).

12. CZA S6/42969, report dated 11 January 1942; HA 14/712, report by one of the *Struma* immigrants who disembarked in Istanbul on 1/20/42; FO 371/32665 W8572/657/68, testimony of David Ben Yaakov Stoliar, survivor of the sinking on 5/3/42; testimony of Perah Gani, J.A. Groups of Betar members from the provinces reached Bucharest and demanded to be included among the passengers.

13. CZA S6/42969 dated 1/11 and 1/21/42 and HA 14/712, testimony of Stoliar.

14. *Ibid.*

15. *Ma'ariv,* 5/14/65, Israel Dinari in "Interview of the Week," interviewed by Rafael Bashan.

16. FO 371/32665 W9936, statement by Ben-Yaakov Stoliar.

17. My account of the ship's departure and the course of the voyage to Istanbul is based on a number of letters and statements by passengers who disembarked in January 1942. These date from the 8, 9, 11, 13, 21, and 30 January and are in CZA S6/42969 and HA 14/712. There are also recollections of those involved recorded in subsequent years, such as Dinari's statement about Stoliar (see notes 13 and 15).

18. CZA S6/42969, letters from the *Struma* dated 8, 9, and 13 January 1942.

19. HA 14/288, anonymous statement on the *Struma* by an immigrant arriving in Palestine on 2/10/42.

20. Letters from the *Struma* (see note 17).

21. We have two accounts of this event. One is in David Stoliar's statement to the British police; the second is the statement of a Palestine resident who was in Constantinople and received the information from a Turkish eyewitness (see HA 14/288).

22. J. Rohwer, *Die Versenkung der Judischen Fluchtlingstrans porte Struma und Mefkura im Schwarzen Meer, February 1942–August 1944* (Frankfurt/Main: 1964) (henceforth Rohwer 1964.) The results of the study are summarized on pp. 96–99. This is a meticulous and reliable work that sets out to prove that it was not German hands that sank the *Struma*. At the same time, a Turkish merchant vessel was also sunk, as noted in Soviet records. In February 1942, no German warships or submarines were yet active in the vicinity of the Bosporus.

23. CZA, Minutes, 35 I, statement by Shapira.

24. CZA S25/2616, Shertok to Luria, 1/13/42, and appeals sent to Shertok from Turkey, London, and the rabbinate in Palestine. Cf. S25/4296, correspondence with Luria, 1/13/42; S25/2515, cables dated 21 and 23 January 1942.

25. *Ibid.,* Minutes, 35 I, 1/25/42: Shertok reports on his meeting of 1/19/42 and reveals his basic approach. He was still optimistic, pointing out that one of the passengers had been granted a tourist visa for Palestine, which might be used to set a precedent in further talks with McPherson. Cf. S6/2496 on 1/30/42.

26. CZA, Minutes, 35 I.

27. *Ibid.,* especially the statements of Rabbi Fishman, Ben-Zvi and Dobkin.

28. *Ibid.,* S25/2616, Shertok to McPherson, 2/13/42, and S6/42969a on 2/12/42, both reports of delegations.

29. It should be noted that the activities of the Agency representatives in London were not entirely without influence. That week, there was a growth of feeling in the Foreign Office in favor of greater flexibility and the suggestion was made to bring the

matter to the Cabinet on February 18. On that session and the preceding Eden-Moyne discussion, see below. Cf. the passage from Weizmann's letter cited in Avneri 1985, p. 313.

30. CZA S26/2616 on 2/14/42.

31. *Ibid.*, 2/15 and 2/22/42.

32. CZA S25/2616, statement by the *Struma* captain.

33. Interview with Avigur, Tel Aviv, June 1977.

34. HA, Shind testimony, 14/714, p. 2; also 14/319, memorandum of conversation between Slutsky and Shechter (Yehieli), 10/22/41, and a cable from Goldin authorizing the purchase on 11/6/41.

35. *Ibid.*, Shind testimony, 14/714, which is the main source for reconstructing this phase of the events.

36. *Ibid.*, p. 5.

37. FO 371/29162 W5097, from the CO to the refugees section, report dated 5/15/41; and FO 371/29162 W6030, 5/10/41; the high commissioner to the colonial secretary, 5/19/41; FO 371/29162 W6039, reply of the colonial secretary to the high commissioner on 5/27/41. This correspondence contains reports on a group of refugees from Budapest and its efforts to reach Palestine, with the help of HIAS and the JDC. Reported as well are attempts to arrange contracts with Bulgarian and Greek shipping agents; workshops for the production of forged passports and entry visas for Latin American countries; and in FO 371/29162 W6600, the activities of the *Pizet* in aliyah bet work as well as those of a second boat, the *Crainuo,* which brought twelve passengers from Constantsa to Palestine.

38. FO 371/29162 W4734 and FO 371/29162 W2180. There are no corroborating sources for this contention.

39. *Ibid.*, and see officials' handwritten comments on MacMichael's proposal, from 10/12/47 to 10/27/41.

40. *Ibid.*, FO 371/29162 W5313 on 12/20/41.

41. *Ibid.*

42. *Ibid.*, 12/22/41.

43. *Ibid.*

44. FO 371/291612, W15313, Boyd to Edward Walker on 12/23/41.

45. FO 371/29162, W15571 on 12/24/41, Moyne to Low.

46. FO 371/29162, W15313. It ought to be noted that a handwritten note to Moyne's letter states that for reasons connected with public opinion in the United States, it would be unwise for Britain to appear to request that the Turks turn away refugees. The signature, dated 12/26/41, is unclear, but was probably Snow's.

47. FO 371/29162, W15571.

48. FO 371/29162, W15313: "I said that H.M.G. saw no reason why the Turkish Government should not send the *Struma* back into the Black Sea *if they wished*" [emphasis added].

49. FO 371/29162, W2093.

50. *Ibid.*

51. *Ibid.*

52. *Ibid.*

53. *Ibid.*, comment by Randall, handwritten, 2/12/42.

54. *Ibid.*, comment, handwritten, 2/11/42.

55. *Ibid.*, Snow's remarks of 2/11/42, and Baxter's handwritten notes.

56. FO 371/29162, W2482 on 2/16/42.

57. FO 371/30/260 W9915 P.M., Eden to the prime minister. There were some

Foreign Office officials who opposed bringing the issue before the Cabinet because of Lord Moyne's hostile and firm position and his considerable influence among his Cabinet colleagues.

58. *Ibid.*, Passport Control Office (PCO), Istanbul, to the Foreign Office.

59. Turkish government policy has until now been alluded to only indirectly, in the context of discussions on British or Zionist policy. It nonetheless seems worthwhile to examine briefly the steps taken by the Ankara government to formulate policy guidelines. The analysis here is based largely on the British and Zionist records. Turkish sources, though perhaps crucial to this discussion, are unfortunately inaccessible.

60. Barlas, 1975, appendix, documents 232 and 234; regulations broadcast by radio and in the press explaining the implementation of the Council of Ministers' decision on 1/30/41 to permit refugees to travel through the country.

61. CZA A203, private papers of Shimon Brod, on his contacts with the Turkish authorities and their attitude to his activities.

62. FO 371/29161 W2503/11/48, the Foreign Office to the secretary of the embassy in Turkey, 3/26/41.

63. CO 733 430, the Foreign Office to Rendel in Sofia, and notes by Foreign Office officials in response to the Bulgarian charges against Turkey. Cf. *ibid.*, the correspondence between Istanbul and the high commissioner in Palestine about the survivors of the *Salvador*.

64. *Ibid.* The three boats did not get provisions in Istanbul and required assistance at Greek ports; cf. FO 371/29161 W2661/11/48, Bennett to Knatchbull-Hugessen, 3/6/41.

65. CZA S25/2616. I have not been able to locate this letter, but large extracts are quoted in a second letter by the captain, dated 1/10/42. The first had been written on 12/24/41, nine days after the ship arrived in Istanbul. British records also allude to two letters.

66. FO 371/312662 W3593, Knatchbull-Hugessen to the Foreign Office on 3/2/41. He describes the Turkish approach and their attitude.

67. CZA S25/2616, the extension of the war.

68. *Ibid.* Reports to that effect based on Turkish sources are cited in the report of the journalist Agronsky concerning his visit to Turkey during the period following the sinking of the *Struma*, 3/24/42; cf. FO 371/32661/9915 W3027, Knatchbull-Hugessen to the Foreign Office on 1/26/42.

69. *Ibid.*

70. FO 371/32661 W9923. A letter from the Foreign Office to the Washington embassy on 3/4/42 hints that the Germans were behind the deportation and the Turks' refusal to allow children to disembark, out of anti-British motives. The British documents themselves are divided on this point, however. There is no substantiation in German records, though at this stage there is clearly no possibility of resolving the question, particularly without examining Turkish records.

71. A more detailed analysis of Turkey's position, as Knatchbull-Hugessen saw it, is contained in his letter to the Foreign Office, FO 371/32661 W9923, W3593, on 3/8/42. He was asked to offer a further explanation of the affair for public consumption, and he demonstrates a remarkable understanding of the Turkish position.

Chapter 9

1. Information on the small boats may be found in scattered reports on Rumanian emigration: CZA S25/2492, 2493; HA 14/60; and British records FO 371 CO 733, the

report of the high commissioner, and reports by consulates and the embassy in Turkey to the Foreign Office.

2. CZA S25/2492, Aliyah Department, Bulletin no. 8.

3. *Ibid.*, and S25/2616, the report by Agronsky (reporter of the *Jerusalem Post*) on his trip to Turkey, 3/23/42.

4. The Turks contended that the refugees were causing deliberate damage to the boats in order to linger in Turkey rather than continue by sea.

5. HA 14/60.

6. *Pinkas*, vol. 1, p. 183; C. Browning, 1978, pp. 170–74.

7. On American Jewish opinion and its influence, especially after the *Struma* incident, see: the detailed report of the British ambassador, Lord Halifax, dated 7/2/1942, FO 371/32680/9609 W4048, in which he is presenting public opinion polls among American public since February 1942. The main conclusions of the polls were that the *Struma* disaster placed Britain in conflict with all of its earlier declarations, with its efforts to win American sympathy, with the Atlantic Charter, and with the struggle for human rights.

8. FO 371/32680 W3963.

9. *Ibid.* It is worth noting the remark by N. Butler, of that Foreign Office section: "From the point of view of North American Department, Lord Cranborne's solution is clearly the preferable one, though the statement does not strike me as a good propaganda document. For American consumption I would have preferred it to start with a general statement, viz., that the development of the war and the calculated brutality of Axis authorities . . . had rendered a modification of the policy necessary."

10. *Ibid.* Note the bluntness of the statement: "If we antagonize the Arabs they are free to change sides so to speak, and throw in their lot with the Axis who will certainly be ready to welcome them. If on the other hand we antagonize the Jews, they have no such alternative, and will be forced still to adhere to our cause, since the whole of their racial future is wrapped up in our victory. Every Jew must realise this, including the Zionists in the U.S.A."

11. *Ibid.*, especially note by Randall.

12. *Ibid.*, summary of the Cabinet meeting and its decisions, 3/5/1942.

13. *Ibid.*, Parliamentary Question—Loss of *Struma*, March 10, 1942.

14. CO 733/445/76201-1942, Luke, 3/13 and 3/18/1942.

15. FO 371/32662/9221 W3820/625/45, 3/19/1942.

16. FO 371/32662 W4351/652/48.

17. CO 733/445/76201-1942. MacMichael's reply contains the following interesting statement: "I think that your suggestion in effect amounts to saying that while we must firmly maintain the ban on illegal immigrants, avoid the issue by making it legal."

18. *Ibid.*, cable to MacMichael, 3/21/42.

19. FO 371/32662/9221 W4486/652/48, Randall, 3/24/42; *ibid.*, W4632, 3/26/42; *ibid.*, letter from Lady Dugdale to the Colonial Office, 3/24/42.

20. *Ibid.*, and the reply by Baxter of the Foreign Office: "To ask the Turks to allow these people to proceed overland would mean that we should be definitely encouraging illegal immigration (and not merely refraining from discouraging it)."

21. *Ibid.*, Cranborne to Gregg, 3/28/42, and notes to a discussion with representatives of the Board of Deputies of British Jews, 3/31/42 (notes continuing to 4 April); *ibid.*, W7320/104/48, memoranda and notes by Foreign Office personnel referring to the proposals of 5/14/42 and 5/15/42; and CO 733/445/76021-1942, notes dated 3/28/42 and 4/10/42, in connection with a suggestion to raise the issue of refuge at a conference of East African leaders; Luke's summation of opinion at the War and

Foreign Offices on this matter, dated 4/17/42, and CO 733/448/76155, MacMichael to Colonial Office, 4/23/42.

22. CO 733/445/76021–1942, notes by Luke, Boyd, and others during 4/8/42 to 5/4/42.

23. FO 371/32665 W7549/652/48, Randall to the foreign secretary, 5/8/42, and Cranborne's reply. It should be noted how much weight he assigned to the opinion of the high commissioner, both within the Colonial Office and in presenting his position to other departments. Shertok was undoubtedly correct in his assessment that much of Britain's inflexibility was the result of MacMichael's stance.

24. For example, in Cranborne's proposal he stated that "batches" of refugees ought to be released from detention. This was corrected to refer not to groups but to individuals, and stress laid on the requirement for security clearance prior to release of such refugees: FO 371/32665 W6531, from the War Office to the minister in Cairo, 4/28/42; *ibid.*, W7459, Harvey to the Colonial Office, 5/6/42, notes on style regarding the secrecy provision.

25. FO 371/32665 W7846, 5/26/1942, and Foreign Office response, *ibid.*, 5/29/42, cable from the consul-general in Izmir to the ambassador in Ankara regarding the public auction of the *Euxine*. The Jewish community wished to purchase it, in order to furnish refugees with funds to reach Cyprus, but hesitated because collective fund-raising was illegal. They therefore turned to the consul asking for assistance. See *ibid.*, W9805, Knatchbull-Hugessen to the Foreign Office, 7/11/42, on obtaining a vessel for the refugees of the *Dordeval*.

26. See Luke's report of his talk with Berl Locker on funding the transfer of the *Euxine* refugees to Cyprus: CO 733/455/7602-1942, 7/21/42. After submitting a detailed report on the discussion, he summed up: "I record my strong impression, in which Mr. Boyd concurs, that Mr. Locker did not seem to think much of the proposal but rather was trying to turn the situation to his own account with a view of [*sic*] getting these refugees into Palestine." See also Luke's report on a discussion with Professor Namier on the question of two refugee boats that arrived from Rumania on 9/9/42. When Luke portayed Britain's position, that it would neither take responsibility nor an active role in determining the refugees' fate, "Prof. Namier at once brushed this point aside as of no importance. He said that he quite understood when concessions were made, that it was always necessary to explain that they were not to be regarded as precedents . . . " See also the colonial secretary's letter to MacMichael, 6/2/42: FO 371/32664/9929 W4459/652/48; *ibid.*, W7608, Boyd to Linton, 6/3/42.

27. FO 371/32666 W12420, Knatchbull-Hugessen to the Foreign Office, 9/12/42.

28. *Ibid.*, reply of the Foreign Office to Ankara, 9/19/42; and *ibid.*, Boyd to Randall on the same matter, 9/18/42. Boyd asks Randall to draft a clearer text, so there should be no doubt whatsoever in the Turks' minds that the refugees were not to be deported.

29. *Ibid.* Note that this was written by Boyd, from the Colonial Office, whose extreme opposition to concessions over aliyah bet was well known up to May 1942. In a draft of the letter to be found in Colonial Office files (CO 733/445/76021) Boyd concluded this passage with the following emphasis phrase: "We realise the embar-rassing implication of this action, but we have gone so far already in interesting ourselves in the fate of the illegal immigrants who may be landed in Turkey that we have already assumed, as was recognised in the *Dordeval* and *Euxine* and other more recent cases, responsibility for their welfare. . . . "

30. FO 371/32666 W12988, Knatchbull-Hugessen to the Foreign Office, 9/29/42; and especially Randall to Boyd, FO 371/32667 W13686/653/48, 10/14/42.

31. *Ibid.,* 10/13/42. Tension was caused by news of the *Vitorul* and four other boats that were about to depart, and by the arrival of the *Dora* (see above).

32. FO 371/32666 W11413, 10/16/42, Helms (of the embassy) to Randall at the Foreign Office.

33. FO 371/32667 W13686.

34. CO 733/445/76021-1942.

35. FO 371/32662 W15790/652/48, the Foreign Office to Angora (Ankara), 12/8/42; the reply from Ankara, *ibid.,* W17422, 12/23/42.

36. For further discussion, see Chapter 10.

37. *Haboker, Haaretz, Davar,* and *Hatzofeh* of 3/11/42.

38. It should be noted that the high commissioner believed that the Yishuv was capable even of revolt against Britain should another incident like the *Struma* occur. See FO 371/32663/9929 W4486, cable to Cranborne, 3/20/42.

39. On the *Darien,* see above; on cooperation with the Allies in the Balkans, see Gelber 1983, vol. 3, pp. 133–207. For information about the envoys and emissaries, see: HA 14/60, on events in Turkey, signed by Z. Dani (code name for Ze'ev Shind), June 1942.

40. *Ibid.,* 14/492, meetings of 7/30 and 8/7/42.

41. *Ibid.,* meeting of 8/7/42, meeting of 9/12/42.

42. CZA, Minutes 35I, 2/26/42. It is interesting that the British believed that the Zionist leaders would seek to use the incident while it was fresh in order to win political concessions: "The Jewish Agency are [*sic*] trying to take advantage of this situation," Baxter suggested (PRO FO 371/3266/9915 W3116, 3/6/42).

43. CZA, Minutes 35I, 2/26/42.

44. *Ibid.,* meetings of 3/19 and 4/14–16/42 and 6/14/42; FO 371/32662/9921 W3820, Abba Hillel Silver's discussion with Randall 3/16/1942, in which he stated explicitly that the injustices done in the *Struma* case might be righted with the release of the *Darien* group. Dr. Silver spoke of Jewish opinion in the United States: "Some of the harm that had been done in the United States would be undone if we could deal with the refugees who had been languishing in a cage in Palestine for the last ten months." See the letter from Lady Dugdale to Cranborne, 3/24/42. See also Discussions in the Mapai secretariat, BBA 42/42, 11/9/42.

45. See FO 371/32663/9924 W4632, notes, 3/24/42; and *ibid.,* position of the Middle East desk; and *ibid.,* W4608, see the letter from Lady Dugdale to Cranborne, 3/24/42.

46. CZA, Minutes 35II, 5/31/42, Shertok on the Agency's assistance in transferring refugees to Cyprus.

47. *Ibid.,* 6/14/42.

48. CZA, Minutes 35II. On the lagging formal talks of this kind, see D. Ofer, *Pe'ulot 'ezra vehatzalah shel ha-mishlahat ha-Eretz Yisraelit lekushta, 1943* (Hebrew), (*Help and Rescue Activities of the Palestinian Delegation in Constantinople, 1943*), Master's Thesis, Hebrew University, Jerusalem, 1972, Chapter 6, Par. 3.

49. A thorough discussion of the Hebrew Press reports appears in Y. Gelber, "Ha-itonut ha-ivrit beEretz Yisrael al hashmadat yehudei Europa 1941–42" (Hebrew), ("Hebrew Journalism in Palestine on the Destruction of European Jewry 1941–42,") *Research Papers on the Holocaust and Resistance,* New Series, Collection A, Tel Aviv, 1970, pp. 30–58.

50. CZA L22/134; see also L22/10; L22/103, Lichtheim's letters to Linton in London.

51. CZA, Minutes 35II, 8/16/42.

52. *Ibid.*

Chapter 10

1. Arad, Yizhak, Gutman, Israel, and Margaliot, Avraham (eds.), *Documents on the Holocaust,* New York, 1982 (henceforth Arad 1982), p. 116.

2. C. Browning 1978, pp. 67–73.

3. YVA TR 3–573, Killinger to the German Foreign Office, and cf. Rohwer 1964, pp. 36–37.

4. YVA, TR3-141, Luther, 2/25/42; also Luther to the embassy in Paris, 3/5/42.

5. *Ibid.,* TR3-571.

6. See Chapter 9.

7. Rohwer 1964, pp. 38–41, and see the table of boats in the appendix.

8. It should be noted that, through Radu Lecca, the Rumanians were directly involved in planning the deportation of Jews. On Lecca's role, see Jean Ancel, "Plans for Deportation of Rumanian Jews and their Discontinuation in Light of Documentary Evidence (July–October 1942)" in *Yad Vashem Studies* 16, 1984, pp. 299–333 (henceforth Ancel 1984). An interesting aspect of Lecca's proposals is the option of deporting some to Palestine as part of the overall plan for deportation to the east. Cf. YVA TR 3–178, Killinger to the Foreign Office, German department, 8/28/42; on Lecca's visit to Berlin, see Browning 1972, *op. cit.,* pp. 125–127.

9. *Ibid.*

10. YVA TR 3-178 and TR 3-401, Killinger to the Foreign Office, 12/12/42.

11. Hilberg 1967, p. 505.

12. It is difficult to assess the precise effect of the German reverses at the Russian front on Rumania's attitude toward the Jewish issue. By the end of 1942, Antonescu no longer believed in an eventual German victory. This does not necessarily explain his attitude in the late summer and early fall of that year, however. Recent scholarship tends to focus on Antonescu's reluctance to deport Jews from the Regat and, therefore, on his willingness to consider the legal and nationalistic arguments against the deportations raised by Filderman and others. This did not prevent him from allowing the respective German and Rumanian representatives to pursue joint plans for deportations (see note 9, above). Jean Ancel, in the essay cited above, considers U. S. Secretary of State Cordell Hull's message to Bucharest appealing for an end to the Transnistria deportations to have been particularly important, as was the New Year's message to the Jews of Rumania. For further discussion, see Ephraim Ofir, *Ha-tenu'ah ha-ztiyonit beRomaniah bemilhemet ha-olam ha-sheniyah* (Hebrew), *(The Zionist Movement in Rumania During the Second World War)*, Ph.D. thesis, The Hebrew University, Jerusalem, 1984 (henceforth Ofir 1984); Aryeh Steinberg, *Ha-hebetim ha-benleumim shel ha-hagirah ha-yehudit miRomaniyah vedarkha, 1938–1947* (Hebrew), *(International Aspects of Jewish Emigration From and Through Rumania, 1938–1947)*, Ph.D. thesis, University of Haifa, Haifa, 1984 (henceforth Steinberg 1984). See also Martin Broszat, "Das dritte Reich und die rumaenische Juden Politik" *Gutachten des Instituts fur Zietgeschichte,* I, pp. 102–183 (1958).

13. Wilhelm Filderman (1882–1963) dedicated his efforts throughout the war years to a political and legal battle to save Jews. A lawyer by profession, he was a political activist and former classmate of Ion Antonescu, and head of the Union of Rumanian Jews. He also served as the representative of the JDC in Rumania and was the non-Zionist representative of Rumania on the expanded board of the Jewish Agency. In

March 1943, he was deported to Transnistria for protesting government policy, and he helped organize a wide-ranging rescue operation there.

14. For the Transnistria episode, see *Pinkas*, pp. 349–388; numerous reports in HA 14/418; Hava Wagman Eshkoly, "Tokhnit Transnistriyah: hizdamnut hatzalah o hona'ah?" (Hebrew), ("The Transnistria Plan: Rescue Opportunity or extortion?") *Yalkut moreshet* 27 (1979), pp. 155–171; Ephraim Ofir, "Ha'im nitan hayah lehatzil 70,000 yehudei Transnistriyah?" (Hebrew), ("Was it possible to Save the 70,000 Jews of Transnistria?") *Yalkut Moreshet* 31 (1981), pp. 108–128 (Henceforth Ofir 1981). Ofir examined sources not previously investigated by other writers on the subject. Dina Porat, *Hanhagah bemilkud* (Hebrew), (*An Entangled Leadership*,) Tel Aviv, 1986, (henceforth Porat 1986), pp. 309–328.

15. It should be noted that the negotiations were not conducted directly by those Rumanian figures who generally aided and profited from Jewish emigration, such as the interior ministry and the Siguaranza (the Rumanian secret police). The only official personally connected with the negotiations from 11/22 on was Radu Lecca. Lecca, in charge of Jewish affairs for the Rumanian government, was also at this time a German agent who furnished information to Richter. Tester and Burstyn, too, were apparently German informants, though there is no clear proof. From conflicting versions it is difficult to determine what the official line actually was. The information given to the Jewish organizations in Constantinople on 11/26 and in Geneva on 12/4 indicates, however, what the Jewish leaders understood the offer to include.

16. YVA TR 3-401.

17. *Ibid.*, TR 3-402.

18. Ofir 1981. Fildermann proposed the idea to K. Bursan, who had first approached him on the Transnistria plan, in the hope he would use his connections with Mihai Antonescu.

19. YVA TR 3-402.

20. On these emigration plans, see Chapter 8 and Chapter 12.

21. YVA TR 3-667 and TR 3-830. On personnel changes in the German section of the Foreign Office, see Browning, 1978, pp. 147–154.

22. YVA TR 3-400; cf. Browning, pp. 170–174.

23. CZA L 15/110, Barlas to Linton, 3/18/43; YVA TR 3-200, Eichmann to the Foreign Office, 3/10/43; *ibid.*, TR 3-232, Killinger to the Foreign Office, 4/4/43; *ibid.*, TR 3-949, Richter and Killinger to Eichmann, 4/9/43.

24. *Ibid.*, TR 3-232, Killinger to the Foreign Office, 4/4/43.

25. *Ibid.*, TR 3-231. In addition, the same report noted that the Turks had granted 20,000 transit visas to Bulgarian Jews. These incorrect reports were based on partial information. Thus, the transit camp idea was constantly but unsuccessfully raised by Jewish organizations in discussions with the Turks. The 20,000 figure is vastly exaggerated.

26. YVA TR 3-981, Sofia to Berlin, 4/10/43; cf. Browning, pp. 170–174.

27. YVA TR 3-1038.

28. Ibid., TR 3-982, Eichmann to the Foreign Office. Jewish sources mention the *Smyrni* only in the fall of 1943, but at this time there is already discussion about a ship in the port of Braila. See Chapter 13.

29. Rohwer 1964, p. 41; Barlas 1975, pp. 190–191.

30. YVA JM–2218/K 212749; Rohwer, 1964, p. 43. It is stated here that the permit for the children's departure was granted by the foreign minister, but elsewhere it is asserted that Hitler himself gave his approval: see Joseph Tennenbaum, *Race and Reich*, New York, 1956, p. 315.

31. Rohwer 1964, pp. 42–43.

32. YVA TR 3-398; Barlas 1975, p. 268; NAR Ref. 840.48/5348, memorandum of the American ambassador in Turkey to the State Department.

33. The document is quoted in German by Rohwer 1964, p. 45, and in Hebrew by Barlas 1975, p. 191. Cf. YVA TR 3–398, von Thadden to Killinger, 6/1/43. In his reply, Killinger emphasized that he constantly assured the marshal that the German government was prepared to accept all "superfluous" Jews for labor camps in the east.

34. For a full discussion of the problems involved in bringing Jews out, from the Jewish and Allied points of view, see Chapters 12 and 13.

35. YVA TR 3-743, Wagner to the Foreign Minister, 7/21/43.

36. The plan, mentioned in German records, has not received wide scholarly attention. It apparently began with the British government's request that Switzerland, which represented British interests in Germany, intercede with the German authorities to secure safe conduct for the rescue of children from Bulgaria. The material we have does not make it clear whether there was any connection between the various requests that reached the German ministries. The Germans seem to have ascribed them to a concerted effort by the Allies to take Jews out of Europe, and were determined to oppose such an effort.

37. YVA TR 3-743.

38. *Ibid.,* TR 3-220, von Thadden reports on his discussion with Eichmann, dated 5/14/43. Eichmann explained that if the agencies concerned did not make a decision quickly, there would be no young Jews left in Europe to trade for German citizens. There are those who connect the transfer of 1,000 children from Bialystok to Theresienstadt in August 1943 with such an exchange plan. See, e.g., Livia Rotkirchen, *Hurban yahadut slovakia* (Hebrew), Jerusalem, 1961 *(The Destruction of Slovak Jewry)*, pp. 31–32 and n. 127.

39. For a detailed discussion, see Chapter 13.

40. There are various sources on the *Tari* affair. Apart from correspondence between the German Foreign Office and the embassy in Ankara, and the correspondence on the matter between the Foreign Office and the RSHA, there are the records of the U. S. State Department—correspondence with its envoy in Ankara, with the Red Cross, and between the War Refugee Board and its special representative, Ira Hirschmann. Jewish sources include Barlas's correspondence and Mossad records. The subject is extensively covered in British Foreign Office records, too. Turkish records were unavailable, so the Turkish position has been outlined here from other sources.

41. For a detailed discussion of the War Refugee Board and American policy, see Chapter 14.

42. YVA TR 3-667 and TR 3-1397, von Thadden to von Papen, 3/25/44; NAR 840.48 Ref/ 4-1744, Hirschmann's report on his contacts with Ambassador Steinhardt regarding the ship.

43. YVA TR 3-667.

44. *Ibid.*

45. Rohwer 1964, pp. 46–56. Rohwer himself does not indicate the link between General Doenitz's order and Marshal Antonescu's position.

46. YVA TR 3-667, Killinger to the Foreign Office.

47. See note 116 in Chapter 13.

48. On the organization of these ships, see Chapter 13, and on the *Mefkura* itself, see Rohwer 1964, p. 63.

49. Rohwer 1964, pp. 92–93.

50. HA 14/67; YVA *Mefkura* file; M. Resel, *Tik Mefkura* (Hebrew), (*The Mefkura File*,) Tel Aviv, 1981 (henceforth Ressel 1981).

51. Rohwer 1964, pp. 68–69; YVA TR 3-1527: Killinger urged Antonescu to strictly enforce the Jewish policy agreed to between himself (Antonescu) and the Führer.

Chapter 11

1. Michael B. Weissmandl, *Min ha-maytzar* (Hebrew) (*From the Straits*) Jerusalem, 1960 (Origin Brakhot 5,2).

2. CZA, Minutes, 36II, 11/22/42, Shertok.

3. The press of the time is full of proposals by individuals and organizations spelling out what might be done to help the Jews of occupied Europe, including dispatching volunteers to the ghettos to organize resistance, and other means of demonstrating the Yishuv's desire to join its brethren in their hour of need. There are letters to the kibbutz central offices, to members of the Jewish Agency executive, and to the executive committee of the Histadrut offering to serve in a personal capacity and outlining plans of action. The opinion of many historians is that the Yishuv was prepared to do a great deal, but the leadership found it difficult to formulate concrete plans. See Porat 1986, pp. 2–101; Shabbtai Beit Zvi, *Ha-zionut ha-post ugandit bemashber ha-shoah* (Hebrew), (*Post-Uganda Zionism in the Crisis of the Holocaust*), Tel Aviv, 1977.

4. I reach this conclusion based on my analysis of countless utterances of Jewish Agency executive members, members of the Mapai central committee, and the Histadrut executive. This also emerges from discussions of the small Zionist executive council meeting of 1/18/43: CZA S25/259.

5. David Frankel, *Beterm shoah: Ha-mediniut ha-zionit khlapei metzukat yehudei Europa lenokhah shilton ha-nazim beGermaniyah* (Hebrew), (*Pre-Holocaust Zionist Policy vis-à-vis the Distress of European Jewry in the Face of the Nazi Regime in Germany*,) Master's Thesis, Hebrew University, Jerusalem, 1983.

6. Porat, 1986, pp. 2–101.

7. BBA, 24/43, meeting of 4/22/43.

8. LA, secretariat meeting, 2/10/43.

9. CZA S25/259, meeting of the small Zionist executive council, 1/18/43.

10. *Ibid.*, and LA, meetings of the Histadrut executive, 2/10/43.

11. *Ibid.*

12. BBA, 24/43, 4/24/43; CZA, Minutes 36II, 11/29/42, 37II, 9/12/43.

13. BBA, 24/43, meeting of 2/10/43.

14. Toward the end of 1942, reports about the fate of European Jewry were being received so frequently, and from such a variety of sources, that they could not be dismissed. On 10/7/42, Lord Cranborne informed the House of Lords of the formation of an Allied war crimes commission to investigate Nazi atrocities. Mass extermination of Jews by gassing was brought up at a meeting of the Cabinet during November, in a general discussion of war crimes. Pressure mounted for Britain to officially condemn the Nazis' crimes against Jews. In December, this was discussed in London by Foreign Secretary Eden and the Soviet ambassador, Ivan Maiskii. Jews stepped up their pressure on the American embassy in London, and the Archbishop of Canterbury demanded a public British condemnation of the Nazis, accompanied by threats of postwar retribution. During those weeks another report was submitted, this time by the Polish government-in-exile, which clarified and further substantiated (through several

sources) the facts about the mass murder of Jews. Winston Churchill took up the matter with Anthony Eden, undoubtedly spurring intergovernmental consultations about a joint declaration. Eden submitted a draft declaration on 14 December, which was duly approved by the Cabinet. The declaration was issued in the name of the eleven countries at war with Germany, including the Free French underground. The declaration was read in Parliament by Eden in response to a prearranged interpolation by Sidney Silverman, MP.

15. A wide-ranging discussion of the organization of the committee appears in Porat, 1986, pp. 101–117.

16. See H. Barlas, "Mivtsah Aliyat Lita" (Hebrew), "Operation Lithuanian Aliyah," *Dapim leheker ha-Shoah vehamered* (Hebrew), *Research Papers on the Holocaust and Resistance*, New Series, Collection A, Tel Aviv, 1970, pp. 246–255. (henceforth Barlas 1970) We use Constantinople instead of Istanbul when the sources use the Hebrew name "*kushta*."

17. CZA, Minutes 36I, of meetings of 11/23 and 29/42 and S25/1833, meeting of the Zionist executive council of 1/18/43; also BBA 23/43, secretariat meeting of 3/24 and 3/30/43; see also Porat, 1986, pp. 202–209.

18. Wasserstein 1979, pp. 122–134, and see note 15.

19. BBA, Mapai central committee, 24/43. Especially noteworthy are the remarks by Shertok on 4/22/43.

20. *Ibid.,* 24/42, secretariat and central committee meeting of 11/24/42, especially the remarks of Dobkin; *ibid.,* 24/43, meeting of 4/23/43; CZA S25/1833, meeting of the Zionist executive council of 5/28/43, especially remarks by Shertok; *ibid.,* L-15 110I, cable dated 1/7/43, opposing the agreement to transfer refugees to Cyprus.

21. BBA 24/43, secretariat meeting of 4/27/43, remarks by Shertok.

22. Discussion of the mission's approach to rescue matters appears in Ofer 1972, pp. 28–46.

23. For a full discussion of these rescue plans, and of the "trucks for blood" plan, see Porat 1986, pp. 309–392.

24. BBA 26/44, meeting of the political committee, 1/26/44.

25. See Chapter 9.

26. YVA M20/36, Neustadt and Pomerantz to Zilbershein, Schwalb, and Posner.

27. For further discussion on this, see Porat 1986, pp. 217–234.

28. YVA M20/36, see note 26: "As previously, monies sent by the executive are not to be pooled with funds collected by the Histadrut for the sake of the movement. These are two separate agencies, both fiscally and organizationally, and separate accounts must be kept and rendered for [what is spent on] the activities of each. The funds of the executive are intended for aid to all parts of the movement recognized by the Zionist Organization (the World Zionist Organization, Hehalutz, Hano'ar Hatziyoni, Hapo'el Hamizrachi). The funds of the Histadrut are earmarked only for the use of labor Zionist causes." See also Moreshet Archives (MA) D1730, Bader to Bornstein in Geneva, 1/22/43 and 3/9/43.

29. CZA L15/188, letters of David Zimend and Akiva Levinsky to the rescue committee from August to October 1943, especially Vanya Pomerantz, of distorting the historical record in order to play up the role of the left-wing movements in rescue and resistance in Europe.

30. *Ibid.,* Barlas to Magnes, 7/6/44, and to Artzi, from Constantinople, 7/17/44; see also the decisions for joint action with the JDC; the agreement between the Mossad and Barlas dated 7/17/44; and Barlas to Gruenbaum, 8/2/44.

31. Barlas, 1970, pp. 18–26; Ofer 1972.

32. CZA, Minutes, 37II, meeting of 9/19/43 and 38II, 12/19/43 and 1/23/44.

33. Optimism regarding the chances of aliyah from the Balkans, including Croatia and Slovakia, is expressed in a report submitted by Kaplan following a visit to Constantinople. CZA Minutes, 36II, 3/28/43. Kaplan was particularly hopeful on the score of arranging sea and overland transport from the Balkans to Turkey, and was most concerned about preventing a bottleneck between Turkey and Palestine (see p. 8 of the minutes).

34. See Chapter 9.

35. For a full description of the Parachutists Plan, see Gelber 1983, pp. 133–206.

36. *Ibid.*, Yehieli to colleagues, 11/30/42, 12/12/42 and 12/23/42; Shaul Avigur to the Histadrut executive committee, 1/15/43, and 2/2/43.

37. *Ibid.*, Kadmon to Rami, 4/8/43.

38. On the problems relating to the Transnistria Plan and alternatives proposed, see Chapter 10.

39. CZA L15/110, Barlas to Linton, 3/17, and 3/23/43; L110/189, 12/17/43; L15/188, Barlas to Kaplan, 2/15/43, and a summary discussion in letter from Geiger to Barlas, 2/11/44.

40. HA 14/60; and see the letter of Shind to Kadmon, 3/17/43, and Braginsky's criticism of procedures, 7/25/43.

Chapter 12

1. CO 733/436/75113, the high commissioner to the Colonial Office (CO), 12/2/42

2. FO 371/36655 W4236, Foreign Office (FO) to the Washington ambassador, 3/18/43. The cable exemplifies the British approach just prior to the decision to convene the Bermuda Conference (April 1943).

3. See Chapter 10.

4. Zweig 1986, pp. 137–140.

5. FO 371/36677 W4102 3/10 and 3/8/43, NAR 840.48 Ref/3665, 3/16/43, Cordell Hull to the London ambassador.

6. FO 371/36655 W4236, Cable to Washington explaining aims of the plan.

7. PRO, PREM 55/2.

8. FO 371/36676 W850, from Bern (Norton) to the FO, 6/14/43. With hindsight we now know that this step saved the Jews of Bulgaria in the face of German pressure to deport them "to the east," which lasted until September 1943. The German Foreign Office reached the conclusion at that time that only a change in the military situation would convince the Bulgarians to change their minds. On August 30, 1944, the Bulgarian government repealed all anti-Jewish legislation. For a detailed discussion, see Hilberg, pp. 473–484.

9. FO 371/36677, Namier to Boyd, 3/25/43. See the proposals of the Board of Deputies and notes on the talk with Mr. Brodetsky (June 27 and 29) in FO 371/36694 W1178.

10. Boyd wrote to Randall on 3/4/43 that the Colonial Office considered Bulgaria to offer the best chance given the advantage of rail transport to Palestine: FO 371/36621 W4070.

11. FO 371/36676 W850, the FO to Ankara, 1/16/43.

12. FO 371/36654 W3468.

13. *Ibid.*

14. FO 371/36654 W6476, report by Walker on his meeting with Namier and Lady Dugdale.

15. FO 371/36707 W2138, esp. Randall's comments, Walker 1/26 and 2/6/43.

16. FO 371/36707 W5444.

17. FO 371/36607 W3860.

18. FO 371/44082 R2527, Mr. Camp to Mr. Clutton in the FO, and *ibid.*, FO 371/44082 R 4699, FO to Ankara, 3/14/43.

19. *Ibid.*, 36677/W5041, Boyd to Randall, 3/29/43, FO 371/36621 W4070, and letter from Boyd to Randall of 3/9/43, in which he stresses the contradiction between strategic and commercial difficulties and the refugee issue.

20. *Ibid.*, 3/17/43.

21. FO 371/36677 W4329, 3/15/43 Bern to FO; FO 371/36670 W4546, 3/18/43, Ankara to the FO.

22. FO 371/36670 W5444, 3/15/43, Ankara to the FO.

23. For detailed discussion, see Chapter 10.

24. HA, archives of the executive committee, letters from pioneer movement members. Two in particular are clear in the fear of deportation: one signed "Lici," 2/13/43, and another 2/22/43 signed Levana. All letters express the degree of desperation. For more on this, see H. Kechales, *Korot yehudei Bulgaria* (Hebrew), *Annals of Bulgarian Jewry*, Tel Aviv, 1970, vol. 3 (henceforth Kechales 1971, Vol. 3), pp. 89–150.

25. FO 371/36654, Joint Foreign Committee Anglo-Jewish Conference, 4/4/43, and FO 371/36678 W5521, reply to Lord Melchett, 4/9/43; and FO 371/36678 W5719, report of the high commissioner on a meeting with the Va'ad Leumi (Palestine National Council) on April 9; and FO 371/36678 W60101, cable from the Jewish Agency to the colonial secretary, 4/17/43.

26. FO 371/36678 W613.

27. FO 371/36654 4/4/43; FO 371/36636 W9631; FO 371/3662 W8192; and FO 371/36659 W6369; all 4/15/43.

28. FO 371/36678 notes from 4/15/43 to 4/18/43.

29. FO 371/36679 W7309, 5/13/43. Knatchbull-Hugessen referred specifically to his support of Eliezer Kaplan's request, as early as March, that the Turks permit the use of Turkish-owned vessels for refugee transport; and to his joint request (with American Ambassador Steinhardt) to the Turkish authorities to permit temporary refugee transit camps to be erected in Turkey.

30. FO 371/36679 W7064, Bern to the FO, 5/7/43, and FO 371/36679 W7706, 5/21/43; cf. comments by FO officials on the cable from Bern. See also the memorandum of the CO, "Immigration from Bulgaria" (CO 733/449/76028), 5/11/44.

31. FO 371/36679 W6863, War Transport Office to Randall, 5/4/43; FO 371/36680 W2294, FO to Bern, 6/11/43, and dispatch of the same date to Ankara; FO 371/36680 W10282, Henderson's discussion with Namier, 7/14/43.

32. FO 371/36679 W7454 5/17/43, from Ankara to FO; and CO 733/449/76208, Randall to Boyd, 5/17/43, cf. notes on the discussion with Lord Perth (FO 371/3662 W8192). They particularly wanted to avoid a planned interpellation regarding extension of the lease of five British boats (known as the Adana boats) to Turkey.

33. FO 371/36680 W1147, cable no. 1858.

34. For further discussion, see M. Cohen 1978, pp. 160–187.

35. CAB 66/38 Cabinet meeting, and decision 65/35.

36. CO 733/436/55113 (1943).

37. CZA Minutes 36II, 3/28/43, report by Kaplan on his visit to Constantinople;

ibid., S53/230, Epstein's diary of his visit to Constantinople; *ibid.*, L15/110I, Barlas to the Jewish Agency executive, 7/20/43, a concluding report.

38. HA 14/714, report by Shind; *ibid.*, 14/60, "Rami"—i.e., Shind—to colleagues, 3/1/43; unrecorded oral testimony of Teddy Kollek; FO 371/36680, Ankara to the Foreign Office.

39. HA 14/46, Rami to colleagues, 5/17/43.

40. Browning 1978, pp. 170–174 (esp. 174), on the children arrested in Sviligrad; and Chapter 10.

41. HA, archives of the executive committee, 9 March 1943, signed by Nansin and Marco Cohen; 2/12/43, signed by Lici; 2/22/43, signed by Levana; many other letters, unsigned apart from "from the youth organizations," and unclearly dated.

42. *Ibid.*, 14/60 and 14/59, series of letters from Shind to Palestine, especially those written in May, expressing his concern over the situation; CZA L15/110I. Barlas reported this to London in May, emphasizing the difficulties being created by the Bulgarians and the uncertainty regarding their policy.

43. MA D.I.7111, Bader to Venya, 2/22/43; CZA L15/110I, Barlas to Linton, 5/8/43, 5/11/43, and 5/18/43; Kechales 1971 (see note 6, above). Browning 1978, p. 172, letter from Beckerle, the German official assigned to Jewish affairs at the embassy in Sofia, stating that the government would officially permit emigration but would in practice obstruct its implementation and render it impossible.

44. *Ibid.*, 5/7/43 and 5/8/43, signed by Israel.

45. *Ibid.* Particularly noteworthy are the words of Levana and her appraisal of Spasov; *ibid.*, 6/3/43, signed by Israel and, the same date, by Toury.

46. *Ibid.*, 14/60, Rami to colleagues, 7/9/43, and CZA L15/110I, Barlas to the Agency in London, 7/20/43; *ibid.*, L15/86, Barlas to Palestine, 8/9/43.

47. HA 14/714, report by Shind; A. Romano, Y.J. Ben, and N. Levi (eds.), *Encyclopedia shel galuyot* (Hebrew), *Encyclopedia of the Jewish Diaspora*, vol. 10: The Jews of Bulgaria, Tel Aviv, 1970, pp. 856–885, 891–894.

48. CZA L15/86, Barlas to the Agency executive, 9 July 1943; HA 14/59, Teddy to Palestine.

49. FO 371/36680 W9737, Ankara to the FO.

50. *Ibid.*

51. FO 371/36680 W9819, Linton to Henderson, 7/5/43, and Henderson's reply, 7/9/43. FO 371/36680 W10282, conversation with Namier.

52. *Ibid.*

53. *Ibid.*

54. FO 371/36681/W10594, FO to Bern, 7/23/43.

55. *Ibid.*

56. FO 371/36681 W11118, Ankara to the FO, 7/29/43; and, CZA L15/86, Barlas report on the discussion in the embassy in Ankara, 7/30/43.

57. FO 371/36681 W10897, 7/24/43; W11327, Namier to Randall, 8/3/43.

58. FO 371/36681 W11124.

59. FO 371/36681 W11118, 7/29/43; a second, more sharply worded, letter of the same date, FO 371/36681 W11742.

60. FO 371/36881 W11223, 8/4/43; and FO 371/36881 W11511, 8/6/43, all from FO to Ankara.

61. FO 371/36881 W11105, 7/30/43, from Bern to FO.

62. HA 14/714, report by Shind; 14/60, Rami to colleagues, 7/9/43; MA D.I.713, Bader to Barlas, 6/11/43.

63. Efforts to put the *Lilly* into service had been made since it was purchased in

the fall of 1941. The main difficulty was finding a neutral registry for the boat. At the end of 1942, it was decided to register it in Palestine and to use it commercially, as well as a training vessel for seamen. This fit into the plan to train professional crews who would be able to fill the needs of the Yishuv for aliya and other purposes. In the fall of 1943, when the Mossad renewed its work in Constantinople, it was thought that the *Lilly* would serve as one link in the transport bridge between the Black Sea or Turkey and Palestine. This plan, too, however, like others that depended on the cooperation of British intelligence agencies, was never implemented. It sank in a storm in the summer of 1943. There is an interesting correspondence between Yudl Marmer, who worked aboard the *Lilly*, and his friend Venya Pomerantz of the rescue mission, in the KMA (Kibbutz Hameuhad archives), foreign files II, 23/4 May–June 1943.

64. HA 14/714, report by Shind, and 14/60, Meir to colleagues, 11/28/43.

65. MA D.I.899, 11/15/43, signed "the redhead."

66. HA 14/60, Artzi to colleagues, 11/18/43.

67. HA 14/60, Rami to colleagues, 10/18/43.

68. *Ibid.*, 14/492, Braginsky to the secretariat of the Histadrut executive council, 7/25/43, with the notation "urgent."

69. FO 371/36679 W7454, Ankara to the FO, 5/17/43.

70. FO 371/36682 W11960, from the FO to Bern, 8/20/43.

71. FO 371/36682 W1281, memorandum of Lady Rathborne, 8/9/43, and notes to the memorandum until 9/3/43 by ministry officials.

72. FO 371/36682 W9840, and the foreign secretary's reply to Halifax of 8/30/43.

73. FO 371/36683 W15379, 11/2/43.

74. FO 371/36684 W16201, to MacMichael from the colonial secretary, 11/29/43.

75. FO 371/36682 W13557, see, e.g., the letter from Henderson in the FO to Clark in the CO, 9/25/43.

Chapter 13

1. The new Rumanian ambassador in Turkey was Alexander Cretzianu. See CZA S25/261, report on the situation in Rumania, signed by Segal; David Wyman, *The Abandonment of the Jews: American Policy and the Holocaust 1941–1945* New York, 1984 (henceforth Wyman 1984), pp. 219–221; Bauer 1981, pp. 353–355, 405–407.

2. Theodore Lavi, *Yahadut Romaniya bema'avak hatzalatah* (Hebrew), (*Rumanian Jewry in the Struggle for Survival*), Jerusalem, 1965. pp. 42–57, 90–99. On the attempt to disgrace Filderman, and Zissu's report of his own position at the time, see CZA L22/88, Zissu to Lichtheim, 8/15/43.

3. HA 14/148, to Venya, Yulek, Moshe Tabenkin, Idelson and others, from Dov, 8/23/44; *ibid.*, 14/67, 6/16/43, signed by Ze'ev, and again on 7/27/43; *ibid.*, interviews of passengers arriving on the *Milca* and the *Kazbek* between April and July 1944.

4. CZA L15/188, Barlas to Benvenisti, 5/4/43; HA 14/60, Kinarti, 12/43; Barlas to Zissu, 7/21/44, and Avigur to Zissu, 7/21/44.

5. HA 14/67, Bucharest, 6/14/43, signed by Ze'ev.

6. *Ibid.*, 6/14/43, signed by Yanko.

7. *Ibid.*, reports of interviews with passengers reaching Palestine between April and July 1944.

8. CZA 526/1186, Torda, 5/30/44, signed by Aryeh.

9. *Ibid.*, 6/11/44, signed by Aryeh and 5/26/44, signed by Zvi Bassy, Aryeh, Benno, Moshe, and Zvi.

10. HA 14/67, letter to Constantinople, 11/21/43.

11. *Ibid.,* L15/83, to members, 10/2/43.

12. These matters became clear during interviews with the passengers of Mossad boats. See HA 14/67, interviews with passengers, 5/10/44: "Rumania, Through the end of April 1944."

13. CZA L15/188, Benvenisti to Barlas, 5/14/44, and L15/149, Kolb to Gilbert Simonds, the Red Cross representative in Istanbul, 11/4/43.

14. HA, signed by Kinarti. For reactions produced by the letter, see CZA L15/ 179, Geiger to Barlas, 1/10/44.

15. CZA L15/179, Geiger to Barlas, 1/2/44.

16. HA 14/60, Marmer to colleagues, 10/18/43; *ibid.,* Rami and Itai (Ehud Avriel) to colleagues, 10/24/43; CZA L15/179, Kolb to Simonds describing the *Smyrni*: 53 meters long, 8 meters wide, 4 meters in height, steel hull, and in good condition.

17. CZA L15/732, 12/1/43, Enzer (apparently) to Zimand, and 526/1186, 11/14/ 43, Yaakov (Yaakov Rosenzweig) to colleagues. Rosenzweig was a member of Ihud and close to youth movement circles.

18. HA 14/67, discussion with Wellfeld, 1/11/44; *Pinkas Kehillot Romaniyah*, p. 180. The documents mention the names of people who in the past had supported aliyah bet as candidates to organize the transport. Such, for example, was B. Grupper, who was the Panamanian consul in Rumania until December 1941.

19. CZA L22/82, 10/23/43. In October 1943, Geiger and Enzer appealed to Switzerland and asked Lichtheim's help in obtaining a Swiss flag of registry for the boat. They thought to transfer legal ownership to a Jewish Swiss citizen, one Kalmanovich, who was known as a past supporter of aliyah bet, as a means of obtaining the Swiss registry. At the same time, the opponents of a sea transport on the *Smyrni* and of assigning the boat to Pandelis contacted Kalmanovich directly and asked him to help find an alternative boat. They wrote that the *Smyrni* would not cut it as a passenger vessel: it was just an old crate. The master of the vessel was a known pirate, responsible for the *Struma* disaster.

20. HA 14/60, 10/18/43, Meir to colleagues.

21. *Ibid.,* 14/67, discussion with Wellfeld, 1/11/44.

22. *Ibid.,* 14/60, Rami and Itai to colleagues, 10/24/43.

23. *Ibid.* For criticism of the decision to work with Enzer, see CZA S26/1866, Yaakov to colleagues, 11/25/43. Apparently, this was Yaakov Rosenzweig: "You have appointed a new committee, Enzer and Geiger. Geiger is Benvenisti's greatest foe and will do anything to aggravate him, for no reason. This is a lost cause with us— Geiger versus Benvenisti. You have inserted yourself into the middle of this and have strengthened Geiger."

24. *Ibid.*

25. *Ibid.,* 14/62, 11/26/43.

26. On the announcement, see below, and HA 14/62, transcript of a discussion between the British and Barlas, 3/22/44.

27. *Ibid.,* 14/67, discussion with Moritz Geiger, 4/19/44.

28. *Ibid.*

29. On the criticism of Barlas by members of the British embassy staff, see Chapter 12.

30. HA 14/60, Meir to Artzi, 11/3/43 (or 2/3/44—the date is unclear); CZA L15/ 188, agreement between the representative of the Mossad for Aliya and the representative of the Jewish Agency, 7/17/44.

31. HA 14/60, 1/28/44, Meir to Eldad; Moreshet D. I. 700, Bader to Avramek, 4/9/44. It was reported that the Soviets promised not to molest Jewish immigrant boats, and departure information was therefore supplied to them in advance.

32. HA 14/60, Meir to colleagues, 2/5/44 and 2/20/44; Venya to the kibbutz secretariat, 2/22/44; CZA S25/7831, report of the investigating office in Haifa on Hans Volti, 9/22/44; *Pinkas,* pp. 187–188; PRO FO 371/42881, interrogation of Bondy and Gross. The matter of the arrests and releases was a particularly painful issue between the young and old leaders in Rumania. Many veterans felt that impetuous and reckless behavior by the young Zionists had disclosed the incriminating evidence, while many of the young people harbored resentment over their perceived abandonment after older Zionists were released from prison. This came to light in debriefings of young immigrants and in letters. See, for example, HA 14/67, on the arrests in Rumania, 4/26/44; *ibid.,* 14/151, two letters to Venya, undated, but on the basis of their content dating roughly from early April 1944. On the parachutists and the fate of Lova Gokovsky, see Gelber, vol. 3, pp. 133–206. For a summary discussion, see HA 14/67, discussion with M. Geiger, 4/19/44.

33. HA 14/62, Barlas to London, 3/13/44.

34. *Ibid.,* and 3/18/44; and 3/22/44, discussion with Maivie.

35. On the position of the United States on immigration and on the War Refugee Board, see Chapter 14.

36. HA 14/60, Meir to Artzi, April 11, 1944.

37. *Ibid.,* and 14/625, Simonds to Kolb, undated. The content indicates that it was before April 8.

38. HA, Zissu to Barlas, 3/29/44, and Romtouros (ORAT) to Barlas, 4/2/44.

39. HA 14/151, 152, to Dear Venya, undated and unsigned. An examination of the contents reveals that the letter was written at the end of March or the beginning of April. Another letter was written in early to mid-May, again undated and unsigned, but relating to Venya's letter of 4/19/44.

40. For further details, see Chapter 14.

41. *Ibid.* The writer's comment about Zissu and the Left is interesting, especially coming from an Ihud man, because there were those who accused him of being too close to Revisionist ideas. On Zissu's personality, see Schraga Amiel, *Ha'asui lebeli hat* (Hebrew), (*The Undaunted*), Tel Aviv, 1964.

42. HA 14/67, Interviews bureau, "Romania, April-May 1944, *aliyah* matters."

43. *Ibid.,* 14/60, full report on Rumanian Jewry, 1/19/44; 14/67, report of the interviews bureau in Haifa—"Romania, April 1944." The sources for this episode, as for the entire story of aliyah from the Rumanian side, are incomplete. The reconstruction of the events is based on the following: Participants' accounts, taken down in Haifa in 1944 (HA 14/67, 14/62, 14/60, 14/151/152); letters of the parachutists from July to September 1944, in the same files; the Rumanian ministerial committee decision of 6/9/44, *ibid.,* 14/151/152; the letters and cable sent by Zissu to Barlas and Shind during April–August 1944, in the same files; Zissu's letters to Lichtheim, CZA L22/88, July–August 1944. The possibility of error in this reconstruction cannot be ruled out; however, the overall progress of events appears to be accurate, and the conclusions to be drawn appear valid.

44. It should be noted that problems cropped up in the selection of immigrants, apart from differences between Zionists, non-Zionists, and young pioneers. One of the regime's methods of repaying collaborators was to help them leave the country among the other immigrants. Pandelis received a great deal of money from these

people and he added them to the lists. The interviews bureau in Palestine regularly made mention of this in its reports.

45. HA 14/151/152, declaration of the Rumanian government regarding Jewish emigration, 6/9/44.

46. *Ibid.*

47. HA 14/61, Meir to Artzi, 5/19/44.

48. *Ibid.*, 14/60, Ze'ev to colleagues, 5/31/44.

49. *Ibid.*, 14/67, 6/19/44. The letter is unsigned, but from its content and from the fact that it is mentioned in a letter to Palestine (8/24/44), it is clear that Rubin is meant.

50. CZA L22/82, Marton to Lichtheim, 7/29/44; S26/1186, letters from Aryeh (member of Dror), who was active in smuggling refugees over the border from Hungary at Torda, June 1944; *ibid.*, Zvi, 6/21/44.

51. *Ibid.*

52. HA 14/62, Meir to Artzi.

53. *Ibid.*, 14/148.

54. *Ibid.*, 14/62 and 14/61, letters from Kaplan and Avigur to Kinarti (parachutist's code name).

55. CZA L22/88.

56. *Ibid.*, L15/179.

57. *Ibid.*, L15/88, Barlas to the Jewish Agency executive, 7/19/44. Note that the distinction between legal and illegal is in this case a matter of who was organizing the operation, and not a substantive distinction.

58. HA 14/62; the announcement was received in Palestine on 8/15/44.

59. *Ibid.*, Meir to Artzi, 7/29/44.

60. *Ibid.*, 14/67.

61. Lichtheim in Geneva was also informed by cable and letter. CZA L22/88.

62. HA 14/151/152, Rudolf to colleagues, 8/8/44.

63. Rohwer 1964, p. 62; HA 14/62, Artzi to Meir, 7/26/44; *ibid.*, Zaslani to Meir, 7/13/44. The last letter raises the question of continuing to travel on the Black Sea.

64. HA 14/148, Frantz (parachutist's code name) to Kinarti and Dani.

65. *Ibid.*, 14/151/152, "Dear comrades," from Rudolf.

66. Only a few members knew about the parachutists. One of them was Zissu. See Resel, p. 29; HA 14/148, testimony of Zvi Goldwad, one of the *Bulbul* passengers, 8/25/44.

67. HA 14/59 contains a copy of the document. It is dated 8/3/44.

68. The sources on the sinking of the *Mefkura* include testimony taken from the survivors and reports sent to Palestine from Constantinople, and reports to the War Refugee Board. The latter is in the Roosevelt Archives, WRB Box, Evacuation, "Report on the Circumstances of the Sinking of the Turkish Motor Boat 'Mefkura,' " by Eri Jabotinsky, 8/18/44. Testimony by the ship's captain, Kuzim Turun, 8/24/44; discussion with the people of the *Bulbul*, 8/14/44, unsigned. Hirschmann to Pehle, 9/13/44. A translation from Hungarian of a letter by Lazurlov Filoph to a fellow member, 9/5/44. Record of a meeting of 8/17/44, participants: Ira Hirschmann, Katzky, Shind, Resnick, Schweitzer, Barlas; meeting of 8/12/44. Report by Gilbert Simonds, 8/13/44; report on the sinking by the British embassy in Ankara, PRO FO WR1099, 8/28/44.

69. The committee's findings were reported on 9/9/44. The material is in YVA, *Mefkura* file, and was published in full in Resel, pp. 44–48.

70. HA 14/59.
71. *Ibid.*, 14/151/152.
72. *Ibid.*
73. *Ibid.*, Kinarti to Frantz and Theo (parachutists).

Chapter 14

1. For a comprehensive study of the War Refugee Board, its members and its place within the framework of America's rescue policy, see Henry L. Feingold, *The Politics of Rescue. The Roosevelt Administration and the Holocaust, 1938–1945* New Brunswick, 1970, and Wyman 1984, chapters 10–13. Chapter 12 of the latter contains the text of the Board's authorization. On the establishment of the Emergency Committee to Save the Jewish People of Europe, and the individuals involved in it, see chapter 8.

2. See FO 371/36678, W5521, Lord Melchett to Lord Cranborn, 3/26/43, and FO 371/36682 W12841, memorandum and reply to Lady Rathborne, August–September 1943.

3. National Archive (NAR) 840.48 Ref/5041, State Department cables of 1/25/1944 to the embassies in London, Ankara, Madrid, Stockholm, and Bern.

4. FO 371/42727 W1381, 2/4/44, Foreign Office to Washington, and *ibid.*, W1953, from the foreign secretary to the cabinet committee on refugee affairs, 2/7/44.

5. FO 371/42727 W2214, from the Washington embassy to the FO, 2/22/44.

6. Franklin D. Roosevelt Library (Hyde Park): FDRL WRB/Box 40, 2/22/1944.

7. NAR 840.48 Ref/5041, State Department to Steinhardt, 1/25/1944.

8. *Ibid.*, Ref/4460, 9/1/1943, and the ambassador's reply, *ibid.*, Ref/4444 9/7/1943. Hirschmann wrote his memoirs in two books, Ira Hischmann, *Life Line to the Promised Land*, New York, 1946; *Caution to the Winds*, New York, 1962.

9. FDRL WRB/Box 45, Evacuation; and see also the letter to Pehle, *ibid.*, 2/18/944, outlining guidelines for activity.

10. *Ibid.*

11. FDRL WRB/Box 39, Evacuation, Steinhardt to the State Department, 3/15/1944; and *ibid.*, Hirschmann to Pehle, 3/21/1944.

12. *Ibid.*, Steinhardt to the WRB, 4/12/44.

13. *Ibid.* He also said that the Turkish foreign minister threatened to hold a press conference to expose American recalcitrance in pledging a replacement ship. After long delay, Steinhardt received confirmation of this from the Board on 4/19/1944.

14. *Ibid.*, Hirschmann's diary.

15. FDRL WRB/Box 39, Evacuation, Steinhardt to the State Department, 3/16/44.

16. *Ibid.*, Memorandum from Hirschmann, 4/5/1944, and a second appeal later that month; cf. NAR 840.48 Ref/5599, report of the Red Cross; *ibid.*, Ref/5797, Hirschmann to the State Department, 4/22/1944, summarizing all the efforts made to date and expressing optimism.

17. NAR 840.48 Ref/6398, Johnson to the State Department, 6/25/1944, involving the *Bardalanda*, a Swedish ship that supplied food to Greece and enjoyed a safe conduct from the Germans and the other belligerents for this purpose.

18. *Ibid.*, Ref/5784, Steinhardt to the State Department, 4/19/44.

19. *Ibid.*, Hirschmann to Pehle, 7/27/1944.

20. FDRL, Hirschmann's diary, notes of 3/11/44. This passage epitomizes his point of view, illustrating his feelings of excitement and trepidation, and his consciousness

of participating in something of momentous historical significance. See also, regarding the transfer of the orphans from Transnistria as promised to Filderman, NAR 840.48 Ref/5376.

21. FDRL, Hirschmann's diary, notes of March 3/11/44. See also 3/16/44.

22. *Ibid.,* notes of 3/18/44.

23. NAR 840.48 Ref/5391, and *ibid.,* Ref/5367, 3/23/44.

24. *Ibid.,* Ref/5393, Hirschmann and Steinhardt to the WRB, 3/20/19. Cf. *ibid.,* Ref/5487 to the WRB, from Hirschmann and Steinhardt, 3/30/44. It should be noted that a balanced and objective evaluation of these contacts can be made only after Rumanian records have been examined. Both Hirschmann and Steinhardt, and the WRB in Washington and the State Department as well, credited the matter to the contacts between Hirschmann and Cretzianu.

25. *Ibid.,* Ref/5408, WRB to Hirschmann, 3/20/44, and Ref/5393.

26. *Ibid.*

27. NAR 840.48 Ref/81944, Hirschmann's report of 8/19/44 stating that in April a boat had been sent to Bulgaria to take on refugees. The boat returned empty. No other sources support this account. It is likely that Hirschmann was referring either to the *Firin* or to the *Vita,* two Bulgarian-registered boats that Mossad people had prepared in April 1944 but that they were unable to use.

28. *Ibid.,* Ref/4041, the embassy to the State Department, 1/7/44.

29. FDRL WRB/Box 29, Evacuation, Hirschmann to the State Department 4/19/44.

30. *Ibid.,* Hirschmann's diary.

31. NAR 840.48 Ref/5415, Hirschmann to the members of the WRB 3/23/44 and, FDRL WRB/Box 40, Hirschmann's correspondence with the WRB in the matter, 8/19/44.

32. *Ibid.,* Hirschmann's report of 8/19/44, which includes a detailed description of how this was accomplished. The example given is that of the *Kazbek,* but he writes that this is a general pattern.

33. *Ibid.,* memorandum to the ambassador, 4/5/44.

34. FDRL WRB/Box 39, report of 4/20/44 on the Adana ships; and cf. a second memorandum (undated), apparently written in May; NAR 840.48 Ref/6137, Dobkin's appeal to the Board, 5/25/44; *ibid.,* Ref/6139, Gruenbaum to the Board, 6/12/44; *ibid.,* Magnes to the Board, 6/15/44. All of these appeals asked the Board to recommend to its representatives, in Turkey in particular, to agree to sailings without any safe conduct. The main reason put forth was that the dangers of sea travel were more than balanced by the immediate danger of the deportations in Hungary. The appeals also stressed that, with the conquest of Hungary by the Germans, there was the added fear that Rumania might likewise be occupied. In the face of these circumstances, the Mossad had succeeded in saving hundreds on small boats without any safe conduct, and therefore the WRB ought to instruct its representatives to act accordingly.

35. FDRL WRB/Box 39, Evacuation, Steinhardt to the State Department, 4/5/44.

36. *Ibid.,* Hirschmann to the Board, summary report, 8/19/44; *ibid.,* Board to Steinhardt, 5/31/44. The Board leaders suggested the advantages of using small boats as opposed to large ships, which were more conspicuous to the Germans. In reference to the small boats, the names of the *Akbal* and the *Anadula* were mentioned—two boats in which Barlas and the Mossad had taken an interest as early as winter 1944, but use of which the Turkish government had refused.

37. *Ibid.,* Marks to Friedman in the State Department, 4/5/44; *ibid.,* embassy to WRB, 5/2/44.

38. FDRL WRB/Box 40, Evacuation, Hirschmann Report 8/19/44. A good summary on the contacts with Balabanov appears on pp. 13–14.

39. *Ibid.,* p. 10.

40. *Ibid.* On p. 12 he noted: "We are awaiting momentarily the arrival into Rumania of Hungarian refugees who will receive priority by us in being evacuated by sea or rail."

41. Wyman 1984, pp. 255–260.

42. For a wide-ranging correspondence on the matter, see FO 371/42728 W4519 and the notes made during March 1944.

43. *Ibid.,* and also FO 371/42728 W4586, Henderson's report of a discussion with Brodetsky, reference to British policy and the WRB, 3/21/44.

44. *Ibid.,* FO 371/42724 W5702, a particularly angry letter, 4/3/44, reflecting the derision and jealousy of the Ankara embassy.

45. *Ibid.,* W5424, to Boyd from the refugee desk, 4/7/44 and 4/17/44, W5050, the FO to Cairo, 4/11/44, and also 5/13/44; after the arrival of the *Kazbek,* W2453, MacMichael to the CO, 7/17/44 and 7/20/44; the FO to the CO, 7/28/44.

46. *Ibid.,* FO 371/42724 W5424, refugee desk to Boyd, 4/7/44.

47. Wasserstein 1979, pp. 262–266. NAR 840.48 Ref/7.1944, from Ankara to the State Department, July 19, 1944. The numbers of potential emigrants referred to by German sources were far smaller than those mentioned by the Hungarians to the Red Cross, or by representatives of the Yishuv. In any case, the figures of 7,000 passport holders and 1,000 children cited by the Germans were still higher than those cited in the past by German sources.

48. PREM 44/574, 8/6/44.

49. *Ibid.,* report of 8/19/44.

50. JDC Archives, Turkey, report of Resnick, 3/27/44, pp. 3–4.

51. FDRL WRB/Box 40, Evacuation, memorandum of Hirschmann, 8/19/44, last page.

Chapter 15

1. Total immigration for the period was 3,317.

2. When the Soviet Union was drawn into the war, it began to display an interest in the Zionist question and in Palestine. Yishuv representatives made an effort to meet with Soviets almost as soon as fighting broke out on the eastern front, to discuss the problem of refugees on Soviet territory. The Soviet interest lay in the potential political advantages of a "Jewish connection" in terms of securing public support for the Soviet struggle against Nazi Germany. This was part of a general propaganda offensive the Soviets mounted in the West, supported by Soviet Jews through the Anti-Fascist Committee. Meetings with Zionists were held in London, Cairo, and the United States, and covered such broad topics as the postwar future of the Jewish people and the political role of the Yishuv and Zionism in the "Jewish Question." Questions related to a postwar settlement took on relevance, the Soviets increased their involvement in Middle East affairs, and the political calculations that led them to take the Arab countries into account became weightier. Nevertheless, messages transmitted to the Zionists were inconsistent, reflecting what must have been a continuing ambivalence within the Soviet leadership. The Yishuv leaders were therefore unable to feel very confident about Soviet intentions. The Yishuv's position in this

context has not been thoroughly examined, but for the Soviet side, see Yaakov Ro'i, "Maga'im Sovietim 'im ha-yishuv ha-yehudi baaretz ve'im manhigim zionim (yuni 1941–februar 1945)" (Hebrew), ("Soviet Relations with the Jewish Yishuv in Palestine and with Zionist Leaders, June 1941–February 1945,") *Shalem* I (1974), pp. 525–602.

3. CZA, Minutes, 39II, 9/29/44; LA, meeting of the executive council, 10/4/44; BBA, 24/44, section 2, Mapai central committee meeting, 10/17/44.

4. CZA, Minutes, 39II, 9/29/44, statement of Eliyahu Dobkin.

5. On this group, see Haim Avni, "The Zionist Underground in Holland and France and the Escape to Spain," in Y. Gutman (ed.) *Rescue Attempts During the Holocaust*, New York, 1978, pp. 550–590.

6. CZA, Minutes, 39II, 9/29/44.

7. *Ibid.*, and statement by Shaul Avigur at the same session.

8. *Ibid.*, minutes of 10/14/44.

9. *Ibid.*

10. *Ibid.*

11. *Ibid.*, 12/16/44, statement by Ben-Gurion after his return from Bulgaria.

12. *Ibid.*

13. *Ibid.*, statements by Shertok and Weizmann.

14. *Ibid.*, 9/29/44, Shertok and Dobkin.

15. *Ibid.*, 10/27/44.

16. *Ibid.*, and also LA, Histadrut executive council session, 10/11/44.

17. *Ibid.*

18. HA 14/62, 9/13/44, CZA, Minutes, 39II, 9/9/44, report by Elias.

19. *Ibid.*

20. On this see the letters of Venya Pomerantz, CZA S25/3879, 9/27/44 and 10/27/44.

21. LA, Histadrut executive session, 10/11/44, Avigur.

22. CZA S25/3879, Venya to colleagues. Pomerantz met with the Bulgarian minister of information a few days after he arrived in Sofia. After this discussion, in which Pomerantz explained the nature of his mission, he received permission to broadcast each Friday. Most of the programs were published in Hebrew translation in the Tel Aviv newspaper *Davar*.

23. On the attitudes of Zionist leaders in reports about these meetings, see CZA, Minutes, 39II, 9/21/44, 10/17/44, and 12/17/44.

24. For a general description of the Jews' situation in Rumania after the war and the Rumanian government's policy, see J. Ancel, *Yahadut Romaniyah bayn 23.8.44 levayn 30.12.47* (Hebrew), (*The Jews of Rumania between 23 August 1944 and 30 December 1947*), Ph.D. Dissertation, Hebrew University, Jerusalem, 1979) (henceforth Ancel 1979).

25. CZA S25/3879, "Brother Jews," signed by the Hehalutz youth movements (undated); and "To the Jewish Youth," signed: "Labor Youth Movement," Dror, Habonim (also undated).

26. On the parachutists' mission, see Yoav Gelber 1983.

27. HA 14/148a, testimony of N. (Uriel Kenner), p. 12.

28. *Ibid.*, and also 14/62, letter to Palestine from Meir, 10/14/44; *ibid.*, 14/67, emissaries to the Histadrut, 11/14/44.

29. *Ibid.*, 14/67a, Dov to Hakibbutz secretariat, 10/31/44; *ibid.*, to the Histadrut from the Hehalutz central office in Rumania, 11/4/44.

30. *Ibid.*, reports of the parachutists upon return to Palestine.

31. On the Jewish Council, see Ancel 1979, pp. 66–75.

32. HA 14/148a, testimony of N. (Kenner), p. 15; and CZA S25/8904, Aryeh Fischman.

33. On the question of the parachutists' remaining in Rumania and their status as British soldiers, see HA 14/148, letter by Avigur, 11/12/44, and Gelber 1983, pp. 269–289.

34. HA 14/67a, Agami to Meir and Artzi, 10/23/44.

35. *Ibid.*

36. *Ibid.*, Moshe to Hannah and Ehud, 10/5/44. The letter deals with the threat of confiscation of large boats by the authorities.

37. CZA S25/3879, from Agami to Palestine, 11/25/44. The deal was concluded, but the Russians intervened and nullified it.

38. HA 14/67a, Moshe to Hannah and Ehud, 11/5/44.

39. HA 14/67a, on Rumanian aliyah through December 1944; Bauer 1973, pp. 23ff.

40. HA 14/397, from Moshe, 12/7/44; *ibid.*, Ehud to Moshe, 12/1/44.

41. *Ibid.*, 14/62, from Artzi, 12/31/44. The expenses for the *Taurus* trip were also borne by the Mossad, as Jews with means in Rumania were not prepared to risk a semilegal sea voyage.

42. *Ibid.* Agami transmitted a personal greeting to the Rumanian government minister, Patrascanu, from a friend (name unknown) who had immigrated to Palestine. The note was meant to serve as a letter of introduction for Agami.

43. *Ibid.*, a very sharply worded letter, 11/17/44; *ibid.*, 14/397, letter dated 1/23/45.

44. *Ibid.*

45. *Ibid.*, detailed letter from Agami to Ehud, 1/23/45, describing the difficulties being posed by the Russians and the promises broken at the last minute, apparently without reason.

46. HA 14/60, from Constantinople to Artzi, undated; cf. PRO FO 371/3148 W2150, Foreign Office to the envoy in Sofia, explaining in detail the arrangement regarding immigrant permits mailed during the war.

47. HA 14/62, Constantinople to Artzi, 11/25/44. On Kladovo, see above, Chapter 3.

48. HA 14/397, Ehud to Moshe, 12/7/44.

49. FO 371/42825 WR2125, 12/26/44; and 11/22/44; 11/28/44; NAR 840.48, Ref 12–20.44: correspondence between the embassy in Ankara and the Foreign Office.

50. FO 371/42825 WR2125, 12/26/44.

51. For a summary of the British position, see FO 371/42825, WR2150, Foreign Office to the ambassador in Sofia, 1/3/45; and NAR 840.48 Ref 12–13.44, Steinhardt to the State Department.

52. CZA, Minutes, 39II, 2/26/44; and 39II, 10/17/44.

53. Ben-Gurion Archive, Sdeh Boker, Ben-Gurion's diary on his visit to Bulgaria.

54. The description here is based on Ben-Gurion's diary; on his report to the Agency executive, CZA, Minutes, 39II, 12/12/44; his report to the Mapai central committee, Mapai Archive 24/44, section 2, 12/14/44; Venya Pomerantz's letters, CZA S25/3879; report by Ehud Avriel on the visit, Avriel 1979, pp. 150–156. On Ben-Gurion's concern for the rescue of children, see Tuvia Frieling, *Me'uravuto shel Ben-Gurion befarashat hatzalat ve'aliyat ha-yeladim uvepulmus ha-klita, november 1942–mai 1945* (Hebrew), (*The Involvement of Ben-Gurion in the Rescue and Immigration of Children and the Absorption Controversy, November 1942–May 1945*), Master's Thesis, Hebrew University, Jerusalem, 1984.

Bibliography

Bibliographical Abbreviations and Sources

Archives

Museum and Archives of the Labor Movement = Labor Archives = LA
Minutes of the Executive Commitee of the Histadrut.
Minutes of the Secretatiat, Executive Committee.
Minutes, Central Committee.
Minutes of Histadrut Councils.
Correspondence with Emmissaries.

Jabotinsky Archives = JA
Files, Aliyah Bet.
Presidential Files.
Files of the Rescue Committee (contained within these), Files of Joseph Klarman.

Yad Vashem Archives = YVA
Files of the ships "Struma" and "Mefkura" – 011.
Files of the Abraham Silberschein Bureau – M20.
Files of the Eichmann Trial – TR.
Files of the German Foreign Office – JM.
Microfilm, listed under: (G. Kent, Catalogue of Files and Microfilms of the German
    Foreign Office Ministry Archives. 4 Vols. Stanford, 1967–1972.
Testimonies of Immigrants and Aliyah Organizers, according to country – 03, 033.
Testimonies on Aliyah Bet from Germany in the Ball-Kaduri collection.

Moreshet Archive, Giv'at Havivah = Moreshet Archive = MA
Constantinople Unit, Bader Files – D.I.

Labor Party Archive, Beit Berl = Beit Berl Archive = BBA
Minutes of Labor Party – 23.
Minutes of the Secretariat – 24.
Minutes of the Political Department – 25.

Minutes of the Political Department – 26.
Files of Emmissaries – 3.
Files of the Union (Ihud) Party – 101.

Central Archives for History of the Jewish People = *CAHJP*
Files of Vienna Archive AW

Central Zionist Archives = *CZA*
Minutes of the Executive of the Jewish Agency.
Minutes of the Rescue Committee.
Files of the Aliyah Department – S6.
Files of the Political Department – S25.
Files of the Office of the Zionist Organization in London – Z4.
Files of the Office of the Zionist Organization of America – Z5.
Files of Correspondence With Representatives in Geneva, principally Lichtheim –
    L22.
Files of Representatives in Istanbul – L15.
Personal Files, Simon Brod – A203.
Files of the Revisionist Movement – F17.

Archive of the United Kibbutz Movement = *Kibbutz Meuhad*
Minutes of the Secretariat, United Kibbutz.
Correspondence with Emmissaries.
Files of the Diaspora Committee – Diaspora Unit.
Personal Archives; Braginsky, Tabenkin, Zisling.
Diary of Y. Idelson.

Archive of the Haganah = *HA*
Files of *Aliyah Bet* 14.
Personal Files.
Ships Files.
Archives of the Executive Committee.
Oral Testimonies.

Archive of the Joint Distribution Committee, New York (JDC)
Correspondence according to name of country – 1.
Reports and Accounts of Representatives in Europe – 4–19.

Franklin D. Roosevelt Library (Hyde Park) = *FDRL*
Files of the Board of War Refugees – 38–42 Box W.R.B.
Personal Files of Ira Hirschmann.

Library of Congress
Personal Archive of the U.S. Ambassador to Turkey – Laurence A. Steinhardt Papers.

National Archive U.S.A. = *NAR*
Refugee Unit – 840.48 Refugee.
Correspondence with the Consulate in Jerusalem – R659, M34.

U.S.-British Relations – N867.
U.S.-Turkish Relations – N687.

Public Record Office London = PRO
Files of the Foreign Office – General Correspondence (Political) FO 371.
Colonial Office Palestine – Original Correspondence CO 733.
Files of the Prime Minister – PREM.
Files of the Cabinet – CAB Papers.

Daily Journals

Ha-aretz
Ha-boker
Davar
Ha-Tzofeh

Published Reports and Accounts

Reports and Accounts of the Zionist Executive and the Jewish Agency to the 18th to 21st Congresses, Jerusalem 1933, 1935, 1937, 1939.
Reports and Accounts on Activities, 1940–1947, Statements of the State Department, the Aliyah Division, the Relief Commission on Behalf of the Jewish Agency for Palestine, London 1936.

Oral Testimonies

The majority of the testimonies used were in the Oral Documentation Center of the Institute for Contemporary Jewry = Oral Documentation Center = ODC.

A portion of the testimonies were found in archives, as indicated above.

I spoke with many of the witnesses about their testimony, but I did not compile comprehensive new material. I indicated only new testimonies, which were given for the purpose of this work and can now be found in the Oral Documentation Center: Ehud Avriel (of Blessed Memory), Pino Ginsburg, Reuben Hecht, Ephraim Frank, Alexander Shapira.

Books and Articles

Aliav, Ruth, and Peggy Mann. *The Last Escape*. New York: Doubleday, 1973.

Amiel, Schraga. *"Ha-'asui lebeli hat"* (Hebrew), *The Undaunted*. Tel Aviv: B'nai B'rith Organization, 1964.

Ancel, Jean. *Yehadut Romaniyah bayn 23.8.44 levayn 30.12.47* (Hebrew), *The Jews of Rumania Between 23 August 1944 and 30 December 1947*, Ph.D. Dissertation, Hebrew University, Jerusalem, 1979.

———— "Plans for the Deportation of Rumanian Jewry and their Discontinuation in Light of Documentary Evidence (July–October 1942)," *Yad Vashem Studies* 1984, pp. 299–333.

Arad, Yizhak, Israel Gutman, and Avraham Margaliot (eds.), *Documents on the Holocaust*. New York: Ktav, 1982.

Arendt, Hannah. *Eichmann in Jerusalem: The Banality of Evil*. New York: Viking Press, 1964.

Avigur, Shaul. *Im dor ha-haganah* (Hebrew), *With the Haganah Generation*. Tel Aviv: Ma'arakhot Publishing, 1962.

Avneri, Aryeh Levi. *Mivelos ad taurus* (Hebrew), *From Velos to Taurus: The First Decade of Jewish Illegal Immigration to Mandatory Palestine 1933–1944*. Tel Aviv: Hakibbutz Hameuhad, 1985.

Avneri, Yizhak. *Ha-histadrut ha-zionit vehaaliyah ha-bilti legalit leEretz Yisrael* (Hebrew), *The Zionist Organization and Illegal Immigration to Palestine*, Ph.D. Dissertation, Tel Aviv University, Tel Aviv, 1979.

Avni, Haim. "The Zionist Underground in Holland and France and the Escape to Spain," in Y. Gutman (ed.), *Rescue Attempts During the Holocaust*. New York: Atheneum, 1975.

Avriel, Ehud. *Open the Gates*. New York: Atheneum, 1975.

Bader, Menahem. *Shelihuyot atzuvot* (Hebrew), *Sad Missions*. Tel Aviv: Merhavya, 1954.

Ball-Kaduri, K.Y. *"Ha-aliyah ha-bilti hukit miGermaniyah ha-nazit leEretz Yisrael"* (Hebrew), "The Illegal Immigration from Nazi Germany to Palestine," *Yalkut Moreshet* 1963, pp. 127–142.

Barlas, Haim. *Hatzalah beyemei ha-Shoah* (Hebrew), *Rescue in the Days of the Holocaust*. Tel Aviv: Hakibbutz Hameuhad, 1975.

———— *"Mivtsah Aliyat Lita"* (Hebrew), "Operation Lithuanian Aliyah," *Dapim leheker ha-Shoah vehamered* (Hebrew), *Research Papers on the Holocaust and Resistance*, New Series, Collection A, Tel Aviv: Hakibbutz Hameuhad, 1970, pp. 246–255.

Bar-Zohar, Michael. *Ben Gurion: The Armed Prophet*. Englewood Cliffs, N.J.: Prentice Hall, 1967.

Bauer, Yehuda. *American Jewry and the Holocaust*. Detroit: Wayne State University Press, 1981.

———— *From Diplomacy to Resistance: A History of Jewish Palestine, 1930–1945*. Philadelphia: The Jewish Publication Society of America, 1970.

———— *Flight and Rescue: Brichah*. New York: Random House, 1970.

———— *My Brother's Keeper: A History of the American Jewish Joint Distribution Committee, 1929–1939*. Philadelphia: The Jewish Publication Society of America, 1974.

Beit Zvi, Shabtai. *Ha-zionut ha-post ugandit bemashber ha-shoah* (Hebrew), *Post-*

Uganda Zionism in the Crisis of the Holocaust. Tel Aviv: Bronfman Publishers, 1977.

Ben-Elissar, Eliahu. *La Diplomatie du III Reich et les Juifs (1933–1939).* Paris: C. Bourgois, 1981.

Ben-Gurion, David. *Bama'arakhah* (Hebrew), *In the Battle.* Tel Aviv: Mifleget Poalei Eretz Yisrael, 1950.

Bethell, Nicholas. *The Palestine Triangle.* New York: Putnam Books, 1979.

Bondy, Ruth. *Elder of the Jews.* New York: Grove Press, 1989.

Braginsky, Yehuda. *Am hoter el hof* (Hebrew), *A People Striving for the Shore.* Tel Aviv: Hakibbutz Hameuhad, 1965.

Braham, Randolph. *The Destruction of Hungarian Jewry.* New York: 1963.

Broszat, Martin. "Das Dritte Reich und die rumaenische Juden Politik," (German), *Vutackten des Instituts fur Zietgeschichte* I, 1958, pp. 102–183.

Browning, Christopher. *The Final Solution and the German Foreign Office.* New York: Holmes and Meier Publishers, 1978.

———— "The Final Solution in Serbia: The Semlin Judenlager—A Case Study." Yad Vashem Studies 1983, pp. 55–90.

Chary, Frederick B. *The Bulgarian Jews and the Final Solution,* Pittsburgh: University of Pittsburgh Press, 1972.

Cohen, Gavriel. *Churchill ushealat Eretz Yisrael, 1939–1942* (Hebrew), *Churchill and the Question of Palestine, 1939–1942.* Jerusalem: Hakibbutz Hameuhad, 1976.

———— *Ha-kabinet ha-Briti ushealat Eretz Yisrael april-yuli 1943* (Hebrew), *The British Cabinet and the Question of Palestine: April–July 1943.* Tel Aviv: Hakibbutz Hameuhad, 1976.

Dobkin, Eliyahu. *Ha-aliyah vehahatzalah beshnot ha-shoah* (Hebrew), *Immigration and Rescue in the Holocaust Years.* Jerusalem: *Ha-mahlakah le'inyenai ha-noar shel ha-histadrut hatzionit behotza'at Mas,* 1946.

Documents of German Foreign Policy, Series D, Vol. 5, Washington: U.S. Government Printing Office, 1953.

Dinur, Ben Zion. *Zakhor: devarim al ha-shoah velikhah* (Hebrew), *Remember: Stories of the Holocaust and its Lesson.* Jerusalem: Yad Vashem, 1958.

Encyclopedia shel galuyot (Hebrew), *Encyclopedia of the Jewish Diaspora,* Vol. X. *The Jews of Bulgaria.* Albert Romano, Joseph Ben, Nissim Levi (eds.), Jerusalem: Hevrat Encyclopedia shel galuyot, 1970.

Esco Foundation, *Palestine. A study of Jewish[,] Arab and British Policies,* Vol. 2. New Haven: Yale University Press, 1947.

Esh, Shaul. "*Bayn haflayah lehashmadah*" in *Iyyunim betekufat ha-Shoah veyahadut zemananu*" (Hebrew), "Between Discrimination and Extermination," *Studies of the Holocaust Period and Contemporary Jewry.* Jerusalem: Institute for Contemporary Jewry, 1973, pp. 262–274.

Feingold, Henry. *The Politics of Rescue.* New Brunswick, N.J.: Rutgers University Press, 1970.

Fraenkel, Josef (ed.). *The Jews of Austria.* London: Vallentine Mitchell, 1967.

Frankel, David. *Beterem shoah; Hamediniut ha-zionit khlapei metzukat yehudei Europa lenokhah shilton ha-nazim beGermaniyah* (Hebrew), Pre-Holocaust Zionist Policy vis-à-vis the Distress of European Jewry In the Face of the Nazi Regime in Germany. Master's Thesis, Hebrew University, Jerusalem, 1983.

Frieling, Tuvia. *Me'uravuto shel Ben-Gurion befarashat hatzalat vealiyat ha-yeladim uvepulmus ha-klita, november 1942–mai 1945* (Hebrew), The Involvement of Ben-Gurion in the Rescue and Immigration of Children and the Absorption Controversy, November 1942–May 1945, Master's Thesis, Hebrew University, Jerusalem, 1984.

Galezer, Eliyahu. *Beterem zarhah ha-shemesh* (Hebrew), *Before the Sun Rose*. Jerusalem: Makhon Jabotinsky, 1984.

Gedaliah, Bata. *"Shnei kaisarim umalekah hagadat kladobo—perek mekupah metoledot ha-ha'apalah"* (Hebrew), "Two Kaisers and Queen Kladovo—A Chapter from the Annals of the Illegal Immigration," 1948–1978 Collection, Research Studies and Memoirs, Thirty Years of the State of Israel and Organized Aliyah from Yugoslavia, Tel Aviv, 1978, pp. 115–129.

Gelber, Yoav. *"Ha-itonut ha-ivrit beEretz Yisrael al hashmadat yehudei Europa 1941–42"* (Hebrew), "Hebrew Journalism in Palestine on the Destruction of European Jewry 1941–42," *Research Papers on the Holocaust and Resistance*, New Series, Collection A, Tel Aviv: Hakibbutz Hameuhad, 1970, pp. 30–58.

――― *Toledot ha-hitnadvut*, (Hebrew), *The History of Volunteer Work*, Jerusalem: Yad Yitzhak Ben Zvi, Vol. 1, 1979, Vol. 3, 1983.

――― "Zionist Policy and the Fate of European Jewry 1939–1942," Yad Vashem Studies 1980, pp. 129–158.

Gilbert, Martin. *Exile and Return*. London: Weidenfeld and Nicolson, 1978.

Golomb, Eliyahu. *Hevion 'oz* (Hebrew), *Refuge of Strength*. Tel Aviv: Hoza'at Mifleget Poalei Eretz Yisrael, 1950–53.

Gorni, Yosef. *"Ha-'otzmah shebehulshah—demuto shel Haim Weizmann kemanhig ha-tenu'ah ha-tzionit"* (Hebrew), "Strength in Weakness—Haim Weizmann as Leader of the Zionist Organization," Bauer (ed.), *Ha-Halom ve-hagshamato: Haqut u-Ma'as Bezionut* (Hebrew), *The Dream and Its Fulfillment: Meditation and Action in Zionism*. Tel Aviv: Misrad ha-bitahon, Hotza'ah Laor, 1979, pp. 132–141.

Greger, Rene. *"Zur Identitat einiger judischer fliichtlingsschiffe im Schwarzen Meer,"* *Marine Rundschau* 12 (1983).

Gruenbaum, Isaac. *Beyemei hurban veshoah* (Hebrew), *In the Days of Destruction and Holocaust*. Jerusalem: Hotza'at Haverim, 1946.

Habas, Brakha. *Portzei ha-shearim* (Hebrew), *The Gatebreakers*, Tel Aviv: Hotza'at Ma'arakhot, 1960.

Ha-Cohen, David. *Time to Tell*. New York: Cornwall Books, 1985.

Heller, Joseph. *Bema'avak lemedinah* (Hebrew), *The Struggle for Statehood*. Jerusalem: Zalman Shazar Publishing, 1984.

Halevi, Nadav. "The Economic Development of the Jewish Community in Palestine 1917–1947." Research paper, Falk Institute of Economic Research in Israel, Jerusalem 1970, pp. 31–41.

Halevi, Yehoshua. *Habaytah* (Hebrew), *Homeward*. Tel Aviv: Vaad Olei Pencho BeYisrael, 1950.

Hilberg, Raul. *The Destruction of European Jewry*. Chicago: Quadrangle Books, 1961.

Hirschmann, Ira. *Life Line to a Promised Land*. New York: Vanguard Press, 1946.

Hohne, Heinz. *The Order of the Death's Head*. London: Coward-McCann, 1970.

Horowitz, Dan and Lisak, Moshe. *Miyishuv lemedinah, yehudei Eretz Yisrael betekufat ha-mandat ha-Briti kekehillah politit* (Hebrew), *From Yishuv to State: Change and Continuity in the Political Structure of Israel*. Jerusalem: Hebrew University Papers in Sociology, 1972.

Hurewitz, Jacob Coleman. *The Struggle for Palestine*. New York: Norton, 1950.

Jabotinsky, Eri. *The Sakariya Expedition, A Story of Extra Legal Immigration into Palestine*. Johannesburg: Jewish Community of Johannesburg, 1945.

Jabotinsky, Vladimir. *Ketavim, baderekh lemedinah* (Hebrew), *Writings, On the Way to Statehood*. Tel Aviv: Eri Jabotinsky, Amihai Publishing, 1959.

Joseph, Bernard. *Ha-shilton ha-Briti beEretz Yisrael* (Hebrew), *The British Empire in Palestine*. Jerusalem: Mossad Bialik, 1948.

Katznelson, Berl. *Ketavim* (Hebrew), *Writings*, Vols. 7 and 9. Ein Harod: Hakibbutz Hameuhad, 1948.

Kechales, Haim. *Korot yehudei Bulgaria* Vol. III (Hebrew), *Annals of Bulgarian Jewry*, Vol. III. Tel Aviv: Davar Publishing, 1971.

Konfino, Barukh. *Aliyah bet mihofei Bulgaria* (Hebrew), *Illegal Immigration from the Shores of Bulgaria*. Tel Aviv: Ahiasaf Publishing, Ltd., 1965.

Krausnick, Helmut. *Anatomy of the S.S. State, Part I: The Persecution of the Jews*. New York: Walker, 1968.

Kulka, Dov and Azriel Hildesheimer. *Documents Zur Geschichte der Reichverein-ingung der Juden in Deutschland* (German) (in press).

Kuperstein, Leib. *Megillat struma* (Hebrew), *The Struma Charter*. Tel Aviv: Hitahdut 'olei Romaniyah beEretz Yisrael, 1942.

Lavi, Theodore. "The Background of the Rescue of Rumanian Jewry During the Holocaust," in Mosse, George L., and Bela Vago, (eds.), *Jews and Non-Jews in Eastern Europe*, New York: Wiley, 1974.

——— (ed.), *"Pinkas kehillot Romaniyah, Alef"* (Hebrew), "Records of Rumanian Communities, A," Jerusalem, 1970.

——— *Yehadut Romaniyah bema'avak hatzalatah* (Hebrew), *Rumanian Jewry in the Struggle for Survival*. Jerusalem: Yad Vashem, 1965.

Laurence, Bruce. *"Sippura shel pencho 1940–1942"* (Hebrew), "Story of the Pencho 1940–1942." *Yalkut Moreshet* 20, April 1976, pp. 35–52.

Lazar Litai, Haim. *Af al pi, sefer aliyah bet* (Hebrew), *In Spite of All: The Book of Aliyah Bet*. Tel Aviv: 1959.

The Letters and Papers of Chaim Weizmann, Series A, Jerusalem, 1979, Vols. 19, 20, M. J. Cohen, (ed.), Vol. 21 J. Heller (ed.). London: Oxford University Press.

Melzer, Emanuel. *Ma'avak medini bemalkhodet: yehudei Polin 1935-1939* (Hebrew), *Political Strife in a Blind Alley: The Jews in Poland 1935–1939*. Tel Aviv: Tel Aviv University Press, 1982.

Mardor, Munia. *Secret Mission*. New York: New American Library, 1966.

Milstein, Uri. *Kadmon veheverato* (Hebrew), *Kadmon and his Associates*. Tel Aviv: Am Oved, 1974.

Nicosia, Francis. *The Third Reich and the Palestine Question*. London: I.S. Tauris and Co., Ltd., 1985.

Niv, David. *"Bema'arkhot ha-irgun ha-tzvai ha-leumi* (Hebrew), *In the Battles of the Irgun*, Vol. II. Tel Aviv: Klausner Institute, 1967.

Ofer, Dalia. *"Mimas'a aliyah el ha-mavet"* (Hebrew), "From Immigration Journey Unto Death," H. Weiner and D. Ofer, *"Parashat Kladovo Sabac"* (Hebrew), *Undertakings on the Illegal Immigration in the Name of Shaul Avigur* (in progress).

——— *Pe'ulot ezra vehatzalah shel ha-mishlahat ha-Eretz Yisraelit leKushta 1943* (Hebrew), Help and Rescue Activities of the Palestinian Delegation in Constantinople 1943, Master's Thesis, Hebrew University, Jerusalem, 1972.

Ofir, Ephraim. *Ha-tenu'ah ha-zionit beRomaniyah bemilhemet ha-'olam ha-sheniyah* (Hebrew), The Zionist Movement in Rumania During the Second World War, Ph.D. Dissertation, Hebrew University, Jerusalem, 1984.

——— *"Aliyah bet miRomaniyah"* (Hebrew), "Illegal Immigration from Rumania," *Yalkut Moreshet* April 1981, pp. 38–74.

——— *"Ha'im nitan hayah lehatzil 70,000 yehudei Transnistriyah?"* (Hebrew), "Was it Possible to Save the 70,000 Jews of Transnistria?" *Yalkut Moreshet* April 1982, pp. 108–128.

Otiker, Israel. *Tenu'at hehalutz bePolin, gidulah ve-hitpathutah, 1932–35* (Hebrew), *The Hehalutz Movement in Poland: Its Growth and Development, 1932–35*. Tel Aviv: Hakibbutz Hameuhad, 1972.

Perl, William. *The Four Front War From the Holocaust to Promised Land*. New York: Crown Publishers, 1979.

Porat, Dina. *"Anshei ruah beEretz Yisrael nokhah ha-shoah, 1943–45"* (Hebrew), "Intellectuals in Palestine in Face of the Holocaust," *Ha-Zionut* 8, 1983, pp. 245–287.

——— *"Hanhagah bemilkud"* (Hebrew), *An Entangled Leadership*. Tel Aviv: Am Oved, 1986.

Resel, Moshe. *Tik mefkura*, (Hebrew), *The Mefkura File*. Tel Aviv: Hitahdut 'olei Romaniyah, 1981.

Rohwer, Jurgen. *Die Versenkung der Judischen Fluchtlingstransporte Struma und Mefkura im Schwarzen Meer Feb. 1942-Aug. 1944*, Frankfurt/Main: Bernard Graefe Verlag fur Wehrwesen, 1964.

Roi, Ya'akov. *"Maga'im Sovietim im ha-yishuv ha-yehudi baaretz veim manhigim zionim (yuni 1941–februar 1945)"* (Hebrew), "Soviet Relations with the Jewish Yishuv in Palestine and with Zionist Leaders, June 1941–February 1945," *Shalem* I 1974, pp. 525–602.

Rose, Norman Anthony. *Baffy. The Diaries of Blanche Dugdale 1936–1947*. London: Vallentine Mitchell 1973.

Rosenkranz, Herbert. *Verfolgung und Selbstbehauptung*. Munich: Herold, 1978.

Rotkirchen, Livia. *Hurban yehadut Slovakia* (Hebrew), *The Destruction of Slovak Jewry*. Jerusalem: Yad Vashem, 1961.

Ruppin, Arthur. *Three Decades of Palestine*. Jerusalem, 1936, Westport, Conn.: Greenwood Press, 1975.

Sarid, Levi Aryeh. *Hehalutz vetenu'at ha-noar bePolin, 1917–1939* (Hebrew), *The Hehalutz and Youth Movements in Poland, 1917–1939*. Tel Aviv: Am Oved, 1979.

Schechtman, Joseph B. *The Life and Times of Vladimir Jabotinsky*, 2 Vols. New York: Thomas Yoseloff, 1961.

Shapira, Anita. *Berl*.: Cambridge: Cambridge University Press, 1984.

Sharett, Moshe. *Yoman medini* (Hebrew), *Political Diary*, Vol. IV. Tel Aviv 1975, Vol. V. Tel Aviv: Am Oved, 1979.

Sheffer, Gabriel. *"Shikulim politim bekevi'at mediniut Britania beshealat hagirat yehudim leEretz Yisrael"* (Hebrew), "Political Considerations in the Process of British Policymaking With Regard to Jewish Immigration Into Palestine." *Ha-Zionut* 5, 1978, pp. 182–226.

Sikron, Moshe. *Ha-aliyah leYisrael 1948–1965* (Hebrew), *Immigration to Israel 1948–1965*. Jerusalem: Lishkah ha-mercazit lestatistica, 1967.

Slutzky, Yehuda. *Seder Toledot ha-haganah*, (Hebrew), *History of the Haganah*, Vol. 3, Tel Aviv: The Zionist Library, 1967.

Steinberg, Arie. *Ha-hebetim ha-benleumim shel ha-hagirah ha-yehudit miRomaniyah vedarkha, 1938–1947* (Hebrew), The International Aspects of Jewish Emigration From and Through Rumania, 1938–1947, Ph.D. Dissertation, Haifa University, Haifa, 1984.

Stern, Eliyahu. *Korotahem shel yehudei Danzig meaz ha-emancipaziyah vead ha-girush beyemei shilton hanazim* (Hebrew), *The Jews of Danzig, 1840–1943. Integration, Struggle, Rescue.* Tel Aviv: Ha-kibbutz ha-meuhad, 1983.

Tabenkin, Yitzhak. *Devarim* (Hebrew), *Collected Speeches*, Vol. 2. Tel Aviv: Hakibbutz Hameuhad, 1967.

Tenenbaum, Yosef. *Race and Reich*. Westport, Conn.: Greenwood Press, 1976.

Vago, Bela. "*Mercaz ha-yehudim beRomaniyah bayn begidah le hatzalah*" (Hebrew), "The Center of Jews in Rumania Between Betrayal and Rescue," Y. Guttmann, (ed.), *Demut ha-hanhagah ha-yehudit beartzot ha-shelitah ha-nazit* (Hebrew), *Patterns of Jewish Leadership in Nazi Europe.* Jerusalem: Yad Vashem, 1979, pp. 239–259.

⸺ "*Ha-mediniut ha-yehudit shel ha-dictatura ha-malkhutit beRomaniyah 1938–40*" (Hebrew), "The Jewish Policy of the Governmental Dictatorship in Rumania: 1938–40," *Zion* 29, 1964.

Wagman-Eshkoly, Hava. "*Tokhnit Transnistriyah—hizdamnut hatzalah o hona'ah*" (Hebrew), "Transnistria Program: Opportunity for Rescue or Extortion," *Yalkut Moreshet* April 1979, pp. 155–171.

Wasserstein, Bernard. *Britain and the Jews of Europe, 1939–1945*, Oxford: Clarendon Press, 1979.

Weiner, Hanah. "*Rezah ha-kevutzah*" (Hebrew), "Murder of the Group," H. Weiner and D. Ofer, *Parashat Kladovo Sabac* (Hebrew), *The Kladovo Sabac Story*. Tel Aviv: Am Oved, in progress.

⸺ "*Latzet bekhol mehir—ha-reka lefarashat Kladovo Sabac*" (Hebrew), "To Leave at Any Cost—The Background of the Kladovo Sabac Story," H. Weiner and D. Ofer, *Parashat Kladovo Sabac* (Hebrew), *The Kladovo-Sabac Story*. Tel Aviv: Am Oved, in progress.

Weiner, Hanah, and Dalia Ofer. *Parashat Kladovo Sabac* (Hebrew), *The Kladovo-Sabac Story*. Tel Aviv: Am Oved, in progress.

Weissmandl, Michael B. *Min hamaytzar* (Hebrew), *From the Straits*. Jerusalem: Hotza'at Emunah, 1960.

Weizmann, Chaim. *Trial and Error*. Westport, Conn.: Greenwood Press, 1972.

Wyman, David. *The Abandonment of the Jews: American Policy and the Holocaust 1941–1945*. New York: Pantheon Books, 1984.

Yahil, Leni. *Ha-shoah, goral yehudei Europa 1932–1945* (Hebrew), *The Holocaust: The Fate of European Jewry 1932–1945*. Jerusalem–Tel Aviv: Schocken Books, 1987.

⸺ "Select British Documents on the Illegal Immigration to Palestine 1939–1940," *Yad Vashem Studies* 1974, pp. 241–276.

⸺ "Madagascar: Phantom of a Solution for the Jewish Question," Mosse, George L., and Bela Vago (eds.), *Jews and Non-Jews in Eastern Europe, 1918–1945*, New York: Wiley, 1974.

Yisraeli, David. *Ha-reikh ha-Germani veEretz Yisrael* (Hebrew), *The Palestine Problem in German Politics 1889–1945*, Ramat Gan: Bar Ilan University Press, 1974.

⸺ "The Third Reich and Palestine," *Middle Eastern Studies* 7, 1971.

⸺ "The Third Reich and the Transfer Agreement," *Journal of Contemporary History* 6, 1972.

Yogev, Gedalia, and Yosef Gorni (eds.), *Medinaim be'etot mashber* (Hebrew), *Statesmen in Times of Crisis*. Tel Aviv: Hakibbutz Hameuhad, 1977.

Zariz, Ruth. *Hatzalat yehudim meGermaniyah beemtzaut hagirah november 1939–*

1945 (Hebrew), The Rescue of German Jews through Emigration, November 1939–1945, Ph.D. Dissertation, Hebrew University, Jerusalem, 1986.

Zweig, Ronald W. *Britain and Palestine during the Second World War*. London: Royal Historical Society, 1986.

The photos are taken from the Central Zionist Archives.

Index